British and Irish Salmonidæ

BRITISH AND IRISH

SALMONIDÆ.

BY

FRANCIS DAY, C.I.E., F.L.S., & F.Z.S.,

KNIGHT OF THE CROWN OF ITALY, HON MEMBER DEUTSCHER FISCHEREI-VEREIN, AND
OF THE AMERICAN FISHERIES' SOCIETY, PRESIDENT OF THE CHELTENHAM NATURAL
SCIENCE SOCIETY, VICE-PRESIDENT OF THE COTSWOLD NATURALISTS' FIELD CLUB,
ETC , DEPUTY SURGEON-GENERAL MADRAS ARMY, (RETIRED,) AND FORMERLY
INSPECTOR-GENERAL OF FISHERIES IN INDIA.

IN ONE VOLUME.
WITH TWELVE PLATES

WILLIAMS AND NORGATE,

14, HENRIETTA STREET, COVENT GARDEN, LONDON,
AND 20, SOUTH FREDERICK STREET, EDINBURGH

1887

LONDON
J. NORMAN AND SON, PRINTERS, HART STREET,
COVENT GARDEN

To

JAMES RAMSAY GIBSON MAITLAND, BART., F.LS. & F.ZS.,

WHOSE PRACTICAL KNOWLEDGE AND UNWEARIED ENERGY

HAS ENABLED HIM TO INAUGURATE

A FISH FARM AT HOWIETOUN OF UNRIVALLED EMINENCE,

BOTH AS A SCHOOL FOR FISH-CULTURE

AND ICHTHYOLOGICAL RESEARCH,

THIS WORK ON THE BRITISH AND IRISH SALMONIDÆ

IS DEDICATED BY HIS OBLIGED FRIEND,

THE AUTHOR.

PREFACE.

So MANY publications upon the subject of the British Salmonidæ, treated by Fishery Inspectors, Zoologists, Field Naturalists and Fish-culturists, have been published during recent years that it appears almost presumptuous adding another to their number. But owing to the opportunities so freely given me by Sir James Maitland, Bart., for collecting information at his unrivalled Howietoun fish-farm, and his kindness in instituting many and costly experiments among this class of fishes when he deemed them likely to obtain valuable results, I have considered it might not be inappropriate to lay those results along with other investigations before the public, in the hope that they may conduce to further research.

It has been increasingly evident to me for some years that one of the main reasons militating against the successful cultivation of trout (and possibly char) in this kingdom by riparian proprietors, has been the confusion into which these forms have been thrown by naturalists, who, in order to give greater accuracy to their descriptive treatises on Museum specimens, have subdivided them into many species. The consequence of this has been, that fish-culturists who have accepted the statements made, have been constantly attempting to introduce new species into their waters in order to improve the native race. For the zoologists who have been most active in raising local varieties to specific rank have been compelled to admit

that they all very commonly interbreed, but that the young revert
to one of the original parents

External form or colour, or internal organization (as the number
of cæcal appendages), have been adduced as reasons for considering
certain trout as distinct species In the following pages, however,
I have brought forward instances which, I believe, show that all
these appearances are consequent upon local surroundings, and how
such may be modified at will by changing the abode of the fish.

That hybrids do occur among Salmonidæ has been known in this
country for upwards of two centuries, and Sir James Maitland's
experiments distinctly prove that they may be fertile for, at least,
three generations, but time has yet to show for how long this will
continue, and, likewise, what the result of hybridization may be So
far as investigations have gone they tend to demonstrate that hybrid
races do not revert to the original colours of either parent.

Artificial fish breeding has given conclusive evidence that with
the maturity of the mother the size of the eggs of these fishes
augment, and that the progeny obtained from the largest ova
produce finer and more quickly-growing offspring than in such as
are raised from smaller eggs, or those given by younger or more
badly nourished mothers. This is a subject of great importance to
the fish-culturist, as showing that if he requires fine races pedigree
breeding must be resorted to; and that skill, combined with opportunity, can produce far larger trout than can be obtained by simply
collecting eggs from these fish while living in their native streams
It also tends towards the conclusion that a race may deteriorate
when they are the offspring of young parents

Riparian proprietors probably may improve their local races by
the introduction of fresh blood, but when numerous small and
possibly lean trout are present in a stream or lake, such may be
consequent upon insufficiency of food caused by its absence or due

to there being too many trout present to prey upon it. Mere numbers in a fishery do not invariably give a true indication of its condition.

In the following pages I have collected, and, so far as space would admit, have inserted the opinions which have been held from time to time in this kingdom upon the Salmonidæ, and in order not to confuse them with the text, have placed them in the form of notes. Many of the experiments or investigations, with the evidence on which my conclusions were made, will be found fully detailed in the columns of *The Field*, or in *The Proceedings of the Zoological Society of London*, to which the reader must be referred.

The cause mentioned below,* and which has not (so far as I am aware) yet been removed, must be my apology for the illustrations having been drawn by myself. The fish were coloured from nature by Miss Florence Woolward, whose accuracy in delineation needs no remark as it speaks for itself Also I have to thank Messrs. Hanhart as the chromolithographers, and Messrs. Norman & Son as the printers of this publication.

I must offer my best thanks to Sir James Maitland without whose assistance this work would never have seen the light, he has afforded me every information during the course of my inquiries, and furnished me with specimens for examination and delineation.

---

* From the *Secretary to the Trustees of the British Museum*.—" Dear Sir, Having referred your letter of the 13th to Dr Gunther, I learn from him that as both you and he are engaged in preparing a publication on British Fishes, he thinks it inconvenient and against the interests of either work that the same artist should be employed on both He has therefore intimated to Mr Mintern, that if he is working cuts for you, he will engage another artist for himself This is a matter which cannot be considered to concern the Trustees —Yours, &c , E Bond. August 20th, 1880 " Seven years have now elapsed since Dr. Gunther, *Keeper of the Zoological Collection of the British Museum*, induced Mr Mintern to break his agreement and cease engraving for me on the above plea Dr Gunther's work, stated then to be in the course of preparation, has not yet been advertised !

While Mr J. Willis-Bund, M.A., has given me the opportunity of investigating some Cardiganshire streams, and furnished me with considerable information during the progress of my work through the press. Mr. Andrews has likewise helped me in my inquiries at his famous fish-farm at Guildford.

In short, many whose names will be found mentioned throughout this work, have assisted me in various ways, and to all of whom I tender my hearty acknowledgments.

Likewise I have to give my sincere thanks to my old and valued friend A. C. Brisbane Neill, Esq., of the Madras Medical Service (retired), for his invaluable help in carrying this work through the press

CHELTENHAM,
September 15th, 1887

SALMONIDÆ

OF

GREAT BRITAIN AND IRELAND.

———————✥◈✥———————

AMONG the indigenous fishes of the British Isles, those belonging to the salmon family are universally admitted to rank second to none in value, whether regarded as food, as affording sport, or interesting objects for study either in their natural conditions of life or subsequent to changes accidentally effected in their habits or purposely caused by fish-culturists   Composed of forms that pass the whole or a portion of their existence in salt or in fresh water, they are distributed from a high inland elevation (in some countries even the snow-line) through the lakes and other large pieces of water, the rivers, the streams, and the neighbouring seas   Dispersed over such a wide and varied area the different species frequenting the littoral districts, estuaries, or fresh waters, show, as might be anticipated, many local peculiarities in size, form, and colour, generally dependant on the character of the waters they inhabit, the food available for their subsistence, the circumstances of temperature to which they are subject, or to temporary conditions in the fishes themselves

In searching the literature of the ancients respecting the salmon family, we do not observe that *Salmo salar* appears to have been known to the Greeks Ælian[*] alludes to a spotted fish in Macedonia that in his days was captured by means of an artificial fly, the mode of manufacturing which he detailed   It is not unlikely that he referred to the trout, or possibly the char, while the species he called *Thymalus*, found in the Ticino and Adige, is doubtless the grayling, still existent there   The name suggests the thyme-like odour that some poisons have observed to be given off by these fish when fresh from the stream.

If we turn to the Latins we find that Pliny, the elder, in the first century of the Christian era referred to the salmon,[†] remarking that in Aquitaine it was preferred to all the fishes of the sea   In the fourth century, Ausonius, a native of Bordeaux, one of their poets whose writings have descended to our times, descanted in the most favourable terms on this fish   He mentioned it in his poem "Mosella," being a description of the river Moselle, and he observed that it has red flesh, and springs by strokes of its broad tail from the lower into the higher waters above it   He alluded to three species, the *salar*, or our brook trout —

> "Purpureisque *Salar*, stellatus tergora guttis,"

to the salmon in the lines—

> "Nec te puniceo rutilantem viscere, *Salmo*,
> Transierim,"

and to the sea-trout, or as some have termed it the salmon-trout—

> "Teque inter species geminas, neutrumque et utrumque,
> Qui necdum salmo, nec jam salar, ambiguusque
> Amborum medio *Fario* intercepte sub ævo?"

It is clear that Ausonius referred to two distinct species, the brook trout and

* Ælian is supposed to have been born at Corycus, or at Anazarba in Cilicia, and is said to have flourished about A D 180
† It has been surmised that the term *Salmo* was derived from "Salmona," a tributary of the Moselle, mentioned by Ausonius, and that *salar* had its origin from "salire," "to leap"

1

the salmon, but was undecided as to whether the third, which was a silvery form, might not be a hybrid between the two others. The hybrid origin of this last may be rejected, as investigations of late years tend more to the conclusion that although we may augment the number of local races, our indigenous *Salmones* are restricted to two species, the salmon and the trout, which last has almost endless variations, some the result of a fresh-water, others due to a marine residence.

In the British Isles salmon appear to have been known to the Celts as "Ehoc," "Eog," and "Maran," terms in 1776, still in use among the Welsh, and which may have been partially adopted by the early Saxons, although one searches almost in vain for allusions to them among such ballads as have descended from Anglo-Saxon periods to the present day. The word "salmon" as applicable to its adult condition is supposed to have been of Latin origin and introduced by the Normans.

During the time of the Anglo-Saxons and Normans, it would seem probable that when founding Abbeys and Monasteries the clergy were not unmindful of the necessity for taking precautions in order to secure good water carriage for themselves and their goods, and it may be for this reason that monastic establishments were very frequently situated on the banks of the best streams where a continuous supply of fresh-water fish would be available, tending to alleviate the pangs of hunger during the periods of rigorous fasts, while an additional advantage must have been gained when they produced the rich and goodly salmon.

Of the two Archbishoprics and twenty-five Bishoprics in England in 1873, Buckland observed that the following were situated on salmon rivers. Llandaff on the Taff (founded the beginning of the sixth century). Salisbury on the Avon. St Asaph's on the Elwy (A D 560). *Canterbury on the Stour (A D 597). *Rochester on the Medway (A D 604). *Bath on the Avon (A D 607). London on the Thames (A D 610). York on the Ouse (A D 622). *Winchester on the Itchen (A D 634). Exeter on the Exe (A D 636). Gloucester on the Severn (A D 657). Hereford on the Wye (A D 676). Worcester on the Severn (A D 680). Carlisle on the Eden (A D 686). Durham on the Wear (A D 1040). *Oxford on the Thames (A D 1545). Chester on the Dee, and Ripon on the Ure, or 18 out of 27 were created on salmon rivers, in six of which these fishes have become exterminated.

The various species of Salmonidæ inhabiting the fresh waters of Europe have been described by naturalists from the earliest times, but respecting them many divergent views have been and are still held. Artedi (*Genera Piscium*, 1738, page 37, &c.), in his dissertation on the soft-rayed fishes, or Malacopterygii, placed together *Coregonus, Osmerus*, and *Salmones*, as genera in all of which two dorsal fins are present. Linnæus divided the family of Salmo into *Truttæ*, or those having the body variegated or spotted, *Osmerus*, with the dorsal fin placed opposite the ventrals (erroneously printed anal), *Coregonus* having minute teeth, and *Characini* possessing only four branchiostegals. Bloch included under Salmo the various species of salmon, trout, char, smelt or *Osmerus*, grayling or *Thymallus*, and *Coregonus*. Cuvier removed *Characini*, owing to their wanting teeth on the tongue, from among the forms placed by Linnæus under this head. Valenciennes (1848-1849) included the following genera in the family of Salmonoides, the dentition of each of which was taken from what exists in the adult. *Salmo*, salmons and char in which the body of the vomer is toothless, teeth if present being only on the head of that bone. *Fario*, the salmon or sea trout or *Torelles*, head of vomer toothed and a single row along the body of the bone. *Salar*, the fresh-water trout or *Truttæ*, in which the head of the vomer is toothed and a double row also exists along the body of that bone. *Osmerus* or smelts, *Mallotus, Argentina, Thymallus* or grayling, *Coregonus* or gwiniad, *Curimatus, Leporinus, Epicyrtus, Parolon, Salminus, Prochalodus, Citharinus, Piabuca, Hemiodus, Tetragonopterus, Brycinus, Piabucina, Gasteropelecus, Distichodus, Alestes, Myletes, Tometes, Myleus, Mylesinus, Chalceus, Chalcinus, Serrasalmus,*

Pygocentrus, Catoprion, Hydrocyon, Cynopotamus, Xyphorhynchus Agoniates, Xyphostoma, Salanx, Gonostoma, Chauliodus, Argyropelecus, Sternopteryx, Odontostoma, Scopelus, Saurus, Saurida, Parionella, Aulopus, and *Alepisaurus.* Fleming (1838) classed the following genera among the British Salmonidæ: *Salmo, Osmerus, Coregonus* including *Thymallus* and doubtfully *Scopelus.* Jenyns (1835) adopted the same classification, except that he placed *Thymallus* as a distinct genus. Dr. Günther (1866) divided the family of Salmonidæ as follows:—*Salmo,* including salmon, trout, and char, *Onchorhynchus, Brachymystax, Luciotrutta, Pecoglossus, Osmerus* or smelt, *Thaleichthys, Hypomesus, Mallotus, Retropinna, Coregonus* or guiniads, *Thymallus* or grayling, *Argentina, Microstoma* and *Salanx.*

In the following pages I shall restrict my remarks to what may be termed the "game fishes" of this family found in the fresh waters of the British Isles, and which include the salmon, various forms of trout and char, and also the grayling.

SALMON PASS.

Family—SALMONIDÆ, *Müller*.

Pseudobranchiæ present   The margin of the upper jaw formed mesially by
the premaxillaries, and laterally by the maxillaries. Barbels absent   Two
dorsal fins, the anterior containing rays ' the posterior, which is the smaller,
being adipose   Pyloric appendages, as a rule, present and usually numerous
Body scaled, head scaleless   Air bladder large, simple, and with a pneumatic
duct. The ova pass into the cavity of the abdomen before being extruded

This family is characterized, among bony or teleostean fishes, by the large size
of its blood discs.

Geological appearance —No fossils representing fresh-water forms have as yet
been discovered ; but the marine smelt, *Osmerus*, is found in the greensand of Ibeln-
busen and the schists of Glaris and Licata   A species of *Mallotus* is also present
in the clay nodules in Greenland, whose age has not been determined   Some
supposed marine forms have likewise been recorded from the chalk at Lewes,
co-existing with fossils of the genus *Beryx*, and they have been located in the
genera *Osmeroides, Acrognathus,* and *Aulolepis*

Geographical distribution —The Salmonidæ consist of marine and fresh-water
fishes, the latter being normally restricted to the Arctic and temperate portions
of the Northern hemisphere with the exception of the genus *Retropinna*, found in
New Zealand rivers   Absent from India and Africa, they have during the present
century been artificially distributed to many portions of the globe where they are
not known to have existed previously   In the Northern hemisphere the fresh-
water forms are present between the latitudes 45° and 75°, and one species has
been captured so far north as 80°   In fact they are residents of cold and temperate waters and do not normally extend to where the water is very warm.
The species of some of the genera, as *Argentina*, which are included in this
family, do not enter fresh waters   others again as the smelt, *Osmerus*, ascend so
far as the tide reaches but rarely beyond, while the salmon is an anadromous form
which passes up rivers even to their higher portions and here it forms its nest,
deposits its eggs, and its young are hatched and reared   Trout, char, and grayling
may pass their entire existence in fresh waters, but all these forms have been
captured in salt water *   Consequently it becomes evident that some species of
the same genus may be living in the sea while others are exclusively resident in
fresh waters, demonstrating how anadromous fish may change into resident fresh-
water ones   Also in certain species, as the common trout, some examples may be
found residing a great part of the year in fresh or in brackish waters, others in
fresh   We are thus able to follow an unbroken chain connecting sea forms of the
salmon family with others that appear to normally pass their entire existence in
fresh water, but which latter have in every genus furnished examples that have
been captured in the ocean
This gives rise to the inquiry whether the Salmonidæ are descended from a
marine or fresh-water ancestry ? a question of importance to the fish culturist
should he be debating upon the possibility or rather probability of successfully
rearing and subsequently breeding salmon in fresh waters without deterioration,
provided they are unable to migrate to the sea
That strictly fresh-water fishes are intolerant of saline water is well known,
thus carps are deleteriously affected, usually dying on the addition of salt water,

* Specimens of several deep sea genera belonging to this family have been secured by our
exploring expeditions

and this intolerance acts as a barrier against their diffusion   Consequently if the inland waters of oceanic islands are examined true fresh-water forms are absent, unless at some former period a land connection had existed with a continent or these fishes had obtained access accidentally or been imported by man   But there are certain forms of fish life in our fresh waters which are evidently descended from a marine ancestry as eels or perches, and these are much more tolerant of salt water than are those which are of purely fresh-water descent   •

But while it is difficult to show fresh-water forms that have changed to a marine residence, it is very easy to find sea fishes as temporarily or permanently residing in fresh waters.   Malmgren drew attention to certain marine species as the four-horned bullhead, *Cottus quadricornus*, a sucker, *Liparis barbatus*, and a variety of the common herring, *Clupea harengus*, being present in the northern portion of the Baltic, where the sea is now least saline, whereas they seem to be absent from its southern extremity where they might well be looked for had they obtained an entrance from the North Sea   These forms are smaller when residing in the Baltic than are those of the same species living in the Arctic Ocean, and it has been reasonably concluded that they are the remnants of a fauna which at one period was common to both localities   During the latter portion of the glacial epoch most of Finland and the middle of Sweden were submerged, so the Baltic must have been a gulf of the glacial ocean, for the entrance to the south at the Cattegat had not then been opened   As the Scandinavian continent became elevated, the Baltic became cut off by this raised land from the Arctic Ocean to the north, but it opened to the south through the Cattegat into the North Sea, and its fish-fauna even now retains representatives of its former marine northern glacial fauna, as well as such immigrants as have arrived through the Sound *

The foregoing must be classed among instances in which marine forms have inadvertently become imprisoned in water which has steadily changed its character from true saline to that which is only a little more than brackish ; here some live and breed, one can scarcely add thrive   But we shall presently have to allude to the land-locked salmon of Lake Wenern which demonstrates how an anadromous form may be similarly imprisoned in fresh water and still flourish †   Even British waters possess, besides members of the salmon family, anadromous forms, or such as ascend our rivers for the purpose of breeding, as shad, *Clupea alosa* and *C finta*, also flounders, *Pleuronectes flesus*, while many other marine fish, as bass, gray mullet, turbot, soles, plaice, and smelts have been naturalized in fresh water where some have continued their kind

When we find that some members of a genus inhabit the sea and others are restricted to the fresh waters, as among the Coregoni, we are probably not far wrong should we conclude that their ancestry was marine   The houting, *Coregonus oxyrhynchus*, is found along some of the European coasts, and it ascends into fresh water, while Mr Ogilby has observed the pollan, *C pollan*, in Ireland descending to the sea   Respecting the salmon, trout, and char, the most diverse opinions have been and are still held as to whether their ancestry was marine or fresh water ‡

* Inherited instinct appears to induce those Arctic forms to seek a passage to the north   while, due to the alterations in the physical character of the water in the Baltic, which is continuously decreasing in salinity, they are a smaller and more miserable race than are their relatives which still reside and thrive in the Arctic Ocean

† In tropical countries, as India, it is not uncommon to find marine fish detained in pieces of fresh water, to which they obtained access under varying circumstances   Some forms of fishes enter inundated grounds during high spring tides, or are carried over banks, and often find it impossible to return to the sea ; here they live until the succeeding rains cause floods and allow them to escape   The probabilities are that species of gar pikes as *Belone cancila*, some herrings as *Engraulis telara*, the pretty globe fishes, *Tetrodon cutcutia*, and numerous other forms now entirely confined to fresh water in India, must have descended from a marine ancestry, for representatives of the same genera are numerous in the contiguous seas

‡ Pennant (*British Zoology*, iii, 1776, p 288) observed that "the salmon is a fish that lives both in the salt and fresh waters, quitting the sea at certain seasons for the sake of depositing its spawn in security"   Fleming (1828, p 179) considered the salmon as a "migratory fish from the sea"   Parnell (1838, p 279) remarked "there is no doubt that the true abode of the salmon is in the sea, for as soon as it has entered the rivers it begins to deteriorate in condition,

The fact must not be lost sight of that, if salmon ever depended for their entire subsistence in the fresh water they ascend, the amount of food they would require would be so great in a river as to constitute a nuisance, and cause pollution were it left unconsumed

The number of cæcal appendages present in each form of Salmonoid has been considered a criterion by which the various species may be differentiated, but, on a more careful investigation, they have proved to be inconstant in their numbers. Still, the broad fact that all the species possess many of these appendages is important, for, if we examine the true fresh-water fishes as the carps, we find them destitute of these appendages, while those fresh-water forms which possess them in any number, as perch and ruffe in the Percidæ and burbot in the Gadidæ, appear invariably to have marine relatives, consequently, their presence in the salmon family tends towards a supposition as to their also having a marine ancestry

It may reasonably be asked on what grounds it can be held that a species of fish as the brook trout, *S fario*, in which sometime teeth are normally present throughout its life,* could be a retrograde descendant from a salmon *S salar*, in which these teeth are shed as the adult stage is obtained ? If we look at the very young salmon, as when in its par stage we find the same distribution of colours as are present in many adult trout or the immature livery of the salmon continued throughout the life of the more minute *S. fario* While in America the land-locked salmon, *S salar* which occurs in some lakes and only attains a few pounds in weight, would seem to be somewhat arrested in its development, and par bands are visible even in adults on the scales being rubbed off In the larger lake Wenern variety of the land-locked salmon although the par bands do not continue through life, the fish is extensively spotted

It must be admitted that these finger marks are usually lost in adult trout, but when they pass their existence in small streams these immature marks may be continued through life, in fact the trout has not arrived at the silvery stage of the smolt And what we find in colour we similarly perceive in dentition the double row of sometime teeth, so indicative of the fresh-water trout, are invariably seen in the immature par, or to put it in another way a sign of immaturity in the trout is a persistence of the infantile dentition of the salmon Consequently, it is to be expected that if this permanence of sometime teeth is symptomatic of a change from a marine to a fresh-water state of existence we should expect to find such occurring in anadromous sea trout, whether *S trutta* or *S cambricus*, did they commence residing in rivers and lakes And this is exactly the difference which we perceive does occur, in such forms becoming more persistent through life than if the fish had retained its anadromous propensities

Salmon on entering rivers, as a general rule, deteriorate in quality, similarly to what has been shown takes place in sea fishes, prevented migrating to the ocean, unless under peculiarly favourable conditions, therefore it becomes a question of what is the effect on salmon debarred from going to the sea ? Here doubtless the reply of all observers is to one effect—that they sensibly dwindle in size, and generally the breed dies out, for even the land locked salmon is a dwarfed race—in fact, similar in its character to the dwarfed breed of herrings imprisoned in the brackish Baltic sea

---

the scales lose their brilliant silvery lustre, and the flesh becomes soft and pale   Dr Gunther (*Catal* xi 1866, p 8) placed the fish of the genus Salmo as "inhabitants of the fresh waters of the Arctic and temperate parts of the Northern hemisphere, many species descending to the sea after having deposited their spawn" In 1866 he stated of the char "none of which migrate to the sea as far as our present knowledge goes" (*Catal* vi,| p 145) while in the *Zoological Record* for 1861 the char he remarked "the origin of which cannot be deduced from a marine species" Frank Buckland, on the contrary, observed, "I consider the salmon a sea fish proper, nevertheless, this sea fish ascends the rivers and streams in order to deposit its eggs, for, unlike other sea fish, it does not breed in the sea" (*Familiar Hist Brit Fish* p 321)

* Char do not possess teeth on the body of the vomer, and possibly those systematists are correct who place them in a distinct genus from the salmon and trout But this work not being intended to refer to any extent to such disputed points, I have considered it unnecessary to enlarge on this question and followed those authors who have suppressed the separate genus *Salvelinus*

As to the varieties and hybrids of trout If, as seems probable, we merely possess one very plastic species subject to an almost unlimited amount of variation, that its largest race is found in the ocean, while in order to breed it ascends streams, but usually (to which there are many exceptions) not so far as the salmon, unless it permanently takes up its abode in the fresh waters, we at once obtain a clue to the characters of the various so-called species, and relegate these different trout to a single form, in which numerous local races are to be found * This also accounts for the hybrid theory, or numerous hybrid trout stated to exist in our waters, for they should be regarded as really changing local races, as to whether they are assuming a fresh-water existence from a saline one, or *vice versa*

Here it will be necessary to slightly digress for the purpose of discriminating between local races or varieties and species, because what one naturalist considers a variety another may look upon as a species Two primary characters have been selected as demonstrating the true position of a specimen, either the morphological or that relating to its structure and development, or secondly, the physiological as relating to its functions Even within the limits of a single species no two are found to be exactly similar, but a tendency to diverge from the original type appears to exist, which power of divergence is in such a direction as will be most likely to preserve and increase useful variations For it seems to have been conclusively shown that there exists a law in animal life of an hereditary tendency to follow the specific type, while there is likewise a law of variability by adaptation which is destined to modify every organism so as to fit it for new conditions of existence Owing to a knowledge of this latter tendency, by means of judicious selection and breeding from individuals that are possessed of some desirable variation, such may become permanent through future generations † while natural selection (perhaps assisted by some as yet unknown factor) would similarly tend to favour the continuation among wild races, of forms which possess variations favourable to the life of the fish and thus produce and continue

* The descendants of the common brook trout sent to Tasmania have shown in most localities very great disposition to vary Mr Arthur informed us that " In the Shag river the largest trout are near the tideway, and small trout numerous above In the Leith the large trout are only found during spawning time " Also, " That as large trout are not now seen in the Leith except during winter, they must live in the brackish water at its month, or in the bay itself, for nine months out of the twelve And this is further borne out by the fact of many large fish being netted by the fishermen in the bay with the characters, more or less, of the brown trout ' In short, the brook trout are here migrating seawards, and becoming anadromous

A trout, *Salmo fario*, of 25 lb weight, 32 2 in long, and 2 ft in girth, from Waimakiriri, New Zealand, as silvery as a salmon and marked with X spots, was taken by Mr Farr to the British Museum where it is preserved in spirit In the same river the trout caught previous to 1878 were marked with red spots, but they are never seen there now (*The Field*, Dec 20th, 1880) Thus we are able to trace in the Antipodes not merely changing colours, but varying habits in the descendants of the non migratory brook trout, which in a few generations has assumed more or less of the sea dress and anadromous habits of the European sea trout

Respecting the char, *S alpinus*, we are told by Dr O Reuter, in his *Fishes of Finland*, that it is met with on the coast of the Arctic Sea and in the rivers, which they ascend to spawn, but in Sweden it is known exclusively as a fresh water fish, while it is quite clear that the American trout, *Salmo fontinalis*, belongs to this division of the genus Salmo Professor Jordan observed the common Rocky Mountain trout, *S purpuratus*, is so known when taken in rivers and brooks, and as salmon trout when taken in the sea or river's mouth, for sea run specimens are more silvery, the only difference being temporary, and dependent on the water and possibly on the food (*Bull U S Fish Com* 1885, p 310) The British char has been said to have descended to the sea in Wales after it had been driven out of Llanberis Lake by poisoned water, and Mr Jackson observed upon two which had escaped from a fresh water tank in the Southport Aquarium and were captured many weeks afterwards by some boys fishing in the contiguous salt water, there does not seem any more reason why char should not be of marine origin than trout or salmon, while he would be a bold reasoner who could maintain that char, trout, and salmon are descendants from more than one ancestry, that, in short, the salmon was a marine and the trout and char strictly fresh water forms.

† The experienced fish culturist is aware how varied are the changes observable in some piscine forms, as for instance in the gold carp, *Carassius auratus*, wherein may be found differences in form, proportions, colours, and in many ways, but all sprung from a single original stock and capable of being reproduced by artificial culture Similarly the various races of common carp, *Cyprinus carpio*, as the leather carp, the mirror carp, &c , are merely local races of one species, and possibly some of our Salmonidæ have similarly shown local peculiarities which mistaken zoologists have believed to constitute species

certain local varieties or races. If, however, the variations are not of a persistent
character, nor exceed the differences between the limits laid down for a species,
these cannot be considered as indicating a distinct species : for to render such
valid, we must have a *permanence of variation* from the original form. Thus,
among the sticklebacks we find in the ten-spined form, some possessing ventral
fins, others destitute of them ; but this difference not being permanent merely
resolves itself into a local race or inconstant variety. The number of vertebræ
and the cæcal appendages have been considered as characters which may
materially assist in fixing the locality of a species among the *Salmonidæ*, and it is
proposed investigating in detail some of the various structural and functional
differences that have been brought forward for the purpose of establishing species
among the true salmon, *Salmones*. It has occurred that owing to too great
importance having been given to inconstant variations the number of species
among this family has been unduly augmented, and varieties have been accorded
specific rank : while every little variety of form, colour, or structure has also
been reckoned as possibly demonstrating hybridity.

The proportions of different parts of the body vary with age, season, or
locality,* and this may be augmented in some anadromous forms which have
been subjected to unnatural retention in fresh water, insufficiency of food, or
sickness from any cause. The head of the male is generally longer than that of
the female, especially in old examples, but these proportions are liable to variation
should the example be barren.

* Young Lochleven trout, raised by Mr. Andrews of Guildford, from eggs sent from Howietoun,
are found to grow more rapidly in their southern home, become deeper in form, while the colours
are not very far removed from those of the local brook trout : and other as remarkable deviations
from the original type will be alluded to when this local race is described.

Synopsis of British Genera

1 *Salmo* —Maxillary long dentition strong and complete Scales small Anal rays in moderate numbers (14 or less) Pyloric appendages numerous

2 *Thymallus* —Maxillary short small teeth in the jaws, vomer, and on the palatine bones Anterior dorsal fin many rayed Scales of moderate size Pyloric appendages numerous

3 *Coregonus* —Maxillary short teeth if present minute Anterior dorsal fin with few rays Scales of moderate size Pyloric appendages numerous

4. *Osmerus* —Maxillary long dentition complete, with fang-like teeth on the vomer and tongue Scales of medium size Pyloric appendages few

5 *Argentina* —Maxillary short teeth absent from jaws Anterior dorsal fin with few rays Scales rather large Pyloric appendages few or in moderate numbers

Of the foregoing my remarks will be restricted to species belonging to the two first genera, or those of *Salmo* and *Thymallus*, forms in which their eggs are much heavier than the water, and are mostly deposited beneath sand or gravel

The blood discs of the fishes of this family are of very large size, those of the salmon being nearly equal to such as are found in the cartilaginous sturgeon Gulliver (Proc. Zool Soc 1872, p 834) recorded the average diameter of the red corpuscles of the blood in the following species—L D signifying the "long diameter" and S D "short diameter" —*Salmo salar*, L D $\frac{1}{15.4}$, S D $\frac{1}{1400}$ *S fario*, L D $\frac{1}{15.74}$, S D $\frac{1}{1800}$ *S feroa*, L D $\frac{1}{15.24}$, S D $\frac{1}{1900}$ *S fontinalis*, L D $\frac{1}{14.56}$, S D $\frac{1}{2180}$ *Thymallus vulgaris*, L D $\frac{1}{1481}$, S D $\frac{1}{2000}$. These corpuscles appear to be at least a third larger than the corresponding corpuscles of most other osseous fish

Genus I —SALMO, *Artedi*

Furio and *Salar*, Cuvier: *Trutta* and *Salvelini*, Nilsson.

Branchiostegals from nine to thirteen pseudobranchiæ present Eyes lateral. Cleft of mouth deep, the posterior extremity of the upper jaw reaching to beneath the hind edge of the eye or even beyond Teeth conical, present on the jaws, vomer, palatine bones and tongue, absent from the pterygoids Anterior dorsal fin with a moderate number of rays (10-15) anal with rather few (10-13) Scales small and cycloid Lateral-line straight. Cœcal appendages numerous A pancreas present

Geographical distribution —These physostomatous fishes, found in the fresh and salt waters of Europe, Asia, and America, are most abundant in the Arctic or colder regions, in contradistinction to the distribution of the carps and siluroids, which augment in numbers the nearer we approach the tropics Temperature would appear to limit the distribution of these fishes to the colder and temperate regions, or we should find them extended to the Mediterranean in, where Davy remarked he had only known a stray salmon captured off the coast of Malta *

The indigenous species belonging to this genus have been divided into (1) *Salmones*, or true salmons, wherein the body and the head of the vomer are toothed at some period of their lives, and (2) the *Salvelini* or chars, wherein the vomerine teeth are restricted to the head of that bone.

* Davy (*Physiological Researches*, 1863, page 82) gave the result of some investigations that he had made on the temperature of salmon captured with an artificial fly.
Sept 1862—Temper of river, 56° of male salmon, under liver, opened immediately, 59°. in the heart still pulsating, 58°
Sept 1862—Temper of river, 58° of salmon, under liver, opened immediately, 60°
      ,,   58° of grilse   ,,   59 5
In all these three instances the thermometer was introduced into the wound made by the gaff in the thick muscles of the back from which blood was exuding

A. *Salmones or true salmon.*

1. *Salmo salar.* (*See* Fig. 1.)
2.   „   *trutta*, with its sea and fresh-water varieties or local races. (*See* Fig. 2.)

B. *Salvelini or chars.*

3. *Salmo alpinus*, British char. (*See* Fig. 3.)
4.   „   *fontinalis*, American char (introduced).

FIG. 1.—FRONT VIEW OF TEETH ON   FIG. 2.—FRONT VIEW OF TEETH ON   FIG. 3.—SIDE VIEW OF TEETH
VOMER OF SALMON GRILSE.   VOMER OF BROOK TROUT.   ON VOMER OF BRITISH CHAR.

With such plastic forms as trout whether fresh-water or marine, and such diversified appearances as some of these fish assume at different ages, it is not surprising what diverse views have been and are still held as to the number of species existing in our waters.*

* Willoughby, *Historia Piscium*, 1686, enumerated (1) a salmon; (2) *Salmulus*; (3) the gray; (4) "the scurf and bull trout," *Trutta salmonata*; (5) *Trutta fluviatilis*.

Ray, *Synopsis Methodica Piscium*, 1713, gave (1) *Salmo*, "a salmon;" (2) *Salmulus*, "the samlet;" (3) *S. griseus seu cinereus*, "the gray;" (4) *Trutta salmonata*, "the salmon trout," or "bull trout," or "scurf," (5) *Trutta fluviatilis*, "a trout."

Pennant, *British Zoology* 1776, described (1) the salmon; (2) the gray trout, *Salmo eriox*, which he believed to be the sewin; (3) the sea trout, *S. trutta*; (4) the trout, *S. fario*; (5) the white salmon; and (6) the samlet. He alluded to that from *Llynteisi*, a lake of South Wales, termed *Coch y dail*, and marked with black spots as large as sixpences; to a crooked-tailed variety in the Einion, a river not far from Machynlleth, and also to a similar form being in the Snowdon lakes; to the Gillaroo trout of Ireland, remarkable for the great thickness of its stomach, though it does not otherwise differ from the common trout; and to the Buddaghs of Lough Neagh, in Ireland, some of which have been known to weigh 30 lb.

Donovan, in his *British Fishes* (1802-1808), referred to the (1) sewen or *Salmo cambricus*, of which he stated, among other indications, that the head was shorter than in the common salmon, and the tail more forked—this he considered to be an anadromous form peculiar to Wales; (2) the common salmon, *Salmo salar*; (3) the trout, *Salmo fario*, which he observed to be subject to many variations: and, lastly, to some in Scotch lakes, spotted very differently from the common sorts, which he suspected to be a distinct species, but of which he makes no further mention. He likewise observed how trout vary in size, and referred to the Fordwich form, in Kent, which attains to nearly that of the salmon. He also remarked upon the flesh of trout captured during the same season in two contiguous streams in Cardiganshire, the names of which he omits to give, one of which invariably produced the red and the other the white variety.

Turton, 1807, admitted into his *British fauna*—(1) the salmon, *Salmo salar*; (2) the shewen, *Salmo eriox*, to which he referred Donovan's sewen; (3) the salmon trout, *Salmo trutta*; (4) the common trout, *Salmo fario*; (5) the white salmon, *Salmo phinoc*; and (6) the samlet, *Salmo salmulus*.

Sir Humphry Davy (*Report of Parliamentary Committee on the Salmon Fisheries of the United Kingdom*, May 5th, 1824) gave the following species of the genus *Salmo*, as captured in the salmon fisheries of Great Britain and Ireland, evidently meaning the sea fisheries: (1) *Salmo salar*, or the common salmon, and (2) *S. eriox*, known under different names in different districts as salmon-peal, sewen, bull trout, but most correctly as sea trout.

Fleming, in his *History of British Animals*, 1828, enumerated first those anadromous forms that have a forked tail, as (1) the common salmon, *Salmo salar*; (2) the bull trout, *Salmo hucho*, which is little inferior to the salmon in size, but more elongated, and has white and insipid flesh, but which he stated had no teeth on the vomer; (3) the phinock or white trout, *Salmo albus*,

Prior to commencing a detailed description of the various species of British Salmonidæ, it will be necessary to take a brief but general survey of the fishes of which it is composed, especially as regards their external form, internal organization, and some of their natural functions

which seldom attains to a foot in length, and is common in the seas and rivers of Scotland and the North of England   Secondly, anadromous forms with even tails, as (4) the sea trout, *Salmo trutta*, of which he considered the samlet or par to be the young of this or of the salmon, the migrations of the two almost coinciding , (5) the gray trout, *Salmo eriox*, including *S cambricus*, and found in the sea and in rivers   Lastly forms stationary in rivers, as (6) the common trout, *Salmo fario*, remarking of the Gillaroo variety that when it fed on shell fish the coats of its stomach acquired a thickness similar to the gizzards of birds

Agassiz, in the *Reports of the British Association* for 1834, only admitted (1) *Salmo salar*, (2) *S trutta*, (3) *S fario*

Jenyns, in his *Manual of British Vertebrate Animals*, 1835, included (1) the common salmon , (2) the bull trout or gray salmon, *S eriox*, (3) the sea trout, *S trutta*, inhabiting the sea and rivers, identical with the salmon trout of the London markets and the white trout of Pennant and Fleming , (4) the common trout, *S fario*, with its variety the Gillaroo, (5) the great lake trout, *S ferox*, which he believed to be identical with *S lacustris*, of Berkenhout, though Agassiz believed not of continental authors

Yarrell, in his *History of British Fishes*, 1836, gave (1) the salmon, *Salmo salar* , (2) the bull trout or gray trout, *S eriox* and *S cambricus* , (3) the salmon trout, *S trutta* , (4) the par or samlet, *S salmulus* , (5) the common trout, *S fario*, and (6) the great lake trout, *S ferox*, and in a later edition (7) the Loch Leven trout, *S levenensis*

Parnell, in his prize essay on the *Fishes of the Firth of Forth*, 1838, entered very fully into his views respecting the *Salmonidæ*   He admitted (1) the salmon , (2) the bull trout, *S eriox*, of which he enumerated and figured the following varieties which he had obtained in the Firth of Forth —a salmon spotted bull trout, a few spotted bull trout, a thickly spotted bull trout, a large headed bull trout, a curved spotted bull trout, a crescent tailed bull trout, a Norway bull trout, and a salmon bull trout identical with *S trutta* of Jenyns and Yarrell, (3) salmon trout, *S trutta*, which is likewise the same as *S albus* of Fleming, (4) the par, (5) the common trout, (6) the Loch Leven trout

Jardine, in his *British Salmonidæ*, 1839, figured (1) the salmon, (2) the phinock or gray trout, (3) the great lake trout, (4) the common trout and five principal varieties , (5) the Solway migratory trout or herling, (6) the salmon or sea trout, (7) the par, of which he had not any hesitation in considering not only distinct, but one of the best and most constantly marked species which we have

White, in the *List of the specimens of British animals in the National Museum*, enumerated in 1851 (1) the common salmon , (2) the sea trout, (3) the bull or gray trout, (4) the common trout , (5) the great lake trout

Knox in 1855 added *Salmo estuarius*

Thompson, in his *Natural History of Ireland*, 1856, gave (1) the salmon, including the par , (2) the gray or bull trout, *S eriox*   (3) the salmon trout, (4) the common trout, including the Gillaroo, which variety he recorded having met with in most fresh water races, (5) the great lake trout

Dr Gunther, in a *Catalogue of fishes in the British Museum*, 1866, divided the genus *Salmo* as follows —*Salmones* (=*Truttæ*, Nilsson, also *Fario* and *Salar*, Cuv and Val) having teeth on the head of the vomer and also along its body, the posterior of which latter become lost with age and *Salvelini* or chars with the vomerine teeth at all ages are restricted to the head of that bone   The former were subdivided in accordance with their habits into "anadromous" forms or such as migrate from the sea into fresh water to breed, and the non migratory fresh water forms   He described the following as species —Anadromous forms (1) *Salmo salar*, Vertebræ, 59 60, Cæcal appendages, 51 to 77, (2) *S argenteus*, Cæc pyl 61-67, (3) *S trutta*, Vert 59-60, Cæc. pyl 43 61, (4) *S orcadensis*, Vert 56 57, Cæc pyl 50, (5) *S brachypoma*, Vert 59, Cæc pyl 43 47; (6) *S cambricus*, Vert. 59, Cæc pyl 33 52   While of the non-migratory fresh water forms, he admitted —(7) *S levenensis*, Vert 57-59, Cæc pyl 49-90, (8) *S fario*, northern variety *gaimardi*, Vert 59 60, Cæc pyl 33 46, southern variety *ausonii*, Vert 57-58, Cæc pyl 38 47 , (9) *S ferox*, Vert 56-57, Cæc pyl 43-49 , (10) *S stomachicus*, Vert 59 60, Cæc pyl 44 , (11) *S gallivensis*, Vert 59, Cæc pyl 44 , (12) *S nigripinnis*, Vert 57-59, Cæc pyl 36 42

Couch, *Fishes of the British Isles*, 1864, also augmented the nominal species of salmonidæ, describing the following —(1) *Salmo salar* , (2) *S trutta*, which he termed *Peal*, and observed that under several names it exists in considerable abundance through the whole extent of the British Island , (3) *S cambricus* or sewin, (4) *Sea trout* from the Fowey in Cornwall, evidently identical with the so-called hybrids of the sewin, (5) *S trutta* no 2, termed salmon trout, which he asserted to be more a fish of the north than the generality of this genus, and seemed to be identical with *S eriox*, Yarrell, or a compound of *S albus* and *S cambricus*

Day, *British and Irish Fishes*, 1880 84, believing many of the reputed British species to be simply local races, or unstable varieties, decreased the number to—(1) the Salmon, *Salmo salar*, (2) sea trout, *S trutta* and its several varieties, as the brook trout, Lochleven trout, &c , (3) the char, *S alpinus*, and (4) the American char, *S fontinalis*, which had been acclimatized by fish-culturists

The head, which is comparatively large, is divided from the body by the gill-openings, while the eye (fig 4 e) sub-divides it into two parts, that in front of this organ being termed the ante-orbital and that behind it the post-orbital region, in

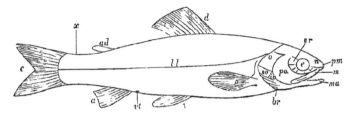

Fig 4   Outline of a young Lochleven trout a anal fin ad adipose dorsal fin br branchiostegous rays c caudal fin d rayed dorsal fin e eye io interopercle, ll lateral line m maxilla ma mandible n nostrils o opercle p pectoral fin pm premaxilla po preopercle so sub opercle s.i. suborbital ring v ventral fin vt. vent τ peduncle or free portion of the tail.

the former is the snout wherein are placed the nostrils (n) and the mouth   The region between the orbits is known as the inter-orbital space, while that below the orbit is the infra- or sub-orbital, with its ring of bones (s r)   The mouth is somewhat oblique, and rather protractile   The gill-covers or opercles consist of four pieces, the posterior and upper of which is the opercle or operculum (o)   In front of it is the preopercle (po)   While of the two lower pieces, the posterior is known as the sub-opercle (so), and the anterior, situated below the preopercle, as the inter-opercle (i o)

The body or trunk, which commences just behind the head, passes by almost imperceptible degrees into the caudal or tail portion, the vent (vt) separating the two regions   While the finless part between the adipose or dead fin of the back (ad) and the tail fin (c) is termed the peduncle or free portion of the tail (τ)

The skin is scaled, and the row of pierced scales that passes along the side is known as the lateral line (l l), the number on which may be useful in assisting in discriminating a species

If the composition of the fins in fishes of this family is examined, we perceive them to consist of soft rays that are either simple and undivided, or composed of numerous pieces articulated

Fig 5   Caudal ray of trout

to one another by transverse joints, and which rays may have their outer extremities branched   A ray is essentially formed of two lateral halves fastened together, with the basal ends more or less separated, as seen in fig 5, which represents the caudal ray of a trout where the divided basal extremity embraces both sides of an hypural bone   Fin rays when broken may reunite, if lost they may likewise occasionally be reproduced, but often in an incomplete manner *

The fins are divisible into such as are single and unpaired, hence termed "azygous," as those along the median line of the back or dorsal (fig 4, d and ad)   The tail or caudal fin (c), placed vertically at the posterior extremity of a fish, where it may be seen of two very distinct types, in the generality of the finny tribes when the two lobes are equal it is termed "homocercal," as in the perch or carp, whereas in the sharks and some other allied classes the vertebral column is

* According to M M Philipeau's investigations and experiments made on gudgeons, Gobio fluviatilis, he found that the fins were reproduced only when the basal portion at least is left intact   Having removed the left ventral fin on a level with the abdominal surface, it became completely restored in eight months   In another example he repeated the operation, also taking away the small bones which supported it, but at the end of eight months there was no trace of the fin's regeneration   (Comptes Rendus, March 15th, 1869, t lxviii, pp 669 670)

prolonged into the upper half of this caudal fin, rendering it unequally lobed or "heterocercal." Among the salmonidæ the character of the last two or three of the vertebra is somewhat intermediate between these two forms of fin, although externally it is of the homocercal or equally-lobed type The anal (a) commences behind the vent (vt) and passes along the median line of the lower surface * The functions of the dorsal and anal fins are mostly restricted to increase or diminish the extent of the lateral surface, by means of their being elevated or depressed, and so preventing violent lateral oscillations or the body being turned upside down

These fishes possess two pairs of horizontal or paired fins, one on the breast (p) or pectorals (also known as chowk fins), corresponding with the anterior extremities of higher vertebrata, while the second or ventral pair (v), the homologues of the hind pair of limbs, are abdominal, so termed as being near the hind end of the body The pectoral can assist in a forward movement by rapid strokes towards its body, and likewise in a backward movement by means of reversed or forward strokes Under certain circumstances the upper rays of this fin are useful in respiration, as should a deficiency of air exist in the water, when they are constantly in motion, sending a current towards the gills, thus in very young fish, as salmonoids, prior to the absorption of the umbilical vesicle, they are ceaselessly employed in assisting respiration In some localities a considerable development of this fin appears to be constant, but it is generally largest in males † Variations in its size are of insufficient character upon which to constitute species.

Experiments have demonstrated that should both the dorsal and anal fins be removed, the fish rolls from side to side if one pectoral is cut off, it falls over to the side from which such has been taken if both are abstracted, the head sinks should the pectoral and ventral of one side be gone, equilibrium is lost while removal of the tail fin interferes with progression

The form of the caudal fin amongst these fishes alters very considerably with age, being more forked in the young than in the adult ‡ while non-migratory varieties of trout sometimes have it less so than do the young of the anadromous races But the variations are exceedingly numerous, and attention has to be paid to the age, sexual development, and locality from whence the specimen was procured, for this fin would be required to possess much greater power in rapid than it would in sluggish streams, while although excessive use might, and probably would augment its extent, the same influence might also curtail its size by wearing off its extremities, more especially its corners, as will be more fully entered upon when arriving at the description of the various forms of trout

Prior to examining these questions some fixed method on which to proceed when investigating the conformation of this fin is desirable, for it is evident that the wider it is expanded the less will be the comparative emargination at its centre To illustrate this the following figure of the caudal fin is given Here the fin is placed so that the depth of the free portion of the tail, from A to B, about equals the distance from C to E, and E to D, or half the length of the expanded fin (C to D), and when in this position it is seen to be but slightly cleft But should the distance from C E D be extended about one half more, or from C' to E and on to D', the fin then becomes merely emarginate. Or in the first position we find it very slightly forked, in the second scarcely concave, and

* These median or unpaired fins are considered by some to be appendages to the skin, but believed by Balfour to be the specialized and highly developed remnants of a once continuous lateral fin along either side

† In the opinion of Agassiz, trout inhabiting rapid rocky streams have their fins always much developed (Richardson, *Faun Bor Amer* p 169) "This opinion is not founded on observations in nature Salmonoids inhabiting such streams are distinguished by short fins, the delicate extremities being worn off by constant activity of the fish, whilst individuals inhabiting still waters show the fins proportionately longer Hence mature specimens have the fins more rounded and shorter than the sterile ones, on account of their greater activity " (Gunther, *Catal* vi p 149)

‡ Widegren likewise believed that sexually mature individuals have the caudal fin less deeply cleft than immature ones of the same age and size

this is a very noteworthy fact, as in some instances in which there exists a discrepancy in the accounts of two authors as to the shape of this fin, such may be owing, not to an error in facts, but to a difference in the method in which the examination was conducted.

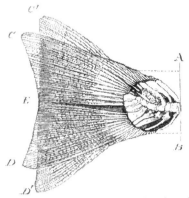

Fig. 6.   Caudal fin of a sea trout, expanded half and two-thirds.

Locomotion is the main use to which the fins of fishes are put, but even in locomotion other forces are frequently or rather generally brought into play to assist the fins, whether such is for the purpose of swimming, or for leaping as in the salmon while ascending rapids when the muscles of the tail are of great assistance.

The skeleton* or endo-skeleton of Salmonoids, consists essentially of a skull and a vertebral or spinal column (to which are certain appendages) these forming a protection to the cerebro-spinal nervous system and large blood-vessels present in the long axis of the body. The vertebræ, of which the spine† is made up, consist of a varying number of bones, the bodies of each of which are excavated at either end causing them to be bi-concave or amphi-coelous. The cavity produced by the apposition of the two concave surfaces is filled up with gelatinous substance the remains of the notochord, while it is covered in by connecting ligaments. Consequently, between the vertebræ are elastic balls of semifluid consistence which enables them to move freely one upon another.

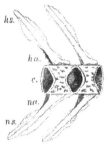

Fig. 7. Section of two caudal vertebræ of a salmon. c. cen-trum; ha. hæmal arch; hs. hæmal spine; na, neural arch; ns. neural spine.

---

* The numerals employed for the various bones in this work are almost identical with those of Cuvier and Owen, being as follows:—1. Frontal. 2. Prefontal. 3 (Ethmoïde, Cuv.), Nasal. 4, Postfrontal. 5 (Basilaire, Cuv.), Basioccipital. 6 (Sphénoïde principal, Cuv.), Basisphenoid. 7, Parietal. 8 (Interpariétal ou Occipital supérieur, Cuv.), supra-occipital. 9 (Occipital externe, Cuv.), Paroccipital. 10 (Occipital latéral, Cuv.), Exoccipital. 11, Alisphenoid. 12, Mastoid. 13 (Rocher, Cuv.), Petrosal and Otosteal. 14, Orbitosphenoid. 15 (Sphénoïde antérieur, Cuv., Ethmoïd and Ethmoturbinal, Owen), Basisphenoid (Huxley). 16, Vomer. 17 (Intermaxillaire, Cuv.), Premaxillary. 18, Maxillary. 19 (Sous-orbitaire, Cuv.), Infraorbital ring. 20 (Nasal, Cuv.), Turbinal. 22, Palatine. 23 (Temporal, Cuvier, Epitympanic, Owen), Hyomandibular (Huxley),

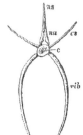

The abdominal or trunk vertebræ have two superior or dorsal processes, which passing upwards coalesce and form an arch (*na*), termed the neural arch which protects the spinal chord. At the summit of this arch the bones join and form a spinous elongation, the neural spine (*ns*). Two epipleural spines (*es*) pass outwards from the body of each vertebræ, while from either side a rib is directed downwards.

Fig. 8. Abdominal vertebra of salmon. *c.* centrum or body : *na.* neural arch : *ns.* neural spine : *es.* epipleural spine.

The caudal vertebræ (fig. 7) are furnished superiorly with neural arches, (*na*) and spines (*ns*), but well developed transverse processes are absent, while along the lower surfaces of the bodies of each is a second or the hæmal arch (*ha*) which serves to protect blood vessels, while inferiorly from this arch springs a hæmal spine (*hs*).

Along the median line of the body, between the neural or hæmal spines certain vertically directed dagger-shaped bones are inserted, to which are attached the bases of the dorsal and the anal fins.

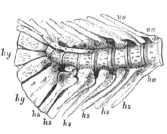

The hindmost caudal vertebra, which is of a small size, articulates posteriorly with a fan-shaped bone, which along with the last few hæmal processes are similarly enlarged and flattened, and termed hypural bones (*hy*), which support the main portion of the caudal fin. The last two vertebræ are generally counted as one, a course I shall follow, as in specimens when fresh or in spirit it sometimes becomes difficult to distinguish the line of separation between these two bones. The epipleural in the embryonic stage is connected with the termination of the notochord which lies beneath.

Fig. 9. Hind end of vertebral column of a salmon. *ha.* hæmal arch : *hs.* hæmal spines : *hy.* hypural bones : *na.* neural arch : *ns.* neural spine.

24 (*Os transverse*, Cuv.), Pterygoid. 25 (*Pterygoidien interne*, Cuv.), Entopterygoid. 26 (*Jugal*, Cuv., *Hypotympanic*, Owen), Quadrate (Huxley). 27 (*Tympanal*, Cuv. *Pretympanic*, Owen), Metapterygoid (Huxley). 28, Opercle. 29, Stylohyal. 30, Preopercle. 31 (*Mesotympanic*, Owen), Symplectic. 32, Subopercle. 33, Interopercle. 34, Dentary. 35, Articular. 36, Angular. 37, Epihyal. 38, Ceratohyal. 39 and 40, Basihyal. 41 (*Os lingual*, Cuv.) Glossohyal. 42 (*Queue de l'os hyoïde*, Cuv.), Urohyal. 43, Branchiostegal rays. 46 (*Surscapulaire*, Cuv. *Post-temporal*, Parker), Suprascapular. 47 (*Supraclavicula*, Parker), Scapula. 48 (*Humeral*, Cuv. *Clavicula*, Parker), Coracoid. 49 and 50 (*Coracoid*, Cuv. *Postclavicula*, Parker), Epicoracoid. 51 (*Cubical*, Cuv. *Coracoid*, Parker), Radius. 52 (*Radial*, Cuv., *Scapula*, Parker), Ulna. 53, Carpals. 53 bis, 54, and 55, Basibranchials. 56, Inferior Pharyngeals. 57, Hypobranchial. 58, Ceratobranchials. 59, Upper Epibranchials of first branchial arch. 61, Epibranchials. 62 (*Pharyngobranchial*, Owen), Superior Pharyngeals. 68, Abdominal vertebræ. 69, Caudal vertebræ. 70, Hypurals. 72, Rib. 73, Epipleural spines. 74, Interneural spines. 76, First Interneural. 79, Interhæmal spines. 80, Pubic.

† Owen considered that the skulls of these fishes are originally composed from four vertebræ irrespective of bones of the splanchnoskeleton and dermoskeleton : while Stannius, Parker, and others have arranged them in accordance with their development.

As already remarked the number of vertebræ in the spinal column of Salmonoids is not invariably identical in every individual of any given species, and this inconstancy may be natural or consequent upon accident or disease. Occasionally a very large one may be seen occupying the space where two naturally exist, as shown by the number of neural or hæmal arches and spines (figure 7) for two bones being present, or even the bodies of several vertebræ appear to coalesce into one as will be more fully observed upon when the description of the hog-backed-trout is arrived at   On the other hand two or even three small vertebræ may take the place of one large one   In fishes wherein the number of these bones is normally about sixty an extreme variation of four or five, especially when such has not been shown to be constant, cannot be looked upon as beyond what might reasonably be anticipated in a single species, and inconstant variations, unless conjoined to other differences, would scarcely justify the creation of new specific names for their reception

The skull, or that portion of the skeleton which articulates posteriorly with the first vertebra, encloses the brain as well as forms the face, and although it contains too many component parts to be fully discussed here, still a few remarks are necessary respecting such bones as more or less constitute the orbit, mouth, and respiratory organs, while it must be noted that the bones especially of the head, undergo great changes with age, even after the maturity of the fish has been arrived at

The upper jaw is formed of two main bones, the premaxillaries (Plate 1, No 17), which are furnished with teeth and placed at the anterior end of the snout in the middle line of the head   The posterior portion of the bone passes upwards and backwards, while the anterior or the tooth-bearing portion forms the upper and front edge of the mouth   The maxilla (18) is likewise toothed and articulates with the palatine bone   it is somewhat dilated towards its distal end, where a small, ovoid-shaped, supplementary bone (18') rests upon its upper and outer surface and has been likened to an ossified labial cartilage   The maxilla and premaxillary are connected together by a narrow membrane, causing them to move parallel to each other   The width and strength of the maxilla in adult fishes depends to a considerable extent upon the food on which the fish has subsisted during its lifetime, it being comparatively stronger in the trout than in the salmon and in fresh-water than in anadromous races   If it has been much called into action it may greatly exceed in size and strength what is present in examples in which it has been less employed   It appears to be almost the invariable rule that the jaws are larger in adult males than in females, while in old examples the lower jaw is provided with a hook at its extremity, that is seasonably developed during the breeding period, but is always more or less present in old specimens

The mandible or lower jaw, consists of two branches or rami, connected together anteriorly in the median line by ligament, where it is called the symphysis and which union becomes ossified in old fish   Each branch of the jaw is made up of several pieces in the young, which are solidified into one by age   The upper and anterior being the largest portion of the jaw (34), bears teeth and is termed the dentary part, its inner surface is deeply excavated in order to receive a cylindrical cartilage or "Meckels cartilage," the remains of an embryonic condition, the small angular (36) and articular (35) portions of this bone being ossified portions of that cartilage   Behind the dentary portion and along the upper edge is the articular bone which on its upper and posterior edge has an articular cavity which receives the quadrate (26) and also sends up a coronoid process to which a ligament from the maxillary and masticatory muscles is attached   this bone anteriorly is more or less sheathed in the rougher dentary portion.

The suborbital ring of bones (19) passes round the lower edge of the eye, and consists of several pieces, the anterior of which is often termed the pre-orbital or lachrymal

The opercular pieces or those bones forming the gill-covers (28, 30, 32, 33) have already been referred to (page 12 ante) the most anterior or innermost the preopercle (30) articulating with the tympano-mandibular arch of the skull, or the hyomandibular (23) and the symplectic (31)   When remarking upon the form of the opercular bones it must not be overlooked that three, 28, 42, 33, at their edges, often more or less overlap one another

The scapular arch which supports the pectoral fin is joined to the occipital bone, and contains the following bones commencing from above   the supra-scapular (46), articulating with which is the scapular (47), next the coracoid (48), and attached to it is the epicoracoid (49, 50), while it is united below either by suture or ligament to the same bone on the opposite side   To the coracoid (48) are articulated two others, the radius (51), and ulna (52), and two rows of small bones placed between the forearm and the fin, or the carpals (53) and meta carpals

The form of the preopercle varies among individuals belonging to the same species, sometimes the change being merely due to age or sex, but in some races the development of its lower limb is much more pronounced than it is in others obtained from a different locality   This merely shows that in the marine as well as in the fresh-water races there are fish subject to variations in the shape of this bone   The lower limb is very short in the young, elongating with age in some forms, but not so in others, while an arrest of development may easily take place even on opposite sides of the head of a specimen, which, were this the sole criterion of species, might, and sometimes does, produce forms said to be typical of *Salmo trutta* on one side of the head, and *S albus* or *brachypoma* on the other

The hyoid arch which is composed of a central and two lateral portions, is attached to the temporal bones by two slender styliform ones termed stylo-hyoids (29)   The bones along the two branches commencing from behind forwards are the epihyal (37) to which the stylo-hyoids are affixed   the ceratohyal (38) to which the branchiostegal rays are attached at their bases, next two small bones termed basihyals (39, 40) between which the small glossohyal (41) extends forwards to the tongue, while a single bone, the urohyal (42), passes backwards

Of the five branchial arches, four bear gills and one is destitute of them, bounded externally by the hyoid arch   they are attached inferiorly and along the median line to a chain of bones, the basibranchials (53, 54, 55), which are situated above the urohyal (42) and are anteriorly connected with the body of the hyoid   These branchial arches pass upwards, and are attached by ligaments to the under surface of the skull   The three anterior branchial arches are each composed of four pieces of bone, which commencing from their inferior attachment are known as the hypobranchial (57), ceratobranchial (58), and the epibranchial (61)   In the fourth arch the epibranchial piece is wanting, and superiorly the more expanded upper piece which generally bears teeth, is known as the superior pharyngeal bone (62)   while the fifth arch is composed of the ceratobranchial (58) only, and known as the inferior pharyngeal, and likewise is furnished with some fine teeth

The chief masses of muscular structure are seen in the four great lateral muscles of the body, which are arranged longitudinally, but divided by oblique tendinous bands of a gelatinous character (and which dissolve on boiling) into numerous flakes or semi-conical masses termed myocommas   These four longitudinal layers of muscles have the tendinous bands directed much as follows   the upper series passing downwards and backwards, the succeeding layer downwards and forwards, the third downwards and backwards, and the lowest downwards and forwards   These flakes are arched backwards, being convex anteriorly   The number of tendinous intersecting bands correspond with the vertebræ into which they are inserted *

The nervous system in these fishes in proportion to that of the general mass of the body is comparatively small, while in the adult the brain doesnotfill the cranial cavity

As regards thirst, it would seem either to be unknown to these creatures ; or living as they do in a watery medium it may be quenched by means of endosmosis through the skin   Were this not the case it would be difficult to conceive how such a longing could be satisfied while residing in salt water

* For an account of the various muscles employed for the movement of the fins, the jaws, eyes, breathing, &c , the student must be referred to treatises on comparative anatomy

The skin, excluding that of the head, is scaled, the scales being cycloid and partially imbedded at their bases, the posterior or external portions of each over-lapping its neighbour like tiles, and consequently they are termed imbricate They have then free edges directed backwards, thus preventing their being any impediment in the water when swimming Scales increase in size in proportion with the growth of the body of the fish consequently the adult has the same number as the young, and also they are imbricated to much the same extent   The number of rows existing along the lateral line is subject to considerable variation, while those in a line passing from the hind edge of the adipose dorsal fin downwards and forwards to the lateral-line afford one of the most constant characters by which these fishes may be discriminated there being from 10 to 11 in *S salar* and its varieties and 13 to 15 in the various forms of British trout

Although fishes do not periodically shed or change their scales as buds do their feathers, still such as have been lost by injury can be renewed   Special organs of touch are developed in fishes in several different manners   Even papillæ, as round the mouths or on the lips, of some forms are highly sensitive, and as has been shown by Leydig and others they are abundantly supplied with nerves

The lateral-line consists of a series of tubes along either side of the body, and is often known as the muciferous system, but although from it mucous is excreted, it is essentially an organ of sense, and as such is variously modified, while the inside of the canal is lined with epithelial cells, and here nerves ramify, and terminate in an expansion

Intimately related to the tegumentary system and the composition of scales is the subject of colour   Among the finny tribes the display of colour may be of the most varied description, some tints being permanent, many transient, and others again of periodical occurrence   Certain of these colours are due to the influence of light* while they may vary in the same fresh-water species owing to the character of the water they inhabit, for should the latter be opaque and muddy, fish as a rule are darker than when obtained from localities where it is clean, those in running streams are generally lighter and brighter than when from stagnant pools, or such as are from shallow pieces of water than from those that are deep, while if captured in dark caverns they are frequently destitute of both colour and vision

Age and season likewise exercise an influence in this respect, as do also the state of health and temporary local emotions   In the very young but few markings or colours are present but these rapidly develop themselves by the time, or even before, the first breeding season has been reached, when the brilliancy of the individual has often attained to its maximum   This nuptial adornment is generally acquired a short time prior to this period, subsequent to which it usually disappears   Some see in the markings on these creatures grounds for assuming the probability of the descent of many forms from some common ancestral progenitor   Thus, among the young of the members of the *Salmonidæ*, dark bands or bars down the sides are almost universal, being evidently hereditary throughout the family † These bars, as well as the black and red spots, are almost lost in anadromous forms when they are in a condition to migrate into salt water, for then they assume their silvery smolt stage   In large rivers it is rare for bands to be retained in adult trout, while most of the black and red ocellated spots as a rule remain, although instances have been recorded in which they have entirely

---

* Pouchet and others have pointed out that the changeable tegumentary colours of fish depend more especially upon two conditions *Firstly*, we have iridescence effected by an interference with the rays of light, owing to the presence in the scales of thin plates or ridges, and in these forms the tints change with great rapidity in accordance with the angle at which they are viewed such lamellar colouring is common among insects, crustacea, and some fishes—it is beautifully seen in the Dolphin, *Coryphæna*, and the scale of a common herring furnishes a good example *Secondly*, a distinct anatomical element, as chromatophores or colour-sacs, which are often highly coloured may be present and capable of changing their form under special influences, which are apparently directly connected with impressions of colour received by the eye and brought about by the reflex action of the nervous system

† This same banding of the young is seen in some species of the horse mackerel or *Caranx*, flying-fish or *Trocerus*, the gar fish or *Belone*, &c , in which they are usually a sign of the immaturity of the individual

disappeared   While in some mountain streams they are present in fish weighing as much as half-a-pound

We may generally anticipate non-migratory forms being more vividly-coloured than such as are periodically residents in the sea, or brackish water, which seems, as a rule, to cause a fish to assume a general silvery* or steel colour with or without X-shaped or starred† black spots, and these latter are not surrounded by a light circle   On the other hand, as will be more fully referred to under the head of "trout," some examples from lochs and also from fresh-water localities where access to or from the sea is impossible, are found to be of a silvery colour, due to local circumstances or possibly sterile conditions of the specimens

The sense of taste in fishes is popularly considered to be but slightly developed, a conclusion to a great extent arrived at because most fish bolt their food   On the other hand, the angler, line-fisherman, and pisciculturist perceive that they will often ravenously devour one kind of food, rejecting another, that they have their likes and dislikes, which must have some connection with the character of the object or else with its taste

That fishes possess the sense of smell has long been known, and in olden times anglers employed certain essential oils to add zest to their baits   Some Salmonoids are now and then captured which, due to accident, disease, hereditary malformation or want of development, are found totally devoid of vision, and yet are in good condition and well nourished, and the question arises how did they obtain food ?   In addition to the sense of touch they are provided with organs of smell to enable them to receive impressions from the surrounding medium, directing them to their food or warning them against impurities in the water   These organs are situated much as we perceive them in the higher animals, but they do not communicate with the mouth, nor are they related to the function of breathing, for were their delicate lining membrane subject to incessant contact with currents of water, it would doubtless have a deteriorating effect, owing to the density of the respired element   The nostrils are depressions or cavities, lined with a large amount of a highly vascular pituitary membrane, packed into as small a compass as possible, while there are two external openings situated on either side of the median line of the snout

Hearing is developed in fishes, and it is very remarkable how any diversity of opinion can exist as to their possessing this sense   Lacépède relates how some fish, which had been kept in the basin of the Tuileries for upwards of a century, would come when they were called by their names, while in many parts of Germany, trout, carp, and tench were summoned to their food by the ringing of a bell   The internal auditory apparatus is placed within the cranial cavity, its chief constituent parts are the labyrinth, which is composed of three semi-circular canals and a vestibule, which latter expands into one or more sacs, where the ear-bones or otoliths are lodged   A tympanum and tympanic cavity are absent   They possess fontanelles between the bones forming the roof of the skull, and which, being closed by very thin bone or skin, sounds from the surrounding water may be readily transmitted to the contiguous internal ear   But the chief mode in which hearing is carried on must be due to the surface of the fish being affected by vibrations of the water, and the sounds are transmitted directly to the internal ear   or else by means of the air-bladder acting as a sounding-board

The methods adopted by fish to communicate with one another are various, thus in some forms a distinct sound is emitted, as in the horse-fishes, *Hippocampi* while among the Salmonidæ it is not unusual for the angler, when the water is

---

* Mr Lockington (*American Naturalist*, May 1880, p 368) observed somewhat the same phenomenon in the Western hemisphere, where the *Salmo irideus*, a resident in all Californian brooks and rivers, descends in the autumn to the sea, and when in salt water changes its colour to a steel blue, while its spots mostly disappear

† It cannot be admitted that the black X shaped or starred spots are invariably due to the influence of salt water, as we see them present in our strictly fresh-water grayling, *Thymallus*, also salmon grilse reared entirely in fresh water have many more spots then the marine visitant (*see* plates III and IV)   While in Willoughby (p 194) we find, 'in Salmonum et Truttarum speciebus distinguendis nimium ne crede colori," and we may also apply the words of Ovid concerning the Polypus to these fishes, "Sub lege loco mutatque colorem"

2 *

even moderately clear and ho has alarmed a trout, to observe that it first ceases feeding in order to watch him, subsequently, if unsatisfied, it darts away, and immediately all which may be within sight do the same, apparently alarmed at the movements of the first fish

Before offering remarks upon respiration as effected among these fishes, some observations appear to be desirable respecting their air- or swim-bladders This organ may be likened to a sac placed in the abdominal cavity above the centre of gravity where it lies beneath the backbone or vertebral column from which it is separated by the kidneys, while inferiorly the peritoneum lies between it and the intestines In the embryo it originates as an offshoot from the dorsal surface of the upper portion of the alimentary canal, and subsequently elongates into a blind tube, the terminal portion of which finally enlarges into what constitutes the air-bladder

The air-bladder is generally considered to be homologous with the lungs[*] of some of the higher orders of vertebrates,[†] being a sac with an outer fibrous and glistening coat, and an inner mucous and vascular one   A pervious pneumatic duct, the remains of the embryonic structure, exists throughout life, connecting it with the dorsal surface of the alimentary canal   Its uses are mainly mechanical, as a hydrostatic organ or for the purpose of flotation as by a contraction or distention of its walls it is able to condense or rarify the contained gases, thus enabling its possessor to maintain a desired level in the water   The fish has likewise the power of renewing, expelling, compressing or dilating its gaseous contents, so that it can rise or fall as necessity or inclination dictates   It has also acoustic uses, being partially employed for hearing, owing to its connection with the internal ear

During respiration the blood is oxygenated at the gills, by means of the oxygen (of the atmospheric air which is normally present in water) and carbonic acid gas passes off.   For the purpose of breathing the fish takes or gulps in water by its mouth, this passes backwards to the gills, and is then discharged outwards by the gill-openings.   Should anything prevent the water passing as described, or should the delicate fringes of the gills become dry so that they adhere together, or should they be choked by mud, the blood cannot be oxygenated   While various causes, as heat, or the water being at a very high elevation, may occasion an insufficiency of air being present in it, thus impeding or even entirely stopping respiration, as would also be the case were the fish in distilled water   Both an arterial and venous circulation are present, one for nutrition, the other for excretion as by respiration or other means, while a portal system also exists

The heart is situated a short distance behind the lower jaw and between the branchial and abdominal cavities, it consists of an auricle or atrium having thin walls and into which a large venous sinus that is situated outside the pericardiac cavity, and which receives the blood from the venous system, empties itself It also possesses a strong muscular ventricle and an arterial bulb, this latter being a pear-shaped enlargement situated at the base of the arterial system and termed the " bulbus arteriosus " which is destitute of contractile power

According to the experiments of Dr J Davy, when water in which trout were placed was artificially raised to 75° or more they became very active and tried to leap out, on the contrary when a char was similarly treated with water of 80° it went to the bottom with its head downwards as if seeking a cooler stratum ‡

---

* Among Dipnoids it is double, lung like, and communicates throughout life by means of a duct and glottis with the œsophagus or pharynx and on its ventral side   In the sturgeon this organ does not appear to be employed for respiration, while it opens on the dorsal surface of the alimentary canal and is not guarded by a glottis

† Professor Albrecht, of Brussels, remarked (*Physiological Society of Berlin*, Jan 16th, 1885) that " many naturalists were of opinion that the swimming-bladder was homologous with the lungs, which likewise represented a tube in communication with the intestinal tract, an opinion however decidedly opposed to the views of the speaker, for in all fishes the swimming bladder was placed supra-intestinally on the dorsal side, while the lungs are invariably situated infra-intestinally or on the ventral side of the intestinal canal "

‡ In August 1882, Dr Davy (*Physiological Researches*) placed a common trout of about a quarter of a pound weight into a good volume of water at 62°, which was pretty rapidly raised

The teeth in the salmon, trout, and char are of a conical shape and used more for capturing than masticating their prey : they are present in both upper (*m*) and lower (*ma*) jaws, on the vomer (*v*), palatine bones (*p*), and tongue (*t*). They are frequently shed and as constantly renewed by others

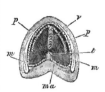

appearing from beneath or else on one side of the discarded ones. As age creeps on the number of their teeth become more and more reduced, the teeth-bearing portion of the bones diminish in extent more rapidly in such forms as frequent the sea than those which pass their time in fresh waters.

Fig. 9. Diagram of teeth inside mouth of trout: *m*. maxilla: *ma*. mandible: *p*. palatines: *t*. tongue: *v*. vomer.

The size and arrangement of the vomerine teeth are somewhat varied, as they diminish more or less rapidly in number with certain conditions, especially the character, whether saline or fresh, of the waters in which the fish live. They also vary greatly in different specimens of even the same universally admitted species, from what exists in the earliest period of their lives when they are in a double row, to old age when all may be absent, consequently it would be unsafe to base specific differences upon this dentition. When the teeth-bearing ridge commences to become narrower, the teeth are at first forced into a more or less irregular single line, and subsequently this ridge becomes absorbed commencing from behind and gradually extending forwards and the teeth as a consequence fall out.

The teeth in the jaws are comparatively stronger[*] in fresh-water trout than in salmon or sea trout, as will be subsequently more fully alluded to.

The lingual teeth or those on the tongue are in a row of about five or six on either side of the middle line and the largest in the mouth : they are curved backwards and thus prevent the escape of prey after it has been once seized.

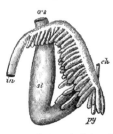

They are shed and renewed similarly to the other teeth in the mouth of these fishes, and are more commonly in reduced numbers or absent in marine than in the fresh-water forms.

Fig. 10. Teeth on tongue as seen from in front.

The mouth, situated at the commencement of the intestinal canal, is the receptacle both of water passing to the gills for respiration and of food transmitted to the stomach for nutrition. The gastric portion of this canal consists of an œsophagus (*œs*) and a stomach (*st*), between which is a constriction—the cardiac—

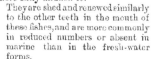

while at the inferior extremity is a second constriction termed the pylorus. But due to the stomach having a siphonal shape, or one which somewhat resembles a bent tube, its two orifices are more or less approximated and cause food to be retained there as in a cæcum. The length of the intestines is shorter

Fig. 11. *œs*. œsophagus : *ch*. chylopoetic duct : *in*. small intestines : *py*. pyloric cæca.

to 75° by additions of warm water, when it became very active, and tried to leap out. In an hour the temperature was increased to 80°, and after a few more minutes to 85°, when it became convulsed, and, although transferred to cool water, died. When the water had sunk to 70°, a smaller trout and a minnow were put in, and although the next morning the temperature had sunk to 67°, the trout was dead, but the minnow had not suffered. A par of the salmon, about four inches long, was similarly treated, the water in half-an-hour being raised from 60° to 70°, and now it tried to escape. The water was raised to 80°, and it became torpid and convulsed ; at 84° it seems to have died. A char of about the same size had the water gradually raised to 80°, when it appears to have succumbed. The trout tried to escape by leaping out of the water, while the char kept to the bottom with its head downwards, as if seeking for a cooler locality.

[*] "The trout," observed Dr. J. Davy, "when it feeds principally upon fish, must be extremely active and strong ; consequently, from its predatory mobile habits, acquires large teeth, large fleshy fins, thick skin, and great pectoral fins for turning."

than that of the body, but the lining membrane is puckered with transverse folds thus increasing the extent of its secreting and absorbing surface, which is still further assisted by the presence of cæcal appendages The commencement of the small intes-

tine is marked by the orifice of the chylopoetic duct (*ch*) while at the beginning of the large intestine is a circular valve which is succeeded by several others which are completely or incompletely transverse (fig 12)

Fig 12. Cast of a part of the interior of the lower portion
of the intestinal tube in salmon showing the valves, :

It is curious to observe how, when some of these fishes select hard substances for their diet, the coats of their stomachs, especially in its lower portion, may become thickened, as in the gillaroo trout and other salmonoid forms

The cæcal* or pyloric appendages or pyloric cæca (*py*), already alluded to, are secreting tubes closed at their outer end and situated at the commencement and along the edge of the first part of the small intestines, where they begin in three or four rows, which in the trout are gradually reduced to two, and finally to one Into these tubes food does not enter, but in the rich secretion which flows from them it is very common in the salmon to find a species of tapeworm (*Bothriocephalus*) These pyloric cæca are generally considered as the representatives of a modified pancreas in addition to the very rudimentary form of that organ which opens into the small intestine in close proximity to the chylopoetic duct (*ch*)

The number of these cæca are variable, fifty-one to seventy-seven having been observed in the common salmon, and to differ largely in the various races of trout as will be subsequently alluded to They are capable of distension, of subdivision, of amalgamation between two or more, and of being longer or shorter than is ordinarily the case The difficulty does not appear in discovering variation in number, but in determining within what fixed limits they exist in a given species The eggs sent from the brook trout of Hampshire and Buckinghamshire, by Mr Frank Buckland and Mr Francis Francis, to Tasmania, developed into a large race in which these cæca seem to have normally reached fifty-two. showing a considerable increase in number and proving such to be inconstant and consequently of little if any value for the purpose of discriminating a species Marine species and varieties of Salmonidæ appear to generally possess more of these appendages than do the strictly fresh-water races,‡ as would also seem to be the case in brook trout when transferred to a warmer clime

The urinary organs are composed of the kidneys as an excretory apparatus, the ureters, the bladder, and the urethra §

These organs are distinctly separated anteriorly one from the other they are placed close to the vertebral column, but divided from the abdominal cavity and the intestines by the air-bladder, and the peritoneum

Salmonidæ, in common with other teleostean or bony fishes, are diœcious, the sexes being present in different individuals In the male the reproductive organs or the testes are symmetrical, distinct one from the other, placed beneath the

---

* These appendages are more readily separated one from another and counted after they have been a few hours in alcohol ; while if first inflated with air by means of a blow pipe or with spirit the cæca will be rendered more distinct

† Parnell, struck with the number of these cæca in the Lochleven trout, termed it *Salmo cæcifer* Dr Gunther considered of the number of pyloric appendages that " there can be no doubt that this character may materially assist in fixing a species," and at page 11 ante, can be seen the numbers he attributed to each form

‡ This is in accordance with what it has been already stated (page 6), that cæcal appendages are more common in marine than in fresh water fishes, and almost confined to such as have a marine ancestry

§ The kidneys, according to Vogt and some others, appear to be composed of the Wolfian bodies, structures persistent among fishes, but which are not permanent among other vertebrate animals, whereas other authors deny this The anterior portion or head contains no malpighian bodies and was regarded by Balfour as a lymphatic gland.

vertebral column and the "vasa deferentia," as their ducts are termed, uniting near the termination of the urethra, while their contents or the seminal fluid, which is white and of a thick, milky consistence, is popularly known as the soft roe or milt. Under the microscope this substance is found to be composed of an infinite number of microscopic organisms, termed spermatozoa or zoosperms, which consist of a small head and an elongated tail-like termination. These organisms are exceedingly active during the period of their existence, the duration of which has been computed by different investigators at from two and-a-half to thirty minutes, but should they be placed in water then lives are rapidly cut short, although a good deal depends upon temperature at which this takes place. They are found to be surrounded by an alkaline fluid composed partly of phosphates and partly of other constituents, and in it they will live for some days, even after removal from the fish, provided no water be added, M Vrasski having kept them alive six days in a tightly-corked bottle. The reproductive powers of this milt may be sufficiently matured in some Salmonoids at the termination of their second year to be capable of fertilizing eggs although the progeny may possibly be weak, sickly, or even imperfectly developed.

In the female, the ovaries which are symmetrical organs are destitute of a closed covering, while their internal surface is lined with stroma and transversely plaited. Here the development of the eggs takes place, each of which is invested by a fine membrane, and by it they hang suspended to the ovary, the length of the pedicle decreasing as the egg augments in size. But as the ovaries are destitute of oviducts it necessarily occurs that when the investing membrane bursts the ovum falls into the abdominal cavity from whence it is extruded through the abdominal pore.

There is a considerable seasonable augmentation in the size of the procreative organs in such of these fishes as are not sterile, while certain external secondary sexual characters are also observable. In the male a knob appears at the upper end of the extremity of the lower jaw, while the skin on the surface of the head and along the back becomes thick and spongy. At these periods also the colours generally become more brilliant, and the fish takes less food, or even ceases feeding. As eggs given by late breeding fishes cannot hatch out for some time subsequently to those of the early breeders, much of the summer may be consumed before the yolk-sacs of these alevins are absorbed, and as a consequence the fry may be backward as winter sets in. Although the climate has much to do with the period at which spawning* occurs, it would appear that the organs of generation may be stimulated by certain kinds of food† while, should their diet be unduly reduced, such may cause seasonal sterility‡ by

---

* The term "spawn" is generally employed as denoting the eggs and milt that are extruded from fishes, but in some localities it is likewise used when referring to the young of these creatures prior to the absorption of the yelk sac. While even in Acts of Parliament it is not clear if this latter was not what was alluded to in the two following among many other instances, more especially as the eggs of eels were then unknown. "None shall use any Net, Device, or Engine whatsoever to destroy, kill, or take the spawn or fry of eels, pike, salmon, or of any other fish," &c , 1 Eliz cap 17. "Every person who between the first day of March and the last of May shall do any Act whereby the spawn of fish shall be destroyed shall forfeit the instruments," &c , Stat 3 Car 2, cap 9

† At Howietoun the clam *Pecten*, and mussel *Mytilus*, having been scalded are used as food for the purpose of stimulating the breeding fishes

‡ At Howietoun it was observed in 1884, that the American Char (*Salmo fontinalis*) suffered a good deal from fungus, owing, it was believed, to their over-feeding. Consequently, in 1885 their diet was reduced, and that with the best results as regards fungus , but when the breeding season came round it was found that large numbers were sterile. That this is solely a question of food a most interesting instance in pond No 5 may be quoted. Here the hybrids were kept and fully fed and one female *fontinalis* was placed along with them. She attained to a large size, and in November, 1885, was found to be full of eggs. In August, 1886, my attention was directed to two ponds at Cowley, near Cheltenham, which, after having been drained, mudded, and puddled with clay, were stocked in December, 1884, and January, 1885, with yearling Lochleven trout, received from Mr Andrews of Guildford. Due to causes which will subsequently be fully referred to, those in the upper pond did not exceed seven inches in length, and were sterile, those in the lower pond were much better nourished, averaging about eleven inches in length, and had the generative organs well developed

preventing the development of the ova, or should they be present in the ovaries
by arresting, or retarding their further increase in size.

Among these fishes—at least in the salmon—the female is normally one year
later than the male in attaining to a breeding condition, while it has been
observed at Howietoun that the extrusion of milt or ova may be retarded even
for several weeks in ripe fish if placed in a box having smooth sides, and through
which a sufficient stream of water passes. The eggs are ovoid, or nearly circular,
elastic bodies of a clear white, pink, or coral colour, the outer coat which is
porous, possessing much toughness and elasticity, properties most important to
its future existence in the localities where it is naturally deposited, or in the
subsequent movements which it may have to go through. On the surface of each
egg may be seen a microscopic orifice (looking like a healed ulcer on the cornea
of the human eye), termed the micropyle, which allows the entrance of the
spermatozoa, without which it would remain unfertilized, and consequently
barren.

The eggs, as extruded, are soft, but rapidly absorb water which fills up the
interspace between the outer shell and its delicate inner lining, and as soon as
this period of absorption has passed by, which has been considered not to exceed
thirty minutes in trout eggs,* it is impossible for the ova to be fertilized. Should
these eggs have milt added to them in the water, it is evident that unless
fertilization rapidly occurs the spermatozoa may have perished. On the other
hand, should eggs be obtained from a fish and expressed into a dry pan (or one
into which no water has been placed), and milt added in their own fluid and
thus stirred up among the ova, the supposition would be that these organisms
would more likely be active when thus employed than in water which rapidly
destroys their vitality. And fish-culturists have found in practice that this which
is termed the "dry process" is far more successful than when water is first used
or the "moist process" employed.

A difference of opinion respecting the persistent or variable size of the eggs of
Salmonidæ appears to prevail, which could not continue to exist if contending
parties would take the trouble to measure them when freshly removed from the
parent fish, or as lying in the hatching-troughs. For they do not increase in size
during the process of incubation, although such as die in fresh water become
sodden, white, and somewhat distended † While the observations recorded below
and which have been since made conclusively show that the eggs of these fishes

---

* Mr James Annin (*American Fish Cultural Association*, 1883, page 110) observed that during
the past winter he had made an experiment with eggs taken from a fine healthy brook trout,
Salmo fontinalis, impregnated by a number of good males of the same species. First 350 eggs
had milt added, and then washed off as quickly as possible, and 45 seconds after extrusion
they were placed on the trays in the hatching troughs. Next 350 more eggs were expressed from
the same fish, and were allowed to stand three minutes before the milt was washed off. The
rest of the eggs from this fish, 935 in number, were allowed to remain thirty minutes in the
spawning pan. The three lots were carefully placed on the trays, the bad ones were daily
removed until the eyes became visible, when the results were as follows.—Of the first lot only
six were unimpregnated, or about one in 58, of the second lot 31, or about 1 in 11, and of the last
lot about 1 in 1 $\frac{1}{16}$. Max von dem Borne observed (*O.-U. Fischerei-Zeitung*, Vienna, 1880) that he
had sent salmon eggs and milt from Basle mixed together in a hog's bladder without the addition
of water. The journey lasted three days, and the temperature was high, in spite of which they
arrived in good condition, while some eggs treated in the ordinary manner, and similarly sent,
were almost all received dead.

† Harmer in 1767 (*Transactions of the Royal Society*, " On the Fecundity of Fishes ") gave
a table showing the number of eggs which he had observed in certain forms of fishes, among
which the Salmonidæ were not included. He remarked, "From this table it appears that the
size of the eggs is nearly the same in great and small fishes of the same species, at the same time
of the year." And these observations may be found, with but little variation, in the writings of
authors from that period up to recent years, as perhaps in no branch of biology are assertions
once made more dogmatically adhered to, and that without re-investigation, than in Ichthyology.
Passing on to the *Zoological Record* of 1864, p 170, we find that Professor Malmgren having
observed that certain Salmonoids in a lake in Finland were descendents of the common Salmon,
whose access to the sea had been cut off owing to an elevation of the land, mentioned as one of
the present differences that this fresh-water and dwarfed breed gave smaller ova than *Salmo salar*.
In this conclusion Dr Gunther did not coincide, remarking that " the last character [or size of
the ova] will be considered very significant by all who may have a more extended knowledge of

undoubtedly differ in size The following figures which will be more fully entered upon when considering the various species, are here given from measurements made at Howietoun   Diameter of eggs of grilse 0 20 to 0 22 of an inch ; of a 16 lb salmon, 0 24 in , Lochleven trout at Howietoun, 2 and 3-year-old, 0 17 in , 6-year-old, 0 18 to 0 19 in , 8-year-old, 0 20 to 0 24 in   American char, 2-year-old, 0 14 in , 3-year-old, 0 17 in , 4-year-old, 0 18 in

The above are only some out of the many measurements which I have made, and show very conclusively that the diameter of the eggs in salmonoids increases, at least up to a certain period, with the age and probably the condition of the parents ; thus the ova of grilse are inferior in size to those of the salmon   And in large trout as in the older Lochlevens there is an augmentation in the thickness of the shell, a rather important question to the fish-culturist, because such shells require a strong embryo in order to readily hatch , this, however, may be obtained by giving an increased supply of water during their eyed period.   It was also found, as a rule, that trout eggs obtained latest in the season were of rather larger size than such as had been taken in the earlier months, while in nature these larger eggs generally produce more rapidly growing young and thus to a certain extent counterbalance any bad effects from late hatching

Next is the consideration of whether any difference is perceptible in the eggs of two parents of the same age that have been kept under identical conditions ? Among the young salmon reared at Howietoun from eggs obtained from the same parents, and reared in the same pond, some taken on December 1st, and again on the 13th, 1884, averaged 0 22 of an inch, some from similar fish on December 9th averaged 0 20 of an inch, while others taken the same day were 0 22 of an inch   The same phenomenon has been observed among the Lochleven trout, wherein, although the diameter of the eggs of fish at eight years of age was generally 0 24 of an inch, in some it was 0 22, in a few 0 21, and in three or four 0 20 , also in six-year-olds it has been observed to vary from 0 18 to 0 19 of an inch   That such variations might theoretically be anticipated most of us must admit, for whatever causes deficiency of nutrition might occasion diminution in the size of the ova   Also the size of the parent ought possibly to be taken into account, for disease, crowding them when young, and other causes may dwarf these fishes, and such would probably give comparatively small eggs.

Can we detect any variation in the size of the eggs given by a single fish ?   I have already adduced instances of this among salmon or rather grilse and Lochleven trout   In November, 1884, I placed 80 unimpregnated eggs of one of these fish in a tub of water, wherein they were kept for a week, the water being

fishes, as the size of the ova is not only invariably the same in individuals of whatever size, but, as far as our experience reaches, is even often characteristic of the species of a genus "   This opinion, slightly modified, Dr Gunther still apparently held in 1880, for he asserted (Introduction to the Study of Fishes, p. 159) that " the ova of Teleostean fishes are extremely variable in size, quite independently of the size of the parent species   The ova of large and small individuals of the same species, of course, do not differ in size "

On the other hand, Mr E Blanchard in 1866 (Poissons des Eaux Douces de la France, p 461) observed that the ova " of the grilse are always sensibly smaller than those of the adult Salmon "   Livingston-Stone, 1877 (Domesticated Trout, 3rd edition), remarked that in American Trout (Salmo fontinalis) that reside in spring-water, which is equivalent to a diminished supply of food, smaller eggs are developed than in such as reside in brooks   On the McCloud river (Report of United States Fish Commission) "it was noted, in 1878, that the parent Salmon were unusually small, their average weight being under 8 lb "   This small size was stated to be undoubtedly caused, in whole or in part, by the fishery at the canneries of the Sacramento, where the 8-inch meshes of the innumerable drift-nets stopped all the large Salmon, but let all the small ones through   The eggs when taken proved to be at least one-third smaller than those of most previous years, and the average number of eggs to the fish was about 3500 against 4200 in the previous year   Livingston Stone in 1882 (Bulletin of the United States Fish Commission, ii, p 11) writing respecting the eggs of Salmo fontinalis observed that those from the small fish of the elevated rivulets are not so large as those of the finer breeds from warmer streams, concluding that the ova of these last are fully twice as large as those found in the race residing in mountain rivulets   Also that " large eggs are the result of keeping the breeders in water that warms up in the spring and summer   It is true, if it becomes too warm, say above 70°, it is injurious , but water that stands at 65° in the summer will make larger eggs than water at 55°, and very cold spring water will always develop small eggs "   (Page 183)

changed daily At the end of this period I measured each ovum, and found 75 were 0 25 of an inch in diameter, three were 0 20 of an inch, one was 0 175 of an inch, and one 0 15 of an inch Looking through the hatching-troughs at Howietoun it appeared that from 4 to 5 per cent of the eggs are less than the normal size of the remaining 95 or 96 per cent

It has been observed that the offspring from large eggs are superior to such as are reared from small ones, consequently fish-culturists should be careful to obtain their stock from the best sources, unless the water in which they are going to be transferred is deficient in amount or in food when the source from whence the supply is obtained becomes of little practical moment *

The immediate and possibly remote result of employing eggs from young fish for stocking purposes is one which requires the earnest consideration of the fish-culturist For it is evident that by selection a more rapidly growing race may be reared, and I now purpose demonstrating that small eggs from young parents may give bad results† as to the number hatched or the quality of the young In short the great mortality from the eggs of young mothers appears to be during the incubating stage, while from the progeny of young males one season older it seems to show itself among the fry , passing over another year, there is not so great a mortality among the eggs nor disease of the offspring Bearing on this I may allude to the ova of American chars having been milted from a Scotch char in November, 1882 , one of the progeny gave 146 eggs on November 12th, 1884, or a little under two years of age Only six feeble little ones hatched on February 3rd,

---

* Two batches of Lochleven trout were spawned November 2, 1882, at Howietoun, the parents of one lot having been hatched in 1875, and of the other in 1876 , the eggs were similarly treated, and the young came out during January and February, 1883 At Craigend are two ponds, which have been constructed for the reception of young fish, each of the same width and 100 ft long , one is nearly on a level with the other, and the identical stream passes through both Into these two ponds the two lots or fry were turned, those from the older (1875), or seven year old parents, having the lower pond , those from the younger, or six year old fish, having the upper pond, while they were fed and otherwise similarly treated At the end of November, 1883, those in the lower pond were about one-fourth larger than those in the upper pond, and it seemed as if the produce of the older parents, or larger eggs, were decidedly superior to those from the younger parents, or smaller eggs A second experiment was tried in the same two ponds, which were stocked with young Lochleven trout bred from parents of the same age, spawned the same day, and hatched in the same room I saw these fish both in August and also in November, 1884 but no difference in size or appearance was perceptible between them It would, consequently, seem that the larger eggs from older parents produce fry which grow faster than do those from the smaller eggs furnished by younger parents Also, Mr Francis Francis (Fish Culture, Appendix, p 309), when alluding to the salmon fishery at Doohulla, in Ireland, noted that big smolts make big fish One that was peculiarly fine was marked, and on the shoals returning from the sea this very fish was caught, and as he was the largest smolt, so he was the largest grilse, and weighed 7½lb

† For several seasons it had been remarked at Howietoun that eggs from young mothers were subject to a greater percentage of deaths than those taken from older fish On November 13th, 1881, about 500 eggs, having a diameter of 0 17 of an inch were obtained from a rising two-year old Lochleven trout, and they were impregnated from another of the same race of the usual size Out of these eggs only about a dozen hatched on January 28th, and seven lived to be turned into the rearing-pond In this instance the immaturity was on the mother's side On November 29th, 1883, 4500 eggs of the Lochleven trout (of the season of 1875) were milted from the par of a salmon raised at Howietoun, and which had been hatched in March, 1881, and consequently were a little over 2½ years of age The mortality during incubation was only about 2 per cent , but this by no means gave a true index of the experiment, for when the young hatched January 15th, 1884, nearly all were seen to be suffering from what has been termed dropsy or blue swelling of the yolk sac (Day, Proc Zool Soc 1884 p 376) Among these 1000 dropsical fish only about 100 lived out the year As the same cross had been made December 24th, 1881, but with older parents, and that without occasioning dropsy, one is irresistibly led to the conclusion that hybridization had nothing to do with these results, but that they might reasonably be attributed to the immaturity of the male pars As a further confirmation of this view, pars in 1884 taken from the same lot were found prolific but with comparatively few cases of dropsy occurring On November 11th, 1884, about 12,000 Lochleven trout eggs were milted from a salmon smolt hatched in March, 1881, and though about 8000 hatched on January 28th, 1885, by March 12th about 1000 had died, they having mostly shown signs of dropsy Subsequently the mortality ceased In this case the male was one season older than in the last experiment Dropsy did not set in so rapidly neither were so many affected , but it must be clear that there was deficiency of vitality in one of the parents, and that would most probably have been in the male, which was thirty one months old

1885   At the same time milt was obtained from some of these hybrids and used to impregnate 4500 eggs of Lochleven trout, these hatched on February 2nd, but the mortality was large, being upwards of half the eggs, while there were many deformities and some dropsies among the offspring   Males are evidently more matured for breeding-purposes than are females of the same age   I would here advert to a remark I published in 1883,* that in the fresh waters of India due to indiscriminate net-fishing the young (of many forms of fish) have to be raised from ova of such as are merely one or two seasons old, while the younger the parent the smaller the eggs, and this is probably one mode in which races of fish deteriorate.

Although it is known that among mammals, breeding from two nearly related parents—as brother and sister—frequently gives rise to deteriorating offspring, it has not been shown that this consanguinity deleteriously effects to so great an extent, or even at all, the lower classes of vertebrates   Reasoning from analogy we must suppose that the infusion of fresh blood improves piscine races, and instances have been adduced when from local circumstances fish have deteriorated and an improvement has occurred on the cessation of the deleterious conditions, sometimes aided by eggs from a fresh stock having been introduced   It would appear that from young parents or deteriorated breeds small offspring are raised, but unless other circumstances combine, fine fish kept in suitable water have been raised from eggs of normally small breeds, but doubtless large eggs are most likely to produce larger and more rapidly growing offspring   Possibly if eggs are insufficiently aerated while incubating the resulting young are stunted, while similar results ensue on crowding alevins

The period at which breeding takes place can be affected by many circumstances, the chief of which may be briefly enumerated as follows —the age of the parent   the race or variety as to whether it is strong or weak, healthy or unhealthy   obstructions, whether natural or artificial, but which occasion difficulty in obtaining access to the breeding grounds   their habitat, as residents of the colder north or more sunny localities   the range of waters through which they can rove   climatic and seasonal variations whether such are normal or abnormal   the character of the water   the geological formation of the country   its elevation ·   the abundance or the reverse of food   whether the fish are kept in confinement or in a wild state, and if disturbed or not

This brings one to consider whether seasons or changes of temperature exercise any marked influence on the time of the year when these fishes spawn ?   If they do we ought to be able to observe such among the trout and *Anadromous Salmonoids* despatched in the form of ova to Tasmania from this country   Turning to Mr Allport's account (*Proc Zool Soc* 1870, p 25), we find a most marked instance of such a result †   We know the cold season in that portion of the globe corresponds with our summer, and the first brook trout which were spawned

---

* *Indian Fish and Fishing*   Great International Fisheries Exhibition, 1883 series, p 27

† Sir Humphry Davy, writing from Southern Austria, on May 28th, 1827, remarked that "the char I got this morning with mature eggs was just about to spawn, yet in England they spawn in the winter   If summer is the spawning time of the char and trout of the lakes of Southern Austria, it is connected with or owing to the waters at that time being of the temperature best fitted for the purpose, most of these lakes being fed by mountain streams, frozen in the winter, and full in summer from the melting of the snow "   Herr Geistbeck (*Nature*, 1886, p 375) remarked of the German Alpine lakes, that " small depths and large affluent streams are causes of a higher temperature in summer and a lower in winter   Cooling in autumn goes on more rapidly than heating in spring, for in the autumn the upper layers of water get heavier consequent upon cooling and then sink, being replaced by others, till the entire mass reaches the temperature of the greatest density, but in spring the circulation fails   Large affluents, too, by promoting mixture cause rapid heating   Down to 6 or 8 metres' depth in midsummer the fall of temperature is very slight , thence to 18 metres a rapid fall, which continues to about 50 metres   below 50 metres the temperature is about constant "   In Sweden, Artedi observed that the salmon spawned in the middle of the summer   Livingston-Stone (*Bulletin United States Fishery Commission*, 1882, ii, p 12) observed of *S quinnat*, that, raised in the United States it did not spawn in the Californian time, but in the *S salar* time, November or very near so   We also know that, as a rule, in very hard winters when the spawning grounds are frozen spawning is usually deferred, and when very cold weather has unexpectedly set in, salmon have been observed to stop their ascent of rivers and return to the sea

in Tasmania occurred on July 3rd, 1866, by the 7th of August fourteen females had been stripped, and shortly afterwards five pair of trout were observed constructing redds in the River Plenty During June, July and August, 1867, the trout were again stripped of their ova artificially In this country, trout spawn at different periods in different rivers, from about September to February The very first Tasmanian bred trout hatched from English trout eggs have not selected for spawning the months adopted by their ancestors in this hemisphere, but have chosen others which are better suited for their purpose, clearly demonstrating the possibility of trout being capable under changed conditions of varying the period of the breeding season *

The ova having been extended by the female in a suitable spot, are subsequently fertilized by the milt of the male brought into contact with them in the water when the spermatozoids effect an entrance into the egg at the micropyle But it must be very apparent that numerous causes may be in existence either to prevent fertilization, or, should such have taken place, to subsequently destroy the ova Among these deleterious agencies are the character or polluted state of the water, or that when the eggs are being deposited in running streams they escape the influence of the milt, or even be carried away by the current, or overwhelmed by mud Or the water may subside to that extent that they are left uncovered, and perish by drought or frost, or else consumed by fish in the vicinity, who will even root them up for this purpose. When safely deposited in redds they still have enemies to contend with, floods may sweep them away, or, should such a state of the rivers continue for any length of time, the fish may not be able to avail themselves of their usual breeding grounds, they being too deep in the water This may compel them to drop their eggs in the swollen stream, when they would become smothered by mud or otherwise lost, or the fish might push up higher to smaller water courses, which would render the chances considerable of the eggs being left uncovered upon a subsidence taking place Irrespective of the seasons, the eggs have numerous enemies, as fish, the larvæ of the Dragon-flies *Labellulida*, the May and stone-flies, *Ephemeridæ*† and the caddis-flies, *Phrygancidæ*, some birds, as the dabchick, or little grebe, *Podiceps minor*, the water ouzel, *Cinclus aquaticus*,‡ ducks and swans, while the house-rat, mice, also the vole or water-rat, *Arvicola amphibia*, join in their destruction § Besides the enemies to fish ova which have been enumerated, they have many more in our streams, and so enormous is the loss which occurs among the eggs and young that in such a river as the Severn the annual produce of salmon and grilse at the present time consists of about 20,000 fish Or were all the ova of one female salmon of about 20 lb weight to be hatched and attain maturity they would suffice for keeping up the stock to its present condition

As the mortality among the eggs left to hatch in rivers and streams is so enormous, while it is impossible to destroy their enemies which exist there, it has become obvious that great gain might accrue were the ova to be collected and artificially incubated‖ and thus placed out of reach of many causes of destruction,

---

* The Black Swan, introduced from Australia, breeds here in our spring

† Brown (*Stormontfield Experiments*, page 33) remarked that in the spring of 1854 Mr Buist took some eyed salmon ova, and placed a dozen of the grubs of the May fly (*Ephemera*) taken from the same locality along with them in a vessel which was supplied with water by a syphon of thread In a few days the grubs had devoured one of the eggs, and in a few days more the whole were devoured They were carefully watched when feeding, and five or six grubs were found firmly fixed to an ovum which they never left until totally eaten up Messrs Ashworth, of Galway, one year deposited 70,000 salmon ova in a small pure stream adjoining a plantation of fir trees, and they were entirely destroyed by the larva of the May fly —(Buckland, *Fish Hatching*, 1863 page 51)

‡ I gave an account in *Land and Water* of February 28th, 1885, how, on one of these birds being shot near Howietoun five or six trout eggs were found in its stomach

§ At the *Great International Fisheries Exhibition* of 1883 the vole eat the eggs of the Salmonidæ placed in their cage and since then they have been observed taking them from the redds (*Field*, January 5th and 19th, 1884)

‖ It would be obviously impossible in a work of the present scope to enter fully into the various modes of artificially propagating these fishes Such information may be obtained in the *History of Howietoun*, by Sir James Maitland, now in course of publication, also in *Domesticated Trout*, by Livingston-Stone, *Fish Hatching*, by Frank Buckland, 1868, *Fish-*

as in properly constructed hatching houses, where the water might be maintained at a suitable temperature, and whatever is known to be injurious to the eggs excluded as far as possible

The discovery of how to collect and artificially fecundate fish ova has been claimed by many different persons in various ages and in widely separated countries * During this century the French Government in Europe † first turned fish-culture into practical channels Commencing experiments in 1842, their establishment at Huningue came into existence near the Rhine and Rhone Canal in 1848, and from it the rivers and lakes of France were re-stocked In Great Britain, where the importance of Jacobi's re-discovery of how to propagate Salmonidæ was recognized during the last century by the British Government, who granted him a pension and at the present time maintain five Inspectors of Fisheries, their assistants and clerks, but the only connection they have with fish-culture is the keeping up of a few tanks in the South Kensington Museum Although Mr T Shaw first succeeded in 1836 in artificially hatching salmon eggs in Scotland, it was not until December 20th, 1852, that this process was first tried on a large scale in Ireland by the Messrs Ashworths by the proprietors of the Tay, in Scotland, in 1853, and by Mr. Fisher, of Richmond, Yorkshire, associated with other gentlemen of that town and county who in the same year commenced breeding salmon artificially in the River Swale

For the purpose of obtaining the eggs of Salmonidæ, in order to undertake artificial fish-culture, three sources, irrespective of purchase, are available direct from the fish living in a wild state, or else from such as are kept in breeding-ponds, or robbing the nests or redds in rivers or streams Anyone who has been practically concerned in capturing fish in a wild condition for spawning purposes knows the vast amount of trouble, exposure, disappointment, and expense which this entails, and in trout, at least, the most practical plan has been found to keep breeders in suitable ponds,‡ well separated one from another,§ while a very great advantage

culture, 1865, and the *Practical Management of Fisheries*, 1883, by Francis Francis , *Trout-culture*, by C Capel, 1877 , *Fish culture*, by Francis Day, Great International Fisheries Exhibition, series 1883

* In the fifteenth century a monk, Dom Pinchon, bred fish from eggs placed in boxes, lined at the bottom with sand and gravel, and having their front and hind ends protected by basket work, and through which a stream of water flowed Stephen Ludwig Jacobi, a landed proprietor, residing at Hohenhausen, a small town in Westphalia, as early as 1733, or thereabouts, made many experiments respecting the artificial breeding of trout, adopting much the same methods as Dom Pinchon, except that the ends and upper covering of his troughs were constituted of fine gratings, and these were deposited in streams, at suitable depths His account of the results of his 30 years' experiments appeared in 1763 in the *Hanover Magazine*, and a translation exists in Yarrell's *British Fishes*, second edition, vol ii, page 87 Jacobi's experiments were deemed so important that the British Government granted him a pension See also a *Treatise on the Propagation of Salmon and other Fish*, by E and T Ashworth, 1853, pages iii and iv, for a full history of this paper

† The artificial breeding of salmon was placed by the French Government under the Minister of the Interior, of Agriculture, and Commerce, and directly under M Coste, and the two engineers of the Rhone and Rhine Canal, MM Berthot and Detzen. The results of their labours, together with a history of the experiments of Shaw, Andrew Young, Boccius, and Milne Edwards were detailed in a work by M Coste, entitled *Instructions Pratiques sur la Pisciculture, suivies de Mémoires sur le même sujet*, 1853

‡ The private fish-cultural establishments in Scotland are at Houretown, near Stirling, belonging to Sir James Maitland, Bart , F L S and F Z S , commenced in 1873, and by far the most complete in existence, especially for trout, and upwards of ten million ova are annually incubated there Every 24 hours about one million gallons of water flow through the ponds, which are 32 in number and employed either for breeding fish or raising the young, or experimental work The *Solway Fishery*, established by Mr Armistead in 1881, and capable of hatching one million ova, has 19 ponds *Stormontfield Ponds*, erected in 1853 near Perth, now nearly superseded by the *Dupplin Hatchery*, instituted in 1882, where young are hatched for the Tay also smaller ones at *Loch Leven*, *Linlithgow Palace*, at *Culzean* in Ayrshire, *Benmore*, at Kilmun, Argyllshire, *Lochbuie*, Isle of Mull, *Aberdeen*, for the rivers Dee and Don, *Moriston*, in Invernesshire, *Caithness* on the Forss, and a few others. While in England there are Mr. Andrew's at *Guildford*, Mr Capel's at *Cray's Foot*, and the *National Fish Culture Association* at Delafore Park, and some few others, mostly of a private character

§ Ponds should not be too large, while excavated ones are safer than such as are formed by dams, these latter being more liable to give way. A fall from one to another is desirable, but they have to be constructed in accordance with, if intended for breeders, fry, or fish for the market, also with the

is thus secured in that care can be taken to select these breeders in accordance
with their age, for, as has been shown, the size of the eggs increases, up to a
certain point, with that of the parent and from these larger eggs finer and more
rapidly growing offspring are produced   In this manner and by constant selection, breeds may be improved, as has been proved by Sir James Maitland at
Howietoun   Although salmon have not yet been kept in suitable ponds for the
purpose of obtaining their eggs and stocking our rivers, much has been done in
other countries *

The mode of how to artificially spawn these fishes† requires time in learning
and considerable practice in being an adept at, consequently a skilled manipulator
will obtain a larger amount of eggs from one which is ripe than will an inexperienced or a careless one   Whether a fish captured for this purpose is in a
suitable condition may be ascertained by making gentle pressure along its
abdominal surface, commencing from the ventral fins and stroking it rather
heavily towards the vent   If sufficiently forward eggs from the female or milt
from the male will, as a rule, be extruded, but in some cases females will not at
first be induced to part with their ova and require a little coaxing or even
deterring the operation for a short time   Should the ova not be quite ready, the
distended abdomen feels hard and the eggs do not move under pressure as they do
in ripe fishes, force should never be employed, because not only are immature
eggs valueless but injury may be occasioned to the spawning fish especially if
some ova mixed with blood are expressed   Sometimes only fish of one sex may
be obtainable, and it becomes necessary to retain those which have been captured
until some of the other sex have been procured, and this may be done in tubs of
water, contiguous pools, or even by fastening a large fish, as a salmon, by means of
a cord being affixed around its tail, and thus securing it to a stake on the bank of
a river, or placing it in a well-boat

amount of the water supply and should the latter be plentiful, shape is of little consequence , if,
however, it is restricted they should generally be deep and narrow   Some employ planks in
forming both inlets and outlets, others prefer brick or stone laid in cement   At the intake a
means should exist of entirely shutting off the water when required, while the outlet should allow
the passage of all the water at the highest possible flood and making allowance for the screens
being clogged   These screens should be placed both at the entrance and outlet of each pond, and
may be constructed of perforated zinc, or copper or iron wire plates, fixed into wooden frames,
which securely block both channels , and in order to obviate clogging from descending débris an
inverted V shaped frame may be built out in front of the screens   Capabilities ought to exist
enabling the water from the ponds to be drawn off when it is necessary to repair or clean them

The results of experiments made in fish cultural establishments where segregation is not
perfect must always be accepted with the greatest caution   Fishes if allowed the slightest chance
will range out of the pond in which they are placed   Irrespective of this, if herons, gulls, or
dabchicks are about, the chances are increased of a little admixture being occasioned by their
dropping fish from one pond into another as they are flying off with their slippery and struggling
prey

* In Canada Mr Wilmot had salmon captured in the sea in May and impounded in a tidal
pond, until they became ripe in October or November when they were artificially spawned   They
have also in the United States been imprisoned in rivers for this purpose with more or less
success   As such an undertaking in this country would be costly it is improbable that it will be
carried out by private individuals, being, in fact, more of a national than private requirement

† An ingenious plan, were it sufficiently successful, has been invented by Mr Ainsworth, of
the United States, in order to induce the trout to naturally spawn in a trap so that the eggs can
be readily collected   The channel or race, which supplies water to the pond where the breeders
are kept, is left open in order to allow them to ascend but this they can only do for a certain distance,
as it is closely fitted by a wooden framework   This has a floor of perforated zinc raised about a
quarter of an inch above the bed of the stream consequently permitting a circulation of water
from below, but the perforations are not sufficiently large to permit eggs to fall through, any
which would find their way there from above being thus unable to escape below   A little above
this perforated zinc floor is a second similar tray, thus forming a closed chamber   This is likewise of perforated zinc, but in it the holes are sufficiently large to allow eggs falling through
it into the chamber which has been formed between these two zinc trays, On the upper surface
of this upper tray are placed two inches in depth of coarse gravel, which is too large to drop
through, and here the trout spawns, and as it forms its redd with its tail stirring up the gravel,
the eggs fall through the perforations in the upper tray, into the receiving chamber, and can
be removed when required   Mr A S Collins has made an improvement by substituting an
endless apron for the lower tray, where by means of a roller which is turned by a handle,
the eggs can be received into a pan that is removable at will   (Day, Fish Culture 1883,
pages 29, 30, plate I fig 1, 2, 3)

The fish while being spawned* is held with its body somewat sideways, its tail obliquely downwards, and its abdomen turned slightly towards the manipulator, if large its body may also be a little bent. A pan to receive the eggs is placed on the ground as near as convenient to the fish's vent, then gentle pressure is exercised commencing from the ventral fins and continued downwards towards the vent. The ova which are thus pressed out may be treated either by the moist or the dry process. In the moist some water is first put into the pan which is to receive the eggs, for it used to be held that if ripe milt and ova were mixed together in water the fish-culturist would be most closely following the operations of nature. In the dry process (inaugurated by M. Vrasski in 1856) the use of water at this time is dispensed with, the eggs being expressed from the fish directly into a dry pan (into which of course a little water will fall from the surface of the fish), over these eggs, milt from a male is distributed, the pan is now tilted backwards and forwards, causing the contents to be well mixed. After allowing time for this comingling to take place, water is added to the depth of two or three inches, this is gently stirred with the hand and then allowed to stand until the eggs harden or "frees" as it has been termed, being a period from one- to three-quarters of an hour according to the temperature, taking longest in cold weather. In the moist process the average success in fertilizing eggs was about 50 or 60 per cent, by the dry process as many as 95 per cent are not uncommon, and even all have been fertile.

The ova as extruded are soft and adhere to whatever they come in contact with, apparently owing to the absorption which is going on through their shells, for water is gradually imbibed as seen most distinctly in eggs of such species as the gwiniad or *Coregonus*, and first observed by Ranking in the egg of the common stickleback. When the interspace between the outer and inner coat is filled absorption necessarily ceases, and when this occurs the ovum no longer adheres to contiguous objects but ' frees " itself and is seen as a hard, almost round, and elastic body. Now more clean water has to be carefully poured over the eggs and continued until no effete milt remains, and so soon as the water is no longer discoloured they may be transferred to the carrying can in the proportion of about one-third eggs and two-thirds water. They are then removed to the incubating house and gently distributed by the aid of a feather over the bottom of the hatching tray.

There are some points respecting the conveyance of the eggs of these fishes which may well be discussed in this place when recently taken they will bear

* Different modes of spawning fish have been adopted in this country. Shaw, in 1836, obtained salmon ova from a redd which he placed in gravel and hatched in a stream of pure spring water. He in 1837 took two spawning fish and having dug a trench in the gravel, he directed a stream through it two inches deep, the fish were then held side by side and the eggs and milt pressed out into the stream, and after a few minutes they were removed to another stream where they were hatched. Boccius, in 1848, in his *Treatise on the Management of Fish*, observed that " the principle of artificial spawning I have been acquainted with as far back as 1815.   Should the fish be all right, take a large earthenware pan, with about two quarts of spring water at the bottom, and holding the female fish up by the gill-covers, draw your hand downwards from the pectoral fins to the anal point." The milt was to be similarly obtained from the male, the whole agitated with the hand for about a minute and the eggs were now to be spread on the shingle in the hatching apparatus, being careful one was not above another, then two inches of shingle was to be placed above the ova and spring water permitted to flow freely over them. Messrs Edward and Thomas Ashworth's experiments were made in a similar manner to Shaw's, they commenced December 20th, 1852, at Outerard, in Galway, as related by themselves, and their manager, Mr Ramsbottom, added the advice to keep the eggs submerged, which must always be attended to even when the ova or milt is flowing from the fish. Buckland (1863, *Fish Hatching*) advised the same process as had been advocated by those who had preceded him, and it was not until an article by Livingston-Stone in *The New York Citizen and Round Table* of March 9th, 1872, first drew attention to the dry process of M. Vrasski that any considerable change was made and this plan generally adopted. Prior to this time the use of gravel in hatching trays had been abandoned by most fish culturists as being a great source of mortality among the eggs due to the elements of mischief it introduced in spite of the greatest care. It was also ascertained that placing covers on the hatching trays and thus excluding the light, or else hatching the eggs in darkened rooms, were sufficient for the necessary exclusion of light during the period of incubation.

travelling,* thus some trout were spawned at Howietoun on November 27th, 1884, the eggs were at once packed in a cigar box between layers of muslin in damp moss and sent by train to Cheltenham, arrived the afternoon of the 28th, after experiencing very rough usage on their way, the box even being broken, still they hatched satisfactorily, and there was not a single monstrosity   The next year, on November the 26th, some salmon eggs were obtained in the Teith, and also some trout eggs from Howietoun fish, but were not packed sufficiently early to reach me before starting for the train on the 27th   They were sent by train on the 28th, and arrived at Cheltenham on the 29th, about three days after they had been obtained from the fish, but all died, doubtless owing to the shaking they had sustained at this period, or while segmentation was in progress †

It is dangerous to the existence of the embryo within the egg to permit them to travel subsequent to the first twenty-four or forty-eight hours after they have been removed from the fish, unless a swing can is employed or some contrivance to prevent shocks, for such interfere with the vital processes which are going on and usually occasion its death   It is not in fact until the ova are "eyed," as it is termed by fish culturists, that they can travel in safety except certain precautions are observed   This eyed period commences somewhere about the fortieth day of incubation in trout eggs, when the outline of the fish, also the eyes, are visible

The appearances presented by salmonoid eggs have been already described, but certain changes may take place owing to morbid conditions   It is very common to observe large or otherwise abnormal ova, some of which are popularly termed 'wind eggs,' passed from a fish among the first which are extruded, while there are often some small hard white and opaque ones that have remained attached to the ovaries or in the abdominal cavity from the previous season   Unimpregnated eggs when left unmoved in hatching trays mostly continue clear, but concussion may cause them to assume the white and opaque appearance of dead ova   In salt water fertile eggs which die become clear in the shell and the embryo contracted in size is visible within, but if in this condition it is transferred

---

* At Huningue eyed ova were first sent in the following manner   a thin layer of damp moss was placed inside a wide mouthed bottle and pressed down to the bottom, then a layer of eggs, next one of moss and so on up to the top of the shoulder of the bottle, its neck was then filled with damp moss and a paper cover full of holes to admit air, tied over the top   One or more bottles were then packed in a box with damp moss, while this box was placed in an outer wooden case which was also lined with damp moss   In warm weather ice was added

† Mr Brooks, F L S , has kindly furnished the following note on the development of the embryo " 1 The contents of the egg envelope essentially consist of two portions, a comparatively small quantity of living protoplasm and a large quantity of food yelk, to be drawn on as required 2 A comparatively thin but continuous film of protoplasm surrounding the whole of the yelk   As the yelk is immediately coagulated when in contact with water the supposition is that the film-like sheet of protoplasm prevents coagulation 3 Five or six hours after fertilization the bulk of the germinal protoplasm collects at one pole of the egg forming a lens shaped mound, the blastoderm, which thins off at the periphery and is continuous with that portion which envelopes the yelk   4 During the formation of the blastoderm and prior to its subdivision, its surface is irregular and shows amœboid movements 5 The blastoderm then becomes divided into two nearly equal parts by a vertical furrow   a few hours later a second is formed at right angles to the first, so that the blastoderm now consists of four segments 6 Next follow stages, usually during the second day, in which there are eight or sixteen segments but slight irregularities are frequent 7 During the succeeding days these subdivisions are continued until at the end of a week the blastoderm consists of a cap-like mass of small cells, known as the mulberry mass or morular 8 The blastoderm now consists of a circular plano convex mass of small cells at one pole of the egg   During the second week this disc begins to spread out over the yelk, thinning out near the centre 9 About the 15th or 16th day when the blastoderm envelopes about a quarter of the yelk, a thickening appears near one point in the margin, which is soon recognizable by its opacity and constitutes the first trace of the embryo   It extends inwards as a somewhat triangular streak and increases in length and importance during the next few days   The posterior portion of this streak is where the tail of the future embryo grows free from the yelk, while the anterior part soon becomes raised from the blastoderm and forms the head 10 With the formation of this more opaque and thickened streak the axis of the embryo can be recognized   The extension of the blastoderm over the yelk continues, but progresses more rapidly from the anterior than from the posterior margin   About the end of the third week the yelk is almost entirely enveloped by the blastoderm, the last trace of yelk being seen as a circular spot a little below the posterior end of the embryo   This in turn also becomes closed in by the growth of the blastoderm over it "

to fresh water it becomes white and opaque, but returns again to its clear glass-like appearance if re-immersed in salt water, and this alteration on changing fluids may be seen on being repeated for several successive times

Dead eggs are sources of great injury to the contiguous living ones, whether in the natural redds or in the hatching trays of the fish-culturists, being liable to byssus, a product or decaying animal substance   This, which is of a fleecy appearance, develops long tendrils that branch out in many directions, attaching themselves to all the eggs in the vicinity and mostly ensuring their destruction   Its existence renders it necessary to remove* all opaque and dead ova, which should be done not less frequently than three or four times a week.   Another form of fungus must likewise be remarked upon, this species is allied to the *Saprolegnia ferox*, so destructive to many of our fishes, and when it once shows itself all the eggs will probably perish, or should any young emerge they will be sickly and worthless   Difficult to perceive on account of its fineness and absence of colour, it may obtain a firm hold on the eggs before the fish-culturist is aware of its presence, and the cause of its existence has yet to be discovered   Dirty water will not invariably bring it, nor clean water keep it away, the rapidity of its growth is diminished by darkness, and increasing the flow of water and also decreasing the temperature have been found in some instances to be checks, but the most likely preventive is to char the inside of the trays and every piece of wood over which the water which supplies the hatchery flows, or use paint or other similar expedients, and keep the eggs in the dark.

The water most suited for a hatching-house† is that from an inexhaustible spring‡ of sufficient capacity throughout the year at a low temperature, as from 41° to 45° Fahr and free from all forms of pollution; that which rises from a limestone source is preferable   When the water supplying the hatching-house, as the Mill-Holme one at Howietoun, comes from an underground source it is not subject to fluctuations of temperature or to floods, consequently filtering beds are unnecessary, a few settling pits distributed along its course being all that is required

The water which is intended for hatching purposes is now conducted into a supply trough, and from thence distributed to the hatching-trays, and whatever plan is adopted they ought to be in such a position that the attendant can obtain easy access to the eggs and readily examine them in order to ascertain their condition, and, when necessary, remove the dead ones

Hatching-trays of various forms and sizes are employed, in accordance with the water supply, and either contain one layer of ova resting on the floor of the tray, or placed so that a current of water§ flows under as well as over them, or there may be several trays placed one above another within a large one, while from 1¼ to 1½ inches of water should always be present above the eggs   The

---

* One of the best plans for this purpose is the bulb syringe, as employed at Howietoun, and several other modifications are in use, also tweezers or nippers of fine wire, a miniature spoon, or even a leech glass

† The hatching-house has to be modified in accordance with the locality and requirements, in cold places a more solid construction being necessary to keep out frost, or it may even be necessary to place it under the lee of a bank   If it is desired of large size it should be erected on a slope, in order to permit the hatching trays to be placed in stair-like sequence, so that a considerable fall of water may exist between the one above and that next below it   But, as has been frequently observed, however adequate your house and water supply are, you are not secure unless all your joints, screws, taps, &c, are kept in good working order

‡ Of course this is not always available, and water may have to be obtained from streams or other sources rendering filtering necessary, but filtering, although it may clarify water, does not always remove all its injurious ingredients, while, although clear water, destitute of animal and vegetable impurities, is best adapted for incubating eggs, its very absence of life renders it unsuitable for young fish   River water is liable to droughts and floods, while in winter it often brings down ice, leaves, sticks, and other *debris*

§ At Howietoun, where the average temperature of the water is from 41° to 45° Fahr, the supply is 10 gallons a minute to every 100,000 eggs, which flow is increased in the later stages of incubation, while the hatching trays are about 6 ft 8 in long and 19¼ inches wide, inside measurement, after the eggs are hatched one foot of the lower end is kept vacant, and divided off from the remainder of the tray by a screen   Where the water enters is a screen of perforated zinc, placed about 8¼ in from the upper end, but it slopes obliquely downwards to the floor of the tray, so that no space is lost

3

trays may be made of slate, stone pottery, or wood, being careful that, should the last be selected, no odorous form is employed. Wood should be thoroughly charred inside, or covered with tar or asphalte varnish or paint, which aids in preventing the formation of fungus. Glass grilles are largely employed by those who are desirous of raising strong and healthy fry. Metal substances are liable to undergo chemical changes in some waters, and should perforated zinc trays be employed they should have a sufficient covering of paint or varnish * Copper should be rejected for trays.

It has been held that deep or still waters are unsuited to the incubation of the eggs of these fishes,† but, although this may be the case in natural conditions, it is not found to be invariably so in artificial fish-culture.

The eggs having been safely deposited in the hatching-trays, the fish-culturist has to be careful that the supply of water is continuous and nothing occurs, so far as he can obviate it, which would cause injury during the process of incubation. The room should either be dark or the trays fitted with covers, as light is injurious and ova subjected to it are liable to be small-eyed and weakly if hatched. Of course the more perfect the impregnation has been the greater the proportion of fertile eggs, and this saves a large amount of manual labour in removing the useless ones. To save space, some fish-culturists have advocated several successive layers of trays, a plan objected to by the majority as tending to produce weak young. others again suggest that as soon as the eggs are eyed all should be washed in a pan, when most of the unimpregnated ones and bad ones will turn white, and then the good and clean ones might be placed in one of these trays in several layers. The water should not swirl about the eggs as if they were boiling or bubbling up, as such concussion would be fatal to many, while if no appearance of the embryo is observable by the fiftieth day the best plan is to throw the ova away as any chance of their ever hatching is past.‡

I have already alluded to the forms of fungus to which eggs are liable, while small eyes as seen in the embryo is a sign of weakness and observable as the result of an excess of light or excess of cold. If it is desired to pack eggs after

---

* When fish-culture was first commenced, it was considered necessary to follow nature and deposit the eggs under gravel, which was first sifted to about the size of a large pea and then boiled to destroy deleterious agencies, while such as contained much iron was rejected. Next, simply charred boxes, with covers to keep out the light, were used. Glass grilles or hollow rods were easily employed, fixed in wooden frames or resting on a strip of perforated galvanized zinc, and going across the entire width of the tray, being sunk to about an inch from the bottom, where a ledge of wood prevented their sinking lower and a catch precluded their rising above a desired level, as from 1¼ to 2 in below the surface. These glass rods do not quite touch one another, while a passage is secured for water both above and below the eggs. Frank Buckland objected to glass grilles because ‘parent fish do not find glass bars at the bottom of the river, but they do find gravel.’ (Nat History of British Fishes, 1880, p 390.) While Livingston Stone remarked that simple charcoal or carbonized troughs are equally as efficacious as grilles and infinitely more economical. He considered the first to be the thing for business, and the second more suitable for rich men's experiments. Or the trays to receive the eggs may be made of perforated zinc and the supply pipe fixed under the bottom of the box, so that the water ascends through the eggs. Similarly, these trays may be in a single, double, treble, or even in four tiers. For an account, with illustrations, of a large number of processes now in use, see Day's *Fish Culture*, 1883.

† Ephemera (*Handbook of Angling*, 3rd edition, 1853, p 233) asserted that "salmon never deposited their spawn in deep or still waters if they did it would not be vivified. To vivify salmon ova impregnated by the milt, the combined influences of running water, atmospheric and solar action are necessary." Sir Humphry Davy ('*Salmonia*') considered that all which is required for the production of *fishes* (as salmon) from the impregnated egg is a constant supply of water of a certain temperature furnished with air. "The precipitation of water from the atmosphere, its rapid motion in rivers, and its falls in cataracts, not only preserve this element pure, but gives it its vitality, and renders it subservient even to the embryo life of the fish" (page 85)

‡ Livingston Stone very clearly explained how to recognize good from bad eggs, for although it had been generally held that until the spinal column showed itself the difference between the two was almost undiscernible, he remarked that this is not strictly true, because there is a period, within forty-eight hours of the taking of the eggs, when the good can be distinguished from the worthless ones. In the unimpregnated a small annular disk with a round dot in the centre is seen at the top of the egg and continues until the egg turns white. In the impregnated egg the disk will disappear within twenty four hours. Eggs which after the first day show the disk are unimpregnated. those without the disk are impregnated (*see page 32 ante*)

they have eyed, they may be left for twelve or more hours in damp moss, when the weak ones will often be distinguishable by their pale appearance

When the eggs commence to hatch considerable attention is necessary, while somewhat different treatment may be required in accordance with the method which has been adopted   In the glass grille system the young slips through between the rods on to the bottom of the box, but as it then comes in contact with the discarded egg-shells, which are decidedly injurious, one plan is to turn all the eggs off the grilles on to the box and slightly raise the depth of the water Or, if perforated zinc trays are employed, the use of the watering-pot may be necessary in order to remove the discarded egg-shells and other impurities Some fish are seen to hatch by the egg splitting down the line of the back, others emerge tail first or head first, this last being frequently effected at the great danger of a portion of the sac becoming forced before the head at the risk of suffocating the alevin   Some on emerging are lively and strong, while others on the contrary are listless and weak, occasionally a little assistance is necessary in order to help the little fish out of the shell, and for this purpose some fish-culturists recommend the use of a camel-hair brush   If the trays are sufficiently large, the young salmon and trout may be kept two or three months in the hatching-house, and char still longer

Although experiments have shown that eggs may be successfully incubated in damp moss, it would seem that a sluggish current of water may be equivalent to a diminished supply of proper aeration, and merely sufficient for the slow development of the embryo   On December 12th, 1885, a number of trout eggs, which had been obtained from the fish the previous day, were received in a swing tin can at Cheltenham, from Howietoun they were placed inside a coach-house in hatching-trays supplied with a slow stream of water from a tub, filled twice or more daily from a contiguous well   As the water was only sufficient to pass in the form of a small stream from thirty to forty times a day through each incubating tray, it is clear that they must have received merely a minimum of aeration   On December 21st, Mr Ogden had about 200 of these eggs, which he took to Matlock and put in hatching-trays in a good stream of water, where they hatched upwards of a month before those which were kept at Cheltenham.* Consequently deferred hatching, or protracted incubation, may not invariably be a good sign or the certain forerunner of strength in the young †

It has been shown that the temperature of the water employed exercises a considerable influence upon the time required for incubation, and Seth Green

---

* Another subject of interest was the date at which the trout eggs hatched during the season of 1885-86, at Cheltenham, for in 1884 85 they commenced on the 82nd day, but not in large numbers until the 87th day, while in the winter of 1885 86 the first emerged on the 103rd day, and the main body began to show themselves on the 106th day   As during these two seasons the eggs were incubated in the same house, with water obtained from the same pump and likewise in nearly the identical apparatus, the conditions were almost similar But doubtless a lower temperature was one of the causes, and I have been furnished by my neighbour, Mr Tyrer, with the following comparative statements of the temperature of the two seasons under review —

	Season 1884-85	Season 1885-86
December	40 1	38 0
January	36 6	35 0
February	43 1	33 6
March	40 1	39 6
Mean monthly temperature	39 9	36 5

Although the mean temperature of the four months in the open air, in 1885 86, was 3 4° below that of 1884 85, that of February, 1886, was nearly 10° below that of 1885 The figures show that in the latter season the temperature was 3½ degrees colder than in the former one, or a difference of about 17½ days, computing by Seth Green's table, which was within 1½ days of the actual period

† In the course of my experiments carried on during the season of 1885-86, at Cheltenham, it must not be taken for granted that everything invariably went on smoothly, for accidents occasionally took place   Thus, one Sunday it was thought that instead of fresh water being pumped in order to fill each reservoir tub, that which had passed over hatching eggs would do just for that day only   This water, however, had the usual appearance seen at this period, being covered with a sort of soap suddy foam, and highly deleterious for this purpose, it, however, was tried, and with the result of a large number of deaths resulting

seems to have been the first to point out in America, that although for this purpose the eggs of their common char, *Salmo fontinalis*, normally require fifty days when the water is at 50° Fahr., every degree warmer or colder makes five days' difference, the warmer water acting in expediting the period of hatching, and the colder in protracting it * But while this is generally correct, it must also be borne in mind that the size and rapidity of the flow, as well as the character of the water, must be taken into consideration.

Not only will these eggs incubate in damp moss under the conditions described,† but even should they from any cause become dried, such may not necessarily occasion death unless it is continued to some time. On March 13th, 1886 at 3 P.M., a trout egg was removed from a hatching-tray where it had been ninety-one days, and the contained young was seen to be very active. It was placed in a dry glass tube, and subsequently forgotten until 7 P.M., when the shell had become dry and somewhat shrivelled, its upper surface having a cup-like depression, which had contracted the size of its interior to about three-quarters of what it had previously been. On examination, the heart of the embryo was seen to be rapidly but feebly pulsating, so it was at once transferred to water, and after little more than half-an-hour the egg had regained its original shape. It hatched seven days afterwards, the little fish emerging in a lively condition ‡

It may be as well to here advert to the result of placing the eggs of the Salmonidæ in salt water, for the idea, or conjecture, periodically appears to be revived that salmon can breed in the sea, or at least that it has not been proved that brackish water is deleterious to their eggs § It is useless pointing out to the advocates of this opinion, who are mostly prejudiced or ignorant not fishermen, that could they do so, why do salmon push up into rivers for breeding purposes, and that often as far as they can ascend from salt-water influences? They do not choose a spot between high and low water-mark along our inlets and bays, for in such localities their nests would be liable to be disturbed by the ebb and flow of the tides, whereas if they selected the deeper portions of the ocean possibly the eggs would be insufficiently aerated

Rondeletius, who wrote upon the salmon *upwards of three and a quarter centuries ago*, was an upholder of the doctrine that salmon spawned in the sea, one which,

* Seth Green likewise pointed out, that in the above fishes, when hatched in fifty days, the yolk sac remains thirty more, but if incubation has extended to seventy days, the sac remains at least forty-five

† The foregoing experiments show that eggs may be kept in damp moss, or other situations destitute of any flow of water, if the conditions of cold, damp and darkness are observed while the period of hatching may be retarded by the judicious use of ice It would, consequently, appear practicable to carry on incubation with varying degrees of rapidity, and so suit the time of evolving the young to the capacity of the hatching-house, or even to do without the latter, should the fish-culturist possess proper shallow ponds fed by streams in which to turn the eyed-ova or hatching eggs, a subject which will be again alluded to

‡ Dr John Davy, in 1853, made some interesting observations on the subject of temperature on ova and young fish, in each instance the experiment being carried on in a thin glass vessel of the capacity of about four ounces, nearly full of water, and this vessel was placed in a water bath of the temperature required An ovum was two and a-half hours in water at 70 deg, which rendered its circulation languid, kept two hours more, and increasing the heat of the water to 80 deg, no further apparent ill effects were seen The vessel was now removed from the bath, and allowed to cool gradually, and ten hours later a vigorous young fish was found to have burst its shell An ovum and a young fish were kept in water between 68 deg and 72 deg for about eight hours when the egg was found to be hatched and a tolerably active young fish was produced Next day both were exposed to a temperature between 70 deg and 80 deg, rarely reaching 80 deg, and at the end of the day they were languid, or if in motion disposed to irregular movements Removed from the water bath the next day they were active, and subsequently showed no ill effects from their treatment A young fish and an ovum were put into water raised to 82 deg, and after an hour to 85 deg, when the water was gradually cooled, but the circulation in the young fish was found to be languid, and the following day it was dead The egg did not suffer materially for three days, subsequently a vigorous young fish was produced An ovum kept in water for two hours at from 90 deg to 95 deg died, as did also one put for half an-hour in water at 100 deg

§ In January, 1882, Mr Douglas Johnstone recorded in a Montrose newspaper that a beautifully marked salmon smolt, six inches long, had been taken from the stomach of a whiting caught in the deep sea fishing two miles off the Forfarshire coast Having sent the specimen and necessary information to Professor Huxley, F R S, H M Inspector of Salmon Fisheries, he was informed by him that this raised the novel and interesting question whether salmon spawn in the sea or not?

were it believed in and acted upon, would be disastrous to our salmon fisheries, as it might be advanced that these fishes could breed as well in the ocean as in rivers, consequently no necessity on their behalf arises for keeping our fresh waters pure, or having free passes in our streams in order to allow them to reach their spawning-beds It was probably from such views the notion of the par being a distinct species sprang, and even now there are some who assert a doubt whether our "last-springs" are the young of *Salmo salar* * Willoughby followed Gesner, and in his *History of Fishes*, published in 1686, lib iv, adduced reasons for disputing the correctness of Rondeletius's opinion, while Pontoppidan, in 1755, in his *Natural History of Norway*, returned to Rondeletius's view, asserting that he was well assured that salmon chiefly eject their roe at the mouths of rivers, where they empty themselves into the sea, or else a little above the salt water †

I thought it well worth making investigations on the point, which was done by placing the ova in tumblers and changing the water once daily for eggs similarly placed in tumblers of fresh water hatched Two trout eggs kept in brackish water at the specific gravity of 1008° (except for two days at 1019°) from January 9th hatched, one on February 28th the other March 1st, but one had dropsy of the sac, apparently due to the medium in which they had been kept, still as a rule salmonoid eggs placed for a day or two in salt water, i e of a salinity of 1020° and upwards, invariably died, as will be fully detailed when discussing "breeding" of salmon and trout.

Among the many agencies that tend to limit the geographical distribution of these fishes is that of temperature, the Salmonidæ, with few exceptions, being confined to an area possessing a cold or temperate climate, while the salmon, trout and char deposit their eggs during the winter months It is a matter of history how Mr You‡ first proved that eggs of fishes of this family could be transmitted even to the Antipodes by the agency of cold scientifically utilized, and although some authors have contended that freezing ova will not destroy the life of the embryo, such a contention is most probably incorrect Dr John Davy ascertained that impregnated salmon ova are capable of resisting a degree of cold sufficient to freeze water and imbed them in ice, while in 1881 it was stated that a large amount of salmon eggs in rivers in the highlands of Scotland had been destroyed by frost

Circumstances occurred which permitted the effects of freezing fish-eggs to be watched by myself on rather a large scale during the winter of 1885-86§, about 10,000 Lochleven trout ova that had been taken from the fish on the 10th, having been sent from Howietoun to Cheltenham and arriving on December 12th They were transmitted in water in a swing tin can, suspended to a strong wooden frame, and when received the lid was found to be tightly frozen down, while even

* A history of this controversy in the British Isles during the present century as regards salmon will be given under the head of the "breeding" of this fish

† As bearing on this question of the effect of saline water, I may notice the paper of M Emile Young (*Ann and Mag Nat Hist*, January, 1884, xiii, page 74) "On the influence of Physico-chemical agencies upon the development of the Tadpoles of *Rana esculenta* " He concluded they were developed the more slowly the greater the degree of salinity of the water

‡ M Pouchet has given reasons based upon experiments that no vertebrate animal which has been completely frozen is susceptible of resuscitation, owing to the blood having become disorganized, although it has been abundantly proved that fish may be revivified after they have been surrounded by ice without being entirely frozen Even partially frozen fishes if resuscitated often subsequently succumb from the injury their constitution has sustained Livingston Stone (*Domesticated Trout*, p 158) observed that he has frozen alevins several times so that they were glued tight on to the ice and could not stir, and in most instances it did not seem to hurt them at all

§ In the above instance 2454 eggs were accidentally frozen, at least every one of them was imbedded for some time in ice, 565 being quite dead when thawed out, and without enumerating the daily mortality it will be sufficient to give it in periods of ten consecutive days each, and which were as follows —89, 45, 173, 69, 199, 121, 193, 197, and the remainder subsequently succumbed, not a solitary ovum hatching A small opaque white spot in most instances showed itself or else a white semi-circle, subsequently the entire egg became opaque Those which survived the longest or until the embryo became sufficiently forward to be examined, were in every instance found to possess a badly developed head, and very small black eyes, apparently evidencing a want of development in consequence of the injury received from the amount of cold to which they had been subjected.

the air-holes were plugged with ice, for a very severe frost had existed for several days. Agitation of the can had prevented the surface of the contained water freezing, but on emptying out the eggs which were free, it was found that the entire inner surface of the can was a solid incrustation of ice, wherein about one-fourth of the consignment of eggs were imbedded. The next morning there was no change, although the temperature of the contained water had risen from 31° to 34° Fah., still it was not until 6.30 p.m. that the ice in which the eggs were imbedded could be extracted, or about 54½ hours after the can had left Stirling. Here was a case in which eggs were frozen in such a manner as might be expected to occasionally take place when in their natural redds, but although some survived longer than others, the contained embryos were insufficiently developed, and none lived to be hatched. On January 19th, 1886, thirteen ova were taken from a hatching-tray wherein the unfrozen eggs were, and these were placed in water in an unglazed flower-pot saucer, and left out-of-doors to freeze. The next morning the surface of the water was frozen, and by the evening, at 8 p.m., it was a solid block of ice, in which the eggs were imbedded. On the 26th a thaw set in, and by mid-day all the eggs were thawed out, one was found dead, and the rest were placed in a tray in the hatching-house. On February 24th, two died, nine during the first seven days in March, and the last within forty-seven days after then having been frozen. It would thus seem that freezing is fatal to these eggs, either immediately or after a varying period, and that ova once embedded in a block of ice cannot be expected to survive. Consequently a very severe frost may prove to be most destructive to salmonoid eggs, should the water in the redds be frozen.*

The depth of water at which these eggs may be incubated is also important, for when redds are disturbed the contained ova must be washed away down stream, and should they not be consumed by their enemies, more especially voracious fishes, it has been surmised they perish, due to the depth into which they have been carried. In some experiments which were tried† it appeared that trout eggs may be incubated in still water, changed daily, at least as deep as 26 inches, the greatest depth at which such was attempted.

Deposits of various kinds, some noxious, others merely acting mechanically on the egg by smothering it, and thus causing its death by the process of preventing the due aeration of the contained embryo, may be occasioned in various ways. These sediments if excessive, may be immediately fatal to the embryo or to the young fish, causing their destruction by suffocation, or such may be deferred owing to its being incomplete. Consequent upon certain legal questions involving the inquiry whether peaty water could do injury to trout eggs, a series of experiments were undertaken at Cheltenham, and from which it appeared that only about 50 per cent of the eggs were fertile in peaty water, while 90 per cent hatched in water wherein there was no peaty solution: also that spates of peaty water are more fatal to these eggs than their being continuously in a peaty solution: while the effect of the sediment is to arrest development, especially in the head, and increase the size of the eye‡

* December 28th, 1885, twenty trout eggs were taken from a hatching tray and placed in an artificial redd constructed of fine pebbles, which had been previously boiled for some time, and for periods from four to six hours daily, until February 25th, this redd was kept uncovered by water. On March 27th the two first eggs hatched on the same date as those in the trays wherein a constant supply of water had been kept maintained.

† On December 24th, 1885, a paraffin cask, which had been well chained inside, and subsequently kept filled with water for a month, was placed in the hatching house at Cheltenham. For the purpose of the following experiment a blacksmith made an iron rod 34½ inches long, and half an inch in diameter with cross bars every six inches projecting three inches on either side. Three small trays of perforated zinc were securely fixed to these cross bars, the upper being two inches below the surface of the water, the next fourteen inches, and the lowest 26 inches. The water in the cask was changed daily until February 22nd, or for about seventy days, when the zinc trays were transferred to a hatching-tray. In the eggs from the upper tray the first hatched March 24th, two on the 25th, and two on the 26th, while two died. Of those from the middle tray the first hatched March 23rd, the second on the 24th, the two others died. Of those on the lowest tray, or 26 inches below the surface, one hatched March 25th, three on the 25th, one on 26th, and one died.

‡ Having obtained some moist turf or peat cut from the vicinity of Earls Burn, near Howietoun,

Irrespective of sediments occasioning destruction to the eggs, and concerning which the foregoing shows the general cause, there are pollutions more or less poisoning the water, and which if sufficiently potent of course destroy the vitality of the eggs, or perhaps occasion the young to be a sickly race. Some pollutions, however, may be present which do not act in so direct a manner, such as paraffin. Doubtless this product of wood-oil or tar-oil stearin, when in a pure state, is inodorous, tasteless, and insoluble in water, but in its commercial condition, as used in lamps and employed in the following experiments,* its odour was pretty strong. It would, however, seem that in a strong flow of water, especially when of moderate depth, this oil floats away without being immediately fatal, although very injurious, to incubating salmonoid eggs while I have known it accidentally tried on a large scale where a good current of water was present, but the ova hatched fairly well, it being only when the flow became weak that the eggs appeared to suffer.

Although in fish-culture a good and sufficient stream of water is considered highly desirable, and that the depth above salmonoid eggs should be at least from one to one and a quarter inches, such is not indispensable for incubation, as they may be hatched in water in which there is but a slight current, as well as in that which is only occasionally changed, or even in damp moss, and this brings one directly to the question of what are the changes occurring that enable the impregnated egg to exist? Two theories have been held, the first by Vogt, that aerated water obtains access through the shell of the egg to the embryo, when the carbon conjoins with the oxygen of the contained air and passes off as carbonic acid gas. The second theory is that the oxygen gas alone obtains access through the shell of the egg, and then conjoins with the carbon. Whichever is the correct theory, it is evident that the excretion of carbon must take place, or the embryo will die. Likewise that, even if carbonic acid is given off, it must not remain in the vicinity of the ovum, which its presence would poison. It has been pointed out

$7\frac{1}{2}$ lb were placed in large masses in $18\frac{1}{2}$ gallons of water, which was filled up twice or thrice daily. The water was led from this in the usual manner to a hatching tray, where on December 15th, 1885, 230 eggs were placed, from these some were from time to time removed, but 91 were treated continuously in this manner until February 22nd, or for sixty nine days, when they were transferred to clean water, and commenced hatching on March 27th, at the same time as the eggs which had been thus treated from the first. Of the foregoing 91 eggs 45 were hatched, the young being rather smaller and thinner than those entirely incubated in fresh water. Possibly one reason they were not suffocated was that every now and then the eggs were washed by means of a watering can, a process which otherwise was doubtless destructive to some or injurious to others (see Hog-backed trout). The amount of peat remaining in the reservoir on February 22nd was $1\frac{1}{4}$ lb, consequently $5\frac{3}{4}$ lb had passed over the eggs, or been lost in the amount of 3830 gallons of water which was consumed. The experiment was varied to see whether spates of peaty water would or would not have the same influence on the eggs as a continuous flow of it. On December 30th, some of the above ova were transferred to a hatching-tray supplied by clean water, which would have been equivalent to them having been subjected to the spate of fifteen days' duration in a peaty stream. Having been there 22 days I took some to my friend Mr. E. Wethered, who most kindly photographed them when under the microscope, as well as others kept all the time in fresh water, or in a peaty solution. The difference between these embryos was very apparent. Those treated from the first in fresh water were normal, such as had experienced the fifteen days' spate of peat water were soft and badly developed, so that it was with the greatest difficulty that any photograph of them could be obtained; while the embryos kept continuously in peaty water could not be taken at all, they almost seemed to melt away. On March 18th, successful photographs were made of embryos in those developed in fresh water, the interspace between the eyes equalled the horizontal diameter of that organ, whereas such as had been exposed to a fifteen days' spate had large eyes, and the distance between them only equalled one-third of their horizontal diameter, showing badly developed heads and extraordinary large eyes, and although in these last the embryos lived nearly to the period for hatching, none were sufficiently robust to emerge from their shells, for although some came out partially, none did entirely, they died in the process.

* January 13th, 1886, at Cheltenham, a bucket was fitted with a wooden tap, near its bottom, and then filled with spring water, into which 12 drops of paraffin were added to each quart, and 15 trout eggs were placed in a small hatching tray, into which the water from the bucket slowly dropped. On the 16th they were removed to clean water, but none lived to hatch. This was repeated several times, and the average number of eggs that hatched was one in ten. The final experiment was made on Feb 3rd, and continued until the 11th, ten eggs were employed, and the paraffin was gradually augmented up to 22 drops to every quart of water. One egg died March 27th, one hatched March 28th, but the remainder died.

that shortly after extrusion from the parent some eggs at once largely increase in size by the direct imbibition of water, but this does not prove that there is a constant current through the shell, while the following experiments distinctly show that such could not invariably be the case   Eggs, it is well known, are sent long distances, as to the Antipodes, in moss,* and, if necessary, kept cool by means of ice, in such cases sufficient dampness is present to enable imbibition to occur through the egg-shell, but there is water whereby a current could be kept up, yet the embryo develops, thus clearly demonstrating that moisture without immersion is sufficient for incubation, provided the eggs are kept cold, dark, and damp   In such cases oxygen or gas alone could be absorbed, while the presence of moss would assist in carrying off excreted carbonic acid   Should the egg be placed on a piece of glass or other smooth substance, and kept moist, it soon dies, the water which attaches it by its base to the glass probably becomes charged with the excreted carbonic acid, which, reacting on the embryo, is as a poison to it

In order to ascertain whether this absorption of oxygen occurs solely at the micropyle, or throughout the general surface of the egg-shell,† the shells of two trout eggs were emptied of their contents, and the portion where the micropyle‡ is situated was removed, and in each instance a solution of preocarmine passed through the shell showing its permeability

Salmonoid eggs may even be successfully incubated in water that is not flowing, thus—on December 15th, 1885, ten trout eggs were placed in a tumbler wherein the water was changed daily, one died, the remainder hatched between March 25th and 28th   On February 4th, one egg was similarly treated, except that the water was changed on alternate days—it hatched on March 26th   On February 12th, six more trout eggs were placed in a tumber in which the water was renewed every third day, and all hatched between March 27th and April 6th

The influence of light upon the eggs of Salmonidæ has a decidedly deleterious effect, while during incubation the embryo is a rule, appears to he with its eyes uppermost   Should an excess of light be allowed, the contained young seems to be badly developed, and has small and dark eyes, while any alevins that are hatched are, as a rule, weakly   It may be for this reason that redds are constructed, in order to keep the eggs in the dark, or it may be also for the purpose of preventing movement in their earlier stages

The dangers of transporting salmonoid eggs, except at certain periods and under exceptional conditions, have already been alluded to (pp 31, 32 ante), and here the effects of injuries or shocks which ova can sustain and yet survive have to be considered   Slight shocks may be reasonably anticipated to frequently

---

* Feb 27th, 1886, I was shown at Howicktoun some hundreds of eggs of the Lochleven trout, and a few of the salmon, the former of which had been taken from the fish on December 19th, when they were placed in a hatching-tray   On January 22nd they were removed to damp moss, on which a little ice was laid and had been subsequently kept in a room in which the temperature only varied between 40 and 44° Fahn   I took the box of eggs as they were to Cheltenham, and on March 2nd placed a few in a hatching tray, leaving the remainder in the moss   Those in the trays commenced hatching on March 20th, on the 106th day, when ten came out, and two days subsequently, on looking at the eggs which had been left in the moss, in which the temperature stood at 55° Fahn, one was found hatched, twelve dead, so the rest of the ova were placed in a hatching tray, and came out in due course, whether of salmon or trout   Some of the foregoing eggs were removed from the damp moss on March 9th, and placed in tumblers of water in a warm room, and commenced hatching on the 16th, or 96th day   (For a detailed account see The Field May 8th 1886)

† Respecting whether the air in solution in the water is or is not conveyed directly to within the ovum conflicting opinions have been held   Dr John Davy (Physiological Researches) questioned if the shell of the egg among the Salmonidæ, when in a sound state, before putrefaction had commenced, could be pervious to water, as asserted by Vogt, but both agreed that the death of the impregnated ovum or embryo is clearly demonstrated by the coagulation of the yelk from penetration into its substance

‡ To see whether, after death, water obtains access to the interior of the egg through the micropyle, the experiment was tried of placing ova in water just sufficient to cover them two thirds up their sides, leaving the micropyle dry, but the changes were similar to those in other eggs in which the micropyle was submerged

occur to fish eggs, although deposited under favourable conditions, when floods or other causes might disturb the redds, while even the artificial fish-culturist is sometimes compelled to remove ova from one tray to another, to wash them when covered with mud or other sediment, or even to send them to distant places Sometimes the deposit on the eggs is so great that were it not removed the embryos would be suffocated, and the consequence of draining the trays and cleansing the ova, by means of a watering pot,* is different in accordance with the period of incubation at which it takes place   The capacity for receiving slight shocks with a considerable amount of impunity, ceases after about the first twenty-four or forty-eight hours subsequent to extrusion from the fish, and does not return until at least one-third of the period of incubation has been completed, and even then some slight injury may be occasioned

Experiments† were undertaken in order to ascertain the effects of direct concussion on these eggs, which influences would be identical with what they must experience if carried over rapids or steep inclines   They were either placed in a bottle of water and dropped from various heights, or direct into water, when it was found that in those in which this was tried within twenty-two days after having been obtained from the fish, none lived over eight or nine days   But in eggs dropped from even a greater height, after they had incubated forty-seven days, some lived to hatch, demonstrating what a much larger amount of motion and concussion eyed ova will bear than eggs in their earlier stage

Among the various experiments of shocks and concussions made during the first days of incubation no single monstrosity was observed   neither were any hatched from the eggs which had been subject to frost and cold, which will again have to be referred to

It is now about thirty years since Dr John Davy experimented upon the fertilized eggs of these fishes,‡ with reference to their capabilities for diffusion, and what adverse circumstances they might be subjected to, but retain their vitality   Living and incubating, as I have shown they are able to do without immersion in water (*see* page 35), they might be conveyed from one piece of water to another adhering to the feathers or feet of birds, or the fur of mammals, even fish which have swallowed impregnated eggs might be the vehicle for their conveyance when carried off by rapacious birds.

---

* January 5th 1886, trout eggs in tray No 2, at Cheltenham, containing about 2500, were transferred to another tray, and by 3 P M 24 were dead, while the average number of deaths up to this period had been one daily, now the pick rose to 31, 2, 7, 7, 2, and then the mortality reverted to what it had previously been   The eggs in trays Nos 1 and 3, placed under the same conditions, showed no increase in the daily average of deaths, consequently the above experiment may be adduced as an example of the effect of slight shocks in the very early (not earliest) condition of embryonic life   January 18th, the eggs in tray No. 1, likewise containing about 2500, were similarly changed, but the deaths were scarcely increased thereby, as only five were picked out during that and the succeeding 13 days, whereas 26 had been removed during the previous 36 days   February 5th, the eggs in the trays where they were treated by a solution of peat, were washed without any deaths resulting   February 21st, the eggs in tray No 2 were again washed, and soon five opaque ones were seen, but no such mortality took place in the other trays   February 23rd eggs in tray No 1 were washed   for the preceding ten days only two had died, and during the next six days they occurred as follows, 2, 5 0, 1, 1, 1

† January 2nd, 1886, at 10 15 A M, a trout egg, on the 22nd day of incubation, was dropped from a height of 2 ft into the water, and by 12 A M it was dead and opaque, a second was similarly dropped on to a board, it also was dead by 1 P M   Next, five eggs were dropped from the same height into the water and subsequently returned to a hatching tray   the first died on January 12th, and the remainder by March 8th   On December 30th, 1885, at 1 25 P M, ten eggs were taken from tray No 2 and placed in a quart brandy bottle which, when empty, weighed a little over 1¼ lb, but when full of water and corked, 3 lb 4 oz   Thus filled it was dropped from a height of 2 ft on to the grass, and by January 1st, 2 were dead, 2 died in February, and the remainder by March 7th   On January 27th, eight eggs, on the 47th day of incubation, were placed in a bottle similar to the foregoing, and dropped 4½ ft   one died the same day, one on the 15th, 3 hatched on the 25th or 26th, and the remainder succumbed

‡ Dr Davy in his experiments upon salmon eggs ascertained that when exposed to dry air at the ordinary temperature they rapidly died, that their vitality was as well preserved in moist air as in water, while ova placed in ice were not affected unless lowered many degrees below the freezing point   If the water in which the eggs were, became heated to 80° or 82° Fah, they could stand it with impunity for a moderate period, but 84° or 85° was fatal

Packing the eggs of these fishes for the purpose of sending them long distances, as to the Antipodes, must be adverted to in order to give a connected history of what has been accomplished in this country respecting the Salmonidæ, for various plans have found favour for conveying these ova from place to place in Europe, and also for transporting them long distances across the sea.* In 1862, Mr Youl's discovery that the French mode of conveying salmonoid eggs in moss could be adapted to sending them in safety even through tropical heat, was a great advance. Some eggs will almost invariably die when travelling far, however well they may be packed, although the safest time is to transmit them during the eyed stage, still they have been conveyed earlier. The main principle is to employ thin layers of well-picked and pressed moss in trays with perforated bottoms,† the eggs being separated from the moss by muslin,

* Ephemera, writing in *Bell's Life* (December 11th, 1858), observed "Earl Grey did, and the Duke of Newcastle does, favour and support an attempt to transfer salmon to the rivers in Van Diemen's Land by artificial means, under the direction of Mr Gottlieb Boccius One attempt has failed, Mr Boccius says, through the retention, beyond the day fixed for sailing, by more than a month at Plymouth, of the ship, on board of which impregnated salmon ova were placed in tanks prepared with due care This is not to occur in a second attempt about to be made shortly " In the year 1854 the attention of Mr. Youl was first directed to this subject, and he concluded that the fry or ova alone could be successfully conveyed through the tropics, but for which the assistance of iced water would be indispensable On February 25th, 1860, about 35,000 salmon ova were shipped in the "Curling" for Melbourne They were in a swing tray, through which a stream of water flowed from a tank on deck, the connection being by small tin pipes placed inside and around an ice-house which contained upwards of fifteen tons of ice On the sixty fifth day the ice had become exhausted, the temperature of the water suddenly rose to 71°, and the last of the ova died On March 4th, 1862, a second venture was made in the "Beautiful Star," packed as follows —A wooden tin lined tank, holding two hundred gallons of water, was built on deck and surrounded by a casing of charcoal Directly under it was the ice-house constructed to carry twenty five tons of ice, at the bottom of which was a flat iron tank holding one hundred gallons, connected to the upper tank by an iron pipe which passed nearly through the centre of the ice-house The cooled water was conducted by iron pipes to the vivarium where the ova were placed on two sets of swing trays with gravel, and the stream which flowed out of the vivarium, ran into a receiving tank, from which it was pumped back to the large wooden tin-lined tank All the pipes were regulated by stop cocks attached to flexible gutta percha piping at their extremities, and from five hundred to two thousand gallons could be passed through at discretion during twenty four hours It was in this vessel Mr Youl first turned to account the mode of packing fish ova which was then in use Having seen in Paris moss employed for this purpose, and in which they successfully travelled short distances, at least after their eyes had become developed, he packed some similarly in a wooden box made of inch pine and having its sides perforated , this he deposited in the centre of the ice house On May 15th the ice was very low, the box came to light and in it were nineteen living ova , nine days subsequently the ice was exhausted, and although the ova perished, the method of successfully conveying them through the tropics had been solved

† The following is the plan as employed at Howietoun, taken from the *Sporting and Dramatic News* —" The packing is managed so as to subject the eggs to as little handling as possible A large sink stands at the foot of the staircase of the principal hatching house, a lead basin is placed at one end, and a box a little larger than a grille is floated in this sink, partly resting on the edge of the basin One end of the box is open, and water rises through it to a depth of three inches So soon as the embryo in the salmon ova is sufficiently formed to show as a thick white line, the ova may be moved with impunity, the grilles are lifted out of the boxes, and reversed, one by one, into the wooden trough After 50,000 eggs have been thrown off, a waste valve is opened, and the water draws all the eggs into the lead basin

" They are then scooped with a glass measure into frames covered with coarse peach netting, an undulating motion is given to the floating frame, and the eggs spread as if by magic one into each mesh A thin square of felted or compressed moss is laid over the frame, and a small piece of muslin over the moss A frame covered with some soft material is placed over the muslin, and the whole reversed When the first frame is removed the eggs are seen beautifully arranged on the moss in rows corresponding to the meshes of the net The muslin is then lifted into the travelling tray, and a second square of moss gently laid over the eggs Each travelling tray holds three layers, and six are usually placed in a box It requires two hours to pack 100,000 eggs for New Zealand For shorter journeys eggs are thrown off the frames on to swan's down, which takes little more than half the time, and greatly facilitates the unpacking at the end of the journey Livingstone Stone (*Domesticated Trout*, p 147) observed that "the usual way in practice to pack trout eggs for transportation in small quantities is in circular tin boxes, with perforated ends, not over three or four inches in depth, and one six inches in diameter is supposed to be able to hold about 5000 eggs These boxes are packed in a tin pail of somewhat larger circumference, and the interspace between the two is filled in with sawdust For packing, he advised as follows —Fill a large pan, a little deeper than the packing box, with water. Take a

mosquito-netting, swan's down calico or butter cloth, and that each tray contains two or three layers. These trays, the lowest being empty to receive the drip, are then piled inside a larger outer case with sawdust filling up the interspace between the two cases, which prevents any sudden change of temperature, and subsequently the whole can be placed inside an ice-house or a cold current of damp air may be kept constantly passing through the trays which retards the hatching of the eggs * When the eggs are going to be unpacked, the bulb of a thermometer should be inserted into the middle of the package, and should it be within 6° Fahr of the water in the incubating trays they may be transferred at once if not, this may be gradually altered by adding water Eggs are not injured by exposure to air, provided it is not for too long a period, and that they do not become warm, dry, freeze, or be subjected to great vicissitudes of temperature

Artificial redds may be constructed in suitable spots near to the ground most adapted for young fry, and where the water is shallow and with a slight ripple and of a proper temperature Here eyed-ova may be deposited, being careful that the localities shall be where floods and discoloured water do not injure the eggs or the alevins when hatched

Reverting to the period when the young are hatched as "alevins" to commence their new mode of existence in a world of waters, we see a large bag, the yelk- or umbilical-sac, dependant from their under surface a little behind the gill-opening, and which contains the nourishment whereon they have almost wholly to subsist for a period varying from three weeks to three months in accordance with the temperature of the water and some other disturbing causes During this or the alevin time, they are not difficult to keep alive, provided they have a fair amount of care combined with a sufficiency of pure water of this last some are in favour of its being shallow with a strong ripple, while others prefer it to be deeper by one or two inches than what was employed for the incubation of the eggs, and with a slow current, while in rivers and streams they remain in shallows at this period, localities where they are moderately safe from their larger enemies When in hatching or rearing-trays they seek dark places in which to hide, they get into every crevice and push into any hole which they can find, consequently numerous precautions have to be adopted to prevent them obtaining access to where their existence would be cut short. Likewise the fish-culturist has to be careful that every screen is in working order, and that the fish are not too crowded

During the first few days of their existence alevins incessantly employ their pectoral fins, in order to promote a current, which not only assists respiration, but carries away from their vicinity any deleterious substances which may be floating about Even subsequent to this period, should the water from any cause be insufficiently aerated they again use these fins for the purpose † of assisting

---

bed of moss, about half-an inch deep, on the bottom of the box, and sink the box in the pan of water The bottom layer should be a single bunch of some kind of the finer common mosses, while the subsequent layers should be the damp rank moss which grows in the swamps, and is known by the name of sphagnum " They may also be packed in baskets Packing is usually done under water, by which means eggs are more readily spread, but they can be exposed in air, so long as it is damp and moist and the room dark, for some hours without doing them any injury

* The hatching of salmon eggs was retarded, in the vaults of the Wenham Lake Ice Company, in 1865, until the 144th day, and at the Crystal Palace until the 148th day The Times observed (January, 1884), that the eggs sent to New Zealand by Sir James Maitland were packed on an entirely new principle in order to keep down the temperature It is a modification of Haslam s refrigerating machinery, and by an ingenious contrivance, the air is kept at a steady temperature of 30° to 34°, low enough to retard the development of the eggs without freezing them, while it is also so saturated with moisture, that a piece of dry flannel being hung up in the chamber in which the eggs are deposited, becomes quite damp in the course of a few hours The air, reduced to this condition, is driven into the chamber and expelled again on the other side at regular stated intervals of time so that all possibility of " mouldiness " and of too great saturation is prevented on the one hand, and of too dry cold or too great heat on the other They arrived at their destination in excellent condition

† At Cheltenham on March 14th, 1885, the alevin of trout now twenty days old, had ceased using their pectoral fins for aiding breathing, but as soon as the water supply was reduced they again

respiration*, while in some instances the gill-covers are abnormally small, leaving a portion of the gills uncovered and consequently immersed in the surrounding water, but more usually this seems to be the result of deficiency of development or even of disease as gill-fever

Although alevins are able to subsist on the contents of their yolk-sac, so long as it lasts, it is imperative when this source of supply has become exhausted that they should obtain natural or artificial nourishment, and now it is that most of the monstrosities succumb, being generally unable to consume food having been up to this period in the same condition as chickens within their shells, prior to being hatched   It is, however, very advisable to commence feeding alevins before the yolk-sac has become quite absorbed, and as soon as the little fish appear to be searching for nourishment themselves , at this time they seem to require more air and energetically push up stream   The food should consist of the finest particles, while that which is tainted or diseased must be avoided as absolutely poisonous to them   Opinions differ as to what is the most suitable nutriment, and different fish-culturists advocate various constituents as being the best   Hard-boiled eggs and fillet of horse are employed at Howietoun, six of the former, which had been boiled twelve hours previously, to $\frac{1}{4}$ lb of the latter   or nine eggs to 1 lb of fillet, subsequently passed through perforated zinc of No 8 size, being a diameter of 0 25 inch , it has a long and stringy consistence, and many fish get hold of its ends, as its thread-like bands are agitated in the water   Some employ liver and curd made from sour milk, in equal parts, or two portions of the former to one of the latter, and all reduced to the finest particles   yolk of eggs boiled for half an hour, and subsequently finely powdered   boiled liver by itself   Alevins will live for a long time in water which is unchanged, and consequently can be transported with comparative ease   they are likewise said to bear cold well

In some localities alevins are turned out into a stream or other suitable rearing pond, protected from their enemies, while should they be put into an unprotected piece of water they fall victims to all the vermin in the neighbourhood †   But even if it is considered desirable to turn these alevins out such is not always practicable thus snow may be still present on the ground, and were it to suddenly melt, floods injurious to these young fish might be occasioned

When the umbilical sac has become absorbed these fish commence to be known as " fry, ' and now a period of greater danger to the artificially reared ones commences   Looking more like fish, as they are no longer weighted down by the large sac, they are seen to collect less in masses, in short, to lead more separate existences, looking out for food   They rise from the floor of the

---

employed them for this purpose   Alevins of the trout 0 85 in. long, and also a salmon 1 25 in long, of about the same age, were placed in a tumbler of still water taken from the tray where it stood at 42° Fahr , at 11 7 A M   and which, on being carried indoors, rose by 11 20 A M to 45°   In seven minutes the pectorals of the trout began to be used for accessory breathing purposes, at the rate of three times to every once of the gill-covers, this went on for fifteen minutes, when the fish was returned to the tray   The salmon alevin breathed faster, but did not employ its pectoral fins

* In 1884 some little blennies, mostly shannies, *Blennius gattorugine*, were placed in a small salt water aquarium, the contents of which had been accidentally left unchanged, and the water as a consequence had become very foul   The little fish until the water was changed could be seen employing the upper rays of their pectoral fins in order to assist respiration, for in these fishes the character of the rays differ, the upper seven being shorter, thinner, and more elastic than the lower six, which are thicker and stiffer   Although the entire thirteen may be employed simultaneously during locomotion, the upper ones, when the fish is stationary, may be used to assist breathing, while the lower stiff ones are employed to support   In gobies the ventral fin under the same conditions was observed to be used in order to attach the fish to the aquarium, while the outer pectoral rays were also placed against the glass, as a person during an asthmatic paroxysm fixes his elbows on the table or window sill while he gasps for breath   During this period the gill covers were spasmodically working at about 10s times in a minute

† Andrews, *Badminton Library*, "Salmon and Trout Culture," page 435, observed that " most fishing clubs not being able to provide suitable rearing-places for their young fish turn the ' fry ' that they produce or breed direct into the rivers, which already contain trout, the probable consequence being that 90 out of every 100 go down the throats of the larger fish   a few hundred yearling fish would cost far less and make a much better ' show ' in the water "

tray and balance themselves in the water, with their heads directed up stream, and are ready to seize any suitable passing object   Now it is absolutely necessary that they should be fed,* commencing with one meal a day, and being careful that no remains of food shall be left to corrupt at the bottom of the tray   Some believe that at this period there is more danger of over-than of under-feeding, while others warn the inexperienced against the fry being too crowded, as such is very productive of disease   Care has likewise to be taken against their dividing themselves into two sets, and the stronger taking forcible possession of the best places, where food is most plentiful, and driving the weaker ones away to herd by themselves, generally to the lower end of the tray, and here some may be found lying dead against the screen †   Should they subsequently become languid, cease feeding, avoid the current, and commence to die in numbers, such is possibly due to decomposition of uneaten food in the trays, or because the diet is unsuitable, and for the first Livingston-Stone advises as a remedy the free application of common earth, covering the bottom of the tray to half-an-inch or more   What has already been enumerated as suitable food may be given, also microscopic forms of animal life—as the larvæ of gnats, *Daphnia*, *Cyclops*, &c , which may be skimmed from the surfaces of ditches or obtained from stagnant pieces of water

After a varying period, the fry, if kept in the trays, will commence springing out of the water, evidently desirous of changing their abode, and they can be turned into larger rearing boxes, or transferred to suitable ponds where there is a constant supply of the purest water and they are protected from their enemies   If crowded in this stage they are subsequently usually stunted   These rearing ponds, or boxes, should afford shade to the fry

When turned into rearing ponds fed by a stream of water, weeds or other forms of shade should be present, while such as contain the natural food as *Daphnia*, *Cyclops*, fresh-water snails or *Limnæa*, or fresh-water shrimps or *Gammarus pulex*, are best adapted for them thriving in   But the locality may be too cold or too far north for sufficient nourishment to be present, and then artificial feeding‡ must be continued

The period required in order to prepare young trout for travelling varies from three or four days in the case of yearlings to as many weeks for larger examples   While for stocking purposes yearlings§ are better than those which are younger, because they can find their own food which younger ones are often unable to accomplish   No difficulty is now experienced in conveying these fish alive for a distance which does not take more than twenty-four hours if the water is iced, but unless the water into which they are going to be transferred is of a similar temperature some loss will probably arise from gill-fever, and cold weather is most suited for their conveyance   Aeration of the water may be assisted by the forms in which some of the transporting cans are now made, or by the use of an aerating pump or other suitable contrivance

Some of the enemies or vermin which attack the fry have already been referred to as inimical to the eggs (*see* p 28), for these little fish are esteemed as delicate morsels by rats and mice, also by birds, as swans, geese, ducks, moor-hens, water-ouzels, and kingfishers, while as they get larger, sea-gulls and terns join in the

* A simple and very effective feeder is employed at Howietoun, consisting of a long wooden handle, at the end of which is fixed at right angles the feeder which resembles a tumbler made of perforated zinc, into this the food is placed, and as it is agitated in the water it gradually escapes

† Livingston Stone observed that "*there is no need whatever of this*.   If they get against the screens it is because they are weak, and you may know that their weakness has come either from their being too much crowded, too little fed, or from being actually sick " (page 174)

‡ Irrespective of the forms of food alluded to, Kuffer has suggested for growing fish, meat or fish being boiled, ground up and mixed in the proportion of three parts of it to one part of flour   Haack proposed horse-flesh even if salted, chopped with a meat cutter, for forms up to one-year-old, and cut into cubes for larger   sheep's liver ground through a fine sieve and mixed with water   sheep's or calves' brains passed through a wire sieve   dried ants' eggs likewise ground fine   or sheep's lungs boiled in salt water   The ova of other forms of fish has also been used   English dog-biscuits, worms and maggots

§ When coarse or large fish are present in the water it is intended to stock, two year old fish are found to succeed best

work of destruction   Frogs will likewise prey on them, also many fish as bull-heads, sticklebacks, perches, eels, river trout, and other forms of Salmonidæ. Among their invertebrate enemies[*] which have been recorded, it does not seem improbable that some, as the fresh water shrimp, *Gammarus pulex*, may be useful in consuming surplus food, which might otherwise tend to putrefy and cause disease, as well as by eating any dead fry, although they may likewise destroy some few of the living, especially such as are weakly

There are numerous diseases alevins and fry are subjected to when artificially reared, among which the following have been enumerated —Constitutional weakness occasioning arrest of development in the young, which is sometimes induced by breeding from young parents or inter-crossing species , from the same causes deformities may arise, although some, as spinal affections, may be due to injuries sustained by the embryo in the earlier stages of its development   This also seems to be one predisposing cause to blue-dropsy of the sac, as well as those cases in which small black eyes, so indentive of bad development, are perceptible in the unhatched young   Too much light, likewise, seems to be injurious to the brain, acting through the medium of the optic nerves   In some instances eggs which had been attacked with fungus will hatch, but the young are mostly weakly   while it is not infrequent to observe the alevin suffocated when attempting to emerge from the egg, or should it succeed in its endeavours, to subsequently die from the effects of weakness   The water itself may be injurious, owing to its being too warm, insufficiently aerated or polluted   Crowding the young is likewise a fertile source of disease, while insufficiency of nutriment may occasion starvation   Still excess often sets up fungus, owing to a portion of the unconsumed food remaining in and polluting the water   Sometimes the fry are choked by trying to swallow pieces of meat which are too large, while fungus may show itself among them

Considerable attention has been devoted of late years to the hybridization of animals and plants, and many assertions, which formerly passed current as undoubted facts, have been ascertained to be partially or wholly erroneous   At the present day we cannot admit the theory of Ray, that "any two animals that can procreate together, and whose issue can procreate, are specifically the same " nor the 'statement of the elder Flourens, that hybrids can only be produced between individuals belonging to the same genus   In short it has been conclusively proved that hybrid offspring are not invariably sterile,[†] their degrees of

---

[*] Mr Daubeny, of Redhampton Rectory, observed in *The Field* (March 22nd, 1881, p 106), as follows — ' I he most deadly enemy to young fish I believe to be leeches (*Piscicola geometra*), and in some streams it seems to me a puzzle how any of the fry, when just emerged from the egg, can escape them   The ponds in my garden and the streams round are alive with leeches about one-third of an inch in length   they devour everything   It is impossible to set a night-line   A large lob worm is eaten in a few minutes by them, and even a mouse used as a bait by one of my boys for eels had nothing but the tail left the next morning   A piece of meat an inch square, after being left in the water an hour, was found to have 1300 attached to it   On a warm day they may be seen crawling on the bottom of the water in every direction   Hardly a square inch this time of year but has a leech or two on it   I think that they will not touch trout own the shell being too tough for them, but fry a few days old, on being placed in a saucer, with some of these tiny leeches by way of an experiment were at once seized upon and devoured   Their powers of locomotion are too feeble to afford them a chance of escape from their ubiquitous foes "

[†] Hybridization has been observed between two quadruna pertaining to different families of Catarhina   Thus an offspring was born in the Regent's Park Zoological Gardens on October 13th, 1878, which was a cross between a male ape *Macacus cynologus* and a female baboon *Cynocephalus mormon*   It died December 20th 1879

All are aware of the existence of mules and hinnies between the horse and the ass, and although some of these mules have been observed to produce offspring, Columella (M de la Malle, *Ann des Sciences Nat*, xxvii, page 237) and others have remarked that they do not have fertile crosses among themselves, but only when interbreeding with one of the primitive species from which they had been derived   Mr Bartlett (*Proc Zool Soc*, 1884 page 399, pl xxxiv, xxxv) has described a cross made in the Regent's Park Zoological Gardens, which includes the races of Zebra, Gayal, and Bison, and in which communication he gave descriptions of other hybrids between mammals kept in a semi domesticated state   Another instructive instance has been recorded by Professor Kuhn, of Halle, respecting the interbreeding of the Gayal, *Bos frontalis*, and some of the ordinary breeds of the domestic ox of Europe   A young bull and a cow Gayal were received from Calcutta, June 18th, 1880, the bull paired readily with cows of every variety

fertility graduating from sterility to perfect fertility and what occurs in other divisions of the vertebrata has been shown to likewise take place in fishes. Pallas held that in some instances domestication tends to the elimination of sterility while Morton considered that it merely evolves the capacity for being prolific.

Evidence has been handed down to us from early times that the existence of hybrid fish was believed in, as may be seen by referring to Willoughby and Ray in 1686, while Pennant (*Brit. Zool*, 1812) alluded to " hybrid fish, for that such exist, those persons who had paid most attention to the subject in ichthyology have not a doubt "

The ova of these fishes have to be fertilized by the milt of the males diffused as a rule in the surrounding water, and it may occur, especially in streams, that milt comes in contact with, and perhaps fertilizes, the eggs of a female of a different species, genus, or family, thus giving rise to a hybrid offspring * But the size of the micropyle of the ovum, and that of the spermatozoid of the milt, must be of conforming capacities, or fertilization would be a physical impossibilty

of domestic cattle, and numerous hybrids were born, nine males, and ten females, of these, the older ones of both sexes have already (*Field*, Jan 15, 1885) been used for further experiments Females on being paired with an ordinary European bull, in every case proved fertile, so far conclusively proving the fertility of the hybrid Gayal cows when paired with European bulls of unmixed blood But the hybrid Gayal bulls, without exception, have proved absolutely sterile although they have readily paired both with hybrid females and cows of unmixed European races Likewise, it was remarked (*Field*, May 16th, 1885) that the same experimentor, Professor Kuhn, has also crossed the domestic sheep with the moufflon, *Ovis musimon*, the wild sheep of Corsica and Sardinia The results were equally favourable with the various European, Asiatic, and African breeds of domestic sheep and uniformly successful, whether ewes of the domestic sheep were crossed with moufflon rams, or the reverse Their descendants proved fertile in both instances when crossed with each other This was the case with animals of close consanguinity and even with twins, and in (1885) lambs of mule crossings have been born which belong to the fourth generation of these animals crossed exclusively between themselves

Among birds, Eyton crossed the Chinese goose with the common goose, from which he reared two hybrids, but from separate sittings, while from these two hybrid offspring he obtained a hatching of eight hybrids, the grandchildren of the original unmixed parents Darwin procured two of these hybrids, and from them (brother and sister) raised five extremely fine birds from two hatches, which in every respect resembled the hybrid parents Pheasants, also, are known to cross freely In this class, kept in confinement, many interesting facts on this subject have been recorded, and which seem to have more analogy to what obtains in fishes than the instances observed in the higher grade of mammals Hybrids have been raised from a hen Canary and a cock Goldfinch. from a hen Canary and a cock Siskin, the young of this cross resembling the Siskin in shape from a hen Canary and a Linnet Most of the foregoing have proved fertile, and no great trouble has been experienced in inducing the parents to pair, but the difficulty increases in proportion to the remoteness of the relationship between the species A hen Canary has also been crossed with a Bullfinch, but the eggs, says Bechstein, seldom prove fruitful, still Dr Jassy found a plan of making other Canaries sit on the eggs and bring up the young A hen Canary paired with a Nightingale in Bechstein's presence, but the eggs did not hatch The reason why the Canary has been selected as the mother is, because she will lay her eggs in an artificial nest, which wild birds are not readily induced to do Some, at least, of the foregoing hybrid progeny of birds were fertile—as crosses between hen Canaries and Goldfinches, Siskins and Green finches The first eggs of these hybrids were said to be very small, and the young hatched from them very weak, but the eggs of the next season were larger and the nestlings stronger and stouter

* Leuchart observed that, " if, however, it be true, as Fraisse asserts in his work on *Scientific fish breeding*—and we have no ground on which to doubt it, *primâ facie*—that he has been able to effect, by artificial fecundation, a hybrid offspring between the brook trout and the burbolt, which is between two forms which belong to two totally different groups, then the limits of hybridization must be greater than we have hitherto been inclined to assume " In the bulletin of the United States Fish Commission for 1882 is an account of a hybrid between a fish belonging to the herring family, an *Alosa* or *Clupea*, which furnished the eggs, and the striped bass, *Roccus lineatus*, that pertains to the perches, and which supplied the milt (Some doubts have since been thrown on the latter experiment, it having been questioned whether fertilization took place as described, and the young were not kept, while the first seems to require confirmation)

Passing on from instances of hybrids which have been recorded as bred between fishes belonging to distinct families, we come to intercrossings effected between species belonging to two different genera Livingston-Stone observed in 1869 how he had artificially crossed the eggs of the yellow perch, *Perca flavescens*, with the milt of a glass eyed perch, *Lucioperca*, both pertaining to the percoid family The embryos continued to develop until the seventh day, when all at once they ceased to do so Mr Roosevelt, *Proc Amer Assoc for Adv of Science, 1884*, recorded that in the United States *Salmo confinis* had been bred with the white fish, *Coregonus albus*, the brook trout with the fresh water herring, *Coregonus clupeiformis*, the brook trout and

If we now almost entirely restrict ourselves to the recorded instances respecting hybridization among the Salmonidæ in Great Britain, we find some of our earliest ichthyologists, down to those of the present day, have observed upon their occurrence while fish-culturists have conclusively shown its possibility by artificial breeding, from which fertile or sterile offspring have resulted   And further on I shall adduce successful instances of intercrossings, in addition to those here noted, which were effected by Sir James Maitland, at Howietoun, between the salmon and trout, trout and char and how the offspring were prolific *

the California trout, *Salmo irideus*   Mr G Berney, writing from Morton Hall, Norfolk, on April 28, 1883 to the committee of the Great International Fisheries Exhibition, remarked as follows ' Baron Clock informed me that he had a few fish, a cross between the golden tench, *Tinca vulgaris*, var , and the common carp, *Cyprinus carpio* He clearly did not wish to give me any of them, and I had no desire to introduce a mongrel fish " Pennant, in the last century, alluded to hybrids between the carp and tench, and also to having heard of some between the carp and the bream   They have also been observed between the roach, *Leuciscus rutilus*, and the bream, *Abramis brama* between the rudd, *L erythrophthalmus*, and the bream and between the chub, *L cephalus*, and the bleak, *Alburnus lucidus* while Pritchard remarked that "Defay mentioned a hybrid between a barbel (*Barbus*) and a carp (*Carpio*) "

Crosses have likewise been obtained from between turbot and brill, plaice and flounders, but it is among the carps that probably the most hybrids, bred in a wild state have been observed Hessel stated that he placed a female of the common carp with a male crucian carp, *Carassius vulgaris*, also a female crucian carp with a male of the common carp, and a female *Cyprinus kollarii* (a cross between the common and crucian carps) with a male of the common carp   In the two first instances the young became identical with *C kollarii*, some approaching more towards one parent and some towards the other, while in the last experiment the offspring was with difficulty to be distinguished from the genuine carp   The roach has been observed interbreeding with rudd, and also with the chub

* Willoughby (1686) remarked that he was persuaded that the salmon and the various forms of trout interbreed   and many authors in this country have erroneously asserted that pai were hybrids until the question was set at rest by the fish culturists   Mr Shaw, on April 26, 1841, informed Mr Scope that his "experiments with the ova of the common trout and salmon had been quite successful, and that the hybrids had hatched and were in good health Again, in October, he observed that they were all in a very healthy state, the cross not having in the slightest degree affected their constitutions   Those produced between the salmon and the salmon trout appeared to partake more of the external markings, silvery coating, and elegance of form of the par than any of the others   Those produced between the salmon and the common trout, and between the common trout and the salmon trout, had in every respect more the appearance of the common trout than the former "   "In the Dunrobin Museum is a large series of stretched skins of trout collected by the late Mr Young of Invershin, which are called crosses between sea and river fish as labels on the fish or notes respecting them do not exist " (J Harvie Brown, MSS) These probably refer to Mr Young's preparations of the skins of the salmon he alluded to in his work as remarked upon by Ephemera, in *Bell's Life* of December 11th, 1853

Edmund Thomas Ashworth (*Propagation of the Salmon* 1853, page 19), observed that "the ova of trout fecundated by the milt of the salmon, by the care of MM Barthot and Detzem, and forwarded from the banks of the Rhine, were hatched in their laboratory   Also ova of salmon fecundated by the milt of trout gave the same results   Davy (1858) remarked that "it had been ascertained that the ova of the salmon can be impregnated with the milt of the common trout ' and subsequently, that "Mr Reynolds mixed together the roe of the lake trout and the fluid milt of the char, which he placed in his breeding boxes in November   In seventy days some of the ova were hatched , the young fish had a hybrid character, the fish themselves having much the appearance of the char of the same age ' I received from Howietoun (January, 1885), three figures of hybrid Salmonida in colours from fish in spirit in the ' College of France at Paris   The label asserts ' these were from Professor Coste's fish house 1866 67   The water became bad when they were about eighteen months old and killed them   They had milt and roe " They seem to be of two sorts—trout and salmon, and American char and trout

Dr Gunther (1866), while he admitted that from the time of Willoughby till now the existence of hybrid Salmonidæ had been believed in, continued, "yet no instance had been clearly made out until we were enabled, through the liberality of the Rev Augustus Morgan, to convince ourselves of the existence of a hybrid between the sewin, *Salmo cambricus*, and the river trout, *S fario* " In 1872 he observed, "I am not quite sure but that milt and ova might be found in a hybrid , it has been found in pars, and my theory is that where this is so the fish is the produce of a hen salmon and a male river trout   This hybrid would come to maturity sooner than a pure-bred salmon, and thus give the appearance of roe or milt being found in a par " Professor Rasch in 1867 instituted experiments in order to practically test the question of hybrids among the Salmonida , he found that the ova of the sea and river trout were developed regularly, whichever form were the parent one, and that the offspring were fertile   That of the ova of the char, fertilized by the milt of the trout, 30 to 40 per cent were developed, but many young fish perished after being hatched   Trout ova, fertilized by the milt of the char, only gave 10 per cent of young, many of which were mis shapen   Salmon ova, fertilized with trout milt, yielded

Until recent times the opinion has been very generally accepted that the sterility of hybrids is Nature's mode of preventing the intermingling of species; for it is apparent that, did not some means exist by which the commingling of forms could be prevented, in a short space of time all distinctions would become obliterated—families, genera, and species would be inextricably mixed up * But among fishes causes exist, as to seasons, localities, ova, and milt, but which it is unnecessary to again detail, that greatly tend to circumscribe such commingling

40 per cent of young fish, but more if the milt of the char were employed The ova of a hybrid between a trout and a char could not be fertilized by means of trout milt Carl Peyrer (1876) stated that in Upper Austria "artificial fish-culture had produced many cross breeds, especially of the char, *Salmo salvelinus*, with the trout, which excel the pure breed in many respects In Upper Austria the eggs of the char are mostly impregnated with the milt of the brook trout."

Leuchart remarked that in January, 1878, some salmon ova were fertilized with trout milt, and the offspring were kept in a private brook, well protected from the ingress of strange fish In the beginning of 1879 seventy of them were transferred from the water in which they then were, into a small perfectly inclosed pond, wherein they remained until January, 1880 On taking the fish from the pond only fifty four were found, and a portion of the larger ones had effected their sexual development Only one example was a female, while twenty five milters were counted (possibly the missing ones were females which had jumped out of the water at night-time and been carried off by vermin) On Feb 7 the ova of the female was milted from one of the males In the middle of March the eyes of the embryo were visible, and shortly afterwards the hatched fry, along with their parents, were brought to Berlin in spirit In this instance the male parent was a trout, and trout of both sexes commence breeding at two years of age, as was here observed to be the case, the importance of which has been referred to In the Berlin Fishery Exhibition (1880), were some lovely fish, crosses between the char and the trout, and shown by Professor Hanck, who is said by Leuchart to have observed a capacity for impregnation of the ova of hybrid salmon with one of the parent species

The Hon Robert B Roosevelt observed (*Proceedings of the American Association for the Advancement of Science*, vol xxxii, 1884) that "the crosses made under the New York State Fishery Commission have been very numerous The first was that of the California salmon (*Salmo quinnat*) and the brook trout (*Salmo fontinalis*), this was in the year 1876 Then came the cross of the salmon or lake trout (*Salmo confinis*) with the brook trout then the California trout, *Salmo irideus* and the brook trout and thereafter the entire range of the salmon and trout families as far as they were within the reach of the operators, were combined in many and curious proportions "

The earliest hybrids to mature their ova were the cross between the male California salmon and the female brook trout This took place in the year 1879 They not only became gravid but ascended the spawning races as naturally as those of either distinct species But as they deposited no eggs and did not appear to mate, an examination was made, and it was ascertained that they were all females To remedy this a number of male spawning brook trout were admitted to the same race way The nests had been constructed but no eggs had been deposited in them A further examination proved that the eggs were too large to pass the ovarian opening When they were extruded by force, as in the stripping process, the shells were crushed and a few which were obtained by the use of the knife, a sort of modified Cæsarean operation and were brought into contact with the milt of the trout, failed to impregnate and perished. In all subsequent operations, however, the proportion of each sex has been about equal

The cross of the male brook trout and the female salmon trout, the *Salmo fontinalis* with the *Salmo confinis*, matured ova in October, 1880 There were about 72,000 eggs cast which hatched as readily as those of either parent, although it was found that a larger percentage of them could be impregnated with the milt of the male brook trout than with the milt of their own kind The percentage of fertility was good, and the young proved to be perfectly healthy and as able to stand the struggle for existence as any of their brethren of pure strain At the first cross one-half of the salmon trout was eliminated, their young impregnated with the milt of the male brook trout left only a quarter of the coarser parent, and then came those which were seven eighths brook trout to one-eighth salmon trout, which is as far as we have got at the present time The young of each of these generations show the effects of the cross The first in descent had none of the carmine specks which are the distinguishing feature of the "speckled trout" of our brooks In the second generation the spots began to appear, and in the last they are distinctly visible, although fewer in number than in the trout of *Sangre Azul* In the year 1883 there were distributed to the brooks of the State 45,300 hybrid fry which were one half salmon trout and one-half brook trout, and in 1884 a second planting of 70,000 three-quarter brook trout was made The first, which were deposited in wild waters, were found in six months to have attained a growth of four and a half inches in length, equal to the growth of a brook trout in the same water for an entire year

* Mudie observed (*Popular Guide to the Observation of Nature*, 1832) that " the mules of whatever they are hybrids, will not breed as a race, though they generally can with either of the parent stocks, and the result is a partial return to that stock and if the system were continued, the ultimate progeny would be again assimilated or identified with the pure blood " Dr Gunther

4

Changing the conditions of life in an animal, however slight that change may be, might affect the reproductive organs. Thus carnivora, excluding plantigrades, breed freely in confinement, but carnivorous birds under the same conditions rarely lay fertile eggs, while intercrossing animals of the same species, but belonging to different local races or varieties, generally adds vigour to the mongrel offspring. But if still greater changes are tried, as between two distinct species, a mule or hybrid race is produced which is more or less sterile. The reproductive organs in hybrids are supposed to be in an imperfect condition, which would account for such fishes being more difficult to breed from than the pure species. Geoffroy St Hilaire's experiments proved that unnatural treatment of the embryo occasions monstrosities, while the experiments at Howietoun show that numerous malformations occur when no direct injury or unnatural circumstances (except hybridism, or causes connected with age or consanguinity) could have taken place. Also young parents give weak and often diseased offspring, as well as some monstrosities, which are certainly influences that would affect hybrids as well as pure species.

Darwin was evidently correct in advancing that the sterility of first crosses with pure species, where the reproductive organs are perfect, depends (often, not always) on the early death of the embryo, while the sterility of hybrids having imperfect reproductive systems, he considered allied to that sterility of pure species in which the natural conditions of life have been disturbed. But something in addition seems to be necessary in order to account for the monstrosities and diseased forms seen among young hybrid fishes.

The question arose whether, should an anadromous form of the Salmonidæ be crossed with a non-migratory species, the tendency to migrate to the sea would be lost? Experiments showed that in such hybrids, until their eggs commenced developing, this migratory habit was in abeyance; but with the development of the eggs it at once prevailed.

The question of the prepotency of the sex of either parent in the colour of the offspring, or the period when it breeds, will be deferred until the Howietoun hybrids are considered.

A thorough investigation into the various forms of Salmonidæ present in our waters possesses more than a passing interest, for if, as some suppose, we have many species of trout and char, and they intercross, it becomes a first consideration as to what are the probabilities of sterility occurring in the hybrid offspring? On the other hand, should trout or char from two (asserted to be) separate species be crossed and no unusual phenomena occur, except improvement in the breed, while sterility is absent and monstrosities or malformations few in number, the supposition must be raised whether we are not dealing with local races instead of with distinct species, and if the young are not in reality mongrels instead of hybrids. Also should hybrid offspring be fertile, it becomes important to ascertain to what extent this fertility extends, and through how many generations it may be found to continue.

The question of species is also one which greatly concerns the fish-culturist, while systematic zoologists who constitute new forms of trout and char on insufficient grounds, are occasioning great injury to fisheries. For when successful in promulgating their views, they have induced fish preservers to believe that a diminutive race is not the result of poverty of food, or some local cause, which therefore has remained unsought for. While they have also occasioned the eggs or fry of large varieties to be obtained from a distance, often at a great cost, and the deteriorated progeny (due again to the effects of local causes) has been supposed to show that the purchaser had been imposed upon by the vendor, thus inducing trouble and needless vexation.

(*Introduction to the Study of Fishes*, 1880, page 631) when alluding to the Salmonidæ, stated that "some of the species interbreed, and the hybrids mix again with one of the parent species, thus producing an offspring more or less similar to the pure breed," and a few pages further on he remarked that 'the hybrids are sexually as much developed as the pure breed, but nothing whatever is known of their further propagation and progeny" (*l. c.* page 638)

THE SALMON,[*] Plates III and IV (*male, female, grilse, smolt, and par*).

Salmo, Salvianus, Aquatilium Animalium Historiæ, 1600, page 100, Belon, De Aquatilibus, 1553, i, p 277 e fig, Gesner, Fischbuch, Edition 1598, page 182 cum fig, Schonevelde, Ichthyologiæ, 1624, p 64, Aldrovandus, De Piscibus, 1638, iv, p 483, Willoughby, De Historia Piscium, 1686, p 189, t N 2, fig 1, 2, Ray, Synopsis Methodica Avium et Piscium, 1713, p 63 *Salmo*, no 1, Artedi, Bibliotheca Ichthyologica, 1738, Genera, p 10, Synonomia, p 22, and Descriptiones Specierum Piscium, Edition 1793, page 48 *Salmon*, Pennant, British Zoology, Edition 1776, iii, p 303, pl lix, Edition 1812, iii, p 404, pl lxv

Salmo salar, Linnæus, Systema Naturæ, i, p 509, O F Muller, Prodromus Zoologiæ Danicæ, 1776, p 48, Bloch, Allgemeine Naturgeschichte der Fische, 1782-95, i, p 175, t xv (female) t xcviii (male), Gmelin's Linnæus, Edition 13, 1788, p 1361, Bonnaterre, Encyclopédique Ichthyologie, 1788, p 159, pl lxv, f 261, 262, Bloch by Schneider, 1801, p 398, Lacépède, Histoire Naturelle des Poissons, 1749-1804, v, p 159, Turton, British Fauna, 1807, p 103, Fleming, History of British Animals, 1828, p 179, Faber, Naturgeschichte der Fische Islands, 1829, p 156, Nilsson, Prodromus Ichthyologiæ Scandinaviæ, 1832, p 2, and Skandinaviska Fauna, 1855, p 370, Jardine, Edinburgh New Philosophical Journal, 1862, viii, p 46, and British Salmonidæ, pl i, ii, vii and viii, Richardson, Fauna Boreali-Americana, Fishes, 1831-37, p 140, pl xci, f 1 (head), Jenyns, Manual of British Vertebrate Animals, 1835, p 421, Yarrell, History of British Fishes (Ed 1) 1835-36, ii, p 1, e fig (Ed 2) 1841, ii, p 1 (Ed 3) 1859, i, p 155, Parnell, Wernerian Memoirs, vii, 1838, p 258, and Fishes of the Firth of Forth, 1838 p 118, pl xxx, xxxi, and xxvii, f 1, 2, Swainson, The Natural History and Classification of Fish, 1838, ii, p 287, Agassiz, Histoire Naturelle des Poissons d'eau douce de l'Europe, 1839-42, pl i and ii, White, Catalogue of British Fish, 1851, p 74, Gronow's Fishes, edited by Gray, 1851, p 151, Kroyer, Danmarks Fiske, 1838-53, ii, p 540, Mitchill, the Fishes of New-York, 1814, p 434, De Kay, Fishes of New-York, 1842, p 241, pl xxxviii, fig 122, Thompson, Natural History of Ireland, 1856, iv, p 113, Schlegel, Natuurlijke Historie van Nederland, Visschen, 1862, p 126, pl xiii, f 1, Blanchard, Les Poissons des eaux douces de la France, 1866, p 448, Gunther, Catalogue of the Fishes in the British Museum, vi, 1866, p 11, Storer, Fishes of Massachusetts, 1867, p 142, pl xxv, fig 2, Collett, Norges Fiske, 1875, p 155, Malm, Fauna, 1877, p 534, Moreau, Poissons de la France, 1881, iii, p 525, Day, British and Irish Fishes, 1880-84, ii, p 66, pls. cx and cxi, Brown-Goode, Game Fishes of the United States, 1879, p 5, fig and Fishery Industries of the United States, 1884, p 468, Garman, American Salmon and Trout, 1885, p. 8, fig 2, 3, 4

Salmo salmo, Cuvier and Valenciennes, Histoire Naturelle des Poissons, xxi, 1848, p 169, pl 614

Salmo salmulus, Ray, l c p 63, Turton, l c p 104, Jardine, l c xviii, p 56, Jenyns, l c p 426, Parnell, Wern Mem vii, p 278, pl xxxii, fig 1 and pl xxx, and Fish Firth of Forth, p 138, pl xxxii (*Par* or *Smolt*)

Salmo nobilis, Olafsen und Povelsen, Reise durch Island, 1774-75, i, p 83, Pallas, Zoographia Rosso-Asiatica, 1811 and 1831, iii, p 342

Salmo hamatus, Cuvier, Regne Animal, Cuv and Val l c xxi, p 212, pl. 615 (*old male*)

Salmo gracilis, Couch, Report, Royal Cornwall Polytechnic Society, 1859 and Fishes of the British Isles, 1865, iv, p 216, pl ccxvi (*a thin deteriorated race*)

Salmo argenteus, Gunther, Catal vi, p 86 (not Cuv and Val) (*a helt*)

The Salmon,[†] Russell, 1864, pp 234, Couch, l c. iv, p 163, pl ccxi

[*] The literature relating to this fish is so extensive that it has been found necessary to omit a considerable number of the references

[†] The synonymy of the land locked races of this species will be given when the Lake Wenern variety is described, but it must here be remarked that *Salmo scinernensis*, Gunther, was named by that gentleman upon the erroneous supposition that he was examining this form, whereas his specimens were those of lake trout The Penobscot and Sebago salmon of the American continent are likewise varieties of *S salar*, but do not attain to the dimensions of those present in Lake Wenern.

4 *

B xi—xii, D 13-14 ($\frac{3\cdot 4}{10\cdot 11}$), P 13-14, V 9, A 11 ($\frac{2\cdot 3}{8\cdot 9}$), C 19, L 1 120-125,
L tr $\frac{11-14}{19-22}$, Vert 59-60, Cæc pyl 53-77

The body is rather elongated, with the abdominal profile more curved than that
of the back. But the proportions of one part to the remainder in this fish vary
considerably, not merely consequent on the locality it inhabits, but likewise with
its age and the season thus in the young there is a comparatively large head
and eyes, a short snout and rounded body, but as the adult stage is attained
there is greater depth of the body due to a more prominent abdomen * After
breeding, the kelts are recognizable by low, lanky bodies and long heads. The
length of the head varies with the age and sex of the specimen, being
comparatively slightly longer in the par than in the female grilse or salmon, in
which latter, as age advances, the head becomes comparatively shorter, whereas
in the male it is longer than in the female. The length of the head is from
$4\frac{1}{4}$ to $4\frac{3}{4}$ or even 5 in the par and male salmon to 5 or $5\frac{1}{4}$ in the female salmon
and grilse, the caudal fin is from 6 in the par to $7\frac{1}{2}$ in the salmon of the entire
length while the height of the body (which is greatest beneath the origin of the
dorsal fin) is from $4\frac{1}{2}$ to 5 in the total length. Eye—situated slightly in front
of the middle of the length of the head in the par (fig 13), or nearly in the middle
of that length in breeding males (fig 14) and comparatively much smaller in
adult than in young fish interorbital space convex and equal to about 2/3 the
length of the postorbital portion of the head in young, but more in old fish
Snout much produced in the male, and during the breeding season the extremity
of the lower jaw is provided with a strongly curved prominence which in old
specimens precludes the closure of the jaws. The posterior extremity of the
maxilla reaches to beneath the middle of the eye in the par, but beyond its
posterior extremity in the adult while it is comparatively wider in the young
than in the adult. Operele higher than wide, from about 1/5 more in the par, or
1/4 in the grilse or young salmon to 1/3 or even more in large salmon, (Plate 1)
suboperele from 1/2 to 1/3 of the height of the operele, while its posterior margin
forms a semi circular curve along with that of the operele. Preoperele with its
angle rounded and having a rather distinct lower limb. Yarrell observed that
what distinguishes *Salmo salar* from all other British species is the form of the
opereular bones, which have a rounded outline to the posterior edge of the
gill-covers, the longest diameter of which to the nose would be in a line *through
the eye*, while in all other British migratory species the same line would pass
below the eye. And this definition, although not absolutely correct in all
instances, will be found to be so in the great majority, as shown in the lines
A to B in figures 13 and 14 of the par and old male salmon

Fig 13. Head of par, natural
size

Fig 14 Head of old male salmon,
two elevenths the natural size

* Professor Benecke (*German Fisheries Association*, March 4th, 1886) adduced some
interesting figures regarding the weight and corresponding length of some German salmon,
wherein he showed that one measuring 15 7 inches in extent, can in the same water weigh from
16 lb to 30 lb which would occasion considerable difference in the various proportions of the body
to that of the entire fish

Teeth—in a single row in the jaws and palatines: the premaxillary ones being rather stouter than those in the mandibles, while the maxillary and palatine ones are still smaller. In adults the teeth are often larger in the jaws of males than in those of the females, while there are from one to three teeth (unless all are absent) on or just behind the head of the vomer*: in grilse, should teeth be present, there are from one to three on the head and one or more in a single row along the body of that bone. But the numbers are very various so soon as the fish arrives at an age to commence its migrations sea-wards. In the par and smolt a double row exists along the body of

Fig. 15.
Teeth on vomer of par, 7 in. long.

Fig. 16.
Teeth on vomer of grilse, 3¼ lb. wt.

the vomer, while the hind edge of the head of that bone is armed with three or rarely four teeth placed in a single row: some of these commence being shed as the par is becoming a smolt,† and the loss rapidly increases in the grilse stage. As a rule there are less teeth on the head of the vomer of a salmon than exists in that of a trout of similar size. There are three to six recurved teeth on either side of the tongue.‡

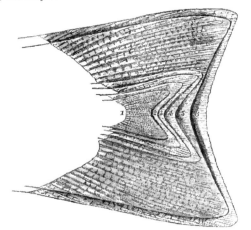

Fig. 17. Outlines of tail fins of salmon at various ages :—
1. Male par, 4·2 inches long; 2. Par, 5·2 inches long; 3. male par, 6·4 inches long; 4. male smolt, 7·8 inches long; 5. Grilse, 3¼ lb.; 6. Grilse, 4½ lb.

* July 12th, 1886, a grilse of 3¼ lb. weight had two teeth on the head of the vomer and one on its body: vertebræ 59 + x: one of 4¼ lb. had only two on the hind edge of the head of that bone; while a large male salmon, 26 lb. weight, had one tooth on the hind portion of the head of the vomer and a second on the commencement of the body of that bone.

† In several par seven inches long taken in September, 1886, the teeth on the body of the vomer were commencing to take on a single row in all, for out of nine sets originally of two each only four pairs remained, the rest having become single.

‡ In June, 1883, a female salmon of 10 lb. weight had three teeth on either side of the tongue: July 21st, 1886, a female salmon 12 lb. weight had the lingual teeth all shed. Parfitt, *Fauna of Devon*, 1875, page 9, observed, "Notice is taken by Mr. Couch and others of salmon having teeth on their tongue; but, so far as I know, no one has taken notice of salmon of the same size

Fins.—The rayed dorsal fin in mature fish is a little longer at its base than its highest ray is. Pectoral in adults as long as the head excluding the snout, and does not reach half-way to the ventral, whereas in the par it extends 2/3 of that distance: in the par it is rather pointed, the third to the seventh from the upper ray being the longest. In par and grilse it is about one-sixth longer than in brook trout of the same length. Ventral in adults reaches half-way to the base of the anal, in the par 2/3: anal one-fourth higher than its base is long. The form of the caudal alters with sexual development: in the young par it is deeply cleft, and varies with age in par and grilse (*see* fig. 17); at 2 or 2¼ feet in length it is as a rule truncated, and becomes more square* with advancing age. The free portion of the tail is comparatively finer in grilse than it is in adult salmon, and the corners of its tail fin more pointed. *Scales*—in the caudal portion of the body they are larger in this than any other British species of the genus, there being from 11 to 12 rows in an oblique line running from behind the adipose dorsal fin downwards and forwards to the lateral-line. Although it has been stated that when the par becomes a smolt a new layer of scales overlaps the old ones, this is erroneous, the silvery pigment which lines the inside of the scales becomes more developed, thus concealing the subjacent colouring.† It has also been said that the grilse possesses a diamond scale, but this alludes to the appearance of the fish when fresh captured.‡ The following figures will show the form of the scales at various ages. (Fig. 18 *a*,

Fig. 18,*a*. Scale of par 32 months old, magnified 2½ times.　　*b*. Scale of grilse 46 months old, magnified 3 times.　　*c*. Scale of salmon 16 lb. weight, magnified 4½ times.

b, and *c*.) The skin on the back of old males, both during and subsequent to the breeding season, being thickened and spongy, causes the scales to be more or less imbedded.

Colours.—In adults superiorly of a steel blue, becoming lighter on the sides and beneath. Mostly a few rounded or x-shaped spots scattered over the body above the lateral-line and upper half of the head,§ being more numerous in the

and apparently the same age, having no teeth on the tongue, this organ being perfectly smooth. I have examined many this season, and I find almost as many smooth-tongued ones as those having teeth. This is not a sexual peculiarity, as I find them about equal. The first I examined weighed on an average from 8 lb. to 14 lb. or 16 lb. each." Frank Gosden, *Land and Water*, November 28th, 1885, wrote on this subject: "I have restricted my examinations to salmon from the Exe and the Dart in Devonshire." . . . "Mr. Couch. I am aware, as well as many others, has taken notice of the teeth on the tongues of salmon: but I do not know of anyone having remarked upon salmon of the same age or about, some having teeth others no teeth upon the tongue. For several consecutive seasons I have examined numbers of salmon varying from 6 lb. to 30 lb. each and have found it immaterial whether they be large or small."

* The existence of valves in the large intestines has already been alluded to (page 22 and fig. 12). The gut was removed from the fish, hardened in a solution of chromic acid, and injected the next day with plaster of Paris.

† This will be more fully considered under the head of the "life history of the smolt."

‡ Mr. Anderson (September 30th, 1885) wrote: "I think you mistake me when I say the grilse has a *diamond* scale. It is only this appearance upon the fish when you see it newly caught, but loses it in a few hours; it, as well as the salmon scale, takes on a different appearance after six hours."

§ March 26th, 1884, I was shown three salmon, all males, and about 12 lb. weight each, and all caught in the Severn the same day by one gang of fishermen. One had no spots on the head, one ten, and the third twenty, showing how dissimilarly these fishes may be marked at the same

female than in the male The dorsal, caudal, and pectoral fins grayish black ventral and anal white, the former grayish internally. Prior to entering fresh waters salmon are of a brilliant steel blue along the back which becomes changed to a muddy tinge after they have remained in rivers When these fish have passed into fresh waters for the purpose of breeding, numerous orange streaks appear in the cheeks of the male, and also spots, or even marks of the same, and likewise of a red colour on the body It is then termed a "red-fish " The female, however, is dark in colour and known as a "black-fish " In *grilse* the pectoral fins are often of a bluer colour than in large salmon *Smolts* are bluish along the upper half of the body, silvery along the sides, due to a layer of silvery pigment being formed on the under surface of the scales, while they have darker fins than the yearling pink but have similar lateral bands and spots which can be seen as in the par if the example is held in certain positions of light *Par* have two or three black spots only on the opercle also black spots and orange ones along the upper half of the body but usually no dark ones below the lateral-line, although there may be orange ones along its course On the side of the body are a series (11 to 15) transverse bluish bands wider than the ground colour and crossing the lateral-line, while in the upper half of the body the darker silvery colour of the back often forms an arch over each of these bands A row of spots exists along the middle of the rayed dorsal fin, the adipose is leaden coloured, and, in rare instances, after death or under peculiar circumstances has a narrow orange tip *

Varieties —Although among the British *Salmonidæ*, when not kept in any unnatural condition, the salmon is perhaps the form in which the fewest variations are seen, still some, affecting either its shape or else its colour, are occasionally present

In form —Are more commonly perceived among the young artificially hatched, two or even more heads may be found, one with three heads was born in the spring of 1879, but as soon as the yolk sac was absorbed the fish died (*Anglers' Note Book*, p 79) Arrests of development, as of the upper or under jaw, of one or more fins, or spinal portions of the body, or spinal curvatures are occasionally observed It may be mentioned that a few fish salesmen and some fishermen believe they can tell from external appearances the river the various salmon have come from *Salmo argenteus*, Gunther,† is a kelt-like form, its elongated condition probably owing to disease or starvation, possibly the latter as it had been kept in a fresh-water pond. Another form is *Salmo gracilis*, Couch, examples of which I had the opportunity of examining at Teignmouth and Torquay in 1882 and 1883 ‡

In colour —Occasionally quite brown salmon are captured in fresh waters, especially towards the close of the season, which would appear to be due to a prolonged fresh-water residence Mr Ffennell recorded having taken them of a copper colour in the early lakes having the ova not very far advanced.

Opinions differ as to whether local races of salmon § distinguished by well

time, age, and locality At Howietoun the grilse raised and kept in fresh water are more spotted than those which have visited the estuaries or seas

* Young Lochleven trout have their adipose fins usually without a trace of orange in them

† The spots on the head, dorsal fin, and body are more what is generally seen on *Salmo trutta* or a grilse reared in fresh water, otherwise the fish is identical with *S salar*, but reliable characters would scarcely be expected to be well marked in a fish either ill or nearly starved, anyhow as lean and lanky as a kelt

‡ In a male were 61 and in a female were 71 cœcal appendages their flesh was rather pink, and as food they were not so rich as salmon from northern rivers, while they are said sometimes to be hard, woolly, and deficient in the curdled richness that is present between the flakes of fresh run Severn salmon. The reason why these fishes are of this elongated description is locally said to have first been due to the river having been poisoned with mine water, and it seems to be generally believed that this has been the cause of the present inferior race As already observed, great differences are seen in these fishes thus, a salmon 50¼ inches long was netted in the Severn, near Worcester, in June, 1884, which weighed 50½ lb , while a short time previously one was taken in the same place 48 inches long, which only weighed 35 lb In the Tay, July, 1886, one 53 inches long weighed 54 lb , and in March an Irish fish 34 inches long weighed 14¾ lb

§ In the *Report of the Salmon Commission* for 1824, Mr James Wilson asserted of the North and

marked characters, exist in our rivers, and if fish from their appearance could be clearly referred as having been received from certain waters   Speaking generally, there would be nothing very remarkable in the existence of peculiarities in local races due to local circumstances   Thus we are told that the higher the latitudes, as a rule, the smaller the fish, possibly one result of cold and a diminished food supply affecting their size ; the form of the body is much deeper in some races than it is in others*   and local causes may modify the taste as to its richness or dryness for food, &c , also the external colour or that of the flesh internally †

South Esks at Montrose, that " the species of salmon is quite different in these two rivers, one is a large coarse scaly fish, and the other a smaller and finer fish" (p 11)   Mr Bell stated that the " Aberdeen fish is quite different from the Tay, different in the scale" (p 28)   Mr Little stated that, ' I believe that every river has a peculiar kind of fish attached to it, both as to salmon and grilse   We have three fishings that fall all into one bay in Ireland the Bush, the Bann, and the Foyle , and we can easily distinguish the fish of all the different rivers when we take them   The salmon in the Bush is a long-bodied round salmon nearly as thick at the head as he is at the middle   The salmon that we kill at the Bann is what I call a very neat made fish, very broad at the shoulders, and the back fin tapering away towards the tail, and quite a different shaped fish from the Bush fish   The Foyle is a river that we seldom get any large salmon in " (p 112)

In the *Report of the Committee on the Salmon Fisheries* for 1824, the following evidence was given by witnesses   Mr J Wilson deposed "I am fully of opinion that every river has a peculiar breed of salmon they all return to the same river where they were bred   I have attended a few weeks in the year at Montrose there are two rivers , the South Esk is about four miles from the North Esk, and the species of salmon is quite different in the two rivers "   J Bell deposed as his reason for believing distinct races of fish came from, and returned, to the same river "because there are different sizes because the Esk fish is not above 7 lb or 8 lb in weight the Tay fish on the average is from 12 lb to 14 lb weight," and in his opinion the fish always ascended the river where they are bred   "Fish take their own rivers the Aberdeen fish is quite different from the Tay, different in the scale "   J Proudfoot thought that fish bred in a river will endeavour to return to that river again one reason being on account of the weight of the fish in the Tay, which were rather above what he had seen in the Tweed, and that the stake nets being placed along the shore, to the eastward of the mouth of the Tay there are fish of about the same average weight caught there as in the Tay   Small fish were deemed Isla fish, larger ones Tay fish, but were he to take fish in the Firth, he could not say to which river they belonged   J Halliday stated that he could not distinguish between the fish caught in one river from those caught in another if they were of exactly the same size and make, and taken at the mouth of the river, and he did not believe in the stated differences (l c page 87)

Mr. Loch remarking of the Shin river in Sutherlandshire observed that ' the river is divided into three nearly equal parts   The upper and lower portions having a fine gravelly bottom and full of excellent spawning beds   The central portion consists of a series of rocky rapids terminating in a considerable cataract, up which none but the most powerful fish could make their way this impediment, together with the absence of all cruive dikes until the year 1788, appears to have produced an uncommonly large breed of fish for up to a recent period many salmon, weighing from 30 lb to 40 lb were caught in this river but as it became more closely fished then size diminished "—*Mag Nat Hist* 1, 1837, p 208

Mackenzie (*Salmon Fishery of Scotland*, 1860, page 16) considered that every river, and even every branch and tributary stream of a river in which salmon are produced, has a variety of the species peculiar to itself, and which return regularly to it from their migration to the sea   He remarked that " in some rivers they are long and narrow or lank , in others broad and short—so broad and so short that when cut up they are nearly circular   In one river we find all the salmon straight in the back—in another round or hog backed   In some rivers their heads are all large and clumsy—in others small and neat   Even in the spots and scales, there is often a visible difference   In short, the distinctions are so numerous that it is needless to detail them   The salmon of some rivers are so strongly marked that a stranger would recognize them at a glance, while he would only be sensible of the distinctions between them and others by comparing them, when the difference would strike him at once " (p 17)

Mr Willis-Bund considered that in the Lower Severn " different kinds (or races) of salmon are met with   There is the ordinary Severn fish a longer and lanker fish is said to be a Wye fish a short thick fish that the fishermen speak of as " Uskers"   The two last he has not seen above Tewkesbury Weir, but forms so vary that he considers it as " almost impossible even for the most experienced to say positively that such a fish belongs to a particular river " (*Salmon Problems*, p 146)

* Norris tells us that at Pulaski, "there were formerly three salmon streams in this vicinity—Grindstone Creek, Deer Creek, and Salmon River, and each stream had a different type of fish.   An experienced fisherman would readily tell from which stream a fish was caught, though they were but four miles apart   In Deer Creek the fish were long and slim in Grindstone short and chubby, and in Salmon River large and heavy " (*American Angler*, p 177)

† Superior forms may be inherited, or else be owing to the greater abundance and more nourishing character of the food present in the sea feeding grounds of some than it

If early ascent is inherent in a race, it must be evident that were the eggs of such transferred to a "late" river, it would cause the introduction of an early-ascending breed of salmon *

Sexual distinctions.—The male at the breeding season has a hook, knob, or kype developed at the upper surface of the end of the lower jaw, which disappears by degrees, often by the time it has become a well-mended kelt, unless the fish is a very old one,† when the bony portion of this swelling cannot be absorbed (Plate 1) The cause of the existence of a knob on the lower jaw of male salmon and trout has been a fruitful cause of discussion from early ages down to the present day We find that male pars or smolts whose milt is capable of fertilizing eggs possess no such knob, but as years pass, one becomes more and more prominent It annually augments at the breeding season and partially diminishes in size subsequently, as age advances that portion of the head which is anterior to the nasal valves seems to double its previous proportional length or what is seen in the female At first the lower jaw increases in length more than do the bones of the snout, consequently, the prenasal portion is found to be only one-half of the comparative length to what obtains in very old fish, but as the knob grows on the upper edge of the extremity of the mandibles it is placed when the mouth is closed anterior to the front edge of the snout, where there is often a sore spot caused by abrasion But after a few years the snout and upper jaw commence growing more rapidly than the mandibles, and as a result, the knob becomes overlapped by the snout, and then it presses against and is received into a large depression, situated between the two ascending portions of the premaxillaries which are freely movable Thus, although the hook may press against the palate, it can do so without occasioning any injury, because the parts give way before it But should any irritation occur at this spot it might ulcerate through the soft parts, when it would appear above the snout or on the upper profile of the head When this takes place, movement in the upper jaw would be difficult or impossible, and the fish would as a consequence become starved

The knob appears to be entirely composed of connective tissue,‡ so cannot fall off, but may be more or less absorbed,§ as it doubtless is after the breeding season

---

is of others to the temperature of the water or to the unwholesomeness of some rivers either acting directly on the contained fish, or in a secondary degree through the medium of their offspring which may be a weakly race It may also be worth inquiring whether the present continuous modes of fishing estuaries and capturing all the large salmon which are ascending, leaving the smaller fish mostly to continue their kind, may not be causing deterioration of breeds

* Some rivers may possess an early and a late breed (i e , if fish always return to the stream of their birth) should it have tributary streams in which these fish can breed early or late, still all must ascend the main channel

| July 31st, 1886, a large salmon, in fair condition, was in a fishmonger's shop at Cheltenham having a very large hook, but no orange colouring, here the knob was probably persistent from age the succeeding month (August 24th) there were three more, but all had orange markings on the head and body On June 6th, 1886, a fine 36 lb fish had only a small and soft knob, either increasing or diminishing

‡ Professor Gadow, who was so good as to make sections of one and stain it with carmine, thus remarked, "The hooks consist entirely of fibrous connective tissue, without any traces of cartilaginous cells in it, the whole being surrounded by the epiderm Therefore the hook cannot be looked upon either as an outgrowth of the bones of the lower jaw, or as a sort of horny excrescence like horns, nails, or pads such as toads possess on the palms of their hands But as a periodical outgrowth of the cutaneous connective tissue which surrounds the body, being situated between the epiderm and the bone, without, however, having any relation to the periosteum This cutaneous connective tissue nature explains why and how the hook can again be absorbed, or rather re-absorbed after the season is over Certainly it cannot be shed "

§ Several authors speak of this knob "falling off 'subsequent to the breeding season, but it can only be gradually absorbed, and when the bone itself grows (as seen in plate 1, fig 1) the bony tissue cannot be removed The statement made in *The Field* by Mr George, February 16th, 1884, must evidently have been written under some extraordinary error "When the fish has reached a certain stage in the kelt state, the hook gradually loosens at what seems on examination to be a kind of joint just where the point of the nose should be in the fish, a slight tap when it has arrived at this stage, or slight pressure on the gravel, will dislodge it I have dislodged many

Old females frequently show small knobs, and instances have been recorded in which large ones* have existed, and still the fish has been fertile Other sexual distinctions have already been referred to (page 23 *ante*)

Names —Speaking generally this fish in its full-grown condition is known as the *salmon*, in the Severn, one on its second return from the sea is often called a *gerling* or *gillion* or *gilling* (this term seems to be one which is mostly used in order to refer to the size of the fish, as from 8 lb to 15 lb) or a *botcher* on its first return when under 5 lb weight, although the more general designation is *grilse* (Pennant termed them *gilse*), when under 2 lb weight it is usually termed *salmon-peal* by fishmongers   From one to two years old, before it has gone to the sea it is known as a *par*,† *pink*, *smolt*, *smelt*, *salmon-fry*, *sprag*, or *salmon-spring* (Northumberland), *samlet*, *brandling*, *fingerling*, *black-fin*, *blue-fin*, *shed*, *shegger*, *gravelling*, *hepper*, *laspring*, *gravel-lasping*, *skerling*, or *sparling* in Wales, *spawn* (in the Dart, A Pike) *moor-ged* (Exmoor) *morgate* (Somersetshire) *streamer* (in the Tamar, W Mason)   Isaak Walton used the terms *tecon*, *samlet* and *skegger* for the young of the salmon A third-year salmon is known as a *pug* (Halliwell) In Northumberland a "milter" or spawning male is known as a *summer-cock* or *gib-fish*, and a salmon as a *simen*   In the Severn, a salmon which has remained in fresh water during the summer without going to the sea is termed a *lauret*, but usually applied there to a well-mended kelt   After spawning it is a *kelt* or *slat*, but a male is generally termed a *kipper‡* and a female a *sheddler* or a *baggit*, this latter term according to Jameson means "pregnant" or "gravid" fish   also at Inverness as *macks* and *shags* (Fraser)   In the Ribble, according to Willoughby, salmon of the first year were termed *smelts*, of the second year *sprods*, of the third year *morts*, of the fourth year *fork-tails*, of the fifth year *half-fish*, of the sixth year *salmon* § Dr Davy also observed that *mort* and *sprod* were names used in Cumberland indiscriminately to the salmon and salmon-trout   In an old work we are told that in the north of Scotland the fry were termed *brood* and *cockspcr*, and Stoddart mentioned the largest and most compactly built ones being called *grey-schule* which ascend for spawning in October until February   In the Tay those exhausted during spawning-time are termed *Moffat-men* (*Parliamentary Commission*, 1824, p 61)   The designation *bull-salmon* and *bull-pinks* employed in the Kirkcudbright Dee has been said to refer to well-mended kelts   In Ireland Sampson remarked upon a *samlet* or *penkin* which Tighe termed a *ginkin*, but the term *par* was more frequently employed to the north and *gravel-ing* to the south   Par are also termed *rack-riders* or *sprats* and larger ones *leaders* (Miller)   At Kerry a kelt is termed *judy*, and Rnity stated that a grilse was called a *gravel*, and Johnston said that it was known in Lough Foyle as a *grayling*   Welsh, *caug*, male salmon *cemyu luyddell*, female salmon spawning, *maran*, or a *salmon* on his third return from the sea (Severn) (*glersicdyn*, *cog*, and *maran*, Pennant)   De Zalm, Dutch   Le Saumon, French

A correspondent of *Land and Water* (*Scotus*, March 27th, 1880) gave a list of the Gaelic names for salmon in the Highlands of Scotland as follows —

The fish after this is rather snub nosed, and the point is rather indented and light coloured, but it soon wears smooth and resumes its proper shape "   The *slight tap* to render a salmon, such as I have figured "snub nosed," would have to break off most of the premaxillary bones (No 17) and the anterior end of the mandibles (No 34), and even then, should the fish survive, its snout would never "wear smooth and resume its proper shape "

* In 1884, when fishing a river in N W Ross-shire, I killed a salmon having most fully developed the "horny projection," and the same day another salmon was killed by a friend, also having the same horny projection   These two fish on being cut up were both found to contain well developed ova, and were undoubtedly female fish   A third friend who had fished the same river for ten years, said to us, that only once before had a similar case come under his notice   The first two fish weighed about the same, viz , 11 lb (J Harvie-Brown, *Zoologist*, May, 1886, page 215)

† Jameson in his Scottish Dictionary spells this form *par*, and *parr* appears to be a modern innovation

‡ In Acts of Parliament passed in the time of Queen Anne, *Salmon strikes* or *kippers* are mentioned

§ Prior to 1861, when angling for young salmon was stopped in the Severn above Shrewsbury, the March, April and May shoals formed of pars or pinks were known as *salmon fry*, and the autumn smolts as *samlets*

Salmon—*Brădan, Glas-bhreac* grilse—*Gealag Bànag* he-salmon—*Brădan-firionn* she-salmon—*Brădan-cheirionn* clean salmon—*Brădan-glan, Urbhreac* · foul salmon—*Brădan-salach* male unspawned salmon—*Brădan-inchragach* female unspawned salmon—*Brădan-inhealagach* male spawned salmon—*Brădan-ruithte* female spawned salmon—*Brădan-claidhte* a lean or spent salmon of either sex—*Bhonach, Mathach, Bluanay, Dubh-bhrădan* parr, *Breem* *

Habits—The salmon, as already observed, is an anadromous fish, which enters rivers mostly for the purpose of depositing its spawn in a locality where its eggs will be hatched and its fry reared During the summer months it roams along our coasts in search of food, and may be found close in shore many miles from where any fresh water enters the sea, loitering in estuaries and also at the mouths of rivers up which it purposes ascending †

The migrations of the salmon at its various ages and during different seasons of the year have long been themes for discussion at every stage of their occurrence These fish are "anadromous" or terms which enter our rivers chiefly for the purpose of perpetuating their race, for this cause they select suitable spots wherein to deposit their eggs, here the young are hatched, and remain in the stream for the first years of their existence Consequently during their youth they live and feed in fresh water, as they grow older they descend as smolts to the sea, from whence after a time they return as grilse and salmon to the rivers, thus the waters they select for their residence differ from each other in their specific gravity, taste, temperature and products

Where these fish pass their sojourn in the sea has not yet been satisfactorily cleared up,‡ neither does the practical fisherman much concern himself with this question as he is unable to capture them there, while the fish-culturist is aware that their eggs will not hatch if deposited in salt water

It will be necessary prior to following out these migrations to observe upon the terms "early" and "late" rivers, for among the many problems respecting salmon and their fisheries there is none which exceeds in importance how to legislate for these different classes of streams These terms "early" and "late"§ are employed in two different senses, one person alluding to the ascent of clean fish in relationship to the time of the year, while another does so as regards their ascent for breeding or the period of their spawning, a sense in which it is not understood in the following pages

Early rivers are those in which clean-run salmon, fit for the market, ‖ ascend during the first months of the year, as in February, or even in January, while these ascents are deferred much later in other, and occasionally even in contiguous streams, and this gives rise to the inquiry of at what time sufficient numbers of

---

* J Josselyn writing in 1675 refers to the salmon of New England as in the first year a *salmon-smolt*, the second as a *mort*, the third as a *spraid*, the fourth as a *soar*, the fifth as a *sorrel*, the sixth as a *forket-tail*, and the seventh as a *salmon*, showing that even in those days differences had been observed in the various stages of growth of this fish

† Pennant asserted that the salmon quitted the sea to free itself from parasites, and Dr Anderson considered that they again quitted the fresh water owing to being infested with another form of vermin

‡ In the Baltic, Judge Fiedler observed that a salmon about 18 lb weight was caught in a seine in the Great Belt, south of Korsor, in which was a somewhat compressed brass hook, similar to those formerly described by Malmgren, so no doubt the salmon must have swallowed it and carried it from the North German coast of the Baltic (*Bulletin, United States Fish Commission*, 1885, p 185)

§ Russel (*The Salmon*) observed that "there are great differences between rivers regarding the periods in late winter or early spring at which they contain *clean* fish in quantities sufficient to render fishing profitable, and have got rid in any considerable degree of the foul fish, spawned and unspawned" He suggested terming the rivers "short-seasoned" and "long seasoned," as he was not of opinion that there is much difference between rivers at the end of the season—the season at which a greater or less proportion of the fish begin to get gravid and out of condition Likewise, it has been considered that breeding commences somewhat earlier, or that the fish complete their spawning operations in a shorter time in some rivers than in others , in either of which cases they would return earlier into condition than in localities where reproduction was deferred until late, or extended over a longer period

‖ Clean salmon are much earlier in some rivers than they are in others G Little, giving evidence before the *Parliamentary Commission* in 1824, observed " that the Eden is earlier than

clean fish may be present in a river which might be reasonably captured for food without injuriously affecting future years' supply?* These fish are well conditioned, and some may be observed ascending during almost every month of the year

the Esk or the Annan, the fish enter it earlier than they do the others by nearly six weeks Fishing in the Solway, the Eden and the Dee at Kirkcudbright, might commence on the 2nd of February but in the Annan, the Esk and the Nith, should not begin earlier than the middle of March The salmon that are caught in the Dee are quite out of season fully a month before they are in the Nith and the Annan these are two very late rivers" He likewise stated that in the Nith last season his tenant commenced on the 11th March He was informed that he then killed upwards of 200 salmon, some of them positively not spawned J Proudfoot deposed that, ' in the spring of the year the fish always occupy the north side of the Tay (i e , the sunny side of the river) The north-side fishing kills far more fish than the south side" (*Report of Commission* for 1824, p 28)

In Yorkshire their ascent as fresh-run fish varies greatly, and is dependent upon the state of the rivers, if either July, August, or September are wet the salmon commence running from the sea, if otherwise, then ascent is delayed until the autumn rains set in (*Yorkshire Vertebrata*, p 126)

So *William Jardine* observed that the causes influencing ascent are as yet undecided, and where the time varies much in neighbouring rivers they are less easy of solution With but few exceptions the northern rivers are the earliest, and it has been suggested that this variation in the season may be dependent upon the temperature of the water, and that such Highland rivers as have their origin in large lochs are all early owing to the great mass and warmer temperature at their sources, and that the eggs in such localities are earlier hatched Thus the Oykel in Sutherlandshire, springs from a small Alpine lake, perhaps about half-a-mile in breadth while the Shin which is a tributary of it, coalescing at about five miles from its mouth, takes its rise in Loch Shin a large and deep extent of water, and connected to a chain of other lochs The river Shin, from its course between the loch and the tideway of the Kyle, has its temperature several degrees higher in winter than the waters of the rivers Oykel and Cassley, with which it mingles on entering the Kyle, and the temperature is several degrees lower in summer than the waters of the long run, hill collected, and sun-heated rivers "To be sure respecting the temperature, a thermometer was regularly kept The salmon soon finds out the warmer side of the estuary, and the river from which that warm water flows It is well known that salmon during the winter and spring months, when the water of the warmest river is cold always run on the sunny side of the estuary, that is as much as possible on the north side, and there during that time the run of fish is to be found In the summer months, that is, after the 1st of May, the fish run on the opposite side of the estuary The high temperature of the water at that time induces them to seek as much as possible to get under the cool shade of the south banks, where there is the least influence of the sunbeams Of the many rivers going into the estuary, the only one which produces early fish is the warm Shin"

Buckland considered that clean scaled, well-developed, fat fish run up some rivers during February and March, possibly earlier, that these ascending fish must meet the descending kelts Or in short that there is a small *spring migration* ascending in contradistinction to the usual large *autumnal migration* for breeding purposes He found that the amount of fat upon the pyloric appendages of these spring fresh run fish, less than what is seen in such as migrated later for breeding purposes Denying that they are barren he considered that they would not breed the season they ascended the stream, or in fact that they were temporarily sterile He thought they had laid up sufficient fat in the sea or estuaries to take a run into fresh water, fancying they might be the early kelts of the previous year, which having reached the sea in January, re appear as clean fish in thirteen months, or February the next year, or even very large fresh-run fish in twenty five months, or February the succeeding year He likewise remarked that it is impossible to convert a "late" into an "early" river

* According to *Isaak Walton*, "so there are some few rivers in this nation that have Trouts and Salmons in season in winter, as 'tis certain there be in the river *Wye* in *Monmouthshire*, when they be in season, as *Camden* observes, from *September to April*"

In the *Report of the Salmon Commissioners* for 1861 is a Table showing, as far as could be ascertained, the periods at which the local justices fixed the close time for rivers in their respective districts Thus, in the Trent and Somersetshire Avon it began on August 12th, in the Ribble August 31st, in many rivers in September some in October, others in November, a few in December, and in the Devonshire Avon in the middle of January, ceasing on May 6th These varying periods would seem to show either that the salmon bred at different times in different rivers, or were variously in season at different places, or that the close time was not arranged solely in the interests of the spawning fish, some having probably been selected in order to allow the trout to get into condition before being fished for

It is unnecessary to enter upon a detailed examination of how, up to 1858, three different close seasons were in force in Scotland, and which period was supposed to be fixed in accordance with the time at which these fishes bred, as for instance in the Solway, the Tweed, and the fisheries to the north of the latter river How in England and Wales up to 1861, the close season commenced in various localities from August 12th to the middle of January How after 1861 this season was arbitrarily fixed between September 1st and February 1st, and how in 1873 an

An instance has been adduced how a river that was originally an early one was found to become a late one,* and which was considered to be a result of the drainage works so extensively carried on for agricultural purposes, causing the summer floods to run off in a few hours instead of in several days, as had been previously the case, or else caused by other obstructions

Irrespective of these early rivers, so termed owing to the period at which clean salmon ascend, we have the migrations of these fishes up rivers in a gravid condition, and which do so solely for spawning purposes † The secondary causes which induce them to enter streams have been variously defined by different authors,‡ but more especially the warmth of the water in the river as compared with that in the ocean, while of two rivers that which is the least cold will generally be selected, and I propose to briefly consider a few of these as to whether they have an influence in certain rivers being early or late

Act was passed permitting the commencement of the close season to be varied between certain limits, provided it did not begin later than November 1st For treating all rivers in an identical manner, whether clean fish were present early or late in the season, and insisting upon fishing beginning or leaving off on a specified day in all, was, as illustrated by a Highland Laird, when before the Salmon Commission of 1824, about " as sensible a plan as it would be to prohibit the farmers of England from cutting their crops till the harvests were ready in the Highlands "

* The *Earl of Home*, in 1837 observed "that in the Tweed a very great change had taken place within these twenty or thirty years , a considerable portion of the breeding fish not arriving into breeding condition until long after the time they had formerly been in the habit of doing so " The first inquiry here should be whether this had happened consequent upon any changes in the river, the placing of artificial obstructions in its course, or an alteration in the natural spawning time in the fish irrespective of the condition of the water The river itself, it was observed, "had changed, due to the draining of the sheep farms on the hills, the effect produced being that a little summer flood which, previous to 1795, took a fortnight or three weeks to run off, now (in 1837) became completely run out in eight hours The bogs on the hill sides, which were the feeders to the river, have the water at once carried off by drains, causing sudden but short floods, which have all run off before the river has had time to clear itself " *Sir H Davy* compared the Tweed district as it was prior to these drains, to what it had become subsequent to their construction— to two houses, the one covered with thatch, and the other with slate , the first dripping for hours after the rain has fallen, the other ceasing when the rain stops

† Professor Huxley (*Report of H M Inspector of Fisheries*, 1884, page 26) suggested that " we may call the interval between the ascent of the earliest and that of the latest fish in any given river the ' anadromous period' of the river " But however applicable such a designation might at first sight appear, very strong objections must occur to restricting such a term to migrations of anadromous Salmonidæ In some rivers these fish only ascend during the spawning time, while char migrate at the same season for breeding purposes, from the depths of lakes or large pieces of water, to suitable streams and shallows, in order to deposit their ova and milt , and this time with the char would be as completely their " anadromous period " as when similar conditions in the salmon caused similar movements , but char are not usually considered to be anadromous forms even carps in Asia similarly migrate at spawning time, as well as many other fish, and to term such migrations " anadromous periods " in some fish and not in others would clearly be erroneous

‡ *James Gillies* deposed in 1824 respecting the Tay, where he had fished for twenty six years, that " when I first went to Perth, most of the river was over with spawning in December, but you will now scarcely see one fish come there to the redd, till about the end of November, and the spring time for spawning is generally in the months of December and January "

Mr Bust (1832) stated that, " from his own observation or from the testimony of others who have had opportunities to observe it very minutely, that the fish begins to spawn about the middle of October and continue until about the end of January "

The *Commissioners* appointed in 1861 to investigate the Salmon Fisheries of England and Wales came to the conclusion that, "the great breeding season in England and Wales of all fish of the salmon kind is in the months of November, December, and January   and believe it will not vary more than a fortnight in any river   in some seasons it may commence a little earlier, or be continued a little later, but the principal breeding operations are performed chiefly in the three months mentioned "

Yarrell considered that "rivers issuing from large lakes afford early salmon, the waters having been purified by deposition in the lakes, on the other hand, rivers swollen by melting snows in the spring months are later in their season of producing fish, and yield their supply when the lake rivers are beginning to fail " The general impression seems to have been that the temperature of the river water exercised some influence in acting upon the time at which they were ascended by salmon when desirous of entering for breeding purposes, they usually first selecting such as were the warmest

Dr Heysham was of opinion that in Cumberland salmon at first spawn in the warmer streams, leaving the snow-fed ones until later on, consequently, during the winter and spring, they

The existence of lakes near the sources of rivers has been held to influence the earliness or lateness of its waters In England and Wales we find such conditions present in the Eden, 70¼ miles long, with a catchment basin 916 square miles in extent, the Dee, 93 miles long, and with 850 square miles of catchment basin,

prefer the Eden to the Esk, the Caldew, or the Peteril The two first rivers enter the same estuary, their mouths being merely separated by a sharp point of land, yet there is scarcely an instance of a new salmon ever entering the Esk until the middle of April or beginning of May The fishermen assert that the Eden is considerably warmer than the Esk, the latter having a more stony bed, shallower stream, and broader expanse When snow-water comes down the Eden the fish will not ascend, by the beginning of summer the temperature of the two rivers is about the same The Peteril joins the Eden a little above, and the Caldew at Carlisle, yet up these rivers the salmon never run unless in the spawning season, and even then in no great numbers

As Inspector of Fisheries, Professor Huxley in his *Annual Report* for 1884, entered upon his views regarding "early" and "late" rivers Having quoted Yarrell's observation, "that some rivers are much earlier than others, the fish in them coming into breeding condition and beginning to spawn at an earlier period," he continued "I am not aware of the grounds on which Mr Yarrell made this statement, and I am unable to discover any satisfactory evidence that it is well grounded"

Yarrell's observations on this point, as remarked by himself, were based on those of Sir W. Jardine, who had remarked in *The Edinburgh New Philosophical Journal* of 1835, from which Yarrell quoted, that "it is a mistaken opinion to suppose that the spawning season is only between October and February In many rivers it would commence in the end of August, if the grounds and entrance to the rivers were left open and unmolested, and in some of the Sutherland streams which have been left undisturbed for the last two years, the spawning season has been advanced by a month or six weeks" (pp 18, 19) But he seems to have subsequently changed his opinion, as, in the *Report of the Salmon Commission* of 1861, of which he was President, a contrary view was held, as already quoted

"All the evidence," continued Professor Huxley, "to which I have access tends to show that, taking all the salmon rivers in England and Wales together, the spawning season covers more or less of November, the whole of December and January, and more or less of February It is rare for fish to spawn as late as March, and I know of no conclusive evidence that they spawn earlier than November" (p 28) He concluded that the "earliness" or "lateness" of a river being affected by artificial conditions is devoid of foundation, while there is no evidence that any 'early' river was formerly made "late" by late fishing, or that any "late" river has since been made "early" by early cessation of fishing He instanced the Cumberland Derwent, where the coops at Salmon Hall Weir used to be fished until October 10th, but from 1861 have been closed on September 1st annually, but there is no evidence that the fish have become any earlier than they formerly were He considered the problem not so much why some rivers are late as why so many are early—why fish should ascend months prior to any breeding necessity rendering such advisable In the same Report the Inspector observed, ' In the Tamar, peal are said to be ready to spawn in August, and salmon in September In the Tavy the salmon are said to be ready to spawn in October, but the peal seldom spawn before November I very much doubt, however, whether anyone ever saw a salmon or a peal actually spawning so early as August, September, or even October The opinion that they are ready to spawn' is inconclusive Against this evidence may be cited the case of a neighbouring river, the Plym I am informed by Mr Henry Clark, one of the conservators, that the fishermen fishing for herrings and *course fish in the tidal waters* of the Plym, in December last, caught at the same time spent peal just returned from spawning, and fresh run salmon going up to spawn, and that about the same time several salmon, weighing from 14 lb to 24 lb, killed by otters, were picked up below the weir at Cann Quarry, 'full of peas, nearly ripe,' while in March last year some fresh-run peal going up, and spent salmon coming back, were caught together between the weir at Cann Quarry and the tidal waters" In these instances it is to be regretted that neither the Inspector of Fisheries or his assistant took any steps to personally ascertain the condition of the fish in these rivers at the period referred to, but accepted information received at second hand

"As to the cause of early and late rivers for salmon," remarked Mr Pike, the Secretary of the Dart Fishery Board (*Land and Water*, March 28th, 1885), ' my theory is that a 'late ' river is only caused by the inability or difficulty of salmon getting to the upper waters to spawn This may arise either upon a small river where the water is insufficient till the winter floods come, or it may arise from artificial obstacles to the passing of the fish, such as weirs The Dart is a marked instance of the latter cause The Totnes Weir entirely prevented fish getting up For a great many years the river had been netted in close time to pass salmon over, but it is only four seasons ago that this netting was permitted before the rod fishing ended on October 31 Ever since the salmon were passed up early in September they have been seen spawning high up on Dartmoor as early as the first week in October, and young salmon have been hatched out the first week in January"

Mr Willis Bund, in *Salmon Problems*, 1885, remarked "Mr Huxley says there is no evidence that it (i e, salmon which come into the river in January and February) will spawn before November. The evidence of the Severn goes to prove it would spawn in October" (p 166) "I can only say I have in several years seen fish spawning in October, and the Severn Superintendent

the Derwent, $35\frac{1}{4}$ miles long, and 268 square miles of catchment basin, the Ehen, $14\frac{1}{3}$ miles long, with 59 square miles of catchment basin, the Irt, $16\frac{1}{4}$ miles long, with 48 square miles of catchment basin, and the Leven, $6\frac{1}{3}$ miles long, and with 123 square miles of catchment basin. The two first, with the longest course, are early rivers, but not so the remainder, which are rather late than otherwise. Irrespective of which some of the earliest and some of the latest rivers are among such as have no lakes in their course, and are of very different lengths

Buckland held that large estuaries at the entrance of salmon rivers must have the same influence as lakes near their sources, or in their course, but detailed investigations hardly bear out this theory, while it has been remarked that in a single estuary, as of the Severn, three rivers with different degrees of earliness enter. It has also been suggested that the conditions which occasion the early or late ascent of fish into fresh water may have some connection with the circumstances of the marine life of the salmon, the food which it is able to obtain, or the enemies from which it has to escape

What the temperature or other conditions of the water in the river, or the food that is present therein at various seasons of the year, have to do with the period at which salmon ascend into it from the sea, are worthy of study * Jardine, Yarrell, and others have remarked that the temperature of the river-water exercises some influence in the time of the ascent of these fish, they usually first selecting those that are warmest (of course in moderation), while in most streams the eggs would be more rapidly hatched, thus, other things being equal, the young fish would be hatched earlier in the warmer than in the colder streams. The *Salmon Commissioners of the Tweed* remarked in 1867 that it was stated by several witnesses that salmon do not enter the river freely when full of

---

tells me he has constantly done so" (p 20) "This year (1885) I have heard of fish spawning as late as the end of March, and one year I heard of fish, full of spawn, being caught in April. On the Usk, on the 18th of May, 1861, a fish was taken full of spawn" (p 59) Mr John Anderson informs me that in the Teith, above Callender, he has seen plenty of salmon spawning during the last week in October. Fraser (*The Salmon*, 1833, page 7) that in the upper rivers that feed Lochness they spawn from the middle of October to the middle of November

The *Usk Board of Conservators* reported in 1885, "that the Usk has undoubtedly become an earlier river than formerly. Twenty years ago but few salmon spawned in November, the first great run was at Christmas, and the second in January, considerable numbers spawned in February and a few in March. Now occasional fish spawn in October, large numbers in November and December, comparatively few in January, and only occasional fish in February. In consequence the additional water-bailiffs are put on earlier and discontinued earlier. The change has been gradual." There has been no change in the condition of the water. Mr Armistead (*Land and Water*, Nov 10th, 1885), remarked on the foregoing "Possibly the fact of their having more to eat and less to do may have something to do with this, but I believe that temperature has more to do with the time of their spawning, and with apparent deviations from rule than we are at present inclined to suppose. In the case of our river here, the Nith, salmon, after a run of a few miles, arrive at a fork called the Cluden. They spawn earlier in the Cluden than in the Nith, and I had thermometers carefully placed in both streams and examined daily at the same hour all through the spawning season, and the Cluden water proved to be rather warmer than the Nith. It would be interesting to know, if from any change, say in the drainage of the land, warm springs from mines, or any other cause, the Usk water has in any degree risen in temperature the last few years. I have known cases in which the cutting down of wood has had considerable influence on streams. Those who have had much experience with domesticated trout know well enough what an influence the weather has upon them, if from any change, a warm or cold rain making a great difference, for that day, at least, in the yield of eggs. It is now known, for instance, that a trout or salmon when ripe, and even partially spawned, can still hold its ova for a month if desired in certain cases, indeed, I have known them to do it longer. On the other hand, pisciculturists know how to make fish spawn earlier than they would do if left to nature"

* Temperature has often a direct connection with the food which may be present, while because that of a river exercises a manifest influence as to the when and where the eggs of the Salmonidæ are deposited, it does not follow that temperature is the sole cause which induces salmon to enter certain rivers

Livingstone Stone in the *Bulletin of the United States Fish Commission*, 1882, vol ii, page 12, observed of *Salmo quinnat* that when raised in the United States it did not spawn at the Californian time but at the *Salmo salar* time, November or nearly so. When investigating the ascents of carps in Asia into hill rivers for breeding purposes, I observed that it was an almost invariable rule that they turned aside from the main snow-fed streams into the side affluents in order to deposit their eggs, this being probably done in order that the young should be hatched in water not replenished from melting snows because such would be deficient in food

ice or snow-water, while on the other hand, a high temperature of the river-water equally deters them from entering it * Mr. A Young, Inspector of Fisheries in Scotland, remarked that as a general rule such Scottish rivers as fall into the German Ocean and Portland Firth are "early," while those emptying themselves into the Atlantic are "late" And he suggested that as the German Ocean is a cold sea, so the slight difference between the temperature of its waters and those of the rivers induces salmon to ascend early Whereas rivers on the west coast mostly descend from snow-fed sources, and are therefore cold much colder than the Atlantic, consequently the salmon wait until the snow floods have ceased It is also evident that the same comprehensive rule extends to the English and Welsh rivers, and those on the east coast falling into the German Ocean are earlier than those on the west, or of the south Coast of Devonshire and Cornwall, where the warmer Atlantic or the English Channel would have the same influence as pointed out by Mr Young in Scotland

But there are also differences in degrees in the temperature of the waters of rivers to be considered, which may be influenced by the extent of their course, and the nature of the country through which they pass, as well as by the amount of rainfall Thus rivers which have their rise in mountains, and after a short and rapid course fall into the ocean, would be colder than such as are longer and more sluggish, and as Sir W. Jardine's and others' observations pointed out, that in the cold months salmon naturally select the warmer streams as well as their most sunny sides Rainfall has been observed to afford an index to the temperature of rivers, for its distribution is dependent on the level of the land, the result being that such as pass through districts with the heaviest rainfall, would, Professor Huxley observed, be late rivers, while those traversing lowlands where the rainfall is less, would be early rivers According to this view the waters of the Severn should be warmer than those of the Wye, which latter should be of a higher temperature than those of the Usk, and the salmon would ascend these rivers in the foregoing order, which is the order in which they are tabulated among early and late rivers † But it must be observed that this theory respecting rainfall does not stand the test of examination throughout Scotland and Ireland.

Can any conditions of salmon ascending "early" or "late," or breeding earlier or later, or completing their ova depositing within a shorter period of time, be attributed to constitutional peculiarities affecting the local race of fish ? Two main branches of inquiry would seem to be here indicated First, are all these early fish ascending in order to breed the same year ? Secondly, what are the constitutional peculiarities of early salmon ?

It would seem from the few investigations which have been made that it is by no means improbable that some of the early-ascending clean fish may be seasonally sterile, although it is generally held that in many ova and milt may be discovered on a microscopic investigation to be a very little developed, and although these last would probably be among such as push on to the upper waters, it seems still to require proof why it is that they should desire to remain so many months in the stream, away from the sea This gives rise to the very important question of how frequently do salmon breed ?‡ In the United States Mr Atkins has been

---

* February 28th, 1886, a severe snow storm set in, and as a result clean salmon were checked ascending rivers, consequently but few catches were made, as may be seen from the following London market prices of this fish Of course floating ice and cold likewise impeded the fisherman's work February 26th, salmon 1s 4d to 1s 8d per lb 27th, 1s 8d to 2s 28th, 1s 9d to 2s 3d March 1st, 2s 2nd, 1s 9d to 2s 3d 3rd, 2s 4d to 2s 8d 4th, 2s 2d to 2s 6d

† In the United States Professor Brown Goode observed that salmon spawn on a falling temperature, yet they seem to enter rivers on a rising temperature In America the Southern streams seem to yield the earliest fish They are not sensitive to sudden changes, and are capable of enduring a range of at least 45°

‡ We may dismiss as untenable one consideration which has been advanced, that they may do so twice yearly, still we possess the evidence of Mr Burst that he spawned a particular fish on two successive seasons, and of Mr Brown, who treated another similarly on two alternate years, but where it was during the intermediate period of course it is impossible to say Lastly, we have Mr Frank Buckland, who stated before a Parliamentary committee in 1877, that

able to prove from a series of experiments, extending over several years, that in the Penobscot the salmon, *Salmo salar* var , breeds every second year   (*See* page 79)

As to any constitutional peculiarities in an early or late race, although summarily disposed of by several authors, it does not appear improbable that such may exist   Many excellent observers have held that the descendants of early-ascending fish would similarly give rise to a form having the same peculiarity   And if this early habit is capable of transmission to offspring, it would be sound economy to stock a late river with an early breed, in order to try and convert it from a late into an early one , while it has been advanced, and with a show of reason, how in the Dart Fishery the obstructions have converted an early breeding river into a late one, and now when these causes are being modified the river is becoming earlier   On the other hand how in districts where the back end of the season has been shortened—for instance, on the Blackwater and the Tay—the spring fishing has been greatly improved   At the same time attention must be drawn to the fact that it has not been proved that it is the early breeders that produce the early ascending fish,* and it has still to be shown whether the parents of these early forms do not deposit their milt and ova at the same time as salmon whose descendants have the late instincts , while there is a want of evidence respecting the condition of the early-ascending fish as regards their fertility or sterility

It is clear some rivers have early ascending fish, while in others they may be late, and all the intermediate grades are seen, as well as several ascents in one stream during the year   While differences in the size and length of their course will occasion variations in the mode of ascent, thus, up the smaller streams these fishes, as a rule, can only migrate late in the season and merely remain a sufficient time to deposit their spawn

---

" a salmon does not breed every year, but once every three years," and whose further remarks I have already quoted   It is asserted in *Nature*, 1877, page 376, that a gentleman who at different times had marked hundreds of kelts during the months of February March, and April, while they were descending to the sea had never seen one returning to spawn in the river that autumn, but he had met with individuals he had marked coming back the next year   He believed that " they frequent the fresh waters from habit, although there is no sign of milt or roe," and that these fish are biennial breeders   On this point one looks in vain through the reports of our Inspectors of Salmon Fisheries for any facts, but in such there is absolutely nothing to the point except bare opinions, and those often crude

* The *Commissioners* for 1861 observed " Experience has fully proved the fact in Ireland, where the enforcement of an earlier closing season has produced within a few years a corresponding early supply in certain rivers" (p xxviii)   They also concluded that as to " the alleged difference of season in certain rivers, we think that artificial causes have much more concern in producing such anomalies, than the laws of nature   In order to enable the upper waters to be fully stocked, it is necessary to afford a free run to the early spawning fish, which are naturally impelled to seek the highest parts of the stream to breed in   If, however, in consequence of an undue extension of the fishing season, these fish are cut off in their passage up, it follows that no stock will be left to replenish the river, except those later fish which make their ascent under the protection of the close time   It is in this way that some rivers are artificially made later, and the fact accounted for " (p xxviii)   *Professor Huxley* seemed to consider that, just as the capture of the early fish in early rivers had not tended in the least degree to make them late, so the preservation of the late fish in the very late rivers had not tended to make them later than they were ' I cannot say," he continued, "that I can discover any good ground for the belief that any kind of human interference is competent to affect the earliness or lateness of a river   Differences in the habits of fish in the same river have been and are still observed where the artificial conditions are constant," and he instances weirs, but denies that their presence has altered the inherited instincts of these fish as to their times of ascent

Mr Pike, secretary to the Dart Fishery Board, remarked in *Land and Water*, March 28th, 1885, that the Totnes Weir entirely prevents salmon ascending the river "For a great many years the river had been netted in close time to pass salmon over, but it is only four seasons ago that this netting was permitted before the rod fishing ended on October 31st   Ever since the salmon were passed up early in September they have been seen spawning high up on Dartmoor as early as the first week in October, and young salmon have been hatched out the first week in January   The result is that early spawned fish have returned again to the sea before Christmas, and a goodly number of large fish from 12 lb to 20 lb have been taken in the nets throughout the month of March " This instance, the correctness of which I assume, is one showing that the lateness in spawning in a certain river may be consequent upon the presence of an artificial

The migrations of the salmon from the sea towards inland fresh waters are, broadly speaking of two kinds *first*, what may be generally described is the great autumn and winter ones, for the purpose of spawning, and *secondly*, much more irregular ascents, consisting of a few or many fish, occurring throughout the year, or restricted to certain months This inquiry would embrace several considerations, such as the following —How do salmon return from the sea to our coasts? How do they enter and continue in estuaries prior to their ascent into the stream? How do they ascend rivers? How do they return to the sea?

As a general rule, is I have observed upon under the head of ' early and late salmon rivers," these fish migrate towards rivers sooner from cold seas, as the German Ocean on the east coast of the British Isles, than they do along the west coast, presumably because the Atlantic is warmer than the German Ocean, while among the latest rivers they ascend are those of Devonshire and Cornwall, where the temperature of the sea is the highest

With the object of attaining the estuaries or mouths of rivers up which they purpose ascending, salmon in small assemblages or schools keep along the shore, only a short distance from land, swimming rather high in the water, and betraying their presence by occasionally leaping out of the sea as if they were endeavouring to reconnoitre their way, or else they throw off a ripple in a calm as they move along the surface, while, as Mr Sinclair of Donegal remarked (*Field*, March 29th 1884) then tracks are as well known as those of cattle returning to the farm-yard Mr D Mackenzie in his *Salmon Fisheries of Scotland*, 1860, page 43, his also observed that along the coasts of Scotland salmon shoals pass a short distance from the land, and when a shoal meets with a stake net some of the fish are caught in the traps or cruives, or what are called its chambers, others start off, in short, the shoal is broken and dispersed The scattered fish, however, always guided by their instincts, gather in again to the land, singly or in groups, and continue their course with the tides, until they meet with another similar engine, when the same capture and dispersion is repeated " While packs of seals, porpoises, grampuses, and other enemies have been observed to deter salmon from entering rivers, and also to break up and scatter the shoals of fish

Salmon appear to possess a homeing instinct which induces them to endeavour to return to the river where they were originally reared,* but instances are occasionally brought to notice when such could not have been the case Thus almost yearly we hear of a grilse or of a salmon being captured off the mouth of the Thames or Medway, sometimes even attempting to ascend, but from which localities all these fish have long since been destroyed, consequently they could not be descended from eggs hatched in those rivers

obstruction to ascent, remove that obstruction or pass the breeding fish over it early in the breeding season, the young are earlier reared, and the breeders return sooner into condition than had they been left to wait to a later period before spawning This and other examples which I have adduced, go to prove that artificial causes may convert an early breeding into a late breeding river, that after the conditions and the fish may again breed in the earlier months, but more evidence is requisite to show the result of this on the early ascending fish

Mr Francis Francis, having remarked ' The Erne and the Bundrowse are only a few miles apart, their capabilities are very similar, both have large lakes for shelter, yet one gives fish in February and the other not till May " the Editor of *The Field* observed, " Where there are heavy spring runs which are left solely to the rod and never netted, those runs keep up in almost undiminished numbers, but as soon as the nets are brought to bear, they sooner or later die out altogether "

* Buckland recorded how a friend of his, who owned a well-known island on the west coast of Scotland, netted a certain pool in his fishery, and out of a number of fish which he captured he marked twenty or thirty He then put them on board his yacht where they were kept alive, and he sailed with them almost round his island, then up a creek to the mouth of a river, and turned them into a lake about half a mile from the source of the stream from which they had been originally captured, but with which it was in no way connected, the two rising from different watersheds It was as though the salmon had been carried from one heel of an enormous horse-shoe round to the other heel, and then taken right into the middle of the horse-shoe, and there let loose During the *same season* some of these marked fish were caught in or near their own pool, to do which they must have come back a circuit of at least forty miles, and passed by six or seven tributaries

Mr D Milne Home, when writing about the Tweed, observed that marked fish from that river

Were the homeing instinct in these fishes very strongly marked, such as were hatched from eggs brought from a certain river might (like the Blue-rock Pigeons reared from eggs obtained from another dovecote) return to the locality where the ova were originally deposited. But if such were an invariable rule, the re-stocking of salmonless rivers from distant sources would be useless, while experiments have demonstrated the procedure to be almost invariably satisfactory

Still a very strong opinion exists, and which observations have proved to be to a certain extent correct, that salmon return to the river they were originally reared in Mr Willis-Bund has, however, adduced several instances in which if salmon return to a tributary river in which they were bred, they must have always come as breeders, for clean fish hardly ever enter Some have imagined that they select the purest waters, or recognize the taste or smell of their native stream, but, on the other hand, it has been asked, how could the purity of the water induce salmon to enter certain rivers, for they generally ascend during a flood, when they are most full of mud, but at which times the fish are keenest to pass up

Irrespective of salmon having died out of a river, instances have been adduced in which it has been stated that they have deserted* streams, but the statements of H M Inspectors of Fisheries that sea-trout have driven salmon out of the Coquet is wanting in one particular There does not seem to be evidence that they were ever there habitually in any numbers, so much so that sea trout appear to be locally termed *salmon*

The foregoing are instances in which such desertion cannot be ascribed to pollution or artificial impediments to ascent, but owing to some as yet unascertained cause Possibly the numerous drainage works in the agricultural country through which these rivers pass have had some effect in rendering them less suitable than formerly for the residence of these fish, as the surface water, instead of gradually percolating through the soil, and so by degrees obtaining access to the main stream, is now rapidly carried off in a short period by these means ; while I have previously alluded (page 61) to an " early " river having changed to a " late " one, possibly from this cause

had been taken in the Frith of Forth, the Don and Dee, while to the south at Holy Island, the Tyne, Shields, and even Yarmouth This last was a so called 'bull trout," caught in the Whit adder, a tributary of the Tweed, on March 29th, 1852, it was netted at Winteston, near Yarmouth, April 2nd, 1852, or nearly 300 miles distant, within four days A second, marked in the Whit adder, March 10th, 1860, was taken at Yarmouth, May 5th, 1860 He considered it certain that salmon, after having frequented particular rivers from time immemorial, have abandoned them, and the inference is that they betake themselves to other rivers which they deem preferable As an example of this, the Whitadder may be referred to it has a course of about forty miles from the Lammermuir Hills this river joins the Tweed at a distance from its mouth of about three miles, so that all the higher waters of the Tweed must have passed the Whitadder The tide flows into it as well as into the Tweed, going up the latter for six or seven miles Formerly the true *Salmo salar* frequented the Whitadder, but during the last thirty years none of that species has been seen in it It is now only frequented by bull trout In the Midlothian Esk, he also remarked that about fifty years ago he had seen hundreds of true salmon wriggling up over the mill weirs, but for the last twenty years there has been no such fish in that river

Mr Willis Bund, in *Salmon Problems*, observed that " in one week in December, 1872, the water bailiff caught and put into the Severn forty fish from the Dowles Brook, and in a few hours the fish had all returned to the brook " (p 26)

* In 1864, Russel observed (p 71) respecting *bull trout*, that the Aln and the Coquet are full of that species to the almost entire exclusion of salmon and grilse And a few years later it was suggested by *H M Inspectors of Fisheries* that this latter was owing to the presence of " bull trout," consequently, if they were destroyed salmon would again flourish ! From 1868 to 1872 the annual close time for migratory trout was suspended, and the destruction of these anadromous forms ruthlessly carried on The amount of trout was soon reduced, then stock was rapidly diminished, but the salmon would not increase, so the massacre was stopped And now again, in 1885, the Inspector observed of the Coquet that it " is a much later river than any of its neighbours in the east, but this may be accounted for by the fact that that river is infested by bull trout, whose habits are different from those of the true salmon " A correspondent of the *Kelso Mail* observed that " the Coquet trout is the common yellow fin or *Salmo fario*, and the bull trout are the salmon of the river There are no true salmon, *S salar*, in the Coquet, the only fish frequenting the river being the bull trout, but with Coquet-side fishermen the term salmon and bull trout are synonymous hence ' salmon' with them means *S eriox* or bull trout, and trout *S fario*, or common river trout " (See *Badmin Series*, p 151)

It has been suggested that along the colder seas of our eastern coast salmon do not remain in the ocean, but ascend the warmer rivers, and consequently do not hang about the rivers' mouths; while, on the contrary, they behave differently along the Atlantic, or on our southern shores. Thus off the "late" river Fowey, Buckland remarked that "a larger number of salmon than are due leave the sea and play about the mouth of the river. These fish come in from the north, south, east and west. They are big fish, from 25 lb to 30 lb in weight. They come late in the year. They are very fat and greatly different in every way from the native salmon of the Fowey. In these warmer seas, with abundance of food, these fish may continue in the sea until compelled by the near approach of the reproductive period to ascend rivers towards their spawning beds, or they may be fish which are sterile for the season." None seem to have been examined on this point, and only vague surmises have been offered.

The evidence taken in 1824 went to show that in Scotland, as in the Tay, the salmon were more abundant in dry seasons along the shore and in the estuaries, but in rivers they abound most in wet seasons. For in dry seasons the rivers are smaller in size irrespective of their being too heated to retain them in health.

It has long been a vexed question as to the manner in which salmon enter estuaries and ascend rivers on their arrival from the sea, and although doubtless local circumstances may occasion certain differences, still the mode of migration would probably in all places be somewhat similar were it unchecked. Mackenzie remarked of the Scottish rivers that the "salmon proceed with the flood tide, and rest during the ebb in eddies and in easy water, hence great numbers are always caught in the flood traps of the stake nets placed in their course, while comparatively few are got in the ebb traps. If the ebb sets in, and the water becomes shallow from the receding of the tide, they drop down with the tide into deeper water, until the return of the flood tide enables them to continue their course, and in this dropping down some fall within the range and are caught in the ebb traps of the engines in question; but it is in the summer season, in dry weather, that by far the greatest number are so caught." At this period the water in the rivers is so low that they swim about with the tide, awaiting a flood.

Admitting that the foregoing distinctly proves that in some localities, at least, large numbers of fish ascend with the flood tide, it does not disprove that a great many also descend with the ebb, and that in times or places when the very low condition of the water could hardly be deemed a sufficient cause to obstruct ascent. In the Severn, in the stretch of tidal water from Newnham to the railway bridge, there are about seven sets of puts and putchers on the right bank, all being fixed with their mouths *up stream*. On May 26th 1885, I visited two of these sets of engines, and saw seven fish taken, all with their heads fixed in the puts and directed *down stream*, and when captured they must have been descending the river with the ebb tide. The lave-net fishermen carry on their occupation during the ebb tide, more especially in the slack water, rendering it evident that in this river these fish both ascend and descend with the tides *

In the Severn these fish are observed to swim up with the tide, which regulates their pace, as they rarely get in advance of it, and follow a fixed track, probably the channel of the river, but as the tide turns they leave the track by which they ascended, and are found in the shallows. If once disturbed or frightened from their regular course, they would appear to be slow to again return to it, thus Mr Willis Bund remarked that there used to be a good fishery just above the place where the tunnel passes under the river Severn. In consequence of the boring operations, chiefly the blasting, the fish have left that part of the river, and the fishery is almost worthless; and although the blasting has now (October, 1885) ceased for some time, the fish do not return. In the McCloud River the blasting operations of the Constructive Corps of the Central Pacific Railway Company

* Three views concerning these migrations were held at a meeting of the Dee Conservators at Chester in December, 1884.—(1) That salmon run up with the flood tide; (2) That they rest during the flood tide, and run up with the ebb; (3) That they allow themselves to be carried up with the stream of the flood tide, with their heads towards the sea, and that when the tide begins to ebb they turn, and continue their upward course against it.

prevented the parent salmon ascending the river as usual (Livingston-Stone, *Bull U S Fish Comm*, 1885) But the remarks of Sir W Jardine and others must not be overlooked, that temperature in estuaries is occasionally, at least, a cause as to the side they select when migrating, for they have been observed to choose the sunny side during the cold months, and the shady during the warmer portions of the year

But the period arrives when these fish consider it necessary to migrate from the tidal portions of a river and ascend into the fresh waters, where, instead of going with the tide, they have to pass on against the stream, and fishermen, at least in the Wye, appear to consider that it is a rule, excepting during a fresh, that these migrations take place chiefly during the night-time—in fact, so strong on this point is the opinion of some, that they do not hesitate to say that, were night-fishing in this river to be put an end to, their occupation would be gone It may be worthy of investigation, whether the constant netting to which these fishes are subjected is not one cause of their selecting to ascend during the night-time

During this period they require shelter, and even if they are found near ledges of rock or large stones there is almost certainly some gravelly spot in the vicinity where they can rest

The salmon having while in the ocean stored up fat, which is most readily seen on and around its pyloric appendages, and possibly, especially if in the autumn, being in such a condition that within a definite period its roe or milt must be deposited, commences its migration towards its breeding-grounds in the fresh waters One reason why the fish maturing its eggs has an excess of fat over one not so engaged, is supposed to be the great amount of nourishment which is required by the females while the eggs are rapidly maturing.

In November, 1885, being with Sir James Maitland searching for salmon eggs in the Teith, near Stirling, we took a female, 15 lb weight, so injured by seals that it succumbed It was a clean silvery fish,* with ovaries 4 7 inches in length, the two weighing $2\frac{1}{4}$ ounces, and each egg being 0 1 inch in diameter It is clear that a salmon having eggs one-tenth of an inch in diameter at the end of November could not have its ova sufficiently ripe to spawn within the next two months, while experience tells us that no other period for depositing eggs will normally come round before this time the succeeding year November 26th, 1886, out of nine salmon netted in the same place three were clean newly-run fish It has long been accepted as a physiological necessity that a female smolt must descend to the sea before it can develop eggs, the reason advanced being, as stated by Rasch, in 1866, that the development of ova requires far more nourishment than that of milt, that in the ovary of the female the eggs are formed nearly simultaneously, and their development is uniform, one being enveloped in as large an amount of albumen as another But in order to produce this albumen, a far greater quantity of food is needed than the fish can normally procure in fresh-water rivers On the other hand, grilse at Howietoun, both last year and during the present season (1884-85 and 1885-86) have given eggs without going to sea, and the land-locked salmon breeds in fresh water without descending to the ocean

I think that the explanation of these apparently contradictory facts is possible Thus, it is generally admitted that salmon, while residing in rivers, do not increase in weight, but rather fall off the longer they are absent from the sea, existing as they mainly do upon the fat which they have accumulated while feeding in the salt water, and such food as they can procure is sufficient for nutrition of the body but insufficient in females for breeding purposes If this is so (and of it I think there can be no reasonable doubt), they would be unable to obtain enough nourishment wherewith to develop eggs so long as they continued in the river, that, in

---

* Three similar ones were likewise captured that day, but being uninjured were at once returned to the Teith On December 23rd, 1884, five clean fish were taken when obtaining salmon eggs in the same river These must not be considered exceptional occurrences, as clean fish at this time are invariably netted when seeking for gravid salmon In the Rhine, Barfurth observed in 1874, that spawners ascend from September to November, while there is likewise a barren winter variety coming sporadically and for a brief season from September until May.

short, they could not do so without another visit to the sea, consequently these early ascending salmon, until they have again descended to the salt water, cannot be those fish from which we have to expect ova for replenishing the stock in our rivers Knox, in 1854, observed that a smolt, after first descending to the ocean and tasting its marine food, never again resorts to its infantile food as a constant mode of nourishment

This brings me to the question of how it is possible to prove that insufficient nourishment can impede or prevent spawning among the Salmonidæ, or, in fact, render a fish temporarily sterile An instance will be adduced further on to show how fungus among the American char was checked by decreasing their food, but as one result these fish at Howietoun became sterile for the season

Deficiency of food may, therefore, occasion sterility by an entire arrest of development in the ova, or, should the eggs be formed in the ovaries, it may stop (possibly not entirely) their further augmentation in size, as cold will retard the development of the embryo in eggs that have been deposited, as has been abundantly proved by transmitting them to distant countries by the assistance of ice Possibly in some few instances these early-ascending fish may find a locality where food from some cause is unusually abundant, allowing the ova to augment in size, and that this is the explanation of occasionally a female salmon with large eggs being captured at the end of the summer, but normally these fish will be sterile during the year of their ascent in the condition described, at least until after they have revisited the sea

But it may be advanced, if this is so, how do land-locked salmon breed ? Here we have an entirely different set of circumstances to deal with The fish have never been to the sea-feeding grounds, but have been compelled to adapt themselves to local conditions Thus, in large lakes, as Wenern and other suitable places, where food abounds, they breed, or else they become "demoralized salmon," as Agassiz remarked ; or, finally, they may die out, due to sterility, the nourishment which they are able to obtain being insufficient or unsuited to allow them to perpetuate their race

There is hardly a month in the year when fresh-run salmon may not be found in our rivers, but the main run for spawning purposes occurs as a rule from October to January or even later Some of the December and January fish, however, are in that condition, as I have shown, that they could not spawn for many months to come; and I am disposed to think that it is only autumn and winter ascending ones that breed, but experiments are much needed to test this

The various runs of salmon which ascend our rivers,* do not appear to be quite the same in each, but still there is a general resemblance, as will be seen

---

* Mr Willis Bund, in his account of the Severn (Salmon Problems), shows at least eight distinct runs during the year They may be summarized as follows :—(1) End of December or January, the largest run of the season, and spawning fish (2) End of January or February, or later spawning fish fewer in number, but generally large in size (3) A run in February of large clean fish but at the end of the month of gillings (4) February and March, a spring run of gillings which press up to the head-waters of the river, and are the early spawners for the next season (5) A small run of grilse, and some small salmon, during April. (6) June and July, the main run of grilse (7) Autumn run of Michaelmas gillings (8) Great run of spawn ing fish, in October and November But it must be noted that all the foregoing do not take place invariably every year—thus grilse or gillings may be absent , but there are, as a rule, three distinct runs of spawning fish, and five runs of clean fish, and irrespective of the fore going, there are individuals moving about Fish which are ascending alone do not appear to be so eager to press up, but stop at the foot of weirs in the pools, while the largest run of salmon is on a spring tide Possibly male fish pass up sooner than do the females, for at certain times in the Usk the higher up the river the netting takes place, the greater is the percentage of males to females which are caught

Mr Anderson writes to me respecting the Forth, and the migration of salmon and grilse therein, remarking that his observations extend over a period of fifty years (1) The first run of salmon, the beginning of December till nearly the end of February, should there be a fresh in the river, they are coarse looking fish, from 16 lb to 30 lb (2) About the middle or second spring tide in February, clean spring run fish, the fish 3 lb or 4 lb in weight, increasing in weight every week until the end of April, when some are from 8 lb to 10 lb (3) The summer salmon enters with the first spring tide in May, or earlier should the river be in flood , they are from 12 lb to 20 lb (4) The first run of grilse, from 1½ lb. to 3 lb , enters the rivers in May, in 1881, the

from the observation of Mr Willis-Bund, made in the Severn, and Mr. Anderson in the Forth, and Mr Russel in the Tweed, which are recorded below From these it is apparent that, contrary to the movements of the adult salmon, the grilse or young fish may be said to ascend all at once, commencing about June, doubtless owing to their having then attained sufficient strength for the purpose The later in the year these grilse ascend the larger (comparatively) they are Young fish, as has been pointed out by Russel, are apt to live in shoals and if we refer to his table respecting Salmonidæ in the Tweed, we see that the trout suddenly increase in numbers in June, but decrease in proportional weight, owing to the ascent of young fish

Heavy rains occasioning floods may not only increase the take in the rivers and

first were recorded on June 28th, and in 1883, a week later (5) The second run of grilse ascends about the middle of June, or during the second spring tide, they are from 3 lb to 5 lb (6) The "autumn salmon" ascend at the end of June, are from 16 lb to 40 lb (7) With the first spring tide in July, quantities of grilse ascend (8) With the first spring tide in August, grilse from 8 lb to 16 lbs ascend in shoals, and many are heavy in spawn (9) "The gray schule salmon," or the regular breeders, ascend with the first spring tide in September, or later if the water is low Many are from 20 lb to 50 lb , some are very dark, others very red (10) There is also the "gray schule grilse," the most are ugly-looking fish, and very shiny all over their scales

Russel (The Salmon, 1864) remarked that the reason salmon ascend rivers more or less every month of the year, while grilse only do so at certain periods, or so to speak come all at once, must be owing to one being an adult form capable of ascending at any time, while the other is a young fish which first attains to that capacity at that season when its ascent is practically bound to begin The following return shows the proportions of salmon, grilse, and trout to every 1000 of each kind caught on an average of years in the net fisheries of the river Tweed —

	SALMON	GRILSE	TROUT		SALMON	GRILSE	TROUT
February (2nd half of)	22	0	8	July	233	371	254
March	56	0	7	August	151	408	164
April	89	0	23	September	113	154	129
May	128	1	56	October (1st half of)	71	53	186
June	138	13	173				

Salmon ascend in every month of the year, in numbers comparatively not very unequal Grilse, speaking roundly, do not ascend in the first half of the year, and all but a fraction within two consecutive months in the middle of the year , subsequently, their ascent is checked Forms ascending throughout the year being adults , those coming in shoals being the young of the same species That this is so is further borne out by the trout column, wherein are comprised both old and young, and in June they suddenly increase by 300 per cent , and another 50 per cent in July, during which month a fourth of the whole of the year's captures were recorded, while the average weight falls off during the months when the young appear to be ascending The increase of trout in October is due to fish ascending to spawn, when the average weight of the fish increases Russel has also shown that in examining some returns of takes of grilse and salmon from the Tweed, he found that the proportion which the grilse of any one year bore to the average number of grilse, was found to be just about the proportion which the salmon of the following year bore to the average number of salmon. Taking a series of years, the average weight of grilse captured in the Tweed was found to be in June, 3 lb 11¼ oz , July, 4 lb 5¼ oz , August, 4 lb 15 oz , September, 5 lb 12½ oz , October, 6 lb 11¾ oz · the late comers having been longest in the sea

The following are the figures supplied me at Inveran on the Shin by Mr Mackay, and which include the takes by anglers for the four years ending 1886 in that river —

	SALMON	GRILSE		SALMON	GRILSE
February	37	0	June	88	48
March	124	0	July	38	131
April	143	0	August	17	34
May	286	13	September	41	18

Dr Fri came to the following conclusions respecting the migrations of the Bavarian salmon (he omits the grilse), among which he observed three distinct times of ascent from the sea A Not ready for spawning when ascending (1) At the end of February under the ice, or March until May Large and strong fish from 35 lb to 50 lb (avoirdupois), famous as "violet salmon " (2) From the middle of June till August, if the rivers are not too low From 12½ lb to 22½ lb Flesh reddish, and known as "rose salmon " B Ready to spawn on arrival (3) First half of September until the end of November, and in mild winters until December Weak fish from 3 lb to 10 lb , or even 15 lb Flesh pale, and known as "silver salmon " (U S Fishery Reports, 1876, p 607)

estuaries, but likewise along the sea coast, which would seem to show that some effect had been produced which induced these fish to press onward toward the spawning beds *

Bad takes in a given year may be often due to causes which have acted generally upon the fishes, or else been locally detrimental to their appearance off the coast, or to their entering estuaries or ascending rivers, while on the other hand a good season may be mainly owing to a successful breeding season three or four years previously. It has been observed by Dr Mime that in the year 1867 there was a general absence of grilse throughout the waters of Great Britain, and in 1885 H M Inspector of Fisheries observed " that it is remarkable that while so large a run of grilse was obtained in the Tyne on the east coast, this description of fish was exceptionally rare in the rivers of the Bristol Channel on the west coast "†

During their migrations up river these fish have to overcome many obstructions, whether natural obstacles or artificial impediments, as weirs, and frequently these can only be surmounted during a heavy flood. While in the Severn, although salmon ascend every tide, the shoals seem to do so mainly during the six or eight spring tides preceding and following the highest spring, while the most do so just prior to the highest tide. If the water in any river is very low, possibly the pools would contain no safe resting places for ascending salmon, and spring fish would be very unlikely to accomplish their ascent, for they would most probably be captured by man or destroyed by vermin ‡

It has been observed by Mr Willis-Bund (Salmon Problems) that supposing a clean fish were interrupted in its journey up stream in fresh water, it drops back. Thus he remarked that a poacher who has missed gaffing a fish, first looks for his lost game in the pool below, not in the one above. It has also been observed of the Californian salmon, that when a rack is placed across a river the unripe fish drop back. In November, 1885, with the aid of Sir J Maitland, we investigated this on a small scale in the Teith, and when netting salmon for the purpose of obtaining ova, so far as was practicable, each fish on being returned into the river, had an elastic band slipped over its tail, and out of eight shots with the net, and a total take of forty-three fish, three of which were clean, we only recaptured one marked specimen. We worked down stream, except for the last two shots, and it was at shot No 7 that the marked fish was taken. Consequently it would appear that spawning fish, when captured below where they

* In the Birmingham Daily Post, July 17th, 1882, it was stated that " for the last ten days, owing to the heavy rains, the takes of salmon in the principal Scotch rivers have been extra ordinarily large, and the stake net fishing on the sea coast has also been unusually productive On Tuesday, on a stretch of coast not longer than eight miles, between Montrose and Bervie, from seven to eight tons of salmon, grilse, and trout were landed, and were at once despatched to the southern markets "

† Mr Willis-Bund (Field, August 7th, 1886) remarked, with reference to the laws which regulate the migration of fish in connection with weather, that a good year for one kind of anadromous fish in our waters is usually also a good year for the other kinds, while if it is a bad season for one kind, it is usually a bad season for all. It therefore seemed to follow that the same cause which leads to a large migration of one kind of fish will produce a large migration of the other kinds, always opining that the stock of each kind of fish is kept up in the same proportion. Isolated migratory salmon ascend on almost every tide, but the shoals in the Severn only on spring tides, and mainly on the six or eight spring tides preceding and following the highest spring, while the largest is just before the highest tide. At the very highest tide there appears to be a partial or entire cessation of migration (but on other rivers this is said not to be so) more fish run during the change from neap to spring than during the change from spring to neap, while a series of high spring tides generally give a larger run of fish than a series of moderate spring tides. Anglers are aware that with a falling barometer fish usually will not rise, it may be because they are moving. The different elements in the Severn required to bring about a good run of fish are the following (1) A high spring tide, (2) S W wind, (3) higher temperature of water in the estuary than the land water in the river, (4) low but steadily rising barometer to a height of 29° 50', and (5) moderate use of land water. The result of an examination of the four types of weather leads to a conclusion that fish run better during weather of a southerly or westerly type than they do when the weather is northerly or easterly

‡ Dr Brookes, Art of Angling, 1799, observed, " where the salmons have not dams to stop them they will change the salt for the fresh water several times during the summer " (p 170) and Dr Gunther believes that a salmon changing from salt to fresh water, and vice versa, several times in the year, only occurs in rivers falling into the Moray Firth

intend to construct their nests, may be expected, on being returned into the stream, to ascend it *

During their ascent these fish must keep to the middle, or deepest and safest part of a river, where, however, they are constantly pursued by the netter, and this causes them to become shy   They will not lie up, but seem more disposed to push on to their breeding-grounds   This question of rapidity of ascent is one by no means settled, while it is of the greatest consequence to the upper riparian proprietors †   Mr Willis-Bund considers that in the Severn they go up stream very leisurely, as two or three miles an hour, consequently, in a river having a long course, the weekly close time merely changes the locality where they are captured, for he believes none attain to the upper waters during the netting season   As a corroboration of this, it is observed that, except under exceptional conditions, it is some days after the nets are off rivers before the upper proprietors have much chance of hooking a fish

In some places it has been remarked that the male fish appears to ascend more rapidly than the female, and the sexes have even been observed to migrate in distinct companies ‡

In their course up stream it is very remarkable what difficulties they will overcome §   While at impassable cascades they have been observed to die, consequent upon repeated but fruitless exertions in attempting to ascend, a clear jump of six feet being probably as much as a salmon under ordinary conditions could accomplish

In the Severn it has been remarked that after the exertion of crossing a weir or ascending a rapid, they take a rest, for the best draught of these fish are captured *above* the obstruction in the dead-water   Kelts when obstructed in their course down a river are said to strike up stream, thus, we are told that at Powick weir, which solely captures ascending fish, kelts are often taken in the spring, and usually when there is a slight fresh in the river

For the purpose of assisting salmon to surmount natural or artificial obstructions which hinder or prevent their ascending rivers or attaining to their natural spawning beds, fish-passes,|| or fish-ladders, are generally erected, especially where

* In April, 1886, it was reported to the Severn Fishery Board (*Field*, April, 1886) "that but little progress has been made in the matter of fixing labels on salmon returned to the river, the labels not having been secured until late in January   All the nineteen fish secured for spawning operations had, however, been marked before returning to the river   Several of the marked fish had been recaptured, and in all cases higher up the river   One fish liberated at Worcester was caught two days afterwards at Lincombe, nine miles higher up the river, and had passed over two weirs "

† Livingston-Stone, speaking of *S quinnat*, says that "their rate of progress up the rivers varies between very wide limits.   The earliest runs are the longest time on their way up the river   The latest runs make the journey more quickly   The fish seem to regulate their speed according to the forwardness of their eggs "   While Professor Benecke (*German Fish Assoc*, March, 1886) could not observe in the Kuddow or Rheda during two years' investigations any law governing the migrations of these fishes

‡ Some fishermen consider that the larger fish head the ascending shoal, because should any such be netted a good haul generally follows, whereas, if smaller fish are first taken, the main body seems to have passed

Livingstone Stone remarked that "it frequently happened that a whole run of salmon for several days will be composed almost entirely of males, the effect of which, of course, is to leave the females together by themselves, whether they take an active part or not in bringing about the separation   In fact, in hauling a seine frequently in a river for some time, it is generally very noticeable that the sexes alternate in turning up the river about the spawning season, a large body of males being followed by a large body of females, and these by a run of males again, and so on through the season " (*Bull, U S Fish Comm*, 1885, p 468)   Mr Willis-Bund has also observed "that the male fish swims up the river more quickly than the female, at all events, the higher up the river the netting takes place, the greater percentage of males to females caught " (*Salmon Problems*, page 156)

§ Fleming asserted that he had known a salmon leap up over a fall of 30 ft, but probably he intended to mean in a succession of jumps from one pool or resting-place to another, Twiss (*Travels in Iceland*) declared that from personal observation he knew they were able to dart themselves nearly 14 ft perpendicularly out of the water   Professor Landmark has stated (*Nature*, August 16th, 1885) that he had witnessed their jumping 16 ft perpendicularly, but continued, "Such jumps are rare "   Scrope, after making a number of observations, came to the conclusion that 6 ft or 7 ft came nearer the truth

|| The *Commissioners* in 1861 reported that "every fact elicited during our inquiry bears

weirs exist in which there is no free gap However efficient these passes may be they are not complete cures for the injuries inflicted by the obstructions, for here, except during very high floods, the salmon will often loiter while ascending, and the kelts descending, as if they were hesitating prior to trusting themselves to these unnatural roadways

Fish passes are constructed of wood, stone, concrete, or iron, and may be classed under such as assist the fish by means of steps or pools to ascend over or even round any obstacle, or else by means of a succession of lochs to pass through the obstruction But from the year 1830, when Mr Smith of Deanston invented the first salmon ladder used in this country until the present day, many improvements have been made, but in all it would seem that the most effective are such as improve a natural passage, while if steps or stairs are employed the gradient should not exceed an incline of 1 in 8 The second class of passes, or such as are intended to assist fish passing through the body of an obstruction, are few in number and scarcely in favour at present *

When descending† seawards, it would appear that the salmon usually pass gradually into the salt water, but a heavy flood sometimes carries weak fish down stream Many observations have been made that none but kelts ever descend salmon rivers, and I have experienced net fishermen in the Teith hold this opinion, as they consider all clean fish will be killed; but, as I have already observed, if not killed (see page 69) some must descend to the sea before they will be in a condition to spawn, a view confirmed by the experiments made in the United States (see page 79), that salmon in some rivers only breed in alternate years The pinks or smolts keep to the sides of the river, but having once arrived at the tideway would seem to seek the deep water, to return again at a future date as breeding grilse

witness to the conclusion that an open river is the best for all, and that a recurrence to the ancient and clearly pronounced policy of the country by the removal of obstructions from the water is the sure and only road to the restoration of the fisheries"

* The reader must be referred to works on "fish culture" for full details as to fish passes

† Mr Stephen deposed, before the *Committee on the Salmon Fisheries*, in 1824 that, "Our cruives in the River Don are so constructed that salmon of 10 lb weight can at all times go up, but none can descend past the cruives We fish generally in the pools above the cruives, and if the unspawned salmon returned again down the river we would undoubtedly catch them there, which is never the case They are never seen to descend the river, except as kelts, after having spawned"

James Halliday deposed that salmon which enter rivers at any period, but not for spawning, would return again to the sea at times, were such return not cut off by want of water on the shallows, but if floods occur they descend He continued, respecting the Sand Pool in the Annan 'Although we had fished this pool quite clean of fish before the rain came on, yet whenever the rain did come on we then continued fishing constantly, until the water rose so high that we could not manage it, and we got the salmon and grilses coming down the river all the time into the pool, some of them had the appearance of having laid long in the water, and were very much exhausted—quite changed in the colour, as if they had hung in a smoky chimney for some time, others were very red in the skin, by having been in the fresh water for some time I have known us take 103 fish in one night in that pool after the rain commenced, although we had fished it clean immediately before Our opinion was that the fish came down from the river above, out of the rocky waters of the Bridekirk, Loos, and Hoddam The reason for fishing the pool at that particular time, was that the river at the foot of it parted into three small branches, and the pool itself was very deep When the water was using the fish could not find their way so readily down there, and they turned into the deep pool, and we kept drawing constantly as long as we could manage the water"

Mr Durst (*Quarterly Journal of Agriculture*, 1832, p 624), criticizing Hogg's paper, remarked —"He, however, is wrong in stating that clean salmon return to the sea in great numbers from Glenlyon, on the upper part of the Tay, without having spawned After the salmon leaves the tideway of the river, it pushes upwards to the smaller rivers, and when these subside, it may return downwards to the pools in the larger rivers We seldom or never see a salmon 'that has been long in the fresh water return unspawned through the bridge at Perth, which is nearly about the boundary of the tideway Men are stationed on the bridge to observe every fish that passes in the ordinary state of the river Below that, among the many thousands of salmon that I have seen taken, few or none bore the appearance of having been long in the fresh water While many hundreds of foul or newly spawned fish are hauled ashore every year, we get none with milts or roes returning to the sea, or that have the emaciated appearance, and maggots in the gills which characterize the fish that are found far up out of the tideway and have been long in the fresh water"

Before passing from the migrations of salmon, it is necessary to observe upon what have been termed "pool-bound" fish,* or those which have been some time in the river, remain in the pools, but refuse to rise to the angler's lure, consequent upon the absence of floods while, owing to their having been some time from the sea, they are generally of a more or less red or rusty colour

Marking fish is of ancient date Isaak Walton alluded to observations made by tying ribbons on the tails of some numbers of young salmon which were taken subsequently at the same place The reasons for thus marking fish are various, as for the purpose of tracing their growth or their migrations, or facts as to their breeding, such as whether they do so annually, biennially, or otherwise And while it is necessary that the marks should be distinct, in order that the fish may be unmistakably recognized at any future date, even by common fishermen,† it is also desirable not to occasion any serious injury It would be better did the skin remain unbroken, as abrasions might be the means by which the spores of the dreaded saprolegnia may obtain admittance, also external pressure long continued may set up irritation, ulceration, and so induce fungus, while any markings must not be allowed to interfere with the movements of the fish

Cutting part of the fins has been advocated, such as one of the lobes of the tail, or removing part of the bases or lower portion of some of the rays in the back fin or else employing the dead or adipose fin for this purpose, as dividing it into two, cutting a notch out of it, or even removing it entirely; but it is difficult to obtain such a variety in sections of these fins that we could distinguish any particular fish so as to be positive as to the period when it was last marked Also some forms of incisions, as for extracting the lower portion of rays, may occasionally be seen in fishes captured in the wild state, while removing portions may be due to the attacks of enemies

Branding is open to many objections, and although Buckland suggested a burn from a match on the cheek would be indelible, such is doubtful, while even were an indelible scar there, its origin would always be open to question In short, branding, to be efficient, must cause mutilation

Cross-cupping kelts has been advised, but cannot be recommended

Puncturing a hole in the gill-covers was not found to be a success at Stormontfield, as the place rapidly filled up again (*Brown*, p 68)

Elastic bands round the free portion of the tail so far have been a failure I tried them in 1885, using both elastic bands punched out of a flat sheet, and likewise bands cut from tubing, but the result was unsatisfactory, the pressure occasioning fungus On netting a pond at Howietoun in October, 1886, in which several fish had been so marked, none were found, and some are known to have died from fungus which these bands evidently caused One sent to an aquarium even lost the whole of its caudal fin, but still lives Possibly the fish thus marked in the rivers of the United States were not again recaptured, because they had all died

It seems to be generally considered that a metallic tag is necessary, having a number stamped upon it, and attached by a wire to one of the fins ‡ A silver wire has been placed in the form of a loose ring through the dead fin, but it seems very questionable whether it would not most probably ulcerate through, and so be lost § A wire has also been placed round the bases of the first or last few of the dorsal rays In the United States, the first tag employed was a thin aluminium plate, $\frac{1}{2} \times \frac{1}{4}$ of an inch, attached to an india-rubber band, which encircled the free portion of the fish's tail but no fish thus marked were recaptured. Next an aluminium tag was attached by a platinum wire at the base of

---

* See article by Mr Senior, Red Spinner, *Field*, September 25th, 1886

† It is almost needless to point out that care should be taken that they cannot be imitated for the purpose of obtaining rewards

‡ At Stormontfield, Brown observed that no ringed fish were retaken, so he questioned whether a foreign substance could be inserted into a smolt in fresh water, that would remain for any length of time attached to the fish after it had gone to the sea

§ Plated tags, with numbers engraved on them, are employed on the Severn; but it is very doubtful if they will be a success The fish is held in the lave net at the side of the boat while the wire is passed through its fin Zinc labels, of course, would be destroyed by sea water.

the last few dorsal rays, the wire being threaded to a needle, and so readily passed through, the ends being twisted together in a loop But the aluminium tags became brittle after being a short time in water, and fell off, so platinum wire and tags were substituted, and seem to be durable

The subject of early ' and "late" rivers has been already remarked upon, whether these are coincident with the ascent of clean fresh-run fish or the period at which they breed, which latter occurrence generally takes place in Great Britain between the middle or last week in October until the middle of February or even later * Those eggs deposited early in the cold upper waters of rivers would take longer hatching than such as are in warmer affluents lower down and nearer to its mouth Instances have been adduced (page 63) wherein these fish have been observed going to the redd in March , but it is not improbable that the progeny from such late breeders would be few, even if any survived, as the redds are often prepared in unsuitable places For the late migrants are mostly fish which are weakly or have been detained en route, and consequently have to be satisfied with forming their redds in the lower portion of the rivers, where disturbing influences are most prevalent † The time during which salmon remain in our rivers for spawning purposes is rarely less than three months, but such must be regulated by many causes as distance to be traversed, accessibility, temperature, &c , while there are certain fishes in which abnormal development occurs by having eggs at unusual seasons ‡

Prior to following out these periods more in detail, several questions in the life-history of these fishes require solution, while others which it is believed have been solved may perhaps be found to be worthy of still further investigation We have had it proved that salmon eggs deposited in the sea necessarily die from the direct injurious effects of the saline water , we know that young salmon or grilse give smaller ova than older and more mature salmon , while we are also aware that the size of the eggs in the ovary of one of these fishes are not all the same   The age at which these fishes first breed has been a disputed point, while the experiments made at Howietoun may be open to discussion as to whether fishes artificially raised, and subsequently retained semi-domesticated in fresh waters without being able to descend to the sea, carry on this function similarly to those in a wild state   Can it be that the breeding in the females under such conditions, it may be asked, is deferred for a season but, no data on which to base such a theory actually exist

It must be evident that forming conclusions as to age simply from observing fish in rivers at different times of the year but believed to be the same brood, would be liable to give rise to more or less error While, as already observed marking fish should be done more carefully and systematically than at present to furnish reliable facts On the other hand when care is taken, as at Howietoun, to segregate the fishes forming the different experiments, data are obtained which must, as a rule, be more or less doubtful among fish in a river The Howietoun experiments have shown that young male and female salmon kept in suitable fresh-water ponds, may develop milt or ova Some were hatched in

* In the Tay, spawning is said to usually commence about Martinmas (November 11th) , but in 1881 fish were not found ripe by the Stormontfield fish culturists until December 22nd or 23rd , while in 1883 it was not until December 31st that the hatchery was fully stocked Tenth salmon are said to spawn a little later than those of the Tay , and Mr Napier, the local superintendent, observed that as a rule, the period is from November 22nd or 23rd, and lasts until the early part or middle of January

† Late fish when forming their redds frequently root up those which were existing in the same spot, and consequently many ova are carried away down stream It has been remarked that this procedure permits of any diseased eggs being washed away and not left to contaminate the good ones , but it does not seem improbable that such treatment is worse than the disease In some seasons when the water in the rivers is too low for breeding fish to ascend, they deposit their ova at the mouths or in the sea, occasioning the loss of the year's supply of eggs For when the ova are ripe for extrusion, the female even by the muscular exertion of swimming or partaking of food, and so distending the abdomen, may cause their expulsion

‡ In The Field of April 30th, 1881, an account was given of one 15 lb weight with ova the size of No 6 shot captured in the Severn above Shrewsbury

March, 1881, and most of the male pairs had milt in November, 1883, or when 2 years and 8 months old, also two or three smolts of the same age had ova, which probably would have matured but they jumped out of the pond and so met with their deaths. In November or December, 1884, or at 3 years and 8 months age, all these fishes seemed ready to breed, and young were bred from their spawn * Consequently, descending to the sea prior to depositing ova is not a physiological necessity for young salmon †

Whether simply the heat of the water, unless excessive, exercises any deleterious effect upon the breeding fish we have but little evidence on which to rely, but in the *United States Fishery Reports* for 1876 Mr Atkins remarked of the Atlantic salmon, *Salmo salar*, in the Penobscot in 1873, that the temperature in the ponds in which those for spawning were confined, "between June 28th and August 13th there were only five days when the water at the bottom of the pond stood below 70° Fah., and on one occasion, July 31st, it rose as high as 76° Fah. Not only did no salmon die during this heated term, but at the succeeding spawning season they came out in perfect condition and yielded eggs of the highest degree of health and vigour."

At the spawning time‡ these fish are in a poor condition, covered with slime, and often nearly as slippery as eels, for at this period they almost cease feeding, living upon the fat which has accumulated in their system during their residence in the salt water, where the supply of food was abundant. Possibly the fat in the salmon's system may be more rapidly used up in cold rivers than it is in warm ones.

The eggs of the salmon are small, nearly round, elastic bodies, of a clear white, pink, or even coral colour § Due to their tough outer coat they are very elastic, as may be seen by throwing one on the ground, from whence it will rebound like an india-rubber ball. This strength and elasticity we know must be an exceedingly important property if we remember where these eggs are deposited and what an amount of pressure they have to undergo. The following are the sizes observed in some salmon eggs (see page 25 *ante*) of Howietoun grilse up to 1¼ lb weight 0 20 to 0 22 of an inch in diameter, while of these fishes from the Teith, taken Nov 26th, 1885, a 10 lb grilse had them 0 20, a 16 lb salmon, Nov 1884, 0 24 of an inch, a 15 lb salmon, Nov 26th, 1885, 0 27 of an inch and the eggs of one large salmon in 1884, weight not noted, were up to 0 30 of an inch. Here we observe a considerable variation in size from 0 20 of an inch in the diameter of the eggs of a grilse, to 0 30 of an inch in that of a salmon, while these eggs have been obtained of a still larger size ‖

* Grilse, it has been asserted, in some rivers breed earlier in the cold season of the year than do salmon, which it has been surmised is due to their being fish in which the time of reproduction has been deferred from February or March until October or November. As at the period grilse spawn fertile male pars would be present in the rivers, it would appear not improbable that they might perform the necessary marital office

† Many have held the opinions which Rasch so fully detailed in 1866 when he commenced by the inquiry why it is that all the male fish, including those that have gone to the sea and those that remain behind in fresh waters, have their reproductive organs fully developed, while the female is under the necessity of making the journey to the sea before being able to spawn (*see* page 60 *ante*) He considered that if smolts were prevented going to the sea they would readily accustom themselves to a fresh water home, if the piece of water were sufficiently extensive, and "should the water be a very large lake such as Ladoga, Wener, Peipus, and as rich in nourishing food, the fresh water salmon will then attain about the same size as the salmon of the sea" He also observed that Hetting hatched out numbers of salmon ova, which he subsequently turned loose into the Tyri fiord and during the last two years fish had been caught in that lake resembling in every respect salmon proper

‡ It has been suggested that a sojourn in fresh water, even if such be merely temporary, may give the first impulse towards bringing the sexual organs to maturity, but there does not appear to be any evidence on which to base such a theory, and the breeding of the land locked races and the Howietoun experiments clearly demonstrate that the maturity of the breeding organs may occur without any migration from the fresh waters in which the fish were originally hatched

§ The micropyle in the salmon's eggs from the Teith had nine pits or depressions around the opening in such as were examined

‖ Stoddart, *Angler's Companion*, 1847, held that the eggs were fertilized before they were extruded, and that it was a "false but popular notion that the ova of the salmon, previous to its being emitted, is in an unimpregnated state" (page 188)

Some authors have laid great stress upon the weight of the eggs in these fish at different stages as compared with that of the mother, but very unnecessarily so, for such affords but little, if any, useful information The eggs up to a given point constantly increase in size and weight consequently their comparison with that of the body of the parent, which remains the same or even diminishes in weight, must be almost daily changing

Salmon are provided with numerous eggs in order to meet the destructive agencies to which the ova and young are subjected, and these are as a rule sufficient to counterbalance natural waste, which, however, must be enormous,* for the number of eggs which each female salmon produces has been estimated at about 900 for every pound weight of the parent fish, but they may exceed these, thus one weighing 20 lb contained 27,850 eggs † It is very obvious that the number of young reared from fish left to nature is far less than what obtains in those artificially propagated In the Tay, so soon as artificial propagation commenced, the augmentation was as much as 10 per cent, an increase not apparent in rivers in which this mode of fish cultivation was not carried on This is now adopted in many rivers where the eggs in their natural state prove unequal to the destructive agencies that affect them While the number removed for this purpose from streams is but a small percentage to what remains ‡

It has already been observed (p 26) that immaturity of parents may occasion sterility of the eggs or disease, as dropsy, of the offspring, while, although, as I shall have subsequently to observe, it has been stated that the milt of young pars has all the properties of that from adult fish, such is contrary to my experience §

Doubtless the prejudices of many persons were formerly in favour of not interfering with nature, and permitting salmon to breed as best they could in our rivers and streams, but some of the latter had already been deprived of these fish through the greed of the fishermen, poisoning of the waters or other causes, and it appeared that if the rivers could not be restored to their pristine condition, artificial attempts at propagation should be attempted   (See pp 29-36 ante)

It has been disputed as to whether salmon are annual breeders,‖ breed on alternate years, or every third year as suggested by Buckland, or merely do so once in their existence This last proposition may be well dismissed, because if such were so, fertile pars or grilse would be subsequently sterile which is not the case The young males kept in fresh water having milt for two successive seasons has been observed at Howietoun while the experiments made on the Penobscot River would seem to show that there at least the fish breed every alternate year,

---

* It was calculated by Stoddart and others that if salmon eggs are left to nature the produce is about four or five fish fit for the table for every 30,000 ova deposited, whereas the same number are obtained from every 800 eggs artificially protected Mr Ashworth stated it as his opinion, in which Mr Ffennell coincided, that not above one in 6000 salmon ova deposited naturally in the bed of a river arrives at the grilse or salmon state and becomes marketable He argued that more than 24,000 fish of various ages annually ascended the river, half being females, or 12,000 fish from 6 lb to 12 lb , which would give 72,000,000 ova, or one from 6000 ova deposited naturally in the river (Brown, *Stormontfield Experiments*, p 65) These figures, however, are founded upon calculations some of which may be fallacious, for instance, if the number of adults left in a river are taken as the basis it was probably computed they breed every year, but if some only do so on alternate years this would considerably alter the number

† We are told that a Penobscot salmon, *Salmo salar*, of about 8 lb weight does not give more than 5000 or 6000 eggs

‡ Eggs have been found to still return their vitality in a female salmon that had been dead two hours or even more, having been successfully vivified by the milt from a live male

§ As corroborative of the above view that the milt of these young salmon pars was deficient in marital powers, I may mention that on Nov 29th, 1883, 1000 eggs of the common brook trout were milted from a Howietoun salmon par which had been dead a few hours But not a single egg fructified , only three turned white in December three in January, and fifteen in February, or a total of twenty-one On March 12th the remainder were still quite clear, but destitute of any sign of a contained embryo

‖ Mr Burst, writing to *The Field*, observed, " a few years ago a fine male fish of about 20 lb was used for spawning purposes at Stormontfield A mark was put on him by means of a copper wire, and two years afterwards he was got when nearly 30 lb weight on the same ford, and at the same season and after doing duty again, was returned to the river hale and strong, but he was not traced afterwards "

while, unless there is a very great difference in the distance of ascent from the sea to the redds, it would be most probable that what this species does in one locality it also does in another *

Although observations have already been made that salmon do not spawn in the sea, or should they do so, their eggs will not hatch or the young succumb (*see* pages 36, 37), some of the opinions or statements recorded have been collected and will be found below Mackenzie, *Salmon Fisheries of Scotland*, page 13, observed that "one of the luminaries of the Scottish bar, distinguished by his grave eloquence, declared that if all the rivers in the kingdom were blocked up, salmon would become more plentiful than ever, as they would then be *forced* to spawn in the sea "†

* Mr Atkins observed before the *American Fisheries Society*, respecting experiments made since 1872, at Bucksport, on the Penobscot River, that in November, 1873, 391 salmon were marked in a secure manner, each fish being first measured and weighed and supplied with a numbered tag Several of those fish came to hand in the spring, and were found to have lost weight very much, and were otherwise in poor condition, showing that they had not been to their feeding-grounds Those captured in the second year, however, were enormously increased in weight and were in prime condition A female, placed in a breeding pond, yielded some 11,000 eggs In 1875, 357 salmon were marked and released, and of these a number were taken in the spring of 1876, without exception all in poor condition In the spring of 1877 three of the 1875 fish came to hand, and, like the second year's fish of the 1873 lot, were very fine When placed in the water in 1875 the three weighed together 41½lb , and when recaptured in 1877, 90lb exactly Thus the second experiment coincided exactly with the first In 1880, 252 salmon were marked and released Those recaught the next year showed poor condition, three-fourths having actually fallen away In 1882 five were recaptured These when released weighed together 45¾ lb , when recaptured 90½lb These three experiments conclusively proved that the salmon of the Penobscot, at least, spawn every other year only

† If we refer to the *Report of the Committee of the House of Commons on Salmon Fisheries*, in 1824, we find them asking a witness, Mr Johnstone—"Is the Committee to understand that there are salmon which frequent the friths, and go out to sea again without going up the rivers?" To this he replied, "Yes " He also remarked that although they generally spawn above the influence of the tides, they may spawn where the tide reaches And they subsequently interrogated Mr Halliday thus—"Are there a great many salmon which come into the friths that do not go to the rivers but return again to the sea ?"—"There are a great many " While Mr Steavenson, of Forth ose, deposed " that there cannot be a doubt that salmon spawn in the sea "

During the winter of 1824 Mr Hogarth found that salmon ova taken from the river Don and put into salt water never came to life, from which he inferred that if salmon spawn were deposited in the sea it would not be evolved (*Parliamentary Committee on Salmon Fisheries*, 1824, page 62) Sir Humphrey Davy observed of the salmon "Sometimes, indeed, in very small streams it deposits its spawn almost close to the sea in gravel, where the stream meets the waves at high-water mark " (l c , p 144) Sir James Mathieson, in Davy s *Physiological Researches* (p 261), has recorded at the mouth of the Greamster, in the island of Lewis, a similar instance, continuing that the spot is covered with "brackish water " only for about two hours at each high tide, but not at all during the neaps, while this brackish water is so diluted as to differ but little from fresh water in specific gravity, the tide serving as a dam to the river water, and by obstructing its free outflow, caused its accumulation and overflow The foregoing instances occurred near the mouths of small rivers, and should their state be such—due to pollutions or insufficiency of water—that *Salmonidæ* are unable to ascend, they may drop or deposit their ova in the sea or at the mouths of rivers, but suppose it is thus deposited, experiments have, as I shall show, proved that the presence of salt water is fatal to the fertilizing property of the milt, as also the unpregnated egg, should it come in contact with it Doubtless, salmon and sea trout will drop their spawn in salt water at times, but should an investigation be instituted such is usually found to be consequent upon a want of sufficiency of water in the rivers to enable them to ascend to their spawning beds, while they cannot retain their ova for an indefinite period Mr Jackson (*Land and Water*, June 10th, 1876) recorded that " the salmon-trout cast their ova in the salt water at Southport Aquarium, without assuming the appearance of kelts, or even leaving off feeding greedily on shrimps They did not attempt to make a bed, and the spawn was immediately eaten by their fellows " It would seem in this case that the fish, aware of the uselessness of forming a redd, did not take the trouble to do so About 1862 Mr Sinclair made some experiments in Ireland on the effects of salt water on salmon ova, remarking, in *The Field*, 1882, upon having taken about one hundred eyed salmon ova, of which two portions were enclosed in wicker baskets, and buried in separate streams, one of which was reached every tide by salt water whereas the other was entirely fresh They were examined in about three weeks after one set of spring tides, when all which had been reached by salt water were found to be dead not so those in which the stream was entirely fresh water The remaining third were hatched in a wash-hand basin, in which was fresh water changed once a day He subsequently observed (*Field*, March 7th, 1885) that since then he had two or three times seen salmon redds in the same tidal water, and had been assured by his head water bailiff that he had seen one a quarter of a mile lower down, where the gravel was covered over by neap tides , also he had been told that in another river, on a particular

During the winters of 1884-85, and also of 1885-86, experiments were instituted on this question at Cheltenham (*see p* 37), all of which fully corroborated the view that salt water is fatal to the eggs of salmon

It has been asserted, and is still maintained by some that redds are formed by salmon burrowing into the sand or gravel with their heads, or the male with his hooked jaw

When one considers the structure of this fish, it must be evident that it would be impossible the male could dig a hole in the bed of the river with the hook on the lower jaw, because it possesses no neck, nor the power of moving its head up and down, as observed by Mackenzie (*View of the Salmon Fisheries of Scotland*, 1860, p 175), without a corresponding movement of its entire body While even if the fish retreated a few yards to give it an impulse, it would still be necessary for it to raise its tail out of the water at an angle of 45° to enable it, like a pickaxe, to knock its snout against the gravel, or, for anything the poor creature knows, against a stone   Irrespective of the injury such a proceeding would occasion to the fish, the gravel disturbed by the snout would enter the fish's mouth to the detriment of its respiration   and the knob cannot be a necessity for this work, for in how few trout or char do we see it, yet they all form a redd or nest

Of course the nearer the sea suitable spawning grounds are, the more valuable do they become to the fishery at the mouth of the river. Salmon eggs are deposited in rivers, rarely near their mouths, where the tide or the current would be too strong for the young fish to live in, but often in small and even mountainous streams, where the water is pure and shallow, having a gravelly bed which permits the redd or nest to be constructed,* while deep pools in the vicinity allow the breeding fishes to retire into them for rest   The salmon ascends our rivers to a suitable spot, and in the gravel at the bottom of the stream constructs its redd, which work would seem to be the occupation of the female   She lies on one side,

ford, which is affected by spring tides, but only in a slight degree, half-a dozen redds are generally to be found every winter   Mr J Jackson (*Field*, December 20th, 1884), writing of the Yorkshire Esk, recorded, respecting salmon ova that "it is an interesting question, however, as to what amount of brackish water will destroy it, and as we have a lot of spawning fish depositing their ova in the stream, just below Ruswark Mill dam over which they cannot get when heavy in spawn, and up to which spring tides rise about two or three feet, covering the spawn beds for about two hours each tide for some three or four days at each period of high tides   Some ova from fish spawning there was procured and placed in a box in the gravel at that spot   This was done in order to ascertain whether they would come to life   Though nothing came of the experiment for the first two years, it was asserted that this year (1884) a good portion of them were hatched   Another account, however, stated that some of the ova were removed from this box, and hatched in a basin of fresh water in the village brook, whereas all that were left in the box died

Sir T Matheson, during the winter of 1861 62, had two portions of impregnated salmon eggs used one for trial in brackish water of specific gravity 1015°, the other in fresh   They were held on a wire cloth in a glass vase with a tap at its bottom, and the water was changed daily   During the first ten days the ova in the brackish water did not appear to suffer, but no longer , no further development was observed in them   and they all died, while those in the fresh water made progress, and in due time were hatched   Dr Davy (*Physiological Researches*) tried the effects of a solution of common salt in water, having a specific gravity of 1026°, on a salmon egg, the embryo in which appears to have succumbed in a few hours over two days   The ovum of a Dee salmon in similar water, or a specific gravity of 1007°, was hatched at the end of about forty-eight hours , the young was very languid, but at the end of the fourth day was still alive   Brown in his account of the *Stormontfield Experiments*, 1862, observed — ' We have also taken ova which had been recently manipulated upon, and dropped it into sea water, which destroyed it almost instantaneously, only a few of them becoming opaque, in the greater portion of them the yolk became shrivelled up and contracted " Mr Brander, in *The Field*, remarked upon having observed some holes scooped out in the gravel close to the mouth of the small river Lossie (near the Spey), and within the reach of the salt water, and here he found in January, 1882, a few salmon working at their redds, which were within a mile and a half of the sea, and covered once a fortnight at spring tides with quite salt and undrinkable water, for perhaps an hour's time

* Very complete accounts have been given as to the manner in which the salmon redd is constructed   Captain Francks (*Northern Memoirs*, about A D 1656, p 167) recorded how he watched a female until she arrived at a bed of sand where she was scarcely covered with water, certainly not exceeding a foot in depth, here, with her tail, she wriggled to and fro so long and oft until he saw a flat blueish stone, over which she oft times contracted her body and ejected her eggs   The male having arrived at the same spot dilates his fins, and flutters about, and

and, by moving her tail rapidly from one side to the other, fans up the gravel* until she gradually sinks into a kind of trough, the male remaining near ready to give battle to any intruder   Perhaps for this purpose his lower jaw is furnished at this period with an offensive weapon in the shape of a cartilaginous, hook-like process   The female (waited upon by the male) now deposits her eggs in the trough she has made, and these are fertilized by the male, and subsequently covered with gravel to some feet in depth, the whole forming a redd

It has been remarked that should there be plenty of water to let the fish into rivers in time, salmon are many days constructing their nests, doing a little every night, but if prevented ascending until quite ripe they are much more rapid in their operations, and if much disturbed they have been known to forsake the spot, while a little frost or fall of temperature will hasten the deposition of eggs

When the salmon has formed her nest and deposited her first instalment of eggs she falls back into one of the deep pools, until she has acquired sufficient strength to again shed more eggs   The places selected by salmon for their redds are sometimes the localities where trout have previously deposited their eggs, which now become rooted up and carried away down stream to be devoured by every hungry fish   The absence of frosts is favourable to the eggs in the redds (*see* p 39), while although floods may sweep away redds, moderate ones protect them from poachers   Mild seasons and late spates seem best adapted for preventing mortality among the breeders †

probably with his nose rooted as a swine, or something like it, and fecundated the eggs   The milter having retired to the depth of the water gives place to the spawner, who works a trough like a cistern in sand or gravel as near as he could guess about her own proportions, into which she jumbles and tumbles her eggs and gently covers them over with sand   Shaw (*Development and Growth of Salmon Fry*, in the Transactions of the Royal Society of Edinburgh, xiv, 1840, page 551), stated that " on January 10th, 1836, he observed a female salmon of about 16 lb and two males of at least 25 lb engaged in depositing their spawn   The two males kept up an incessant conflict during the whole day for possession of the female, and, in the course of their struggles, frequently drove each other almost ashore, and were repeatedly on the surface, displaying their dorsal fins and lashing the water with their tails   The female throws herself at intervals of a few minutes upon her side, and, while in this position, by the rapid action of her tail digs a receptacle for her ova, a portion of which she deposits, and, again turning on her side, she covers it up by renewed action of her tail, thus alternately digging, depositing and covering the ova, until the process is completed by the laying of the whole mass, an operation which generally occupies three or four days " In the *Report of Salmon Commission*, 1824, we read, Mr Halliday stated " they generally spawn in the running water, at the foot of fords and the top of fords, where the gravel is fine, and low down in the foot of pools where the water begins to run, so as to assist the salmon in removing the gravel " (p 60)   " When they proceed to the shallow waters, which is generally in the morning or at twilight in the evening, they play round the ground two of them together   When they begin to make the furrow, they work up the gravel rather against the stream, as a salmon cannot work with his head down the stream, for the water going into his gills the wrong way drowns him   and when they have made a furrow, they go a little distance the one to one side and the other to the other side of the furrow, and throw themselves on their sides when they come together, and, rubbing against each other, they shed their spawn both into the furrow at once "   " It requires from about eight to twelve days for them to lay their spawn "   Mr *Atkins* in the United States observed a land locked salmon excavating her nest by turning on her side and flopping violently against the bottom with her tail, while the male was engaged in driving away rivals and predaceous foes   Mackenzie (l c page 13) observed that in forming redds the exertions of the spawners are greatly assisted by the action of the water in the streams   " they commence their operations at the lower extremity, shedding the ova and milt as they proceed, so that, in working upwards, the gravel thus stirred is carried down by the strength of the current and covers the spawn as it is deposited   In still waters this would not be the case, nor, unaided by the current or action of the water, could the fish make the necessary furrows   Their instincts, therefore, which in all animals are perfect, points out to them the proper place for their operations "   But the foregoing and evidently correct accounts have not passed unchallenged, and many persons still believe that the use of the knob on the jaw of the male fish (*see* page 80) is to rout up the gravel and form or complete the redd   We find Mr *Andrew Young*, of Invershin, 1840, referring as follows to this subject.
" A salmon bed is constructed thus   the fish having paired, chosen their ground for bed making, and being ready to lay in, they drop down the stream a little, and then returning with velocity towards the spot selected, they dart their heads into the gravel, burrowing with their snouts into it   This burrowing action, assisted by the power of the fins, is performed with great force "

* Possibly one reason for the Salmonidæ covering their eggs is to prevent them being moved for some days after they have been deposited, as such is a very potent cause of mortality among ova
† " Piscator " in the *Fishing Gazette* of March 6th, 1886, observed   " There were about six or seven male fish (salmon) surrounding a female.   There was one fellow who appeared to be king

G

The period salmon eggs take incubating is subject to considerable variation (see p 35 ante), thus it has been found that at 45° Fahr they take 90 days, at 43° 101 days (Shaw), at 41° 97 days (J Maitland) and at 36° 114 days (Shaw), while their normal period of hatching has been deferred to the 148th day by placing them in ice vaults (see p 43 ante), but freezing them is probably fatal (see p 37) Mr Bartlett, *Proceedings of the Zoological Society*, 1859, p 125, observed how some of these eggs under his supervision at the Crystal Palace were taken on February 5th and deposited in boxes with gravel and water which averaged 37° Fahr, and the young hatched on March 7th, or in thirty days

But salmon eggs, even in redds,* are not permitted to rest in peace and hatch in security they have many accidents to escape from and numerous enemies whose vigilance must be evaded, and which have been already enumerated (p 28)

When these little fish emerge from the eggs as *alevins* (see p 43), they have a large bag (the umbilical sac) attached to their under surface a little behind the gill opening, this contains the nourishment which is to serve them from three weeks to two months for their subsistence, and they do not commonly take in much food by the mouth until it is absorbed Weighed down by it they lie quietly among the stones at the bottom of the stream and seek concealment from fish larger than themselves, water insects, and other enemies which now commence to feed on them Living in shallows many forms of large fish are unable to follow them, but floods may carry them down to their enemies At about the end of two months the alevins are about $1\frac{1}{4}$ inches long, at four months $2\frac{1}{8}$ inches, and at six months $3\frac{3}{4}$ inches, but there are great individual variations in size among them The yelk or umbilical sac in young salmon is generally of a much more orange colour than is seen in the alevins of fresh-water trout Monstrosities are not rare, and being similar to those occurring among trout they will be alluded to together

The alevin stage, or that which begins when the fry is first hatched, passes after a few months into that of a parr or pink, when the fish becomes adorned with brilliant colours, as has been already described These young fish reside two years in our rivers migrating seawards in their second or third spring, and occasionally in the autumn as smolts Many discussions have arisen as to whether the parr is or is not the young of the salmon, or even a hybrid between it and the trout, and though there exists a strong family resemblance between the young of the salmon and trout, still it has been abundantly proved that the *Salmo salar* passes through a parr stage In fact it was long ago pointed out that in rivers destitute of salmon there were no parrs, while wherever they existed there parrs were present This point has now been most conclusively decided by hatching out eggs and milt taken directly from salmon and artificially rearing the progeny, the result being parrs It has also been shown that similar parrs can be raised from the eggs of smolts fertilized from parrs, or salmon similarly fecundated, from grilse and salmon, from pure grilse, and from pure salmon

Whenever one attempted to come too near the female he made a rush at him, seized him and shook him as a retriever would shake a hare This game was carried on for a considerable time, until every one was more or less torn to such an extent that in a few days several of them were found lying dead on the bank, and I had no trouble in identifying them as those engaged in the combats'

* Mr Brander examined a redd that appeared to have been left dry, but on opening it found that a little water was trickling through the stones and gravel which was sufficient to keep the ova healthy Having scraped a hole, he obtained a considerable number of eggs, and these he transferred to a pail of water, where two thirds hatched within periods varying from five minutes to twenty four hours About a week subsequently he returned to the same spot, and had another dig for salmon eggs (no rise having occurred in the river during the interval) He collected more, and putting them into the water, they hatched as the former ones had done He advanced that this may be a provision to prevent ova deposited in localities where the depth of the stream is liable to considerable fluctuations, from becoming lost or killed, as must occur unless a delay, to obtain suitable time, could be provided for But there are no means of knowing whether these ova were all deposited at the same time While at p 38 ante, will be found the account of experiments made at Cheltenham with eggs in artificial redds, and although they were kept several hours daily uncovered by water they hatched on the same day as others which were kept all the time with a stream flowing over them

The young of the salmon in Acts of Parliament were formerly designated as fry and smolts, while of late years the term par has been commonly used, and which has been said to be calculated to mislead, because there are salmon par and trout-par This brings us therefore to the consideration of what is a par ? And I think a short history of the controversy this question has raised will be interesting, for in such, zoologists, fishermen, learned divines, doctors, lawyers, poachers, in fact almost every class has joined * Arguments for and against their being

* We find Willoughby, *Historia Piscium*, 1686, p 192, giving a description of the *Salmulus* or "samlet" of Herefordshire, which, he tells us, inhabits the Wye, and all which he has examined were males ; he however places it as a distinct species In the next page he gives it as *branlins* or *fingerins*, and asserts that he is persuaded that they interbreed with the salmon, and are only found in such places as are frequented by the salmon Willoughby was persuaded that all the various species of the genus *Salmo* interbred
Ray, *Synopsis Methodica Piscium*, 1713, p 63, classed the samlet of Herefordshire and the branlin and fingerin of Yorkshire all as one species, and of which he affirmed all were males Isaak Walton, *Complete Angler*, 1653, remarked that "in divers rivers, especially that relate to or be near to the sea, as *Winchester* or the *Thames* about Windsor, is a little trout called a 'samlet' or 'skegger trout,' and that these be by some taken to be young salmons " Captain Francks, *Northern Memoirs*, 1658, page 301, described "the various brood of salmon, so to distinguish them according to mode, or as some will have it the custom of the country In the south they call him 'samlet,' but if you step to the west he is better known there by the name of 'skeggar,' when in the east they avow him 'penk,' but to the northward 'brood' and 'lockspen,' so from thence to a 'tecon,' then to a 'salmon'" J Williamson, *The British Angler*, 1711, page 138, considered 'the 'samlet,' or 'salmon smelt,' or, as they are called by some, 'salmon-fry,' are only so many different names for the 'young salmon'" But, in *Letters from the North of Scotland*, page 126, writing of the Ness about 1730, remarked on a small fish the people call a little trout, but of another species "called in the North of England a *Branlin* These are so like the salmon fry that they are hardly to be distinguished, only the scales come off the fry (Smolts) in handling, the others (Pars) have none It is by law no less than transportation to take the salmon-fry but in the season the river is so full of them that nobody minds it, and those young fish are so simple the children catch them with a crooked pin Yet the townsmen are of opinion that all such of them as are bred in the river, and are not devoured at sea by large fish, return thither at the proper season , and as a proof they affirm they have taken many of them, and by way of experiment, clipped their tails into a forked figure, like that of a swallow, and found them with that mark when full-grown and taken out of the crures "
Pennant, *British Zoology*, iv, 1776, page 303, said the samlet is the least of the trout kind, it is by several imagined to be the fry of the salmon, but from which he dissented, first, because salmon fry vanish on the first vernal flood after they have been born, and which sweeps them into the sea, leaving scarce one behind ; and secondly, because the growth of the salmon fry is so quick and so considerable as suddenly to exceed the size of the largest samlet That the salmon attains to a considerable size before it breeds, while samlets on the contrary are found male and female, although it has been vulgarly imagined that there were no other than males of this species That they are present all the year round in the rivers, and spawn in November and December He concluded "these fish are very frequent in the rivers of Scotland, where they are called 'pars,' they are also common in the Wye, where they are known by the name of 'skinlings' and 'lasprings'" He gives a short extract from Mr Potts respecting the salmon of the Tweed,— "about the latter end of March the spawn begins to exclude the young, which gradually increase to the length of four or five inches, and are then termed 'smelts' or 'smouts' About the beginning of May the river is full of them, it seems to be all alive, there is no having an idea of the numbers without seeing them , but a seasonable flood then hurries them all to the sea, scarce any or very few being left in the river "
Turton, *British Fauna*, 1807, page 104, admitted *Salmo salmulus* as a distinct species
Should we now turn to the *Reports on the Salmon Fisheries of the United Kingdom*, drawn up by a select committee of the House of Commons, in 1824 and 1825, we find a considerable amount of evidence as to what par were considered in those days One witness (G Little, page 113), on being asked if he had ever known them found in any river where there were no salmon ? replied, "I do not know that I have, I never took particular notice as to them, but I consider them a fresh water fish, unconnected with our salmon fisheries altogether " But on being asked at what season of the year does the salmon fry begin to go down to the sea ? he at once answered that "when the natural warmth comes into the water in the month of March, the fry generally rise, and they continue going down from that time until the 1st of May , sometimes I have seen them going down till the month of June " (p 115)
Mr Hogarth, in May, 1824, when samlets were descending the Don, had a number of them captured and marked, by cutting off the *mort* or dead fin During the month of July several grilses were taken without that fin, whence he inferred that they were some of the fishes which he had previously marked Not only did samlets thus become grilses in a few weeks, but in the following year, 1825, he got three salmon, marked in the same way, which he also considered to be some of those individuals he had marked originally as samlets In September, 1824, he caught ten or twelve grilses which were put into a salt-water pond Owing to high tides some

the young of the salmon have been employed, invectives against opponents have been freely indulged in, and all because no one would hatch the little fish from the ovum, and ascertain the various changes it went through in the course of the first few years of its life

escaped, but there were three alive the following May, these were taken out and examined in the presence of many competent judges, who were decidedly of the opinion that they were real salmon These experiments showed not only the growth of the smolt or samlet into grilse or botcher, but also that of the grilse into gilling or salmon of one year's growth

One must, however, decline assenting to some of Mr Ellis's conclusions ("Natural History of the Salmon," in the *Edinburgh New Philosophical Journal*, 1828, p 250 et seq), viz , that salmon "frequently propagate their kind during the first year of their age," or that "in the first five months of its existence, that is, from April to August, both inclusive, it reaches, in favourable circumstances, to about 8 lb in weight, or grows at the average rate of about 1 lb 9¾ oz a month , that from September following to March, seven months, it acquires 7 lb additional weight, which is at the average rate of about 1 lb 1½ oz per month , and lastly, that through the next twelve months it gains 10 lb. more, or weighs 35 lb., which is somewhat more than 13½ oz per month "

Fleming, *History of British Animals*, 1828, p 179, speaking of the young of the salmon, remarked, "The fry leave the spawning groove about March, retire to pools, and proceed according to circumstances in myriads along the easy water at the margin of the river, with their heads against the stream, until they reach the tide in the estuary where, like the kelts, which frequently go down at the same time, they retire to the deepest part of the channel and disappear in the sea These samlets, smoults, or smouts, are regarded by many as reappearing in the estuaries a few months afterwards in the character of 'grilses,' of from 3 lb to 4 lbs weight, according to the lateness of the season "

Sir Walter Scott, *Fair Maid of Perth*, 1828, observed, "Eachin resembles Conachar," said the glover, "no more than a salmon resembles a par, though men say they are the same fish in a different state "

Sir Humphrey Davy, *Salmonia*, 1832, p 68, considered par to be hybrid offspring of a salmon and a trout also that "pars are exceedingly numerous in those rivers where they are found, which are never separated from the sea by impassable falls , from which I think it is possible that they are produced by a cross between sea and river trout " (p 70)

Stoddart, *Scottish Angler*, 1831, strenuously advocated the theory that par are the young of the salmon

Mr Burst *Quarterly Journal of Agriculture*, 1832, observed that Mr Hoggs' novel theory of pars being the young of salmon, astonished him, as the par differed from the smolt in many essential particulars "the par is a compact fish, with firm scales, small head and eye, and from every appearance a fish come to maturity The smolt is evidently a young tender fish, its scales come off with the slightest touch , its head and eyes are large, like other young creatures that are destined to be of a much greater size But the greatest and most decided difference is this, that pars are found in our rivers *at all seasons of the year*, and 'smolts,' or what we reckon salmon fry, only from March to about the middle of June The difference between the fish, even in this respect, is almost sufficient to prove that they are not the same species "

A correspondent in *London's Magazine of Natural History*, vii, 1834 p 209, observed "The opinion there, on the Wharfe, is, that if a female salmon gets up, even if no male accompanies her yet her eggs are fecundated by the male smolts "

Sir W Jardine, *Edinburgh New Philosophical Journal* 1835, p 56, stated of the *Salmo salmulus*, or par "the greatest uncertainty, however, latterly resolved itself into whether the par was distinct, or a variety, or young of the common trout, S *fario* With the migratory salmon it has no connection whatever "In the markings they are so distinct as to be at once separated from the trout by any observer " "I have no hesitation in considering the par not only distinct, but one of the best and most constantly marked species we have, and that it ought to remain in our system as the S *salmulus* of Ray " He also said, "From the *migratory salmon* it is separated entirely by its habits. The correct distinguishing marks to be seen by a person who has not leisure to make a minute examination, are the great size of the pectoral fins, the shortness of the maxillary bones, and consequently the small gape, and the narrow breadth between the rami of the lower jaw" (*Berwickshire Naturalists' Field Club*, 1, p 84)

Jenyns, *Manual of British Vertebrate Animals*, 1835, p 426, gave the *Salmo salmulus*, which he remarked is now pretty well ascertained to be a distinct species, always remaining of a small size It is called in some places a "par," in others a "skirling" or "brandling " According to Dr Heysham, *Catalogue of the Animals of Cumberland*, p 31, the adult fish go down to the sea after spawning, which takes place, as in the other migratory species of this genus, in the depth of winter

Sir John Richardson, *Encyclopedia Britannica*, Ed 1835, p 205, stated, "The ova continue covered by the gravel during the winter, and begin to vivify from about the end of March to the commencement of April The fry remove from under the gravel when nearly an inch in length, with the ovum still attached , and at this period, if the spawning bed or furrow be turned up, it will appear in motion When disengaged from the ova the fish increase in size more rapidly, and about the end of April and during May commence and perform their first migration or journey to the sea At this time they are from four to six inches in length "

As, however, the changes these fish undergo will be fully alluded to under the head of salmon bred in fresh waters, and which have not descended to the sea, such will not be described in this place

Yarrell, *History of British Fishes*, Edition I, 1836, i, p 15, observed of the fry of the various species of *Salmonidæ* that "it is this similarity in marking and appearance of the fry which has caused the difficulty in distinguishing between the various species when so young, and experimenters, believing they had marked young par only, have been surprised to find some of them marked fish return as grilse, young bull trout, or whitling, salmon trout, river trout, and true par" "The laspring of some rivers is the young of the true salmon, but in others, as I know from having had specimens sent me, the laspring is really a par" At page 42 he gives a good figure of the par, and remarked "that this little fish, one of the smallest of the British *Salmonidæ*, has given rise to more discussion than any other species of the genus" Continuing that it has frequently been insisted upon as the young of the salmon, and local regulations have as generally been invoked for its preservation That the par is not the young of the salmon, or indeed of any other of the larger species of *Salmonidæ*, as still considered by some, is sufficiently obvious from the circumstance that pars by hundreds may be taken in the rivers all the summer, long after the fry of the year of the larger migratory species have gone down to the sea and the greater part of those pars, taken even in autumn, do not exceed five inches in length, when no example of the young of the salmon can be found under sixteen or eighteen inches, and the young of the bull trout and salmon trout are large in proportion" He also alluded to an opinion which prevailed that pars were hybrids, and all of them males Heysham found 190 females out of 395 Yarrell likewise remarked the "skegger" of the Thames is the par or samlet

Russel stated that about ten years before what were really the first decisive experiments (1824 or 1825) were made, Mr Scrope (*Days and Nights of Salmon Fishing*) wrote a long letter to the Right Hon T F. Kennedy, M P, in which the theory or rather fact that the par is the young of the salmon was stated with positiveness and argued with great clearness and force Also "the finding in spring of the distinctive marks of the par under the silver scales of the smolt" About eight years later, and still previous to the decisive experiments, he continued, "James Hogg, the Ettrick Shepherd, gave the world some very good reasons of his own for holding the par to be young of the salmon, reasons founded on observation and experience, partly on his having observed the gradual assumption of the migratory dress by the par in the spring months, partly on his having caught a grilse fish which he had marked when par, or when in their transition-state from par to smolt" Previously he had held a different opinion, believing the par not to be the young of the salmon, but was convinced to the contrary by Mr Scrope

Shaw, *Edinburgh New Philosophical Journal*, 1836, p 99, communicated certain experiments which he instituted on the par as to what its relations really were, for he had always believed it to be the young of the salmon On July 11th, 1833, he caught seven pars, and put them into a pond supplied with a stream of wholesome water In April, 1834, they became of a beautiful blue on the back, and a delicate silvery appearance on the sides, while the scales came readily off on their being handled In March, 1835, he took twelve more pars, averaging six inches each in length from the river, which assumed the smolt dress in April, 1835, which species he concluded these fish to be "The salmon fry has hitherto been erroneously supposed to grow to the size of six or eight inches in as many weeks, and to take its departure for the sea after this brief period has elapsed The rapidity with which the par of two years old assumes the appearance of the salmon fry has led to this error, the par taking about the same time to perfect its new dress, as the young salmon is supposed to take in attaining the growth at which it has arrived at the period of its migration" In May, 1834, he caught some young about one inch in length with a gauze net, and put them into two separate ponds provided with a proper supply of running water In May, 1835, they averaged 3½ inches long, and corresponded to the par of the river, and in the second week of that month assumed the smolt livery and measured about 6½ inches in length each On January 10th, 1836, he saw a female salmon about 16 lb weight, and two males of at least 25 lb engaged in depositing their spawn, and these days subsequently he obtained ova from the spot where he had observed these fishes, and which ova he placed in gravel under a stream of pure spring water On April 8th he found they had hatched, and after 140 days more corresponded with the little fishes he had taken away in May, 1834

Mr Shaw read a paper before the *Royal Society of Edinburgh*, December 18th, 1837, in which he observed that his former paper on ova taken from the Nith had been objected to as there was not sufficient evidence that these were the eggs of the salmon, the same stream being accessible to other fish So he repeated his former experiments, preserving the skins of the parent fish, also laying his experimental basins dry, not only for the purpose of removing any young fish which might remain, but likewise to fit them up on such a principle as would exclude the possibility of confusion, either from the overflowing of the ponds themselves, or from the flooding of the river Nith, on the banks of which they were situated On January 4th, 1837, he captured a pair of salmon engaged in depositing their spawn Before proceeding to take the fish he formed a small trench in the shingle at the edge of the river, through which he directed a small stream of water two inches deep At the end of this trench he placed an earthenware basin of considerable size for the purpose of ultimately receiving the ova Having drawn the fish ashore he placed the female, still alive, in the trench, and pressed from the body a quantity of the ova Then the milt was similarly obtained from the male, thoroughly impregnating the eggs The eggs were now transferred to the earthenware basin, and deposited in a stream connected with a pond previously formed for its reception On the 28th of April, or 114 days

In October, 1886, I received from Mr. Willis Bund a fish 5½ inches long taken in the Teme, and which the fishermen asserted was a *scagger*, and neither a samlet nor

after being removed from the parent fish, the eggs hatched   On May 24th, or twenty seven days after being hatched, the young had absorbed the yelk sac, they died a few days subsequently, caused he supposed, from a deposition of mud, the same result having been more than once produced when the pond had not been sufficiently embedded with gravel

The next experiment was conducted with more success   The parent fish were similarly captured on January 27th, 1837, subsequently killed, and their skins preserved   The male when taken weighed 16 lb , and the female 8 lb   On May 7th, or 101 days after removal from the parent fish, the eggs hatched   He gave illustrations life size, from examples ten days old, forty eight days, two months, and six months of age, while no marked difference could be observed between them and the par in the river of a corresponding age

Shaw stated, *Transactions of Royal Society of Edinburgh*, xiv, p 561, that in January, 1837, he took a female salmon, weighing 14 lb , from the spawning bed, from whence he also took a male par weighing one and a half ounce, with the milt of which he impregnated a quantity of her ova and placed it in a stream connected with a pond, where, to his great astonishment, the process succeeded in every respect as it had done with that which had been impregnated by the adult male salmon, and exhibited, from the first visible appearance of the embryo fish, up to their assuming their migratory dress, the utmost health and vigour   In January, 1838, he took another female salmon weighing 14 lb and two male pars from the same spawning bed and impregnated two lots of their ova with the milt from the two pars, and afterwards placed them in two different streams enclosed in boxes, open at the top, temperature 45°   In December, 1838, he took a female salmon from the river weighing 11 lb , and four male pars from the same spawning bed After impregnating four different lots of ova, one lot to each individual par, he placed the four pars in a pond, where they remained until the following May, at which period they assumed the migratory dress   The ova were placed in streams to which no other fish had access, and where they became mature in a similarly progressive manner to those already detailed, thus clearly demonstrating that the young salmon of 18 months old, while yet in the par or early state, actually performs the duties of a male parent before quitting the river   While the males of the three several broods which occupied ponds No 1, 2, 3 continued in a breeding state, which lasted throughout the whole of the winter of 1838 39, he impregnated the ova of three adult female salmon from the river with the milt of a male taken from each of the three ponds, and the whole of these ova matured   This, he deemed at once, removed any doubt which may have been entertained regarding the constitutional strength of individuals reared under such circumstances

At Stormontfield, in the season of 1857 (November or December) milt from a par was used to fertilize the ova of a 16 lb salmon, and in 1858 they had fry of salmon, fry of grilse and salmon, fry of grilse, and the fry of the salmon and par   "On the closest inspection, no difference was perceptible either in the form, colour, size, or markings of any of these fish   There were larger and smaller fry to be seen amongst all these hatchings" (Brown, *Stormontfield Experiments*, p 74)

Parnell, *Fishes of the District of the Forth*, 1838, page 298, gave the *Salmo salmulus*, or par, as a distinct species, observing " that if we compare a young *salmon* of eight inches in length with a *par* of equal size, both taken from the same river in the month of May, we shall find them to differ in the following respects   the form of the salmon is long and narrow, the snout pointed, and the caudal fin acutely forked   the body of the *par* is thick and clumsy   the snout broad and blunt, and the caudal fin much less forked   The operculum of the salmon is beautifully rounded at its posterior margin, with the basal line of union with the sub-operculum much curved   in the par this part is rather produced, with the line of union nearly straight   In the *salmon* the maxillary is short and narrow, in the *par* it is longer and broader, particularly at the posterior free extremity   The teeth of the *salmon* are long and fine, when recent easily bent   those of the *par* are shorter and stouter, and resist much greater pressure   In the *salmon* the pectoral fin is short, not quite one seventh part the length of the whole fish, with the fourth ray the longest   the same fin in the *par* is very long, not quite one-sixth part the length of the whole fish, with the fifth ray longest, giving a form to the fin totally different from that of the salmon   The pectoral, dorsal, and caudal fin in the *salmon* are black   those fins in the par are dusky   The flesh of the salmon is delicate and pinkish, the bones soft, and the coats of the stomach thin and tender   the flesh of the *par* is white and firm, the bones stout and hard, and the coats of the stomach and intestines thick and tough "   " It is generally supposed that those small fish, from four to five inches in length, which are found so plentiful in many rivers during the autumn months, and which are marked on the sides with from ten to eleven transverse dusky bands, and a black spot on each gill cover, are either all pars or the young of the salmon   But from a minute examination of several hundred of these fish, taken in various rivers in England and Scotland, I am induced to consider them as not all of one species, but the young of various species or varieties of migrating trout, in company with the young of the salmon, with the *Salmo salmulus* or par, and with different varieties of the common fresh water trout , all of which have received the names of *Heppers*, *Brandlings*, *Samlets*, *Fingerlings*, *Gravellings*, *Lasprings*, *Skirlings*, and *Sparlings* "   " There are still great doubts as to the par being a migratory species since no instance has been recorded of its capture in the sea   Nor does it appear to me to be so common a fish as is generally considered "

Mr Jenkins of Hereford (January 29th, 1840), observed that " the lasprings or samlets seen in the autumn in the Wye, are the young of the salmon, but some think they are hybrids "

Mr Young of Invershin, *Book of Salmon*, 1850, observed that Shaw's calculations on the age

a smolt. It was a salmon par, rather thin for this time of year, and its generative organs only half mature In colour it was similar to many which I have seen from

of the par " were wrong by one whole year that there were no salmon fry to be found in salmon rivers with transverse bars at the age of eighteen months, that they became smolts at the age of twelve months, and then migrated seawards, and not at the age of twenty-four months according to Mr Shaw's experimental theory" (p 163)

A Committee of the Tay Proprietors, on May 2nd, 1855, was held at the Stormontfield ponds, " to consider the expediency of detaining the fry (which had been hatched March 31st, 1854, and were 3 or 4 in in length) for another year or allowing them to depart A comparison with undoubted smolts of the river then descending seawards, with the fry in the ponds, led to the conclusion that the latter were not yet smolts and ought to be detained Seventeen days afterwards, viz , on the 19th May, a second meeting was held in consequence of the great numbers of fry having in the interim assumed the migratory dress On inspection, it was found that a considerable portion were actual smolts, and the committee came to the determination to allow them to depart Accordingly, the sluice communicating with the Tay was opened and every facility for egress afforded Contrary to expectation, none of the fry manifested any inclination to leave the pond until the 24th May, when the larger and more mature of the smolts, after having held themselves detached from the others for several days, went off in a body A series of similar emigrations took place, until fully one half of the fry had left the pond, and descended the sluice to the Tay As the shoals successively left the pond, about one in every hundred was marked by the abscision of the second dorsal fin A greater number were marked on the 29th of May, than on any other day, in all about 1200 or 1300 Within two months of the date of their liberation, viz , between the 29th of May and the 31st of July, twenty two of the young fish so marked when in the state of smolts on their way to the sea, have been in their returning migration up the river, recaptured, and carefully examined This fact may be considered as still further established, by observing the increased weight, according to date, of the grilse caught and examined those taken first weighing 5 to 9½ lb , then increasing progressively to 7 and 8 lb , whilst the one captured 31st July, weighed no less than 9½ lb In all these fish the wound caused by marking was covered with skin, and in some a coating of scales had formed over the part "—Report of Committee on Stormontfield Ponds to the British Association, 1856, page 453

Thompson, Natural History of Ireland, 1856, being a reprint of many of his papers, written at various dates, termed the par or gravelling, the young of the salmon (vol iv, p 113) "The remark of Pennant, that ' the adipose fin is never tipped with red, nor is the edge of the anal white,' can only be considered as generally correct Two of my pars do, though very faintly, show red on the adipose fin and one half of them have the base of the anal fin white " " The three most striking characters of the par in contradistinction to the common trout, are—its tail being more forked, its having only two or three spots on the opercula, and its want of dark coloured spots beneath the lateral-line The pectoral fin of the par is larger, and the hinder portion of the operculum less angular than in the common trout "

Yarrell, British Fishes, 1841, ii, p 14, &c , stated, "In order to prevent any misconception of the terms employed, I shall speak of the young salmon of the first year as a pink , on its second year, until it goes to sea, as a smolt , in the autumn of the second year, as salmon peal or grilse , and afterwards as adult salmon " 'Mr Shaw's experiments have gone very far towards convincing many that the par, as a distinct species, does not exist" (p 84)

In the List of the Specimens of British Animals in the Collection of the British Museum, "Fish" was written by Mr Adam White in 1851, and at page 76 the par was given as the young of the salmon and sea trouts

In the evidence given in the case of Galbraith versus Shaw, held at Dunblane in January, 1858, some river watchers deposed as follows,—"I have not seen a female par with spawn at all The male par will spawn, or, as I mean, have milt the first year of its existence " "I have seen smolt go to sea in shoals I won t swear that I ever saw par going down with them " "Par sometimes remain more than a year in the river after they are hatched They then become smolts with a silvery skin, and in that state descend to the sea When a smolt is stripped of its scales, it is a par below" (James Mathie) "The marks of a par are finger marks The number of marks vary I have found eleven, and I have found sixteen. The pars thus observed were of the same ages The number of marks does not depend on the size I never saw par with fewer than eleven I have never seen par taken from any river but the Tay " "The par of the trout has the dead fin orange , the rudder fin is white at the bottom and yellow at the top They have not so many par marks as the par I do not think they have ever more than six marks" (Peter Marshall) "There is not a pool or stream on the Teith where par are not (I confine myself to smolts) Every pool at a certain time has par It is my opinion that pars are the fry of salmon They assume the silvery scale when they go down the river I have seen kelts taking on the same silvery coat at repeated times, in the end of March and April, preparing to descend the river , but before this I have seen them of a different colour " (James Greenhorn)

Of the 1854 salmon hatching at Stormontfield, Mr Buist reported "that the first of the fry that left the ponds as smolts in 1855 was on the 19th of May , the last on the 7th of June No more left that year The first of the same brood which remained as par all last season assumed the smolt scales in August, 1856 The first division went off on the 28th of April, and the last on the 20th of May In both years they went off daily in divisions from the first to the last day About 1300 were marked in 1855, and several returned, as stated in my report. The number marked in 1856 was 300 with rings, and 800 with cuts in the tail Taking one in each hundred

Wales and the south, in which the finger marks are distinct along their upper edge from the colours of the back into which they do not run as is mostly the case

At Stormontfields, a suggestion which had been advanced that the anomaly of

as marked it may be reckoned thus —Left the pond in 1855, 130,000, in 1856, 100,000, total, 230,000 ' Although many grilse were reported to the superintendent as captured, having this year's mark, not one having the ring was among those taken The grilse in 1856 were very numerous but marked ones were not detected A few of the fry that left the pond in May or June, 1855, were reported as having been caught this season as salmon

Dr J Davy, *Physiological Researches*, 1863, p 221 concluded "that a par—a distinct species—is a creature of the imagination, and that the idea of such a species ought to be opposed, both as founded in error, and as affording a pretence to allow of the wasteful, mischievous capture of the salmon and sea trout fry "

Russel, *The Salmon*, 1864, p 33, observed that the chief questions are, or have been — 1st Is the par the young of the salmon in earliest infancy ? 2nd At what age does the smolt emigrate to salt water? 3rd After what length of absence does the emigrant return to fresh water ? 4th In what state does he return, "grilse or salmon?" Continuing "that the par is the infant young of the salmon was a fact so clear, or a conclusion so inevitable, before the experiments (Shaw's) were made, that it would not be hard to conceive how it could ever have been in doubt Were it not that, even after the experiments have furnished the most ample demonstration, there are still to be found a considerable number of people who, instead of having been convinced, have only been enraged " "Every schoolboy on the banks of the Tweed (where almost alone the *S salar* and *S eriox* are found together in plenty) knows at a glance the difference between the smolt of the salmon and of the bull trout—the black fin and the orange fin "

Couch, *British Fishes*, iv, 1865, p 245, observed, "The question at present, therefore is not whether the young of the salmon—and, we may add, of some others of the same family— may not remain in fresh water for more than a year, during which they may bear on the sides a series of dusky marks at this time, denominated Par-bands, but whether there be not also a distinct species which bears those marks, and which, by something like arrested development, is never deprived of them " "Mr Shaw's conclusions, in some particulars, appear to be far from satisfactory and, as regards the true nature of a fish he terms the par, the question appears to be exactly where he found it "

Bertram, *The Harvest of the Sea*, 1865, p 105, remarked "Indeed, the experiments conducted at the Stormontfield ponds have conclusively settled the long-fought battle of the par, and proved indisputably that the par is the young of the salmon, that it becomes transformed to a smolt, grows into a grilse, and ultimately attains the honour of full-grown salmonhood The anomaly in the growth of the par was also attempted to be solved at Stormontfield, but without success In November and December, 1857, provision was made for hatching in separate compartments the artificially impregnated ova of—(1) par and salmon , (2) grilse and salmon (3) grilse pure (4) salmon pure It was found, when the young of the different matches came to be examined early in April, 1859, that the sizes of each kind varied a little Mr Buist, the superintendent of fisheries, informing us that—(1st) the produce of the salmon with salmon are four inches in length, (2nd) grilse with salmon, 3½ inches , (3rd) grilse with grilse, 3½ inches , (4th) par with grilse, three inches, (5th) smolt from large pond, five inches These results, of a varied manipulation, never got a fair chance of being of use as a proof in the disputation , for owing to the limited extent of the ponds at the time, the experiments had to be matured in such small boxes or ponds as evidently tended to stunt the growth of the fish "

Another theory at this period obtained some notice respecting why merely half of the par descended as smolts one year, for this, it was asserted, must be in consequence of the first batch being the progeny of pure salmon and the second the offspring of grilse—a theory which on investigation proved to have no foundation

Dr Gunther, *Catalogue of the Fishes of the British Museum*, vi, 1866, pp 11 34, placed the *Salmulus* of Willoughby as the young of a variety of sea trout, which he termed *S cambricus*, while the *Salmulus* of Ray he considered an immature salmon, observing in a note that " under these names the young not only of the salmon, but also of other salmonoids, have been described " Ray's description was almost verbally identical with that of Willoughby, and in the *Introduction to the Study of Fishes*, by Dr Gunther, 1880, it was observed that " the Historia Piscium, which bears Willoughby's name on the title-page, and was edited by Ray, is clearly their joint production " He also said "Shaw has demonstrated in the most conclusive manner that those small Salmonoids, generally called *Par*, are the offspring of the salmon and that many males from seven to eight inches long have the sexual organs fully developed, and that their milt has all the impregnating properties of the seminal fluid of a much older and larger fish That this par is not a distinct species—as has lately been again maintained by Couch—is further proved by the circumstance that these sexually mature pars are absolutely identical in their zoological characters with the immature pars, which are undoubtedly young salmon, and that no par has ever been found with mature ova But whether these par produce normal salmon, impregnating the ova of female salmon, or mingle with the river trout, or whether they continue to grow and propagate their species as true salmon, are questions which remain to be answered "

In 1869 commenced the case of the Tay Fishery Board *versus* Miller, who was accused " in so far as, upon Saturday, the 16th June, 1869, or about that time, the said Robert Miller had in his possession nine smolts or salmon fry " This was first decided against the Fishery Board,

some pars migrating at one year the remainder after two seasons was owing to
the first being the produce of salmon and the second of grilse was refuted *
While observations made in the same establishment also clearly proved individual
par from one hatching may greatly vary in size,† and that when half the par
descended‡ from the breeding pond as smolts one year, those which remained for

who appealed, when the case was remitted back to the sheriff to inquire whether " par were
salmon fry "? On the 8th of October, 1869, the sheriff found that " the defendant had in his
possession certain fish commonly known as pars, but which are not named in the prohibitory and
penal clauses libelled, but finding it not proved that he then had any fish known as smolts, the
only fish named in the same section of the statute libelled, and declines to inquire and decide
the question in natural science, whether par be, or be not salmon fry " The sheriff substitute,
July 12th, 1870, " finds it not proved that, in the popular and well understood sense, any of the
pars found in the possession of the accused on the day libelled were salmon fry " He, however,
admitted that the evidence as a naturalist " would have led him to decide, as a point of science,
that par, or at least certain of that family, were the young of salmon " Another appeal was now
made on July 20th, 1870, that as the pars " were the young of salmon, or salmon fry, the sheriff-
substitute ought to have given effect to said proof by a judgment against the respondent " The
case was tried at Perth, September 7th, 1870, and the defendant was finally convicted

June 4th, 1872, an individual was summoned before the sheriff in so far as, on the 24th of
April last, he did, on the right bank of the river Allan, by means of a rod and line, take or have
in his possession six smolts or salmon fry As the first witness observed, salmon fry meant the
smolt of the salmon proper The yellow-fin was the sea trout smolt One witness, Mr G Young,
of Berwick, deposed that the orange-fins of the Tweed were identical with the yellow fins of the
Allan, and that they were the par or young of the sea trout Very extensive experiments had been
made in the river with regard to these fish He was a Tweed Commissioner, and also belonged to
the experimental committee They had marked these fish for a great number of years, and had
traced them into all stages of their growth, from the egg to the full-grown bull or sea trout The
orange fin is the young of the sea trout They were known as " black-tails," just before passing
from the orange-fin into the whitling or bull trout Mr Bruce remarked " They have par to
account for the young salmon, the small yellow trout to account for the young of the yellow trout,
and it seemed to him that the yellow-fin could be nothing else than the young of the sea-trout "
Dr Gunther deposed that " there is a distinction between the young of Salmo salar (the salmon)
and a member of the Farios (trout) In the par of the former I have counted as many as nine or
ten cross bars, and in the latter only six or seven " " I am not quite sure but that milt and ova
might be found in a hybrid It has been found in pars, and my theory is that where this is so,
the fish is the product of a hen salmon and a male river trout, and it was frequently found that a
hen salmon was spawning on the same gravel bed with a male river trout This hybrid would
come to maturity sooner than a pure bred salmon, and thus give the appearance of ova or milt
being found in the par "

Mr Buist, Stormontfield Piscicultural Experiments, 1867, altered his mind with respect to
pars, due to his having been engaged at the Stormontfield ponds, where experiments were being
carried on, and affording him the opportunity of observing the transformations in the par with age
After remarking that at one time he was an advocate of the popular dogma that the par was a
distinct fish by itself, one proof being that in the month of November, 1842, a male par had been
brought to him with the milt flowing out " The par in question was really the young salmon of
the second year, which had not then gone to the sea At Stormontfield we have repeatedly seen
a young salmon that remained in the rearing pond till the time of migration in the second year,
though not the size of a man's finger, yet with such a state of milt in the breeding season that we
have impregnated eggs of the full-grown salmon with it, and thereby produced young fish Such
is not the case with the sister fish of the second year in the pond, as not even the rudiments of
roe can be traced in them."

* The whole of the fry, numbering about 200,000, were the produce of 19 male and 31 female
salmon spawned in 1859, some remained as par while others migrated as smolts

† While as to variation in size among par, Peter of the Pools remarked, in the Field of April
25th, 1863, " as another instance in the strange anomaly in the growth of salmon, I send three
specimens taken from the Stormontfield pond on April 1st As the label on the bottle tells, they
were spawned from salmon roe about the end of December, 1861, they came to life and were
hatched in April, 1862, they have been fed in the same pond, and you will observe what an
amazing difference there is in the size and growth, the largest being 6½ inches and weighing 6⅙
grams the second 3½ inches, weighing 135 grams, and the third 2¼ inches, weighing 26 grams
No 3 is a tiny little creature with the par marks on it, no 2 has the incipient scales on it, and
no 1 with these scales far advanced I have no doubt that at least no 1, had he been left in the
ponds, would with others of like size, or even smaller, have gone to the sea this year, and returned
as a grilse No 2 is doubtful and may perhaps have remained till another season, while no 3,
would we allow him, would keep his habitation in the pond "

‡ Ramsbottom, The Salmon and its Artificial Propagation, 1854, remarked of these fish, that
" at eighteen months of age, an ounce and a half is their average weight, nor do they much
exceed two ounces in weight, and seven inches in length, when about to assume the migratory
dress at the age of two years and a month or thereabouts " (p 17) " Two years after their

another season consisted of fish of both sexes, consequently females do not migrate, as had been suggested, one year earlier than the males * The statement of Dr Davy, *Physiological Researches*, p 221, that when kept in confinement the milt of these fishes is shed prior to their assuming the smolt livery was not found to be generally correct at Howietoun

Having now traced the produce of salmon eggs up to and through their par stage, it is necessary to follow out their further progress towards attaining the condition of becoming a salmon The par on assuming the smolt livery, as it does as a rule when commencing its seaward journey, changes from its brilliant golden and spotted colours with its brilliant finger-marks, which have been described (p 55), to take on a bright silvery appearance, both on its opercles and body As Howietoun fish showed this change without leaving the ponds, it is clear that such must precede or be coincident with, but not consequent on, migration seawards † This silvery colour is not owing to their acquiring an additional coating of scales, as has been asserted, but due to the deposition of a silvery pigment on the under surface of the scales and opercles,‡ which latter could not be so overlaid because of being scaleless

These silvery smolts, at least after they have been some time so, may be turned directly and without injury into sea water, while the scales are not nearly so adherent as when the fish had the par livery, and the fish itself seems more susceptible of injury

Although the great seasonal migration of smolts is during April, or May and June,§ this is not the only period at which they descend seawards, as some do so during the autumn months, as well as probably throughout the year As the

exclusion from the ova, the pinks begin to assume the silvery coat prior to their migration At this period their transverse bars and pink spots gradually disappear and give place to bright silvery scales In three or four weeks the change is completed With the variation of their external appearance a striking alteration in their habits also takes place Pinks are invariably *solitary* previous to their transmutation into smolts After that event they are *gregarious*, and assemble in numerous shoals shortly before the commencement of their descent to the sea "

* Mr W Brown, *Stormontfield Experiments*, 1862, p 7, observed upon having in February, 1836, caught a dozen and a half of par in the Tay He kept them confined in a stream of running water, and by the month of May the whole of them had become smolts, but some had leaped out of their confinement in their struggle to find their way to the sea, and were found dead upon the side of the pond It has also been remarked that whether a river is an early or late one, the descent of the smolt generally occurs during the spring, between March and June Mr Dunbar, who annually hatched about 500,000 in the Thurso river, in the county of Caithness, informed Mr Young that about eight per cent became smolt at the end of the first year, and about 60 per cent at the end of the second year, and the remainder, or 32 per cent, at the end of the third year

† There seems reason to believe that occasionally par ascend rivers, being found in localities above where any breeding salmon have been seen I have received one of a large size which was taken in Wales above a cascade up which sea-trout were known to ascend, but where salmon had never been seen

‡ Davy, *Physiological Researches*, 1843, p 230 suggested "that the young remain in fresh water until they have acquired not only a certain size and strength, but also additional scales, fitting them in their smolt stage to endure without injury the contact of the saline medium " Dr Davy considered the scales of the smolt to be new productions, not mere alterations of the former scales (*Angler in the Lake District*, p 209) Couch, in 1865, demurred to such an opinion, observing that the silvery colour of smolts is not due to their acquiring additional scales, but owing to a deposit of bright soft matter which shines through the transparent scales Dr Gunther (*Introduction to the Study of Fishes*, 1880, p 632) remarked respecting the river trout, that they "frequently retain the par marks all their lifetime at certain seasons a new coat of scales overlays the par-marks, rendering them invisible for a time, but they reappear in time, or are distinct as soon as the scales are removed When the Salmones have passed this par stage a new coat of scales overlays the par marks " It was likewise stated in one of the conference papers read at the 'Great International Fisheries Exhibition " in 1883 that the young of the true Salmon "do not venture into the sea till another skin of glistening scales has been formed over their first skin They then receive the name of *smolts* If put into salt water before getting this silvery dress they die " (*Salmon and Salmon Fisheries*, by D Milne Holme, p 4)

§ We are told that in the exodus of the smolts from Stormontfield in 1857 of the fry of 1856, the first shoal left the 12th of April, a week earlier than the first hatching in 1851, which appeared to be owing to the winter of 1856 57 having been much milder than that of 1854 55 (*Stormontfield Experiments*, pp 61 63)

accuracy of my statement of this being the case has been challenged, the opinions of various observers are recorded below.*

* Pennant, *Brit Zool* in, p 304, remarking on the samlet said, "near Shrewsbury (where they are called *samsons*) they are found in such quantities in the month of *September*, that a skilful angler, in a coracle, will take with a fly from twelve to sixteen dozen in a day " Mr Young, of Invershin, observed, respecting the migration of smolts being generally from the middle of April to the end of May, continued "oftentimes their migration takes place earlier, and frequently later in the year Late migration is caused by late spawning, which is the result of a late 'close' time, or not allowing salmon to ascend the rivers freely in the early autumn months " (*Book of the Salmon*, 1850, p 19) Shaw (*Edinburgh New Philosophical Journal*, 1836, p 99) remarked "to enable me to watch the progressive growth of the par, I caught on July 11, 1833, seven pars " Parnell, in his *Essay on the Fishes in the District of the Forth*, 1836, stated, "the largest specimen (*Salmo salmulus*) I have met with, measures 9½ in in length It was taken in the North Esk, Forfarshire, September, 1835, by James Wilson, Esq " (p 298) Among specimens of par (*S salmulus*) from Parnell's collection is a skin 5½ in long, taken from the Cumberland Esk in the month of August, it is the young of *Salmo salar*, while there are likewise some similar skins from the North Esk in Forfarshire, but the date of capture is not recorded The foregoing, however, show the capture of salmon smolts in the Cumberland Esk in August, and their reported capture during the same month in the Forfarshire Esk. Russel, in his work on *The Natural History of the Salmon*, 1864, observed, "in the months of May, June, and July, full-sized pars are to be got in the rivers, but in numbers much smaller than in either the preceding or the following months of the year" (p 44), but these he considered did not descend to the sea during the summer season This autumn smolt is probably the form referred to by Thompson, *Natural History of Ireland*, 1856, vol iv, p 148, who, remarked Mr Sinclaire, "is of opinion that a small fish, which is taken in rivers during every month from March to November inclusive, and which he calls the par, is a distinct species " Thompson having been shown some of these specimens, considered them to be young salmon Murie, *Proceedings of the Zoological Society*, 1870, stated, on the authority of Buckland, that "there is good evidence of a second migration of smolts in the month of September" (p 42)

In the second volume of my *British and Irish Fishes*, 1882, p 69, I observed, "Years ago, when I used to fish in the Severn, at or near Shrewsbury, we knew the younger stages of salmon, especially the March, April, and May shoals, formed of the par, as salmon fry, and the autumn smolt as the samlet " I may mention that those were times prior to the capture of these young fish being stopped, when the taking of par was an ordinary amusement for the fly-fisher We divided the "salmon fry" from the "samlets " (for my especial attention had been directed to this subject of inquiry by the late Professor Rymer Jones, when lecturing on "natural history" at Shrewsbury) The salmon fry were the fishes which constituted the great seasonal migration during the first two quarters of the year, and were of diverse sizes, but, about September to October, a second appearance of these finger-marked fish occurred, comparatively few in number, but as large as the largest of the earlier migratory "salmon fry " They were rather deeper in form and stronger when hooked The foregoing was not, so far as my recollection serves, merely a solitary occurrence about Shrewsbury, but took place annually In *Salmon Problems*, Mr Willis Bund remarked that in December, 1884, he found a few samlets in an affluent of the Severn descending to the sea; but "an autumn migration of smolts is a thing hardly ever heard of, indeed, its existence is denied Yet, here it was, and, but for the merest accident, would have passed by unrecorded The importance of it to fishery boards is considerable To give an instance They have power to make bye-laws to determine the times of the year at which gratings shall be placed at the head of channels to prevent smolts being led astray on their seaward migration " (pp 9 and 10) "If there is such a thing as an August migration, equal necessity exists for maintaining the gratings in the autumn as well as in the spring" Since then he has observed that "the water bailiffs who declare that there are distinct kinds of samlets, and that the one that migrates in the autumn (they now say they have noticed autumn migrations for some years) is a distinct kind of salmon from the small smolt which migrates in the spring" (January 5th, 1886)

In Professor Huxley's *Report on the Salmon Fisheries* for 1884, when referring to the migration of smolts in the Severn, and the time for retaining gratings at the canal feeder at Aberbanat, it is observed "The period from Feb 14th to May 31st was agreed upon as the 'smolt season,' during which the narrow grating was to be retained " He also referred to Mr Fryer's report, wherein it was remarked of the period "when the smolts are in the river At such time, however, there are no leaves falling ' (page 12)

The foregoing extracts would seem to clearly show that neither the Inspector of Fisheries nor his assistant had the slightest idea of there being any autumn migration of smolts in the Severn , but now attention has been directed to the subject, because the chairman of the Severn Fishery Board had witnessed such an occurrence, and naturally inquired whether such is or is not normal?

A correspondent of *Land and Water* (February 21st, 1885) observed "During last autumn in the Severn, or rather one of its tributaries, when the first autumn floods came down, and they were unusually late this year in the Severn district, and the eel nets and eel traps were set to intercept the usual migrations of eels seaward, there were caught among the eels in the Teme a number of smolts, not samlets, but fully developed silver scaled smolts This, however, is the first instance recorded of the existence of smolts in the Severn or Teme at this late period of the year—the beginning of December,"

The smolt,* as Old Log observed in the *Field*, January 24th, 1885, goes out to sea on the autumn floods, returning next year as grilse But they also descend to the salt water during other months in the year When at Montrose at the end of June, 1882, I saw several smolts taken from the stomach of a saithe, *Gadus virens*, captured in the sea a couple of miles from the coast A similar occurrence was noticed at the same place in December, 1881, the fish which had eaten the smolt being a whiting When at Aberdeen in July, 1882, Mr Sim showed me some smolts similarly procured from the stomach of a marine fish In fact this has been observed at different localities, proving conclusively that the migratory smolt passes into the ocean

It has been asserted that while these fish retain the parr livery they are unable to live in salt water, and that on some being so transferred they at once died and became of a beautiful carmine colour, but such does not appear to be invariably the case, as was shown by Mr Francis Francis, who observed in *The Field*, May 10th, 1879, that at the Brighton Aquarium about twenty small salmon parr were placed in a fresh-water tank, and in the next May, about eight months after they had been received, most commenced to assume the smolt livery, but four remained golden parr Salt water was gradually introduced, but this did not prove fatal to the parr, as it had been feared it might, while the smolts became rampant with pleasure as the water became more and more salt When no fresh water remained, the parr began to assume the smolt livery, and the change was described as being truly marvellous They ate five times as much as previously, were in incessant and rapid motion all day, and then growth became perfectly astonishing Curiously enough, there was at the time among them a common trout He too took to the salt water very kindly, and fed smartly and grew very rapidly

Smolts that have descended rivers have been shown to re-ascend as grilse,†

H M Inspector of Fisheries for 1885 now joined in and asserted that having inquired respecting this subject " the answer was more or less in the negative from every district except the Dee, the Seiont, the Wye, the Avon, the Eine, the Trent and the Severn" (Annual Report for 1885, p 4), concluding with the novel observation and interesting application thereof that " one swallow does not make a summer, and care should be taken not to assume a general fact from isolated instances " Since then the Chairman of the Severn Fishery Board marked about two dozen smolts one day in October 1886 The water bailiffs consider the samlets which migrate down the Teme in the autumn to be a distinct kind of fish from the salmon fry that migrate in the spring, or the same idea which prevailed many years ago higher up in the Severn.

* Scotus remarked *Land and Water*, " I have seen them on a fine spring morning going down the slack water in shoals of eight or ten head first, going about twice as fast as the water that they might breathe I have no doubt but that in four mile an-hour water they go tail first They are safer, and if the water was running four miles, except they went six or eight miles an hour, they could not breathe When the river is small and clear I have never seen smolts running down during the daytime, only early in the morning, just about sun-rise No doubt when the river is coloured they run all day " " In some waters, as where they are quick and rough, smolts have been observed to descend tail first, but in smooth slow water, as a mile an hour, they have been seen to go down head first "

Owing to certain legal proceedings two individuals acquainted with fish or fisheries, were deputed in 1809 to examine into the migrations in the Tay of smolts seawards, and the results are given in detail in the *Report of the Fish Committee* for 1824 It seems they inspected the whole stake nets in which they never found either salmon fry or small fish of any kind except flounders, but saw a large quantity drawn ashore at Stockgreen by the nets used in the net and-coble fishing Below Carpow bank they found no salmon fry, although they fished the river with the small meshed nets both in the eddy water and in the stream, and never found them in the spirling nets although it is believed some fry descend in April while spirlings are being taken They saw the fry in the Tay first on April 29th, immediately below Perth, in thousands, and found them downwards all the way till within half a mile above the junction of the Larn with the Tay At high water and at the first of the flood, the fry were observed in the easy water near the side of the river, and when the tide ebbed, they appeared to go into the current, and the last fry which they caught with the net in going down the river was in the channel opposite to Carpow bank, from which point, down to below Bronghty, trials were made in every part of the Tay for salmon fry but none were found Every means were employed to capture them in deep water between high and low water-mark, but without success, and one of the men considered that the surf or agitation of the water between high and low water-mark in the Frith compels them to go into deep water, and the swell in the deep water forces them to go deeper down

† Fraser *On the Salmon, &c*, 1833, pp 15, 16, remarked " In April (1825) I marked several of the fry (of the salmon), and only one of them came to my hands in July Two of them were

although some excellent observers are still disinclined to believe that it is possible these fish can increase so rapidly in size that one descending in May a few ounces in weight could be capable of returning within two or three months as a 4 lb or 5 lb grilse But it is not impossible that as we see differences in the periods of descent of smolts, so some may return in one season, the remainder in the succeeding year * It is remarkable that grilse do not commence ascending until two or three months subsequent to the descents of smolts, whereas had they been upwards of a year in the sea it would appear strange why some few at least had not previously put in an appearance, this invariable absence from the nets almost seeming to point out the probability that they are entirely absent

It has been maintained that grilse are a distinct species of the Salmonidæ, but at Howietoun, as I shall have to observe under the head of " salmon raised in fresh waters," the par turned to smolts, and subsequently to grilse,† and from these last

however, caught about the same time at Inverness by Mr Hutchinson, and each weighed about 5 lb In the river Berridale, in Caithness, Mr Alexander Morrison in the year 1794, in the month of May, marked five smolts or salmon fry, in such a manner, that if ever any of them returned to the river, and were caught, no doubt could remain as to their being of the number so marked Two of these smolts, then become grilse, he caught in six or seven weeks after they had been marked, when they weighed about 3½ lb each In April following, he caught another of the number, then a salmon, which weighed between 7 lb and 8 lb , and in the month of August he caught a smolt weighing 8 lb " He also stated " I ascertained by experiment that a grilse which weighs 6 lb in February after spawning, will, on its return from the sea in September, weigh 13 lb " (p 13)

Sir W Jardine writing in 1835 respecting the fisheries in Sutherlandshire, in the *Edinburgh New Philosophical Journal*, p 47, observed " Last spring several thousands of fry were marked in the different rivers, among others, by Mr Baigrie, in the Laxford and Dinard, on the west coast In the Laxford, the first grilse (marked in April as fry) returned on the 25th June, and weighed 3½ lb Many others were got during the season from this weight to 6½ lb , returning to the rivers where the fry were marked, which was known by a particular mark being used in each, and showing that a return to their breeding ground was as frequent, or rather as constant, as among the higher animals "

Mr Young of Invershin, in 1843, observed that " in the months of April and May, 1837, he marked a great number of the descending smolts by making a peculiar perforation in the caudal fin with a pair of small nipping irons constructed for the purpose and in the months of June and July he caught a considerable number on their return to the rivers, all in the state of grilse, and varying from 3 lb to 8 lb according to the length of sojourn in the sea Again in 1842 similar experiments led to similar results In *the Tweed* numbers of smolts have been marked by a silver wire having been passed through and fastened to the back part of their tails None were obtained the same year, but the experiment was repeated the succeeding season, and several were taken as grilse The *Duke of Roxburghe*, on May 14th, 1855, had a smolt marked by the insertion of a peculiar shaped wire through its gills , it was retaken July 21st, 1856, as a grilse, weighing 6½ lb Brown, *Stormontfield Experiments*, remarked that in May, 1855, 1300 smolts were marked at Stormontfield by cutting off the adipose fin, and 22 were recaptured as grilse the same summer, the first on July 7th, 1855, when it weighed 3 lb , one on the 20th, 5½ lb , 24th, 5 lb , 30th, 7½ lb , 31st, 9½lb, August 4th, 7½ lb , and on the 14th, 8 lb

Those left in the pond, continued Mr Brown, though healthy at the end of the year had not increased in size very much, many male pairs were full of milt and some of the fry were very small, not being much above three or four inches in length (pp 49, 51) Also, that in 1859 " the first marked grilse was taken six weeks after leaving the ponds and had increased from not more than 1 oz or 1½ oz to 3 lb 3 oz " (p 78) That " the experiments here have shown that marked grilse of one year return as salmon the next that all the smolts of one year do not return the same year as grilse, the one half returning next spring and summer as small salmon " (p 92, 93)

* *Buckland* (Nov 9th, 1879) remarked that in his opinion some may return to the river the same year they go down as smolts, but that some stay one, if not two years in the sea " Grilse have even been captured of the extraordinary weight of 14 lb Such a striking augmentation of size has, in all probability, resulted from the operation of several causes A longer stay than usual on the feeding grounds, or a richer and more abundant supply of food, would have a marked effect in the acceleration of growth Other causes on the contrary may tend to *retard* their natural development It is not unlikely that grilse leave the sea in shoals on their return to the fresh water On such a supposition it is easy to understand how straggling fish may return in their company, which have not been on the feeding-ground more than one-half of the time which the shoal itself has spent in the ocean To such circumstances the small size of occasional grilse of only a single pound in weight may, with much probability, be ascribed" (Ramsbottom, *On the Salmon*, 1854, p 22)

† Brown, *Stormontfield Experiments*, observed that " these experiments have shown that smolts were caught, marked as grilse the first season, and salmon the second " (p 94) *Ramsbottom*,

eggs have been obtained, and young in the form of salmon par have since been raised It has also been advanced that grilse cannot be young salmon,* ignoring the fact that only in salmon-rivers are there true grilse, and wherever they exist there also are salmon Now, although it has been shown that grilse may be reared from salmon eggs, still, it has been pointed out that salmon and grilse of the same size can readily be distinguished one from another In the evidence taken before a *Committee of the House of Commons*, in 1824, Mr Johnstone stated the difference between a grilse and a salmon† to be as follows —"The grilse is a much less fish in general, it is much smaller at the tail in proportion, and it has a much more swallow tail, much more forked, it is smaller at the head, sharper at the point of the nose, and generally the grilse is more bright in the scale than the salmon"

Doubtless there is a difference in the appearance of a small salmon and a grilse of the same size, but such is probably due to the former from some cause not having got into condition and so lost a season That grilse frequently re-ascend rivers at irregular periods has been constantly observed ‡ while they have also been entirely absent for a whole season, as in 1867 as has been already remarked (*see page 72*)

At p 71 I have recorded the captures made by anglers in the Shin, which tend to show that grilse commence running up the river at the end of May or commencement of June, while the greatest number ascend in July, after which there is a decrease The average weight of each fish captured in the various months in 1886 were as follows —February, *salmon*, 9 lb March, 11 lb April 13 lb May, 12½ lb June, 14 lb July, 12¼ lb August, 10 lb while September was not fished Of *grilse* the average weights of fish were in May, 3 lb June, 4½ lb July, 5½ lb August, 6 lb September not fished These figures agree to a con-

---

in 1859, deposited 18,000 salmon ova at Doohulla, they hatched in February, 1860, only a few were ready for sea when about thirteen months old, the great majority migrating at twenty seven months old, they stayed from thirteen to fifteen months at sea, when they returned as grilse at two years and four months old (*Irish Culture*, by Francis Francis, 1865, Appendix, page 311)

* In 1860, Mr Mackenzie, when publishing his father's treatise on the *Salmon Fishery of Scotland*, did not accept the view therein held that the grilse was a young salmon, but gave his reasons in an appendix under the title "do grilse grow to be salmon ?" And he asserted that they did not, that "its instincts in some respects are different, though its habits are precisely the same " His arguments being that the salmon's instinct impel them to ascend rivers in winter and spring, but the grilse do not leave the sea for the fresh waters until the summer, one in short being a spring, and the other a summer fish That salmon and grilse do not spawn promiscuously , and when the grilse appear in May or June, their roe is in precisely the same stage of growth as in the salmon when they appear in rivers in January, but as they spawn about the same time, it shows that the roe of the grilse requires only half the time which that of the salmon requires to bring it to maturity Also, that grilse in May weigh from 3 lb to to 5 lb , in July, from 10 lb to 12 lb , and instead of finding them in August and September 16 lb or 20 lb , which would be natural if they continued to grow in order to become salmon, they apparently begin to grow backwards, as in October they are as small as in May The river Shin produces salmon, but very few grilse , the Oykell few salmon, but shoals of grilse The tail-fin of a grilse tapers off to a finer edge than in the salmon *A Committee of the Commissioners of the river Tweed*, ignoring some of the experiments previously conducted in that river, reported in 1863, as follows —"Our opinion from the experience of the last twenty years, is, that grilse never become salmon at any stage whatsoever"

† Fraser (*l c* , p 37) observed, "A large grilse is a breeder the first season A small salmon may be of the same age with the large grilse, but it has never spawned, owing to its not getting in its season to the proper feeding ground, and before the young fish it feeds upon have grown strong and left the ground These (salmon) fry not only lost the season, but lost their ordered food, and are only in condition to return to rivers, some early and some from first to last of every season " Professor Brown Goode (*Natural History of Aquatic Animals*, p 474) observed of the grilse and adolescent salmon, that the two may be easily distinguished, even though both should be of the same size as not infrequently happens "The male grilse is sexually mature, but not so the female in America , in Europe the same is claimed for the male par and the female grilse " (smolt)

‡ Mr J Miller, *Land and Water*, May 10th, 1879, reported on having caught in 1879, four grilse weighing 20¼ lb , all in the scale together, the largest 5½ lb , the smallest 4 lb These Galway grilse were ascending at the latter end of April, and such an early run, it was supposed, had not happened for twenty five years the main run generally occurring in May and June In 1881, the first grilse in the Forth was recorded on June 25th, but in 1882 they were a week later

siderable extent with those given by Russel for the fisheries of the Tay (*see* p 71), and tend to show that in the Shin the grilse which first ascend in May are the smallest, but that they gradually increase in weight until September, when the fishing ceases *

I have endeavoured to trace in the preceding pages how the grilse are sprung from salmon, that from their eggs salmon par are produced indistinguishable from those raised when both parents had been large salmon   These grilse return to the sea as grilse-kelts and re-appear in our rivers as salmon †

As to the rapidity of growth in salmon, various experiments have been instituted in different localities which would tend to the conclusion that generally it is rapid   But for the purposes of observation on this point there have been two classes of fish marked, kelts which were out of condition and grilse or salmon in good condition   It must be evident that in the first set of experiments considerable allowance has to be made for the fishes getting again into condition

It seems from investigations made in various places (*see* p 79) that undoubtedly some salmon do not breed every year, in fact if this were the invariable rule it would be impossible that any clean ones, unless possibly as small grilse, could be captured during the months of July and August ‡

* From the above notes in the Hotel record to which I was allowed access, I found that during the season of 1883, the salmon taken had an average of 12 lb per fish   in 1884, nearly 13 lb   in 1885, about 13½ lb   and in 1886, about 12½ lb   While the grilse in 1883 averaged nearly 6½ lb   in 1884 6 lb   in 1885, 5½ lb   and in 1886, 5 lb

† Mr Mackenzie, *Second Parliamentary Report*, p 21, stated that in March, 1823, he marked a grilse kelt of 3½ lb weight with a brass wire, and caught it again in March, 1824, then a salmon of 7 lb. weight   A fish which weighed 3½ lb as a kelt ought to weigh 5 lb or 6 lb when in good condition again, so this instance is hardly one which leads to the inference of rapidly increasing in weight

Mr Fraser, *On the Salmon*, &c , 1833, pp 11-15, observed "In February, 1829, I marked several grilse after spawning, by cutting off the fin above the tail   On the 1st of September following I caught one of them, which then weighed 13 lb   On the 10th of the same month I caught another weighing 14 lb   both were very fine salmon and charged with spawn   None of these could weigh above 5 lb or 6 lb at the time I marked them , they were taken very near the ground where they were marked   In February 1830, I tied a wire round the tail of some grilse returning to the sea, and only one of them came to my hands in the following August   Macleod of Macleod, Mr Fraser of Culduthell, and other gentlemen saw this salmon, and the mark produced on it by the wire   Mr Mackenzie of Ardross tied wire round the tails of some breeders returning to the sea in March, 1821, and about the same time next year, in March, 1825, he caught one of the fish thus marked, doubled in size, and the wire nearly out of sight " Mr Young stated that a grilse kelt of 2 lb weight was marked on March 31st, 1858, and recaptured on August 2nd of the same year as an 8 lb salmon   *Ramsbottom* remarked in 1854 that " the Duke of Athol, when Lord Glenlyon, captured on the 31st of March, 1845, a kipper fish of 10 lb weight, to which he attached a zinc ticket for the purpose of ascertaining the amount of its increase during its stay in the sea   In less than six weeks it was again caught and found to weigh 21½ lb " (In this case we are not informed how the *zinc* label continued legible after being kept in salt water)

Mr Scrope, in his work entitled *Days of Salmon Fishing*, 1851, gave the following experiments as having been made in the river Shin in Sutherlandshire —

Weight of grilse kelts when marked		Date retaken the next year		Weight
Feb 18th	—4 lb	June 23rd		9 lb
,,	4 lb	,, 25th		11 lb
,,	4 lb	, 25th		9 lb
,,	1 lb	,, 25th		10 lb
,,	4 lb	,, 27th		13 lb
,	1 lb	, 28th		10 lb
March 4th	—4 lb	July 1st		12 lb
,	4 lb	,, 1st		14 lb
,,	12 lb.	, 10th		18 lb
,	4 lb	,, 27th		12 lb

In 1859 the Duke of Athol had three salmon captured, while migrating seawards, weighing 10, 11½, and 12½ lb respectively   These were marked by a copper wire being placed round their tails, and six months subsequently they were recaptured as they were returning to fresh water, and their weight was ascertained to have augmented to 17, 18, and 19 lb respectively

‡ Fraser, *On the Salmon*, &c , 1833, p 17, observed, respecting the salmon of the Ness, that " breeders of this season, after remaining all summer in the sea, partly return as breeders in the months of August and September to spawn in the following winter   The greater part, however, return to the Ness in November and December, barren and averaging 16 lb each in weight "

Having now briefly detailed the salmon's history from the egg to the adult fish, it becomes necessary to revert to those forms which have completed their spawning Commonly known as *kelts* or *slats*, or if males, as *kippers*,[*] they drop down stream, from pool to pool, in a very thin and exhausted condition, the males much more so than the females However, they generally remain in the river in a debilitated state, feeding upon whatever fish comes in their way, not rejecting the young of their own species At this period they are readily captured, and, owing to their weak condition, very prone to attacks of disease, often dying in vast numbers, while a heavy flood carries them off towards the sea, but as a rule they continue some time in the brackish water of the tideway before seeking the ocean Although, doubtless, a few of these kelts mend in the rivers, recovering their silvery lustre prior to reaching the sea, and others return at a future period in a healthy state from the salt water, it seems questionable whether too many are not now permitted to mend, possibly to a great extent, upon the salmon fry, thus reducing the amount of stock in the river In olden times fishermen took all spawned fish as their own perquisites, consequently but few descended to the sea in some rivers also poachers, assisted by otters and other vermin, kept the number of kelts in check

If for the benefit of the fishing in a river, it were deemed advisable to permit the capture of salmon kelts, such would have to give rise to many other considerations Were it legal to sell them, how would such a permission end ʳ for soon grilse kelts would be accused of occasioning damage, and assuredly their capture would before long be legalized

These concessions granted it might next be advanced that many fresh-run clean salmon were in the river and which if not captured would be lost as food [†] Still we have to consider facts as they exist, and without doing more than just touching on this subject it seems as if it might be divided as follows —That the salmon subsequent to the spawning season becomes sickly, and is as well destroyed as kept, and while mending it consumes more young salmon, trout, and other fish than it is worth, that possibly kelts might be eaten

After spawning, salmon doubtless become exhausted and more easily susceptible to disease and capture, and it has been proposed to kill all the male kelts from the commencement of February, and all of either sex from the commencement of March Now, although there can scarcely be a doubt that some at least of the kelts return to rivers[‡] after recovering their strength in the sea, still many

He continued that these early, clean, and barren salmon have inside them several grains of the ova of last season still undischarged

[*] The hook, or kype, in the lower jaw of the spawning male is doubtless the origin of this term, while it has been surmised that they were first known as "kipper" salmon Mr Dunbar Brander remarked (*Field*, October 20th, 1886), that "A kip-nosed man, in Scotch, means a man with a turned up pug nose As these kip-nosed or kipper fish are soft and flabby, they are generally dried and smoked, and the process they undergo has been named from the fish that are utilized in this way It is almost impossible to cure and dry a fresh run fish during March, April, May, and June In July and August they are so full of oil, curd, and fat, that they spoil in the process, but by the month of October the fish get kip nosed, and they can be dried and cured The curd and oil is very much absorbed Reference to a Scotch dictionary will show that anything turned up at the corners is said to be 'kippered '"

[†] Such arguments as the following would soon be again brought forward, that "another cause of disease may be the spring-run fish remaining fully a year in the river, which must be injurious to them Could all these early run fish be captured, and the late autumn fish strictly preserved, the markets would benefit and the breeding stock would not be diminished " Or that "I cannot help thinking that, with regard to kelts, our laws might be revised with considerable benefit alike to anglers and rivers Have any of my readers ever tasted these fish when well made up? So well mended are they at times that some experience is positively necessary to detect them when caught from new fish I have tasted them, and, although I do not pretend to say they are equal in delicacy of flavour, yet, as respects an article of food, they are perfectly wholesome and good eating "

[‡] It has been shown that salmon after having spawned die, as has been asserted by Stella, Pallas, and Sir John Richardson when writing respecting the salmonoids of Kamtschatka and North Western America Although this, no doubt, is found to be true in some parts of the world, it is not invariably so here If all kelts died how could grilse or even male par which have been known to breed ever reach salmonhood? Still many old kelts succumb from exhaustion and

observers are of opinion that they never come back, consequently as mending kelts they have been consuming food, but in return for which they will not subsequently benefit the river *

Certainly, were all the salmon kelts destroyed the probabilities are that the breed in the river might decrease in size† (see p 27), but that the destruction of a number will have this effect, is not so sure, thus during the winter season of 1881-82 the salmon disease seriously affected the Tay and its tributaries, killing vast numbers of kelts, and by some people a greatly diminished catch was prognosticated for the season of 1882-83 But the spring and summer fishing was fairly favourable,‡ while in August there was a large increase both in grilse and salmon the effects of the mortality seemed to show itself in the decreased weight of the individual salmon and the paucity of exceptionally heavy fish, none attaining 40 lb until the commencement of June This would go towards favouring the contention that kelts when mended do return to the river, but that a great destruction of them does not necessarily involve a greatly diminished take of salmon the ensuing year

possibly ulceration of the snout (see p 57) Buist observed, "A few years ago a fine male of 20 lb weight was used for spawning purposes at Stormontfields A mark was put on him by means of a copper wire and two years afterwards he was got when nearly 30 lb weight on the same ford, and at the same season and after doing duty again was returned to the river hale and strong, but he was not traced afterwards " Also instances have been adduced of marked kelts having returned to the same river (see p 95) A correspondent, "Blackwater side " writing in Land and Water, May 28th, 1881, remarked " that in the Blackwater we have a class of fish locally termed 'retrievers' or 'recruits ' These fish have the remains of the markings generally of the male kelts and the hook on the under jaw still developed They are usually in company with a good run of fresh fish, as if, having been down to the sea, they met a number of old friends rushing up, and turned back with them Some of them have been so short a time in salt water that the remains of the maggots are found in their gills The gray or 'harvest fish' of this part of the country are also beyond a doubt the kelts which went down early and recovered themselves sufficiently to run up in the autumn and spawn during the following winter "

* "I want to ask your correspondents," observed a writer in Land and Water (November 18th, 1891), writing of the Tweed, "who swear salmon kelts return, and so make the big autumn fish, how is it that for the last three winters they have died by thousands, and yet we have more fish of all sorts, and more big ones than we have had in the river for years, and there are hundreds, perhaps thousands, still ascending the fords every day? It was calculated that in the winter of 1879 80, 50,000 kelts were buried or washed out to sea, the same thing happened last winter when the disease was worse than ever, and equally as many died (in fact I stated at the time that it was worse last spring than was ever known), and thousands were washed out to sea, as we had two very big floods , one the biggest since the year 1826, and in spite of all this we have more fish than ever " Another correspondent remarked of these kelts "They lie helpless in the river in many instances, and though alive, can be hooked out by a stick No doubt when our grandfathers lived on acorns, all these fish were taken out They are diseased, and ought to be killed, as diseased birds and animals are or ought to be killed It is all very well to talk of magnificent 30 lb or 40 lb fish if kelts are preserved, but far better have two fish of 15 lb than one fish of 30 lb When a salmon is over 20 lb he begins to get coarse, and a 40 lb fish is real 'old bull ' No man who has the pick of a hundred fish would select one over 18 lb for his own eating " In another communication to Land and Water, August 23rd, 1883, it was observed, "Kelts were killed and sold previous to the Act of 1857, and no one ever one bit the worse, and yet they are now supposed to be unwholesome Surely they are ten times better than a fish covered with Saprolegnia ferax—in one case the fish are only lean, in the other simply rotten A kelt is not unwholesome , it is foul and unclean, and it is by law protected in the hope that it will return from the sea a clean fish Now they are protected every way for no purpose whatever except to please a few who think they return, and the whole time they are in the river they are destroying smolts and spreading disease "

† Arguments condemning the slaughter of kelts have been adduced, thus one well-known author protested against advocating the indiscriminate destruction of salmon-kelts, observing, "If we were to destroy all kelts in a river, where are the large fish to come from ? The natural consequence of such a proceeding would be that only grilse would be left, and these fish would be on their second run from the sea and would not average probably 8 lb , whereas it takes years to produce the noble 20 lb and 30 lb which have since their first appearance as grilse reproduced their species yearly "

‡ H M Inspector of Salmon Fisheries, Professor Huxley, in July, 1883, reported, "Another very singular fact which has been brought to light by observation, though it certainly sounds paradoxical, is, that even a violent epidemic of disease (Saprolegnia ferax) continued for several years does not diminish the productiveness of a river " Probably the reason is to be found in so many kelts falling victims, and as a consequence the smolts escape, thus it will possibly augment the gross weight of the captures, although it may be more or less fatal to the presence of many very large fish

An experiment of permitting kelts to be destroyed in one river for a single year, and ascertaining the effect on the stock of salmon and grilse the succeeding season, appears well worthy of a fair trial, provided such could be done without entailing greater difficulties as regards the disposal of the captured fish, &c. as I have already pointed out.

It has likewise been proposed that people should be permitted to kill and eat these kelts, which otherwise probably become lost as food. But prior to such a proceeding being sanctioned, it might not be amiss to inquire whether they would be wholesome. Some observations tend to prove that occasionally they are not so,* while it must be evident to anyone who studies our fish markets that a large number of kippered salmon are of this description and have not been accused of entailing unpleasant results.

It has been remarked that kelts may mend in fresh water, and certainly they must do so in the land-locked rivers. Brown, *Stormontfield Experiments*, pp. 111, 112, recorded that a male kipper, no. 78, was caught April 1st, 1861, by Mr Evans above Logierait: it weighed 13½ lb; May 4th, 1861, it was taken again by Mr Brown on the Stanley water, and weighed 16 lb, having evidently improved in condition in the fresh water.

In Parliamentary language the terms "unclean" and "unseasonable," as well as "foul" fish are mentioned and their destruction prohibited: but much discussion has taken place concerning the meaning of these phrases. Probably the first decision respecting what is a "clean" or "unclean" salmon was given in December, 1885, by Mr Fowler, who considered that a "baggit," or gravid but unspawned fish, comes under the term "unclean."

We are told, after the penalties for taking unclean† or unseasonable salmon

---

* *Dr Gerald Boate*, writing from Ireland in 1645, asserted that the leprosy was caused "through the foul gluttony of the inhabitants in the unwholesome devouring of foul salmon when they are out of season, which is after they have cast their spawn, upon which they do not only grow very weak and flabby, but so unwholesome as it would loathe any man to see them." *Buckland* related how a water-bailiff, who was a strong, healthy man, ate a portion of one, and was made so ill that he was confined to his bed for two days.

† In the *Report of the Salmon Commissioners* appointed in 1860 to inquire into the Salmon Fisheries of England and Wales, and consequent upon which report a Salmon Act was passed, it was observed (p. xvii), "With reference to the capture of unseasonable fish, whether in a spent or spawning state, when they are unsuitable if not unwholesome for food," *i.e.*, clearly showing the views they held on the subject. Paterson (*The Fishery Laws of the United Kingdom*, 1863, p. 274), referring to unclean fish in Ireland, gave the following: "If any person at any time wilfully take, kill, destroy, expose for sale, or have in his possession any red, black, foul unclean or unseasonable salmon or trout," &c. (13 and 14 Vic.). Here it is evident that unspawned fish would come under the head of unclean fish. Russel (*The Salmon*, 1863) remarked of a river having "got rid in any considerable degree of the foul fish, spawned and unspawned." In *Chambers's Encyclopædia* (? 1865) we read, "As the time of spawning approaches salmon undergo considerable changes of colour, besides the change of form already noticed in the snout of the male. The former brilliancy of the hues gives place to a general duskiness, approaching to blackness in the females much tinged with red in the males, and the cheeks of the males become marked with orange stripes. Salmon in this state are 'foul fish,' being considered unfit for the table, and the killing of them is prohibited by British laws." The Irish Salmon Fisheries Act enacts that if any person shall take, kill, or have in his possession "any red, black, foul, unclean, or unseasonable salmon," such person shall forfeit, &c. Oke, *Salmon Fishery Acts*, described an unclean fish "as a fish that had not migrated to the sea after spawning." 'A Looker on,' in *The Field*, December 26th, 1885, remarked, "According to my reading of the law the term (unclean) included gravid fish that are about to spawn as well as spent fish that have spawned." Mr Willis Bund (*Salmon Problems*, 1885) defined an unclean fish as one "unfit to be taken, wherever and whenever caught, even if during the open season; thus a kelt would be an unclean salmon." Mr C. Pennell (*Badminton Series*, 1885, p. 114) observed of salmon that "shortly before spawning and whilst returning to the sea as kelts or spent fish salmon are unfit for food, and their capture is illegal." The Editor of *The Field* remarked respecting unclean salmon, in a footnote (December, 1885), that 'we are inclined to think that it is an open question, and very much would depend on the view a magistrate took of it. A baggit can hardly be held to be a clean fish—we do not consider it so—though it is quite possible that an objection might be raised to its being held to be a foul one." E. C. T. (*Field*, December 26th, 1885) observed that "the law enacts that all fish caught by rod in the Aberdeenshire Dee up to October 31st are clean, except kelts or spent fish." "Females full of spawn are killed in the River Dee every October that are clearly unfit for food. The male fish also, though not spent, are red and much deteriorated by the long sojourn in fresh water. They also, in point of fact, are unclean."

have been enumerated, that an exemption is made in favour of any person who takes or is in possession of *such fish* for artificial propagation Mr Paterson, in his work on *The Fishery Laws of the United Kingdom*, 1863, pointed out, when commenting on this section, that the joint consent of the owners or occupiers of the fishery and of the Board of Conservators "always is necessary when a third party takes unclean fish There is no such exemption as to fish that are clean Accordingly we must conclude that the Act includes unspawned fish in the term 'unclean,' or else that the only legal means of carrying on 'artificial propagation' is by the capture of kelts "

Among questions of practical moment among those relating to the breeding of salmon, as well as bearing on the races of so-called "land-locked salmon," is whether *Salmo salar* can be permanently retained in fresh water[*] without ever descending to the sea And if so whether, under such conditions, it would continue its race ? A great obstacle in coming to a conclusion on this point has been that it seemed occasionally to be doubtful whether in the recorded instances of such having been successfully accomplished the observer referred to *Salmo salar* or to a sea trout ?

Some authors have held that could salmon migrate from rivers into large fresh-water lakes where a sufficiency of suitable food existed, they would be able to return to the streams where they had been reared as well developed salmon But doubtless the generally accepted opinion has been that salmon, if retained in fresh water and unable to migrate to the sea, do not increase in weight but die without continuing their race [†] This however I shall be able to show is not, under favourable circumstances, a necessary result, as has been proved by experiments at Howietown,[‡] where smolts or grilse have given ova without descending to the sea, and from which parr have already been reared

---

[*] Dr Gunther (*Catal* vi, p 108) observed, "We have no evidence whatever that a migratory species has ever been changed into a non-migratory one , and persons who bring forward instances of such changes having taken place in the course of a few years, must first prove that they have correctly determined the species of the specimens experimented upon "

[†] In 1653 Izaak Walton published the first edition of his *Compleat Angler*, wherein the opinions of the most reliable authors of previous or contemporary times on salmon-breeding were condensed He remarked that it "is said to breed or cast its spawn in most rivers in the month of August some say they dig a hole or grave in a safe place in the gravel and there place their eggs or spawn, after the milter has done his natural office, and then hide it most cunningly and cover it over with gravel and stones 'Kippers' have bony gristle growing out of their lower jaws, and may live one year from the sea, but pine and die the second year Little salmons called 'skeggers,' which abound in many rivers, are bred by such sick salmons that might not go to the sea, and though they abound they never thrive to any considerable bigness "

Willoughby (*De Historia Piscium*, 1686), quoting a communication to Gesner, tells us that generally about the end of November salmon ascend for breeding purposes up rivers to their affluents, where the eggs are deposited and the young born, these latter are termed "samlets," while the old fish descend to the sea

Ray (*Synopsis Methodica Piscium*, 1713, p 63) observed that salmon are born in the rivers, from which they descend to the sea

Pontoppidan (*Natural History of Norway*, 1755, chap vi, p 131) remarked that Willoughby "also confutes Gesner's opinion concerning the salmon's breeding in the sea he thinks that it is done in fresh water, from whence they afterwards go to the sea , but in this he is certainly mistaken The salmon unquestionably breeds in the sea, though it is not entirely to be denied but that they may sometimes breed in rivers also, for they are found in the midst of Germany, and upper parts of the Rhine, about Basel , but we are very well assured that the salmon chiefly ejects its roe at the mouth of rivers, where they empty themselves into the sea, or a little way beyond, in the salt water, in this manner they bend themselves crooked, in order to eject the roe at an aperture under the belly, and in the meantime they stick their heads down in the sand, that they may have the more strength The male comes presently after, to keep off other fish from devouring the roe, and he then bends his head towards the tail, and ejects his sperm upon the roe "

[‡] Passing over the various authors who have mostly reproduced the opinions of those who have preceded them, we come to Yarrell, *British Fishes* (Edition 2) ii, p 17, who tells us that about the end of 1830 water was first turned into a certain pond, three or four acres in extent, situated in Scotland, and in April, 1831, one or two dozens of small salmon fry, 3 in or 4 in long were taken out of the river and turned in In 1833 the first fishing was allowed, and several salmon were taken with the fly from 2 lb to 3 lb in weight , all were perfectly well shaped and filled up,

7 *

At one time* the search for roe in salmon which had not descended to the sea was energetically carried on, but lately appears to have ceased, so it was

of the best salmon colour outside, the flesh well-flavoured and well coloured, though a little paler than that of new-run fish

Mr Upton, in the autumn of 1835 and the following spring, according to Yarrell, transferred some "pinks," none of which exceeded 3½ in in length from the Lune, to a lake termed Lillymere, and which has neither outlet from other waters by which fish can obtain access, or any obtain exit, and no communication with the sea   In August, 1837, two salmon peal, measuring 14 in in length and weighing 14 ounces, were taken with a fly, in excellent condition in every way, and in July, 1838, another small salmon was caught equal to the first in condition and colour, about 2 in longer and 3 ounces heavier   A "pink" was transferred to a well at White-well in November, 1837, and removed thence as a smolt 6½ in long in July, 1838   These and other similar instances would appear to point out that, as in the trout so in the salmon, the larger the extent of the water in which the fish resides, so much the more probable is it that it will more rapidly attain a large size   He remarked of the subject under consideration that "a knowledge of the growth of young salmon in a fresh water lake may be useful to those gentlemen who possess lakes near salmon rivers, from which they can supply them with pinks   Whether salmon thus prevented going to salt water will still retain sufficient constitutional power to mature their roe, and, by depositing it in the usual manner, as far as circumstances permit, produce their species, would be a subject worthy of further investigation"   (L. c (Ed 2). ii, p 16)

Knox observed in the *Proceedings Linnean Society*, ii, p 358, December 19th, 1854, that "from the time the salmon enters the fresh water it ceases to feed, properly speaking, although it may occasionally rise to a fly, or be tempted to attack a worm or a minnow, in accordance seemingly with its original habits as a smolt   But after first descending to the ocean and tasting its marine food, it never again resorts to its infantile food as a constant mode of nourishment   The absence of this marine kind of sustenance forms an insurmountable obstacle to the preservation of salmon and some kinds of sea trout in fresh water lakes "

Bertram—observing upon having been present at Stormontfield at the yearly exodus of smolts in 1861, when they were found to be large and in fine condition—continued, One fish, which has been detained for three years for the purpose of discovering whether the species will grow in fresh water without being permitted to visit the sea, was found to be fully twice the size of the largest smolt" (*Harvest of the Sea*, 1865, p 110)   It must not be overlooked in experiments of this nature that the extent of the fresh water in which these fish are confined must exercise a considerable influence upon the result, and also on the amount and suitability of the food which is available for their consumption

Buist (1866) published a letter from Mr G Anderson of Glasgow, which appeared in *The Field*, June 20th   With it he sent a salmon par which had not put on the smolt livery and gone to the sea from Stormontfields at the 2 year old migration   It was long enough to be 3 lb in weight, and only weighed 1 lb   Without the possibility of doubt it had been confined to fresh water for six years, and where a sufficiency of food existed

Dr Murie in *Proc Zool Soc* 1868, p 249, gave an account of some Rhine salmon hatched in the Zoological Society's Gardens in 1863, and which lived there in fresh water until 1868   At the usual migration period of May in 1865 those which were smolts tried to escape by leaping out of the tank, while it was remarked that such as had assumed the silvery smolt livery at the beginning of the year, but were unable to go to the sea lost it in the autumn, when they again became par-marked   Only two lived to the fifth year   These fish had been kept in a comparatively small tank with a stream of running water, a subject which it is very necessary to bear in mind, because, although here they were subject to an arrest of development, such may have been due to the small space in which they were confined or the limited amount of water which they obtained, irrespective of which the changes of temperature may have been considerable

Yarrell (*Growth of Salmon in Fresh Water*) remarked "that the rate of growth in young salmon has some reference to the size of the place to which they are restricted, receives further confirmation in these river, lake, and well specimens   The smolt taken from the well in July, 1838, where it had been confined for eight months, was rather smaller in size at that time than the smolts in the preceding April, though both were pinks of the same year, namely 1837   The smolt taken from the lake in August, 1838, which then measured 7¼ in , had also grown more rapidly than that in the well, but had not acquired the size it would have gained had it been allowed to go to sea   Further it may be observed, that the salmon peal from the lake in August, 1837, then 18 months old, though perfect in colour, is small for its age, while that of July 1838, or 29 months old, is comparatively still more deficient in growth, supposing both fish to have resulted from pinks of the year 1836, and put into the lake at the same time, of which there was no doubt, since the lake, the formation of which, though commenced in the autumn of 1835, was not finished till February, 1836, soon after which the first pinks were put in "

The Duke of Buccleuch's gamekeeper at Lowhill was for some years in the practice of putting a few smolts into a fresh water pond, and feeding them regularly with bullock's liver   He reported that the smolts which grew into salmon throve for about three years and then died, but that bull trout smolts kept in good condition for a longer period

"Into a deserted stone-quarry near Coldstream, filled with rain water, two smolts, about 3 in long, were put by boys out of mere amusement   One of these grew into a salmon which when 5 years old, weighing 14 lb , was caught and sent to Mr Stoddart of Kelso, who had it boiled for

intended at Howietoun to re-open the investigation after an interval of forty-five years. But as it was not improbable that objections would be raised were young fish captured in the rivers used for this purpose, it was determined to rear the parr from the eggs and ascertain whether the smolts and grilse thus raised would or would not breed in fresh water.

In such investigations as those which I am about to detail I need scarcely dilate upon the necessity of first being absolutely certain respecting the species upon which these experiments are made; secondly, on there being most absolute segregation of the eggs and young from those of all other forms. That segregation is complete at Howietoun I need hardly remark upon to those who have visited the establishment.

dinner. He reported that it was not unpalatable. The other smolt grew into a bull-trout and lived for seven years. It died during a very severe winter when, on account of the water being frozen, it could not be fed."—Extract from *Report of Experimental Committee to the Tweed Commissioners*.

Dr Gunther (*Introduction, Study of Fish* 1880, p. 639) considered that "the question of whether any of the migratory species of *Salmonidæ* can be retained in fresh water, and finally accommodate themselves to a permanent sojourn therein, must be negatived for the present." Up to 1880 he doubted the instances of successful experiments which had been brought forward, as he was not convinced that the young fish introduced into ponds were really migratory *Salmonidæ* and not hybrids. He had previously recorded (*Fisherman's Magazine*, i, 1864, p. 157) how to test the truth of whether migratory *Salmonidæ* perish if prevented from going to the sea at the proper season, the Rev Augustus Morgan experimented during several years with full-grown sea trout, half grown sewin, and with salmon, but all the specimens died, although there was plenty of food in the pond; the fresh water trouts remained perfectly healthy. The dead specimens presented a remarkable appearance, the body being as lean and elongated as in a lake; all the internal parts were much inflamed.

Mr *Douglas Ogilbie* in 1881 took about 100 sea trout and salmon smolts, which he turned into Lough Ash, Co Tyrone, which has no access to the sea. April 30, 1883, he captured a smolt or grilse 11½ in long in this lake, where salmon had not previously been seen. Its abdomen was so distended that he considered it would have spawned very shortly, more especially as it was taken at the mouth of the only stream that enters this lough. The specimen is in the Natural History Museum at South Kensington, and is evidently a true *Salmo salar*, and as such I described it in the *Proceedings Zool Soc* 1881 p. 584, while the eggs in spirit were each 0.25 of an inch in diameter. Provided there had been a ripe male in the vicinity, there seems no reason why this fish should not have deposited her eggs, and such might have given rise to a land-locked race.

* Shaw remarked that solitary instances have occurred of large female parrs having been found in salmon rivers with the roe considerably developed, and he ascertained that by detaining the female smolt in fresh water until the end of the third winter individuals are found in this comparatively mature condition. Davy (*Trans Royal Soc Edin* 1854, xxi, p. 253) observed that he had examined hundreds of parrs, and had frequently found the males with milt, but never a female with roe correspondingly developed. On the contrary, the females, without exception, had the ovaries so small that without they had been carefully sought for they would have escaped notice. Russell denied that female parrs ever had the roe developed.

Yarrell (*Brit Fish* 1836) recorded that Mr Heysham had sent him an example 7 in long having both lobes in a forward state, as well as notice of a female taken in March with large ova. Mr Couch also informed him of a similar case in the Dart in March.

Brown (*Stormontfields Experiments*, 1862, p. 89) considered that no female parr had yet been discovered with the roe developed, possibly meaning no young salmon in the parr livery had been seen with the ova fully developed, for, as I shall endeavour to show, smolts with parr bands have given eggs at Howietoun. Brown reared the young from eggs to the smolt stage and obtained at Stonehaven a salt water pond for their reception into which the sea ebbed and flowed, but poachers destroyed the experiment.

March 4th, 1859, M Julius Cloquet read a paper before the French *Société d'Acclimation* on the breeding of salmon in a pond without descending to the sea (vol vi, 1859, p. 253). The small pond which was the scene of this experiment was situated in the hollow of a wooded valley, which was not more than a hectare in superficial extent. Its depth was from six metres towards the end where the bound was erected, while in the remainder of its extent its richly herbivorous bottom sloped towards the edges like those of a basin. Some trout were first introduced, and in April and May, 1857, many thousand salmon, which at twenty-two months had an average weight of 120 grammes and from twenty five to thirty centimetres in length. Females were found full of eggs, these were artificially fecundated, and got so far as to be close upon hatching.

Dr Gunther, after remarking how conclusively Shaw has demonstrated that parr are the young of salmon, and that they may contain milt, continued, "No parr has ever been found with mature ova" (*Introduction to the Study of Fishes*, 1880, p. 639). Mr *Gosden* observed that in the Exe parr-marked fish, graveling or smolt, so called, have been taken with ova actually exuding from the fish on being handled for the purpose of removing the hook.

In December, 1880, Sir James Maitland obtained some salmon in the Teith, from which he personally took eggs and milt and in March, 1881, the ova were hatched   In due course the young were transferred to pond No 7 at Howietoun This pond is lined with wood, and its extent 100 ft long by 15 ft broad, 8 ft deep in the centre, and 6½ ft on either side, while the average supply of water passing through it is 1,000,000 gallons a day

In July 1883 in the presence of several of the foreign commissioners to the "Great International Fisheries Exhibition," and other invited guests, this pond was netted, when it was seen that some of the youngsalmon, then two years and four months old, were of a general golden colour, spotted, and in the livery of the banded par stage while others were beautiful silvery smolts similar to such as we generally find descending to the sea, and which, in certain lights, showed par bands   Although, as a general rule, the smolts were the larger, still a few of the pars exceeded the smolts in size

October 10, 1883 one of these fish, which was under 1 lb in weight, in the smolt livery,* but still showing par bands, jumped out † of the pond, and was found dead on the path   On being opened it proved to be a female, with comparatively large ova, which were of a deep reddish colour, thus almost disposing of the statement that "no par has ever been found with a mature ova "   I say almost, because as yet the ova were not quite mature, although they would have become so had not the fish met with an untimely fate   Also the objection might be raised that it was a smolt not a par, and although the par bands were present, certainly the golden tinge seen in the young of the salmon was absent

At the end of November, 1883, several of these fish during the night and early morning were found to have jumped out of the pond, and it was surmised that more might have been carried off by rats or birds   On November 29th two more, one being 11½ in in length, were found dead this latter was a silvery smolt, with par bands, and on being opened proved to be full of ripe milt   A net having been employed, three fish were removed for examination   The first was a silvery smolt 10 8 in in length, which in certain lights distinctly showed the par bands, the generative organs were not developed   The second, 9 in long, was more distinctly par marked, but otherwise very similar   The third was 6 3 in in length, in the par dress, and was a male full of milt ‡   As a rule the females were silvery, although the ova was not ripe, but the males, on the contrary when pressed, gave ripe milt   Generally the smolts appeared to be more spotted than such as are taken in a state of nature in the rivers, the largest was 1 3½ in long Those in the golden par livery seemed to be males, most of which were ripe, while the silvery smolts were mostly females   These fish rendered it very evident that the relative growth of the fry does not depend on the size of the pond, quantity, quality, or variety of food, or amount of water, as all had been treated alike, yet they varied in length from 4 in to 13½ in

During the month of May, 1884 sixteen of these fishes jumped out of the pond and were found dead, and the breeding organs in all were found to be developing in a satisfactory manner   August 28th, 1884, an examination was made of pond No 7, and a smolt 1½ lb in weight and 14 1 in long was removed, it proved to be a female with the ova well forward, the largest being 0 1 of an

---

The beautiful illustrations of grilse in Sir W Jardine's magnificent *Salmonidæ* do not resemble *in colour* the Howietoun fish, which latter are more spotted than his 2 lb 13 oz specimen from the Solway Firth, taken in July, and even more so than his 3½ lb fish captured in August

† Brown (*Stormontfields Experiments*) observed that "in the month of February, 1836, caught a dozen and a half par in the Tay, and kept them confined in a stream of running water, and by the month of May the whole of them had become smolts , but some had leaped out of their confinement in their struggle to find their way to the sea, and were found dead on the side of the pond " (pp 7 and 8)

‡ The teeth in the vomer of a par were as follows —Three on the hind edge of the head of that bone, behind that a par, then two placed one at an angle to the other, and subsequently eight in a single row, but with their points somewhat divergent   There was very little change seen in those of the smolt, while in one 13 in long, that spawned in 1884, the same dentition prevailed

inch in diameter   October 4th, one 13 in long, which had jumped out of the pond, proved to be a female, and the eggs were 0 2 of an inch in diameter, in fact, of mature size

From this time the fishes commenced constantly jumping out of the pond and meeting with fatal injuries, they did so towards the upper end, where the stream of water entered, as if seeking for a place where they could ascend it   Wire netting was now fixed around the upper part of the pond, but against this the fish continued to spring   About the middle of October, fungus, *Saprolegnia ferax*, showed itself, most probably due to the injuries occasioned by their endeavours to escape   It was also observed that they ceased from feeding, so a number of small Lochleven trout were added to vary their diet, but which they did not appear to consume many of

November 7th, 1884, a smolt, 1¼ lb in weight, was found lying almost dead by the side of pond 7, and from it about 100 apparently ripe eggs were expressed   These were milted from a Lochleven trout   On January 23rd, 1885, eighteen of these eggs hatched, and when I first saw them on February 10th the young were looking remarkably well and vigorous, none of them seemed to be in the slightest degree deformed   So far as I am aware this is the first successful attempt in Great Britain made at raising young from salmon eggs the parent of which has never descended to the sea, but passed its entire existence in fresh water

November 14th, 1884, the water was drawn off from pond No 7, as the wood with which it is lined required recharring, and the fish were placed in pond No 5, just done up and previously inhabited by brook trout, but which were now turned into the burn as being too old to be worth further preserving   Sixty-eight young salmon were transferred, the majority being males, while the fishes showed all the gradations in colouring from the golden and banded par to the silvery smolts   These latter, however, had not lost their par-bands, while some of the larger ones were distended with ova   All the fish in the full par dress were males, but so were some of the silvery smolts   About two dozen eggs were obtained from one, but they did not germinate, possibly not being quite ripe   Three smolts were too injured to live   These were opened, then ovisacs were found to be distended with eggs, almost but not quite ripe, being still slightly adherent

As these young salmon became ready for continuing their species, the following ova were obtained in December, and laid down in the hatching-house

December 1st, 1884 (box 104a), 1500 eggs from two smolts, which were treated with the milt of one of the males   These eggs averaged each 0 22 of an inch in diameter   About 400 hatched February 21st, or in eighty-two days

December 9th (box 108a), about 4000 eggs of these smolts were fertilized with the milt of one of the males, these eggs averaged each 0 20 of an inch in diameter   About 2200 hatched February 27th, 1885

As the further development of these experiments is fully followed out by Sir James Maitland, in his *History of Howietoun*, it only becomes necessary for me to observe that I exhibited at a meeting of the Linnean Society in November, 1886, a par 5¼ in long, taken the week previously from a fine shoal of these fish at Howietoun, and which had been hatched there in March, 1885, from eggs and milt of parents that had never descended to the sea, the specimen being twenty months old and in excellent condition   Whether these fishes after a few generations will lose their migratory instincts and be satisfied to pass their lives and reproduce their kind in fresh waters, only time can show, but they afford incontestable evidence that a sojourn in salt water is not necessary in order for a grilse to develop eggs   and that migratory salmon are able to reproduce their kind in fresh water without migrating to the sea, thus removing one great obstacle which has stood in the way of ichthyologists admitting that a land-locked salmon can beget a race of *Salmo salar*

Having thus shown that salmon can be reared in fresh water and also breed without descending to the sea when in suitable localities, the question arises whether such an occurrence is seen in nature, if in fact, there are what may be termed wild land-locked races of this fish

Although it has been denied by Dr Gunther that the land-locked salmon of Lake Wenern* are anything but trout, it is, as I have stated, owing to his unfortunately not having had the opportunity of examining the real local race Scandinavian ichthyologists appear from early times to have considered it to be a local breed of the true salmon (*Salmo salar*), which had become unable, due to physical changes in the conformation of the country at some period long since gone by, to migrate seawards, and had consequently been compelled to pass its entire existence in fresh waters (*see* page 5) This opinion was strongly combated by Dr Gunther in the *Zoological Record* for 1864, for having obtained two forms of trout from Lake Wenern, he came to the conclusion that one must represent the land-locked salmon This statement has possibly deterred fish-culturists from seeking this variety for artificial propagation, as, had Dr Gunther s identification been correct, introducing either of these two races of trout into our waters would certainly have been productive of little, if any, benefit

Having had an opportunity of closely examining a pair of undoubted Lake Wenern salmon in 1883,† I must express my opinion that they certainly resemble

---

* In the year 1863 Widegren gave it as his opinion that the different forms of Scandinavian trout were local races or varieties of one species, while a large salmonoid from Lake Ladoga he considered to be identical with *Salmo salar*, variety *lacustris* of Hardin, and in these views Malmgren concurred Professor Lovén about this time ascertained that certain marine animals still survived at great depths in some of the Scandinavian lakes, as I have remarked (page 5 *ante*) Malmgren believed that anadromous salmon might have had their descent to the ocean summarily stopped, and either themselves or their fry, which latter at least must have been in the fresh water, had to select between extinction or continuing their race under altered conditions

Hetting the *Superintendent of Fisheries* in Norway, wrote to Dr Soubeiran in February, 1866, remarking that the common salmon lives in Lake Wenern, and has done so from time immemorial, that it is now naturalized both there and in the great lakes of Norway, and where the conditions of nourishment are favourable, it loses nothing of its qualities—at least, that the Lake Wenern race rivals the marine salmon in its colour, taste, and size, while every year, from May until the end of autumn, it migrates from the lake towards Klara ely, similar to the sea salmon, which at the same period quits the ocean in order to ascend into fresh waters

In 1866 Dr Gunther, in the *Catalogue of the Fishes in the British Museum*, gave the local species of the genus Salmo (omitting the chars) from the Scandinavian Peninsula and Finland as follows 1 *Salmo mistops* Gunther, 2 *S hardinii*, Gunther, 3 *S. renernensis*, Gunther, and a Lapland *S polyostens*, Gunther, having come to the conclusion that all descriptions published up to that period by preceding authors were insufficient for identification To his second species he appended the synonomy of the land locked salmon of Wenern, *Salmo salar* variety *lacustris*, but with a note of interrogation, as he was naturally doubtful whether the two referred to the same fish In short, the true land-locked salmon of this lake finds no place in the catalogue, and the two forms (*S hardinii* and *S renernensis*) recorded from thence in the work are local races of *Salmo trutta* Owing to this unfortunate confusion, Dr Gunther concluded that the Lake Wenern land locked salmon, which he supposed *S hardinii* might be, had smaller scales (or thirteen transverse rows on the tail) than the true salmon, which has only twelve or less at that spot, but admitted that it never entered the sea, being found in the Lake Wenern, into which no marine fish can ascend, in consequence of intervening cataracts He continued " A fanciful idea has been started that it is a salmon, with some of the characters modified, in consequence of its compulsory residence in a fresh-water lake We cannot see how such a change in the life of a fish has the effect of diminishing the size of the scales ' (p 108) Certainly it must be admitted that, although a lake salmon may vary in appearance as much as might a lake trout from its river relatives still the number of scales would keep within the same limits While having had the opportunity of examining the specimens in the British Museum alluded to in the catalogue, there can be no doubt that the enumeration there given is generally correct But the real question is whether his enumeration of the scales is that which exists in the true Wenern salmon ?

† The male is nearly 31 in in length, has 115 rows of scales, and from nine to ten in an oblique line from the adipose dorsal fin to the lateral line, it possesses fifty-five cæcal appendages, and the milt semi mature The female is between 32 and 33 in in length, has 116 rows of scales, and from nine to ten in an oblique line from the adipose dorsal fin to the lateral line It also possesses fifty five cæcal appendages, while the eggs are semi-mature Further description would be out of place here, and I can only say that these fish, if stuffed, could not be separated from the salmon The cæcal appendages are rather restricted in number, still as few as fifty three have been recorded from a salmon, and we do not yet know the conditions under which these appendages vary in their number, unless as seems possible, those living in the best feeding-grounds and having a large range possess the greatest number The scales on the tail do not resemble in number those of the trout in its various races

S salar in all points, and are not identical with any of the Scandinavian races described by Dr Gunther in the *Catalogue of the Fishes in the British Museum*

There appears to be one remarkable point of divergence between the Scandinavian and American land-locked salmon In the first Malmgren found that the eggs had decreased in number and diminished in size, whereas Mather says of the latter it 'may be noted that though in maturity smaller, in embryonic stages the land-locked salmon are larger, the eggs perhaps being ten per cent greater in diameter" Atkins, however, found them smaller, so they may vary in different localities, possibly in accordance with the food supply

It is certainly remarkable that among the Scandinavian land-locked races some are found in a number of lakes with broad outlets into the sea Also respecting the land-locked salmon of America, Mr Atkins, in 1884, observed that he did not think we have any evidence that the land-locking of the species has occurred during recent geological periods "There is nothing at present to prevent any of these salmon going out to sea from any of those waters where they are now found. There are obstructions to their coming back if they once went to the sea, and these same obstructions would hinder the sea salmon having access to the upper waters, where the land-locked salmon now live "*

Should it be decided to stock† some of our larger and clear lakes with this race of land-locked salmon,‡ it might be worth considering whether eggs obtained from Lake Wenern, which is slightly north of the British Isles, would not be more likely to succeed than those from the United States, where the waters are entirely to the south of Great Britain While a trial of the two forms would be of greater utility than all the theories which could be advanced on the subject

It seems very questionable whether these fishes are suited to our rivers, which

---

* The land locked race of salmon found in the State of Maine and neighbouring portions of Canada, in Lake Sebago, Lake Sabec, and the Schoodic lakes, are also identical in external form with *Salmo salar* That similar conditions in America may occasion the same changes is exceedingly interesting, but only what might be expected These salmon Agassiz considered to be identical with the lake salmon, or *Salmo argenteus* (silverlax) of Sweden

Mr Atkins, who has made a special study of these American forms of land locked salmon, tells us that there are differences which point towards a theory of arrested development, such as the dark par bands which are retained through life, as may be seen by removing the scales Such appearances were not present in any of the Wenern fish as have come under my observation, perhaps twenty or thirty in all In the United States some land-locked forms give fewer and smaller eggs than the anadromous race, while ovarian disease has been found to be frequent They only cease feeding for a few weeks at the breeding time, and undertake two migrations yearly from the lakes to the streams The first is in May, and continues until August, it seems to be for the sole purpose of feeding The second or "fall" migration begins in September, and ceases at the commencement of winter and is for breeding

The land-locked salmon in the breeding season never assumes such bright colours as do male sea or river salmon, while Atkinson observed of the Schoodic lake, Here, as in many other instances that I know of, the salmon move down from the lake into its outlet at the spawning season, instead of up into the tributaries It follows that the young fish, instead of dropping down with the current, as many sea salmon do, are in the habit of ascending their native streams till they reach the deep water above "

These salmon, in the United States, as well as in Canada, are inferior in size to the anadromous race for in the Penobscot the average adult is given at about 13 lb, while among the Sebago race the largest average 5 lb, although a solitary instance has been recorded of one of 25 lb that had been found dead Although these forms seem to thrive best where the waters are very deep, still to this general rule there are some exceptions Large numbers of eggs from this race, some of which are much larger than those of our salmon, have been brought into this country, and many hundreds of yearlings are thriving at Howietoun

† In some cases it has been found that the introduction of salmon into pieces of water frequented by trout has not been conducive to the well-being of the latter species.

‡ In case at a future date the following observation from *Land and Water*, 1886, should raise discussion, I may mention that the fish alluded to below (of which I have a series of specimens) were trout, *S purpuratus*, but not *S salar* The extract alluded to was as follows —

"LAND-LOCKED SALMON Three specimens of this Canadian fish, about 14 in in length, which have been presented to Mr. Thomas Sprechley by the Science and Art Department at Kensington, were taken to Chertsey on Thursday last, and placed in one of the tanks belonging to Mr James Forbes, of Chertsey Bridge, prior to their being turned into the Thames in that neighbourhood "

are destitute of lakes, as they would certainly require considerable range and abundance of food. For in such cases lakes would be to the land-locked salmon as the sea is to the anadromous form, and the decision with which the statements of Norwegian ichthyologists that these fishes were the descendants of *Salmo salar* was received in this country must now be admitted to have been an error.

What are the limits of reproduction among the salmon? is a question which has often been propounded, but to which various replies have been given. Among fishes generally it exists to a very different degree, thus our catadromous eels would seem to pass many seasons in a sterile condition, only reproducing their species when they descend to salt water. In the salmon, although it is evident that the male is capable of producing milt before it is twenty-four months of age such is very deficient in marital powers, while in the female eggs seem rarely to be developed prior to its being thirty-six months old. The trout and the char will furnish eggs and milt when nearly two years of age, but even among these fishes the female is rarely so far advanced as the male.

Among salmon permanent or temporary sterility may occur. Thus in those cases in which it is permanent* such may be owing in some individuals to their not being sexually developed, as observed by Siebold, or to a mechanical difficulty in the ova being extruded or if extruded the eggs themselves may be sterile, due to the spermatozoa being of too great a size to enter the micropyle of the ovum, or sterility may be consequent upon some physiological cause, possibly as close interbreeding deficiency of food, or unsuitable residence,† affecting the reproductive system to such an extent as to preclude the formation or at least the fertility of the eggs. And, lastly, hybridity may be a cause, and which will be considered when the various hybrids are described. Cases of temporary sterility are seen, as in clean-run salmon ascending our rivers every month in the year, while it is manifestly impossible that such as do so, as I have described, in November (*see* p. 69) could breed that season, and they evidently were not kelts that had bred. But in such fish a very slight development of milt or roe may be detected by means of the microscope ‡. These seasonally sterile fish would seem to corroborate the view advanced by Mr. Atkins that salmon breed on alternate years (*see* p. 79).

Hybridism in a natural state is supposed to be rare as regards the salmon, but that such may take place has been proved by Rasch, Sir James Maitland, and others who have fertilized their ova with the milt of the trout and of the char, and *vice versâ*, and obtained fertile progeny, as will be treated of further on. These fish do not lose their anadromous instincts when the period of migration arrives, so could not be utilized as a land-locked race§, on the supposition that they would be sterile and so lose the desire to migrate seawards.

Respecting stocking rivers with "alevins," or young salmon in which the yolk-sac is very nearly or just absorbed, various opinions are held. Some

---

* Widegren considered that the form of the caudal fin and the colours of the fish are connected with the development of the sexual organs as will be referred to when treating of trout.

† Some fish, although apparently in good health, will not breed when kept in an aquarium.

‡ Mr. Ffennell gave evidence before a *Parliamentary Committee* that clean salmon with only a thread of milt or roe in them are found in rivers during December, January, and February, and he considered that these fish do not spawn until the November or December following, remaining ten or twelve months in the fresh water, then ova developing until they are ready to spawn, and that, although discoloured, due to their residence, they are very good eating. Brown (*Stormontfields Experiments*), pp. 94, 95, caught one of these fish in a Sutherlandshire river and gave the same report. He also remarked that the foregoing fish are strong, able to overcome falls and penetrate to the extreme feeders of the rivers, whereas those fish which do not leave the sea until heavy with spawn could not overcome falls or ascend any considerable distance.

§ Professor Baird (*United States Fisheries Report* 1875 76, p. 13) observed "Another subject of consideration by the convention was the hybridizing of fish, with a view of removing the instinct of migration, and by the atrophy of the sexual apparatus, allowing a more rapid accession of flesh and fat, as is the case of hybrids and castrated domestic animals." Professor Brown Goode remarked 1884, respecting hybrid salmonidæ being likely to remain in the head waters of the streams "Such is the theory of certain English experts, but it occurs to me that their theory is without very good foundation."

believe that by this means the number of fishes in a river can be largely increased. Others maintain that such a proceeding merely increases the number of fry which are preyed upon by every species of vermin (p 44) But as this has certainly proved beneficial in some rivers, if not in all, it simply comes to the question of whether their enemies are too great for their being able to survive, and which must always be a question for local knowledge and experience to decide *

The food consumed by the anadromous salmon is somewhat varied, for while living in the ocean they appear to lay in a sufficient stock of fat, which is most readily seen around the stomach and cœcal appendages, to last them when residing in fresh water, or at least until the spawning season has passed I have seen the remains of sand-eels, *Ammodytes*, herrings, and crustacea in their stomachs Jardine remarked that on the Sutherlandshire shores they are often captured on haddock lines baited with sand eels Thompson, in Ireland, also found these fish eating sand-eels, and that they were occasionally taken in Dundrum Bay upon lines baited with pieces of mackerel which were laid for mullet Morrison recorded having captured salmon within flood mark, some of which contained two, others three, full-sized herrings In the British Museum are the remains of a gar-fish, *Belone*, taken out of a salmon captured in fresh water, but evidently only lately from the sea One of 24 lb being opened, two trout (size six to a pound) were found inside it (*Fishing Gazette*, December 20th, 1879) † Parnell (*Fishes of the Frith of Forth*, p 287) observed " in the county of Devon as well as in Loch Lomond in the north, I have seen with the minnow, and the common earth-worm is a deadly bait for the clean salmon On dissecting the alimentary canal of several dozens of salmon that were taken in salt water, I seldom failed in discovering the remains of some kind of food in the lower intestines, the stomach itself being almost invariably empty In one out of five I found the remains of crustacea and bones, apparently of the sand eel and other small fish I have repeatedly found the remains of worms and aquatic insects in the intestines of those salmon that were taken in rivers and lakes , but in those fish which were far advanced in roe both stomach and intestines were almost invariably empty."‡

* Ramsbottom, of Clitheroe, in *The Salmon and its Artificial Propagation*, 1854, observed " What would be the fate of any number of defenceless fry which might be turned into a river ? It would be as reasonable to expect a return of salmon from so many flies as from fry thus recklessly exposed to destruction " (p 61) " To turn one or two hundred thousand *smolts* into a river would afford a vastly different result from exposing the same number of *young fry* Instead of being liable, for upwards of two years, to the attacks of their enemies, their stay in the river would be but temporary " (*l c* , p 61)
† Mr Gosden (*Land and Water*, March 8th, 1886), remarked —" In 1874 I opened 490 salmon and examined the contents of their stomachs , 290 from the river Exe, 150 from the River Dart, and 50 peal from the Dart In these I found eels, minnows, loach, gudgeon, sand eels, shrimps, &c A friend of mine in Exeter called my attention on May 19, 1871, to an eel about a foot long This was partly digested , also to a carp taken from a salmon caught in Hampshire waters, and a half digested grey mullet from an Exe fish " Also another correspondent observed in the same paper on February 20, 1886, as follows —" I have seen salmon feeding in both river and lake and am simply astonished that any person could maintain that they do not Salmon are no doubt heavy feeders while in the sea, and also while in the estuary I have taken no fewer than eleven herrings out of a ten-pound grilse caught at the mouth of the Ayr I saw at Dalmeny five small sprats taken out of a salmon A salmon caught at Kincardine had in its stomach seven sparling, besides other small shrimps; another caught high up the Forth, at Polmaise, contained a smolt and eighteen shrimps , one taken at Craignorth Cruives, twenty-seven young eels , others having swallowed a trout fully half a pound and every imaginable insect, flies, beetles, worms and spiders So it is all nonsense to say that salmon, when in fresh water, live upon love In 1844 two salmon caught on Loch Tay in May had in their stomachs one and two young char quite entire, besides partially digested pieces of others "
Some Severn fishermen believe that elvers are largely consumed by salmon, and in the Usk there is a local saying, " a good year of prides (small lamperns), a good year of salmon "
‡ Dr Davy (*Physiological Researches*) wished to ascertain whether the usually empty condition of the stomach in salmon in fresh water is or is not accompanied by the presence of gastric juice ? He took test papers, considering that if there it must be acid August 24th, he tried on four salmon taken in the sea, about three hours after capture, there was no solid food or liquid, only a little adhering mucus, and no effect was produced on the litmus paper 26th, four more

From time to time discussions arise as to whether salmon do or do not feed in fresh waters, some maintaining that they do while others hold contrary opinions, the argument which is generally adduced against their doing so being that as a rule very little, if any, food is found in the stomachs of those captured in rivers which are far distant from the salt water

Many of those who admit that the male parr or the mending kelt will feed in fresh waters, hold that salmon as a rule do not increase in weight when absent from salt water, but proof in figures is still wanting to uphold this theory as applicable to all salmon, while excreta from the vent may be seen in some and which must be the remains of food that they have consumed *

It seems possible to divide salmon ascending rivers into two classes first such as will breed within a short period after their ascent, and secondly, such as will not do so without again descending to the sea, being clean-run fish This raises the question whether the latter of these classes or the clean-run salmon may not be the feeders, whereas the breeders are more or less abstainers In recording investigations on this subject it is desirable that the sex and condition of the fish should be ascertained, because many piscine forms, such as shad, trout, and char, more or less cease feeding at the period of spawning and subsist on the fat stored up in their bodies At Howietoun, in 1882, as the time for the smolts to give eggs arrived, they were observed to go off their feed, and young fish were supplied to tempt their appetites but only with moderate success, and subsequent to the breeding season they came on their feed again (*see* p 103 ante)

On March 10th, 1886, Mr Olive, fishmonger in the Promenade, Cheltenham, drew my attention to the condition of the belly in a male 12-lb clean salmon received by him the previous day from the tidal portion of the Severn below Newnham   The stomach was very distended, and on being removed from the fish it was found to measure 7 in in length and contained twenty-two entire sprats (*Clupea sprattus*), the smallest being 2 6 in long, and the largest 4½, while all were quite fresh   Their eyes were bright, their fins complete, and their scales as adherent as is generally seen in those fishes as exhibited for sale they had scarcely been acted upon by the gastric juices, tending to show that, at times at least digestion in these fishes is not very rapid   This he informed me was the first instance of fish present in a salmon's stomach, that he Mr Olive, had seen in forty years experience

One modifying circumstance in the feeding of the salmon has been observed to be connected with a muddy state of the river, possibly interfering with respiration, consequent upon the amount of mud which had been swallowed †

---

similarly taken were found to be empty, and only gave a slight alkaline reaction   August 27th, September 3rd and 6th, two salmon and one grilse taken with the fly in fresh waters their stomachs were empty, and reactions the same   In parr and smolts he obtained different results, food was always present in their stomachs and gave an acid reaction, the examination being made so soon as they had been taken from the water   Sea trout taken with fly in fresh water in the majority of instances afforded results similar to those of the salmon in some, which contained food, giving an acid reaction only once in forty two trials did he find an acid reaction occur with an empty stomach   Brook trout gave the same results

* T Harris, in the *Field*, March 29th, 1884, observed that on March 22nd a fresh fish of 32 lb weight had been taken with a rod and line in the Hampshire Stour about four miles from Christ church, the bait used being a dace, 4 or 6 in long and light trolling tackle   This was the second fish killed with a dace bait during the year, and in each case after fly and prawn had failed   Either three or four were killed the previous year with similar bait, the other two fish weighed respectively 11 lb and 19 lb   Mr Robinson sent to the office of *The Field* on September 7th, 1885, a small trout 6 in long, taken from the stomach of a female fresh-run grilse 6¼ lb weight, from Well Pool, Thurso river

† Mr C Pennell observed that "in the Spey, for instance, in Scotland, fish rise most freely and as freely take the fly almost in the tideway which comes up but a short distance   In the Wye, where the tide runs ten miles up, the fish do not take freely till they have run up seventy miles   Does this result from the fact that the Spey fish are never in muddy water? the sea and river being quite clean, and the bottom pebbly, whereas the fish come twenty miles up the muddy Severn and then have ten or more miles of muddy Wye besides to run up before they get to clean water   This may make them so sick that they do not recover before reaching the Hay in Breconshire, and only above that, seventy miles from the mouth, do they take freely" (*Badminton Series*, p 181)

While mud or dirt in rivers may occasion deleterious consequences to the fish owing to its containing injurious ingredients

The young par takes any bait with avidity, and at almost any time, even when the trout refuses to rise, while their stomachs are often found gorged with the larvæ of aquatic insects, even when the milt is exuding from the fish Mr Tegetmeier observed (*Proc Zool Soc* 1868) that the smolts which left the Stormontfields ponds in May that year were much larger than those of the previous season, due to their diet having been changed from boiled ox-liver rubbed down to coarse powder, for this season the aquatic weeds in the ponds had become covered with *Limnea ovata* var ,*peregra*, on which they fed greedily and to which the great increase in size was undoubtedly to be attributed.

The causes of destruction among these fishes may be disease, or consequent upon the modes of capture adopted by man or the lower animals, and can be divided into, (1) those consequent on the condition of the waters they inhabit, (2) atmospheric disturbances and accidents, (3) diseases, (4) misplaced energy in fishing or the work of poachers, and (5) injuries occasioned by the lower animals.

(1) Waters may be of such a directly poisonous character,* as to at once kill the fish in them, or be rendered mechanically unfit for their residence, as by the presence of mud which checks or even stops respiration at the gills   Or the water may be so polluted that the living food which ought to be present has been destroyed   The *Salmonidæ* will perish in waters wherein some fish will live, while possibly bull-heads *Cottus gobio*, gudgeons† *Gobio fluviatilis*, and loach *Nemacheilus barbatula*, will thrive where salmon would die   Also what would be poisonous to the fry may be faced with greater impunity by the old fish   Among the substances which have proved directly poisonous are the refuse of gas tanks, mine washings, chloride of lime, caustic potash, and the refuse from manufactories, paper mills, bleaching grounds, tanneries, or sewers   Also artificial root manure washed into rivers from cultivated fields, sheep dippings, and other destructive agencies   The more rapid the current, the more quickly are the poisons dispersed and diluted , consequently the less chance of their being immediately fatal to the fish, but they may be permanently injured thereby and possibly give rise to a debilitated offspring and infirm race (*see* p 27 *ante*)

(2) Atmospheric disturbances, accidents, and a great rise or a similar fall in the temperature may be destructive, thus a severe frost may freeze the redds wherein the eggs are deposited and destroy their vitality (p 35 *ante*), while too high a temperature is very fatal to the young   Electric disturbances may likewise

---

* "In Ireland, during July and August, brown salmon from the south coast are frequently poisoned and consigned to England for sale   any fish having white gills and white eyes are certainly poisoned fish and naturally unwholesome as food."—*Field*, July 19th, 1884

† I observed in *British and Irish Fishes*, p civ, that "when a river in India becomes unduly full of mud the crabs retire to the banks, and even the eels leave the stream for the wet grass in the vicinity   This attempt to escape from water loaded with ingredients inimical to life has likewise been observed among the invertebrate forms of Europe, as was some years since pointed out by M Geraldin, in France   A series of experiments and investigations showed that colour, taste, odour, or chemical composition cannot invariably be accepted as criteria of whether water is wholesome or the reverse, but that such must be looked for in its effect upon the animals and plants which reside in it   When fish died from river pollution it was observed that molluscs sometimes saved themselves by hiding under leaves and waiting there until the danger had passed away   thus, in July, 1869, *Limnea* remained five days out of the water.

Among plants, one of the most delicate was found to be the watercress, and it was remarked that when some deleterious substance from a starch factory obtained access to the Croult above the cress beds of Gonesse, all these plants died within a few hours ' the pollution removed, the cress-beds again flourished   Pond weeds and veronicas only live in water of good quality , mints, rushes, and water lilies, accommodate themselves to mediocre water , *Carex* is still less sensitive, and lastly, the most robust of water plants is a species of reed, *Arundo phragmites*, which resists the most infected water   Among molluscs, the *Physa fontinalis* lives only in very pure water, the *Valvata piscinalis* in that which is healthy, while others can reside in that which is of mediocre quality , no mollusc will live in what is thoroughly polluted   The phanerogamous or flowering plants thus sketch in distinct traits the character of different streams , but infusoria and cryptogams, and particularly algæ, may also enable one to judge in the matter by the modifications to which they are subject from alterations of the water   Those lower organisms survive after the disappearance of fish, of molluscs, and of green herbs."

be a cause of death among these fishes, thus, on July 3rd, 1866, several salmon in Scotland were reported to have been killed by lightning during the intensely hot weather which was then prevalent   Also thunderstorms may cause a rush of waters from roads, lanes and sewers, sweeping with it every kind of filth, without a sufficient flood in the river to carry it off   Dynamite employed for blowing up the remains of the Tay bridge destroyed fishes as far as a couple of miles away

(3) Diseases may directly attack these fish whether developing in the eggs, in the stage of infancy, or as they mature, while some may be badly developed occasioning monstrosities, or malformed consequent upon accident (p 41 *ante*) Space, however, will not permit an account of the numerous affections to which fishes are subject, especially the young (*see* p 46), from fungus to the many diseases of a contagious or non-contagious character   There are certain animal parasites which affect fish that may be chiefly divided into such as are internal or entozoa, and others that are external or epizoa, also infusoria and parasitic fungi   Entozoa* are very common, and one form (*Bothriocephalus*) is a common resident in the pyloric cæca of salmon   in fact, tapeworms would seem to be numerous, but most of these entozoa undergo transformation after changing their abode the final most frequently occurring in a water bird   Epizoa are likewise seen as small crustaceans, and those which are of most consequence to the salmon are of two classes; first, such as are more essentially surface forms, as fish lice, that are able to move from place to place by means of their hooked and prehensile antennæ, or even leave the fish and swim freely in the water   A parasite of this class, *Lepeophtheirus stromii*, Baird, belonging to the family Caliguilidæ, is found upon salmon when first arriving from the sea,† for they will only live in salt water, while by means of their foot jaws they adhere to the body, on which they are able to move about from one locality to another   They are most commonly found in the gill-cavity or inside the mouth, and they generally die soon after being removed from the water   Muller and Fabricius both supposed that these parasites lived upon the mucus secreted from the fish   The second class of these epizoa are more sedentary forms, belonging to the family Lerneopodidæ, and which frequently have their heads imbedded in their victims' bodies In fresh waters the gills, more especially of kelts, become attacked by a parasite, *Lerneopoda salmonea*, Linn , belonging to this family   Some imagine that it chiefly fixes itself to the *Salmonidæ* prior to spawning, while others believe that it mainly does so to kelts returning seawards   it dies from immersion in salt water

Parasitic fungi may also occur, and of late years one of a contagious and destructive character has been very virulent in our fresh waters, and epidemic since 1878   This is the *Saprolegnia ferax*, which has probably always been present‡ but requires a soil suitable for its germination and growth, and although some of the following are in certain places predisposing causes to this fatal complaint, still it has been observed where none such could have existed   Debility, however occasioned, seems to render these fishes susceptible to the disease, especially after injuries causing abrasions, as in kelts after the breeding season or having been netted, also unspent forms, but young fish may be also affected   Frosts, droughts, and polluted waters favour its extension while, possibly, were fewer kelts preserved and our rivers purer we should see less of the disease, especially where the currents are rapid   Rock salt has been found to be the best mode of treatment in fish ponds and aquaria ; and, while migrating to the sea would seem to arrest the fungus, it is not certain that it will not reappear on the salmon's return to the river Once this fungus has attacked a fish, it may become the nucleus from which infection spreads, and within twenty-four hours, thousands of zoospores, which

* Cooking fish infested with worms destroys the vitality of the latter, while they could not live in the human body
† It has been assumed, and, I believe, with reason, that when salmon are captured with parasitical *Caligi* upon them, they cannot have been long from the sea , still, so far as I know, experiments are still desirable to ascertain whether, if the fish came gradually into brackish and subsequently into fresh waters, these parasites would immediately succumb.
‡ It is mentioned in the Fish Commission Report, 1860, as existing epidemically in the Severn four or five years previously (pp 233, 234)

may be popularly termed minute germs or seeds provided with cilia, rendering them capable of spontaneous motion, may become diffused through the water These germs * arriving at a suitable spot develop into a fungus, and such a locality is found in any abraded spot on the body of a fish, where its roots strike downwards into the flesh and its free extremities come to the surface, forming the white fungus which has been aptly compared to the appearance of a piece of cotton-wool in water or a white furry spot, and is so destructive to fish suffering from this disease, consequent on exhaustion, irritation or suffocation when the respiratory organs are affected

(4) Misplaced energy in fishing, or the work of the poacher, is often very detrimental † to salmon fisheries, but is a subject which must be separately considered   While legislators ought to clearly understand that increased present productiveness may be carried on at the expense of future years' supply, and that multiplying modes of destruction does not invariably tend to the benefit of either the fisherman or the consumer, also that leaving merely young or undersized fish to continue their race is a potent means of fisheries deteriorating

(5) Injuries occasioned by the lower animals are numerous, and differ considerably in the adult stage from what they do among the ova and young   Along the sea coasts, in estuaries and the mouths of some rivers, porpoises, seals, grampusses and their allies commit great havoc among salmon and grilse   While in rivers especially, or spawning beds, otters are very destructive, but they are credited with destroying eels, which are very detrimental to these fisheries   Some also believe that they act serviceably by capturing weak and diseased fish as they come on to the shallows, in a debilitated condition, and so curtail the spread of disease, but on the other hand some hold that they prefer healthy to diseased forms Irrespective of mammals and birds which have been alluded to as detrimental to eggs and young fish (p 28 *ante*) there are some birds that likewise attack adult fish, as the great black-beaked gull, *Larus marinus*, which on account of its well-known partiality is termed a "salmon gull" by the fishermen, in the lower reaches of the Severn   This river falls with great rapidity, while owing to the shifting nature of its sands its course frequently alters and consequently it is not uncommon on falling tide for salmon to be left in a backwater   Now these gulls at once attack and kill them, commencing by picking out their victims' eyes with their powerful bills   Many forms of birds and fish will also eat the young salmon smolts, and at the mouths of some rivers, as that of the Tweed, so many are destroyed by the coal-fish, *Gadus virens*, termed "podles," that men are employed to destroy these members of the cod family as vermin ‡   Trout, as has already been observed, are

---

* Mr Murray experimented upon fish which were inhabiting aquaria at South Kensington, and suffering from *Saprolegnia ferax*, although the fungus was not present in the water supplied He found this fungus in some earthworms which had been obtained from outside the Museum, where the bones of fish which had died of this disease had been buried, and from which spot worms had twice been obtained to feed the aquatic animals in the tanks Mr Murray concluded that "the agreement thus established forces upon me the conclusion that the infectious material was obtained from the dead fish cast out that during the damp weather it remained alive in its resting state, and was spread about by earthworms, and that it was finally conveyed by them into the tanks where the outbreak took place "—*Annual Report of Inspector of Fisheries*

† On the other hand respecting this disease a correspondent of *Land and Water* remarked " In the good old days when ' waters' let at as many pounds as they now do hundreds of pounds when every man leistered and netted and burned and fished as suited his own pleasure when close time was unknown, and fish were killed on the spawning beds by thousands, there were twenty fish at least where there is now one " To this it was replied, that even supposing over-crowding were injurious, the cause of that overcrowding in some rivers cannot be due to over preservation , the number of salmon and grilse having steadily diminished in the Tweed from an annual average of 37,485 in five years, 1851 58, to 25,988 in the five years 1869-74

‡ It has been suggested that swans might be useful in salmon streams, or rather lakes, in order to devour the enormous masses of ova of perch and pike, and so diminish their predaceous foes "Nahanik," in *Land and Water*, September 20th, 1886, observed of the salmon, that " there was a river in that district, a tributary of the Shannon, famous for salmon and white trout   In my boyish days these fish were killed in every way   There were eel weirs on every ford, and, when the salmon and trout were running, they were caught in thousands at the weirs, or were speared by torchlight   Between 1840 and 1850 all the eel weirs were taken away by Act of Parliament, and afterwards all the salmon and white trout disappeared   I took a great deal of trouble

very destructive to salmon eggs, while salmon-kelts destroy trout, and eels have been accused of doing great injury *

Respecting the salmon fisheries of the British Isles no accurate statistics exist, and fancy seems occasionally to have filled in what facts were unable to demonstrate. The annual value of these fisheries has been estimated at the present time to be as follows:—England £100 000, Scotland £250,000, and Ireland £400 000. They are divisible into those of the fresh waters and such as are carried on in estuaries or in the sea. The *Commissioners appointed to inquire into the Salmon Fisheries of England and Wales* in 1860 stated that they "found the fisheries generally in a state of lamentable depression." While *Mr Willis-Bund*, in May, 1880, remarked, "There is no river in England and Wales where each rod fisherman on the present return catches a yearly average of ten salmon." Also it had been observed by Mr Eden, *Fortnightly Review*, Nov 1st, 1881, that taking nine rivers in 1880, those who had bred the fish took 1237, those who netted them 52,563. In the Severn, rods captured 15 fish and nets 16,000, including the estuary.

It has been questioned whether the amount of salmon in our rivers is really much less than was formerly the case. It can be shown that they have been exterminated from the Stour, the Itchen, the Medway, the Avon, and the Thames† in England. In Scotland, the Fifeshire Leven no longer contains salmon, in the Tay district the Almond, Eucht and Dighty are ruined from pollutions, and many other rivers are greatly injured. Mr Blake, in 1874, writing of his Irish district, extending from Wicklow Head to Rossan Point, stated that due to pollutions nearly every river in the County Down had been destroyed as a salmon producer. While stopping pollutions has been found so difficult and expensive, that the polluters appear to have it all then own way.

Although many authors have of late years held that the widely-spread belief that laws formerly existed prohibiting giving salmon to servants or apprentices more than three times a week was a popular fallacy, it seems more probable that it is the recent authors themselves who are in error.† What the reasons may

---

in preserving that river from 1860 to 1880, and some salmon came back to it, but the white trout never. It was full of brown trout, and, in the autumn, of the big lake trout, but the salmon and white trout, that it used to be famous for before "the bad times" (1848 to 1854) never came back. The head waters of these rivers were quite changed in the draining works about that time, and some say this was the reason. This I would believe, but that elsewhere in Ireland there has been a similar failure on rivers where there have not been any drainage works. Taking away the eel weirs I suspect must be detrimental to the salmon and white trout, as there are no greater destroyers than the eels."

* The returns of the number of boxes of British and Irish salmon, averaging 112 lb. each, sent to Billingsgate Market, give the following results for the last ten years:—

	1876	1877	1878	1879	1880	1881	1882	1883	1884	1885
English and Welsh	1508	1608	1224	1908	2028	1890	2186	2271	1600	1897
Scotch	23,615	29,366	27,060	15,564	17,157	23,903	22,968	34,506	27,219	90,302
Irish	7064	6373	4273	5762	9669	10,633	4720	9033	5979	8375

† Captain Richard Franks, in his *Northern Memoirs*, edition 1821, p 133, writing of Stirling in 1658, remarked that 'burgomasters, as in many other parts of Scotland, are compelled to reinforce an ancient statute, that commands all masters and others not to force or compel any servant or an apprentice to feed upon salmon more than thrice a week." At Inverness a century later Burt tells us (*Letters from the North of Scotland*, 1754) salmon which sold at one penny a pound 'was by a late regulation of the magistrates raised to twopence a pound, which is thought by many to be an exorbitant price" (p 121), "the meanest servants, who are not at board wages, will not make a meal upon salmon if they can get anything else to eat" (p 129)—mutton and beef were then about one penny a pound. Sir Walter Scott (*Old Mortality*, 1816) stated, "At that period (1679), salmon was caught in such plenty in the considerable rivers of Scotland that instead of being accounted a delicacy, it was generally applied to feed the servants who are said sometimes to have stipulated that they should not be requested to eat a food so luscious and surfeiting in its quality over five times a week" (cap viii).

In *Notes and Queries* for May, 1857, the following quotation was given from Consell's *History of Gloucester*:—"It was a standing condition of apprenticeship that the apprentice should not be obliged to eat salmon more than thrice a week, the object being to render him less liable to the leprosy, which after the crusades in the Middle Ages was a formidable disease, that was supposed to be brought on or aggravated by the eating of fish." In a *History of Worcester* (1808, p 48), the existence of this proviso was asserted as a well known fact. The late Thomas Bewick, the great wood engraver, in a letter dated April 26th, 1821, wrote as follows to Mr Pease, banker,

have been, whether salted fish were referred to as has been supposed, or whether this prohibition was introduced after the Crusades, because badly salted fish predisposes to leprosy (as it most undoubtedly does), we have now but little evidence to fall back upon   It has also been advanced that this regulation may have been for the purpose of preventing masters giving their apprentices "kelts" as food, which are readily captured after spawning and might have been salted down   This seems very unlikely, for if kelts were prohibited by British Legislators from being used by the rebellious Irish for food so early as 1645,* it is

at Newcastle-on-Tyne, "when a boy, from about the year 1760 to 1767, I was frequently sent by my parents to the fishermen at Eltringham Ford to purchase a salmon   I was always told not to pay twopence a pound, and I commonly paid only a penny, and sometimes three halfpence, before or perhaps about this time   I have been told that an article had been always inserted in every indenture of apprenticeship in Newcastle that the apprentices were not to be forced to eat salmon above twice a week, and the same bargain was made with common servants "

I may here allude to the evidence of Mr Little on this point, given to the *Parliamentary Committee*, in 1824 , he remarked, " I have been told, from mqun ing of people with respect to the fishings in the Severn, that the salmon were formerly very abundant all along the Bristol Channel —so much so that in the apprentices' indentures it was a clause that they should not be fed with salmon more than two days in the week " (p 134)

Murdo Mackenzie, 1860, in *Salmon Fisheries of Scotland*, p 6, also remarked that " servants of farmers used to stipulate with their masters that they should not be obliged to eat salmon except on a certain number of days in the week "

In the *Report of the Salmon Commission*, 1860, it was observed, " We heard also in every locality that we visited that it was in former times a condition commonly made in indentures of apprenticeship that the apprentice should not be obliged to dine on salmon more than twice or three times a week   We endeavoured to obtain a sight of one of these instruments but without success, though we met with persons who stated they had seen them, and the universal prevalence of the tradition seems to justify belief in it " (p vi)

Mr Partridge, J P , when giving evidence before the *Commissioners appointed to inquire into Salmon Fisheries* in 1860, observed " that in all the indentures of apprenticeship of the period there was a stipulation that the apprentices should not eat fish more than so many times a week You will find that in the Hereford charter and in many other places" (p 41)

In M'Culloch's *Dictionary of Commerce*, 1869, we read that " within the memory of many now living, salted salmon formed a material article of household economy in all the farmhouses in the Vale of Tweed, inasmuch that indoor servants used to stipulate that they should not be obliged to take more than two weekly meals of salmon   What is true of Tweedside might also be so of any other salmon-producing district , and I have just heard, on the authority of a lady lately residing near Nairn, that similar stipulations were made in her father's house in that neighbourhood within her own recollection   Although such agreements were, in the case of domestic servants, probably never committed to writing, and perhaps rarely even in that of articles of apprenticeship, it seems not improbable that a custom apparently so common might be incidentally referred to in the correspondence of that period   An examination of the rich collection at Dunrobin Castle has as yet, however, furnished no evidence, save indirectly, in connection with the cheapness of the commodity in question, which seems to have been occasionally sold at less than a penny a pound "

In Kidd's *Companion to Southampton and the Isle of Wight*, it is observed, " Formerly the salmon fishery was carried on here (Southampton) with much success, and a few of them are still occasionally taken   So abundant was the supply that farm servants and apprentices used to stipulate with their masters that they should not have salmon for dinner more than twice a week "

A gentleman writing to me from *France* in 1884 observed, " The story of the apprentice not being compelled to eat salmon more than thrice a week I found current on both the Rhine and the Elbe, showing that the decrease of salmon is general "

I have also been informed by a German lady that in and near the towns of Schlawe and Stolpe, in *Eastern Pomerania*, situated not far from the sea and on the banks of the rivers Stolpe and Wipper, servants of both sexes at the annual hiring before 1850 invariably stipulated that they should not have meals of salmon more than three times a week   This fish was served to them fresh and very rarely cured   But by the year 1854 this stipulation began to be no longer observed, as the price had risen to 5d per pound, flounders to four a penny, and herrings to from six to twelve for a 1½d   Prices after this rapidly increased, salmon rising to 8d a pound, and flounders to two for 1½d   About 1860 a disease broke out among the fishes along the coast, proving very fatal to salmon and flounders. About this period the Government stopped all sea fishing for four seasons, or two years, consequently the only fish in the markets were those from inland lakes   Salmon since 1860 have risen to such prices that they are out of the reach of any but the richer classes, having become a luxury, while their size has much decreased   From 1866, due to the diminution in the number of these fish, their capture has become a lottery, and the Jews have contracted with the fishermen for their takes, which they smoke, pickle, or otherwise cure, and now their very entrails fetch from 2d to 3d a fish

* *See page 98 ante.*

8

improbable they would have permitted masters in England feeding their servants upon them   That such prohibitions were not unknown in other countries can be demonstrated, thus in Western Pomerania on the river Oder and its affluents, the monastic accounts show that a regulation was in force prohibiting salmon being given as food more than three days in a week (*Gadow*)

As regards the price of salmon we are told that about A D 1754 it was raised at Stirling from one penny to twopence a pound, while mutton and beef could be obtained at a penny a pound   *Burt* (p 129) also observed, 1751, that " a Highland gentleman who went to London by sea, soon after his landing passed by a tavern where the larder appeared to the street, and operated so strongly upon his appetite that he went in   That there were among other things a rump of beef and some salmon   of the beef he ordered a steak for himself, ' but,' says he, ' let Duncan have some salmon '   To be short, the cook who attended him humoured the jest and the master's eating was 8*d* and Duncan's came to almost as many shillings "   In a petition from the inhabitants near the Eden in 1805 it was stated that the cost of fish from the Solway, owing to the destruction of the breed of salmon and the monopoly of two persons, had augmented the cost from 3*d*, 2*d* and 1½*d* to 1*s*, 1*s* 6*d* and 2*s* a pound

But there are many disturbing circumstances which render it difficult to compare the price charged a century ago to what obtains at the present time,* thus consequent upon temporary large hauls a local superabundance of salmon must have occurred along the banks of some of our best fishing streams   For want of carriage would have prevented their being distributed throughout the country in ways now practicable by steamers, railways, improved roads, better methods of conveyance, and the employment of ice in packing fish

Thus in or near seaports, as Berwick, Pennant, writing in 1776, informs us that the Tweed fish were sent fresh to London in baskets by sailing vessels, unless the craft was disappointed by contrary winds, when they were relanded, boiled, pickled, and kitted and so dispatched, while other fresh ones replaced them in the baskets   At the commencement of the season, *when a ship was on the point of sailing*, a fresh, clean salmon would sell from 1*s* to 1*s* 6*d* a pound, and the price at such periods was from 5*s* to 9*s* a stone of 18 lb 10½ oz weight, but the value rose and fell according to the plenty or paucity of fish and the prospect of a fair or a foul wind   In the month of July, when they were said to be most plentiful, the cost has been known to be as low as 8*d* per stone, but in 1775 never less than 1*s* 4*d* and from that to 2*s* 6*d*   While to pay the expenses of the Tweed salmon fisheries Pennant estimated it would be necessary to capture 208,000 fish annually

Mr Little in his evidence before the *Salmon Commissioners* in 1821 (p 107) stated respecting the Moy fishery at Balhna in Ireland that the population were hostile because ' before we exported the salmon to England from these fisheries they got their salmon very low, probably not more than ¾*d* or 1*d* a pound   Now that we export them to England a salmon cannot be got there at these prices Locally in the spring months we generally obtain 10*d* a pound   that is during the months of February, March, and April   In other months about 6*d*, say June, July and August   Some we sell as low as 3*d*.   At some of the stations which are away from our ice-houses we cannot get so much for them "   In 1860 the *Salmon Commissioners* reported " it was stated, and we do not doubt the assertion, that salmon was sold fifty years ago in some of the towns in Wales or in Devonshire at 1*d*, 2*d* and 1½*d* a pound   The depreciation in the *rentals* of salmon

---

* Mr Russel wrote as follows :—" There is a fallacy in measuring the difference between former abundance and present scarcity by statements like this or comparisons between past and present prices   Some people seem to forget that even since the least old of the old times with which comparison has generally been made, the number of mouths has at least trebled, and that consequently, even if this represented, as it does not, the whole increase of consumers, there would necessarily be a comparative scarcity, unless the fish had trebled too   But the months have not only trebled, they are incomparably more easily reached   In the old times though there was a glut at Berwick and Perth there might be a dearth at London, and probably an entire destitution at Nottingham and Derby '

fisheries in England and Wales had been great and general and this in the face of a large increase of price and a greatly extended market"

Up to nearly the end of the last century the amount of salmon captured in Scotland was in excess of the local demands for fresh fish, and the surplus was boiled and salted, or kitted, but as the price of salt fish was low there was little or no inducement for over fishing   Mr Mackenzie observed that in many rivers the fishing was over by the end of May, although in some of the later rivers it continued a little longer, but the salmon vats being by this time generally full, and the grilses were deemed of such little importance that one-half of them were not destroyed   About 1780 a Scotch laird, Mr George Dempster of Dunichen, discovered that salmon packed in ice could be conveyed in good condition for long distances, which entirely changed the condition of affairs, for it enhanced the price of the fish by enabling it to be exported to London and other large markets   As a natural consequence this, by enhancing their value, stimulated captures, and from that period some authors, and with a good show of reason, date the decline of the Scotch salmon fisheries   For the inducement to take them became comparatively excessive and their extinction was almost threatened, for more killing modes of capture were brought into use   Stake-nets were introduced from the Solway to the Tay and subsequently to other Scottish friths, increased captures were heralded as owing to augmented productiveness, the estuary and sea-shore fishermen proclaimed that the supply of fish in the sea was inexhaustible, and the public (always ready to listen to those who are bearers of what can be considered as good news) were beguiled   It was useless that the proprietors of the river fisheries asserted that the supply of salmon was really limited, it was of no avail that they pointed out that over-fishing was going on along the sea-shore and in the estuaries, for no one listened to their statements, while the shore and estuary net fishermen boldly questioned the accuracy of their facts   The public did not understand that there was not much positive increase in the quantity of salmon taken, but more a transference of the captures from the river proprietors by whom they had been reared and to whose district they were returning, to the estuary and shore fishermen   As the produce began to decline these latter at once accused the river proprietors of destroying breeding fishes and their fry, while they denied that their own fixed engines could be the cause of the deterioration so apparent to all

Space will not permit my investigating the condition of each river and how in some the very race of these fishes has been annihilated *   Still, a few remarks will be necessary in order to demonstrate how this destruction in some of our finest salmon fisheries has come to pass   For the purpose of minutely inquiring into the condition of a salmon river in relationship to what formerly existed many circumstances have to be taken into consideration, especially the modes in which it is fished both in and near its mouth, as well as throughout its fresh-water course   What natural or artificial obstructions are present, and whether such

---

* Professor Brown-Goode, *Great International Fisheries Exhibition*, 1883, pp 27, 28, remarked, "Up to 1798 large numbers of salmon were caught in the Connecticut river, but from 1870 the fish disappeared entirely from the river, and until about 1875 no salmon whatever were seen   In 1875, however, the salmon began to appear, and this was the direct result of the planting of a large number of eggs in that river three or four years previously"   If we look at the returns from such salmon rivers as the Sacramento we find the following in the *United States Fishery Reports* for 1877, pp 801, 802   "Although the salmon are increasing in the Sacramento, it is nevertheless true, that the yearly supply of young fish comes mainly from the hatching station on the McCloud river, and that consequently that supply must be kept up   If this is neglected the Sacramento will be depleted of salmon"   "So great has been the benefit of this restocking the Sacramento," it is observed in the *Bulletin of the United States Fish Commission*, 1882, ii p 232, "that the statistics of the salmon fisheries show that the annual catch of the river has increased 5,000,000 lb during the last few years"   And Brown Goode l c observed that the catch had increased in five years, from 5,000,000 lb, to 15,000,000 lb, and in 1881 there were more than could be utilized by all the canning establishments on the river   Passing over a few years we read thus in the *Sacramento Union* August 2nd, 1884   "The salmon run in the Sacramento river has decreased until it has proved disastrous to canneries and fishermen   It promises to become extinct   In this dilemma the fishermen threaten to violate the close season and defy the law   Sea-lions are said to destroy many young salmon, and the hatching on the McCloud river is stopped"

could be removed or modified   if the water is polluted   any question affecting the breeding of the fish or the diseases they suffer from, in short, their enemies and their friends in the widest acceptation of these terms   For there is a great difference as to the result of killing these fish when in various conditions, thus a fresh-run clean salmon may be one whose capture is desirable for supplying the market during certain seasons of the year   In short, the destruction of one which has spawned means simply the death of an individual fish, but the killing of one about to spawn is equivalent to the destruction of what may be termed an entire family

It has been the almost invariable rule wherever there existed a market for the sale of salmon that whenever these fish from any cause began to increase in numbers so have the engines for their destruction, and the higher the price of the article the greater becomes the inducement for their capture   Fishermen as a rule mostly act on the maxim to catch all they can, for were they not to do so their neighbours would, while they are very regardless of how future years' supply is to be maintained   The consequences may be seen, as already stated, that these fish are now absent from the Thames,* Medway, and some of our other rivers (*see* p 2 *ante*)

* As regards the salmon fisheries of the *Thames* which were formerly esteemed among the most celebrated in the kingdom, but are now extinct, we find numerous facts detailed   We are informed that for several centuries a tithe of Thames salmon had been claimed and allowed to the Abbot of St Peter's at Westminster, on the plea that when St Peter (according to the legend) came and consecrated that church, he promised the fishermen who ferried him across the river a plentiful supply of fish provided he ceased fishing on Sundays and gave a tithe of his captures to the Abbot   This was paid until 1382 and then stopped, and which is said to be doubtless the reason why salmon have now disappeared from this river   Mr Hepworth Dixon, in a paper on the *Tower of London*, observed that, "One of the points which king John had been forced to surrender to his people was a claim, on the part of his Tower warden, to catch fish in the Thames improperly, by placing kidels in the stream   For three or four reigns, the great kidel question was our chief domestic topic, agitating Essex, Kent, and Middlesex, especially the river side taverns, leading to endless orders in council, and many disorders in the streets   A kidel was a weir, fitted up with nets, in fact, a dishonest fish trap   The king's people not only set their own kidels in the Thames, but sold their rights of dishonest fishing to others, so as to interfere with the legitimate trade, to destroy the salmon and shad, and to diminish poorer people's food   Lionheart tried to settle this kidel dispute   In the eighth year of his reign, being pressed by his wars, he made a merit of giving up his right of kideling the Thames, enacting—as the grant expresses it—that, for the salvation of his soul, for the salvation of his father's soul, for the salvation of the souls of all his ancestors, as well as for the good of his realm, there shall be no more kidels   I am sorry to say his royal word was not kept, and it is to be hoped that the souls of these pious kings do not suffer for his servant's fault   Even after the Great Charter had been sworn, the Tower wardens put kidels into the river, and you may read, in the 'Liber Albus,' that they long continued to vex the fishmongers, not only by taking salmon unfairly from the water, but by seizing on any stray waggons of oysters, mussels, red herrings, and smelts, which they found coming into London overland "

A petition to Edward III (between 1327 and 1377) concluded, "Awaiting which, most redoubtable Lord, if it shall please your Highness thus to make order for the next three years, all your people repairing to London or bordering the river, shall buy as good a salmon for two shillings as they now get for ten "   Mr Lovegrove gave the *Commissioners in 1860*, a list of the salmon captured in the Thames at Boulters Loch and Pool from 1794 to 1821, two having been taken in this last year, but none in 1820   The total numbers of fish for those years inclusive were 483, weight 7316½ lb   Also at p 75 of the *Inspectors of Salmon Fisheries' Report for 1879*, may be found the following —About 1820 a salmon of 20 lb weight was caught by a fisherman named Finmore   It was taken in a deep hole near Surly Hall, just above Windsor   This was sold to the king for a guinea a pound, who then resided at Virginia Water   A salmon was wanted in 1821 for the coronation of king George IV, and 30s per pound was offered   No salmon could be caught in time for the dinner, but the day after two were caught between Blackwall and Woolwich Reaches "   In 1830 Mr Gould stated one was caught at Monkey Island bank by Mr Wilder

In the *Field*, May 23rd 1885, it was remarked—"1860, in which year the occurrence of a salmon in the lower part of the Thames was reported in the press, and following the report was the announcement that the fish was the first that had been seen in the river for twenty years   The *Morning Chronicle* corrected this supposition by stating that a salmon had been caught in 1859   Then it was urged by enthusiasts that salmon were once more coming back to the Thames   It seemed certain that one was caught, though not more than one, in each of the years 1861 and 1862   The Thames Angling Preservation Society, taking the matter in hand, in 1862 hatched their first salmon turning in several thousand fry   In 1863 two smolts were declared to have been caught off Southend at the confluence of the Thames and the Medway, and Mr Buckland, with

For the season 1883-1884 the following comparative return of the salmon caught in nineteen fishery districts in England and Wales was given in the *Twenty-fourth Annual Report of the Inspector of Fisheries*, but in the Twenty-fifth Annual Report these returns were omitted   West Cumberland, 619 ,* Ribble,†

the hopeful confidence that characterised his nature, at once came to the conclusion that they were part of the lot hatched in the previous year   In the same summer a salmon of 5 lb   was caught in the Darenth, which, as our readers know, is one of the lower tributaries of the Thames   In 1864 another consignment of young salmon, to the number of 7000, was turned into the Thames, and in April of that year a fish of 14½ lb was caught in the Medway, where there had been no salmon hatching   In May, 1864, another fish of 12½ lb was caught off Southend   The enthusiasts were again to the fore with their declarations of faith in the salmon-breeding certainties of the Thames "

In Martin's *Natural History of England*, 1785, it was stated of the now polluted and salmonless *Mersey* that it "greatly abounds with salmon, which in spring strive to ascend the arm of the sea, and with difficulty evade the nets of the fishermen before they reach Warrington Bridge, where the river becomes narrower , and the landowners having an exclusive right, each proprietor by his agents, catches salmon, amounting annually to upwards of a thousand pounds   By their capture the towns of Warrington, Manchester, and Stockport are well supplied , and the overplus is either sent to London by the stages, or carried on horseback to Birmingham, and other inland towns "

* In the *Report of the Salmon Commission* in 1860 we are told that half nets were used in the estuary of the *Solway* in the time of Queen Elizabeth, and subsequently a still or fixed engine was employed at Kings Garth where it was a complete barrier to the river   The rent at this spot was £15 between 1706 1718, progressing till 1730 when it was £300, by 1763 it had risen to £597, and continued rising until 1781, when it reached £800   But in May, 1791, this still net was declared illegal, and there do not seem to be subsequent records of this fishing until 1801-1814, when the rent was £32, and rose to £52, and in 1860 it was let at £157 10s   But soon after the commencement of this century traps were invented and placed on the English side of the Solway, being copies of some on the Scottish shore   In fact, so few fish ascended the river that the upper riparian proprietors took to killing the whitlings and very young salmon, asserting that they had now no interest in preserving these fish   By 1811 the captures had decreased one half along the estuary

† The *Ribble* is a very late river, especially when easterly winds prevail, and but few clean fish were reported in 1860 to be taken before May, while those captured during the first week in September in the nets at Walton-le-Dale were full of spawn and said to be utterly unfit for food   In this fishery in 1834, 214 fish were secured, their average weight being 7 65 lb   After a few years, owing to an increased length of the close season, decreased hours of fishing, and never retaining any fish under 6 lb weight, the average rose to 9 70 lb   a fish, and in 1859, 412 were taken   In the *Tees*, about 1830, stake nets were introduced and the fisheries at once commenced to deteriorate   Respecting the fisheries in the *Wear*, which is an early river, the Surtees Society published some records from the archives of two monastic bodies, the Convent of Durham and the Priory of Finchdale   At the latter were twenty-nine monks who disposed of the surplus of their fishery   in 1348 they sold salmon to the amount of £9 12s 8d, and to compare their value with other articles, it is mentioned that they had purchased a bull and two cows for £1 12s   In 1385 their receipts from the Finchdale fishery were £11 2s 1d, and in 1388, £12 5s 4d, in 1137, £5, in 1438, £16, and in 1439, £39 6s 8d

The Convent of Durham in 1532 bought 252 fresh salmon, and in 1552, 306, they purchased every month except January   They gave in the first of these years 6s to 8s a dozen for salmon, either salted or fresh, 2d for each grilse, and 1d for every trout   Also in 1536 they bought in addition to what they obtained from their fisheries, 756 salmon, and 24 grilses, a good deal of which came from the Tyne

Pennant in July, 1775, observed (*Tour in Scotland*, i p 40) of this river at Durham, "The common rents of those (fisheries) are £50 a year, for which the tenants have as much shore as serves to launch out and draw then nets on shore   the limits of each are staked   and I observed that the fishers never failed going as near as possible to his neighbour's limits   One man goes off in a small flat-bottomed boat, square at one end, and taking as large a circuit as his net admits, brings it on shore at the extremity of his boundary where others assist in landing it "   He continued, that "in the middle of the river, not a mile west of the town, is a large stone on which a man is placed to observe what is called the 'reck' of the salmon coming up "   The Dean and Chapter obtained £450 for rent and tithe, this would require nearly 13,500 fish at 8s a dozen simply to pay for   In 1860 it was stated that the Wear was now so denuded of salmon that it was doubtful whether any existed there, while in 1884 it was reported to be almost destitute of fish consequent upon pollutions, and since then the Local Board have omitted to send further returns

In the *Coquet*, which has been said to be a late river, in 1860, the lessee of the fisheries being asked as to what is the earliest date at which salmon comes up this river, replied, "No salmon come up at all   we only caught four salmon during the whole summer, and two of them were caught in April "   He added that they do not spawn in the Coquet, and the lessee of the sea fishery likewise asserted that trout, not salmon, ascended this river (*see* p 67 *ante*)

In the *Tyne*, which is an early river, fixed engines for the capture of salmon were introduced

4054, Clwyd and Elwy, 2400, Conway, by rod, 118, Seiont, 1129, Cleddy, by rod, 250, Usk, by rod, 825, Severn, 20,000, Avon, Brue, and Parrett, 600, Avon and Erme, excluding nets, 116, Teign, 1020, Exe, by rod, 265, Avon and Stour, 1515, Trent, 3150, Yorkshire, 3237, Esk (Yorkshire), 5940, Tyne, 21,286

about 1838-39, and at once the produce of the fishery began to decline, so they were abolished in 1842 by an Act of Parliament within a distance of 4½ miles on each side of the mouth of the river. But the killing "hang-net" now came into use, and stake-nets were fixed beyond the 4½-mile limit. In the river were destructive mill dams and fishing weirs, and the one nearest the mouth of the river at Bywell was most disastrous to the fisheries, but in 1862 a flood carried away a portion of this weir which was not subsequently restored. Fish being able to pass this obstruction had now twelve miles of good water and other valuable breeding grounds. Other weirs were now altered or abolished, and in 1867 it was stated that there had "been a very large increase of salmon caught both by rod and net." It was currently reported and believed that as much as £700 worth had been caught in one flood, which was unprecedented." In 1884 it was suggested as quite possible that the pollutions poured into the mouth of this river being in a more than usually concentrated form owing to the absence of floods, may have had the effect of keeping the fish further away from the most productive fishing grounds near the mouth of the river. The computed annual takes were thus estimated, 1880, 27,406 salmon, 1881, 30,098 salmon, and it was agreed that it was of no further use going to the expense of collecting statistics. In the *Annual Report of the Inspector of Fisheries* we are told that in 1883, 32,566 salmon were taken, and in 1884, 21,286.

The Chester *Dee* is a medium river, few clean run fish being obtained until March or April, while it has every natural advantage of being an excellent salmon stream were it not for the incessant netting and poaching which is carried on. The laws enacted in 1861 resulted in a slight improvement by protection, but this was soon neutralized by an undue employment of destructive implements of capture in the lower waters. It was only in 1878 that trammel nets were legalized which was done because as their employment could not be stopped, the conservators deemed it better to obtain a revenue from them to assist in protecting the river. In 1866 47 draft nets paid for licenses, in 1882-84 there were 63, in 1884, 85, and in 1885, 96. But the licensed trammel-nets had only averaged from seven to eight. The following is the report of this river for 1885, that "the draft-nets have doubled in number in four years, that the profits of the fishermen have decreased that few fish escape them during the fishing season, that the upper proprietors, on whom the preservation of the spawning beds must always in a great measure depend, have become dissatisfied and disheartened, and that, whether the actual decrease of the last years is permanent or not, the stock of fish in the river fails to improve." In the evidence before the Commissioners in 1860, it was stated that during the last fortnight of August there are fish which are not fit to expose in the shops. Respecting the canal, Mr Horsfall observed, "In my opinion there are fry going down every month" (No 8265). While in 1884 it was reported that smolts "had been taken as late as September or October." The average annual captures by nets in three years, ending 1883, were recorded as 11,615, the least being 10,935 in 1882, and the most 12,500 in 1881.

The *Severn* is an early river, and in 1860 complaints were made that subsequent to the erection of the weirs at Worcester and other places the fish had found their ascent more difficult. Shad and flounders had almost ceased ascending to the upper waters, lampreys had been entirely stopped, and the common eels had considerably diminished in numbers; that grayling, which had been abundant up to 1856 likewise had nearly disappeared. A few fine clean run salmon ascend in January and February, while after the middle of May "there are plenty of samlets but no salmon-fly." At Gloucester, one witness considered that clean run fish are shyer in ascending weirs than gravid ones, and consequently do not so persistently push up. Mr W Vmer Ellis observed that, "in 1792, which was a remarkable year, in one week, from 29th of January to the 5th of February, it is on record with us that in four fisheries we caught 292 new fish, weighing 1583 lb." The number of salmon reported as taken in the river for the five years ending 1864 gave the annual average of 30,300 fish, the smallest number being 15,500 in 1882, and the largest 30,000 in 1883. It would seem from the recorded figures that occasionally a good year for capturing salmon is followed by two or three seasons' decline in the takes, while it is sometimes the case that for one or two years prior to a large harvest being secured there have been augmented captures.

The *Wye* is likewise an early river, and, as regards young salmon, we are told in the *Report of the Commission* in 1860, that people were fishing for shillings that very day, while the chairman, on September 20th (Question 2670), asked "Are you confusing the term 'lastspring' to the fish that are going to the sea in the spring, or do you include in it the 'lastspring' that are in the river just now?" Mr J Staunton replied to Question No 2690 on September 20th "I would almost engage to catch 9 lb or 10 lb of lastsprings any day at this particular season, when the water is low" in the small tributaries.

The *Usk* is rather a late river, clean fish are found high up about the beginning or middle of April. In 1860 evidence was adduced that the chief spawning period was from the end of November to the middle of January, that the first great run of breeding fish up the river was in July or August and early in September, that every October there was a heavy run of fish, and that an occasional fish breeds as early as October. Mr Stretton also observed that skirlings or salmon fry were killed "all the way down the river in the spring and later on in the summer."

From early times laws have been enacted in order to prevent the extermination of these fishes, whether from immoderate capture, or to secure a free passage for breeding salmon from the sea to their spawning beds, and a safe descent when unfit for food or too small for consumption, as well as to obviate other deleterious agencies   It has also been found necessary to prohibit each individual proprietor from increasing the efficacy of his methods of capture to the injury of his neighbour or that of the general interest   For rivers only hold a supply to a limited amount, and should a disproportionate capture be made at one spot, this unduly diminishes the share which would otherwise accrue to the owners of fisheries in the upper waters   It has consequently been decided (in theory) that each fishery is merely entitled to its share of the general supply

In legislation there are two main objects to be considered, first that it is necessary in order to prevent the depopulation of our rivers to regulate captures and diminish obstructions in its lower reaches and the contiguous seas, as well as to prohibit pollutions   And, secondly that it is merely in the upper waters and affluents that improvement can be carried out by assisting the breeding of these fishes in every necessary way, and giving them rest during the spawning season as well as by protecting their eggs and young

It is evident that the habits of a salmon compel it to live when in fresh water in a locality where man is able to secure it, or else it has to annually pass through some narrow channel which is capable of being commanded by the fisherman

If salmon rivers are fully stocked, which no English ones are, it would of course be useless to try and augment the number of fish in it, for even if fairly treated they must remain stationary, and will need protection, because as population grows their value as food augments, thus increasing the inducement for their capture and sale   When destruction passes certain limits, tending to rapacity, scarcity sets in owing to the fish being unable to reproduce as rapidly as they are captured

In salmon fisheries there are at least three forces at work   (1) the riparian proprietor who lets them for rent, and sometimes endeavours to realize all he can by them, (2) Fishermen who hire them or ply their occupation in waters that are free, their purpose being to capture all they are able, (3) Fish Commissioners who, if they were competent and did their duty, should be the advocates of the fish to preserve them from undue destruction, and assist in their due propagation in order that the greatest benefits for the community could be obtained from the waters

One peculiarity of the English laws relating to the rights of proprietorship in salmon appears to be that in the sea and in tidal rivers the public have a general right to fish for them (unless some private right overrules the general one), while in such rivers as are not navigable this right is, as a rule, vested in the proprietors along either banks of the stream, but which may from some cause, as by purchase, have become alienated from the owner of the neighbouring land

The many phases through which salmon legislation in the British Isles has passed would require volumes for its full and clear explanation   At first, the primary consideration appears to have been the good of the fisheries, and devices injuriously affecting them were in the earliest periods of English law reprobated as public nuisances   Especial attention was drawn in Magna Charta, A D 1215, to how the Crown had attempted to disregard these laws, and permitted certain

(1752)   The annual average of salmon taken in the Usk from 1871 to 1884 inclusive, and which was effected solely by rods, was 1562, the smallest number being 566 in 1876, and the largest 3556 in 1879

As regards the rivers along the Southern coast, the majority, as has been already referred to, are generally late , but it is remarkable, in the evidence adduced in 1860, what fishermen then considered to be a clean fish, for some believed they might be so up to within a week of spawning Mr Buckland gave a list of the salmon captured in the public waters of the Hampshire rivers, Avon and Stour, commencing prior to the passing of the Act of 1861   It was as follows —
1860, 40 fish , 1861, 70 fish , 1862, 80 fish , 1863, 360 fish , 1864, 380 fish , 1865, 430 fish, averaging 14 lb each , 1866, 460 fish, averaging 11¾ lb , 1867, 317 fish, averaging 12½ lb , 1868, 75 fish, averaging 9½ lb , 1869, 652 fish, averaging 9½ lb , 1870, 873 fish, averaging 12½ lb , 1871, 549 fish, averaging 12¾ lb , 1872, 364 fish, averaging 12 lb , and 1873, 344 fish, averaging 12 lb each

individuals to set up cruives or weirs, and it was enacted that "all weirs from henceforth shall be utterly put down by Thames and Medway, and through all England, except the sea-coast "* What this exception referred to is now a mystery, as no fixed engines existed along the sea-coast in those times It, however, shows that salmon fisheries as early as the time of Magna Charta were being legislated for and protected as property We find especial enactments subsequently in the English statutes respecting allowing salmon a close time The 13th Edward IV, cap 47 (? 1474), prohibited the taking of these fish from Nativity of Our Lady (September 8th), until St Martin's Day (November 12th) in the Humber, Ouse, Trent, Done, Arre, Derwent, Wharfe, Nid, Yore, Swale and Tees

Passing over numerous subsequent Acts and how they were more or less evaded, we find respecting weirs the following decision given at the commencement of this century. The Lord Chief Justice Ellenborough in a judgment (Weld v Hornby, 7 East's Reports, p 195) proceeded to say, "The erection of weirs across rivers was reprobated in the earliest periods of our law They were considered as public nuisances " "This was followed up by subsequent Acts, treating them as public nuisances, forbidding the erection of new ones, and the enhancing, straightening, and enlarging of those which had aforetime existed "

"And, however, twenty years of acquiescence may bind parties whose private rights only are affected, yet the public have an interest in the suppression of public nuisances though of longer standing "

Subsequent to the *Report of the Commission appointed to inquire into the Salmon Fisheries of England and Wales* in 1860,† and of which Sir W Jardine was president,‡ the Act of 1861 was passed which repealed the twenty-one existing Acts and became the foundation of our present laws In it polluting and poisoning rivers and the use of lights and spears for assisting in capturing salmon, the employment of small meshed nets§ and new fixed engines in the capture of

---

* "*Omnes kidelli* deponantur de cetero penitus per Tamisiam et Medwayan et per totam Angliam, nisi per costeram maris " (*See* 9 Henry III, c 23, when confirming Magna Charta) This has been held (Lord Leconfield v Lord Lonsdale) to have been enacted for securing a free waterway, and that the protection of fisheries was merely an afterthought brought up in 1472 "A *kiddle* or *kidel*, a dam in a river to catch fish " (Bailey, *Etymological English Dictionary*, 1747) Halliwell, *Dictionary of Archaic and Provincial Words*, Edition ix, 1878, observed that Blount defined it as "a dam or open wear in a river, with a loop or narrow cut in it, accoming dated for the laying of engines to catch fish " In Act 12 Edward IV, c 7, it recites that one of the reasons for forbidding the use of kidels was "en salvation de tout frye de pesson procreez en lez mesmes "

† The Commissioners reported that the decrease of the salmon fisheries was consequent upon "(1) Obstructions to the free passage of fish (2) The use of fixed engines (3) Defective regulation of fence times or close seasons (4) Illegal fishing, destruction of unseasonable fish, spawning fish ; spent fish, young, or fry (5) The want of an organized system of management of the rivers and fisheries, affording the means of efficient protection against poaching and other destructive and illegal practices (6) Poisoning of waters by the efflux from mines (7) Pollution of waters by manufacturers, gasworks, and other nuisances (8) Confusion and uncertainty of the law, and difficulty of enforcing its penalties against offenders " (Page ix)

‡ Whether this permission to extend the open season after September 1st was a judicious departure from the spirit of the Act of 1861 has been questioned Captain Pinkett, Chairman of the Taw and Torridge Fishery Board, observed (*Field*, December 18th, 1886), "Among those who had studied the case the impression was strengthening that it was an error ever to have extended the open season after September 1st He himself had not the slightest doubt that strict adherence to the close time of the Act of 1861 would have largely increased the summer harvest in the estuary of the Taw, both in number and in size " Although much evidence has been adduced to prove that this extension of the open season has been followed in certain localities by the rivers becoming later, still some assertions on this score which have been advanced scarcely bear examination At p 63 is a statement by the *Usk Board of Conservators* and the present *Inspector of Salmon Fisheries*, that such has occurred in the Usk, but the evidence of Sir W Jardine's Committee in 1860 (*see* p 118) lead to the opposite opinion The accuracy of the former parties having been challenged in *The Field* (January 8th, 1887) has been left unanswered

At p 60 (*ante*) will be found the incidence of the close season in England and Wales

§ It has been contended by some that prohibiting fishing with small meshed nets (even though capable of taking an occasional salmon) and the using of night and set lines during close months has done more harm than good, because trout, pike, and eels were formerly thus captured

fish at mills and weirs was prohibited   Fish passes were to be erected over mill dams, and free gaps and other restrictions were placed on fishing weirs,* also gratings were to be inserted before the inlets to canals during such time as the young of the salmon were descending rivers towards the sea † Unclean, spawning, and young fish were to be protected, and an annual close time was imposed generally throughout England and Wales between September 1st and February 6th inclusive   A weekly close time was also enacted from noon on Saturdays to 6 A M on Mondays, or forty-two hours   But anglers were permitted to continue their sport for some time after net fishing had ceased in order to give persons in the upper portions of rivers some chance of capturing late fish, as now they are hardly visited by salmon except during the breeding season, from too excessive netting in the lower waters   Spawners will rarely take a fly, and as there are always some clean-run salmon in the river, this angling can do very little injury, as unseasonable fish if hooked have to be returned to the water   For the purpose of seeing the law properly enforced, Inspectors of Fisheries were appointed

Among other prohibitions was that against the employment of fish-roe for angling or the possession of salmon-roe or unseasonable fish, and which rendered the individual subject to a fine.

Before long, however, certain defects in the Act became apparent, for, although the sale of salmon during the close season was prohibited, still these fish were captured during this period and exported to France, where they obtained a ready sale   So an Act was passed in 1863 which prohibited the export of any salmon during the close season   Next, it was found that funds were necessary to carry out the provisions of the Act, and also local authorities to see such done , consequently, another Act was passed into law in 1865, which enabled the country to be divided into fishery districts, placed under local boards of conservators elected by the magistrates at Quarter-sessions   By licensing engines for the capture of fish and assessing the rental of fisheries, funds were raised for this purpose   Then a tribunal was constituted of the Special Commissioners of the English Fisheries for ascertaining what fixed engines were legal, in order to diminish the expense of prosecuting offenders   In 1873, another amended Act was passed, in which, in addition to the regulations as to the taking and sale of fish, the issuing of licenses, the powers of water-bailiffs, and rules as to gratings and fish-passes, it added representatives from fishermen who ply their trade in public waters, and allows them to elect one member for every £50 license duty which

and they are detrimental to the young of the salmon   Since then the Fresh water Fishery Act and amendments have become law

* Mr Willis-Bund, *Salmon Problems* (page 10 *et seq*), observed how the Act of 1861 practically introduced the Irish salmon laws into force in this country, irrespective of the climatic differences, and which has had a remarkable effect   The great rainfall and comparatively uniform supply of water in Irish rivers had caused it to be enacted that salmon traps at mills which captured ascending and descending fish, should only be used provided there was a fish pass attached to the dam with a constant supply of water flowing through it   This proviso which was possible in Ireland, absolutely prohibited the use of most of those ancient rights in English and Welsh rivers, where there were days in which no water could flow through the fish passes owing to deficiency of rainfall   But the 20th section of this Act, also copied from that of Ireland, does not work so well, as it provides that the sluices in any dam are to be kept closed when the water is not required for the use of the mill, in order to send it through the fish pass   In large rivers, with plenty of water going over the dam continuously, so as to occasion a strong current which would bring up these fish to its base, it works well, for were there no such provision the miller could raise his sluices so as to allow the water to fall to below the level of the upper edge of the fish pass, which would keep the salmon congregated in the pool below the weir, where they could be readily captured   But in English and Welsh rivers, when no water is coming over the pass, the fish become left in the pools with very little water, where they may be readily gaffed or otherwise poached.   This enactment also prevents the sluices being opened to allow descending kelts to pass through the weir, for were this attempted the miller is liable to be fined   In fact, in some dry seasons the only legal way to let these kelts descend would seem to be by lifting them over the weir

† Complaints are frequently made that constant labour is required at these gratings to keep them free, so, instead of clearing away the rubbish, it is found easier to raise the grating a little, and thus water, rubbish and fish go through together   This may be partially obviated by employing double gratings, only one being lifted at a time

they pay—also, bye-laws can be made by the Boards of Conservators, of which forty-five exist in England and Wales

In fact it was considered inexpedient to have a uniform close time for all rivers, because some were earlier than others By the Act of 1873 power was given to vary the close time, provided such was sanctioned by an order from the Home Office But it was not to be less than one hundred and fifty-four days, and should not commence later than Nov 1st The weekly close time was extended to forty-eight hours, and cannot begin before six on Friday It was not to extend over twelve o'clock on Monday

Here it will be necessary to make a few remarks on the incidence of the close season, prior to and after the passing of the Act in 1861 Early and late rivers (pp 59, *et seq*) and early and late ascents of salmon for breeding purposes (pp 66, *et seq*) have been noticed, and a brief statement has been given as to the time which the local justices fixed as the close time for rivers in their respective districts (p 60) Prior to 1860 it seems to have been considered that gravid salmon should be protected not only just at the period of depositing their spawn, but also for some time previously, in order to allow them undisturbed access to their spawning beds Consequently the earlier breeders were spared where now they are captured, with the result, some observers believe, of making our rivers later, a conclusion not admitted by others

The close seasons existing in 1860* and also in 1884 were as follows.† that which was enacted for each river in 1861, is omitted because it was directed to be uniform in the rivers of England and Wales commencing Sept 1st ‡

Aln, Oct 21st to March 16th (Sept 1st) Avon, Bristol, August 12th (Sept 1st) Avon, Devonshire, Jan 15th to May 6th (Sept 21st), Avon, Hints, Sept 12th to Jan 1st (Sept 21st), Axe, Nov 20th to April 18th (Sept 20th), Ayron, Oct 15th to March 1st (Sept 1st), Bangor Oct 15th to March 10th (Sept 1st), Camel, Dec 24th to May 1st (Oct 1st) Cleddew, Oct 31st to April 30th (Sept 1st), Clwyd, Oct 1st to March 1st (Sept 15th), Conway, Carnarvonshire, Nov 30th to April 30th, in Denbighshire, Oct 1st to Feb 4th (Sept 15th), Coquet, Oct 10th to March 8th (Sept 15th), Dart, Nov 14th to Feb 14th (Sept 1st), Dee, Sept 1st to Jan 25th (Sept 1st), Derwent, Cumberland, Sept 25th to March 10th (Sept 15), Dovey, Dec 14th to April 2nd (Sept. 14th), Duddon, Oct 10th to May 1st (Sept 15th), Eden, Sept 25th to Dec 31st (Sept 1st, lower waters Sept 10th), Elwy, Oct 1st to March 1st (Sept 15th), Esk, Sept 25th to March 10th (Sept 15th), Exe, Sept 20th to Feb 15th (Sept 15th), Fowey, Dec 3rd to May 15th (Sept 1st, lower waters Oct 1st), Itchen, Sept 12th to Jan 1st (Sept 1st), Kent, Oct 10th to Feb 2nd (Sept 15th), Leven, Oct 10th to Jan 2nd (Sept 15th), Lune, Sept 29th to Feb 1st (Sept 1st, lower waters Sept 8th), Mawddach, Oct 1st to March 1st (Sept 1st), Neath, Dec 10th to March 1st (Sept 1st), Nevern, Oct 1st to Feb 1st (Sept 1st), Ogmore Dec 1st to March 1st (Sept 15th), Ouse, Yorkshire, West Riding, Sept 25th to Feb 25th (Sept 1st), Plym, Nov 14th to Feb 14th (Sept 1st), Ribble, August 31st to Jan 28th (Sept 1st) Severn, Glost and Worcester, Feb 1st to Dec 31st, in Salop and Montgomeryshire, Sept. 14th to Dec 31st (Sept 1st), Tamar, Dec 15th to March 15th, Taw, Oct 20th to Feb 20th (Sept 21st), Tees Sept 17th to Feb 14th (Sept 1st), Teifi, Cardigan-shire, Nov 3rd to March 3rd, in Carmarthenshire, Nov 1st to April 1st (Sept 1st), Teign, Dec 3rd to March 3rd (Sept 1st), Test, Sept 12th to Jan 1st (Sept 1st), Torridge, Oct 20th to Feb 20th (Sept 21st), Towey, Nov 1st to April 1st (Sept 1st), Trent, August 12th to Nov 12th (Sept 1st), Trowenn, Sept 1st to Jan 31st (Sept 1st), Tyne, Sept 10th to Feb 10th (Sept 1st) , Usk, Oct 14th to March

* The return has the following note appended " Accuracy cannot be vouched for on account of imperfect information "—*Report of Commission into the Salmon Fisheries of England and Wales*, 1860, p xxxviii

† The names of the rivers are given, first with the dates as existing in 1860, and in brackets as legal in 1885

‡ In 1860 it was found that no close season existed, or it had not been fixed in the Afon, Derwent (Yorkshire) Longhor or Llwshur, Ouse (East Riding of Yorkshire), Parrett, Rhymnu, Taff, Tavy (Devonshire), Tawe, Wyse, and Yealm

14th (Sept 1st), Voryd, Oct 1st to March 1st (Sept 1st), Wear, Sept 17th to Feb 11th (Sept 1st), Wharfe, Sept 25th to Feb 25th (Sept 1st), Wye, Glos Sept 1st to Jan 1st, in Herefordshire, Sept 16th to Feb 10th, in Monmouth-shire, Oct 15th to Feb 14th (Sept 1st), Union, Oct 21st to March 1st (Sept 1st)

Doubtless the early closing of rivers has always been objected to by the salt-water and tidal fishermen* as well as by those who possess fixed engines, and their persistent endeavours to have a portion of the back end of the season abolished has in many instances been met with more or less success In some rivers, as the Taw and Torridge for example, the gravid fish on first commencing their ascent are of a beautiful silvery colour even after they have entered fresh water for breeding, and the net fishermen have held this as a reason for requesting permission to capture them for the market, even when such fishes have been opened and shown to be full of spawn, still they have mostly declared such to be exceptional examples †

It is commonly observed that the interests of the proprietors of salmon fisheries are not identical throughout the entire extent of the stream, occasioning a clashing of views which are inimical to the fisheries, and consequently to the general public The proprietors of fisheries living in the higher waters often argue with justice, that pollutions are permitted unchecked access ; that immoderate netting is almost continuously carried on in the lower reaches,‡ giving the fish,

* *The Commissioners* in 1860, observed the fishermen who got their living by taking salmon on the estuaries and navigable parts of rivers are generally possessed with the belief that the interests of the proprietors on the upper waters are necessarily adverse to their own The measures which they erroneously conceive necessary for their own protection, would only tend more speedily to destroy the breed of fish, the increase of which they, as appropriators of the first and largest share, are above all parties concerned to promote It was likewise remarked that these people were "generally complaining and dissatisfied "

† In investigating such questions it would be well if the investigator were present when the fish are being captured from the river or examples might be brought from other localities and produced in evidence of the fish being clean, as is said to have taken place within the last few years

‡ " Old Log," in *The Field*, January 5th, 1884, wrote as follows — ' We have put a stop to the old practice of spearing salmon on the upper shallows, which used to be so regarded in the light of a fair and legitimate sport, that the penalized salmon spear still figures as an heraldic device in family arms , and we exact a heavy penalty from the riparian owner (who expends much care and money in the protection of his river nurseries), if he takes a dozen or two out of the millions of salmon fry which he may have nurtured , but we still allow the miners to wash their copper ore where the poison shall flow into the salmon stream, if he can persuade an easily satisfied inspector that any remedial measures would be difficult or expensive We flatter ourselves we have made a great advance in salmon culture and legislation , but, after all, I fancy that our fathers had much better salmon fishing, at infinitely less expense, than we can get, and that their predecessors were better off than they were As to the salmon of the future, he will be a rare animal for sportsmen if we do not bring more common sense and justice of dealing in the management of our rivers, and our children's children may perhaps sigh in vain for the ' *Salmo salar* of the olden times ' "

On the other hand, F C S remarked, in *Nature*, September 15th, 1881, that preserving salmon in rivers is an error, and that such has decreased them both in number and size Prior to preservation inhabitants placed large stones across rivers and threw in gravel where deficient—also with forks they loosened the stones They watched the spawning fish and killed all the large ones after they had partially or wholly spawned, and which were said to destroy the fry No pollution in rivers is alluded to, as the number of houses in the vicinity were too few to affect it *Mr Hubert Hall* observed, " It is strange that people should wonder why the salmon disease is a comparatively modern institution The answer is simple Because positive checks to over-crowding were applied in the shape of wholesale extermination Once no man fished seriously unless with a net His living depended on his success he was always at it, there was no check, no limit to his operations When fish failed lower down he shifted his quarters upwards When the stock began to fail there, and the fish grew shyer every year, he appealed to the Crown, or his lord, and found interest to put up weirs and stop the barge traffic Then he commenced anew in virgin waters Take the case of a fishery in the Severn nearly three centuries ago Here it was ascertained that in one length of the river a whole fishing population was at work, renting from the Crown In one pool alone three boats and three long nets were always at work, the result was that they caught every living thing in the river Shads, once absurdly plentiful, had not been seen for five years, salmon very seldom , worse still, their neighbours above them finding most of the fresh-run fish intercepted, cut off in return all the fish that had ascended to spawn They even took out all the salmon fry, and this with the approval of everybody, including the Crown The fact is, we have not, nor have had, any moderation in this matter In one direction we overfish and overflood our rivers , in another we over preserve and pollute them The result is in half our rivers there are no fish to speak of, in the other half the salmon disease "

except in the close time, but little chance of escape ; and that obstructions are not always removed or moderated   Thus the upper proprietors see but few fish excepting during the breeding season, when it is illegal to capture them   They are, in a manner, "clucking hens," whose duties seem to be to take care the old fishes are left undisturbed on the redds, that the eggs are hatched, the fry reared, and to speed the parting guests as they descend to the sea, from whence nets, obstructions, and pollutions in the lower portions of the river will most probably prevent their ever re-ascending ; or else merely in sufficient numbers to maintain a sufficient supply for the lower waters   Under these circumstances it can hardly be a source of surprise if the breeding grounds are not strictly preserved   for the rearing of salmon is commonly asserted to be done at the expense of the local fish, which are residents of the upper waters

The value of the salmon fisheries in Scotland, and the rent paid for a few rivers or fisheries, is recorded in the *Report of the Parliamentary Committee on Salmon Fisheries for 1824*   The Beauly then rented for £1300 per annum ; the greater portion of the Tweed for £10,000 ; one fishery obtaining £1200   While a single fishery on the Tay let for £1205, but the remainder of the others for £8000 per annum   In a *Parliamentary Return* made in 1864 the name of each fishery, of its owner, its value, and the mode of capturing the fish was recorded   Russel, in his excellent treatise on the *Salmon*, 1864, referred to it as follows :—" As this is the first attempt to procure official or authentic information as to the whole of the Scotch fisheries, it is welcome as a beginning, but it has the rudeness and imperfection of a beginning   It both omits and mis-states   Many fisheries are not included at all, of nearly 700 fisheries named, the value of eighty, or nearly a sixth of the whole, is not given "*   As regards the produce of these fisheries, the weight and the contents of each box of salmon sent from Scotland appears to have varied at different periods   Thus in the *Parliamentary Report* (for 1824) already referred to, a witness speaking of the Tweed fisheries stated that prior to 1816 a box contained 6¼ stone of fish, but from 1816 and subsequently 8 stone at least up to 1824, at which it continues now

Mr Young (*British Industries*, 1877, p 298) gave the number of boxes of salmon sent from Scotland to Billingsgate from 1834 to 1875, and which he observed averaged 112 lb each in weight   Adding the numbers received up to 1881, we obtain the following results—a yearly average of 24 214 boxes of 1 cwt each   During the first seven years the annual average was 26,107, during the second period 29,011, during the third, ending 1854, 18,210 ; during the fourth period from 1861 to 1869 20,824, from 1869 to 1875, 24,478 ; and for six years ending 1881, 24,617 boxes   In the *Fourth Annual Report of the Fishery Board for Scotland*, the estimated value of the salmon captured in that country, during 1883, was given at £323,851   The causes which have led to the injury and in some cases to partial but in others entire extermination of this valuable fish in certain rivers in Scotland have been already alluded to (*see* page 112 *ante*)   A few years back the *Scotch Fisheries Improvement Association* observed that there are seven counties in Scotland with thirty-two rivers, which have ceased being frequented by salmon owing to the obstructions or pollutions

Salmon, as has been already remarked, roam along the coast in search of food, and when doing so swim close in shore, enabling them to be intercepted by means of stationary engines during their journeys, as stake-nets or bag-nets, contrivances not sufficiently under control in Scotland, where the injury they do to the fisheries is excessive,† and perhaps as good an instance as could be adduced is the

* The total value of the Salmon Fisheries in 1864, for all Scotland, was set down at £52,613, but Russel remarked that the actual rental of three Scotch Fishery districts—the Tay, the Spey and the twin rivers entering the sea at Aberdeen, amounted at that period to nearly £10,000 a year   Mr James Caird, the chief commissioner appointed to investigate the condition of the British fisheries, in a letter dated March 6th, 1868, estimated the annual value of the river fisheries of Scotland at £200,000, and in 1877 Mr Archibald Young gave them at £250,000

† Dr Sinclair, in his *View of Dumfriesshire*, 1811, gave some particulars with regard to the fisheries, and the rents as they were thirty years previously, which was prior to the commencement of trap-nets in the Solway   " The rents on the Scotch fishings amounted to £876 a year "   These were understood to have been paid for the ancient modes of fishing by half nets, poke-nets,

Solway (*see* p 117 *ante*), and here, although they have been declared illegal, they have never been suppressed

The Tweed is also a river which has been subject to peculiar legislation and for which special Acts are yet in force   The first regulations for the fishing of this river and which are still extant, were made by the Scottish Parliament in the time of King Robert the Bruce, several others succeeded until the first Parliament of James I, when it was enacted "Quha sa ever be convict of slauchter of salmonde in times forbidden be the law, he sall pay four tie scheillings for the unlaw, and at the third time, gif he be convict of sik trespasse sall tyne his life or then bye it"   The mode of purchase is not recorded   Douglas writing of the Tweed Fisheries in the *Proceedings of the Berwickshire Naturalists' Club*, 1863, observed (p 67), that in "A D 1429, in the ninth Parliament of James I, it was enacted 'the waters of Solway and Tweede qu hilkis, sal be reddie to all Scottesmen all time of the yier als lang as Berwick and Roxburgh ar in English mennes handes'   Subsequently they came under the general law of Scotland "*

Further up the East coast of Scotland, and entering a Firth of the same name,

and hang nets, the tenants of the fishings not being acquainted with any other   The trap-net fishings at the mouth of the Nith, possessed by Sir W Giddelin in 1811, let for £1395   (That shows what the effect of the trap-nets had been)   "A comparison of the two rents at different periods, on a nearer inspection, clearly points out the public as well as individual loss sustained by the monopolizing fisheries about the time of the invention of trap nets , but the annual produce of the sea fishings in the north of the Solway amounted to between £600 and £700 "   (In these were included Sir James Graham's and the Solway fishing, which were £376)   "The price of salmon was about 2½d a lb , whereas at present, even in the most plentiful times, it is never below 6d, and is often 1s and earlier in the season 2s, prices never thought of in old times   If to the rents previous to the invention of the above destructive engines, we reckon the immense number of salmon caught and consumed by the small proprietors fishing in the Solway, we cannot hesitate in saying that the cause of the diseases is owing, if not mostly, at least in great measure, to the destruction by such engines   The small proprietors, who follow the old modes of taking fish, I can almost affirm upon oath do not get one tenth part of what was formerly got, when the same means were employed, which clearly shows that the trap nets have taken them almost all "   A recent writer observed that " the avowed principle upon which the old Scotch Legislature acted was this   they decided it was preferable that the Scotch salmon rivers along the Solway coast should suffer damage through the use of fixed machinery rather than permit any chance of benefit to accrue to their English neighbours   For this amiable reason the Solway waters were in ancient times especially exempted from the beneficent enactment of the old Scotch salmon statutes, and upon this ridiculous basis the obnoxious fixtures stand to this day "   Possibly they will continue for some years yet, probably coming under the care of the official appointed to " protect ancient monuments," as a better monument of the savage legislation of times gone by could scarely be found   As such, perhaps, it is interesting to some, but its continuance is very destructive to the salmon, and consequently the food of the public

* Pennant, in 1776, recorded of the Tweed, that there are in the river 41 considerable fisheries, extending upwards, about 14 miles from the mouth (the others above being of no great value), which were then rented for near £5400 per annum   Twelve years later, a writer in *The Edinburgh Magazine* of April, 1788, corroborated a statement of Pennant's, that the expenses of fishing were £5000, to pay which it was necessary to capture 280,000 salmon, exclusive of grilse and trout   In 1811, upwards of 58,000 salmon, excluding grilse, were taken, and in 1816, 54 011 salmon, 120,594 grilse and 67,074 trout, while the rent had risen to its maximum, £13,705 6s 3d In the report of evidence taken before the *Committee of the House of Commons on the Salmon Fisheries*, in 1824, J Wilson deposed that the rental in 1823 was £10,000, but for the last seven years it had averaged £12,000 annually   That the fishing had decreased during the last three or four years, owing to the slaughter of breeding fish   For, he observed, the poached fish " are sent to Edinburgh generally, and there they are protected, from the circumstance of the Scotch fishings commencing so early   they say they come from the Clyde, from fishings which commence in December   at that time they are quite unwholesome food "   The poorer tenants in the upper fisheries were also said to capture fish and sell them   Mr Wilson considered the fish began ascending the river about the middle of August

Douglas, in his paper on " the Tweed fisheries," *Proceedings Berwickshire Naturalists' Club*, 1863, p 67, stated that in 1812 the rental of these was £20,000 per annum, but that they rapidly decreased to £4000   The average estimated annual capture of fish for 18 years, ending 1825, had been, of salmon 54,159, grilse 65,072, and trout 43,384   In five years ending 1858, the average annual take had been, of salmon 10,520, grilse 26,965, trout 26,895   In five years ending 1863, the average annual take had been, of salmon 9141, grilse 18,549, trout 35,518   In five years ending 1871, the average annual take had been, of salmon 10,532, grilse 15,456, trout 28,841   In 1882, 1412 cwt of salmon were sent from the Tweed to London, which, at 10 lb per fish, would give 15,814, but grilse may have been included   The rental in 1875 was £12,173, and in 1876, £12,287

is the Forth, which is joined by the Teith a short distance above Stirling, and a little lower down by the Allan, its length to Queensferry is computed to be about eighty miles, and its drainage area 680 square miles Its chief tributary, the clear and rapid Teith, possessing plenty of fine gravelly spawning grounds, is much preferred by salmon and sea trout to the Forth, while on one of the affluents of the Teith or rather at the outlet of Loch Venachar, is an obstruction to the ascent of salmon to the good spawning grounds above, in the shape of a dam and sluices erected by the Glasgow Waterworks Commissioners *

The Tay is one of the earliest of the Scottish rivers, and has long been famous for the number, size, and quality of its salmon The largest British specimen in the Buckland Museum, and which weighed 70 lb , having been obtained from it In its course of about 150 miles it passes the fair city of Perth on its way to the German Ocean near "bonnie Dundee," it drains 2500 square miles of country, and has the greatest volume of water of any river in Scotland Dr Anderson computed its contents passing Perth to be 3640 cubic feet a second The Dochart, which rises in the extreme west of Perthshire falls into Loch Tay, which is sixteen miles in length, a mile broad and in some places 600 feet deep, and is usually considered the source of the river Tay It ends in a long, bell-shaped estuary, extending from Perth to Drumley Sands a distance of about thirty miles

J Gillies, in 1824, gave evidence that when he "first went to Perth most of the spawning was over by December , but the chief time for spawning now (1824) is generally in the months of December and January "

Among the many instances of injuries inflicted on river fisheries by the existence of stationary engines for catching the Salmonidæ, erected in the estuaries or near the mouths of rivers, few better examples can be quoted than the Tay †

* During the twenty years ending 1882 3 the average annual rents paid for fisheries in the Forth were as follows —The first five years, £2492 , the second quinquennial period, £2158 , the third, £3288 , and during the fourth and last period, £3811   The assessment on the rents for conservative purposes has been about 20 per cent As to fixed nets outside the estuary of the Forth, there were, in 1883, in the twelve miles of coast between Elie and Fife Ness, sixty-four bag and two fly nets The rental of these is given at £760 a year One experienced tacksman put the annual take of fish in the district at about 4000 salmon and 1200 grilse , while about 200 fish were captured by the rod The produce of the fisheries was said to have fallen off of late years

† In the Report on Scottish Salmon Rivers by Mr A Young (Inspector of Salmon Fisheries for Scotland), he remarked that the average yearly rental of the Tay was in 1884 about £20,000 For some years the fishings had been deteriorating, and the estuary was so severely and continuously netted during the open season, that but few fish could reach the upper waters until the nets were taken off on August 21st Four fifths of the rentals of the river fisheries were derived from those existing between Cargill railway-bridge (about 10 miles above Perth) and the sea

Fixed nets were first erected in the Firth of Tay in 1799 and finally declared illegal in 1812 The average takes of the two fisheries immediately above the highest of those nets were as follows —

    10 years before the stake nets, annually 10 871 salmon, 2 211 grilse
        ,, during   ,,   ,,   6,700 , 2,429 ,
        ,, after   ,,   ,, 11,310 , 11 220 ,,

Similarly Bertram informed us that the annual average produce of the Kinfauns fisheries, near Perth, which furnish one-fourth of that of the river, from the junction on the Isla to the sea, and for the same period, were thus —

    1788 to 1797, before the stake nets, annually 8 720 salmon, 1,714 grilse
    1801 to 1810, during   ,,   , 1,666 ,, 1,616 ,,
    1815 to 1824, after   ,,   , 9 010 ,, 8,709 ,,

The number of 100 lb boxes of salmon shipped from the Tay fisheries in 1812, the last year of the fixed nets, was 1175, but in 1819 after they had been completely removed, 5694 About 1821 fixed nets were commenced, being employed along the coast of Forfarshire, and by 1825 the takes in the Tay had become reduced one-half We are further informed that from 1625 to 1834 inclusive, and immediately following the passing of the Act of 1829, was the blackest the tenants ever knew on the Tay

James Bell (Parl Com Report, 1824) deposed that he "gave up his fishing in 1819, as it became decreasing He had paid annually up to then £3 500, but it fell off to £2000 per annum This was at the time Hunter's stake-net fishing along the coast began, when the fishing immediately and very perceptibly diminished '

Russel (1864) remarked of this river and firth that although the rental had not been greatly reduced during the past nine or ten years, this was owing to the price of fish having risen , also the proprietors had anticipated by voluntary agreement the improved legislation to which they

The next rivers that are necessary to mention are two in Inverness-shire * the *Ness*, which has a course of eight miles, in the time of Burt (1730), was said to be much infested by seals, but that they were good signs that the salmon were running he likewise observed that the judges and such other gentlemen ' to whom they do the honours of the Corporation by presenting them with their freedom if it happens to be the salmon season The entertainment is salmon taken out of the cruives just by, and immediately boiled and set upon a bank of turf, the seats the same, not unlike one of our county cock-pits, and during

ultimately became subject Although the Tay fisheries, as a whole, had not materially decreased in money value, the upper net fisheries, situated immediately above the tide, diminished so rapidly that their rental of £3000 sank to £650, clearly showing that the effectiveness of the fishing in tidal waters had reduced the period of a salmon's existence by many months, and his road to destruction by many miles

About 1835 the *Tay Navigation Act* came into operation, one effect of which was the removal of obstructions, and which increased the facility for working the net and-coble industry within the tideway, and Russel gave a return showing the captures of two of the largest proprietors within this space, and these two were generally reckoned as possessing one-half of the entire fisheries of the tideway From 1825 to 1834, before the Navigation Act, the average annual captures had been 6715 salmon and 12,818 grilse, but from 1836 to 1845, after the Navigation Act, it became increased to 8389 salmon and 13,335 grilse But the fisheries next above the tideway now suffered, and their takes decreased nearly 50 per cent

After the passing of the *Home Drummond Act* in 1828, in which it was decided to extend the netting season from August 27th to September 15th, the produce of the river went on diminishing until it had reached its lowest point in 1852, the rents since the passing of the Act having gradually decreased from £11,571 in 1828 to £7973 in 1852

Legislation having thus decreased instead of having increased productiveness, the proprietors about 1852 almost unanimously agreed among themselves to return to what for 400 years had been the commencement of the close season for nets, or August 26th, and for rod fishing, September 24th Rents, which had gone down to £9580 in 1852, now rose as follows —In 1853 to £8715; 1854, £9269, 1855 to £9977 But now one of the upper proprietors broke up the compact, and the law of 1828 resumed its sway, and in 1856 the rental was £10,199, in 1857, £10,772 So in 1858 the great majority of the proprietors united in petitioning Parliament for a local Act, when the close time for the district was fixed by law from August 26th to February 4th, and the rental went on increasing until it reached its culminating point in 1880, when it was £22,518, in 1881 it dropped to £19,579, in 1882, £19,221, in 1883, £17,773, but in 1884 rose again to £19,655, and in 1885, £20,137

In 1853 the *Stormontfield ponds* were erected by the then proprietors of salmon fisheries on the Tay They were situated about five miles above Perth, occupying, roughly speaking, two acres of ground Although now superseded by the Dupplin hatchery, they were useful in their time The boxes are still employed for hatching eggs and the ponds for rearing fish The *Dupplin hatchery* was instituted late in 1882 on the Earn, at Newmill, Dupplin Castle, its capacity is estimated at about 300,000 eggs Here the fry are kept until about forty days old, when they are distributed in the Tay and its tributaries.

In 1864 Russel observed that the Tay furnished about 800,000 lb weight of salmon annually. Mr Buist, in Bertram's *Harvest of the Sea*, 1865, p 111, observed that we find the average number of salmon and grilse taken (in the Tay) in each year is 70,000, but Bertram (p 213) observed " that in some seasons the number of fish taken from the mouth of the Isla down to the sea has ranged from 70,000 to upwards of 100,000 " In p 6 of the Appendix to the 1871 *Report on the Scotch Salmon Fisheries*, the number annually caught in this river was given by one witness at 100,300, and by another at 86,000 Large numbers of clean salmon are captured in the early months of the season in Loch Tay, where they ascend during December and January before the netting begins

T Proudfoot, in 1821, deposed to the fisheries in *the Earn* having decreased very much since 1820, due, he supposed, to two causes " There are a great many stake fisheries up about Montrose (increased about this time), which take a great many of the fish that would come into the Tay, and what they do not take they put off with long leaders , they are of such a length that they put the fish past the Tay," thus affecting the Earn He also complained that close time was not properly observed

The *South Esk* rises in Loch Clova, and after a course of about forty miles, and a drainage area of 245 square miles, it enters the German Ocean at Montrose This is a good salmon river, and between Brechin and the sea there are many gravelly shallows and deep pools Unfortunately it has about ten dams and weirs in its course, while a great amount of pollutions are poured into it The rental of the fishery in this river in 1867 was £1121, 1874, £1536, 1876, £1695, and in 1884, £2475 In 1847 Stoddart gave that on the Rossie fishings at about £650, but stated they had been let as high as £800, of Usan at £50, the station at Boddin Point at £400, and in the Parish of Farnell at £250

The *North Esk* rises in the Grampians, and after a course of about thirty miles, and having a drainage area of 288 square miles, enters the sea in the Bay of Montrose within five miles of the entrance of the South Esk There are five weirs in its course, one of which at Craigo dam is a serious obstacle, and its recent history is very instructive During the winter of 1881 a wide

the time of eating, the heart of the fish lies upon a plate in view, and keeps in a panting motion all the while, which to strangers is a great rarity   The *quires* above the *salmon leap* (which is a steep slope, composed of large loose stones) are made into many divisions by loose walls and have about 3 or 4 feet of water   These render such a number of fish as they contain an agreeable sight, being therein confined, to be ready at any time for the barrel or the table " (p 248)   The assessable value of the fishings in 1876-77 was £3069 11s   The second river is the *Beauly*,* much prized as an excellent angling river   Mudie observed having

breach was made in this dam, and when Mr Young inspected the river above this obstruction in January, 1882, prior to the breach having been repaired, he found that it was full of fish   In fact, this wide and deep gap in Craigo Dike had restored the Esk to its natural condition, and permitted the fish to distribute themselves throughout the entire length of the river, instead of their ascent being arrested by this dam   This erection had been greatly increased in height in 1847-48, since which period the only two good years the upper proprietors have experienced were 1877 and 1881, in each of which it was breached   About 1875 the Fishery Board gained a law suit against the proprietor of this obstruction, and a ladder was ordered to be put in, but it seems that it was erected in the wrong place   Now many fish heavy in spawn are said to be unable to ascend, and consequently drop their ova below this obstruction, where they are lost   This river for its size is an excellent one for salmon, the produce in 1870 having been computed to vary from 25,000 to 30 000, while the rental in 1837 was £3591 along with the coast fishing, and 1882-83 the river fishings let at £5624   Until the nets are off there is scarcely any angling in the upper waters but from September 1st to October 31st the rod fishing is excellent   The number of bag and fly nets in Montrose Bay, from Rockhall to the mouth of the South Esk, in 1883, were as follows — Bag-nets, 74, fly nets, 45, and this in six miles   These nets are on either side of the North Esk, beginning at 400 yards from a centre, fixed mid channel in the river where it joins the sea at low-water mark   The best fishing is on the north side, and the net, which is just without the 400-yard limit, consists, in the height of the fishing season, of three flies and nine bags, combined in the same fixed engine

The *Dee* issues from the "Wells of Dee" on the brow of Ben Macdhive 4000 ft above the level of the sea, and after a course of about 90 miles, and with a drainage of 900 square miles it falls into the German Ocean at Aberdeen where its estuary (which contains a bag net) has been included within the extension of the harbour works   The extent of coast fishing within this district of about 18 miles had, in 1883, an average number of 102 bag nets, of which 91 are to the south of its mouth, and 11 to the north or between it and mouth of the Don, which is within 2 miles   There are also 6 stake or fly-nets to the north of the Dee, the average length of the leaders to the stake-net being 80 yards   In the story of sandy shore 5500 ft long, and situated to the north of the Dee, there were 4 stake-nets and 2 bag nets in 1836, but now there exist 11 bag and 6 fly or stake nets   The assessable rental of this river in 1876 was £8897, and in 1884 £9931, of which £6201 belong to the lower fishings, including the sea coast, and £3730 to the upper river fishings   Stoddart, in 1847, calculated that the quantity of fish captured on an average season at 20,000 salmon, and 40,000 grilses, which included those taken by stake-nets, and at the mouth of the river on the adjacent beach   While between 1813 and 1824 he calculated that the annual take was 52,862 salmon and grilse on the Dee, and 40,677 on the Don   Since then an artificial barrier had been raised   The *Don*, whose mouth is within 2 miles of that of the Dee, had an assessable value, in 1876, of £3361 0s 8d

The *Deveron* is a late river for the East coast, it has a course of 60 miles and has numerous fixed engines near its mouth, the assessable rental is £2566, the average annual capture by rod is about 300 salmon

The *Spey* in 1775 rented, according to Pennant, for £1200 per annum and produced 1700 barrels of fish during the season   It is the most rapid of the larger Scottish rivers, has a course of 120 miles and drains upwards of 1000 square miles of country   In 1803 or 1804, it is said to have let for £6000 a year   The rental of the district which was £6859 in 1863-64, gradually rose to £11,332 in 1875-76, since which period it has steadily diminished until 1882-3 it had come down to £8482   This is said to be partly owing to increased fixed nets

In 1860 the following were stated to have been the annual captures in this river for the preceding nine years   1851 6515 salmon, 33,285 grilse, 1852, 10 980 salmon, 46,041 grilse, 1853, 15,772 salmon, 58,166 grilse, 1854, 29,780 salmon, 36,148 grilse, 1855, 13,194 salmon, 48,740 grilse, 1856, 14 103 salmon 27,528 grilse, 1857, 13,466 salmon, 54,949 grilse, 1858, 30,840 salmon, 35,409 grilse, 1859, 28 608 salmon, 17,263 grilse

There are other good fishing rivers on the East coast of Scotland, but space precludes alluding to all   Mr Young considered in 1883 that it was "not an extravagant estimate to put the total value of the salmon caught in the East coast rivers above described, and on the sea coast, at £120,000 a year, and the number of men employed in net fishing, and in watching the rivers, at 2000   The gross annual value of the salmon caught in the districts of the Tay and Spey alone cannot be much under £70,000 "

* The average takes of salmon, grilse, and trout in this river divided into septennial periods, and ending in 1869, were as follows —

<blockquote>
7 years ending 1815, annual average salmon 3237, grilse 5525
"   "   "   1862   "   "   ,   950, " 3293, trout 284
"   "   "   1869   "   "   "   1304, " 1261, " 350
</blockquote>

seen as many as eighty taken at a single haul in a pool below the falls of Kilmorac, and one of the number weighed more than 60 lb

It will be necessary now to pass on more rapidly through the salmon rivers of Scotland as those on the east coast and the Solway with their stationary engines have been rather fully dilated upon Some are situated in the county of Sutherland and belong exclusively to the Duke of Sutherland, who is consequently able to work them in any manner which he considers most conducive to maintain them in good order, as the tidal fishings one mile seawards from low-water mark, are also his property Among some of the following rivers where artificial propagation of Salmonidæ has been tried, it has been discontinued as not being a success, but it is said not to have had a fair trial

Sir W Jardine in a *Report to the British Association*, 1831, p 613, observed that the Duke of Sutherland* finding his salmon rivers deteriorating, took them under his own direction in 1832, regulating the close time in accordance with the seasons of running The fish were strictly preserved, and in several rivers grilse were all permitted to run· within two years the produce in many streams had doubled It will now be interesting to see whether this improved condition of the fisheries still continues The *Brora* is an early river In 1658 Captain Franck stated that £300 worth of salmon were annually exported from it to France Between 1863 and 1882 the best year was 1874 when 26 025 lb weight of fish were reported to have been captured, and the worst in 1865 when 3971 lb were taken For the nine years from 1863 to 1873 the average take was 8807 lb, and for nine years to 1882 it had risen to 16,404 lb The *Helmsdale* is another very early river in 1876, 5116 lb of salmon and 22,167 lb of grilse were taken by nets in the district, the nets do not commence being worked until

The average annual rents during the first of these periods was £1300, during the second £392, and during the third £768 Severely injured by fixed nets, they have improved since the passing of the Act of 1862, when these engines were removed from Chanonry Point

* Some interesting experiments in *marking salmon* in Sutherlandshire rivers were made by the sixth Duke of Athol, and the results of which were published by the late Frank Buckland in *Land and Water* He commenced, when Lord Glenlyon, in March, 1844, and the lists were continued until the end of 1869 , during this period over 1500 kelts were marked From March 11th, 1844, zinc tickets with numbers on them were used, fastened with copper wire through the dead fin , April 7th, 1845, silver was substituted for the copper wire, and these were employed to March 10th, 1847 , but this mode of fastening wire through the dead fin was now given up as insecure During this period at first the results were not satisfactory, but on March 31st, 1845, a 10 lb kelt was taken, and on May 7th, 1845, it was re captured in the finest possible condition and weighing 21¼ lb

March 20th, 1847, circular copper tickets were commenced, being employed fastened round the free portion of the tail with copper wire, but on this being found to cut the fish, gutta percha cord was substituted On March 10th, 1849, another alteration was tried, the copper labels being sewn on to the tail fin with gutta percha thread March 27th, 1847, a 15 lb kelt was marked and re-captured as a clean fish 20 lb weight on February 20th, 1848 March 28th, 1847, an 11 lb kelt was marked, re-captured July 24th clean and 18 lb March 31d, 1847, a 14 lb kelt was marked, re-caught September 7th clean and 21 lb weight

On February 20th, 1851, the duke adopted flat gutta-percha bands, the ends fastened together with wire On February 26th, the duke commenced with No 21 to fasten the ends of the band with naphtha instead of wire, half an inch of the outside of one end and of the inside of the other end being wetted with naphtha, and then set on fire, and when partially melted the ends were laid one upon the other, overlapping each other half an inch or more When cool, the band formed a firm, complete circle round the fish

On February 26th, 1851, a 10 lb kelt was marked, and re-caught as a clean fish February 17th, 1852, weighing 12 lb March 21st, 1854, an 11 lb kelt was marked, and re caught near Montrose on August 24th, 1854, as a clean 17 lb fish

March 29th, 1859, a 12½ lb kelt was marked, re-caught August 12th, 1859, a clean fish weighing 19 lb , this and other fish were marked by gutta percha tickets fastened round the free portion of the tail by wire, but they were mostly cut to the bone by ulceration

On February 25th, 1861, a 13 lb kelt was marked, re-taken August 11th, 1862, as a clean 26 lb salmon

Mr A Jopp, of Aberdeen, in 1860 published numerous statistics of Aberdeenshire wherein he conclusively showed that salmon had decreased in number and weight since the introduction of stake nets, his results referring more particularly to rivers and not to the sea Several proprietors of fixed nets on the coast very largely increased the rentals of their whole fisheries by giving up the fixed nets The Duke of Richmond removed fourteen from the mouth of the Spey, and in eight years his rental rose from £6000 to £13,000.

May 1st　The *Halladale* is a poor river, and an estuary bye-law permits bag-nets close to the mouth of the river which intercept ascending fish　The best netting year was 1867, when 2139 lb of salmon and 13,634 lb of grilse were captured　The *Naver* is the largest and best river on the north coast of the county and very early, the average captures for twelve years ending 1876 have been as follows —
four years ending 1868, salmon 3342 lb, grilse 6942 lb, four years ending 1872, salmon 3228 lb, grilse 5611 lb, four years ending 1876, salmon 5183 lb, grilse 13,100 lb Mr Murdoch, *Fishing Gazette*, March 20th, 1886, observed　"The Naver is divided into six angling beats which are numbered from 1 to 6, all the rods are on an equal footing, and they severally fish one beat a day, and the whole in regular rotation A fishes on Monday beat 1, on Tuesday on beat 2, and so on, B occupies these beats a day later, and in the same manner the rods follow in succession"
The *Borgie* enters the sea about a mile west of Naver, and its fisheries are said to be deteriorating, the returns give the following results:—four years ending 1868, salmon 2262 lb, grilse 4363 lb, four years ending 1872, salmon 1495 lb, grilse 2992 lb, four years ending 1876, salmon 2361 lb, grilse 7662 lb　With the *Hope* the late rivers commence, as all to the westward of Cape Wrath are, and so on down to the Solway

One river in Caithness, the *Thurso*, which has a course of forty miles, must be more particularly referred to, as it is considered to excel all other rivers in the kingdom for its early fish Bag-nets at its mouth do not commence before June 1st Mr A Young reported that the greatest number and weight of fish killed by the rod in this river since 1853 was in 1863 when 1510 fish weighing 11,777½ lb were captured, and the next best year was 1874 when 1240 fish weighing 13,870 lb were taken　The smallest number was in 1881, when only 236 weighing 2830½ lb were killed　In five years ending 1867 the average weight of the fish was 9 79 lb, in five years ending 1872, 10 54 lb, in five years ending 1877, 11 47, in five years ending 1882, 11 83 lb

The tenure of salmon fisheries in Scotland differs from what obtains in the rest of the British Isles, and the right of capturing *Salmo salar* in the seas to at least one mile (seawards) from low-water mark* in estuaries and in rivers has always been a property distinct from that of the soil, and originally belonged exclusively to the Crown, which, in the exercise of its prerogative, has in most cases sold, or otherwise granted away its rights, or else they have never been enforced Fishing for salmon as a legal right can only be legally conferred by a special grant from the Crown, consequently even the clause *cum piscationibus* in royal charters is not held to convey a right of salmon fishing　Thus riparian ownership may give no right to salmon fishing, even by angling, while salmon fisheries are occasionally held by one who has neither rights along either bank of the river, or in its subjacent soil

Originally the Crown rights in Scotland were principally, if not entirely, such fishings as were carried on as described　While, as all salmon in the sea being in a manner pertaining to the various rivers (as without such the breed would become extinct) it was held by many riparian proprietors that the Crown had long since granted away all its fishery rights, especially is in old times salmon were not commonly captured in the sea　The Crown was believed, and no doubt did, dispose of all modes of fishing for salmon then known and the more recent claim to those of the sea by means of fixed engines† it must be confessed would be open to legal argument were such a proceeding to have been adopted by private individuals who had sold all such fisheries as they believed they possessed from person to person

That salmon have always been cared for by the Scottish monarchs and legis-

---

* In the Statute of Robert I of Scotland, A D 1318, c 12, everything having reference to wears or fixtures applies to such as are "*in aquis ubi mare fluit et refluit*," or as it was subsequently defined in Act A D 1424, c 11, James I "in fresche watteris, quhai the sea falles and ebbs"—*Edinburgh New Philosophical Journal*, 1825, p 357

† Under this new plan or innovation the Crown lets fisheries for salmon along the sea coasts, which fisheries are essentially carried on to intercept and capture salmon and sea trout coming to the rivers where the Crown had previously parted with its rights

lature, abundant proofs are still extant, and although we have no statistics to fall back upon, it has been recorded that pickled Scotch salmon was exported to Flanders and to France, and that it formed a considerable trade so early as 1380   About 1220 it was ordained that from Saturday night to Monday morning it should be obligatory to leave a free passage for salmon in the various rivers, and which was styled the "Saturday's stoppe"   Alexander I enacted at Perth, "that the streams of the water sal be in all parts swa free, that ane swine of the age of three yeares, well fed, may turn himself within the stream round about, swa that his snowt nor taill sal not touch the bank of the water "   Slayers of red fish or smolts of salmonde the third time were to be punished with death, and "sie like he qua commands the famine to be done "

The annual close time for salmon netting in Scotland from 1424 to 1828 was 107 days.   At the latter date it was extended to 139 days, and in 1862 168 days, and the weekly close time from twenty-four to thirty-six hours

By an Act of the Scottish Parliament, passed in the time of James I , in 1424, c 25, it was forbidden that any salmon be slain from the Feast of the Assumption of our Lady until the Feast of St Andrew in winter   The dates of these feast days being corrected according to the new style, the close time enacted by this Act of 1424 was from August 15th until November 30th (N S)

An Act was passed by James VI. of Scotland, A D 1606, against the people polluting lochs and running streams in Scotland, on the ground " that the laying of lint in lochs and burnes is not only hurtful to all fishes bred within the same, and bestial that drink thereof, but also the hail waters of the said lochs and burnes thereby being infected, is made altogether unprofitable for the use of man, and very noisome to all the people dwelling there about, therefore statutes and ordains that no person or persons in times coming lay in lochs and running burnes any green lint, under the pain of forty shillings, toties quoties, for ilk time they shall contravene , and also confiscation of the lint to be applied to the poor of the parish within which the said lochs and burnes lies "

An Act was passed in the reign of James VII , on May 30th, 1685   " Item that all millers that slay smoults or tront with creels or any other engine, or any who dams or laves shall be punishable as slayers of red fish, conform to the (37) Act of Parliament, 5 King James III , and where the transgressor has no means they are appointed to be put in prison, irons, or stocks for the space of one month, upon their own expenses , and if they have it not of their own, to be fed on bread-and-water, conform to the 89th Act of Parliament, 6 King James VI "

In 1828 Act of 9 George IV , c 39, commonly known as the " Home Drummond Act," was made law   In it the annual close time was altered,* that no salmon, grilse, sea trout, nor other fish of the salmon† kind be taken in or from any river, stream, lake, water, or estuary whatsoever or any part of the sea coast between September 14th (instead of August 16th) and February 1st   (This Act did not apply to the Solway, Tweed, or Tay)   This taking off a month at the commencement of the season was found to be very injurious to the fisheries ‡   A man having been prosecuted for illegally taking one of the salmon tribe, the presiding judge found him guilty of killing " whitlings," fish in the grilse stage of the sea tront, but declined to convict, as he could not find the fish referred to in the statute   A

---

* Prior to the passing of this Act, Mr Little gave evidence before the *Parliamentary Committee* in 1824 (p. 114) that " the law then allowed the fishing to commence on St Andrew's Day (Nov. 30th) which was far too early, and permitted fishing to continue till August 16th "   He also observed, " I think, speaking of the habits of the fish, that the seasons are later than they have been when the old laws were made "

† In the Act of Charles II , 1681, "Anent the Salmond fishing in the waters of the Nith " the term *Salmond* is alone employed   In Act 8 of George III , 1790, for regulating and improving the salmon fishery of the river Nith, mention is made of grilse, salmon, trout, sea-trout or herling

‡ Criticizing a late Salmon Act, Fraser (*Salmon*, 1833) remarked, " The new Act has added 28 days to the lawful period formerly allowed the fisherman and, though the present age is indeed an age of wonders and discoveries, it could scarcely be believed that by adding 28 days to the season for killing the breeders of any species the number could be increased   Yet this is exactly what has been attempted by the framers of the Act " (p 31)

further Act was therefore passed in 1844, 7 and 8 Victoria, c 95, wherein whitlings were specially mentioned

The Tweed Act of 1857 seems to have inaugurated a new era in the Scottish salmon fisheries fixed nets were abolished in estuaries and rivers where they had existed more or less for centuries but the legality of those on the fore-shore which have sprung into existence during the present century were not legislated upon Leistering or spearing was prohibited, a weekly close time was enacted, and the mesh of salmon nets fixed at not less than 1¾ in between knot and knot   The period of time and the distance to be observed between the working of nets was likewise laid down, while the killing of foul fish was totally prohibited

In 1862, an Act was passed which was directed among other things against fixed engines, taking care that nothing in the Act should be held to legalize any mode of fishing which had previously been illegal   It formed districts, and appointed Commissioners to lay down all boundaries and local regulations, it fixed 168 days for the annual close time, 36 hours for the weekly close time   It imposed penalties for various offences, and extended the English Act of 1861 as to fixed engines, to the Solway after January 1st, 1865 (but which has not yet been carried out)   This Act does not apply to the Tweed except in three of its sections, illegal fishing (saving clause), possession of salmon roe, and poaching by three or more persons at night-time   But no clause was added repealing old Acts relating to salmon fishing, and some as ancient as 400 years are still in force, causing the law to be very complicated

In 1868 this Act was amended and added to   certain modes of fishing were prohibited in the conjoined Acts,* also the construction and use of cruives, the building and alteration of mill-dams or lades, or water wheels, the size of the mesh of nets   There were penalties for taking, possessing, or dealing in unclean salmon, and the removal of boats or other engines during the annual close time   In 1882 an Act was passed establishing a Fishery Board for Scotland, and an Inspector of Salmon Fisheries was appointed

About the commencement of this century, the fixed-net fishermen began to erect their stake- and fly-nets along the sea-shore and at the entrance to rivers, with probably about equal right to that of manufacturers who have made streams sewers to drain off their deleterious refuse   These nets have been considered to have been at first erected against both the spirit and letter of the existing statutes, and do not appear to have been legalized by prescription as their proprietors now claim them to be   Anyhow, they are causing great injury to the river fisheries directly, irrespectively of what they are causing indirectly by capturing such an amount of fish, that some of the upper proprietors do not see any fish until the nets are off   If they were under more strict control, both as to their position, their size and extent, and their times of fishing, it is probable that the rivers would be better stocked than they at present are

The legal dates for commencing to fish in the Scottish rivers in 1887 were as follows —Thurso, for rods, January 11th to September 14th —Tweed, for rods, February 1st to November 30th , nets, February 15th to September 14th —Tay, for rods, February 5th to October 10th , nets, February 5th to August 21st — Alme, Alness, Annan, Applecross, Arnisdale, Awe, Aylort, Avr, Baa, Badachro, Balgay, Bernedale, Bladenoch, Broom, Brora, Carron, Clyde and Leven, Conon, Cree, Creed (Stornoway), Crenan, Crowe, Dee (Aberdeenshire), Dee (Kirkeudbright), Deveron, Don, Doon, Ewe, Fleet (Sutherlandshire), Forth, Forss, Glenelg, Gour, Greiss, Gruche Ginmaid, Halladale, Helmsdale, Hope and Polla, Inchard, Inver, Kennait, Kilchoan, Kinloch, Kirkaig, Kishorn, Laxford,

---

* Mr A Young, *British Industries*, 1877, p 232, observed of the conjoined Acts of 1862-68, that " as these Acts at present stand stake nets and bag nets may be placed far too near the mouths of rivers , there being at least twenty river with estuaries so fixed by the Commissioners under the Acts of 1862, that such nets may be placed at distances varying from 400 to 150 yards from the mouth of the river on each side, measured from a point fixed in mid channel

No fixed net should, in any case be allowed to be placed nearer than half a mile from the mouth of a salmon river "   While in these Acts " there is no definition of what constitutes a fixed engine "

Leven, Lochy, Loch Duich, Loch Luing, Loch Roag, Lussa, Moidart, Morar, Naver and Borgie, Feochan, Ormsary, Pennygown, Resort, Sanda, Scaddle, Shiel, Sligachan, Snizort, Strathy, Torridon, Ullapool, and Wick, for rods, from February 11th to October 31st, for nets, from February 11th to August 26th — Beauly, Dunbeath, Kyle of Sutherland, Lossie, Nairn, Ness and Spey, for rods, from February 11th to October 15th, for nets, from February 11th to August 26th — Findhorn, for rods, from February 11th to October 10th, for nets, from February 11th to August 26 — Drummachloy (Isle of Bute), for rods, from February 16th to October 15th, for nets, from February 16th to August 31st — Add, Echaig, North Esk, Shira, South Esk, Fyne, Airay and Ruel, for rods, from February 16th to October 31st, for nets, from February 16th to August 31st — Borvie, Carradale, Fleet (Kirkcudbright), Clayburn, Finnis Bay, Avennangeren, Strathgravat, North Lacastile, Scalladale, Mawing, Fincastle, Meaveg, Ballanachist, South Lacastile, Borve, Obb, Guivan, Innei, loisa, livine Laggan, Luce, Stinchar, Ugie, Mullanageren Horasary, Loch-na-ciste, Urr, Ythan, Howmore, Nith, for rods, from February 25th to October 31st, for nets, from February 25th to September 9th

The Irish Inspectors of Fisheries reported that in 1882, 33,885 boxes of salmon of 150 lb weight each were exported to England, in 1883, 59,171, in 1884, 46,955, and the total prices realized were £443,782 in 1883, and £410,856 in 1884. The number of nets which paid duty in 1884, were 305 snap-nets, 811 draft-nets, 363 drift-nets, 36 pole-nets, 51 bag-nets, 0 fly-nets, 55 stake-nets, head weirs 2, box or crib 45, gap, eye, &c 315, sweepers 1, coghills 58, loop-nets 26, but from the evidence given before the Committee of the House of Commons in 1885, there appears to be a large number used, especially in salt water, that do not pay any duty at all. While stake-nets which were put down, as in the Shannon in 1863, are now as, if not more, numerous, than they were at that period.

A few instances of Irish salmon rivers* as they are reported to be at present will be given so as to illustrate the effects of certain modes of fishing, and the reasons adduced by one of the Inspectors respecting legalizing certain destructive modes of netting salmon as the half tram or fixed draught-net, and also the proposition which has been made to reduce the close season and weekly close time, there being, so it has been asserted, too many breeding salmon in the river at the spawning period!

It is remarkable how history repeats itself. In November, 1851, it was asserted in the pages of the *Dublin University Magazine* that a Bill had been introduced in 1842 by the then Government, and which speedily passed into law without

---

* In the Blackwater, *Select Committee of the House of Commons on the Salmon Fisheries*, (*Ireland*), 1885, it was stated that owing to the Act of 1863, the number of standing weirs was reduced from 83 to 8, as a consequence the salmon soon began to largely increase in numbers, and immediately there was an invasion of drift nets in the river and half tram or fixed draught-nets in the sea. Fortunately the Duke of Devonshire and others were able to prove rights to a several fishery in the river and there the drift nets were placed under control as well as reduced from 105 to 45, while to save the fisheries from almost certain destruction application was made and leave given that netting in nine miles of its course should cease. Unfortunately the number of nets seems to be vastly increasing outside the month of the river and with a greater rapidity than is wholesome for the fisheries. *Mr* Slattery deposed (p 77) that in a fishery a few miles above Lismore a tenant holding 120 acres of land on lease (for lives) taken before 1863 for £101 10s never prior to this period obtained a penny for his fishing. The weir was removed in 1865, and the first time he obtained any rent was in 1866 when he got £5 for the year, in 1868 he got £12 annually, in 1871 £25, 1874 on ten years' lease at £40, in 1884 it was let on a seven years' lease at £80 Similarly the Stafford fishery in the same river, which in 1866 was let at £7 annually, now (1885) is hired on a seven years' lease at £80. In another next below, or Meagher's fishery, in 1868 let at £5 a year, but in 1885 at £31. Coleman's, which formerly did not let, now obtains £30, while the Careyville fishery has risen from £100 to £700, and others in proportion. *Captain Francis* observed with regards to the migration of the young of the salmon that in 1868 they, *i e*, salmon fry, were being caught up to the last day of the open season (October 31st) and the water bailiff was directed to continue fishing into the close season to prove this, and on November 27th, six of a much larger size than the February smolt were captured for a meeting of the Conservators.

The *Bandon* river was rented in 1846 at £170 a year, and evidence was subsequently obtained that the produce from 1864 to 1872 had been as follows —1864, 5 tons 6 cwt 3 qr 25 lb, 1865, 3 tons 19 cwt 1 qr, 1866, 6 tons 18 cwt 3 qr 7 lb, 1867, 4 tons 3 cwt 1 qr 19 lb, 1868, 3 tons 4 cwt 3 qr 24 lb, 1869, 7 tons 8 cwt 2 qr 7 lb, 1870, 7 tons 13 cwt 1 qr 8 lb, 1871, 4 tons

sufficient discussion and owing to which Ireland in 1851 had to deplore the prostration and ruin of her salmon fisheries

It was held in 1842, as many assert now, that by extending the period for and means of capturing salmon an augmented supply would be obtained * That fixed engines in a river were a monopoly, to remedy which they legalized a new monopoly by fixtures in the sea and tideway, and thus the last state of monopoly was worse than the first Then came the Act of 1863 which cleared away these fixed engines or bag-nets from the Irish rivers and opened Queen's gaps in weirs where none previously existed The result was that soon a considerable increase became observable in the take of salmon But now a new difficulty set in, for with an increase of fish came a great augmentation of draft-nets, and in some rivers the fisheries are now, and greatly from this cause, said to be hastening towards the condition they were in prior to 1863

A Bill was introduced in 1885, observed the Conservators of No 4 district of the River Blackwater, ' under the auspices of the National Party of Ireland, whose avowed intention is to benefit the poor fishermen of that country; but the inevitable result of which legislation would be eventually to ruin the industry " Its purport was to curtail the annual close season by forty-four days, and the weekly close time by twelve hours,† to legalize the use of the half-tram net which was abolished in 1863 to establish different seasons for different divisions of the same river, and to separate the season for trout fishing with the rod from that of salmon fishing by the same means ‡

---

14 cwt 3 qr 19 lb , 1872, 6 tons 3 cwt 1 qr 7 lb As a ton is of about the average value of £120 this shows produce of between £700 and £800 a year from a river that at first was letting at £170 (Major Hayes, *Select Committee on Salmon Fisheries (Ireland)*, 1885, p. 45) The reasons adduced for the improvement subsequent to the Act of 1863 were, to the additional weekly close season and the restricting of netting to the lower waters

Respecting the Inny Mr Sinclair gave evidence (l c) that the Act of 1863 effected a great improvement for a certain number of years owing to its removing the bag nets that had been legalized in 1842, but since then fixed draught-nets or half tram nets have done incalculable injury, the figures he adduced for the river were as follows —5 years ending 1868, annual average take, salmon 292, trout 1284 , 5 years ending 1873, salmon 1066, trout 391 , 5 years ending 1878, salmon 468, trout 786 , 6 years ending 1884, salmon 245, trout 904

* *See* note, p 131 (*ante*)

† Some sea fishermen went further, in fact proposing to give them the extra twelve hours, but to refuse it to the river fishermen Thus *a coast fisherman* ' Mr Leake, lessee of a considerable net salmon fishery on the coast of Donegal, about three miles in extent, and entirely in the sea, said that he fished with a bag net and a draft net He fished from May to August He was of opinion that he should be allowed to fish until six o'clock, because the sea was a very rough place, and you could not fish more than four days a week As to the rivers, the fishermen could always fish, and he was of opinion the close time for rivers should not be reduced from forty-eight hours to thirty-six The annual close time should remain as it is '—Evidence before *Select Committee of House of Commons*, 1885

‡ "The salmon fisheries are now retrograding towards the condition in which they were found by the Act of 1863, when, as every one knows, the extinction of vast numbers of bag nets and other fixed engines was followed by much increased protection of the spawning grounds, and a consequent revival of the fisheries, although they never entirely recovered from the low condition to which they had been reduced by the legalization of all sorts of fixed engines in 1842 This revival, however, was forthwith followed by an immense increase of legal and illegal fishing at sea, which from the first was so destructive as to discourage the owners of the minor rivers (which are the heaviest sufferers) from resuming the protection of most of those which had been abandoned, and in this district (Ballyshannon) numbered five The earliest of the reports of the inspectors of Irish fisheries to which I have an opportunity of referring to at present is that for 1870 Comparing it with that for 1883, just published, I find that the destructive engines licensed for salmon capture, exclusive, of course, of rods, have increased in number from 1200 in the former year, to 1750 in the latter, that is nearly fifty per cent Of this increase, that of draft and drift-nets is from 790 to 1214, and this increase is annually progressing in every district in Ireland except Ballyshannon, where there is an actual decrease, because drift-nets have not as yet been introduced there, and the draft net men find it more economical to fish without licence, as they have, except in specially circumstanced stations every facility for doing This decrease is from thirty four in 1870 to twenty-seven in 1884, and as of the twenty-seven, about ten belong to river proprietors, it would seem that the sea licences have decreased by about thirty five per cent but they will rapidly increase again if Mr Blake's Bill for allowing boats to fish at half tram becomes law, as all now fishing either draft or drift nets can at once turn them into fixed engines, a ' half tram ' . . . . Boards of Conservators should have power to cause sufficient watchers to be employed on the rivers within their districts, as well as to take possession

There are several improvements very much needed in the Irish Fishery laws,[*] and the modes in which they are carried out, but respecting which readers must be referred to treatises on the subject, the annual reports of Fishery Commissioners, and the evidence in Blue Books   The weekly close time for nets in that country was fixed in 1863 at forty-eight hours, commencing 6 A.M. on Saturday and continuing until 6 A.M. on Monday, while the close season extended for 168 days   But as regards this annual close time for netting, the periods of their incidence are so varied, and the changes so constant, that no good could be attained in detailing the rules at force in different localities; speaking generally it covers the last three months of the year in most rivers, and even four-and-a-half in some   While angling with cross-lines, elsewhere poaching, as a rule has a similar close time to netting   and the open season for angling with a single rod and line varies in its commencement from February 1st to the beginning of June

As regards the means of capture employed for the taking of salmon within the limits of the British Isles, those which are legalized may be classed under three heads —(1) Such as are carried on in fresh waters above tidal influence   (2) in estuaries and tidal portions of rivers and (3) those in the open sea or along the foreshore of the ocean   This may be accomplished by angling in various ways by fixed modes of capture as weirs, puts and putchers, and stationary nets   or by drift-nets, set- or hang-nets, draught or seine-nets, and hand-nets

The estimated number of salmon fishermen in England and Wales, as shown by the actual amount raised in licence duties on instruments used for their capture, was given in 1867 at 3029 net fishermen, and 2350 rod fishermen; these have steadily increased until in 1885 there were 3747 of the former, and 4774 of the latter.[†]

In Ireland, in 1863, there were 9774 persons engaged in salmon fishing   During the quinquennial period ending 1868, they averaged yearly, 10,679, during that ending 1873, 10,336; that ending 1878, 11,570; that ending 1883, 11,596   In 1884 the number of licensed persons employed were—rod fishing, 2460; cross-lines, 226; pollen trammels, 232; salmon nets or traps, 9191; or a general total of 12,109 individuals

Some experiments were made in Ireland, as remarked upon in the *Dublin University Review*, November, 1851, in order to ascertain the size of the members

of such rivers as are now unpreserved, and make them, as they formerly were, nurseries for salmon   To provide for this outlay, they should have power within their own boundaries to fix the tariff of licences, and, in case these did not produce sufficient funds, to lay a supplementary tax on every fishery according to its value, and until something of this sort is done, not only will there be no improvement, but, on the contrary, many more of the small rivers will cease to be protected at all   There is much more of a 'solidarity' of interests between all the rivers of a district, in fact of the entire coast, than is generally supposed   That a certain number of the salmon bred in a particular river will return to it in grilse or salmon state is quite true, but every year brings proof that many of them wander very far, and at all events a much larger number would be found along the shores by the drift and draft-net fishers, who should be called upon to pay something towards their preservation" (W Sinclair, *Field*, September 30th, 1884)

[*] In the *Proceedings of a Committee of the House of Commons* in May, 1855, respecting a proposed new Irish Fishery Bill, Mr Harris remarked, that the owner of a several fishery could in some places prevent a single fish from passing up to the spawning beds   These rights were beginning to operate on *the Shannon*   The public did not altogether realize the change that was gradually depriving them of the rights which they used to enjoy   Draught net fishing on the Shannon lakes was a legitimate mode of fishing, because they could not fish all the waters   Where a man owned both banks of the river he could starve out all who were above him   There would be no chance of a fish getting up except in the close season, or at night-time, and night time was the favourite time for poaching, so that with draught-nets, the Lax Weir, and poaching, the Shannon salmon fishery would be ruined   Several draught nets had been introduced in the last four or five years, and day after day the fishery was becoming reduced "   Also *Major Hayes* concluded his report for 1884, respecting the penalty for wilfully taking, killing, destroying exposing for sale, or having in possession any red, black, foul, unclean, or unseasonable salmon or trout   That "it is understood that spent fish, viz , fish which have recently spawned, would come under the head of unseasonable salmon, but it is most difficult to secure convictions for killing or having them in possession, some magistrates requiring evidence that such fish are unwholesome and unfit for food," so vast quantities are killed with impunity

[†] These are exclusive of men employed under the holders of "general licences"

of the salmon family which could or could not pass through meshes of certain diameters

2 in between bars, 3¼ lb peal will pass   4 lb will not
2¼ „   „   „ up to 5 lb „   „ 5¼ lb will barely pass
Meshes, 1¼ in —3½ lb peal will pass   4 lb will not pass
„ 1⅜ „   5¼ lb ,   „   6 lb   „

As regards angling for salmon, it will be impossible to here enter upon all the various modes of fly-fishing in fresh waters which are recommended for the capture of this king of fresh-water fishes   The reader must be referred for this purpose to cunning treatises on the gentle craft, from whence he may obtain information given by experienced anglers, as to how to wade, fish from a boat or a coracle, or the banks of a river—what rod will be best suited for his purpose, the most appropriate reel or line, and, lastly, the best description of fly   For these latter differ in different waters, and may be said to generally resemble nothing that is normally found in the earth, air, or silvery stream , while the tyro is usually warned not to strike too soon, but when he does so to do it with no uncertain stroke   Lastly, the pros and cons as to whether to employ a gaff or landing net in order to secure a hooked fish have to be considered

In some places fresh or boiled shrimps or prawns are used as a bait by anglers They may be boiled in a saucepan of water to which a handful of saltpetre has been added, removing them as soon as they turn colour, they are then dried singly on a cloth, and, when quite dry, are placed in layers in a glass or earthenware wide-mouthed jar, which is then filled up with glycerine, and they may be kept so for months (see Major Treherne, Badminton Series, Salmonidæ, p 361) Salmon are found to sometimes take them when they will not look at an artificial minnow, which, however, is a killing bait under certain conditions   Live bait is usually tried within tidal influence, where the artificial fly has also been known to have proved successful   Now and again a salmon is taken by a minnow

Rod fishing* is sometimes put a sudden stop to by the unexpected presence of otters, which drive the fish from the fords into deep pools   While poachers† sometimes stone salmon off the shallows while scouring, and an accomplice with a gaff secures the alarmed fish as it dashes down the stream

A form of sport which used to be common in many parts, but is now illegal, is spearing‡ salmon by torch-light, so well described by Sir Walter Scott in "Guy Mannering"

Dogs§ have frequently been trained to assist fishermen in their work, and Yarrell related how a poacher in the Dart used to fix his trammel net at the lower end of a deep pool.   He then sent his dog, which had been trained for the

---

* When illegally fly-fishing for salmon fry a killing bait is said to be a maggot or bit of white kid either on the fly or on a bare hook.

† In some rivers, as the North Esk, a method of illegal fishing was said to have been in existence, even to recent years, and pursued by some anglers, although elsewhere it is generally left to the poachers   It is termed sniggering, sniggling, raking, grappling or dragging, and in England as strokehalling, or snatching, and is thus carried on   When the water is low, and the fish are collected in a pool and refuse the fly, a hook is weighted with lead, or the fly alone is sunk, or even a triangle of hooks or grapples may be used, and these are dragged through the water with the purpose of foul hooking salmon   Or this may be done by using a short line to which a couple of hooks are attached, then sinking the end of the rod in the river, they are dragged along Although some fish are doubtless taken in this manner, many break away injured, often fatally, so , and one can well understand that the District Board of the North Esk are unanimously of opinion that in any new Act steps should be taken to put down this unsportsmanlike practice, which might well be brought to the notice of any Society that cared to interfere where useless cruelty to animals is carried on

‡ Spearing or leistering salmon by torch-light, was thus remarked upon by Fraser (Salmon 1833, p 20), that he had known several fords of spawning ground almost cleared of male breeders in one night   The females are more wary, and if they obtain a single glance of the torch light will at once run into deep water, but in a few minutes will wheel round and return to their beds

§ W , in The Field, November 8th, 1884, observed, " Major Gleig, fishing in the Eamont, a tributary of the Eden, got a 16 lb salmon under very curious circumstances   The fish was fairly well hooked, and gave promise of some excellent play before being brought to book   No sooner did he begin to show himself in the water, however, than a Dandie Dinmont, the companion of

purpose, to dive into the river, like an otter, at the upper end of the pool, on which the alarmed salmon dashed down stream and became meshed in the trammel

In the employment of nets during dry seasons the take of salmon in the tideway is above the average because they are detained and unable to ascend But in such years with low rivers and clear water anglers rarely have a successful time If it is desired to increase the stock of fish in a river both the period during which netting is permitted, the number and size of the nets which are licensed, how they are used, and the localities where they are allowed should be strictly limited But it must always be a question as to what extent the laws are or can be carried out, and whether any local customs exist which are opposed to such It has been already observed (p 69) that some fishermen asserted that were night-fishing in rivers abolished their occupation would be at an end However, the Conservators of the Wye have enacted a bye-law to abolish night-netting and so far it has acted advantageously * In many rivers when the salmon season has legally closed, fishermen substitute fine meshed nets for salmon-nets, and continue fishing as before, pretending to be doing so for coarse fish and in the estuary for shrimps, while in reality they are capturing salmon The nearer the spawning season the more inferior in quality are the fish ascending rivers to breed, and these are the class of salmon which are captured by shortening the close season at its commencement in August and September

But in the fresh waters above tidal influence many different methods of netting may be employed, as by the draft-net which will subsequently have to be considered That *from coracles*† is commonly employed in the Severn and rivers of Wales The shape of the coracle resembles that of a walnut shell, about six feet in length and four feet in width, while it has a seat across its middle It is constructed of basket work, and covered with cloth or flannel which is subsequently overlaid with tar, while a paddle is employed to propel it These boats are very light and portable There are several sorts of nets used by coracle fishermen as the *truckle* net, when there are two of these boats separated by a net about sixteen yards in length There is also a second line, which on being tightened closes the net Each fisherman holds one end of the drag-line and paddles with the other hand, so as to keep the boats as far asunder as possible Directly they feel a fish the drag-line is let go and the second line is at once tightened, the net closed, and the fish drawn into the coracle In the upper waters of the *Dee* these nets are used by poachers, and are so small that they can be carried in a bag or even in the pocket The very darkest nights are the best for the poachers They glide down the river in their two coracles with this deadly net between them and without making the slightest noise except the splash of the captured fish while accomplices are employed to watch the water-bailiffs

Weirs or dams or obstructions in rivers extending partly or entirely across their course, and from their height either impeding or preventing the ascent or descent of salmon and other fish but the injury they occasion has in some localities been partly obviated for ascending forms, by the construction of free gaps or fish passes (*see* pp 73, 74, and 121) Some are for the use of mills or other works or for the purposes of irrigation, or raised by companies for the assistance

---

the Major's excursions, all unobserved, plunged into the stream, with the apparent object of 'beating a hand' in the capture Vociferous calls to return to bank were unavailing, and 'Dandie' vigorously pursued his way towards his intended game, with which he soon came into close quarters, and adroitly laid hold of the dorsal fin, to which he clung with all the tenacity of a bulldog The line became entangled around the dog and the fish, and unable to bear the additional strain soon gave way The gallant angler's feelings at that moment may be more readily imagined than described, but the dog kept his hold on the fish, and, after a struggle with his prey which lasted from eight to ten minutes, Dandie succeeded in approaching sufficiently near to the bank to enable the major to make use of the gaff, and both fish and dog were soon safely landed "

* In the Severn it was illegal from 1766 to 1861

† Coracles were employed so long ago as the time of the Romans, when their outer covering was made of skins They are in use in Southern India, and I have fished from them in the Bowany river in the Presidency of Madras

of navigation, for railways, or waterworks. Many of these weirs are destitute of any traps made especially for the capture of fish, but nevertheless in some mill-weirs the fish are struck and killed while passing beneath the engine, also unless proper care is taken fish, especially the fry descending rivers, often have their course deflected by the mill-lead. In some weirs or dams cruives are inserted into gaps in their walls through which water descends, and into which, on the rat-trap principle, fish can enter, but from which a grating prevents their return. In fact, in fresh waters numerous varieties of fish traps have existed, do exist, or may again be legalized, as cuts, cages coops, slaughters, &c, all being intended for the purpose of capturing salmon ascending or descending streams.

In estuaries and tidal portions of rivers sweep-nets or seine-nets are employed, to some of which a rope is attached being fixed or held on shore, while the body of the net being in a boat is rowed round a semi-circle of the stream, and payed out by the boatman. Drift-nets can be worked down the centre of the stream, and seines from both banks if the river is sufficiently narrow. The *net-and-cobble* industry is largely worked for the capture of salmon at the mouths of rivers and in estuaries, while a modification is used in the Annan, which is termed a *trou*.

In some estuaries and tidal portions of rivers the amount of mud present in the water may render netting difficult, while should a rapid tide likewise co-exist, such a procedure may be impossible at least by long nets, as in portions of the Severn. The presence of ice in rivers likewise interferes with, and may even stop netting. Fixed nets* are by no means uncommonly employed and may be observed in use at the mouths of many rivers.

A destructive mode of fishing but which is now illegal, was formerly common in the Tweed and some other Scotch rivers, and is not unknown in English ones. Its principle is that a net is affixed to the shore or made fast, and a man takes the other end out in a boat and when a fish is observed coming up that part of the river, the fisherman in the boat gives notice to his mate at the shore end and the net is worked round the fish and brought on shore. This is termed "stilling" or stelling †. Or else men are stationed at certain spots where the water is shallow and the ascent of salmon can be noted, they at once give an alarm and a boat containing one of the nets is immediately rowed off, the net being as rapidly dropped into the stream, the other end having been left on shore, and the net is carried round the ascending fish.

There are several modes of netting salmon single-handed, some of which approach in principle very closely to fixed nets, the plan being such as described by Sir J. Richardson for *halve-net fishing* in the Solway. The halve-net consists of a funnel-shaped net or poke-net, ending in a pocket or bag. The mouth is stretched on an oblong frame about three yards wide, to which a handle or pole 14 or 16 ft long is attached. When the tide commences to flow, a number of fishermen proceed over the sands and arrange themselves in a close line across the current of the flood, each with a halve resting on the bottom and its pole against his shoulder. As the tide rises it becomes too deep for the man furthest from the

* The legal definition of a fixed net is "weirs, stakes, bags, stop and still nets" and "whether fixed to the soil or held by hand, or made stationary in any other way."—18th & 14th Vict c 88.
† There are many varieties of this net as the *fixed draught net*, also known as the *half train* or *half tram* net which is employed by poachers in Ireland, either at the mouths of rivers or along the coast. One end is made fast to the shore, it is weighted at the bottom and has corks along its surface, half its length is so fixed between the shore and a boat at anchor, while the other half lies in the boat ready to be used as a seine if a salmon shows itself within capturing distance. In Hamilton's *Letters concerning the Natural History of the Basalts on the Northern Coast of the County of Antrim*, exists an account of a very similar net then employed at Carrick a rede, between Ballycastle and Portrush, the only place along the coast suited for its use. The shore end of the net is fixed, and the outer end is carried out so as to form a slight concavity facing the direction of the expected salmon. From the outer end another rope is brought obliquely to the shore to enable the net to be swept round at pleasure and drawn to the land and a heap of stones is likewise prepared. As soon as the watcher sees the fish coming he gives notice and the obliquely placed rope is manned by the fishermen and dragged to shore so as to encircle the school of salmon. During this period an incessant volley of stones is kept up to prevent the retreat of the fish until the net has been completely pulled round them.

shore, who then raises his net and places himself at the other extremity of the line, where he is presently succeeded by another and another, the whole thus changing places continually   When the halve is struck by a fish, its mouth is instantly elevated above the surface by the fisherman so as to prevent the retreat of the fish until it can be carried into shallow water and secured   During the ebb a similar plan is pursued in a reversed order, the nets' mouths being still turned to the current, but the fishermen constantly change to the end of the line that stands in the deepest water   Flat fish and shrimps are said to be the principal takes, but also salmon occasionally

Stop-nets of the Wye, Usk and some other rivers or "compass nets" of the Claddew are somewhat similar in their incidence, for at the ebb and flow of the tide boats are fixed or moored across a spot which is in the run of the fish   The net is a large bag-net upon a frame of from 25 to 35 ft beam and capable of being easily raised by the fisherman who rests the pole on the gunwale of the boat   The net is sunk so that the bag is carried by the tide or current under the boat, and the open portion meets the stream   At the extremity of the bag is a cord from which floats a cork, or one end of it the fisherman holds in his hand   On a fish striking the net a sensation is communicated by the cord and the net elevated as described

The *lave-nets* of the Severn are very similar to the halve-nets of the Solway, if used in line such is termed "cowing," but usually each fisherman works on his own account and on a falling tide when he intercepts the fish on the shallows

But among the fixed instruments *putts* and *putchers*, otherwise termed trumpets, of the Severn must not be omitted   They are wicker-worked baskets erected on stages the framework of which is 13 or 14 ft high, firmly fixed in a double row to the shore, from high-water mark.   These are bound together by cross bars on which rest the putchers placed one above another, with their wide funnel-shaped mouths directed either up or down stream as they are intended for use with the flow or ebb of the tide   *Putchers* are set upon stake stages having as many as from 300 to 500 several putchers, these take fish on the ebb and flow of the tide as their mouths may be set either way   They consist of rods bound together in the form of a trumpet, the mouth of each being from 3 to 5 ft wide   They capture salmon, also spent fish, but not samlets   any fish which enters is almost sure to be destroyed before it can be removed, as it is wedged in by the force of the tide   In some parts of the Severn there are hedges, termed pens, situated so as to guide the fish to the mouth of the trap   *Putts* take salmon as well as small fish on an ebbing tide   they are made of hazel rods, bound with twigs, and consist of three portions, namely, the kipe or mouth, secondly what is called the butt, has cross bars at his opening and decreases to about 6 inches in width, and thirdly the fore-wheel, which diminishes to a size sufficient to capture a shrimp   They are invariably set with their mouths up the river, and if the inside wheel, or fore-wheel as it is called, is not taken off when the samlets are going down, they are liable to be captured (*see Report of Salmon Commissioners*, 1860, page xi), but do more injury by diverting them into pools where they are taken by the lave-nets

Drift-nets are limited in some districts to 200 yards in length, they are shot across the tide and the fish are meshed in them like herring and mackerel, while set-nets or hang-nets are employed in some places.

There are numerous other forms of nets which are or might be employed, and the Report of the Commissioners in 1860 alluded to raise-nets, bag-nets, mud-nets, drop- or baulk-nets, as names given to various contrivances used at that time along the English or Welsh coasts for fixing up nets, or stakes either to capture these fish or to detain them in some limited space until caught   Some of these nets are attached to the stakes but able to act with the tide, falling with the ebb and confining all within

Stage-nets are employed in the Firth of Forth and elsewhere   A long line of stakes starts from the shore, having a slight curve up-stream, and these are made firm with wicker work, they extend from high to near low-water mark   A narrow gangway leads to the shore   In the weir are couples from 14 to 16 feet asunder, and between them is a poke or bag-net that works on sliders and is used on a flood tide   On the top of the couples is a platform where the fisherman can remain concealed by a straw hurdle and sees or feels, by means of a string attached to the net, when a fish comes in, then he hauls up the net and kills his prey   A leader may be attached to the sea end of the couples for the purpose of directing the fish into the poke-net

The fixed nets when permitted along the sea coast have, as might be expected, a family resemblance to those existing in estuaries, but are more extensive and complicated

Stake-nets are formed by driving stakes firmly into the sands and attaching nets to them   The principle is by means of a leader running to about high-water mark to obstruct or divert the natural course of the salmon and guide them into an opening leading to a trap or chamber from whence they cannot get out   Some of these are of great extent and have many chambers as the Scottish bag-nets, or they even have attached what is termed a fly-net, being anchored and floated by corks with leaders extending a very long distance out

The old weir or *yair* is on much the same principle, being an enclosure situated within tidal influence and which starts from the shore, and made by driving very strong posts into the ground to form a crescent, and this is made firm with wattlings   The open side of the crescent is up stream on the tide flowing over it, consequently on the ebb the fish are left impounded

These bag- and stake-nets are very inimical to the Scotch salmon fisheries, some being situated so close to the mouths of rivers as to impede the ascent of the fish (*see* pp 115, 124, 129)   They keep these fish out of rivers where they could be taken by net-and-cobble fishermen   and it has been a source of dispute as to whether salmon captured in these fixed engines or in seine-nets are best for food *   One party insists that salmon killed by net-and-cobble are knocked on the head as soon as netted and sent off unbruised to the market, asserting that those captured in the stake-nets dash about when in the chambers, endeavouring to force their way out, and thus often become much bruised, also that it not infrequently happens that if left there they swell a good deal, some being absolutely drowned   The stake-net fishermen on the contrary consider their fish the best

As food these fishes are highly esteemed, and although in most opinions they cannot be eaten too fresh, some persons prefer them after they have been kept a day or two, while in selecting them care should be taken, provided there is any choice, to choose those which are bright and silvery, rejecting such as are of a muddy tinge   During the winter those which are out of season are red or dull in colour, their flesh is soft and white, and they are wanting in flavour if dressed   If the fish is newly captured, it is usual, in order to set the curd, to put it into boiling instead of into cold water †   It may be boiled, but should be removed from the water as soon as done, or both its appearance and flavour will deteriorate   It is generally served with cucumber and anchovy, lobster, or shrimp sauce   This fish may be baked, done in slices, or sent up in a hot or cold pudding

Salmon are cured in different ways   as by simply drying, salting or pickling   "Kippered" is well-cleansed salmon which has received several dry rubbings of

---

* In the interests of fisheries and fish-consumers these fixed engines ought to be treated as common nuisances and summarily abolished, leaving the question of compensation to some competent court   Mr Steavenson gave evidence before the *Committee of the House of Commons* in 1824 that previous to the introduction of stake-nets into Cromarty Firth his fishing in the Cannon produced 7656 salmon in one year, while after the Firth was covered with fixed engines he only obtained 633 salmon during a season

Jardine observed (*see* p 107) that in the Friths of Scotland "where sand eels are used for bait, a line is attached to a buoy or bladder and allowed to float with the tide up the narrow estuaries   They are also occasionally taken on lines baited with sand eels and set for haddock '

† Mackenzie, *Salmon Fisheries of Scotland* (p 52), remarked "Salmon are always better for being a few days in their native (river) water   It increases, like crimping, the firmness of the fish, insomuch that while a salmon caught in the morning in the sea is soft enough to be boiled and pickled the same evening, one caught in the fresh water retains its firmness, and would break in the kettle if boiled before next morning   The fish-curers or boilers, who are great epicures, always, accordingly, prefer for their own palates fish that have been some days in fresh water "

pepper and salt, then dried either in the air or artificially by means of the smoke of peat or juniper berries   Those which have a large amount of oil* in them are not best adapted for kippering, but this depends upon the condition of the fish

Habitat —This fish ranges in the northern hemisphere between latitudes 45° and 75°, and examples have even been captured as high as 80° N Lat   In the United States' report it is stated to range from the Polar regions to Cape Cod but their presence in Hudson's Bay and the Arctic coast of America though probable is still doubtful   It extends throughout the seas and counties of Northern Europe, around the British Isles, and also the Atlantic coast of France, but does not occur in rivers which flow into the Mediterranean

It is rare in the Orkneys and Zetland (Baikie), but is found in all suitable rivers of England, Scotland, Wales, and Ireland, where it has not been destroyed by pollutions, or obstructions render its ascent impracticable   In Great Britain most numerous towards Scotland, it is present in all Yorkshire rivers unless excluded by pollutions (Yorkshire Vertebrata), less common down the east coast of Lincolnshire, Norfolk, and round the south coast, the English Channel, but more frequent in the Bristol Channel, while the Severn salmon are among those which are most esteemed

A salmon weighing 23 lb was captured off Lowestoft in a trawl net (Colman, *Land and Water*, May 10th, 1879), being only the second instance since 1849

Sir T Browne, 1662, stated that it was no common fish in the rivers in his time, though many were taken in the Ouse, in the Bure, and in the Waveney   in the Norwich river but seldom and in the winter   Paget observed, respecting Yarmouth, that small ones have very rarely been captured in the mackerel nets   Of late years they have almost disappeared from the Norfolk coast, and one taken December 1st, 1873, in a flooded meadow at Lakenham, was considered such a curiosity that it was sent to London for identification and preservation, it is now in the Norwich Museum (Lowe)   Yarrell remarked that the last Thames salmon was captured in June, 1833, but single ones have been taken in 1859, '60, '61 and since   (*See page 116 ante*)

The size to which this fish attains depends upon the extent and character of the water it inhabits, the quantity and quality of its food, temperature, and other circumstances   A considerable amount of caution is necessary before we accept some of the dimensions and weights which have been handed down to us †   The reason why some Dutch fish are so large is believed to be owing to so many kelts escaping capture

Respecting those taken by angling in Scotland Lascelles, *Letters on Sporting*, gives 54½ lb as the largest he had heard of,   Young mentions one 67lb captured in 1812 in the Nith,   Yarrell one killed by Earl Home in the Tweed which weighed 69¼ lb   Pennant one of 74 lb   Buckland cast one of 70 lb, 4 ft 5 in long, taken from the Tay   In 1885 the largest salmon netted in the Tweed were 56 lb, 44 lb, 43 lb, and of those taken by anglers 46 lb, 44 lb and 43 lb   Mr Hoggan when angling in the Nith in 1885, took a male fish weighing 42 lb, and which was 4 ft long   In 1867 one was taken in the Severn, near Lydney, in July, weighing over 42 lb, another the next month at Beachley, nearly 52 lb, and a third in the Wye, near Tintern, over 40 lb   In 1873 one weighing 70 lb was taken in June at Littleton   In Ireland, Ball recorded two, each weighing 52 lb, captured at the same time at Blackwater   the cast of one of 69 lb taken in March, 1866, in Galway, is to be

---

* Sir Robert Christison, in the *Proceedings of the Royal Society of Edinburgh*, 1871 72, p 695, recorded that on analysis he found as follows —

Salmon kelts, oil in flesh   1 3 per cent   {nitrogenous nutritive principle 17 07 per cent
„   *fresh run fish*   „   18 53   „   „   „   „   19 07

† In Hennesey's *Chronicum Scotorum*, p 317, mention is made as follows —"A D 1109 A salmon was caught at Luimnech (Limerick) this year, which was twelve feet in length, twelve hands in breadth, without being split open and the length of its neck fin was three hands and two fingers "   A correspondent of *The Field*, February 13th, 1886, gave a circumstantial account of one "84 lb" that was taken in a snap net in the Shannon twelve years ago   It was weighed by the station master before being sent off by train   it was also measured "   The succeeding month we were informed that the fish was a *sturgeon !*

seen in the Museum of Queen's College.   One of 57 lb. was landed in 1886 by an
angler on the Suir; several instances of 70 lb. fish are alluded to by Thompson.
It is a disputed point whether the female or the male attains to the largest size.
But it must not be overlooked in such investigations that the mortality among
those of the male sex is greater than among the females, while age has a bearing
on size.

The figure of the salmon in the plate 3, fig, 1, is that of a male 3¼ ft.
long and weighing 22½ lb., from the Teith taken in the month of November: figure
2 is from a female a little over 14 lb. weight, and no. 3 is a Howietoun female grilse
about 17 in. in length.   The figures in plate 4 are, no. 1 from a grilse from the
Severn, of 4½ lb. weight; no. 2 from a Welsh specimen 7·2 in. long; no. 3 par
from Howietoun, 5½ in. long, taken August, 1886.

EEL TRAPS.

TROUT

Although in the general account of the family of Salmonidæ many observations have been introduced respecting both trout and grayling, it now becomes desirable to offer some remarks restricted to the marine and fresh-water forms of British trout, which have been considered by some ichthyologists and fishermen to be anadromous and non-migratory fresh-water species. Before entering upon each in detail it appears desirable to explain why it is that I find myself unable to accept the numerous species that have been described, believing those ichthyologists[*] more correct who have considered them modifications of only one, which, as *Salmo trutta*, includes both the anadromous and non-migratory fresh-water forms.

For it must be evident when looking through the works of systematic zoologists, that the greatest number of false species among fishes are local varieties existing in such genera as are most prolific in forms, and that local races have been taken for distinct species. If among certain specimens an example is found similar to what exists in another so-called distinct species, residing in a different locality, this individual specimen might be an indication that both were descended from a common origin, in short, how it may be an instance of atavism, or reversion towards an ancestral form.

In following out such an inquiry, it is, I think, possible to prove that marine salmonoids may take on a fresh-water existence, also that *Salmo trutta*, *S. cambricus*, and other anadromous so-called species, can be traced into the fresh-water forms of trout. If sea trout which having entered fresh water in order to breed, are prevented returning to the ocean, it may result, as detailed by a correspondent in *The Field* (January 8th, 1881), that they become as he found them, big-headed, lank, and black-looking. But there may have been a reason for this, as insufficiency or inappropriateness of the food, or unfavourable conditions of the water in their new home, which precluded their thriving or even continuing in health. Should, on the contrary, the place prove appropriate, they may thrive even though they are unable to return to the sea.

If we examine the various reputed species of British trout we find them divided into the migratory anadromous forms and the non-migratory fresh-water races, but no one has been able to clearly define where one ends and the other begins. The anadromous forms as sea-trout, *Salmo trutta*, *S. eriox* or *S. cambricus* or the sewin, known in their younger conditions as *S. albus*, *S. phinoc* or *S. brachypoma*, are silvery in colour, with black spots when resident in the sea. But when they enter fresh waters for breeding purposes an orange margin shows itself to the upper and lower edges of the caudal fin, while the adipose dorsal is likewise margined with orange, and some orange spots appear on the body.[†] The

---

* Widegren (*Ofv. Vet. Akad. Forh.* 1863) gave an interesting paper in which he asserted that the anadromous sea trout and non-migratory fresh-water forms were all variations of one species, the differences being due to the localities they inhabited. In these conclusions Malmgren generally agreed, and they appear to coincide with the results of the experiment I have, or shall, allude to, and the series of examples in our national collection and elsewhere.

† Similarly no orange colour is seen on the salmon, *Salmo salar*, after it has once become a grilse, except when returning to the rivers to breed, then some may be present on the body, but more on the males or red fish which are the most exhausted of the sexes, while on their cheeks are orange stripes which have been aptly likened to those present on marine wrasses. But after the debilitating effects of the breeding season have been overcome, the orange colour leaves the fish being in fact restricted to the young and breeding forms, but not in salmon when in their highest condition.

non-migratory forms are in two main primary divisions of colour, as some loch trout are possibly anadromous forms which have become land-locked (see pp 5, 104, 105), and their tints are mainly silvery during the smolt stage, and subsequently golden and spotted, possibly this silvery colour may sometimes be symptomatic of sterility. Thus the Lochleven is normally of a silvery colour, with dark fins between its third and fourth seasons, subsequently nearly resembling the brook trout into which form it may degenerate—it is a somewhat delicately shaped but rapidly growing race, with rather weak maxillæ. While the estuary, lake, river and brook trout are all golden, with purplish reflections and more or less covered with black and vermilion spots.

Commencing with examining the subject of variation in colours, we find that the adult salmon and sea trout, when in their prime, have a beautiful silvery sheen, which is more or less rapidly lost when absent from the sea. This may, in fact, be taken as the normal colour of the *Salmones* when in their highest condition. Should salmon be reared in fresh water, and the smolts debarred from going to the sea, the upper two-thirds of the body and the dorsal fin become densely covered with black spots (see plate iii, fig 3), while sometimes a white edging shows itself on the front margin of the dorsal and anal fins. Likewise, as already observed, the land-locked forms of Lake Wenern are spotted more like sea trout than salmon, and in some par bands are persistent through life (see p 6 ante). Thus, it would appear that a fresh-water residence increases the amount of colour, while the silvery sheen is less highly developed. Here we see a connecting link in colour between the anadromous forms and the young brook or lake trout, with increased colours consequent upon a fresh-water residence.

A very instructive instance is recorded by Mr Nichols in his *Acclimatisation of the Salmonidæ at the Antipodes. Its History and Results*, 1882, wherein he tells us how the eggs and milt of a race (it is not recorded which) of British sea trout were transmitted to Tasmania, and one of the progeny 18 in long was received in the National Collection in 1874. Externally, its form is similar to our northern race *Salmo trutta*, but it only possesses 36 cæcal appendages, numbers more symptomatic of our southern race of sea trout, the sewin or *S cambricus*. The difficulty was met by suggesting the fish to be a hybrid, but as sea trout solely were spawned it could only have been so between our two anadromous races. These salmon-trout eggs arrived in Tasmania, May 5th 1886, were placed in the breeding-ponds, and from them 900 fry were reared. A number of these fry were put into a specially constructed pond, fed by a small rill of bright cool water, where they were disturbed as little as possible. By the middle of October, 1867, many of these par had put on the smolt dress when doubtless feeling the migratory impulse, they leaped upon the bank and perished in numbers. In July, 1869, four pars spawned in the ponds.* It is thus clear that this fish with anadromous instincts was raised from the eggs transmitted from England, and distinctly demonstrates that the number of cæca are subject to variations, consequently they are almost useless as a definite guide to species. Here some change in climate or food had induced such a marked difference, that in the Antipodes two forms of sea trout might be detected in one specimen.

In the National Collection may be seen specimens of what are termed in the *Catalogue* "hybrids between Sewin (*S cambricus*) and River-Trout (*S fario*)' received from Wales through Mr Peel and Mr Morgan. Their colours and general appearance as will be more particularly referred to when describing the sewin, show a graduated series† from the anadromous sea into the fresh-water forms. Similar series likewise exist in that collection which are located as "specimens supposed to be hybrids between *Salmo trutta* and *Salmo gairdneri*" or sea and brook trout, and others likewise asserted (but without any corroborative evidence) to be hybrids between the so-called Galway sea trout, *S gallivensis*, and the brook trout, one form merging into the other. Also I shall allude to a series

* This disposes of the negative evidence of sea trout becoming sterile if retained in a fresh-water pond without being able to descend to the sea

† This series is considered by Dr Gunther to show the effects of hybridization!

from Carlisle passing from the salmon-trout grilse or whitling into that of the fresh-water trout

The next form I propose adverting to is the Lochleven trout, which might possibly be traced in its external appearance to the sea trout In it there is normally a smolt stage in which the fish, subsequent to its par condition and for the third or fourth seasons of its life,* is somewhat silvery, but without any orange edging to the adipose dorsal fin usually present in young trout, and all the spots are generally black

But subsequently, as already observed, it assumes most of the brook trout colours, but without the white black-based margin to the front edge of the dorsal, ventral, and anal fins If the eggs, however, are sent to other and distant localities, as Guildford, or even to Gloucestershire, the young reared from them do not usually assume the colours seen in Lochleven or Howietoun, but take on more or less those of the indigenous brook trout of the locality where they are hatched and brought up (see plates v and vi) But this is not a deteriorating race, because consequent on certain circumstances which will be subsequently detailed (see Lochleven trout) when one of these fishes in Gloucestershire obtained a large amount of food, owing to the removal of many of the others from the pond, it grew more rapidly than its former fellows, and even had the Lochleven colours, previously denied to the rest Also, deteriorated examples at Howietoun assume the brook trout livery, and even the orange edging to the adipose dorsal fin, apparently owing to want of sufficient food or mal-assimilation of it A Lochleven trout having been crossed at Howietoun by a salmon-par, the offspring possessed the orange-tipped adipose dorsal fin which is seen in the young of the sea and brook trout, and it may be asked from whence could such have been obtained, unless the Lochleven possessed blood of one of these races? While the male parent, being only a par, probably occasioned weakness in the constitution of the offspring In colours, then, we have a distinct chain connecting the sea trout with the Lochleven, and so on into the brook trout forms

But silvery trout are not unknown in fresh waters, thus at Loch Crasspuil (see plate vi, fig 3) exists a race of this colour, and in a locality where they are unable to migrate seawards, still it has been surmised that originally they might have been sprung from an introduced anadromous stock While every year silvery trout are captured in inland pieces of water unfrequented by sea trout,† and would seem in some cases to be sterile forms, but in others to be examples reverting to their ancestral colours But we have some evidence to show that such a change of colour might occur owing to local conditions as in the following instance In *Land and Water*, August 15th, 1885, Mr Edon, of the Buckland Museum, remarked upon the appearance of some trout in a loch in Ross-shire, 2200 feet above the level of the sea and entirely fed by springs Up to seventeen years previously it had been troutless, and then Mr Fowler turned in some small black trout In 1885 it held a number of fine fish—"those under 2 lb were beautifully-fed deep fish, silvery with a few faint red spots, more like sea trout (*Salmo trutta*) than *fario*" Lastly, the late Mr Arthur, of Otago, observed that some of the descendants of our common brook trout sent to Australasia apparently have commenced reverting to anadromous habits and colours, thus the largest trout disappeared from the waters of the Leith, except during the spawning season They evidently went to the salt water of Otago Harbour in search of more water and more food than could be got in the river Common trout are being constantly caught in the fishermen's nets in the bay, and these show a tendency to acquire a sea-trout appearance, as they are usually very silvery, and the black spots are often, but not always, X-shaped

I think in the few examples which have been adduced (and they might be largely increased) reasons have been shown for admitting that sea trout might

---

* Dr Gunther has raised the question that Loch Leven some twenty years since was partially restocked with brook trout, but for this there does not appear to be the slightest foundation, as will be more fully entered upon when describing the Lochleven variety

† See paper on *The silvery trout from Loch Lomond*, by Francis Day, *Field*, September 26th, 1885.

breed in fresh waters without descending to the sea. That they can be traced* step by step, and link by link, into the brook trout and vice versâ that the Lochleven trout, which normally possesses a smolt or grilse stage, passes into the brook trout, also that breeding any of these two forms together sets up no unusual phenomena †

Our anadromous sea trout are able to take on a fresh-water state of existence, and breed there, irrespective of which by almost imperceptible degrees we find them in every country passing from one form into the other, which raises the question of which form *Salmo orcadensis*, *S estuarius*, &c (described as new species by Dr Gunther), most resemble, the anadromous *S trutta* or the fresh-water *S fario* Believing the two latter to be merely the extreme limits of one species, it becomes unnecessary to decide whether the diminution in the number of the vomerine teeth is symptomatic of the fresh-water form developing towards its larger relative the anadromous sea trout, or whether it is the sea trout retro-grading towards its par dentition, or that which is often but by no means always persistent in *Salmo fario* Colours, it is true are not very reliable, but these forms more nearly approach the fresh water than the saline varieties, a change which appears invariably to occur sooner or later in anadromous forms which become permanent residents in fresh water

Some of the chief distinctions between the sea and fresh-water forms of trout, consist in the comparatively more complete system of dentition in the fresh-water races, then generally longer heads, blunter snouts, and stronger maxillæ, irre-spective of the decreased number of the cæcal appendages

However, the dentition varies excessively, while we find examples possessing the colours, form, &c, of the brook trout resident in brackish waters or even the sea, but mostly, not invariably, possessing the limited number of vomerine teeth of the anadromous forms On the other hand there are anadromous forms (in colour) in fresh water, with the teeth assuming that present in the brook trout or retaining the par dentition ‡ (*See* p 21 *ante*) It has been asserted and re-asserted that brook trout invariably have a double row of teeth along the body of the vomer, and some authors have gone so far as to insist that these teeth are not deciduous Doubtless it is not uncommon to find trout even up to 2 lb weight or even more with all the vomerine teeth thus remaining intact when a double row is

* An experiment was made on *Tweed Salmonidæ* as alluded to by Mr Brotherston of Kelso, who tells us that a Committee selected 133 examples of orange fins which they placed in Carham pond in May, 1874 The Committee (with the exception of two) as well as practical fishermen, who from time to time personally attended the examination of these fish, were convinced that they had successively changed their character of orange fins for that of black-tails and whitling The two of the Committee who disagreed were Major Dickens and Mr Stoddart, who maintained that they were yellow trout In May, 1879, some were liberated, having had a wire inserted into the flesh behind the adipose fin with the stamp "*Tweed* ii " Two were captured June 4th and 5th, near Birgham on the Tweed, and came into Mr Brotherston's hands, and he found they were brook trout One which had been put into the Tweed on May 21st, 1879, 12 in long and weighing 12 oz , was recaptured June 4th, near Birgham-on the Tweed and when recaptured was 12½ in long and weighed 10¾ oz Mr Brotherston asserted that it was a brook trout A second was recaptured near the same place July 17th, it was 17½ in long and weighed 28½ oz , it also was sent to Mr Brotherston, and was likewise a brook trout, as were some others Both parties stoutly maintained the idea that these young fish were sea trout or brook trout, and it seems to me both were correct, for like the chameleon's colours they were referring to what are merely varieties of one species

† In November, 1886, Sir James Maitland, at Howietoun, laid down some eggs of the sea trout in order to follow out their life-history if kept in fresh-water ponds , 350 hatched in 1887

‡ It is remarkable how erroneous statements in Ichthyology are continued by compilers even after they have been disproved Dr Gunther, in 1866, asserted that in the Loch leven trout the maxillary bone never reaches to behind the eye that there is no knob at the end of the lower jaw in males, and that the tail fin is never rounded which are all merely errors of description In plate vi will be seen a young male with the knob in the lower jaw, the upper jaw also extending beyond the vertical from the hind edge of the eye, while in the woodcut showing the form of the caudal fin in this variety it will be apparent that it becomes as rounded with age as in the other races A most incorrect woodcut (in the *British Museum Catalogue*, vol vi, p 6) of the upper jaw as compared with that of the brook trout has been produced, which even shows maxillary teeth *looking upwards and inwards*, while the size of the bone, as delineated, does not agree with what is normally present in Lochleven trout

present, but it is by no means rare to see only one irregularly placed row While
in very large specimens these teeth (unless they have entirely disappeared) are
always in a single row, and the vomer may be found even toothless or with one or two
teeth at the hind edge of the head of that bone Equally incorrect is the statement
that the teeth disappear differently in different forms, for in all they first assume
a single row and then fall out, first commencing from behind But in the
rapidly growing sea trout the vomerine teeth are shed sooner than in the brook
trout

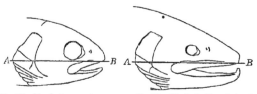

Fig 18 Head of young *burn*   Fig 19 Head of old male *brook*
trout, natural size   *trout*, 1-21 the natural size

If the external conformation of the head is examined it is found very similar
in the young trout, fig 18, to what is seen in the salmon par (*see* p 52, fig 13)
while in the old trout, fig, 19, there are many points of resemblance with the old
salmon (fig 14, p 52) , but should the skulls be referred to (*see* plate 1) the bones
of the trout will be seen to be much stronger and denser than in the salmon,
and this is especially remarkable in those of the jaws and snout At first the
posterior extremity of the upper jaw in the young trout extends to beneath the
eye, but with increasing age it reaches to behind it, and for two reasons, first the
eye with age does not augment in size so rapidly as the rest of the head, so
becomes comparatively smaller in old fish, and secondly the jaw on the contrary
grows proportionately with the rest of the skull · as a rule the jaws are stronger
in fresh-water than anadromous trout As regards the size of the eye, should two
trout of the same length but different ages be examined, the one which is the
younger will have the larger eyes
    Respecting the form of the preopercle in adult salmonidæ, much has been
written, but, as already remarked (p 17), what has been asserted to be specific
differences are often simply such as have been induced by age, sex, or local

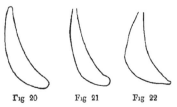

Fig 20   Fig 21   Fig 22

circumstances Fig 22, is that of an adult salmon, fig 21, of a female Lochleven
trout, 19 in long, and fig 20, of a salmon-trout, *S trutta*, also 19 in long, and
having 52 crecal appendages Trout from other localities, of the same size, show
but very little individual differences to what is seen in the above figures * The
forms of the opercles will be subsequently alluded to and figured
    Respecting the size of the fins of trout, those in fresh-water forms are generally
more developed than in marine ones, in young fish than in old ones, and in males
than in females The pectorals, which are shorter in trout than in salmon,

* For figures showing the gradual change of the form of the preopercle with age, *see*
Lochleven trout

10 *

appear to attain the maximum comparative length at two or three years of age,
subsequent to which they somewhat decrease. The caudal fins of large male trout
are usually more rounded than in females of the same size on an average among
many. In investigating the form of this fin it is evident that emargination, more
or less deep, is common to all the various races, and that the depth of that emargination decreases with age, while, as a rule, it is shallower in young trout living
in fresh water than in the marine races (see p. 13 ante).

As regards the number of cæcal appendages, which have been advanced as a
character which may materially aid in discriminating a species, I have already
(p. 22) given reasons against accepting this in respect to our fresh-water trout,
and will adduce further evidence under the head of the respective races.

While it must not be supposed that because British anadromous salmonoids
generally possess more cæcal appendages than are normally found in our indigenous and so-called non-migratory trout, that such is everywhere the case. It
seems that forms in some large lakes have them in great numbers: thus the
Salmo marsilii, from the lakes in Upper Austria, has up to 100; *S. lacustris*,
from Lake Constance, which Siebold considers the same species, has up to 74.
S. venernensis, Günther, from Sweden, which Malm gives, I believe, correctly, as
a variety of the common brook trout, has at least 62, while our larger forms of
lake-trout, *S. ferox*, have been found possessing a few in excess of those which
inhabit streams.

DRAFT-NET BEING HAULED ON SHORE.

SEA TROUT

A Northern Sea Race

Salmon-trout, Plate iv, fig 1.

Trutta salmonata, Schonev Ich p 65, Willoughby, p 193, Ray, Synopsis, p 63 *Salmonata*, Sibbald, Scot no 25 *Truttaceum cinereus aut griseus*, Willoughby, p 193; Ray, p 63 *Salmo trutta*, Linn Fauna Snee p 347, Gronov Zooph no 367 *Salmo*, no 3 and 5, Artedi, Synon pp 23, 24, Gencra, p 12, and Species, p 51, Klein, Pisc Miss V, p 16, t v, f 1 *Sea-trout*, Pennant, Brit Zool (Ed 1776) iii, p 296 (Ed 1812) iii, p 347 *Bull-trout*, Low, Fauna Orcad p 222

Salmo trutta, Linn Syst Nat i, p 509; Bloch, Fische Deuts i, p 143, t xxi, Bl Schn p 399, Gmel Linn p 1366, Bonn Ency Ich p 159, pl lxv, f 263, Triton, Brit Fauna, p 103; Risso, Ich Nice, p 323, Flem Brit An p 180, Nilss Skand Fauna, p 406, Jenyns, Manual, p 423; Kroyer, Dan Fiske, ii, p 582, Jardine, Salmonidæ, pl iii (*half grown*) ix, x, and xi, and Edin New Phil Journ xviii, p 49, Yarrell, Brit Fish (ed 1) ii, p 36, c fig (ed 2) ii, p 77, Parnell, Fish Frth of Forth, p 133, pl xxxiv, and Wern Mem vii, p 293, pl xxxiv, f 11, Thompson, Nat Hist Ireland, iv, p 151, White, Catal p 75, Gronov ed Gray, p 151, Gunther, Catal vi, p 22, Steind Sitz Ak Wiss Wien 1866, liv, p 22; Houghton, British Freshwater Fish, p 93, c fig , Malm, Fauna, p 538, Day, British and Irish Fishes, ii, p 84, pl cxi, fig 2

Salmo argenteus, Bonn Ency Ich p 160, pl lxvii, no 269; Bl pl cii (not Gunther)

Salmo goedenii, Bloch, p 135, t cii (*young*)

Salmo hucho, Flem Brit An p 179 (not Linn *possibly an old male salmon*)

Fario argenteus, Cuv and Val xxi, p 294, pl 616, Yarrell, Brit Fish (ed 3) i, p 250, c fig , Lacepède, v, p 187, Kroyer, Dan Fisk, ii, p 602

Salmo cria, Nilss Skan Faun p 395, Collett, Norges Fiske, p. 157, Feddersen, Danske Ferskvansfiske, p 77

Salmo truttula, Nilss Prod p 5 (*young*).

Salmo microps, Hardm Ofvers Vet Ak Forh 1861, p 383

Salmon trout, Richards Faun Nor Amer. Fishes, p 140, pl xci, f i, A

Trutta trutta, Siebold, Susswasserfische, p 314.

Trutta marina, Moreau, Poiss France, iii, p 537

Also known as *Salmon-trout, Bull trout, gray trout, Scurf* of the Tees, &c (*see* p 158)

(*Immature or grilse stage.*)

Herling, Whitling and Phinoc

White trout, Pennant, Brit Zool (Ed 1776) iii, p. 302, and (Ed. 1812) iii, p 396

Salmo albus, Walb Artedi, iii, p 75, Bonnaterie, Enc Ich 1788, p 161, Bl. Schn p 409, Lacép v, p 219, Fleming, Brit An p 180, Jardine, Edin New Phil. Journal, xviii, p 50, and Salmonidæ, plate no iii, Cuv and Val xxi, p 206, Jenyns, Manual, p 424, Richardson, *l. c* p 141 , Day, Brit and Irish Fish ii, p 85, pl. cxii, f 2

Salmo phinoc, Tuiton, Brit. Fauna, p 103

Herling, Jardine, Berwick Nat Club, ii, p 103

Salmo eriox, Jenyns, Brit Vert An p 422 , Parnell, Wern Mem vii, p 288, pl xxvii, f 3, and Fish Firth of Forth, p 128, pl xxvi-xxxiv , Flem Manual, p 180

Salmo brachypoma, Gunther, Catal vi, p 87 , Houghton, British Fishes, p 107, c fig

Also known as *Sprod, Herling, Whitling* and *Phinoc (see p 159)*

B SOUTHERN SEA RACE *

Sewin, Plate V, fig 2

Salmo griseus, Willoughby, Ich p 193 , Ray, p 63   *The grey salmon*, part, Pennant, Brit Zool (Ed 1776) iii, p 295, and (Ed 1812) iii, p 394   *Salmo*, no 2, Artedi, Genera, p 12, Synon p 23, Spec 50, Linn Fauna Succ p 116, no 307

Salmo cambricus, Donovan, Brit Fishes, iv, pl xci, Richards Faun Bor Amer Fish p 141, pl xci, fig 2 , Gunther, Catal vi, p 34 , Houghton, Brit F W Fishes, p 99, c fig , Day, Brit and Irish Fish ii, p. 86, pl cxii, fig 1.

Sewen and *Blue poll*, Couch, Fish Brit Isles, iv, pp 208, 219, pls ccxiii, ccxvi   *Salmo eriox*,† (Gmel Linn p 1366 , Bon Ency Ich p 159   Tuiton, Brit Fauna, p 103 , Flem Brit An p 180; Jenyns, Manual, p 422, Yarrell, Brit Fish (ed 1) ii, p 31, c fig (ed 2) ii, p 71 (ed 3) i, p 231 , Kroyer, Dan Fiske, ii, p 602, Thompson, Proc Zool Soc 1837, p 57, and Nat Hist Ireland, iv, p 148 , Nilss Skan Fauna, p 395 , White, Catal p 76 *(part)*

Also known as *Peal, Sea trout* and *Salmon-trout*, Couch, Fishes Brit Isles, iv, pp 214, 221, plates ccxiii, ccxv   *White-fish* or *White trout* in Ireland   *(See p 165)*

(Immature or grilse stage)

Also known as *Truff*, Devonshire, *White fish*, Dart and Teign, *Grey* or *Bull trout   Buntlings*, in Wales, also *Blue cap*   *(See p 166)*

The foregoing long list of references to the works of ichthyological authors who have written on the sea trout would seem to demonstrate that either we possess several species, or else that specific names have been bestowed upon various races, or perhaps on the same individuals according to their ages or sexual differences   Anyhow, it is clear that conflicting opinions have existed, and still continue to exist as to the number of forms of sea trout which are present in our seas and ascend into our fresh waters   At the present day the majority of ichthyologists seem to recognize two species, which I term local races, a *northern form* which generally possesses a larger number of cæcal appendages (from 43 to 61) than the *southern race* (from 32 to 52), while the jaws in the former are said to be somewhat less solid than in the latter   Irrespective of the foregoing differences, it is admitted that they pass from one into the other by insensible

<hr>

* Also found in Ireland

† " The term *Eriox* as first employed by Albertus Magnus in the 13th, and by Cuba in the 15th century, was considered by Artedi as referring to the common salmon   Linnæus afterwards employed the term as a trivial name to the ' S maculis cinereis, cauda extremo æquali ' of Artedi, and the *qnay* of Willoughby and Ray   De La Cepéde continued the term in its Linnean sense " (*Nat Hist. Salmon*, Edin Phil Journal, April 1st, 1825)

gradations without showing any definite line of demarcation, while it is not infrequent for individuals of the southern race to be found in the northern portions of the British Isles, and *vice versâ*

Among British Ichthyologists up to the period when Ray's posthumous work on fishes was published in 1713, two forms of sea trout were recognized,* the larger and that most esteemed for the table being known as the gray-salmon *Truttaceum cinereus*, and the Bull or scurf trout *T salmonata*, which was smaller, rarely exceeding 20 inches in length, possessing rank and odorous flesh, as well as a shorter and thicker head than the first

Whether Linnæus in his description of *Salmo trutta* intended to describe an estuary or non-migratory form of this fish has been questioned, for as long ago as Johnston† its variability in colour had been pointed out   But little alteration was made for some years subsequently, except that Pennant introduced as a new species the grilse-stage of the northern form of sea-trout, as the *white-trout*, while Sir Humphry Davy, in 1824, classed all our varieties under one head, *Salmo eriox*

But shortly afterwards more activity in searching for and naming fresh species set in, commencing with Fleming‡ in 1828 and Jenyns in 1835, who recognized a bull trout with a forked tail fin or the scurf, also the northern grilse with a

* Sibbald in his *Natural History of Scotland*, 1684, placed among the river fish salmon trout or *Trutta salmoneta*, and in his list of those from the lakes the great lake trout suggesting whether the last could not be the bull trout   Willoughby, in 1686, gave a brief description of *Salmo griseus*, or the gray salmon, which he considered of a better flavour than the salmon or salmon trout   while the scurf, *Trutta salmonata*, or bull trout, he observed, differed from the gray-salmon in being smaller, rarely exceeding twenty inches in length, having its head shorter and thicker, while its flesh possessed a rank and disagreeable smell, and was not so red in colour as seen in the salmon   also that its tail was rounded, or but slightly forked   Ray (1713) adhered to the views enunciated in Willoughby's work and gave the gray trout, *Truttaceum cinereus*, and the scurf or bull trout *T salmonata*   (See p 10, *ante*)

† Johnson, *De Piscibus*, 1649, offered advice concerning the discrimination of species of these fishes which would not be amiss were it considered in the present time   "In Salmonum et Truttarum speciebus distinguendis nimium ne crede colori   nam is pro tempestate aura, aut aquarum diversitate, mirum in modum variat"   Also, that "a man adventantes in flumina maculis carere, quas postea mora in aquis dulcibus contrahant"   Linnæus (*Syst Nat* 1, p 509), described *Salmo trutta*, but which example appears to have possessed ocellated spots and a double series of teeth along the body of the vomer, this has led to the conclusion that he intended to describe a non migratory fresh water form   Pennant, 1776, suggested whether the "gray salmon" might not be a mere variety of the salmon from which he only separated it on Ray's authority, but he thought it must be the sewin or shewin of South Wales, and *Salmo eriox* of Linnæus   While the sea trout, *Trutta salmonata*, he considered of a thicker shape than the river trout   He also admitted the white trout of the Esk, in Cumberland, which he remarked was "called by the Scots *phinoes*"   Low in his *Fauna Orcadensis*, written prior to 1795, admitted the salmon trout, bull trout, or scurf, *Trutta salmonata*, which he asserted do not grow in the Orkneys to so large a size as the Burn-Trout, were not so esteemed as the flesh was "always white, and but ordinary" (p 222)   Donovan, 1802 1908, figured the sewin or *Salmo cambricus*, which he considered identical with the gray salmon   Turton, 1807, admitted the *Salmo eriox*, or "the shewen," of a deep silvery gray, with purplish gray spots, and a nearly even tail , and the salmon trout, *S trutta*, with black drop like spots on the head, body, and dorsal fin   Sir Humphry Davy, 1824, only recognized one form of sea trout *S eriox*, which he observed was known under different names in different districts, as salmon-peal, sewen, bull trout, but most correctly as sea trout

‡ Fleming, 1828, while recording the bull trout having a forked tail which he considered identical with the scurf, owing to some error placed it under the head of *Salmo hucho*, observing that it possesses no teeth "in the middle on the vomer"   also the phinock *S albus*, also with

a forked tail, common in the sea and rivers of Scotland and the north of Eng land, and seldom reaches a foot in length.   The sea trout, *S trutta*, with a nearly even tail, attaining to about 3 lb weight and 18 in. in

Fig 23   Grey trout, *S. eriox* (Yarrell)

Fig 24   Salmon trout, *S trutta* (Yarrell)

length, and the gray-trout *S eriox*, also with a nearly even tail of much more clumsy shape than the last, seldom entering rivers before July   Fleming's bull trout may have referred to an old male

similarly shaped tail-fin   And two other forms of sea trout with nearly even tail fins, *Salmo trutta* and *S eriox*, the latter being the gray salmon or semif of Willoughby and Ray, the sewin of Donovan and also the whiting or phinoc the grilse of the northern sea trout, showing that these authors united the Welsh sewin with the northern gray salmon and whiting and placed them under the name of *Salmo eriox* of Linnæus   But Yarrell again reverted to there being only two species, but which he considered were both found in the northern and southern portions of the British Isles

During the last quarter of a century much has been written upon our indigenous sea trout, but the number of species has only been augmented (if we omit the estuary forms) by restoring the grilse of the northern form of sea trout to the rank of a species, but ignoring the scientific name *Salmo albus*, which had been bestowed on it a century ago, and *S phinoc* given it by Turton and re-naming it *Salmo brachypoma* Gunther,* while this latter author suggested that

salmon   his phinoc to the grilse stage of the sea trout   his *S trutta* to the salmon trout, and his gray trout to the sewin   Agassiz, 1834, included all forms of sea trout under *Salmo trutta*   Jenyns, 1835, admitted the bull or gray trout *Salmo eriox*, which he considered identical with the sewin of Donovan, having an even tail and sometime teeth confined to its anterior extremity, observing that in the Tweed the young are termed whitlings, while he thought that *S hucho* of Fleming must be identical   He gave secondly the sea trout, *S trutta*, having the sometime teeth extending the whole way and the gill-cover slightly produced behind, with the margin rounded , he considered Pennant's white fish or the *Salmo albus* as the herling, whiting or phinoc, to be the young of this latter race   Yarrell, 1836, believed we possessed two species of sea trout, (1) the gray trout bull trout, round tail or sewin, *Salmo eriox*, the gray trout of Willoughby   He distinguished the gill-covers of these forms as will be seen by comparing the two figures (See last page, figs 23, 24 from Yarrell)   The teeth of the *S eriox* consist in the adult of two or three on the vomer occupying the most anterior part only   the tail becomes square earlier than in the salmon and becomes convex with age, vertebræ 59 or 60   The Warkworth trout and Coquet trout he considered the young of this form (2)   The salmon trout, known also as the truff of Devonshire and white trout of Wales and Ireland, the Fordwich trout, and in its grilse stage as the luling and phinoc, *Salmo trutta*, is excellent as food   the form of its gill covers (fig 21) being intermediate between that of the salmon (fig 14, p 52) and gray trout (fig 23)   The teeth on the vomer extend along a great part of its length   tail fin is less forked at the same age as the salmon, but becomes ultimately square at the end, vertebræ 58   Sir John Richardson, in *Fauna Boreali-Americana*, 1836 gave some notices of British trout (1) salmon trout in which he found in one example from the Nith 59 cæcal appendages and in a second 61   He asserted that this is certainly not *Salmo trutta* of continental authors   (2) Herling, whiting or phinoc, *S albus*, ca ca 49   (3) Sewin, *S cambricus* Yarnell, 1838, while generally following Yarrell, admitted the bull trout, *Salmo eriox*, and asserted that at its grilse stage it was known as whiting in the Tweed, but that such was not the whiting at Berwick   Vomerine teeth confined to the anterior extremity of that bone   When about nine inches in length, has the caudal fin acutely forked , the middle rays elongating with the growth of the fish, and the fin ultimately becoming even at the end, at twenty inches the middle ray is more than half the length in the fin   As regards Yarrell's dependence upon the formation of the sub opercle and its line of union with the opercle compared with the body of the fish   he observed that he had in some examples recognized this character, but in others he had found it to vary too much to form an uniform mark of distinction   He alluded to eight varieties he had observed in the Frith of Forth, the characteristics of which formed the basis for their names (see page 10, *ante*)   Secondly he recognized the salmon trout, *Salmo trutta*, in which the vomerine teeth are not confined to its anterior extremity but extend far back sides with X shaped spots and tail more or less forked   The grilse of this form being the herling or whiting Jardine 1839, gave the gray trout or phinoc   and the Solway migratory trout as herling While White in 1851, and Thompson in 1856 retained Yarrell's nomenclature   In 1863, H Wade given (*Opere Petensk Al ad Imhandl*) considered river, lake, and sea and salmon trout as one and the same species, assuming a different appearance according to the locality it inhabited and local surroundings

*Dr Gunther, 1866, admitted three species into the *Catalogue of the Fishes of the British Museum*— (1) Sea trout (*see* page 10 *ante*), *Salmo trutta*, in the grilse stage known as phinok, herling, lammas-

Fig 25 *Salmo trutta*, reduced to ¼ size (Gunther)

Fig 26 *Salmo cambricus*, reduced to ¼ size (Gunther)

men, white salmon, and gave figures of the gill covers of the two forms (Figs 25 and 26) Found in rivers falling into the Baltic and German Ocean, numerous in Scotland, but less widely distributed

Yarrell's figure of *Salmo eriox (cambricus)*, which was purchased in the London market, "is one of those specimens in which the distinctive characters of the species are very little developed, and it is quite possible that the specimen came from Scotland, and belongs to *Salmo trutta*" (Catal vi, p 37) While, on the continent, Widegren (1863) united the marine and fresh-water forms into one species

Doubtless the popular or, rather, most commonly employed scientific name for the sewin is *Salmo eriox*, but certainly Richardson was right in reverting to *S cambricus*, and for the following reasons —If we turn to Artedi's "*Genera Piscium*," 1738, p 12, we find that he recognized in the description of the "gray salmon" of Willoughby and Ray the gralax of Linnæus, while he admitted as a distinct species the *Salmo trutta* of those authors In the twelfth edition of "Gmelins Linnæus," at p 1366, the "gray trout" of Ray is referred to the *S eriox* of Linnæus, as it had previously been by Artedi, and also by Bloch in his "*Ichthyologie*" at p 172 Nilsson, in 1855, when describing one of the Scandinavian forms of sea trout, imagined that he recognized it in a figure of the "sewin" in one of Sir John Richardson's works, and on these grounds included both under the head of *S eriox*, while Yarrell tells us that he accepted Nilsson's identification, but in 1878, Professor Malm came to the conclusion that the "gralax" of Linnæus was a young *Salmo salar* Consequently, although fully recognizing the inconvenience occasioned by changing the well-known name of a species, I still think it correct to discard the specific term *eriox* from our British Salmonidæ.

For the purpose of fully discriminating the sea trout in its various phases, probably the best plan of proceeding will be first to describe the two races, with the different varieties which have been recorded as species, and subsequently to enter upon a general history of the sea trout as a whole, and in which any peculiarities seen in the various trout forms will be alluded to

in English and Irish rivers, and having observed that Parnell was guided in his identifications by the amount of preservation, of the teeth on the vomer, or possessing the most numerous spots, he continued "It is well known that no distinction of species can be based upon such trivial grounds However, a few of the specimens named *S trutta* by Parnell, deviate so much from the typical form in having a stouter body or shorter fins, or a more perfect dentition on the vomer, that they might be taken for a distinct species But as they do not agree one with another in several characters, it appears to me much more probable that they are hybrids between the Sea Trout and common River Trout " He considered the difference in the shape of the gill-covers very characteristic for the two species, but admitted that numerous variations occur, and that there are specimens of *S trutta* and *S cambricus* which have gill covers of precisely the same shape That the maxillary and mandibular bones are stronger in the latter than in the former, while the number of cæcal appendages he has found in this form vary from 43 to 61 (2) Sewin, the gray of Willoughby, and the Blue Poll of Couch, *Salmo cambricus*, which possesses from 39 to 47 cæcal appendages although he found examples with from 32 to 52 occurring in the rivers of Norway, Denmark, England, Wales, and Ireland (3) *Salmo brachypoma*, consisting either of grilse of the northern form of sea trout or such examples as possess a short head, short lower limb to the preopercle and from 43 to 47 cæcal appendages Of it he observed, as did Jardine when claiming similar specific rank for the salmon par (*see p* 84 *ante*), that ' this is one of the best marked species of *Salmo* " "Parnell named three of our (? his) specimens *S fario*, and a larger one *S eriox* " Couch, in 1864 gave the following as species of sea trout (1) the *peal*, which he identified with the scurf, the *Trutta salmonata* of Willoughby, and the *Salmo trutta* of Linnæus and Yarrell Found in considerable abundance through the whole extent of the British Islands, he remarked on having received one from "Northumberland, under the name of Hirling, *Salmo albellus* " (2) *Sewin*, which he considered a distinct species from the peal, which he restricted to Wales he referred it to *S cambricus* of Donovan (3) *Truff*, sea trout, gray trout, bull trout, or pug trout, which he referred to Yarrell's round tail or *S eriox*, and said to be irregularly distributed throughout the United Kingdom, but only abundant in the rivers of the north of England, Scotland and Ireland (4) *Salmon-trout*, which he again referred to *S trutta* of Linnæus and Yarrell, as he had the peal he considered it more a fish of the north, although occasionally captured in the south and west of the kingdom and also in Ireland Day (1880-84) referred the sea trout to a single variable species, and considered that (1) the sea trout, *S trutta*, was generally a northern form, and the (2) sewin, *S cambricus* (which has likewise been termed *S eriox*) a more southern race, but that they are by no means strictly confined to these localities

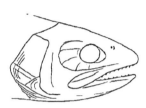

Fig 27   Head, ⅔ natural size of female
salmon trout, 12·3 inches long

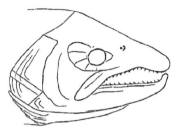

Fig 28   Head, ⅓ natural size, of male
salmon-trout, 20 inches long

The race of *Sea trout** generally considered as our northern one,† is also known
as the *Salmon* or *Bull trout*, *Gray salmon* of the Tweed, *Round-tail* in the Annan,
Scurf, *Scurce*, or *Salmon-scurf* of the Tees, likewise as *Cockrie* near the mouth of
that river, *Fordwich trout* (*cvc* 50), *Candlemas gray*, a kelt in Cumberland and
Westmoreland ‡   In the *grilse-stage* in Scotland, as *Phinoc* or *Finnock*,§ *Herling*,
Mordu-trout, or in the northern English rivers as *Whitlings* or *Whitings* ‖ also
Lammasmen¶ in the Edinburgh market for August ones, while some unclean sea-
trout are termed thus in the river Allan, and *gull of August*, and *mort* of the
Cumberland rivers   *White trout*, Ireland   In the *smolt-stage*, as *Sprod*, in Cumberland, also sea-trout grilse are sometimes so termed, while the parr in Scotland and
those becoming smolts are known as *Orange-fins* or *Yellow-fins*, *Black tails*, *Silver-
whites*, *Silver grays* and *Burn-tails* in the Tyne, and in Cumberland as *Smelt-sprods*
and *Herring-sprods*   A correspondent of *Land and Water* (March 27th, 1880), gave
the following as the Gaelic names of salmon-trout in the north of Scotland   *geal-
bhreac* and *breccan*, and sea-trout as *breac-sail* and *breac-mara*, and salmon-fry as
min-iasg and *siol-bràdain*, and trout of any kind as *breac* or *breccan*—also of
salmon-trout in Ireland as *coligan*

B x-xii, D 12-14 ($\frac{3\text{-}4}{7\text{-}10}$) | 0, P 13-14 V 9, A 11-13 ($\frac{3\text{-}4}{8}$), C 19-21, L l
115-130, L t $\frac{21\text{-}27}{33\text{-}37}$, Vert 57-60, Cæc pyl 33-61

Body rather elongated, but not so elegantly shaped as in the salmon, being
thicker and shorter in proportion   the abdominal profile more curved than that
of the back   The proportions of one part of the body to the remainder vary considerably, while the head is longer in males than in females, irrespective of which,
there appears to be a disposition in some forms to have abnormally longer or
shorter heads, in fact, to form a longer or shorter headed race   The young in
many respects are similar to those of the salmon, but with the pectoral fins always
shorter   Length of head in adults 4¼ to 5¼, of caudal fin from 7¼ to 8, height of
body from 4⅛ to 5⅛ in the total length   *Eyes*—diameter about 6⅓ to 7½ in
examples exceeding 15 inches in length, about 2 to 2¼ diameters from the end of
the snout, and the same distance apart   they are comparatively much larger in the

---

* The term *Salmon trout* was originally employed under the impression that some form (? all)
of sea trout were hybrids between the salmon and the trout
† *Salmo trutta* (*see* synonymy, p 149 *ante*)
‡ *Candlemas*, or the Feast of Candles. held on February 2nd
§ *Phinol*, Mr Orr states, means 'yellow fin"
‖ The term *Whitling* in a few localities appears to be employed for sea trout larger than when
in the grilse stage   while some of the terms given as applicable to smolts of this form are
in other places used for their grilse condition   Stoddart observed that, if breeding, it is called a
Bull in the Tweed and Esk
¶ *Lammas*, loaf, *mass*, or feast, a festival of first-fruits, celebrated on August 1st

young   Interorbital space convex, and equal to about the length of the snout
During the breeding season a knob generally exists at the upper side of the
anterior end of the lower jaw in the males   The posterior extremity of the upper
jaw reaches to beyond the hind edge of the eye in full-grown examples, and it is
stronger in some varieties than in others *   The form of the gill-cover† in this
fish has been held to almost denote species with some authors, to be dependant on
sex according to others, or to be of no signification at all   In some the posterior
edge of the preopercle is somewhat sinuous, while it has a distinct lower limb ;
however, every intermediate form may be found between it and examples in
which there is scarcely any trace of a lower limb, or they may even differ on the
opposite sides of the head in the same specimen ‡   The posterior edge of the
opercle and subopercle form a semi circle, in which the subopercle generally, but
not invariably, forms the most prominent point   Several raised and curved lines
are mostly present upon the outer edge of the subopercle and opercle   Teeth§—
in the young similar to those in the salmon fry   there is a double row along the
body of the vomer, and a transverse row across the hind edge of the head of that
bone   At an early age these vomerine teeth become lost, more quickly in some
examples than in others, but generally along the body of this bone there is only a
single row in examples a foot or upwards in length   and these have their points

* This has been denied by Dr Gunther, who, however, gives proofs of its being so in
nature   In 1866, in the *Catal of Fish Brit Mus*, vi, p 28, he asserted of the *Salmo trutta*,
when criticizing one point of Nilsson's description wherein this author had observed that the
maxillary bone extended to behind the eye, that "this is the case in very old males only ' at
p 30, he described a male twenty inches long, stating the maxillary "extends considerably
beyond the vertical from the posterior margin of the orbit"   Also of a female, 27¾ in long,
that this bone "extends beyond the posterior margin of the orbit" (p 31), and of a male, 18½ in
long, wherein this bone "extends considerably behind the vertical from the posterior margin of
the eye " (p 33)

† 1 have already (p 152 *ante*) referred to Yarrell's definition of the gill covers and given copies
of his figures, while Dr Gunther (1866) observed that the former author generally termed females
with shorter heads as *S trutta* and males as *S eriox (cambricus)*   He believed the maxillary bone
in the latter to be much stronger than in the former

‡ The following are the proportions observed in a pair of salmon-trout from the Teith, which
were used for artificial propagation in November, 1886   *Male*—20 in long, with a well developed
hook to the lower jaw (see fig 29), 47 cæcal appendages, and two teeth in the hind margin of the
head of the vomer and three along its body (see fig 29, No 3)   Length of head 4½, of pectoral fin 8,
of ventral fin 10, height of body 6¼ in the total length   *Eyes*—diameter 6 in the length of the
head, 2½ diameters from the end of the snout, and 3 apart   *Female*—12 8 in long, 50 cæcal
appendages, and two teeth on the hind margin of the head of the vomer and none along its body
Length of head 5, of pectoral fin 7½, of ventral fin 8⅔, height of body 6 in the total length   *Eyes*
—diameter 5½ in the length of the head, 1⅔ diameters from the end of the snout, and 2¼ apart

§ *Jenyns*, 1835, observed of *S trutta*, teeth ' on the vomer extending all along the ridge of the
palate "   Yarrell, 1836, gave the following formula from which to select   In *Salmo eriox
(cambricus)* the teeth on the vomer occupy in the adult the most anterior part only, and are
two or three in number, while in *S trutta* they extend along a great part of its length   Parnell,
1838, remarked that the number of vomerine teeth, when the fish has attained about eighteen
inches in length, are uncertain, varying from three to nine, nor is it possible to distinguish
S trutta by the teeth only, from some of the varieties of *S eriox (cambricus)*, at least not before
the fish has reached the length of twenty inches, when it will be found that *S trutta* has retained
from seven to nine of these teeth, and that *S eriox (cambricus)* and varieties have lost all except
a few, and those confined to its anterior extremity   Di Gunther, 1866, asserted of *Salmo
trutta*, "head of the vomer triangular, as broad as long, toothless   body of this bone with
a longitudinal ridge, armed with a single series of teeth, some of which are bent outwards   the
greater part of these teeth are lost at various ages, so that sometimes only three or four are left
in specimens twelve inches long, whilst others, much older examples of twenty inches, sometimes
show six or eight ; generally only the two or three anterior ones are found in examples of more
than twenty inches in length ' (*Catal* vi, p 24)   And at p 30 when describing a male twenty
inches long he remarked that "the body of the vomer has lost all its teeth, and only three
remain, forming the transverse series across the posterior part of the head of this bone "   Also
at p 33, of a male eighteen and a half inches long, that "all the teeth of the vomer are lost,
except three, which occupy the hinder part of the head of this bone "   Of the sewin *S cambricus* (or *eriox* of Yarrell), he observed, "Head of the vomer triangular, broader than long,
toothless in adult examples, and armed with a few teeth across its hinder margin in young ones
body of the bone with a sharp longitudinal ridge, in the sides of which the teeth are inserted,
forming a single series, and alternately pointing towards the right and left ; in pure (non-hybrid)
specimens, these teeth are lost in the grilse state, so that only the two or three anterior remain
in specimens more than twelve or thirteen inches long " (l c p 35)

turned outwards alternately to the right and to the left, being the remains of a double row that existed here when younger, but with increasing age the dental ridge became narrowed and some teeth have fallen out, as remarked on it p 21 The assertion of Dr Gunther respecting the head of this bone being toothless is possibly a misprint, as it rarely it ever is so naturally in specimens under twenty inches in length, while teeth are often present there in examples exceeding this size

These figures of the vomer in this fish are in No 1 of a female herling or whitling from the Esk, at Carlisle, 8 2 in in length, head 5½ in the total length, the fish having 46 cœcal appendages, and 57+r vertebræ, some of the teeth have already dropped out, but the remains of a double row along the body of the

Fig 29 Vomer and its teeth from 1, *whiting*, 8 1 inches long shown twice natural size, *2*, from *salmon trout*, 17 inches long, from the Oykell, natural size, *3*, from *salmon trout*, 16 inches long, from the Teith

vomer is apparent No 2 is the vomer of a salmon-trout from the Oykell, 17 in long, having 57+x vertebræ, and showing more teeth along the body of the vomer than is usual in a fish of this size No 3 is a salmon-trout from the Teith, 16 in long, with 52 cœcal appendages and 58+r vertebræ Although it has two

teeth along the hind edge of the head of the vomer it only possesses three along its body The teeth in the jaws and palatines are in a single row Three to six strong, sharp recurved ones exist on either side of the tongue *Fins*—in large examples the fins are comparatively shorter than in smaller ones, and the pectoral rarely extends half-way to the base of the ventral, which latter is situated

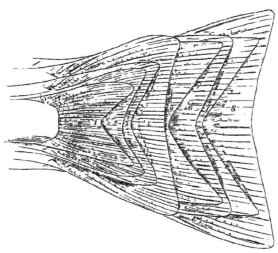

Fig 30 Outlines of tail fins of various sea trout 1 female *whitling*, 8 1 inches long 2 *trup*, 8 2 inches long 3 male *whiting*, 11 inches long 4 female *salmon-trout*, from the Teith, 12 3 inches long 5 female *sea trout*, 15 inches long 6 female *scurf*, 16 6 inches long 7 *salmon trout* from the Oykell, 17 inches long 8 male *salmon-trout* from the Teith, 20 inches long The foregoing tail fins are expanded to twice the depth of the free portion of the tail as shown in p 14

beneath the middle or last third of the dorsal The dorsal fin is comparatively small while the caudal is subject to considerable diversities of form, in fish at about twenty inches long being almost square at its posterior extremity, or in some few instances notched, while in still large examples it becomes convex,* as in what would be termed "round-tails" in the north Scales—fourteen or fifteen rows in an oblique line from the hind edge of the adipose dorsal fin, downwards and forwards to the lateral-line The scales in this species, more particularly in the young, are somewhat deciduous, about twenty-four rows from the lateral-line to the base of the ventral fin Cæcal appendages vary considerably in number thus a Tweed example† possessed only 33, but in other respects resembled this race In those examined in the Tenth this and last year I found from 47 to 50 ‡ As regards the number of vertebræ I have found from 57 to 59+x counted as explained at p 15, i e omitting the last in my enumeration Colours—Black bluish gray, becoming lighter on the sides and beneath, having a purplish gloss when in the highest condition, but which takes on a muddy hue after having been some time in fresh water Small black spots on those fresh from the salt water, mostly of an X-shape, exist along the gill-covers and upper two-thirds of the body, or merely upon the upper half of the gill-covers, where they may be surrounded by a light margin, while on the body they frequently are not seen below the lateral-line But when the fish is in rivers for breeding purposes these spots are usually larger and more numerous, sometimes having a purplish tinge or a purplish or reddish surrounding But some are densely, others sparsely spotted, with every intermediate variety The dorsal fin light gray or even straw-coloured, and may be destitute of spots, thickly or thinly covered by them Pectoral of a bluish lilac, often darkest externally Caudal gray, or even dark coloured, but usually dull straw-coloured in the adult During the spawning season the head of the male is of an olive brown, becoming black on the under surface, and the body of a dingy gray or reddish brown, while the female is of a blackish gray the adipose dorsal fin with from one to three black spots on its edge, also the upper and lower margin of the caudal are usually orange § Sea trout par or orange-fins are marked almost similarly to the young of the salmon, but the dorsal fin has generally a more distinct white upper edge anteriorly, with a blackish basal band, which often passes along almost the entire extent of the upper fifth of the fin, and similar to the colours seen in the brook trout, while its adipose dorsal is tipped with orange In the grilse stage (see whitling, p 159) the caudal is usually blackish,‖ becoming lighter as it gets older, first in its basal portion, which is straw-coloured, and this spreads to the remainder of the fin.

* Fleming stated that the hind margin of the caudal fin in this species is nearly even, Jenyns that it is forked, Yarrell that it is less forked at the same age as the salmon but becomes ultimately square at the end, Gunther that the caudal is square at eighteen or twenty inches, but in rare cases emarginate even at 25 inches

† Mr Brotherston, of Kelso, sent me in August, 1862, a specimen from the Tweed, termed "bull trout," it was a female, with small ova, only two teeth remained on the hind margin of the head of the vomer, its tail was almost square at its extremity, and it only possessed thirty three cæcal appendages

‡ In the British Museum Catalogue, vol vi, we are told of this form "cæcal pylori 49-61, rarely less " while the following are the number of those appendages asserted to be present in specimens in the collection five males from Scotland gave 43 15, 50, 52, 58, twelve females 46, 49 49, 50, 51, 52, 54, 55, 59, 60, one from the Ouse 49, one from the Eden 49, and one from Fordwich 50, showing variations from 43 to 60 Those having less than 47 seem to be considered hybrids, of these there are three, as follows 38, 38, 42, and three more stated to possess from 36-46

§ Thompson alluded to one example which had a series of deep orange longitudinal stripes, possibly a male in the breeding livery, but I have never seen one in the rivers of this colour It has been suggested (see bull trout, p 172) that some of these fish may be hybrids between the S trutta and S salar

‖ Respecting the number of vertical bars or bands, the so called finger marks, the following have been recorded by various ichthyologists in Great Britain Pennant (1776) observed of the samlet or par that " it is also marked from the back to the sides with six or seven large bluish bars but this is not a certain character, as the same is sometimes found in young trout " (p 305, pl lxx, no 119) Fleming (1828) remarked that "the Samlet or Par of Pennant is now generally considered as the young of this species (S trutta) or of the salmon " (p 180) Parnell (1838) described "the lateral-line crossed with from eight to nine, and sometimes ten, transverse

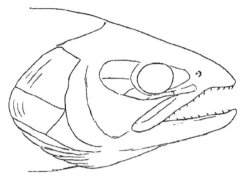

Fig 31   Head natural size of female *scurf*

The *Scurf* of the Tees has, from the time of Willoughby until now, been almost universally considered to be identical with the salmon-trout, *Salmo trutta*   In the following there were, D 13($\frac{4}{6}$), P 13, V 9, A 11($\frac{4}{8}$), C 21, Vert 58 + r   A female received from Mr Grissell, in August, 1855, was 16 6 inches long,[*] and the tail fin slightly concave, length of head $5\frac{2}{3}$ in the total length, form of preopercle as in the figure, while it possessed 56 cœcal appendages, and its tail fin was equally concave with no 5 in figure no 30 (p 156 *ante*)   Another specimen, also termed *Scurf* or *Cockures*, was sent in April the same year, from Turecbridge-on-the-Tees   it also was a female, 16 inches long, and had recently spawned, twenty three full-sized eggs still remaining in the abdominal cavity   Length of head $5\frac{1}{4}$ in the total length (*see figure 31*)   it had 52 cœcal appendages   A third example from the same locality was a male, 18 inches long, with a small hook at the end of its lower jaw   the tail fin was slightly concave   cœcal appendages 52, and the milt well forward   All were of the general colours of salmon-trout, and the black spots extended in from one to three irregular rows below the lateral-line

bluish bands, with an orange coloured spot placed between each " (p 295)   Mr Shaw (1843) gave figures in the *Transactions of the Royal Society of Edinburgh* of young *Salmo salar*, *S trutta*, and *S jario*, showing fourteen in the salmon, twelve in the sea trout, and thirteen or fourteen, some of which were broken up in the middle, in the fresh water trout   He also remarked, with reference to the young salmon-trout, that " on comparing them with the common trout, the resemblance is very striking, the general outline of the fish being less elegant than that of the young salmon or par, the external markings being also more peculiarly those of the trout species, so that, in the absence of the parent skins, it would be a matter of difficulty to determine to which kind of trout they actually belong "   Dr Gunther remarked as follows   *Catalogue of the Fishes in the British Museum*, vol vi 1866, p 25, *Salmo trutta*, " young with nine or ten dusky cross bars "   In his *Introduction to the Study of Fishes*, 1880, he observed, ' the number of bars is not quite constant, but the migratory trout have two (and even three) more than river trout " (p 631)   I may here just allude to the fact that the Lochleven trout Dr Gunther asserted to be " a non migratory species inhabiting Lochleven and other lakes," &c (Catal vol vi, p 101) , con-sequently it ought to have two or three bars less than his *S trutta* (stated to possess nine or ten), but instead of this, it may have from fifteen to sixteen, as observed in a very large number of young examples at Howietoun   In a brook at Cowley, where neither sea trout nor salmon can ascend, the trout pars had from nine to ten lateral bands, similar to the number present in the salmon pars

* In it were numerous eggs up to 0 125 of an inch each in diameter   numbers are said to ascend this river at this period of the year, weighing from 1 lb to 14 lb each   Unless in the kelt stage it is said not to rise to the fly   In a correspondence between Mr Surtees and Frank Buckland in September, 1869, we are told that at Dinsdale-on-Tees they fetch nearly the same price as salmon, for, by the employment of a pair of scissors, the round-tail of the bull trout becomes the more forked tailed salmon   However, Buckland, having eaten one, observed that it had a *very bad taste*

 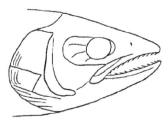

Fig 32 Head, natural size, of
female *whitling*, 8 2 inches long,
cæcal appendages 50

Fig 33 Head, natural size, of male *whitling*,
11 inches long, cæcal appendages 40

The *Whitling* * or *Whiting* of Cumberland has many local names, being the
grilse stage of the salmon-trout (see p 151) Like the salmon-grilse it has proved
a fruitful source of contention to ichthyologists and others † In July, 1885, the
Rev. W Jackson, M A , kindly sent me from Carlisle a series of these fishes,
furnishing a most complete chain of examples passing from *S trutta* on one hand
to *S fario* on the other They were individually between 7 and 11 inches in
length, and seven of them clearly belonged to the white trout, *Salmon albus*, of
Pennant, which is also known as *Spiod* ‡ The following is a brief summary of these
fish *No 1*, male, 11 inches long, cæcal pylori 40, length of head 5¼ in the entire
length, three teeth on hind margin of head of vomer, 12 along its body in a zig-
zag line Silvery with black spots above the lateral-line, and two irregular rows
below it dorsal fin with a few black spots along its summit and base pectoral dark
edged, the other fins diaphanous *No 2*, female, 9 5 inches long, cæcal pylori
46 , length of head 5 the entire length Teeth on vomer as in last Silvery
with black spots, dorsal fin dark-spotted and caudal black edged Many sea lice

* Stoddart observed of the Esk, that " in summer a few sea trout, answering the description
of whitlings, and weighing from 1 lb to 3 lb , push their way up, and are generally killed After
them, in July and August, succeed the herlings, and lastly, the bulls or bulls " . . " The far-
famed bull trout of Tairas, a tributary of the Esk, were merely bills, and, when ' ta'en in
season,' herlings or whitens, the latter being another local name for the same description of fish "
(p 230)
† Pennant, in 1776, remarked that " this species migrates out of the sea into the river *Esk* in
Cumberland, from July to September, and is called from its colour the *whiting* " He observed
upon their having the sea louse adhering to them on their first appearance, that they possess both
milt and spawn, while " this is the fish called by the Scots phinoc," and never exceeds a foot in
length I have already shown that although Turton, Fleming, Jardine, Richardson Gunther, and
Couch have considered it a distinct species , Sir Humphry Davy, Agassiz, Jenyns, Yarrell, Parnell,
White, and Thompson held it to be the grilse stage of salmon trout Parnell, in 1849, believed the ♀
albus to be nothing more than the young of some migratory trout, and having remained several weeks
on the banks of Solway Firth, inspecting several hundred specimens and carefully dissecting two
hundred, he found them to differ exceedingly from one another in their structure, the number of
their scales, the colour of their flesh, and the form and arrangement of the lateral spots He
remarked that shortly after entering rivers they lose their silvery appearance, and the flesh, which
had previously had a reddish tinge and a delicate flavour, now becomes white and insipid, and the
fish soon assumes an unwholesome appearance They return to the sea in January or February,
and are sold in Edinburgh as Lammasmen Hamilton, *Natural History of British Fishes*, 1843,
also held that " Ichthyologists are now agreed it (*S albus*) is nothing more than the salmon-trout
after being for a time in the sea and returning to fresh water, and in this state they are called
herlings or whitings, sometimes phinocks " Fishermen have likewise considered them to be the
young of the salmon-trout Thus Mr Johnstone (1824) deposed before the Salmon Commissioners that
" they are called herlings on the Scotch side of the Solway , they are called *whitings* on the English
side , they are called sometimes *herlings* and sometimes *whitings* at Berwick , they are called
whitelings on the Tay, and *finnocks* in the north of Scotland " While Lord Home, as stated by
Yarrell, observed that " the whiting in the Tweed was the salmon-trout (*S cambricus* or *eriox*),
not the young of the bull trout (*S trutta*), which now go by the name of ' trouts ' simply "
‡ A correspondent of Frank Buckland observed that " the flesh of the sprod, or smelt
(*Salmo albus*) or herling is white, that of the mort (*S trutta*) is pink "

on this fish   No 3 male, 8 2 inches long, cæcal pylori 50   length of head 4⅔ in the entire length   Few spots below the lateral-line   Dorsal fin spotted, its upper-anterior corner black   pectoral very dark   caudal dark edged   No 4, 8 1 inches long   cæcal pylori 40   length of head 1⅓ in the entire length   Only a few black spots below the lateral-line   dorsal fin spotted with black and having its upper-anterior margin with a white edge   adipose dorsal edged with orange   pectoral fin reddish except at its edge   Teeth as in No 1   No 5, female, 7 5 inches long   cæcal pylori 60   length of head 4⅓ in the entire length   Upper-anterior corner of dorsal fin black margined with white   No 6, 7 8 inches long   cæcal pylori 42   length of head 5¼ in the entire length   No 7, 7 5 inches long: cæcal pylori 43   length of head 4⅖ in the entire length   No 8 in colour was a yellow trout, male, 8 8 inches long   cæcal pylori 40   length of head 5 in the entire length ; colour yellowish having numerous large red spots surrounded by a light edging   dorsal fin densely spotted, its upper-anterior corner with a black-based white edging   caudal fin red edged

In the foregoing series (excluding No 8), the colour of the fins graduated towards those of the brook trout   the length of the head of a local example of male brook trout was one-fifth of the entire length of the fish, whereas in these whitlings it varied from 4¼ to 5⅓ in the total   the lower limb of the preopercle in all but one was very short, when the adipose or dead fin was orange   the pectoral was light coloured   and the anterior-superior margin of the back fin from being nearly black in some had a white margin in others, while in two there was absolutely no black spots at all on this fin   As to the vomerine teeth,* in all a row was present along the hind margin of the head of that bone, and in a more or less complete zig-zag line along its body (see fig 29, no 1, p 156)   The cæcal appendages averaged 53, but were of varying numbers from 40, 40, 42, 43, 46, 50, 60   In the one in which the vertebræ were examined, there were 58 + r   It must be evident that in this series we have evidence of a gradual approach from the sea to the river trout

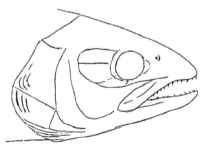

Fig 34   Head, natural size, of female Sewin or southern race

The race of sea trout generally considered as more exclusively our southern and Irish one† has been subdivided by authors in accordance with its size, sex, external appearance   and the number of teeth existing on the body of the vomer

* Parnell observed of the vomerine teeth that " they are from nine to twelve in number, and in about one example out of twenty only three of these teeth are perceptible, and these confined to the most anterior part ' (p 290)

† Donovan, in his Tour in South Wales and Monmouthshire, drew attention to this form, which he termed Salmo cambricus (for synonymy see p 150 ante), observing on its appearing on the sea coast and in the rivers of Wales during the summer months, from May to September, and then returning to the sea

In the Report of the Commissioners appointed to inquire into the Salmon Fisheries of England

Bull trout is a name not restricted to one race, but apparently more used to designate large and coarse examples *Truff* in Devonshire likewise employed for moderately sized fish *Sewin** in Wales *Gwiniad*† in the Teifi *Cove* in the Usk ‡ *Twbs*§ in the Taff *Buntlings*‖ in the Clwyd, Elwy and Chester Dee. *Peal* in Devonshire and along the south coast, of these, several kinds have received names, or else owing to the time of their appearance as *May-Peal*, *Pug-Peal*,

and Wales in 1860 a considerable amount of information was given respecting the sewin In the Severn they were said to be very rare and ascended about July, only a few were taken, and that by chance, in the Wye, while they were absent from the Monnow and the Lugg, and rare in the Usk At Cardiff the rivers were too polluted for fish to reside in, but sewin in the Ogmore spawned as early as September A second form termed "*tobbs*," or *twbs* was believed to belong to a different species of sea trout Mr Lea asserted that sewin from 4 lb to 5 lb in weight ascended in April, those of about 2 lb weight in May, but only of 1 lb weight in August Mr Llewellyn, however, observed that about Christmas there was a run of young fish from ¼ lb to ¾ lb in weight which ascended in couples Near Swansea, the Tawe abounded in sewin and some ascended the Cadly and the Nenth river, while these fish augmented in numbers in the Carmarthen Bay, being very abundant in the Towy, where their average weight was from 2½ to 3 lb and they seldom exceeded 6 lb A fisherman remarked that, from April until August, the sewin vary from 4 lb to 1 lb in weight, and they used a four-inched mesh for their nets, but they generally run very large from April to about the middle of June, in August sewin nets were superseded by those for the salmon Another witness did not know of any fish termed "*twbs*" in the Towy, he considered there was only one kind of sea trout in the river, and that the large ones were salmon Sewin were said to be taken in small meshed nets during July and August in the Cladden and the Teifi In the Taf, the produce of the river upon which fishermen most depended was said to be the sewin In the Nevern at Newport, the sewin commenced ascending in June, and were plentiful The Dovey contained a large amount of sewin until the mine water stopped them to some extent In the Conway sewin were more abundant than salmon, and commenced spawning in September Near Rhyl, in the Clwyd and Elwy, the sewin were termed "*buntlings*," and were in good numbers, perhaps one hundred to every salmon they commenced running up in June to the end of August or September, and by the beginning of October they were out of condition In the Chester Dee these fish were asserted to be plentiful up to July and August As regards size, sewin were said to attain to 12 lb in weight, but bull trout only to 5 lb or 6 lb while it was stated that in some waters which were never netted they scarcely average weight did not come up to 1 lb

* Buckland observed, 'A fish known in the neighbourhood of the Ogmore, Wales, as the sewin, runs up in July, August, and September These are said to be all females, some say that the twb, or in Welsh '*Twbbyn*' (*i e* the sea trout), is the male of the sewin" Continuing that, the Rev Augustus Morgan writes me, "The sewin comes up the river Rhymney, South Wales, just when the oak is coming into bloom *Brith dail* (*Queen* bull trout) come when the leaves in the autumn are beginning to change colour and fall, and the salmon proper (*Salmo salar*) never ascend in any numbers till November or December" *Dr Gunther*, however gave a different interpretation asserting that hybrids are known as "*Twb-y-dail*, literally l'all of the Leaf, indicative of the reddish shade of colour, and of the dark brown spots of the male" (Catal. vi, p 17) While in Owen's Welsh Dictionary this term is locally employed for the chub, *Leuciscus cephalus*

† Captain Benyon, when giving his evidence before the *Salmon Commissioners* in 1860, observed that in Welsh rivers this name was given to the Sewin when in certain conditions, while in the Teifi fry were so called It means "weak fish" Major Treherne also asserted that they were sea trout, that he took them with sea lice upon them, that they ascend the river all through the summer, and he only knew them from trout by their play and the large spots on them, while 1½ lb was the largest he had seen A fisherman, Llewellyn, also deposed that *Gwiniad Ebrill*, or April gwiniad, arrived about the middle of that month, of a size from ¼ lb to 2½ lb. They are a very handsome fish, the marks on them instead of being small like a trout are large brown spots about the size of a threepenny or fourpenny piece Its flesh is as pink as any salmon in the highest season, while the trout in the Ogmore is particularly white

‡ Mr C Pennell says, "I have caught several hundred bull trout myself in the Usk, averaging from 4 lb up to 20 lb, and never remember to have caught one of much less than the first named weight, it is only reasonable to conclude that this is the size at which they return to the river after their first salt water trip" (p 148)

§ Major Treherne giving his evidence before the Commissioners appointed to inquire into the English and Welsh Salmon Fisheries in 1860, remarked concerning the Ogmore, "I know there are fish running down in October called '*twb-y dail*,' they are about nine or ten pounds, and I believe them to be nothing else but the male of the sewin I have never found any milt in what are called sewin In my belief the twb y-dail are all male fish I am certain that the sewin of Wales, the sea trout of Scotland, and the white trout of Ireland are the same fish "

‖ Edwards, giving evidence in 1860 respecting the fish in the Clwyd and Elwy stated, "there are only five sorts of fish in our rivers The first is brown trout, the next is graveling, and where you see graveling there will be no salmon come up to that river at all, then after the graveling there will be the sea trout and the other salmon we call buntling—there are great spots upon them just like a snake,"

Pug-Salmon or *Peal*, if large in the Torridge, *Harvest-Peal* and *School-Peal* in the Devonshire Exe,* *Bourne-Trout* in Hampshire in the Itchen, the Test, the Beaulieu, the Lymington, and other rivers in the county In its *grilse-stage* it is termed *White-fish*, in the Dart and Teign and rivers along the south coast until it becomes about six inches in length, when in some localities it is termed *Peal* (but this latter name is sometimes employed for large fish) while occasionally *white-fish* refers to the smolts In some parts of Ireland they are known as *Trout-Peal* The young are termed *Par* or *Spawn*,† and in Welsh *Sil-bodiam*

B x-xii, D 12-14 ($\frac{2-1}{0-10}$) /0 P 13-14, V 9, A 11-12 ($\frac{3-1}{7-1}$), C 19-21, L 1 115-130 L tr $\frac{3+}{36}\frac{2+}{33}$, Vert 58-60, Cæc pyl 33-52

The form of the body externally is so similar to that of the northern race‡ that it has been deemed necessary to first ascertain the number of cæcal appendages or the strength of the jaws, prior to its being always possible to offer an opinion § It has both its long and its short-headed varieties as seen in the salmon-trout of the east coast of Scotland Although it has been asserted that in the sewin the head is "rather long as compared with its depth," while that of the salmon-trout, *S trutta*, "is rather short as compared to its depth," such does not appear to be the rule if sex is also considered Doubtless it may be so in some examples, but the reader is referred to the outlines of the heads on pages 154, 158, 159, 160 The length of the head in a number of examples was from 4$\frac{4}{5}$ to 5$\frac{1}{4}$ in the total, or rather less than seen in salmon-trout But the proportions of one part of the body to the remainder, and the form of the gill-covers, were so similar to those described for the salmon-trout (p 154) that repetition seems unnecessary *Teeth*—in a single row across the hind edge of the head of the vomer, and in a double row in the young along the body of that bone This last soon changes into a single row, with the points of the

---

* In 1879 a correspondence commenced respecting the *blue poll* and *blue cocks* of the Fowey in Cornwall, also termed *Candlemass fish*, and which were sold in Billingsgate as "Cornish salmon " Some which used to be taken at the beginning of the year were said to have been unmended kelts, while an example sent from that river in December, 1879, to Mr Frank Buckland, proved to be a male with the milt fully developed and ready for extrusion Mr Nott (1860) remarking on the fish of the Clwyd and Elwy, observed that a great many of the " blue salmon ' run up from June to the latter end of August and September, about half were true salmon and half were buntlings In the Towy in Wales, there is a variety termed *salmon glasbach*, "little blue salmon," which largely ascend for the purpose of spawning in the last week in January and the first half of February, and we are told that thirty years ago, prior to the reinstitution of a close season, all the males were crimped and sent to the Severn district as clean run fish, while the females were dispatched there as they were Pennant recorded the Welsh names as *gwyn-iâd*, ' white pate,' and *gloys iâd*, blue pate "

† Pennant gave the Welsh names as follows —Gray salmon, *Penllwyd* and *Idrwlch* sea trout, *Brithyll y mor*, trout, *Brithyll*, white trout, *Brithyll gwyn* Captain Benyon, 1860, observed Bull trout termed *Brochyn* is a very inferior fish and spotted sewin is called *Gwmnal*, is a very superior one, and without spots

‡ Mr Kerr sent from Tan y Bwlch in Merionethshire October 7th, 1885, a sewin 14 inches long length in inches of head 3 5, of eye 0 55, of snout 1 5, eyes apart 1 4, pectoral fin 2 5, depth of free portion of the tail 1 5 cleft of tail 0 6 A male having a small hook on the lower jaw Dorsal fin spotted, vertebræ 58 + r flesh red Mr Kerr observed, "I send you a specimen of the fish we get in this river, it is a fair specimen of what they call here sewin, which I take to be the Scotch sea trout I have caught lots of fish precisely like this one in the rivers flowing into St Andrew s Bay, and from there down to the English border, and we always imagined (though it may be wrongly) that they were all sea trout There is a fish that I have caught in the Tweed and Teviot also very similar to this one, and called there the *bull trout* here they give that name to yellow trout that have gone down to the sea water, but the fish I refer to, which I have so frequently caught, but only in Tweed and Teviot, is a true migratory species, and one which has often puzzled me I have caught a good many sewin in this river this summer, and it has struck me that most of them were much more like, both in appearance and when on the table, these so-called ' bull trout ' of the border than the ordinary type of Scotch sea trout that I have caught in the highlands and elsewhere "

§ In a female sewin 6 8 inches long the length of the head was 4$\frac{1}{2}$, of the pectoral fin 6$\frac{3}{4}$, height of body 1$\frac{1}{2}$ in the total length *Eyes*—diameter $\frac{1}{4}$ of length of head, 1$\frac{1}{4}$ diameters from the end of the snout and also apart The vomerine teeth are shown in figure 35, no 1 In another female sewin 15 1 inches long, the length of the head was 6, of the pectoral fin nearly 9, height of body 5$\frac{1}{2}$ in the total length *Eyes*—diameter 5$\frac{1}{2}$ in the length of the head, 1$\frac{1}{2}$ diameters from the end of the snout, and 1$\frac{1}{2}$ apart The vomerine teeth are shown in figure 35, no 2,

teeth alternately directed to the right and to the left, and subsequently they drop out, commencing from behind. But the age when this occurs varies, as will be seen in figure 35, where a sewin 15·1 inches long still possessed four

along the body of the vomer, while it is by no means infrequent for examples of similar size to retain even more. Occasionally two or three remain across the hind margin of the head of the vomer in examples from ten to fifteen inches in length. The teeth in the jaws and palatines are similar to those seen in the salmon-trout. *Fins*— tions. Anteriorly they are single and undivided, and three or sometimes four

Fig. 35.
1. Teeth on vomer of *sewin* 6·8 inches long :
2. From *sewin* 15·1 inches long.

It has been stated that examples of this fish, retained some considerable time in a fresh-water pond, had their pectorals more pointed and longer than is usual in their sea-going relatives. The anal fin, similar to that found in the more northern race of sea trout, may have a variation in the number of its rays, which consist of two descrip-

in number. The posterior rays are divided, the last nearly as low as its base; of these from seven to nine may be present: the two shown in fig. 36 are from Welsh examples. As regards the form of the caudal fin,* figure 37 shows outline tracings from seven specimens of Truff, White - fish and Welsh sewin, showing how exceedingly variable the depth of the cleft may be, at least in fishes up to 15 inches in length. Had the extent of the cleft in the northern form been invariably at about what is shown in nos. 4, 6, and 8 in figure 30 (*see* page 156) one would be tempted to believe that a specific difference might be seen in the amount of excision in this fin. But extending our inquiries

Fig. 36.
1. Anal fin of *sewin* with 12 rays.
2. Anal fin of *sewin* with 10 rays.

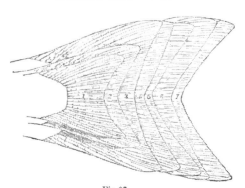

Fig. 37.
Tail fins of female sea trout. 1. *Sewin*, 6·8 in. long, Tivy. 2. *Truff*, 3·2 in., Dart. 3. *White-fish*, 12·4 in., Teign. 4. *Sewin*, 12·6 in., Towy. 5. *Sewin*, 13·3 in., Dysinni. 6. *White-fish*, 13 in., Teign. 7. *Sewin*, 15·1 in. Towy.

* *Yarrell* observed that in old examples the tail became convex and gave a figure of such a fish, which he termed a "Round tail," also a "Sewin" taken from a male specimen 32 inches in length. *Günther* asserted that the caudal fin is "forked in specimens 6 inches long . . . it shows only a slight emargination in specimens in the grilse stage, and is perfectly truncate in adult examples, but never rounded" (Catal. vi, p. 35).

11 *

demonstrates that similar variations are perceived in the northern race, as no 7 in the same figure, where the cleft of this fin from a Sutherlandshire example (from the Oykell), is as great as in any southern specimen of sewin   Although it has been asserted that in Wales the difference in the tails of the sewin and salmon, is that in the former it is not forked, whereas in the salmon it is, I must confess to having generally found the caudal fins forked in these fish, especially among the females (see fig 37)   *Cœcal appendages*—these vary in number, and in those fish personally obtained from Wales or along the south coast of England, they have averaged from 39 to 42 , in the example whose head is figured (no 34, p 160), they were 40) *   *Colours*—silvery, those from the sea generally with black × - shaped spots, the fish, however, becomes of a darker tinge and more spotted when in rivers †   Welsh examples are often more spotted than those taken from Devonshire and Cornwall   The colour of the dead fin varies , in most I have examined, it has had one or two black spots, or a dark upper edge, and just tinged with orange around its posterior margin, but a Tivy fish‡ 6 8 inches long, sent me in March, 1886, by Mr Bowen, had the last third of this fin of a beautiful vermilion   But in that stream, trout are, as a rule, vividly marked

Habits —In the Usk they are early, and the largest ascend about June, but later on, as in the autumn, a number of small sewin are seen, on April 29th, 1873, one of ¾ lb was recorded as of unusual early occurrence in this river, while they have much increased in numbers during the last twenty-five years   The earliest date these fish have been stated to have been seen spawning in the Usk, was September 27th, 1873   The sewin is occasionally found ascending higher up streams than the salmon, but in rare instances, young salmon-par have been observed passing up rivers above where any of their parents have been remarked making redds I have personally obtained sewin along the south coast from Exmouth to Penzance, all of which have been females, and which agreed in every respect with others that I have taken from rivers flowing into Cardigan Bay   The same has been recorded, not only from various portions of the British Isles§ and Ireland but likewise off the Scandinavian Peninsula   Mr Douglas Ogilby, writing from Ireland, says "the variety *S cambricus* is alone found in our northern rivers, and of this, we have a long-headed and a short-headed form , a difference, however, which will be found on dissection to be greatly attributable to sex, the short-headed being, as a rule, females "

1 Sphærium corneum   2 Physa

* In the *British Museum Catalogue* vi, this form is defined as possessing "Cœc pylor 39 17, rarely more," while the following number of appendages are asserted to be present in specimens in the collection   From examples along our south and west coasts, 5 males gave 34, 35, 39, 43, 47 , 3 females 38, 45, 47 , and 11, of which the sex is not recorded, 33, 37, 38, 41, 41, 42, 42, 43 43, 48, 52 , and 1 Irish male example 46, showing variations from 33 to 52   Mr Willis Bund, *Salmon Problems*, p 181, remarked on an example 49 inches long from the Usk, which had 48 cæcal appendages.
† In the *Report of the Commissioners* in 1860, the sewin was said by one witness to be destitute of spots, but the bull trout to be spotted
‡ "In this neighbourhood the brook trout are rather vividly coloured   Rapid streams and rocky beds are the general rule in our brooks, which is against size, but the fish are beautifully marked and of excellent flavour * * the season for the sewin is from June to July "
§ Dr Gunther does not include it among Scotch fishes, but two examples presented to the National collection by Mr. Godman, and obtained from the River Elkey, in Ross shire, are labelled as *Salmo cambricus*

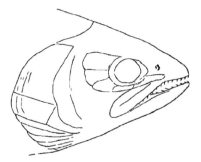

Fig 38   Head of female *Peal*, 12½ inches long

Under the designation of *Peal*, two distinct species of salmonoid fishes along our south coast are recognized, for occasionally the grilse stage of the salmon is so designated, but more frequently the same stage,* or even larger examples of the sea trout. Sir W Jardine considered small ones as identical with the hirling of Scotland and the phinoc of the Eden and the Esk, and in this identification he was doubtless correct   In the British Channel, they are occasionally taken near the surface during April and May in the drift mackerel nets, as the season advances they come nearer inshore, and the smaller ones ascend our southern rivers during the first June floods, where they abound during the two succeeding months.   While from February until June the *white trout* † rarely exceeding six inches in length, is often found in company with the river trout   A peal or sea trout, on its arrival in the Teign or Dart, has been observed to soon have its colours assimilated to those of the pool or stream in which it takes up its abode, while its form is exactly similar to that of the Welsh sewin

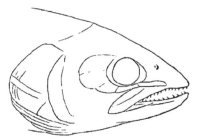

Fig 39   Head, natural size, of female *White-fish*,
12 4 inches long from the Teign.

The *White-fish* of Devonshire streams as the Dart and Teign are generally looked on as a stage of the Truff, some considering the latter the more adult form

---

* It has usually been held to occupy dimensions in size and weight intermediate between smolt and grilse, or the size of the latter, while in rivers where salmon are numerous peal are mostly scarce, but should the stock of salmon become reduced, peal generally soon increase in numbers   J D B , *Fuld*, January 24th, 1885, observed, that "a young 3 lb salmon would be a longer fish than a 4 lb peal, the scale of the salmon three times larger, and the tail very much forked, while the tail of the peal would be almost straight across "

† "The Erne abounds in white fish, peal, and truff, all making their appearance about the time stated by 'Old Log,' and the relative size of these fish being the same as he states, but on

whereas others appear to ignore size, holding the Truff to be a young sea trout. The average weight of white-fish are said by some authorities to be from half to three quarters of a pound. In two examples 12¼ and 13 inches respectively in length from the Teign, the gill-covers and form of the head resemble what has been described in the Truff of the Dart, and likewise agree with small specimens of the Welsh sewin. *Teeth*—in the smaller example eleven are present along the body of the vomer and five along the hind margin of the head of that bone. In the example 13 inches long, there are four teeth along the body of the vomer, and three on the hind margin of its head. One had 30, the other 37 cæcal appendages. *Colours*—the largest had much fewer spots on the body and fins than the Dart Truff.

Some have considered it very improbable that the Welsh sewin, so excellent as food, could be identical with the white-fleshed and insipid* Teign or Dart fish, but alterations as considerable in the value of the flesh of the northern whitling and other local races of sea trout have been observed. While we find as great variations in our brook trout, in accordance with the character of the waters they inhabit and the amount or quality of food they are able to obtain. But, differing as these races do among themselves, whether in size, colour, or even in some structural points, the offspring, if placed in suitable surroundings, may improve, while, on the other hand, the finest breeds will deteriorate in unsuitable places. Should, however, any temporary cause, as mine-water in Devonshire rivers, (see pp 55 ante) have injured the local race of fish, and this cause has been removed, it perhaps becomes worthy of consideration whether it might not be advisable to obtain the progeny of a finer breed from elsewhere and introduce them into the water, instead of waiting for the improvement of the local deteriorated form.

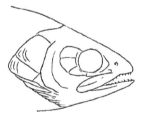

Fig 10   Head, natural size, of female *Truff*,
                  8 2 inches long, from the Dart

the Erme, salmon are never seen above the tidal water, and very few even there. If the above fish were young salmon why should they never appear as full grown salmon in the upper parts of the river ? On the Avon, on the other hand, where salmon have very much increased for the last fifteen or twenty years, the peal and truff are much fewer in number, and the white-fish of the same kind as those in the Erme are now seldom seen, although the river is at all times swarming with the samlets, which are the unmistakable salmon fry. I have not the smallest doubt that the white fish peal and truff of the river Erme are all the same fish in different stages of growth " (G C G , *Field*, February 14th 1885)   *Couch* considered the white-fish to be the only growth of the peal, and believed the Welsh sewin and the blue poll *S albus* to be distinct and separate species   " Old Log," *Field*, February 14th, 1885, observed, that " curiously enough, I find that the old monks, some five hundred years ago, knew the difference between peal and salmon in the Dart, and in official records specify them both by their Latin names—thus ' salmones, trutes, peles, et alii pisces ' "

* Wear Gifford, *Field*, March 27th, 1886 remarked that "if the best specimens are selected and cooked with care, they will not disappoint those who have acquired a taste for eating bread poultices "

The southern race of sea trout are termed *truff's* or *trough's* in Devonshire streams, and also in others along the south coast as the Fowey in Cornwall. Mr. Pike, Secretary of the Dart Fishery Board, observed that these fish however appear only to be known as truff in Devonshire, when they are young in the spring of the year, but that he had seen them in the Dart as large as 12 lb. They commence being taken as soon as the fishing begins on March 1st, and keep on until the end of May, after which very few are killed. Also in March the *white-fish* is captured, which he considered the young of the truff. A female 8·2 inches long from the Dart, received from Col. Tickell in April, 1886, had the form of the head as shown in fig 40, it had 110 rows of scales along the body, 14 in an oblique line from the adipose dorsal downwards and forwards to the lateral-line, 39 cæcal appendages, a double row of teeth in a zig-zag line along the body of the vomer and the caudal fin somewhat forked (see fig 37, no. 2). *Colours*—silvery, darkest along the back, with somewhat large round or ✕-shaped spots of a black or purplish colour on the upper half of the body, and a few below the lateral-line descending lowest anteriorly. Along the lateral-line seven spots, some of which were more or less red. Upper surface of the head spotted with black, and four spots on the opercle and two on the preopercle. The dorsal fin with numerous black spots and a few red ones, as well as a narrow white front edge. Adipose dorsal fin yellow, with the upper half orange, pectoral gray, lightest along its lower rays, ventral with the first few outer rays stained gray, anal yellowish-gray, its front edge white, behind which it had a gray tinge, caudal, pinkish-yellow. (*See Field*, March 4th, 1886.)

---

* Yarrell observed that the salmon-trout *Salmo trutta* "is the Truff of Devonshire, and White Trout of Wales and Ireland; it is found in the Severn, in the rivers of Cornwall, and plentifully in the Esk, the Eden, the Annan and Nith, rivers falling into the Solway, where it is called sea trout, and in its grilse stage Hirling" (vol. i, page 251).

"Old Log," *Field*, November 29th, 1886, remarked that *Salmo trutta*, or the sea trout, familiarly known under its local name of the *truff*, thrives well and breeds abundantly in the Devon and Cornish rivers. He is a glorious fish for sport, and no matter what his size may be as soon as ever he is hooked he springs out of the water, and fights pluckily, contesting every inch of water before he can be brought to the landing net. The young fish, one or two years old, from 6 oz. to ¼ lb., are most abundant in March, when perhaps they are dropping down stream to the sea; but from April onwards they are caught with salmon in the nets on their way upwards from the estuaries, and throughout the summer they may be taken with a fly in the rivers up to 2 lb. or 3 lb. weight, and especially on a summer evening they may be seen rising freely and affording some exciting sport after sunset, together with the peal, with which fish they are often, rightly or wrongly, associated. I have frequently seen them taken in the nets up to 3 lb., or even over that weight, but the netsmen never confuse them with the salmon grilse, and will also distinguish them from the peal, though the size of a small grilse may be less than that of one of the largest of the truff, and the sizes of peal and truff are not widely divided.

While salmon, some still unspawned, were netted on March 1st. *The truff*, however, of which two or three dozen were taken during the first week, in the weir in the Dart, which divides the tidal estuary from the fresh water, were all in splendid condition, and of good size. Now, this would seem to indicate that the truff must spawn earlier, or mend in condition and get out to sea after their spawning is over much more speedily than the salmon, and thus anticipate the general run of salmon in returning to the river, or it may be the more reasonable inference that these fish do not make their first migration until they have sojourned for at least one, and generally for two years in the river, and then are ready to return at the end of the winter. There is no doubt, at any rate, that these *white fish*, as they are called, or young truff, are particularly abundant in the early spring, when they are probably moving down stream on their way to the sea. Later in the season the nets in the weir pool, and the ladder in the weir, still continue to record the fashionable arrivals and departures of the river. They mark the exodus of the last of the kelts, the uncertain return of the grilse, and the regular arrival of the *peal* with the first floods in June. During the summer the salmon come up in gradually increasing numbers, and mingling with them are the full-grown *truff* running to upwards of 3 lb. in size; while here and there an early fish begins to drop down on his return journey, and is easily distinguished by his dull and river stained coat among the others just fresh from the sea, with their scales still glittering like burnished silver.

The question of the peal, as a distinct species of the extensive family of Salmonidæ, must be approached with more caution and considerable diffidence. I am very strongly impressed with the opinion that they are a distinct fish for the following reasons, which appear to me almost conclusive. In the first place, the peal appears to be different in its shape from the truff or sea trout, being deeper and shorter in the body, so that a peal of 2 lb., which is about the largest size attained by only a few exceptional veterans, would be quite two inches shorter than a truff of the same weight, which is by no means an unusually large specimen of the latter species. The peal, in fact, partakes very much of the character and shape of the sewin; and in Welsh rivers, notably in the Dovey, sewin and sea trout may be caught side by side, and the two breeds are easily distin-

The British and Irish sea trout may now be referred to as a whole, with the proviso that it is generally held that the northern form is commonly recognized as salmon-trout, *Salmo trutta*, and the southern or sewin as *Salmo eriox*, now better known as *S. cambricus*. These varieties have been separated owing to certain supposed structural differences, such as the form of the gill covers, the strength of the jaws, the number of teeth on the vomer, and the character of the tail fin; while the northern form has been said to possess from forty-nine to sixty-one cæcal appendages—rarely less—and the southern from thirty-nine to forty seven. It will, therefore, be necessary in this examination first to inquire whether these statements are correct; and secondly, if they are, do these different races pass one into the other?

The shape of the body in the two forms, is admitted to be similar, but the proportions of one part to the remainder differ in accordance with age, season, and locality. In the *young*, the length of the head is to that of the entire length sometimes as little as ⅓, as seen in some whitlings or herlings in the Ouse, and on the east coast of Scotland, and similar examples occasionally are found along the south and west coasts. As the adult stage is reached, this preternaturally shortness of the head is usually but not invariably lost, and along with it there is, as might be

gnished. Again, it will be found that the peal are most regular in their periodical immigrations, which are quite distinct from the sea trout. As sure as ever a flood comes down the southern rivers in June, the first of the *peal* are regularly expected, and they never fail to put in an appearance and to furnish a fresh and very exciting sport. They take a spinning minnow perhaps more freely than the fly at first, but a cunning fly fisher may get his share of them. Their very track along the coast line of the sea is as well known as the period of their arrival, and fixed nets are run out at right angles to the shore, and to a distance of not more than a hundred yards in many places, into which the peal will run their stupid heads as they travel along during the summer nights, but never a sea trout is found among them, though red and grey mullet are occasionally caught. Hundreds of summer visitors, during June and July, visit Anstey's Cove in the bay that shelters Torquay, and many have found, if they are in luck, that an unexpected dish of peal just fresh from the sea is ready to be added to their picnic meal. Then will come the old discussion when the fish is produced, as to what sort of a salmon is this. The delighted cockney will have no hesitation in accepting it as a young salmon, and just the right size to suit the occasion; a patriotic Welshman may imagine that his own familiar sewin has lost its way in the ocean and wandered away to the southern coast; while cosmopolitan anglers who have enjoyed their sport with the sea trout will acknowledge the family likeness, and yet perhaps perceive some difference in shape and structure, and begin to fancy that the peal is a distinct species in the great family of the Salmonidæ.

On December 1st, 'A South Devon Conservator' replied in *The Field* that "near Plymouth we reverse his truff and peal theory, calling the early, thicker fish, from 2 lb to 6 lb, 'truff,' and the later and smaller fish 'peal.' We also find in the Yealm river neither take the fly as a rule, and, I think not in the Plym, except at night, though they do in the Tavy freely. In the Yealm the larger, thicker fish we call 'truff' do not jump on being hooked, they fight hard under water, the ½ lb to 2 lb 'peal' (as we call them) jump vigorously. Fish vary in every Devon river apparently. There is in the Yealm, in spring, a fish larger than the salmon fry ('white fish,' locally called), which does take a fly." "Noss Mayo" concluded the correspondence by observing that "the Fowey and Camel, in Cornwall, may be taken as equally representative salmon streams with the Dart, although their sources are not in the Dartmoor watershed. In these two rivers *truff* are occasionally, but not frequently, met with, the principal branch of the Salmonidæ next to the salar being the *peal*, which is generally acknowledged in the district to be purely and simply the *Salmo trutta*. There seems to be a settled conviction in the minds of some writers that peal rarely, if ever, weigh more than 2 lb. What gave rise to such an idea it is difficult to state, except that probably observations of the river were made when the later or 'school' peal were running. Peal are caught weighing considerably over 6 lb. In *The Field* of October 9th, is reported the capture of one weighing 7½ lb, and the man who took it is a professional fisherman of fifty years' experience. These larger fish are not *truff*, and there is no discernible difference between them and peal of 1 lb, except in size. Does not 'A South Devon Conservator' make the common mistake of calling these first-arriving and larger peal 'truff'? The '*white fish*' of the Yealm, mentioned by the same correspondent last week, I have found by comparison to be similar to the fish in Cornish rivers, which are, in my opinion, more correctly termed '*peal spaun*.' These fish localize themselves in the fresh water for a longer period than the fry of the salmon, which generally drop down to the sea in the spring. Moreover, the so called '*white fish*' never occur in a river where there are no *peal*."

anticipated, mostly a very short lower limb to the preopercle. The general length in the female young is about $\frac{1}{5}$ of the total length, but in males it may be, but rarely is, even $\frac{2}{9}$. When the fish attains 12 or 14 inches in length, the head of the male is generally about $4\frac{1}{2}$ in that of the entire length of the fish, and of the female $\frac{1}{5}$. In adults and breeding fish, consequent upon prominence of the abdomen, the body is deeper than at other periods of the year, or among spent fish. *Eyes*—situated as already described, their diameter varying with the age and sex of the specimen. Interorbital space convex. During the breeding season, a knob shows itself at the upper end of the lower jaw, diminishing in size subsequent to this period. The posterior extremity of the maxilla, reaches to below the middle of the eye in the parr of this form, and beyond its hind margin in the adults. It has been asserted that the strength of the maxillary and mandible* is much greater in the sewin *Salmo cambricus*, than in the salmon-trout *S. trutta*, a conclusion not borne out when a large number of specimens are examined. The form of the gill-covers has been already referred to, but it must be noticed in these bones having a squamous articulation together, that the lower end of the opercle more or less overlaps the upper portion of the subopercle, and this may interfere with the measurements.† In some examples, the posterior or vertical limb of the preopercle is sinuous, in others, more or less rounded, while the lower limb of this bone may be short,‡ of moderate extent and even sinuous. The posterior margin of the opercle and subopercle form a semicircle, of which the lower bone generally, but not invariably, forms the most prominent portion. Several raised and curved lines are mostly present near the outer part of the opercle and subopercle, but which are more visible in dried than in fresh specimens. *Teeth*—in both races of sea trout there exist teeth across the hind margin of the head of the vomer, and also in a double line along the shaft of that bone; these teeth are lost with age, commencing on the shaft from behind, but gradually extending forwards. While it seems to be a general rule that the sewin loses them more rapidly than the salmon-trout. But there are so many variations in this among the sea trout, that no criterion as to species can be deduced from the number or position of the vomerine teeth. *Fins*—speaking generally, the fins in the two races of sea trout appear to be somewhat of similar length, except the caudal, which in sewin up to about 15 inches in length, are mostly longer, and more deeply cleft than in the salmon-trout. The pectoral§ in young fish is occasionally shorter than in adults, being from 8 to 9 in the total length, whereas in specimens over 14 or 15 inches long, it is usually from $7\frac{1}{2}$ to 8 in the same distance, while it becomes more rounded with age. The length of the rays of the dorsal and anal fins varies considerably among these fishes, for although they are mostly comparatively longest in the immature, this is not invariably the rule. It has been asserted that the distance from the front edge of

* Dr. Günther suggested that when a doubt arises respecting a specimen, "only an examination of the internal parts of the maxillary and mandible can decide to what species such individuals ought to be referred, these bones being much stronger and more solid in *S. cambricus* than in *S. trutta*."

† Some authors consider the form of the gill-covers to be affected by sex, others that the modifications which are seen are of no specific value whatever.

‡ Dr. Günther, when re-naming the *Salmo albus*, also known as *S. phinoc*, Turton (which had been long recognized as the grilse stage of the *S. trutta*), *S. brachypoma*, Günther took as his seven examples four skins from Parnell's collection, one of which had been figured on plate 32, fig. 3, as a *bull trout*, three were marked *S. fario*, and one *S. eriox*; one from Yarrell's collection, and two specimens from the Ouse. The length of the head was given as $4\frac{2}{3}$ in that of the total excluding the caudal fin, and 4 times in the males, but no mention was made if the specimen measured was merely a dried skin. He gave the measurements of 5 sea trout, as follows. *S. trutta*, male, $18\frac{1}{2}$ inches long, head $4\frac{1}{4}$ in the total excluding the caudal fin. *S. cambricus*, male, Rhymney, 21 inches long, male, head $4\frac{1}{2}$; a female $22\frac{1}{2}$ inches, head nearly 4; a male, 14 inches, head $4\frac{1}{3}$; a male, $6\frac{1}{8}$ inches, head $4\frac{1}{4}$.

§ The following give the results of some of the measurements made: *salmon-trout*, male, 20 inches long, pectoral $7\frac{1}{2}$ in the total length, at 16.6 in. long $7\frac{1}{2}$, at 16.6 in. long 8, at 14.8 in. long 8, at 12.3 in. long $7\frac{1}{2}$. *Sewin*, at 15 in. long $9\frac{2}{3}$, at 13.3 in. long 8, at 13 in. long 9. *Salmon-trout*, at 12.3 in. long $7\frac{3}{4}$. *Sewin*, at 12.5 in. long 9, at 12.6 in. long 9. *White-fish*, 13.1 in. long 8, at 12.4 in. long $8\frac{1}{3}$. *Whiting*, at 9.5 in. long $7\frac{1}{4}$, at 8.2 in. long 8. *Truff*, at 8.2 in. long 8. *Whiting*, at 8.1 in. long 8, at 7.8 in. long $7\frac{1}{2}$, at 7.5 in. long $7\frac{3}{4}$.

the snout to the commencement of the dorsal fin* differs in the two races of sea trout, but some measurements† which have been instituted, have not confirmed this statement, this space was found to equal about $2\frac{1}{4}$ to $2\frac{1}{2}$ (in one large example $2\frac{1}{2}$) in the entire length of the fish In the anal may be found (see fig 36, page 163 *ante*), 3 to 4 unbranched rays, and from 7 to 9 branched ones (a single sewin-gilse in the British Museum from the Rhymney has 10), and this exists in specimens of the salmon-trout of Scotland and the north, whitling and sewin Thus, clearly showing that as these numbers are susceptible to similar and considerable variations in all the different races of the sea trout, such cannot be looked on as possessing any specific signification ‡ As regards the caudal fin very great discrepancies exist in the statements of different authors, some of whom advert to the length of the fin rays, and that in a manner which wholly fails when tested on specimens. Thus Parnell remarked that "when the fish reaches the length of 20 inches, the middle ray of the tail is more than half the length of the longest ray of the same fin" (p 291) Dr Gunther also remarked of the salmon-trout "the caudal fin is cleft in young examples, in which the longest rays are not quite twice as long as the middle ones " and in a male specimen 22 inches long, taken in the Firth of Forth, we are told that ' the length of the middle rays being not much less than one-half of the length of the longest, &c. These proportions are utterly fallacious if tested on skeletons, but may possibly be intended to refer solely to the exposed portion of the fin's rays This fin from being forked in the young becomes gradually square at the end in examples up to 20 inches in length, but more slowly so in some than in others, continuing forked longest (as a rule) in the southern and western race But in large examples of sea trout it is observed to become rounded, and although Dr Gunther remarks of the sewin, *Salmo cambricus,* that it attains the "length of about 3 feet," its tail fin "is perfectly truncate in adult examples, but never

* *Dr Gunther* (Catal vi, p 27) observed that in the northern race of sea trout, *Salmo trutta,* ' the interneural spine of the first long dorsal ray is attached to the neural of the seventeenth vertebra' And *Dr M'Intosh* in his paper on the "Yellow Fins of the Allan Water," 1872, remarked respecting the burn trout and sea trout, that in specimens "of the same length there is a very appreciable difference in the position of this (dorsal) fin, which is decidedly further forward in the latter—the same variation occurring in the fatty, ventral, and anal, as noticed in the first glance at the fish " (p 231)

† The following give the proportional measurements made in the distance from the front edge of the snout to the commencement of the base of the dorsal fin *Salmon trout,* male, 20 in long, $2\frac{1}{4}$ in the total length, at 16 6 in long $2\frac{1}{2}$, at 16 in long $2\frac{1}{2}$, at 11 8 in long $2\frac{1}{2}$, at 12 3 in long $2\frac{1}{2}$. *Sewin,* at 15 in long $2\frac{1}{4}$, at 13 3 in long $2\frac{1}{2}$, at 11 in long $2\frac{1}{2}$, at 12 3 in long $2\frac{1}{2}$, at 12 6 in long $2\frac{1}{2}$ *Whitling,* at 9 5 in long $2\frac{1}{4}$, at 8 2 in long $2\frac{1}{2}$, at 8 1 in long $2\frac{1}{2}$, at 7 6 in long $2\frac{1}{2}$, at 7 5 in long $2\frac{1}{2}$ *White-fish,* at 13 1 in long $2\frac{1}{4}$, at 12 4 in long 3 *Truff,* at 8 2 in long $2\frac{1}{2}$

‡ The following number of rays existing in the anal fin have been attributed by different British Authors Turton (1807) White Salmon *Salmo phinoc,* A 9, Salmon trout *S trutta,* A 10, Shewen, *S croa* A 12, Fleming (1828) Whitling, *S albus,* A 9, Salmon trout, *S trutta,* A 11 Sewin *S cnor (cambricus)* A 10, Jenyns (1835) *S trutta,* A 11, *S enor (cambricus)* A 11, Yarrell (1836) *S trutta,* A 10, *S enor (cambricus)* A 11, Parnell (1838) *S trutta,* A 10, *S enor (cambricus)* A 10 Thompson (1856) *S trutta,* A 9, *S enor (cambricus),* A 11 In 1866 Dr Gunther (Catal vi, pp 24, 31) attributed to *S trutta* A 11, *S cambricus* A 11 12, which asserted differences in the two races, however, scarcely record with his text For at p 32 he observed of a female *S trutta,* 27¾ inches long from the Tweed, ' that the anal fin is higher than long, and consists of twelve rays, the first and second being rudimentary and covered by skin, the third simple and shorter than the fourth which is branched "

The Fordwich trout has been alluded to by several authors Isaac Walton, who wrote in 1653, remarked that "there is also in Kent, near Canterbury, a trout called there a Fordidge trout, a trout that bears the name of the town where it is usually caught that is accounted the rarest of fish , many of them near the bigness of a salmon, but known by their different colours, and in their best season they eat very white " He likewise observed that it lives and feeds nine months of the year in the sea, and fasts three in the rivers of Fordidge Ja rell remarked that " the Fordwich trout of Isaac Walton is the salmon trout (*Salmo trutta*), and its character for affording rare good meat, besides the circumstance of its being really an excellent fish, second only to the salmon, was greatly enhanced, no doubt, by the opportunity of eating it very fresh It was formerly the custom to visit the nets at Fordwich every evening, to purchase the fish caught during the night " Dr Gunther observed, " All the British specimens of *Salmo trutta* which I have examined (with the exception of the Fordwich trout) are from Scotland " A female specimen 19 inches long, having 50 cæcal appendages, is in the British Museum

rounded " (Catal vi, p 35) This may be merely an error of description consequent upon his not having seen any very large specimen, for he makes the same statement of the Lochleven trout, which I shall show to be incorrect Other authors who record having obtained this form with a rounded tail, he considers must have referred to the salmon-trout, thus showing how very doubtful this asserted difference between the two forms must be in nature

Cœcal appendages —The number present in a sea-trout have been considered sufficient to assist in fixing whether it pertains to the northern, eastern, and Irish salmon-trout, or the southern, west coast and Irish sewin race, differences which Dr Gunther gave as follows —*Salmo trutta* from 43 to 61, *S cambricus* from 32 to 52, while some whose numbers interfere with this division are disposed of as hybrids (see p 157) Parnell recorded from 9 sea trout captured in Scotland that 8 females had 48, 50, 50, 52, 54, 54, 54, 55, or an average of 53 and 50 in one male I have found the following in 13 specimens of male salmon-trout, 33, 40, 40, 42, 43, 46, 47, 50, 50, 52, 52, 56, 60, or an average of 47, and in one female 49 In 6 specimens of sewin from the south and west coast, 36, 36, 37, 39, 40, 48, they averaged 39 One from Ireland had 33 It would consequently appear that in the south (except at Fordwich, where the feeding for trout is said to be exceptionally good) the number of cœcal appendages is less than in the north This is just the reverse of what the British Museum examples of brook trout show, as the northern race are recorded as possessing from 33-46, and the southern from 38-47 (see pp 11 and 157) It is however clear that these organs are unstable in numbers (see pp 22 and 144 *ante*), a subject which will be considered more in detail (see p 188) *Colours*—these, doubtless vary in accordance with local circumstances, for the fish generally become darker and more spotted the longer they have been from the sea, as has been recognized from the time of Johnston, 1649 (see pp 151 *ante*) But even in the same locality great differences of colour may often be observed, more especially if in estuaries* or within the limits of the tides On November 24th, 1886, I examined several of the northern race of these fishes, or salmon-trout, at Howietoun, where they had been kept waiting to be spawned The males had a whitish edge to the caudal, dorsal, and ventral fins, while the adipose dorsal was edged with orange The fins and under surface of the head were nearly black, the dorsal spotted with black, and some purplish-red or purplish-black spots existed on the body On July 26th, 1886, I examined the trout in the tank of the National Fish Culture Association at South Kensington The colours of the sea trout had become so similar to fresh-water forms, that a stranger could not discriminate between them One had been three weeks in salt-water tanks, but still its colours were unchanged, the poor thing, however, was blind, which may have been the reason

Respecting the colours in the par stage of these fishes, one knows of so few well-authenticated instances of such, as to be a little doubtful whether the fish described were the undoubted fry of the sea trout It is true Dr Gunther stated that "the number of bars is not quite constant, but the migratory trout have two (and even three) more than the river trout" (Catal vi, p 3) † This, how-

---

* The *Earl of Ducie*, writing September 2nd, 1887, observed, "I have lately returned from Norway, where I have been fishing in lakes and streams between 61° and 62° N lat The sea trout for which I fished chiefly, were from 10 lb to ⅓ lb Some were thickly covered with black spots, this was the usual type, others had scarcely any spots One sea trout of about 1½ lb weight had three large spots in a longitudinal line on each side, and no other ones. Some of the least spotted varieties might have been taken for salmon, so bright were they Boiling, however, always showed the pale pink flesh of the Norwegian sea trout There was, however, a difference in their degree of merit for the table outward appearance was not always a trustworthy guide in this respect With few exceptions these fish had square tails, but in a few cases, never exceeding 2 lb weight, the tails were forked, we thought that these fish were more cylindrical in form than the others Different types were found in different waters, often two or three types occurred in the same locality, but the variety, thickly covered with large black spots, was common to all places"

† *Dr. Gunther* deposed in the orange fin case, June 4th, 1872, that "there is a distinction between the young of *Salmo sala*, and a number of the *parros* In the par of the former I have counted as many as nine or ten cross bars, and in the latter only six or seven" (p 126)

ever, is one of those broad assertions which require confirmation based on more extended observation In February, 1887, I examined a very large number of young Lochleven trout at Howietoun, and found, as I shall subsequently have to refer to, that they possessed from fifteen to seventeen cross-bands, some being more or less broken up But these bands are not invariably the same in number every year, thus in 1884 I recorded in the *Proceedings of the Zoological Society* (pp 28, 29) how in eight young specimens of Lochlevens at Howietoun they varied between eleven and fourteen, these being four pairs of young trout of the same race raised in the same establishment and under identical circumstances, but which had been some months in the ponds at Craigend in water from a different stream While in some undoubted young brook trout in Gloucestershire I have observed from nine to eleven bars In April, 1887, Mr Andrews showed me his beautiful young fish at Guildford, and among the Lochleven yearlings raised from Howietoun eggs were numerous examples with eight, nine, ten, eleven, and a few with thirteen cross bands Also fifteen on a young local brook trout, but in these the generality ranged from eight to eleven Some of the alevins of both forms showed an orange edging to the adipose dorsal fin, and on both margins of the caudal While in some yearling local brook trout and also in some similar Lochlevens the amount of orange in the dead fin varied In one yearling brook trout there were three brilliant vermilion spots on the dead fin If therefore fresh-water trout can vary, as I have now instanced, in these marks between nine and seventeen, the specific value of the number of such can hardly be great The adipose dorsal fin, although usually margined with orange in the smolt or grilse stage, may be lead coloured *

Vertebræ †—As regards the number present in either race my information from the examination of specimens is not so full as I could desire, because in each case the fish had to be sacrificed In *salmon-trout* I have observed from 57-60 + r and in sewin from 58-60 + a Yarrell has recorded 58 for the salmon-trout and 59 for the sewin, but he apparently rather mixed up his forms, while Dr. Gunther has given *S trutta* 59-60, *S cambricus* 59, and *S brachypoma*, which is the grilse of the salmon-trout, 59

Varieties —These are not very material unless it is considered that two distinct species are included under the head of sea trout In *form*—these may be congenital or acquired, and as they are very similar to what obtain in the fresh-water trout the two will be examined conjointly In *colour*—these are various, from silvery to being as spotted as a river trout, as will likewise be detailed

Sexual distinctions —The male has a knob, hook, or kype developed at the upper surface of the end of the lower jaw and which has a seasonable augmentation in size during the breeding season, there is also a thickening of the skin, especially along the back, as remarked on when describing the salmon (p 57 *ante*), but in the sea trout ulceration though the upper jaw appears to be rare

Names —These have already been referred to (see pp 149, 150 *ante*) *Bull trout* seems to be given to different fishes in various places When netting the Teith, the superintendent, the river watchers, and fishermen agreed that sea trout attain to 5 lb, but are rarely larger but bull trout of 20 lb or 30 lb are seen and believed to be hybrids between the salmon and sea trout It is quite clear that old male salmon-kelts are not infrequently called "bull trout" In some localities sea trout are termed *gray trout* Mr Congreve considered bull trout sterile examples of this species which have ceased breeding and discontinued their annual migrations, while their flesh may be either white or pink

---

* *Dr M'Intosh* (Scottish Naturalist, 1872, p 231) observed that "the reddish edge of the fatty fin is most marked in the common trout, is present in a less degree in the 'yellow fin' (though in some scarcely noticeable) and is absent in the smolt The blackish pigment at the base of this organ is more developed in the 'yellow fin' than in the trout " While in its fully developed migratory condition " the fatty fin, the dorsal and ventral and edges of the caudal are generally bordered with red " (p 230)

† In counting the vertebræ, I adopted the advice given by an old author to boil the fish and detach bone from bone, so as to be sure no mistake occurred in the enumeration As already remarked, I do not in the above count the last aborted vertebra

Habits—This species having much of the habits of the salmon cannot be termed so game a fish, neither is it so powerful, although very active When adult it appears to move more of an evening and during the night than during the day, and frequently selects waters which are more sluggish than suit the salmon, although if the bottom is sandy or even muddy, it is not infrequently found at the tail of a pool or where the current is quiet, but is of a roving disposition When large it appears in some streams to be rather deep in the water, is a wary and sharp-sighted form, and the angler generally requires a long line combined with great caution while attempting to take it, but if it be in the grilse stage, as the white-fish, or up to a few pounds in weight, it dashes at flies It is very destructive to small fish and by no means averse to consuming the eggs or the young of the salmon While ascending to breed the sea trout does not abstain from food as does the salmon

These fish can be retained in aquaria and even thrive there, thus Mr C. Jackson, *Report on the Salmon Disease*, 1880, p 111, in a letter dated June 20th, 1880, observed, " We have in one of our sea-water tanks (Southport Aquarium) two splendid sea trout They came to us a few ounces in weight about two years since and are now several pounds in weight They have not been in fresh water since they came " On the other hand some which had been received at South Kensington from Lochbuie and kept two years in tanks of fresh water are said to have given eggs in the autumn of 1886, showing that absence from salt water had not arrested the reproductive process

Migrations—In many respects those of the sea trout are similar to what occur in the salmon, so far as when the smolts descend to the sea, also when these fish are entering and ascending rivers for several months in the year While there are likewise, as might be expected, certain conditions in the fish which tend to foster these migrations as well as favourable conditions of the rivers In Sutherlandshire* the great run of sea trout is from the first week in June, its height being about the middle of that month subsequent to which it decreases, the small herlings begin about the middle of July, and these are irrespective of the autumn run ascending to spawn While, continued Sir W Jardine, " in approaching the entrance of rivers or in seeking out, as it were, some one they preferred, shoals of this fish may be seen coasting the bays and headlands,† leaping and sporting in great numbers from 1 lb to 3 lb or 4 lb. in weight, and in some of the smaller bays the shoals can be traced several times circling it and apparently feeding "‡

* Sir W Jardine, *Edinburgh New Philosophical Journal*, 1835, p 49, observed that in Sutherlandshire the tacksmen or fishers distinguished the sea trout only as the larger or smaller kinds, and the seasons at which they run This commences the first week in June, is at its height about the middle of the month, decreasing as the season advances, until they are succeeded by the later running fish The smaller sea trout or herling, in Sutherlandshire, he observed commences about the middle of July

† The late Mr Arthur observed that " the Edobaig, in Argyleshire, enters the Holy Loch near Kilmun, and in June has a fine run of *Salmo trutta* from 1½ to 6 lb In August and September a smaller variety ascends known as *blacknebs*, owing to the dark colour of their heads Towards the end of the season a few bull trout Loch Lomond, from June to the end of the winter, has a variety of the sea trout between salmon-trout and sewin On the east side a race like the true salmon trout runs up during August and September "

‡ Mr W Anderson Smith has lately remarked on the migrations of these fish on the west coast of Scotland, which he observed were contrary to the movements of the salmon " Those who seine for sea trout do not find the salmon among their prey " " The sea trout keep close in shore comparatively speaking, and lay themselves open to the operations of the scringers (seine-net fishermen) At regular intervals, more especially at spring tides in June and July, the sea trout pass slowly upwards along the shore to their various rivers, continuing to do so till October By the middle of November they have mostly left the fresh waters not only have the fish of each several stream a character of their own, but they are found intermingled with the *Salmo fario* from the smaller streams that have taken to the sea, and in consequence donned a livery of silver more or less pronounced We have little doubt that the *Salmo fario* takes to the sea at certain seasons when we cannot find a single representative in the small streams that enter the Western Highland Lochs We have found them amidst the sea weed at low water where the stream struggles over the salt-watery shore, while we could not find a single point of specific distinction between the silvered specimens amongst the shoals of sea trout and their dark-coloured congeners in the burns " " We have also taken in certain streams fishes which we

Respecting the migrations of these fish in the Tweed some very interesting figures were given by Russel (*see* p 71 *ante*), who showed the proportionate number that entered that river during the open months of the year. One-tenth were taken in the first 3½ months, or from the middle of February to the end of May and nine-tenths of the remainder during the 5½ months extending from June 1st to the middle of October In June they suddenly augmented by 300 per cent, and in July stood at the highest figure but the average weight of the fish diminished, pointing to a large proportion being young In October a great increase again occurred not only in number but also in size, for now the breeding fish commenced ascending *

In the Kyle of Tongue fine sea trout are found during April and May, while in the Kyle of Durness some of moderate size, as from 1½ lb to 2 lb, commence to show themselves the last week in April and during May The smolt finnocks abound in the Dee near Aberdeen in April, and improve in condition as the season advances In the Forth four distinct runs of sea trout have been recorded (1) Herlings in January, from 6 oz to 12 oz (2) Sea trout in February, from 2 lb to 5 lb (3) Two differently coloured trout in May, from 1½ lb to 2 lb weight, one spotted all over, the other only below the lateral-line, the flesh of one is pale and of the other red (4) Salmon-trout or bull trout, strong coarse fish from 4 lb to 10 lb, and have been taken to 16 lb and are first seen in July While Parnell observed that those which leave the sea about the end of July to enter fresh water do so to deposit their spawn during the months of October, November, and December

Passing on to the migrations of the southern and western sewin we find that in the mackerel drift-nets employed from March until May in the Bristol Channel single examples are frequently taken, also at the mouths of rivers during summer and autumn in hang or moored nets, and in fresh waters some are captured throughout the year But these migrations are subject to considerable variation, thus of late years they have greatly increased in the Wye, while in 1860 they were said to be rare there but numerous in the Usk and common in the rivers to the west The few that ascend the Severn, and which rarely exceed 1 lb in weight, do so mostly in July, in the Usk the largest are about June, but they become smaller in autumn, an abnormally early one of ¾ lb weight and clean-run was recorded in April, 1873 In the Ogmore, fish from 4 lb to 5 lb ascend in April, those of about 2 lb in May, and 1 lb in August, while at Christmas some enter the river in pairs, but they do not weigh above ½ lb to ¾ lb In the Towy and the Teifi† these fish are said to begin ascending in April, but June is the month when they have been recorded as beginning to pass into rivers on the Tâf, Clwyd, Elwy, and Chester Dee, and during July into the Claddw In the month of June these fish would seem to become plentiful in Welsh rivers and the Dee, being mostly so during July and August. In the Towy large ones

should have called sea trout but for their complete absence of silver colouring, the markings pointed to them as bull trout Those we are disposed to consider sea trout that have remained long in fresh water, and lost their silver coat, as the *Salmo fario* acquires it in salt water " The shoals of sea trout he found to be most voracious, having "taken young herring in great quantities and squids also from their stomachs, and this may be the reason they keep towards the shore in their progress riverwards "

* Lord Home wrote an instructive paper on the sea trout of the Tweed to Yarrell, and in it he observed that the bull trout (*Salmo trutta*) take the river (Tweed) at two seasons The first shoal comes up about the end of April and May They are then small, weighing from 2 lb to 4 lb or 5 lb The second, and by far the more numerous shoal comes late in November They then come up in thousands and are not only in fine condition, but of a much larger size, weighing from 6 lb to 20 lb They ascend the Tweed in scanty numbers during the spring and summer season, but are then in excellent condition But the great ascending shoal of these fishes is that which migrates to this and some other rivers for breeding purposes, and this occurs after the commencement of the close season, or between the middle of October and end of November, when, as observed Stoddart, they push up the river to the very sources of its tributaries and their feeders I have already remarked (p 159) that Stoddart recognized sea trout from 1 lb to 3 lb pushing up the Esk in summer next herlings in July and August, succeeded by bulls or bulls

† It has been lately asserted that in the Teth or Tivy, in Cardigan Bay, sewin are now absent, but present in either river on each side of it.

used to be taken from April to June, and from 4 lb to 10 lb by the end of August In the Teifi they were recorded as being from ¼ lb to 2½ lb at the commencement of the season

Along the south coast with the June floods there are usually small peal in the rivers, in fact from February to June, little "white fish," rarely exceeding six inches in length, are generally present   Thus in the Dart the young are present in the spring, and are taken from March 1st till May, of from 6 oz to ¼ lb in weight, after this time very few are captured.   While in some of the Irish rivers they often ascend early in the season

Means of capture—These fish when adults, are very wary, and it has been observed in the Tweed and neighbouring fisheries that they will not freely enter the chambers of the fixed nets, the proportion of them captured there being one for every nine grilse or four salmon   But in the drifting hang-nets at the mouths of the rivers or in the estuaries three or four trout are taken for every salmon, and in about equal numbers with the grilse   The same is observed elsewhere, and in the estuaries of South Wales sewin of from 1 lb to 4 lb weight are secured during March and April   In Ireland a few salmon-trout are taken in the mullet nets   in Belfast Bay they are captured in large quantities early in the morning, if possible before daybreak, by drawing sandy bays

Anglers find in rivers these fish will mostly take a worm if the waters are muddy, as it begins to clear a spinning bait, and when fine a fly   If hooked they often display considerable cunning in their attempts to break the line with a blow from the tail, or impetuously dart off, when a similar result ensues should it not readily run off the reel   Stoddart observed that during the season clean sea trout give more sport than salmon to the anglers, in fact, in Scotland an hour or two's white trout fishing when the fish are in the humour, is esteemed good sport, as they often take a fly well,[*] while in some places they may be taken up to 6 or 7 lb weight, in Wales the sewin also are similarly sought after, especially of an evening, with fine tackle and a small fly   But large examples, as bull trout,[†] appear to generally refuse bait or flies, but kelts are readily hooked   The smaller ones in salt water readily take a spinning bait and are often thus fished for on the west coast of Scotland, while whiffers for pollack on the south coast of England not unfrequently take a sewin

Breeding—The number of eggs deposited by the sea trout in moderately-sized examples is about 800 for every pound weight of the parent fish,[‡] while the size of these eggs show the same variation as will be alluded to under the fresh-water trout.

The observations already made (pp 76, 77 *ante*) as to how reproduction is

---

[*] R B L in *The Field*, October 31st, 1885, gave an interesting account of angling for sprod, which he correctly considered as identical with finnock, whitling, and herling and to be the grilse stage of *Salmo trutta*   Its advent in June and July in the waters of the Eden (Cumberland), Nith (Dumfries), Kent (Westmoreland), and other northern rivers is looked forward to with eagerness as it is too small to be captured by the legal sized nets   It is a free feeder, taking worms well in a spate, or when the water is at all discoloured, even at night time, too, when the streams are low and clear   At the fly it rises far more freely than the brown trout and according to the prevailing condition of the water takes anything from a salmon fly dressed on a no 12 or large hook, to the smallest midge tied on a no 1, and even the spinning minnow is not altogether discarded in deepish pools near the bottom   It arrives in fresh water bright and active as the *Salmo fario* is going out, and the autumn frosts appear to augment its appetite, while it is a bold, hard fighter, and plucky to the backbone   It is often more difficult to deceive than old river trout, and when feeding on a particular fly the most skilful fisherman will scarcely persuade it to rise to any other   "And if for a time the sea fish refuse to rise, just take off your flies and put on a worm line, plenty of lengths of gut, a large hook (14's), and one or two big worms   Use no sinkers, do not let your bait touch the bottom, but fish it almost as you would the fly, with length of line according to circumstances, and if there are sprods or sea trout about the place, manipulating your line properly, the fault will be yours if you catch them not "

[†] "A clean bull trout (*Salmo trutta*) is scarcely ever known to take fly or bait of any description   I venture to say, I have killed more salmon with the rod than any one man ever did, and yet, put them all together, I am sure I have not killed twenty clean bull trout, Of bull trout kelts thousands may be killed " (*Lord House* to Yarrell)

[‡] Mr Willis Bund recorded a sewin taken in October, 1872, which weighed 3¼ lb, and contained 544 eggs for each pound's weight of the parent

carried on among the salmon are so applicable to the sea trout as to render repetition unnecessary The time of year, however, in which these latter fish spawn would seem to be about a month, or even more, earlier than in the salmon, commencing in September or October along with the river trout * On November 26th, 1874, Sir J Maitland netted ten sea trout in the Stirling district, five were males, and five females the first male was nearly spent In some captured in the Teith and retained at Howietoun to be artificially spawned on November 24th, 1886, but few eggs and little milt were found remaining, and on November 26th, 1885, when netting the Teith for salmon (then just commencing to spawn) we took two sea trout kelts On November 12th, 1884, when out for these fish two pairs were seen at their redds in the Stirling district, but the rivers were rather swollen † In a very severe winter, however, Couch found sewin depositing eggs in the Fowey as late as January 22nd Mr Brady observed that in Ireland the white trout spawn a month before the salmon, and the kelts are very ravenous As a general rule these fish commence spawning in the month of October in the Usk the earliest dates recorded have been September 27th and October 1st, 1873

That sea trout can breed without migrating to the sea has been shown (p 113 ante), in fact they may become land-locked similarly to the salmon (see p 103 ante) The eggs of these fish can no more be incubated in salt water than can those of the salmon and of the fresh-water trout Mr Jackson, Land and Water (June 10th, 1876), observed that the "Salmon-trout cast their ova in the salt water in the Southport Aquarium, without assuming the appearance of kelts, or even leaving off feeding greedily on shrimps They did not attempt to make a redd, and the spawn was immediately eaten by their fellows ' While the eggs of this species, similarly to those of the salmon, have been safely conveyed to and hatched at the antipodes ‡

Similarly to the salmon we find sea trout occasionally ready for breeding at inappropriate times, thus "North Countryman," Field, 1883, writing from the Orkneys, observed, having the previous day, July 19th, captured a sea trout with a worm in the sea, "It was a female fish, in good order, weighing 6 lb 2 oz , but was tinged very slightly with a dark shade on the belly When opened the roe was nearly fully developed—in fact, just as we expect to see at the end of September The fish was good and curdy, however "

Sewin would seem to often keep in shoals of females, for several observers have noticed the almost entire absence of male examples among the peal or sewin in salt water, and Dillwyn in his Fauna of Swansea, p 13, observed that "Mr Talbot has found in his streams at Margam that the bull trout are always males, and the sewin females," or in short that in that locality males were termed "bull trout," and females were designated as "sewin" being even thought a distinct species Couch never found a male peal, but observing about thirty forming redds in the Looe river on January 22nd, he had them netted, and all of them were found to be females with the roe running out, except one male which resembled a bull trout rather than a peal Possibly the two sexes may keep separated during periods of migration, for certainly in those I have obtained from

---

* " As each season came round when rods were put aside, watching hundreds of Salmo trutta on the spawning beds in November, working side by side with their cousins Salmo fario, the astonishing fact has been to me that hybrids between the two species are not more common than is actually the case That such do occur, personally, I have not the slightest doubt, though their identification in a natural state still remains to be determined The milt ejected from the male fish of either species cannot fail to fertilize the ova of both, for are they not spawned close to each other on the same bed of gravel, and under exactly similar conditions ?"—R B L , Field, February 14th, 1885

† It is often necessary to wait for a frost, which freezes the small rills and then reduces the volume of water in the streams

‡ In the Proceedings of the Zool Soc 1869, p 473, Mr M Allport, August 10th, 1869, observed respecting the 15 000 eggs of the sea trout sent to Tasmania in 1866, a fair percentage hatched, and most of the smolts were allowed to descend to the sea , " but the Tasmanian Salmon Commissioners retained a few in a suitable pond, having gravelly rapids adapted for spawning grounds attached Twelve of these fish attained weights varying from ¾ lb to 1¼ lb , and during the end of June and beginning of July last, four pairs formed redds and deposited spawn, in which the fish are now distinctly visible."

the sea and in several distinct localities all were females, it is not so, however, in the rivers

The questions of sterility, limits of reproduction and monstrosities, will be discussed along with hybridism

Life history —That of the sea trout, so far as it has been observed and recorded, appears to be very similar to what occurs in the salmon, having its par stage, in which it has been asserted on insufficient evidence, that the anadromous may be distinguished from the fresh-water forms by the number of transverse bands or finger marks along their sides But this method of recognition appears to fail when carried into actual practice* (*see p* 171, 172 *ante*) The par goes through the smolt and grilse stage as whitlings or herlings in the north (*see p* 159) or white fish and peal in the south (*see p* 160) while the young are equally or more voracious than young salmon, for when artificially brought up they will consume pond snails as *Limnea* or *Ancylus* which salmon appear to reject

I have already adverted to the opinion held by others and personally believed in that our sea and fresh-water trout are merely local races of one species That anadromous or fresh-water habits may simply result from local circumstances, and colours be consequent upon immediate surroundings In tracing up these fish then we may well begin by the question, *What is an orange fin ?* The very term speaks for the colour which is, as a rule, seen staining the outer quarter or half of the adipose dorsal fin, or else in the form of distinct orange spots

The rate of growth in sea trout has been investigated by several observers, but as already remarked (*see p* 146 *ante*), in some instances the marked par or smolt has developed into an undoubted fresh-water form of trout I have, therefore, in

* Mr Shaw, of Drumlanrig, observed to the *Royal Society of Edinburgh* in 1843, that having shot a pair of salmon trout while spawning in the Nith, he incubated and hatched the eggs, the young becoming par the first year and orange fins the second year At eighteen months the males have the milt developed at two years, when about 7¼ in long, many assume the smolt dress At this period they are as follows —" Dark brown on the back, passing gradually into a white silvery appearance on the sides and belly the pectoral fins are white, with the extremities (¼) orange ventral fins pure white anal fins white, with a faint dusky mark on each side dorsal fin light brown, inclining to black at the extreme points of the anterior rays, which are tipped with a very little white posterior rays have a faint tinge of orange, and the whole fin is much spotted adipose fin dark brown, margined with red caudal rays of a light colour near the base, running into a dark orange, terminated by a faintly marked double margin of black The spots on the back and sides vary much, prevailing principally along the back, with a few below the lateral line Each spot is surrounded by a circle of a lighter colour than the general surface of the body, and this appears to be a prevailing character of the trout species, and one which the sea trout exhibits, even after having assumed the migratory dress, when every other feature of resemblance to the common trout has disappeared."

But "a certain number of the individuals of both sexes (probably about one fourth of each brood) never assume the silvery exterior, or migratory dress, and even if those which have assumed that appearance be detained in fresh water for a month or two, they will re assume the dusky coating, and in the ensuing autumn both sexes have their reproductive organs fully developed " He observed that "it is by no means improbable that portions of each brood are permanent residents in fresh water, as they are never observed to migrate in a dusky state along with the shoals of silvery fry " Having marked some of these young fish he concluded that the " orange " or " yellow fins " became *herlings* of six or seven ounces after a sojourn of about ten weeks in the sea the first season and ascend their native rivers to spawn and that they return the next and each subsequent season as salmon-trout, with an increase of about 1¼ lb per annum

Dr W M'Intosh, *Scottish Naturalist* (July, 1872, vol 1, no 7, pp 227-233) contributed a paper " on the 'yellow-fins' of the Allan water " At p 227 he observed upon some "yellow fins" which he thought to be young whitlings (*Salmo albus* or *brachypoma*) which had from 43 to 44 crecal appendages and a second variety or species possessing from 49 to 57, while he stated that in the common trout of the Tay, Ericht, Allan-water, and the mill-stream at Stormontfield these appendages ranged from 38 to 56. He also thought that the tail fin of the yellow fin was more deeply cleft than seen in the brook trout The important question of the number of par-bands along the sides is omitted, while it must be evident that if the smolt had the maxillary comparatively slender and the vomerine teeth in a single series they were peculiar He contrasted the young yellow fin smolt with the young burn trout as follows —" The dark back of the 'yellow-fin,' its silvery sides and cheeks, and the silvery and whitish belly, stand in strong contrast with the young river trout The red spots on the sides are much more developed in the latter than in the 'yellow fin '" "In a 'yellow' trout (*S fario*) and a 'yellow fin' of the same length, there is a very appreciable difference in the position of this (dorsal) fin, which is decidedly further forward in the latter, the same variation occurring in the fatty, ventral and anal as noticed in the first glance at the fish," (*See* page 198) the following instances from the Tweed experiments eliminated doubtful cases and restricted my examples to such as have been considered in all stages to have retained their sea-trout characteristics. Among those taken in or near the Tweed,* and if these experiments were not erroneous, we find that a smolt or orange fin 1¾ oz in April, 1873 may be a 1½ lb whitling in June, 1874, or a smolt may become a 3 lb Bull trout in twelve months or in three years weigh 5 lb. While although a Black-tail was observed to increase from 8 oz to 1⅓ lb in seventeen months, another from 9 oz to 1 lb 3 oz in nine months, and a third from 13 oz to 4½ lb in twenty-eight months, on the other hand one example 11½ oz in weight had actually decreased to 10 oz in six months, and a second from 10½ oz to 5 oz in the same time. Among the whitling likewise, one 17 inches long and weighing 1¾ lb increased in twenty-three months to 18¼ inches long, and weighed 2¼ lb, while a Black-tail 12 inches long and 12 oz in weight increased in nine months to 13 inches in length and 17 oz in weight. The foregoing show how very variable both the rapidity of growth as well as the augmentation in weight may be.

Passing on to instances from the same river wherein the marked fish have been captured in distant localities, we find from the observations of the Tweed Commissioners,† that these fish migrate long distances, as one from the Tweed to Yarmouth, in the space of a few days over a month, and during that period it increased ½ lb in weight. But the same variations in increase both in length and weight are shown in fishes thus migrating long distances, just as in those which appear to remain nearer to their native river.

The food consumed by the sea trout is very similar to that of the salmon, but in some respects they seem to be more voracious.

I removed from the maw of a small example (14 in long) from the Aberdeenshire Dee, taken in July, 1882, four sand launces, *Ammodytes*.‡ Sir W Jardine found its common food to be the sand hopper, *Talitrus locusta*. Phinocs in rivers are partial to the fresh-water shrimp *Gammarus pulex*. That they will consume fish eggs is well known, thus Bertram (p 199) recorded how a whitling in 1882 of about ¾ lb weight had been taken in the Tay with 300 salmonoid eggs in its stomach.

Mr Jamieson, *Fishing*, December 18th, 1886, gave an account of some investigations he had made respecting the food of sea trout in the Nether Don and a little above it, extending from the Cathedral of St Machar to where the river discharges itself into the sea.

'The greater portion of this is tidal water, and, consequently many of the stomach-contents of these trout were derived from the sea. During the months

* Orange fin or trout smolt marked April or May, 1851, became a clean Bull trout 5 lb weight, May, 1854. Smolt, May, 1857, a Bull trout, 3 lb, May, 1858. Black-tail, October, 1859, a Whitling, 1½ to 2 lb, March, 1861. Whitling, 1¾ lb, September, 1870 a Whitling, 2½ lb, July, 1872. Bull trout, 2½ lb, Sept 20th, 1870 to a Bull trout, 5½ lb, August, 1871. Black tail, 12 oz, October, 1870, to a Whitling, 17 oz., June, 1871. Black tail, 21 oz, October, 1871, a Whitling, 2½ lb, August, 1872. Orange fin, 1¾ oz, April 1873, a Whitling, 1 lb 8 oz, June, 1874. Black-tail, 9 oz, Sept, 1873, a Whitling, 1 lb 3 oz, June, 1874. Black tail, 11½ oz, Nov, 1877, a Bull trout, 28 oz, August, 1879. Black tail 13 oz, Nov, 1877 a Bull trout, 4½ lb, May, 1879. Black tail, 11 oz, Nov, 1875 a Bull trout 3 lb 12 oz, August, 1877. Black tail, 11½ oz, Nov, 1877, a Black tail, 10 oz, April, 1878. Black tail 11 oz, Nov, 1877, a Bull trout, 2¾ lb, August, 1879. a Black-tail, 10½ oz, Nov, 1875, a Black tail, 8½ oz, March, 1876. Black-tail 11½ oz, Nov, 1877, a Black-tail 10 oz, April, 1878.

† Bull trout kelt, 3 lb, March, 1852, recaptured at Yarmouth, April, 1852, 3½ lb. Bull-trout kelt, 3 lb, March, 1852, recaptured Shields, April, 1852, 4½ lb. three Black tails, Autumn, 1858, recaptured at Aberdeen, one in the Don, and two in the sea as Whitlings from 2 lb to 3 lb. Black-tail, 1 lb, Sept, 1870, as Bull trout, North Esk, 2 lb 1 oz, Sept, 1871. Black tail, 12 oz, Oct, 1870, as a Bull trout, 2 lb 10 oz, at Lamberton, June, 1871. Bull trout, 3½ lb, Oct, 1870, recaptured in Coquet, 1 lb 13 oz, Nov, 1871. Black tail, 1 lb, Oct, 1871, as Bull trout, 1 lb 7 oz, Stirling, August 1872. Black tail, 18 oz, Sept, 1872, as Bull trout, 36 oz, Dee, July, 1873. Black-tail, 12 oz, Oct, 1872, in Whitadder as Black tail, 12 oz, Nov., 1872. Black-tail, 13 oz, Nov, 1875, as Bull trout, Stirling, 28 oz, July 1876. Black-tail, 13½ oz, Oct, 1876, in Firth of Forth as Bull trout, 1 lb 12½ oz, August, 1877. Black-tail, 8 oz, Oct, 1877, in Firth of Forth as Sea trout, 1 lb, July, 1878. Black-tail, 9 oz, Nov, 1877, in Firth of Forth as Sea trout, 2 lb 4 oz, July, 1878.

‡ Mr M Dunn, *Land and Water*, June 24th, 1880, observed that he had found *Peal* feeding on herring-fry in Mevagissey Bay during the months of May and June.

of April and May, August and September, in this river, there is no fish which
will take with greater rapidity, or rise so boldly to a fly or minnow, and no fish,
at such times, shows more pluck or brilliant play During these months the sea
trout is in the very pink of condition, being of greater size and strength at such
times than at others, which is mainly due to its feeding on various species of
insecta and such small fish as the sprat, sand-eel, etc This shows that the trout
is very rapidly affected by the nature of its food

"The following is a list of stomach-contents, extracted from about 300 sea trout
during the last fishing season —I Of Fish —*Clupea sprattus* (common sprat),
Ammodytes tobianus (sand-eel), *Leuciscus phoxinus*, *Anguilla* (small fresh-water
eel), and, in one instance, the skull of a codling. 2 Of Mollusca—*Limnea
stagnalis*, small form of *Mytilus* (mussel), several small species of *Nudibranchiata*
3 Of Crustacea —*Gammarus pulex*, *Thysanoessa borealis*, *Talitrus locusta*,
Amathilla sabini, *Palæmon serratus*, *Palæmon annulicornis*, *Crangon vulgaris*, and
many *Entomostraca*, including *Cyclops* and *Daphnia* and several unnamed species
4. Of Insecta —These are Innumerable, including *Helobia nivalis* and *Sphæridium
quadrimaculatum* (*Coleopterous insects*), spiders 5 Of Annelida —*Sabellaria*,
Nereis, *Lumbricus terrestris* and a small species of black leech 6 Of Polyzoa —
Gemellaria loricata, with small shell-fish attached 7 Of Hydrozoa —*Sertularia
abietina*, *Sertularia operculata*, both with small shell-fish attached

' It is an interesting fact that many of the above-named form part of the diet
of the cod, herring and mackerel, as, for example, the sprat and sand-eel Both
these species are abundant on the Aberdeenshire coast, and in summer are largely
used as baits for other fish, during which time they come close in shore In
August of this year cartloads of them were cast up on the sands at Don-mouth,
and immense shoals ascended daily with the tide and were greedily devoured by
the sea trout, the result being that anglers had a poor time of it, owing to the
fish being so well fed In May and August I found the trout simply gorged with
both of these species

"Of the upper reaches of the river the *Limnea*, a small univalve shell-fish, is
a general favourite, especially where sandy material exists, and in April, May and
August the small black leech forms a grand bill of fare

"The *Gammarus pulex* (fresh-water sandhopper) and *Nereis* (sandling worm)
occur as food throughout the whole fishing season

"To show the varied nature of their food, on April 13th of this year I had
seven sea trout caught with a small 'Professor,' in a swift flowing stream,
unaffected by the tide, and from one extracted the following contents —Nine
Limnea, two red beetles, one black beetle, one spider, three sandhoppers and
several minute *Crustacea* "

As food —Very various opinions are held respecting the value of the sea trout
as food , for while the sewin of Welsh rivers is of a very delicate and superior
flavour, the bull trout* of the Coquet seems to be condemned as worthless, and
large examples, as a general rule, are found to be coarse Several subjects,
however, have to be considered, as (1) the locality from whence the fish was
captured (2) its age and size (3) whether it is clean or near the breeding
season (4) and possibly the length of time it has been in fresh water †

---

* *Lord Home* observed that ' the bull trout (*Salmo trutta*) is an inferior fish and is exactly
what is called at Dalkeith and Edinburgh, Musselburgh Trout." Stoddart remarked that they
ascend in scanty numbers during the spring and summer season but are then in excellent
condition On the whole, however, they are a coarse fish " (p 224) They are very voracious
when ascending to breed and although outwardly they look good they are very inferior as food
In the month of June I found them excellent in the Oykell in Sutherlandshire, also during
August and September in Wales and along the south coast of Cornwall Large quantities are
sent yearly from Scotland to London, and those from Perth, Dundee, Montrose, and Aberdeen
are most esteemed for their colour and flavour

† 'South Devon," in *Land and Water*, June 14th, 1884, observed that above the Totness
weir " hitherto it was a very exceptional thing to take any other than white-fleshed trout now,
however, that the dapping season has commenced, the larger fish in the deep water above
Totness weir have been taken in considerable numbers similar sized fish were last year all white
fleshed trout, but now a large proportion of them are pink I consider this is caused by the fish
feeding in the tidal waters below Totness weir on shrimps and other salt-water food, and they

12 *

Such fish as ascend rivers, prior to the anadromous shoals migrating for breeding purposes, are generally good as food, at least up to 6 lb or 7 lb, and but little inferior to the salmon, especially when they have pink flesh But in some places, as already alluded to, the young fish deteriorate in quality the longer they are absent from the sea In the Usk, however, the core or bull trout are very bad eating although they ascend early While in certain rivers poisonous substances having obtained access appear to have adversely influenced the character of the fish Buckland observed that sea trout are not such a good table fish as the salmon, and the flesh cuts white (but this is not universally the case), while he remarked that the French prefer it to salmon

Legislation —If the sea and brook trout are merely varieties of one species, this might give rise to awkward inquiries of how the former in Scotland have been decided to belong to the salmon proprietor but not so necessarily the fresh-water trout which are placed in a totally different category "In a Tweed Act (15 Geo III c 46) occurs the definition ' Salmon, grilse, salmon-trout, or whitling,' consequently it must be upwards of 100 years since sea trout were legally defined as pertaining to the salmon fisheries "

Diseases —Those affecting salmon (p 109 *ante et seq*) are similarly observed attacking the sea trout Even so long ago as Pontoppidan (*Natural History of Norway*, 1755, p 139) are allusions to disease affecting these fish He asserted the salmon-trout, *Trutta taurina*, to be a very common fish in the fresh lakes and rivers, but many of them are subject to a sort of disease so that they cannot be eaten The head grows very large and the body emaciated, while in their entrails are found pimples resembling millet seed Some ascribed it as due to the sawdust from the mills falling into the river, while others considered it to be retained roe which had become diseased This complaint was asserted not to affect the non-migratory fresh-water trout, and was possibly seen in kelts

Under this head may be included the result of suspending the incidence of the close-season, for I have already remarked (p 67 *ante*), how H M Inspectors of Fisheries, finding sea trout present in the Coquet, but salmon absent, concluded that the former had destroyed the latter, and how if they in turn were eradicated the true salmon would again flourish Acting on this theoretical opinion leave was obtained in 1868 to suspend the close time for bull trout, or in other words, to capture the shoals ascending to breed, and the numbers netted were as follows —

	Open season	Fish	Close season	Fish	Total
1868	Feb 1st to Aug 31st	1757	Sept 1st to Dec 1st	26,350	28,107
1869	,, ,, ,,	1747	,, ,, ,,	15,464	17,211
1870	,, , ,	770	,, ,, ,,	10,687	11,457
1871	,, ,, ,,	4134	,, ,, ,,	9,188	13,622

The massacre was now very sensibly put an end to, but it is interesting as showing how rapidly the destruction of spawning fish entails diminution of the stock in a river Then as to size, during 1868, '69 and '70, the take during the open season averaged 5 lb a fish, in the close season 4 lb a fish in 1871 the average weight of the fish taken during the open season had decreased to 4 lb , while those taken during the close season had risen to 5 lb

Habitat —The sea trout is found in northern Europe ascending rivers falling into the Baltic, North Sea, the seas surrounding the British Isles, and the Seine and the Loire in France

In the Orkneys, Low observed that it is found in great quantities in the Loch of Stenniss, through the whole summer They do not grow so large as the river trout, *Salmo fario*, neither are they so much esteemed, their flesh being white and only moderately good During harvest they ascend to the smallest streams to spawn subsequent to which they return to the sea It is common along the east coast of Scotland, and Russel calculated that in the Tweed it is as numerous as the salmon and grilse combined to the south of the Tweed fifty to every salmon

are able by means of the fish pass to get up again to the fresh water which formerly they could not do except in floods, and that rarely "

and grilse, while in the Forth and Tay and other large rivers difficult of access in the north the bull trout is almost a stranger. It is also present in the rivers along the north-east coast of England, more especially the Coquet, Tyne, Tees, and Wear. It is less frequent on the west coast of Scotland than on the east. In Yorkshire very abundant along the coast and present in all the rivers frequented by the salmon (Yorkshire Vertebrata). In Norfolk it is frequently taken in the Ouse and the estuary (Lowe), and the "Fordwich trout" from Kent is of the northern form. Sewin, *S. cambricus*, is generally found in the south of England and in Wales extending up the west coast of England, but in Cumberland salmon-trout appear to be most numerous. In Ireland it is common around the coast, and there the salmon-trout, *S. trutta*, are likewise found.

In 1873 Frank Buckland, *Familiar History of British Fishes*, having observed that "it has been supposed by some that the sea trout and bull trout are identical," which views he held to be erroneous, although he found it to be impossible to explain their differences in writing, and considered the practical test to be the boiling-pot. The flesh of the sea trout he held to be red and savoury: that of the bull trout white, leather-like and insipid. He believed that the bull trout were gradually gaining ground on the salmon owing to the presence of weirs, the mesh of the nets being too large, and their getting first to the spawning beds. That the bull trout being stronger than a salmon, should some of both species arrive at a weir, the former will surmount the obstacle, leaving the latter below. He observed that there were no bull trout in the Lune, Clwyd, Seiont, Cleddy, Avon (Somerset), Avon (Devon), Frome, Avon (Hants), Stonr. No increase in the Dee, Teifi, Wye, Taw and Torridge, Teign, Tees, Otter, Exe, Camel, Tamar and Plym, Dart, Ribble. An increase in the north Tyne and the Usk. Subsequently (1880), he remarked that the fish-wives occasionally clip the round tail of the bull trout quite square and sell it for true salmon. Also as these fish are not being captured during their autumn run, the netting season ought to be lengthened and the use of "splash-nets" permitted at the mouths of the rivers, and the mesh of the net altered at certain seasons.

As to the size it attains there exists the head of one in the British Museum 10 in. long from the Tweed, which measurement would seem to show the fish must have been nearly 4 ft. in length. Buckland remarked that at the end of November, 1868, the Honourable Charles Ellis caught with the rod at Brigham Dubb, on the Tweed, a male fish, 4 ft. 1 in. in length, weighing 44 lb. This was one of the "Gray skull." One upwards of 21 lb. and measuring 4¼ feet in length, was taken in a small tributary of the Trent at Drayton Manor, and sent by Sir Robert Peel to Yarrell, the skeleton of which is now in the Museum of the College of Surgeons. In the Usk Mr. Willis-Bund has recorded a bull-trout kelt 15 or 16 lb. weight, taken January 3rd, 1870 : one of 28 lb. January 11th, 1873 : and one of 20 lb. taken in a putcher at Goldcliff on April 4th, 1876.

The figures in plate V consist of (No. 1) a male salmon-trout from the Teith, 15 in. long, and which had 57 cæcal appendages, and (No. 2) a female sewin 15 in. long which possessed 40 appendages.

Fig. 41, *Fresh-water Snails*. 1, Planorbis : 2, Limnea peregra. 3, Ancylus (enlarged).

FRESH-WATER TROUT

In the foregoing pages I have advanced reasons for supposing that we possess only one species of sea trout, although our eastern and northern form of salmon-trout, *Salmo trutta*, appears as a rule to have a few more cæcal appendages than the sewin, *S cambricus*, which is chiefly found on the southern and western parts of England and Wales, and along most of our Irish shores Externally so similar are these races, that no naturalist has yet succeeded in pointing out unmistakable differences between the two, while their dentition and the formation of the jaws vary to such an extent that they cannot be relied upon as differentiating one from the other, although generally the vomer has more teeth along its body in the northern than in the southern variety.

Passing, as the sea trout does, by insensible gradations and almost unappreciable differences into the fresh-water races, it becomes necessary to make a rather full investigation respecting whether such is the result of changing their habitation from the sea to fresh waters or the reverse, or if their differences are the result of a hybridizing process carried on between an anadromous sea trout and a non-migratory fresh-water species

As already observed (p 143) Widegren, in 1863, asserted that the anadromous sea trout and non-migratory fresh-water forms were simply varieties of one common species, the differences in colour being consequent upon local surroundings Malmgren, in his account of the Salmonidæ of Finland, came to the same conclusion Collett, *Norges Fiske*, 1875, p 157, likewise held an identical opinion, so also did Malm in his *Fauna*, 1877 p 538, Feddersen, *Danske Ferskvandsfiske*, p 77, and others have likewise held and still maintain the same views * While Shaw, in 1843, gave a short account of having reared sea trout from eggs and how some of the young, probably about a quarter, never assumed the silvery migratory livery, and he advanced the opinion that some may permanently become residents in fresh water But this question of the identity of the marine and fresh-water forms has been already referred to (pp 144, 145)

Opinions still are divided as to whether these two forms are merely divisions of one species, but however this may be, ichthyologists are more agreed in believing that all the varieties of our fresh-water trout are merely local races, in which the differences in this very plastic form are brought about by their surroundings Differences which I have shown (p 145) may disappear on the young being raised under changed circumstances

Jurine, *History of the Fishes of the Lake of Geneva*, 1825, gave what he believed to be sufficient reasons for considering that the local forms existing there and which had been accounted distinct species of trout, as *Salmo trutta*, and *S fario*, and were known under different names as the common trout, salmon-trout, lake trout, river trout, alpine trout, &c, were all referable to differences of sex, age, season, the nature of the water, food, light, &c The distinctive marks taken from the prolongation of the under-jaw beyond the upper, the colour of the flesh, of the skin, with the size and shade of the spots, the form of the tail, &c, being variable, were not to be depended on

Lunel remarking upon the various specific names that had been given to the

---

* Dr *Gunther*, who in 1864 and at other times has given his opinion that these views are the outcome of ignorance or incapacity of the observers, consistently omits all reference to the subject in his *Introduction to the Study of Fishes*, 1880, written according to the *Zoological Record* in order "to serve as a book of reference to zoologists generally, and to supply those who have frequent opportunities of observing fishes, with a ready means of obtaining information" He also refrains from mentioning that some naturalists are unable to admit the numerous species into which he has sub divided trout

varieties of the trout, asserted *Salmo fario*, *S lemanus*, *S rappu*, and *S lacustris*, of Lake Constance all belong to one form which he proposed terming *S variabilis* Steindachner (*Al Wiss Wien*, lii, 1865, Nov 30th) identified *S detea*, Heck with *S fario* Pavesi (*Pesci nel Ticino*) considered the lake and river trout of the river Canton to be merely varieties of one species Fatio observed, ' On fresh-water trout, according as it is more or less confined to small streams or to the deeper waters of our lakes, presents an appearance so different as to have passed hitherto for two perfectly distinct species in the eyes of most ichthyologists It is well known that the size of the basin and the relative abundance of food* have much influence on the dimensions of the fish The little brook trout which most zoologists still distinguish under the name of *Salmo ausonu*, is in fact, in my opinion, nothing more than a form of the great trout of our lakes, which is called according to circumstances *Trutta lacustris*, *T schiffermulleri*, *Fario marsiglii*, or *Salmo lemanus*. Most of the characters proposed for its distinction are those of the early age of the fish In a small stream the trout, which cannot grow for want of room, arrives at an advanced age, retaining more or less the characters of infancy It would be still more surprising to meet with trout of 30 lb in a few inches of water "

Perhaps it will be as well to here refer to the eggs of the fresh-water trout, which have been forwarded to, and been the progenitors of the species in Australasia, and it will be exceedingly important to clearly follow this out, as attempts have been made to show that they may be hybrids† The origin of these fish were due to Frank Buckland having at Admiral Keppel's request collected 1,200 ova from his preserves on the Itchen, and forwarded them as a present from him to Mr Youl Mr Francis Francis also sent two lots, about 800, from Mr Spicer's mill at Alton-on-the-Wey, and about 700 from Mr Thurlow's mill at High Wycombe, Buckinghamshire, and all were picked and dispatched by Mr Youl‡ No subsequent shipment of fresh-water trout ova has been successful, at least up to the date of Mr Nichols' work These original eggs arrived at the breeding ponds in Tasmania, on April 21st, 1864 The first successful trout hatching in Otago, New Zealand, Mr Arthur reported, occurred in October, 1868, from 800 ova obtained from the natural spawning beds of the brook trout, *Salmo fario*, in Tasmania, these and a second lot, the subsequent year, formed the whole of the original stock, some of which were first liberated in the streams in November as was also vouched for by Mr Allport in the *Proceedings of the Zoological Society*

Unless all these gentlemen have been mistaken, it is abundantly clear that the original stock of fresh-water trout in New Zealand came from Tasmania, and were descendants from those raised from the eggs sent out by Mr Youl And now comes the inquiry have these fishes retained the exact characters of those from which they were sprung, or have new surroundings developed differences ? The late Mr. Arthur, c ᴇ., who took so warm an interest in the trout, informed us that in New Zealand they spawned from about the middle of June to the

* Professor Forel, *Nature*, 1886 (p 193), writing of the fauna and flora o Lake Léman, observed that the principal agents affecting life in the lake are temperature and light, of less importance are the shape and capacity of its basin, the matters dissolved in or held in suspension by its waters, and the movements (for the most part superficial) to which its waters are subject Light is a far more important feature than temperature It is at a depth of 30 metres or where chlorophyle-forming vegetation ceases, that he separates the littoral from the deep regions of the lake, the actinic action of light ceases, at 50 metres in summer and at 100 metres only in winter when the water is more transparent In the deep region all tends to calm, rest, and absence of movement, uniformity, monotony, equality, no motion, no variation, and characters only comparable with those of the deep sea The population is denser in the upper part of the deep region than it is in the lower, but even in the deepest part life is present The greater part of the species, invertebrates, are evidently the descendants of the inhabitants of the shallow waters, and differ from them chiefly in being smaller and less brightly coloured, the eyes are wanting in *Gyrator coecus*, and have a tendency to disappear in other species

† " As it is a fact that numerous cross-breeds have been introduced into, and reared in Tasmania, which must more or less interfere with the characters of the pure breeds," Gunther, *Introduction to the Study of Fishes*, 1880, p 612 See also Mr Nichols' work on *The Acclimatisation of the Salmonidæ at the Antipodes*, 1882.

‡ See letter by Mr Youl to *The Fisherman's Magazine and Review*, vol 1, 1864, entitled " Who sent the trout ova to Tasmania " (p 429)

end of September, according to locality, in the coast streams from June 1st
to the end of August, and in the Wakatipu streams in September In certain
rivers the trout now seem to be migratory, so it would almost look as if they
were commencing to be anadromous like the sea trout, for, as observed by Mr
Arthur, migration appears to be the refuge of trout in Otago when planted in a
stream deficient in size, range of water and food   Thus the largest trout
disappear from the waters of Leith, except during the breeding season (see
p 7 ante)   As to the colours and markings of those in the rivers of Otago,
considerable variations are seen, a general feature being that females of any age,
and from any stream, are silvery with black spots, red ones being seldom present
or numerous, while the males are darker with a tendency to yellow on the sides
and belly, at times they are very golden and as a rule they have red spots, sometimes large and numerous, the shape of the black spots always being round on the
gill covers, shoulders, dorsal and adipose fins, but varying on the body from
round to rectangular and ×-shaped spots towards the tail   The theory that a
salt-water residence occasions black spots to become of an ×-shape is not borne
out by facts   For example, trout of both sexes, in clean and white water with a
light bottom, as in the Shag river, Pomahaka, and Wakatipu lake, are silvery and
have black spots mostly ×-shaped, bright silvery females with fine heads and
×-shaped spots may often be seen, that might easily be taken for sea trout
While the Waiwera and Waipaki rivers, which have dark bottoms, produce trout
of the golden variety, with most of the black spots rounded in form   The food
in these four rivers is much the same *

Another experiment on the dissemination of trout may likewise be alluded to
in this place   When at Ootacamund on the Neilgherry Hills in the Madras
Presidency in 1863, I observed a deficiency of fish in the waters of the upper
plateau   These mountain ranges embrace a geographical area extending over
268,494 square miles, their peaks vary from 5000 to 8000 feet above the sea, and
Ootacamund is 7426 feet above the sea level, with an annual mean temperature
of 58°68' Fahr   I proposed to the Governor of Madras attempting to introduce
fresh-water trout from England by means of their eggs, and attempted it in
1866, and although I failed, Mr McIvor, acting on knowledge acquired in my
failure, succeeded in 1868 in bringing out some trout fry from Loch Leven, which
in due time bred in their new home, where, as will be subsequently adverted to,
they developed red spots which are generally absent from the true Lochleven
trout †

* Mr Arthur (Trans Otago Institute, July 9th, 1878) also remarked that unlike the Scotch
trout, which according to Stoddart show a yearly increase of about one-third of a pound in weight,
in Otago they grow so rapidly and are so fat, that they have reached an average yearly increment
of from 1 lb to 2¾ lb   Already the various streams have stamped the trout with local peculiarities   in some they are plump almost to deformity, their proportions are not constant neither are
their colours, while examples have been seen up to 20 lb in weight   In 1882, one 31 inches long
and weighing 10 lb was caught at Temuka, its flesh was of a pale orange   in 1881 Mr Gwatkin
captured one in Canterbury, that turned the scale at 21 lb
The foregoing facts corroborate the view that all our forms of trout are varieties of one species,
and the hybrids we hear so much about are not mules but mongrels, being the result of the
crossing of varieties of one species   Consequently sterility need not be anticipated, but, on the
contrary, improvement is more likely to ensue (should there be no deficiency in food) than when
the stock is bred in and in
† Dr Gunther, in The Zoological Record of 1867, remarked of the above experiment that " an
attempt to introduce trout into the waters of the Neilgherry Hills has failed (as has been foreseen
by all acquainted with the nature of Salmonoid fishes) "   In The Journal of the Linnean Society,
1876, Zoology, vol xii, p 562, I recounted how trout had bred on the Neilgherry Hills, and I
exhibited at a meeting of the Society an example raised at Ootacamund 6 5 in in length   Only
the name of the paper was admitted into The Zoological Record for 1876   In my Fishes of India
and Ceylon Part III, August, 1877 p 504, I gave a short sketch of what had been done in Madras,
and figured the Neilgherry specimen of trout, life size, Plate cxviii, fig 3 but all reference to
it was omitted from The Zoological Record for 1877   Dr Gunther subsequently remarked in his
Introduction to the Study of Fishes, 1880   " Thus, the river trout or sea trout were very proper
subjects for those eminently successful attempts to establish them in similar latitudes of the
southern hemisphere, whilst the attempt of transferring them into the low hill streams of India
ended (as could be foreseen) in a total failure " (p 641)   In these observations Dr. Gunther
appears to have overlooked the following —Firstly, that streams at upwards of 7000 feet above

Colours —Yarrell observed, respecting the distinctions of British Salmonidæ, "too much reliance has been placed upon colour without resorting sufficiently to those external indications founded on organic structure, which may with greater certainty be depended upon." Examples of brook trout have been often found on migrating to the sea, to assume the brilliant silvery livery of the migratory Salmonoids, as well as their ×-shaped spot. Mr Harvie-Brown remarked, June 12th, 1882, on having captured at Darness several so-called sea trout from a sea pool or first pool at the mouth of the river, fresh-water at low tides, salt or brackish at high tides. From their silvery appearance they were known as sea trout, but were the river form acclimatized to brackish or nearly salt water, or periodically visiting such between tides.

Many observers have remarked upon the fact that fresh-water trout may live in salt water. Mr Francis Francis, in *The Field*, May 10th, 1879, stated that when introducing salt water into a tank in the Brighton Aquarium, which was inhabited by some salmon parr, there was at the time among them a common trout It, too, took to the salt water very kindly, fed smartly, and grew rapidly "Aquarius," in *The Field*, July 11th, 1885, stated he had seen the brown trout, *Salmo fario*, taken in the open sea, as have many others, while, that specimens still having their fresh-water dress are occasionally captured in the sea or brackish waters, is known to most persons who fish these latter localities.

I think the foregoing tends to show that the silvery sterile Loch Lomond trout is simply a variety in colour of the common fresh-water species, that this colour has been observed in sterile forms previously, that our brook trout may be found in salt water as well as in fresh without deleteriously affecting its health, that local geological conditions or states of the fresh water in which trout live has likewise been observed to produce this result in their colour, and, in short, that our pretty speckled brook trout may change into a silvery and anadromous form, ascending rivers at certain seasons in order to continue its kind.

I have already (p 145) shown that silvery forms like sea trout may be found permanently residing in fresh water, that our speckled trout may live in salt water and take on the silvery livery of the marine anadromous form, and we now come to the changes perceptible when living in the streams and lakes of the British Isles. For the colours and forms of our fresh-water trout are very dissimilar, at a first glance few would believe that the silvery Lochleven, the large Thames trout and the puny residents of Cornish streams were all one and the same species While, forty years since, Stoddart in his *Angler's Companion*, 1847, p 3, remarked that "unquestionably there exists no species of fish which, judging of it by the external marks, holds claim to so many varieties as the common fresh-water trout In Scotland almost every lake, river, and streamlet possesses a breed peculiar in outward appearance to itself "*

the sea can hardly be correctly defined as "low hill streams" *Secondly*, as the fish have bred on those Madras Hills, the experiments can scarcely be classed among failures Respecting this last, opinions may possibly differ, but that trout have been introduced into the streams on the Koondahs ought to be recorded, or at some future date on examples being captured another species may perchance be added to the present superabundant supply !

* Lord Home in *Yarrell's Fishes* observed of two streams, the Whitadder and its tributary the Blackadder, that the first flows along a very rocky and gravelly bed, while the latter rises in mosses, also goes through them in the first half of its course, but subsequently along a rich and highly cultivated district The trout in the first are silvery in colour, worthless as food while those from the Blackadder are dark with orange fins, but their flesh is excellent The many varieties are dependent upon external causes and chiefly to the abundance or the reverse of food and the nature of the water they reside in or the soil over which it flows Knox, *Lone Glens of Scotland*, 1854, p 10, remarked, "In Scotland there are at least four distinct species of trout" He then enumerated from an angler's point of view the following seven which he recorded as separate species "1, the dark-spotted lake trout 2, the red-spotted estuary trout these are the best of their kind, they have pink coloured flesh and are excellent to eat 3, the red spotted common river trout, with pale flesh and tasteless. 4, the pink-coloured red spotted common river trout, chiefly found in England 5, the parr-trout, rather better, when fed in certain rivers, than the common red-spotted trout, but never equal to the pink-coloured fish 6, the dark-spotted river trout, of whose natural history I know but little, although I believe such a trout exists And 7, the *Salmo ferox* or great lake trout of the north "

In streams where, due to some local cause,[*] the trout are small, it is not uncommon to perceive the par bands, as well as the black and red ocellated spots retained throughout life.[†] I found this obtained among some from brooks near Penzance, similarly so in Scotch burns and Welsh mountain streams. in fact, they were as brilliant as young salmon pars, to which their colours bore a striking resemblance.   Although we must anticipate estuary and fresh-water trout to be more vividly coloured than are those leading a more strictly marine life, still among the former the numerous variations in tints and markings have been explained in more than one manner, as the nuptial season, the effects of temporary emotions, of age, or the state of the fish's health, or its food.

Clear water in rapid rivers or lakes, especially when the bottom is pebbly, is seen to contain somewhat silvery fishes, with black X-shaped spots.   Sir William Jardine remarked that a variety very frequent among trout in small Alpine lochs in Scotland had large dark or red spots placed in a pale or clear surrounding field, these marks being very large, while the principal part of the spotting was confined to the centre of the body.   I have likewise obtained this form of coloured trout from deep holes in the course of burns, but the spots have been present all over the fish, while they have also been recorded from Wales.

The colour, depth, temperature, and character of the water also have an influence on the fish, the presence of moss and peat, or a muddy bottom, causing a dark tint to be assumed, while some captured in dark holes or caves have been seen nearly black.

The colours of the *Salmones* may be shortly summed up as silvery, with or without black spots[‡] among the marine, and some resident in large clear pieces of water, as lochs or rivers   more or less speckled with black and red when non-migratory and living in fresh waters   while, should the race be small, a persistence of the transverse bars or bands on the body, which are present in most of the young, may be observed even in adults.   Irrespective of changes in colour externally, a difference of food may occasion it in the flesh of these fishes, whether the alteration in diet is due to choice or to necessity   Thus crustacea and their allies, which appear to colour it red or pink, may be absent from the locality these fish frequent, or if present they may not relish that food so much as some other which exists in the water   In certain rivers there are trout with white and others with red flesh, the two forms being in good health and equally delicate for the table   This has also been observed in the American char, *Salmo fontinalis*, introduced into this country, and in which it has been clearly traceable to the food upon which it subsists

In some races of our fresh-water trout the males have been said to develop at the breeding season a knob or hook at the upper end of the lower jaw, while other forms have been erroneously stated to be deficient in it.   This sexual development, however, is seen in all races of our fresh-water trout, provided the specimens are permitted to live to a sufficient age, while in some well-fed examples as in Lochlevens at Howietoun, I have observed it at the third season   There is in its mode of development but little difference from what takes place in the

---

[*] Percy St John (in *Wild Sports of the West*, p 240) remarked that he "never observed the effect of bottom soil upon the quality of fish so strongly marked as in the trout taken in a small lake in the county of Monaghan   The water is a long irregular sheet, of no great depth, one shore bounded by a bog, the other by a dry and gravelly surface   On the bog side the trout are of the dark and shapeless species peculiar to moory loughs, while the other affords the beautiful and sprightly variety, generally inhabiting rapid and sandy streams   Narrow as the lake is, the fish appear to confine themselves to their respective limits   the red trout being never found upon the bog moiety of the lake, nor the black where the under surface is hard gravel "

[†] Mr Harvie-Brown has informed me of a dwarf trout said to exist in loch Mulach Corrie in Sutherlandshire which appears to be "a small but apparently adult form about the size of a big minnow and very rarely got   It may be the young of the so called gillaroo, but if so it is a curious departure as it is utterly without par bands "

[‡] We must not forget that brook trout vary greatly in colour even when in the same locality; thus *Lphemera* in 1853 remarked of those in the Wandle that such as "feed under the cover or the trees, or he *perdius* under banks or artificial 'hides,' during sunshine, are dark brown and yellow, those that frequent the unshaded streams with a clean sandy bottom are of a silvery hue " (p 274)

salmon (p. 57 *ante*), this growth, consisting of fibrous connective tissue, increases at the breeding period, and in seven-year-old fish at Howietoun it is in advance of the upper jaw when the mouth is closed, often forming a sore surface in front of the premaxillaries In measuring the proportions of the parts of the head of several specimens I found that whereas the lower jaw was as long or very nearly as long as seen in old fish, the distance from the nostrils to the end of the snout only equalled $1\frac{1}{2}$ diameters of the eye, whereas in old salmon it equals 2 diameters of the orbit At Howietoun my observations had to stop at this point as fish over this age are not kept, but it was clear that should the upper jaw extend in the same proportionate length as in the salmon, the knob would be inside, not outside the mouth. In August, 1883, I received from Mr Arthur,[*] of Otago, an old male trout, *S fario*, weighing 21 lb and 32 in in length, and this completed my series, the upper jaw had elongated as in the salmon and the hook was now inside the mouth Whether this soft hook ever completely absorbs is questionable, but the older the fish the larger the knob, and in very old specimens, due to an elongation of the bones of the snout and upper jaw, it is found inside the mouth ; here it may cause ulceration, impossibility of moving the premaxillaries, and death from starvation In the mandible at its anterior end the rami are ossified together without any appearance of a suture A broad groove (0 3 of an inch) passes from above down the front of the symphysis and having a crest or ridge along each side, this ridge being elevated above the plane of the dentary bone Also anteriorly the foremost portion of the lower jaw has both turned as well as grown upwards and the teeth from one ramus to the other forms an unbroken band The hook or knob is attached to the whole extent of the groove in front of the jaw and also to a small portion of the superior and inner edge of the lower jaw Small knobs are occasionally seen at the end of the lower jaw in female trout

Respecting fins some authors have seen differences in the size and shape of the pectorals, as assisting in discriminating a species, but in all forms of our trout it may be rounded in the very young, become a little more pointed after the second year and again more rounded after the third or fourth season The outlines shown below are taken from fish between 5 6 and 22 inches in length, from a burn in Stirlingshire, a stream on the Cotteswolds in Gloucestershire, and from two examples of Lochleven trout raised at Howietoun the features in all being much the same The number of pectoral rays is unmaterial, as I find in my own collection brook trout, and even in the British Museum specimens labelled as *S. nigripinnis, S ferox,* and *S fario* possessing from 13 to 15

Fig 12 Outlines of pectoral fins of trout 1, from burn trout from Stirlingshire, male, 5 6 in long 2, ditto, female, 6 7 in long 3, brook trout from Gloucestershire, male, 8 in long 4, ditto, 9 6 in long 5, Lochleven trout from Howietoun, male, 12 in long 6, ditto, female, 22 in long

[*] Mr Arthur, of Otago, wrote on February 10th, 1885, respecting "the hook on lower jaw of males I have never missed examining the heads of all trout that I have seen here, and I never yet saw a male, old or young, which had lost the hook You may lay it down as a fact that no such thing has occurred here But I have observed the greater length of this mark and softness of the point during spawning than during summer among trout of equal weights I saw a male lately of 10 lb or 12 lb where the hooked mandible projected a good half inch beyond the inter-maxillary and yet no indication of anything like shedding it as teeth may be cast "

Dr Gunther observed in the yellow-fin case, 1872 (p 127), another important matter is the form of the caudal fins "In *Salmo fario*, which requires a special kind of caudal fin for locomotion in running water, it is different from the same fin in *S trutta*, which are fish which go down to the sea to comparatively still water These fish living in the river require a much stronger caudal fin, and you find that in *Salmo fario* the caudal fin is wholly of strong rays and the lobes become more obtuse and rounded, and it is in fact a short paddle" If the reader will compare the outlines of caudal fins in *S trutta* (p 156 *ante*), so in (p 163 *ante*) and the brook trout (p 199), he will probably see reasons for doubting the soundness of these statements

Cæcal appendages —So many erroneous statements and still more erroneous deductions have been made respecting the number of cæcal appendages present in the fresh-water trout, that it becomes necessary to enter upon the subject a little in detail * Among those personally examined and respecting which notes have been kept, many from Sutherlandshire had from 46 to 50, one from Yorkshire 35, from the stream at Colesbourne in Gloucestershire 34, 34, 38, 38, 39, from the Windrush 39, 42, 45, 45, 49, in six from Cardiganshire from 35 to 44 Dr Hamilton found in two examples in Inverness-shire, 27 and 40 Parnell never found upwards of 49 in Scotland

As regards Lochleven trout, Richardson found 73, Parnell 80, and Gunther from 49 to 90, while at Howietoun I have found them vary form 48 to 82 in the male fish and between 45 and 66 in the female, as will be subsequently given more in detail

Among the examples of *Salmo fario* in the British Museum collection, the number of the cæcal appendages have been recorded as follows —one from the Dee with 44, one from Northumberland, 44, two from Shropshire, 34, 34, many from the Usk, 40 to 45, one from Buckinghamshire, 41, and seven from the Wandle, 39, 41, 41, 42, 47, 49, 51, one from Hampshire, 47, and one from the Erne, 44

Mr G Sim, A L S, of King Street, Aberdeen, has been good enough to make the following observations on the cæca of fresh-water trout he considers that in such wild forms as have been fed luxuriously, these organs are always larger and have thicker walls than ordinary, while underfed ones have them short and with feeble coats Most of the following were taken in lochs or streams where no introduction of other forms has occurred *Males* eighteen from Aberdeen-shire, 29, 33, 38, 38, 39, 41, 44, 46, 47, 48, 49, 49, 49, 54, 55, 55, 56, 69, seven from Kincardineshire, 32, 36, 38, 39, 40, 40, 41 *Females* twenty-three from Aberdeenshire, 30, 36 37, 39, 39 39, 43, 43, 43, 44, 41, 44, 44, 45, 47, 47, 47, 47, 48, 50, 51, 52, 59, sex not recorded, four from Aberdeenshire, 44, 45, 50, 61 *Males* in Aberdeenshire showing an average of 50 cæca, in Kincardineshire of 38 *Females* in Aberdeenshire 44, those of sex not recorded, 50 thus giving a variation between 30 and 69 and a general average of about 46 of these appendages for the 52 examples

Passing on to the number found by the late Mr Arthur to be present in our brook trout raised in New Zealand, we find he recorded that from seven male and twenty-seven female fish taken from nine different rivers, a lake, and the Otago harbour, these appendages ranged from 37 to 55 in the males, with a mean of 48 7, and from 33 to 61 in the females, with a mean of 47 3

It would appear from the foregoing figures that considerable variations are perceptible among trout even when residing in the same locality and under the same conditions Whether deficiency or mal-assimilation of food is competent to reduce the number or size of these organs, or rich living to increase them, are questions that cannot as yet be decided But it is remarkable that forms from the south of England reared in Australasia under warmer conditions and possibly more abundant food have developed from probably 38 to 48 up to 61 That this may be due to this cause a rather corroborative case has occurred for on

* See the numbers of cæca attributed to each form of trout by different British authors (p 11 *ante*)

dissecting a rainbow trout, *Salmo irideus*, at Howietoun, in March, 1887, which had been hatched and reared in that establishment, instead of 41 of these appendages which it is said to possess in its native hill streams, it had 71 And it is common for some continental varieties living in large lakes to have these appendages augmented in number

Again from some cause, as will have to be again referred to when discussing the Lochleven trout, when removed to localities where they deteriorate, the number of these appendages may become reduced

Instances of variation in the number of these appendages are as frequent as variations in the external colours of the fish, probably even more so, for local causes occasion forms to have some colour characteristic of the locality, whereas in the number of cæca no such constancy prevails In the foregoing instances it may be roughly stated* that, excluding the Lochleven race of trout, the number of appendages observed to the south of the British Isles has been found from 33 to 51, and in Scotland from 27 to 69   While the southern form in New Zealand has developed from 33 to 61   As to the Lochlevens they have been recorded between 48 and 90 the only constancy in short to be found in these organs consists in their inconstancy, but taking a wide expanse of rivers and waters for examination, they are as a general rule more in number to the north in the British Isles than to the south, similar in fact to what obtains in the races of sea trout

It has seemed to me that at the commencement of the angling season I have found in some waters where trout subsist largely on water snails, *Limnea*, that the coats of the stomach are thicker at these periods than they are after the May fly season when they have a more varied diet and do not appear to restrict themselves so much to these snails

Vertebræ, respecting the number present in fresh-water trout, I have found from 57 to 59 in Sutherlandshire, from 57 to 60 from the Windrush in Gloucestershire, 57 to 59 from the Churn on the Cotteswold Hills and 56 to 57 in the Tivi Mr G Sim, A L S , examined fourteen examples from Aberdeenshire : in five males he found 58, 58, 58, 58, 59 , in three from Kincardineshire, 59, 59, 59 In six females from Aberdeenshire 58, 58, 58, 59, 59, 60, showing a variation in numbers from 58 to 60

Dr Gunther found in the northern form from 59 to 60, and the southern form 57 to 58 , out of the fourteen examples in the British Museum collection there is one from the Lyne with 59, one from the Isle of Man with 58, one from Northumberland 60, three from Cumberland 58, 58, 59, two from Shropshire 58 and 60, two from the Usk 58, 58, one from the Rhymney 58, one from Buckinghamshire 58, and two from Hampshire 57, 57

The foregoing figures would seem to demonstrate that the number of vertebræ in the fresh-water trout, irrespective of whether it is taken to the north or south of the British Isles, varies between 56 and 60

It is very evident that there is as close a relationship between the anadromous marine trout and the non-migratory fresh-water forms as between the anadromous and the land-locked salmon   Thus the anadromous sewin or sea trout of Welsh rivers crosses with brook trout, and fertile offspring are the result (*see* p 144 *ante*) So also does the so-termed Galway sea trout, *S estuarius* or *gallivensis* while the phinoc or whitling (p 160 *ante*) passes by similar gradations into the brook trout, or as observed by Sir H Davy in *Salmonia*, p 70, " The river and sea trout seem capable of changing permanently their places of residence "

I will now pass on to enumerate the various forms of fresh-water trout existing in the British Isles, and which have been termed species In thus separating them such is done merely for the sake of easy reference to the writings of authors, but not with any idea that most of them even deserve to be classed as distinct races

* Doubtless increased investigations will show far more variations in number than given above

FRESH-WATER TROUT

Variety Brook Trout　Plates V, VI, VII and VIII

Trutta fluviatilis, Will p 199, Ray, p 65, Sibbald, Scot Illus no 25 *Trout*,
Pennant, Brit Zool (Ed 1776) iii, p 297, pl lix, and (Ed 1812) iii, p 399,
pl lxx

Salmo fario, Linn Syst Nat i, p 509, Bloch, Ich. t xxii, xxiii, Gmel
Linn p 1367, Bl Schn p 400, Turton, Brit Fauna, p 103, Bonn Ency Ich
p 160, pl lvi, f 266, Donovan, Brit Fishes, iv, pl lxxxv, Risso, Ich Nice,
p 322 and Eur Mérid iii, p. 460, Flem Brit An. p 181, Jardine, Edin New
Phil Journal, xviii p 51 and Salmonidæ, t v-xii, Richards Faun Bor Amer
p 144, pl xcii, fig 3, Jenyns, Manual, p 424, Parnell, Wern Mem vii, p 304,
t xxx and Fish Frith of Forth, p 144, t xxx, Kroyer, Dan Fiske, ii, p 625,
c fig, Nilss. Skand Faun p 415, White, Catal p 77, Gronov ed Gray,
p 152, Gigholi, Catal Pesc Ital p 41, Steind Ak Wiss Wien liii, 1866,
p 203, Day, British and Irish Fishes, ii, p 95, pls cix, f 3, cxiii, cxiv, and
cxvi, f 1

Salmo trutta, Lacépède v, p 189

Salmo fario, var *forestensis*, Bl Schn p 400

Sular ausonii, Cuv and Val xxi, p, 319

Fario lemanus, Cuv and Val xxi, p 300, pl 617

Trutta fario, Siebold Suss w. f p 319, Canestrini, Fauna d'Italia, Pesci,
p 24, Moreau, Poiss France, iii, p 533

Variety Lochleven Trout　Plate VI and Plate VII, figs. 1 and 2.

Salmo levenensis, Walker, Wernerian Memoirs, i, p 541 (1808), *apud* Neill,
Walker, Posthumous Essays on Natural History (1812), Hamilton, British Fishes,
(1843), vol ii, p 139 Yarrell, Brit Fishes (ed 2), ii, p 117 (ed 3). i, p, 257,
Gunther, Catal vi, p 101 Couch, Fishes Brit Isles, iv, p 243, pl ccxx, Houghton,
Brit Freshwater Fishes, p 123, c. fig, Day British and Irish Fishes, ii, p 92,
pl cxvi, figs 2 and 2a

Salmo taurina, or *Lochleven bull trout*, Walker, Essays, 1 c (large examples)

Lochleven trout, Richardson, Fauna Bor -Amer 1836, p 143, Knox, Journal
Linnean Society, Dec 1st, 1854

Salmo cœcifer, Parnell, Trans Royal Society of Edinburgh, xiv, 1837, p. 154,
pl viii, Fishes of the Frith of Forth, p 306, pl xxx, and Wern Mem vii, p 146,
pl xxx

Highland-trout, Dr Hamilton

Variety Crasspuill Trout.*　Plate V, fig 3

Day, British and Irish Fishes, ii, p 100

Silvery trout

---

* B xi xiii, D 12 13 $\left(\frac{3}{9-10}\right)$, P 14, V 10, A 11 $\left(\frac{8}{9}\right)$, L l 125, L t 27/32 exc psl 16

The fish from this inland Sutherlandshire loch are popularly regarded as land-locked sea
trout because of their silvery colour   Mr Archibald Young, H M Inspector of Scotch Fisheries,
observed (June 5th, 1866, MSS), that " there is a communication between the loch and the sea,

Variety Estuary Trout.*

Salmo estuarius, Knox, Lone Glens of Scotland, 1854, p 29, and The Zoologist, 1855, xiii, p 4662 , Day, Brit and Irish Fishes, ii, p 99, pl cix, f. 3
Salmo gallivensis, Gunther, Catal vi, p 88 , Houghton, Brit Freshwater Fish, p 105, c fig

though now too much blocked up to allow the fish to pass " Their fin rays are similar to those of burn trout , a transverse row of teeth is present across the hind portion of the head of the vomer, and a double row along its body The preopercle has a distinct lower limb in some, indistinct in others, while the shape of the subopercle varies *Fins*—the pectoral is as long as the head excluding the snout *Scales*—125 rows along the lateral-line, 15 from the base of the adipose dorsal to the lateral-line, 25 from the lateral line to the base of the ventral fin *Cæcal appendages* —46 in the one examined Length of head 4⅗ to 5 in the total length *Colours*—silvery, with the upper two-thirds of the body and head closely covered with x-shaped or round black spots, and in two of the examples a few red spots, which were mostly confined to the lateral line Loch Crasspull has a pure white sandy bottom, which probably accounts for their silvery colour When fresh caught their backs are of a vivid green, varying to pale sea green and dark olive, in accordance with the depth of the water in which they live Dorsal fin covered with black spots These fish have the silvery appearance of anadromous forms, and attain to 3 lb or 4 lb weight The Rev Mr Coates, on September 16th, 1886, transmitted a specimen, 13 in long, from Loch Lomond, to *The Field* office, requesting information as to what sort of trout it was He observed that " similar fish are occasionally caught in Loch Lomond, and whether they are loch trout or sea trout is a matter of dispute among local anglers It has been suggested that loch trout may go down to the salt water, and there assume the silvery scales of the sea trout, others hold this to be impossible, and it is a matter of considerable interest to local anglers "

The specimen from Loch Lomond, judging by the dentition, was unmistakably a fresh water trout It had a double row of teeth along the whole extent of the body of the vomer, while its other more distinctive characters were as follows Forty-two cæcal appendages, fifteen rows of scales between the lateral-line and the base of the dead fin, and its maxilla extended to behind a level from the hind edge of the eye The fish was of a silvery colour, with numerous black spots on its head and body, and five red spots on the lateral-line in its posterior half, also a few additional ones both above and below, dorsal fin spotted, but without any white edge, but a slight white edging existed in the front part of the anal fin

Mr J Harvie-Brown (*Land and Water*) observed that at a far inland locality in Sutherland-shire, brown trout, dark and spotted, were caught in 1877, and introduced to a chain of lochs in the same county, which have their sources in innumerable springs of clean water from granite and limestone mountains (principally the former, as the limestone, for the most part, is at a lower level) These fish became, in a single year, silvery and covered with minute bright scales like sea-trout, and grew to the size of 1 lb weight in twelve months, from at most ¼ of a lb The food in the loch is shell fish and tadpoles, and the bottom granite, gravel and sand Did this species run up rivers, doubtless it would take on the colours of the brook trout, as it has its dentition

Habitat—Loch Crasspull, in Sutherlandshire, the example being a female, 9 8 inches in length.

* Knox appears to be the first who elevated yellow trout found frequenting estuaries into the rank of a species in this Dr Gunther appears to have coincided but omitted all reference to Knox's statements and re-named the fish The first author took his at the mouth of the Nith, and also recorded it from the sea in the Kyle of Bute, Loch Fyne, the Forth, and the Esk in Yorkshire. Although he found the dentition similar to other trout he counted 60 vertebræ and 36 cæcal appendages, the longest measuring 1 in (the fish appears to have measured 12 5 in in length) Dr. Gunther described his from Galway specimens, and recorded 59 vertebræ and 44 cæca, the young with 9 par bands The cæcal appendages he considered short, being 1 in in length in a fish 18 in long Some examples sent at the same time from the same place are considered for the greater part to be hybrids Couch, *British Fishes*, iv, p 230, observed, "A well-grown trout has been brought to me, that was caught at a considerable distance from a river or fresh water Under such circumstances a material alteration takes place in the colour of the fish, which becomes of a rich dark brown with an aggravation of the other characteristic tints It is believed that these migratory examples in no long time return to their native river at which season again their appearance is so changed that they have been judged a distinct species, and we believe that they are the same which Dr Knox has denominated the Estuary Trout " Day, *British and Irish Fishes*, figured one from Waterford where they are common They have been recorded from other localities Mr Ogilby, *Royal Dublin Society*, 1885, p 527, observed that the estuary trout about Portrush, in Ireland, is known as *dolaghan*, and appears to be a large brook trout residing the greater portion of the year in tidal reaches, ascending the streams about October Their colours are as follows —"For about two thirds of the length and one-third above the lateral line, the body is thickly studded with *brick coloured* spots, about the size of a threepenny piece, the upper part being covered with similarly sized brown spots, while from head to tail there is a distinct lead-coloured longitudinal band, comprising about four rows of scales below and two above the lateral-line These fish, though living so long in salt or brackish water, never assume a silvery appearance , in fact, some of the most brilliantly coloured and spotted trout that I have ever seen were taken in almost pure salt water, close to the mouth of the Bann "

Variety   Orkney Trout.*

The Salmon, Low, Fauna Orcad p 220 (*part*)
Salmo oreadensis, Gunther, Catal vi, p 91, Houghton, Brit Fresh-water
Fishes, p 121, Day, British and Irish Fishes ii, p 96, pl cxiv, f 1

Variety   Cornish Trout †

Trout, Borlase, Cornwall, p 263, pl xxvi, f 1
Salmo cornubiensis, Walb Artedi, iii, p 65, Bl Schn p 421, Day, British
and Irish Fish ii, p 97, pl cxii, fig 2
Salmo nigripinnis, Gunther, Catal vi, p 96, Houghton, British Fresh-water
Fishes, p 120, c fig, Day, Brit and Irish Fish ii, p 98, pl cxv, f 2

* Mr Low stated that in the Loch of Stennis, Orkneys, as well as in Zetland, were found the
gray trout   also a trout of 36 lb weight or more, along with the common trout   This large form
Richardson considered identical with *Salmo ferox* with saline proclivities, but Gunther found in
it another new species, which he termed *S. oreadensis*   This loch is the largest in the Orkneys,
about 9 miles long and 1½ broad, fresh in the upper portion, brackish or even salt in the lower
Dr Gunther believed the fish very similar to *S nigripinnis*, but distinguished from it by a broader
and stronger maxillary, larger scales on the tail and a greater number (50) of pyloric appendages,
instead of from 36 to 42, while *S ferox* has at least 49   The teeth along the body of the vomer
form a single or double row which are more or less persistent   This fish is an estuary form of
the brook trout similar to that already described

Life history —I cannot here do better than give Low's account of the Orkney Salmon—a fish
which he observed ought almost to be denied a place in his Natural History, because the nature
of the country will not allow salmon fishing in fresh waters as there is not a single stream in the
country where a salmon would be safe, even for an hour, except in the loch of Stennis   There
can be no doubt but that there are salmon in the salt water although he had only heard of four
instances of such, and three (if they were salmon) were killed and brought on shore by otters
from the sea and picked up subsequently by the country people, while the fourth stuck in a
mill wheel and was caught by the miller   In his time, Low had been
informed of a salmon fishery which had formerly existed at the mouth of the Loch of Stennis,
and of heritors who have such fishing in their charters, the old people still showing a place where
cruives were placed, but such had long since been give up   Vast quantities of salmon, he continued,
were caught in the rivers of Caithness, which are right against and only separated from the
Orkneys by the Pentland Firth, and from thence he supposed stragglers came

When Mr A Young held an inquiry into the Orkney Salmon Fisheries in 1860   it was said
that there seems no doubt but that a close time is much needed in Orkney, as the trout were taken
at every time of the year, whether in spawning season or not, and any or every instrument was
used that was the most destructive, from the otter to the sweep net   Some six years ago an
epidemic took place among the fish in the Loch of Stennis, when they were to be found in the
houses of all the small farmers in close proximity to the loch hanging up in the tops of their houses,
like so many red herring   This loch is the largest of the Orkney lochs, it is about nine miles
long by one and a half broad   at its greatest breadth   It is divided by a bridge, called the Bridge
of Brogar   some people call the upper loch the Loch of Harray, and the lower one Loch of
Stennis, but it is generally known as the Loch of Stennis   The water in the lower loch is brackish,
while the upper one is fresh.   The water in the lower loch runs in a rapid stream towards the
sea, which connects it with the Bay of Ireland   A great number of sea trout come up this stream
in autumn for the purpose of spawning   There are many estuaries or burns running into this loch,
where the fish are caught in large quantities, sometimes as large as from 7 lb to 14 lb

Respecting the size attained by the Orkney fresh water or estuary trout, one in excellent
condition was reported having been taken in Graemshall Loch with a fly, early in May, 1886,
which weighed 8 lb 2 oz , about 10 lb seems to be the largest lately recorded   Mr Reid, *Land
and Water*, September 11th, 1886, observed, " Mr Cowan, Kirkwall, in giving evidence, said that
the largest trout he had caught was 4½ lb , but they were got up to 8 lb , 9 lb , and 10 lb   He had
heard of a sea trout caught in a net in Orkney and weighing 20½ lb   and had seen one so caught
12½ lb   Mr Bruce stated that he had seen one so caught weighing 14 lb , and Mr Robert Tulloch,
merchant, Kirkwall, said the largest trout he had caught weighed 4½ lb , but they were taken up
to 8 lb , 9 lb and 10 lb

† The Cornish trout of Borlase is a form mostly residing in small streams, and in which the par
finger marks are continued through life, unless under changed and improved conditions, it increases
beyond its general size, when with augmented size these markings disappear   It and the black-
finned trout of Dr Gunther are evidently nearly if not quite identical and might be included with
the great lake trout, *Salmo ferox*, into which it may develop in suitable localities, a subject which
will be alluded to further on   In six examples of black-finned trout, *Salmo nigripinnis*   the
crecal appendages varied from 35 to 44   In some of these fish the posterior margin of the
preoperele was rounded and had no distinct lower limb   These Cardiganshire fish in the Tivi
are found to 4 lb or 5 lb weight, but rarely if ever take a fly when so large, but are to be caught

Variety **Great Lake Trout.** * Plate VIII, fig 1.

Salmo lacustris, Berkenhout's Syn Ed 1795, i, p 79, sp 3
  Salmo ferox, Jardine, Ency Brit (ed 7) Art Angling, p 142, and Edin New
Phil. Journal, xviii, p 55, and Salm pl iv Jenyns, Manual, p 425, Yarrell

by means of a minnow Small ones removed to a pond attain in about three years to 3 lb. or
3½ lb in size, then flesh is pinkish, and their flavour said to be excellent Out of 8 examples,
6 had no red spots, 1 had them along the lateral line, and the last had them both on the lateral
line and in one or two rows below it

It a trout, normally belonging to a small race, as *S cornubiensis,* is transferred to a lake or
reservoir, as in the one near Penzance, where food is plentiful, it attains a size to which it never
reaches in its ancestral stream, showing capacity for growth to be inherent, and called into action
by luxuriant living

* The great lake trout, or *Salmo ferox,* appears to be simply a large fish, probably an old one,
which prefers to live in lakes at great depths, and, consequently, when residing there is usually of
a dark colour Richardson alluded to a variety occurring in Loch Loyal, in Sutherland, of a
purplish brown above, blackish gray beneath, and the entire body covered with dark sepia-
coloured spots, smallest below the lateral-line, being very similar in colour to the example,
Plate viii, fig 1, from Otago, and likewise to a fish from Mulach Corrie, in Sutherlandshire,
where it is termed a gillaroo (see pl x, fig 2), but its stomach is hardly so thickened as in Irish
examples It is known as *buddagh,* or "big fat fellow," in Lough Neagh and some parts of
Ireland (Harris, *Hist Co Down,* 1744, p 236), and as *ßadh-bhreac* in Gaelic, in the Highlands of
Scotland, and is said to be a deep water form confined to lakes, seldom wandering to rivers or to
the sea, mostly taken by trolling though sometimes with a fly It has been known to return a
second or third time to the bait, even after it has been previously hooked and dragged forty or fifty
yards Thompson found one from 10 to 12 lb weight contained 4620 ova Its flesh is of a dull
orange colour and generally coarse

Among our earlier British ichthyologists we find that Berkenhout called it the "great lake-
trout," *S lacustris* (under which name it appears in Sampson's *Londonderry* and Dubourdieu's
Co Down), supposing it to be identical with the continental variety Jardine and Selby termed
ours *S ferox,* the specific name having been chosen to characterize its size and voracious habits
Moreau (vol iii, p 534) placed among the synonyms of *Trutta* (or *Salmo*) *fario,* "La Forelle du
Lac Leman, *Fario Lemanus,*" and at p 536 observed, "La *Truite feroce, Trutta ferox,* Valenc,
des eaux du Foretz est une simple variété de la *Truite vulgaire,* et nullement une espèce parti-
culière " In fact, the great lake trout of Geneva is the *Salmo ferox* of lakes in Wales, the north
of England, Scotland and Ireland, and merely a form of our fresh-water trout It has been
recorded as attaining to 60 lb in weight

Dr Gunther laid great stress on the "preoperculum being crescent shaped, the hinder and
lower margins passing into each other without forming an angle," but this form is not rare in
undoubted brook trout The example figured from Otago, raised from eggs of our own brook
trout, was 20¾ in long and 16 lb weight (*see* fig 14, p 197)

Dr Gunther likewise asserted that structural difference between it and the brook trout
existed among the specimens in the British Museum, showing that *S ferox* possessed
56 to 57 vertebræ and 43 to 49 cæca, while *S fario* had 57 to 60 vertebræ and 33 to
47 cæca Thompson found 56 vertebræ in a gillaroo I have, however, now shown (p 180)
that examples of *S fario* may have from 56 to 60 vertebræ, and likewise from 38 to 61
cæca, thus overlapping the entire amount of variations ascribed to British forms Sir William
Jardine stated that "the dorsal fin in *S ferox* contains 15 rays, and appears to be constant in
that number," and that "in form it is generally shorter proportionally and deeper than large
specimens of *S fario* " Sir J Richardson distinguished between the great lake trout and brook
trout by the size attained The tail "in adults is perfectly square, or might even be described
as slightly rounded at its extremity, in the young it is slightly forked, and appears to fill up
gradually as the fish advances in age " The relative position of the fins and the number of rays
in the dorsal, were said to vary from 2-4/11 or a total of from 13 to 15 Thompson observed that
he found from 33 to 49 cæca in six examples of *S ferox* from 12 to 17 inches in length

Undoubted examples of our common brook trout have from 13 to 15 dorsal rays Moreau
likewise, in French specimens of the brook trout, found 3 or 4 undivided and 9 to 11 divided rays
in the dorsal fin, also 3 undivided and 7 to 9 divided anal rays, while as to the caudal fin
being square in adults, so it also is in large examples of the brook trout (see p 199) Yarrell
(ed 3 i, p 281) gave an illustration of a large Thames trout (a locality not frequented by *S ferox*
according to authors), in which the caudal fin was as rounded as in any examples of great lake
trout of similar size It was a male, 28 in long, having a hooked lower jaw, while it weighed
11 lb The comparative length of the head and height of the body are almost identical with what
obtains in an example of *S ferox,* 20 in long, from Llanberis, and which is in the British
Museum I examined, a few years since, a specimen (which is still preserved) of trout, weighing
upwards of 13 lb, taken from a large sheet of water at Alresford in Hampshire, which is well
stocked with coarse fish This was one of about a dozen that some years previously had been
transferred from the contiguous stream, to which they could not subsequently obtain access
Without a history of from whence the fish came, I maintain that no ichthyologist could be certain
whether any given specimen is or is not a "great lake trout" The New Zealand specimen

13

(ed. 1) II, p 60, e fig (ed 2) II, p 110 (ed 3) I, p 288, Richards Fauna Bor-
Amer Fish p 144, Nilss Skan Faun p 112, White, Catal p 78, Gunther,
Catal VI, p 92, Day, Brit and Irish Fishes, II, p 96, pl cxiv, f 2 (monstrosity)
Salar ferox, Cuv and Val xxi, p 338
Lake trout or *Buddagh*, Couch, Fish Brit Isles, IV, p 222
Powan-eater, Loch Lomond   *Dolachans* in Ireland when small

Variety   Gillaroo Trout *

The *Gillaroo*, Burrington, Phil Trans Royal Soc 1774, lxiv, p 116, Witson
1 c p 121, Hunter, 1 c p. 210, Sowerby, Brit. Misc t. lxi, Yarrell, Brit Fish,

figured is similar to Sir W Jardine's original form of *Salmo ferox* Pennant alluded to having
heard of Irish specimens weighing 30 lb In Sampson's *Londonderry* they were said to reach
50 lb in Lough Neagh Thompson observed that it attains upwards of 30 lb, and mentioned one
from Lough Melvin, taken October 19th, 1840, of 28 lb, and a second of 32 lb, sent to the Dublin
University Museum

It has been taken in Lochs in the north of Scotland, and as far south as Ulswater and
Derwentwater, up to 50 lb or 60 lb (Heysham) also Llanberris in Wales, and many Irish lakes,
as Lough Neagh, L Melvin, L Eske, L Erne, and, in short, in most of the larger ones

* This has been considered a distinct variety or even species, due to the abnormal thickness
of the middle coat of its stomach otherwise, observed Mr Barrington, there are no exterior
marks by which it can be distinguished from the common trout Pennant asserted that the
increased thickness of the stomach proceeded from the superior quality of shell fish which it
finds in the waters it inhabits, and which may call more frequently for the use of its comminuting
power than is requisite in those of our common trout Thompson (l c) observed that the coats
of other species of *Salmones* than *S jario* (of which only the gillaroo is set down as a variety)
become muscular from the same cause He alluded to having found it in *S ferox*, and asks why
among these the gillaroo should be deemed a species, and other forms of trout not so, in which
the coats of the stomach are similarly indicated, one fails to comprehend Sir J Richardson
observed —" We may here note the existence of a strongly-marked and peculiar variety, called
the gillaroo trout of Galway It is remarkable for feeding on shell-fish, in consequence of which
(it is supposed) the coats of the stomach acquire a great degree of thickness, from which
peculiarity it is sometimes called the *gizzard trout* " Sir H Davy observed that " the char of
the lakes of Southern Austria feeding similarly (to the gillaroo trout) have a like thick stomach "
Dr J Davy remarked that the river trout when feeding chiefly on incased larvæ acquires a
stomach of unusual thickness, like the gillaroo trout of many of the Irish lakes, feeding chiefly
on shell fish While there is a preparation in the Hunterian Museum of the stomach of a
common gull which had been kept alive by Dr John Hunter, who had gradually brought it to live
entirely on corn The muscular parieties were found to be as thickened as those of the common
trout would be did it select shell-fish as its diet instead of softer food In the *International
Fisheries Exhibition* in London, 1883 Mr Capel exhibited two specimens of trout said to be
gillaroos reared from eggs from Lough Melvin, one died and was thrown away, the second I
obtained, on opening it, its stomach was found to be similar to that of the common brook trout
Since then it has been observed that this thickening diminishes or entirely disappears in those fish
raised in new localities It generally prefers a rocky bottom, and is said to breed in the shallower
parts of lakes, and not to ascend rivers for this purpose It is found in the Shannon, Lough
Corrib, Lough Mask, Lough Derg, Lough Melvin, &c The colours of this variety may be due to
the character of the food it indulges in, while in some localities its flavour is considered excellent, in
others quite the reverse In Lough Melvin they are somewhat hog-backed, brick in colour, and well
flavoured in Lough Derg, soft, colourless, and inferior Its stomachs are occasionally served up
in Ireland as gizzards Thompson obtained from the stomach of one example, about 8 inches long,
above 1000 shells of *Limnea peregra*, *Valvata piscinalis*, and a few *Sphærium corneum* Stoddart
observed, this variety is found in a small tarn or loch, situated on a shoulder of Ben More, in
Sutherlandshire, about three miles from Inchnadamph, named Mulach Corrie In June, 1886, I
visited this locality for the express purpose of examining this form, and obtained a good number
of specimens, one of which is figured (see plate x, fig 2) The colours varied, but some examples
were very dark, and the fins, especially of the tail, purplish I found in three examples, 39, 12,
and 45 cæcal appendages, while the stomach was but little thickened in them were small
crustacea, but no shells of any description

A discussion on the gillaroo in *The Field* in 1881, was thus concluded by the editor " To
sum up the facts we have gained, the flavour of the gillaroo no doubt is very much a question of
locality and of circumstances It appears that some are of good flavour, and some indifferent As
to its gameness, it varies also, apparently, some fighting well and some lubberly Both these
things may be said of trout out of the same stream and the same reach With respect to size,
it cannot be doubted that it does attain a large size The fact of its being a very early spawner,
with great power of assimilation as regards its food, would vouch for this, if nothing else would
We think, therefore, on the whole, that it may be fairly assumed that it is a most desirable fish
to cultivate, which was the query started "

(ed 3) 1, p 283, Thompson, Nat Hist Ireland, iv, p 154, Couch, Fish Brit Isles, iv, p 240, pl ccix

Salmo stomachicus, Gunther, Catal vi, p 95, Houghton, Brit. F.-W. Fish, p 125, c fig , Day, Brit and Irish Fish ii, p, 99.

Variety Swaledale Trout * Plate VIII, fig 3

Day, British and Irish Fish. vol ii, p 100, pl CXV, fig. 1.

Mr Sachs, in 1881, thus described the gillaroo from Lough Melvm "When taken out of the water it had a rich orange-coloured belly, its back and sides spotted and shaded with all the colours of the rainbow, pink being predominant Then the shape or form of a large gillaroo is quite different to other trouts—they are more hog-backed, larger mouthed and more lusty looking We always preferred gillaroo trout for breakfast, the flesh being firm, flaky, very pink, and very nice to eat

"The gillaroo trout are usually caught on the salmon casts, or on the rocky points of the islands, and not in the centre of the lake, where the large (Black Lough, so called) or lake trout abound " He continued that there is a gillaroo at the Piscatorial Society of 7 lb , with the shell contents of its gizzard on a heap in the case "This fish, with others of my catching, was exhibited at the Royal Westminster Aquarium in 1877, and was caught from Lough Conn, near Ballina They call them gillaroo, or red trout , but they are quite a different fish to those in Lough Melvin, they are not so hog-backed nor rainbow-coloured at all One at Moy Hotel weighs 14 lb " Another correspondent of *The Field* remarked that "the accounts given of the Lough Melvin gillaroo do not at all apply to that fish in Lough Derg, where they seem to grow to a very much larger size They are rarely taken under 2 lb weight, and are not nearly so beautifully shaped and coloured as the silvery trout of the Lough Nor do they give at all the same sport A silvery trout of 2 lb will make a far better fight for his life than a gillaroo of 6 lb , and is in every respect a better fish In fact, I look on a gillaroo as a most inferior kind of trout, and almost the worst fish that swims His flesh is a pale yellow, is strong, dry, and coarse Our silver trout cannot be beaten by any in the world, and, if cooked and eaten within an hour or two after capture, are as near perfection as it is possible for fish to be Though good next day, and for several days after, still they are very far inferior to the fish when fresh out of the water My boatman, while waiting for me last June, killed a gillaroo of 8 lb , a fine looking fish, but like all his kind I cannot understand how they can be a distinct species of fish, as they are never found of small size in the lough or tributaries, and it seems as if their peculiar habits of feeding on small shell fish had developed a peculiarly strong stomach and a gizzard, as it is often called If one were to judge by appearances, there are several varieties of trout in the lough, and I have often laid out three or four specimens, side by side, that it would seem rash to say were the same species We are also told that in Lough Derg, where I fished many years, and where I have caught, I suppose, thousands of trout, but never, 'to my knowledge,' have I caught a gillaroo of less than 3 lb I have, however, killed them up to near 10 lb , and hooked them much larger I believe they spawn at the same time and in the same way as other trout ' Again, we were told by another angler that "during several years' knowledge of the lake I never saw a gillaroo above a pound in weight, and once only heard of a 3 lb fish Still, there is no reason why this fish might not have attained to greater size than at present "

Mr Francis Francis considered that in Loch Melvin "there are four kinds of trout—the common trout, which is like the lake trout of most lakes, and does not, as a rule, run above ¾lb or 1 lb , the gillaroo, which rarely runs so small as that, the Black Lough, which is the ferox and the young of the ferox (about the only place I know where one often happens on young feroxes) , and a silvery trout, such as may be found in Loch Aid and Loch Lomond, which I believe to be a sea trout which has lost his way and breeds without going to the sea No one can fail to spot the gillaroo as soon as he is taken , his superior size, lovely colour, golden hues, big spots, and handsome shape are at once remarkable out of all the trout, and I have had all four of them in my basket at the same time I say nothing of his superior firmness and flavour, which are quite as remarkable But what I want to get at is, is it breed, or what is it? Do they spawn at the same time as other trout? and, if so, how and where? and what probably would be the effect of introducing them into a stream? Of course, at present they are only known in lakes , can they be advantageously introduced into rivers?"

* B xi, D 12 13 (⁵⁄₇ ₁₀), P 13-14, V 9, A 10 11 (₁₁⁻ₓ ₓ), L 1 125, Cæc pyl 35. vert 58 + x

This beautiful variety, which is comparatively rather broad, was given me in 1882 by Mr G Brooks, F L S , who informed me that it was found in Oxnot Beck, Swaledale, in Yorkshire On July 21st, 1886, I was again furnished with five more specimens by Mr Brooks from the same place

There is a considerable difference in the form and proportions of the several examples *Teeth*—situated in pairs along the body of the vomer, and five across the hind margin of the head of that bone *Colours*—it is the most beautifully tinted form that I have seen, being finely studded with black and red dots placed in a light circle, and likewise with numerous blue marks or spots with bluish borders Its dorsal fin is finely spotted, but the white anterior edge so constant

Brook Trout *   Plates V, VI, VII, VIII, and X

(For synonymy see page 190 ante)

B x-xii, D 12-15 ($\frac{3-4}{9-11}$), P 13-15, V 9, A 10-12 ($\frac{7}{7-9}$), C 19, Ll. 110-130,
Vert 56-60

Length of head† 1$\frac{1}{5}$ to 5$\frac{1}{2}$, in old males has been seen as long as 3$\frac{1}{3}$, and
as a rule it is always longer in males than it is in females, of caudal fin 7 to 7$\frac{1}{3}$
height of body 4 to 5 in the total length   Head much more pointed in some
specimens than in others   Much stress, but very unnecessarily so has been laid
upon the form and size of the pieces of the gill-covers   I have, therefore figured
those of two examples from the Windrush in Gloucestershire captured on June
11th, 1886, and in which the character of these bones was similar on both sides of

No 1   No 2
Fig 43   Gill-covers of brook trout from Windrush, natural
size   No 1, 58 vertebræ and 45 cæca   No 2, 57 vertebra and
49 cæca ┬

the head (which is not always the case)   In the first (fig. 43, no 1), the posterior
termination of the sub opercle is obliquely rounded off, but in no 2 this is much
less the case ‡   Species have even been partially defined by a short lower limb to
the preopercle but it will be seen (*see* fig 44, nos 1 and 2) that this bone becomes
comparatively wider in old examples, and thus the length of this limb becomes
more or less obliterated   All gradations between those two forms may be found
in these fresh-water fishes, consequent upon local peculiarities or age   The comparative size of the opercle, subopercle, and interopercle, to that of the head,
changes very little with age, quite contrary to what is seen in the preopercle   It
is necessary to draw attention to the specimens in figure 43, being from trout taken
where the southern race is considered to reside, while the ancestors of the New
Zealand fish also came from the same area (*see* p 183 *ante*)   *Eyes*—diameter
4$\frac{1}{2}$ to 6 in the length of the head, varying with the size and age of the specimen,
1$\frac{1}{4}$ to 2 diameters from the end of the snout and the same apart   In old breeding

in most fresh-water forms may be distinct, indistinct, or absent   In the specimens received in 1886,
there were distinct finger marks along the sides, and numerous red spots on the body and dorsal
fin, and three on the adipose dorsal   *Scales*—fifteen rows between the posterior edge of the base
of the adipose dorsal in a line passing downwards and forwards to the lateral-line   Stomach
thickened and similar to the variety termed Gillaroo, in the first lot, but among those received in
1886 this organ was not nearly so thickened in a male specimen examined, while in it were tubes
of the Ephemeridæ   *Habitat*—respecting its exact residence, Mr Brooks observed that the upper
part of the beck runs over millstone grit, but as it leaves the moor it gets upon mountain lime
stone, and from this point, for a mile and a half, to where it joins the Swale, it is composed of
numerous small falls with intervening little dark pools in which the trout lie   The beck, which
is in a narrow ravine, is closely overhung all the way (on the limestone) by trees, mostly alder,
silver birch and hazel, but with a good sprinkling of elm, mountain ash, &c   The specimen
figured is a male 9 in long from Swaledale

* *Salmo irideus* from California has been introduced into Britain, the examples at Howietoun
seem to indicate that it will develop into a large species, probably the Pacific coast salmon, the
' steel head," *Salmo gairdneri*

† Length of head is subject to great variations thus in *males* at 32 5 in long, I found it
5 in the total length, at 20 7 in 4$\frac{1}{4}$, at 11 4 in 4$\frac{3}{4}$, at 10 5 in 4$\frac{3}{4}$, at 8 8 in 4$\frac{1}{2}$, at 7 3 in 4$\frac{3}{4}$, at 7 2
in 4$\frac{1}{4}$ at 7 in 1$\frac{1}{4}$, among *females* at 31 5 in 5$\frac{1}{10}$ of the total length, at 19 2 in 4, at 13 3 in 4$\frac{3}{4}$, at
12 in 14, at 11 8 in 4$\frac{4}{5}$, at 10 5 in 4$\frac{1}{2}$, at 10 5 in. 4$\frac{3}{4}$, at 8 4 in 4$\frac{3}{4}$; for a further series of
measurements, see under the head of the Lochleven trout

‡ Colours of these two fish identical, both captured June 11th, 1886, flesh, white.

males the eye is comparatively smaller, and as much as 3 or $3\frac{1}{2}$ diameters from the end of the snout and also apart (*see* fig 19, p 147)   *Teeth*—in a double row along the body of the vomer, placed in pairs in the very young and with a transverse row across the hind edge of the head of that bone   But as age creeps on the dentigerous ridge along the vomer, as already alluded to (pages 21, 146 and

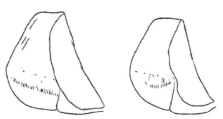

No 1   No 2
Fig 44 Gill covers of brook trout from New Zealand, $\frac{1}{3}$ natural size   No. 1, male, $20\frac{3}{4}$ in long. No. 2, female, 19 2 in long

147 *ante*), begins to lose some of its teeth (fig 45, no 1), and others commence being pushed out from remaining in pairs (fig 45, no 1*a*) as they had been up to this period   For when the ridge narrows (fig 45, no 2), the teeth are of necessity forced to assume a single and zigzag row (fig. 45, no. 2*a*), and now many fall out, commencing with those furthest from the head of the bone, until

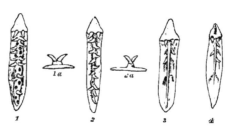

Fig 45   Vomers of brook trout   No 1 from example from Windrush, twice natural size   1*a* transverse section of bone   No 2 from example from Loch Assynt, twice natural size   2*a* transverse section of bone   No 3 from male from New Zealand, half natural size   No 4 from female, New Zealand, half natural size

nearly all become lost on the body of the vomer (fig 45, no 3), and after a time those on the hind edge of the head of that bone as in a male $32\frac{1}{4}$ inches in length   This process may be carried out more rapidly in some forms (especially anadromous ones) than others, and all these figures are from brook trout at different ages, but the process is the same in every variety of trout and even of salmon *   In an

---

* *Jenyns*, 1835, observed that the common trout had "teeth on the whole length of the vomer " Yarrell, 1836, also remarked of the same fish, as well as of *Salmo ferox*, teeth " extending along the whole length of the vomer "   *Parnell*, 1838, of the common trout " vomerine teeth extending the whole way "   Dr *Gunther*, 1866, *Salmo fario*—"vomerine teeth in a double series, sometimes disposed in a zigzag line, persistent throughout life "   *S ferox*, " the head of the vomer small, triangular, broader than long, toothless , the body of this bone armed with a double or zigzag series of teeth, the teeth being alternately placed, forming nearly a single series behind , they are

example 14 inches long from Loch Mulach Corrie, there are two teeth on the hind edge of the head of the vomer and twelve still remaining along the body of that bone

How the jaws in male trout and those of some of these fishes under certain conditions are stronger than is usually the case, and how the teeth of males are often larger than in females, are questions which may well be deferred until considering the subject of the Lochleven trouts The knob on the upper end of the extremity of the lower jaw becomes well developed in old specimens as already described* (see p 186 ante)

Fins—although as quoted in a note (p 13), Dr Gunther denied Agassiz's statement that the fins of trout inhabiting rapid rocky streams are most developed, I find some to be so among a large number of specimens examined while I do not find that in these places the extremities are worn off, at least in fish that are in good health The first dorsal (except in old breeding males), as a rule, commences somewhat nearer to the snout than to the base of the upper caudal ray , the height of the anterior ray usually exceeds the length of the fin's base Origin of adipose dorsal fin about midway between the anterior insertion of the base of the rayed dorsal and the superior extremity of the upper caudal lobe, or the distance from the front end of the snout to the commencement of the base of the dorsal fin, equals about $2\frac{1}{3}$ in the entire length of the fish,† or a similar extent to what is present in the sea trout (see pp 169, 170 ante), disproving the statement alluded to (see remarks of Dr M'Intosh, page 170), that the dorsal fin in the fresh-water races is decidedly further forward than in the marine forms An example from Loch Aird, had $58 + x$ vertebræ and the first dorsal ray was connected to the neural spine of the 15th vertebra Pectoral from 6 to $7\frac{1}{4}$ in the length of the fish, or as long as the postorbital portion, or of even the entire head excluding the snout, in some examples it is more pointed than it is in others Having measured a large number of examples from rivers and lochs, as a rule,

persistent throughout life " *S stomachicus*, vomer with a double series along its body, persistent *S nigripinnis*, transverse series of teeth across base of head of vomer, and in a single row along the body, persistent *S levenensis*, row across base of head of vomer, a single series along its body, persistent through life *S gallivensis* and *S orcadensis*, teeth on vomer in a single series, persistent The above show how some authors have merely examined young or moderately aged specimens, for in all very old ones the vomerine teeth drop out with age as I have figured How conclusions have been come to from the examination of young fish, that the vomerine teeth are persistent throughout life, it is difficult to account for

* Mr Arthur kindly sent me a pair of specimens of New Zealand trout from the Pomahaka river, in April, 1885 *Male*, 16 lb weight, $20\frac{3}{4}$ inches long, length of head $4\frac{1}{8}$, height of body $3\frac{5}{8}$ in the total length *Eyes*—diameter one-seventh of the length of the head, $2\frac{1}{4}$ diameters from the end of the snout, and the same distance apart The maxilla reaches posteriorly to half a diameter behind the orbit Vomer with two teeth on the hind edge of its head Pectoral fin $6\frac{1}{4}$ in the total length Vertebræ 56 58 cæcal appendages the longest being 28 inches *Lateral-line* with 111 scales and 14 rows between the adipose dorsal fin and the lateral line Flesh red as a salmon In a *female* 19 2 inches long, length of head 4, height of body 4 in the total length *Eyes*—diameter one seventh of the length of the head, $2\frac{1}{3}$ diameters from the end of the snout, and 2 diameters apart The mandible reaches posteriorly to $\frac{3}{4}$ of a diameter behind the orbit Vomer with one tooth which fell out on the skull being macerated Pectoral fin 7 in the total length 56 vertebræ , 51 cæcal appendages, the longest of which was 1 9 inches *Lateral line* with 116 scales, and 13 rows between it and the adipose dorsal fin, flesh, white In another pair also sent by Mr Arthur in 1883 from New Zealand, the *male* was $32\frac{1}{4}$ inches long, the length of the head 5, of caudal fin 7, height of body about $4\frac{1}{2}$ in the total length. *Eyes*—diameter $6\frac{1}{4}$ times in the length of the head, 3 diameters from the end of the snout The maxilla reaches to $\frac{2}{3}$ of a diameter behind the orbit *Teeth*—absent from the vomer *Lateral-line*—118 rows of scales. 12 between it and the adipose dorsal fin In a *female* $31\frac{1}{2}$ inches long, the length of the head 5, of caudal fin 7, height of body about 5 in the total length *Eyes*—diameter about 4 in the length of the head, and $1\frac{1}{4}$ diameters from the end of snout *Teeth*—some at the hind edge of head of vomer *Lateral-line*—120 rows of scales, 14 between it and the adipose dorsal fin. All the foregoing four fish are what would be termed *Salmo fario*, yet all were hook trout

† The following are proportional measurements made in the distance from the front edge of the snout to the commencement of the base of the dorsal fin *S fario*, Loch Mulach Corrie in a male, 11 6 in long, $2\frac{1}{4}$, male, Howietoun, 14 6 in, $2\frac{1}{4}$, female, Loch Leven 11 4 in $2\frac{1}{4}$, female, Loch Aird, 11 3 in , $2\frac{1}{4}$, female, River Lossie, 10 4 in long, $2\frac{1}{4}$, male, 10 2 in long, Gloucestershire, $2\frac{1}{2}$, female, 10 1 in long, $2\frac{1}{4}$, male, 7 2 in, long, Stirlingshire, $2\frac{1}{4}$, and male, 6 5 in long, Gloucestershire, $2\frac{1}{4}$ in the total length

this fin is most developed in those taken from running waters.* Ventrals inserted beneath the middle or last third of the base of the dorsal fin. Caudal forked in the very young, emarginate in those of a medium size, becoming square in large examples, or even rounded, as shown in figure 46. While Yarrell (edition 3, p. 281) figured a Thames trout 28 in. long, and 11 lb. weight, in which the hind edge of this fin was slightly rounded. It would also appear that as a general rule the tail fins of trout inhabiting rapid streams are usually more deeply emarginated than in specimens living in more stagnant lakes.

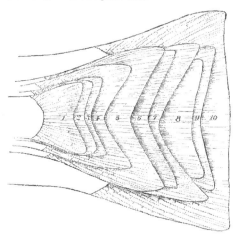

Fig. 46.   Tail fins of brook trout. 1, male, 5·6 in. long, from peat burn. 2, male, 6·2 in. long, from peat burn. 3, female, 6·7 in. long, from same place. 4, male, 8 in. long, Colesbourne. 5, male, 9·6 in. long, Colesbourne. 6, female, 10·5 in. long, Lossie river. 7, female, 12 in. long, Elgin. Tails of brook trout from New Zealand: 8, female, ¼ natural size: 9, male, 20¾ in. long, ⅓ natural size : 10, male, 32½ in. long, ¼ natural size.

Scales.—From 12 to 15 rows are present between the hind edge of the adipose dorsal fin, in a line passing downwards and forwards to the lateral-line : while about 26 or 27 rows are present between the lateral-line and the base of the ventral fin. As regards the appearance of the scales I have had examples from ten races of fresh-water and sea trout photographed under the microscope for comparison one with another, and likewise examined many more, but the variations were found to be so great, even in those from the same specimens, that nothing would be gained by figuring them. The concentric lines in some of those from the sea trout, sewin, and Lochleven seemed in a few examples to be coarser than in the generality of brook trout.

Cæcal appendages.—The number present vary considerably as has been already referred to (p. 188 *ante*), and taking a large number of examples, as a rule trout in the north of the British Isles have more than those in the south. Possibly the number of these appendages will be found under certain circumstances of great value in determining whether the food they can obtain is such that on it they thrive or deteriorate.

* The following give the result of some of the measurements made. Male, Loch Mulach Corrie, 14·6 in. long, pectoral 7¾; female, Loch Ard, 12·8 in. long, 6¼; female, Loch Ard, 10·2 in. long, 6¼; female, Loch Ard, 11·9 in. long, 7; male, Loch Ard, 11·5 in. long, 6½; female, Gloucestershire, 10·5 in. long, or 6 in the total length.

Dr Hamilton, F R Z S, communicated to me the following interesting facts which came under his immediate observation in 1882. In the year 1867 two separate lochs in Scotland were stocked with trout taken from Loch Morar One of these latter localities was situated on a hill, Craigmoor, Inverness-shire, 1500 ft above sea level, it being a mile and a half in circumference, and possessing a sandy and weedy bottom   Here the fish never attain to a pound's weight, but are long and lanky, rise freely to the fly, and give good sport to the angler Externally their sides and under surface have a golden tinge, while they are covered with numerous red spots, having been cooked the flesh cuts white A female 10¼ in long, examined in

Fig 47 Crœcal appendages 49, and also cystic duct of a brook trout from the Windrush, ½ natural size.

1882, was found by Dr Hamilton to have only twenty-seven crœcal appendages, while the length of the head was equal to the height of the body, or 5¼ in that of the total length The tail fin was nearly square at the extremity The second locality also stocked in 1867 from the same loch, and termed Loch Shean Mor, Arisaig, Inverness-shire, is smaller than the preceding one, and not very deep, but the water is dusk-coloured, while the bottom appears to be covered with small rocks

The fish are very game, and rise boldly The head is very dark, nearly black, the sides yellowish olive, and the eyes prominent A few (about ten) red spots are present on each side, and thirteen to fourteen black ones, having been cooked the flesh is yellowish pink Dr Hamilton examined a female 10¼ in long, and found forty crœcal appendages, while the length of the head was one-sixth, and the height of the body one-quarter of the total length The tail fin was nearly square at its extremity Here we observe the progeny of trout transferred from a single piece of water, Loch Morar, in 1867 had so altered by 1882, due to changed conditions of life, that they would be distinct species as recognized by some naturalists If the difference of living in these two localities sets up such changes that only twenty-seven crœcal appendages are developed in one form and forty in the other, that the depth of the body is nearly one-sixth of the length in the first, but a quarter in the second, if one possesses numerous red spots, while the second has but few, but many black ones, it does not appear that we need go so far as Tasmania to prove how inconstant in trout are external colours or form, as well as the inadmissibility of accepting the number of crœcal appendages as a basis for forming species

Colours —Among trout inhabiting fresh waters and estuaries large differences in the tints and markings are perceptible as might be expected* (pp 6, 144, 145) In short, as has been already referred to, we may perceive fresh-water forms approaching sea trout in colour as those of Loch Crasspul (p 190), and of which occasional examples may be seen in Loch Lomond and elsewhere While there are many circumstances affecting colour, as the state of health of the fish, the period of the year if it is in a breeding condition, its age, the quality and amount of food it can obtain, the character of the water and its surroundings, and whether the stream is rapid or sluggish In some of the silvery forms there are merely black spots which may be round, and are often encompassed by a light ring,†

* St John, *Natural History and Sport in Moray*, p 25, observed, " Put a living black burn trout into a white basin of water, and it becomes within half an hour of a light colour   Keep the fish living in a white jar for some days and it becomes absolutely white but put it into a dark-coloured or black vessel, and although on first being placed there, the white coloured fish shows most conspicuously on the black ground in a quarter of an hour it becomes as dark coloured as the bottom of the jar and consequently difficult to be seen "

† Sometimes black spots on these fishes become surrounded after death with a light ring, while in others red spots may appear which were not seen when they were living Also some fish when not in good condition will lose their colours very rapidly

while occasionally, especially when within or near tidal influence,[*] these black spots may assume an x-shape, or be starred

Or the trout may be of gorgeous purple along the back and sides, and of a golden tint along the belly, more especially during the breeding season   These may be spotted similarly to the first variety, except that star-shaped markings are rarer, and red spots more numerous   This colour is frequently seen in such trout as frequent tidal localities, although it pertains more to fresh water

Various causes will occasion these fish to be dark-coloured, and almost invariably with black spots, and often with red ones likewise   This dark colour would seem to be generally owing to the colour of the water in which they reside as when much impregnated with peat   To the depth of water in which they live as in some large and deep lakes, and when char similarly live there, as in Loch Rannoch, in Perthshire, they are equally of a dark colour   Age also is probably a factor inducing darkness of colour

In some forms the finger marks of the parr are found to be persistent in the adult, as is most commonly perceived in small forms, or rather in trout which due to living in small streams have not attained to any size   Sometimes these finger marks appear after death

In many places the dorsal and anal, and often the ventral have a white outer edging, interior to which is a narrow black base   This is most frequent in southern forms, but not so invariable in the loch trout of Scotland, while it is generally absent from Lochlevens, when reared near their original habitat   This deficiency of the white border becomes lost when the fish are removed to another locality where it is the prevailing type   In June, 1886, I examined a large number of trout from the river Loanan, in Sutherlandshire, passing from Loch Awe to Loch Assynt, the cæcal appendages varied between 46 and 50   The white anterior edging to the dorsal fin was very slight, black spots were large and distinct on the body and fins, a few red spots existed along the lateral-line, and a few more were scattered over the body   Examples from Loch Awe were more spotted, had no light edge to the dorsal fin, and were generally purplish with yellow bellies   Here the Loch Awe trout were intermediate in colouring between burn trout and Lochlevens   However, on April 23rd, 1886, I examined some trout at the Windrush in Gloucestershire, the white edge to the front of the dorsal fin was not distinct, neither was the black base, but the fin was closely spotted with black   The opercles of those not quite in condition had a green tinge, but in those in condition it was purple   The stomachs of all were distended with water snails,

---

[*] We find trout assuming a silvery appearance owing to changing their abode to salt water   the fishermen at St Andrews, sometimes after floods in the rivers, capture them in the stake nets in the bay   Mr Dunn observed, May 1st, 1884, upon a fresh-water trout having been taken in Mevagissey Bay   Dr Gunther, *Catalogue*, vi, 1866, p 357, remarked that "specimens of *Salmo fario* frequently descend to the sea and assume a bright silvery colour with numerous x-shaped spots"   While he deposed in the "yellow-fin case," 1872, "I do not know of one single instance in which *Salmo fario* living in running streams assumed the silvery appearance" (p 126)   R B L , writing to *The Field*, March 27th, 1886, remarked on four trout, *S fario*, about ¼ lb each, taken in the Kent, Westmorland, below Sedgwick, immediately below the Basinghall weir   " They were in unusually excellent condition, plump and clean, so much so as to attract the special attention of Mr F Fulton, their captor   In admiring their beauty he noticed that all had sea lice upon them   We all know that the ordinary brown trout lives and thrives in brackish water, but this is the first instance that has come to my knowledge where *Salmo fario* has stayed sufficiently long in the sea to have the parasites mentioned attach themselves to him   On the same river, right away to the bay of Morecambe, I have caught numerous trout, some actually in brackish water, but none of them bore the sea lice "

Mr W Anderson Smith, writing to me the same month from the west coast of Scotland, observed, " My little boy brought in a lot of brook trout from the stream at Nairn yesterday, and all were covered with light silvery scales   They were not far from the sea, and had no doubt been thither   They seemed to be silvered by the salt water "   Mr H G Henderson, March 12th, 1887, observed, " I caught a trout last year in Ireland about 3½ lb , when taken out of the water it had a silvery appearance like a salmon, but the following morning the distinct marks of the trout appeared upon it."   This instance would seem to be one of a fish returning from a sojourn in salt water

Limnea, and tubes of the Ephemeridæ and Phryganeidæ, while there was a fair amount of fat around the pylories   The upper and lower edges of the caudal fin were also generally of a red or orange colour *

The adipose or dead fin in fishes living in clear streams, or where numerous red spots are present on the body, is found to have as a rule an orange or vermilion outer edge   or in some cases it has one, two or even three vermilion spots on it   In some trout this red colour is wanting, while generally this fin has a black spot but may have several   I have already alluded to the presence of this red edging in the young fish (*see* p 172 *ante*)   I examined over 200 taken from the river Loaman, in Sutherlandshire, and orange was present on this fin from the very smallest   Those in peaty water are black, some possessing orange spots on the adipose fin, whereas in others it is orange edged   It would seem that this orange edging in some localities does not show itself until the second year of the life of the fish

What causes the number, size, or form of the spots, cannot with accuracy be determined   On April 4th, 1885, I was shown by Mr Andrews, at Guildford, a number of yearling trout reared from eggs obtained from the Wey   some had brilliant but clear vermilion spots on the rayed dorsal fin, some had none, while some had a few black spots on the body, but in others they were numerous as well as on the fins   There were examples having the body densely covered with black spots, others had none before the dorsal fin, while in some there were only a few spots on the body and those of a small size

The cause of large black spots is difficult to account for, as in some peaty streams where the fish are dark, some have few and very large spots, whereas in others they are of about similar number but smaller   Some captured in deep holes evidently have them of the first description †   In the example figured from Moneyhouse burn near Howietoun, the fish which were captured by Mr Thompson were as follows, but in some finger marks were more clearly defined red along each margin of the caudal fin with a very narrow white outer edge, adipose dorsal with an orange edge round it   Pectoral with a very narrow red and white edged upper margin   and with a reddish white edge   Eight finger marks along the sides much wider than the ground colour   Eight red spots along the lateral-line   Dorsal fin with a pinkish white edge   Ventral straw-coloured, its outer edge white, stained with pink   A purplish hue over the body   The large black spots have a light ring surrounding them

Varieties —Trout, as already remarked, are exceedingly liable to variations of form due to several causes   Some of these would seem to be hereditary, in others the same exciting cause continuing in action occasions results as in previous generations   These will be discussed under the heads of hybridism and malformations

The observations of fish-culturists and field naturalists, respecting the varieties of trout and the modifications to which they are susceptible, have already and may still further prove most valuable in unravelling the confusion which has been imported into this genus

Giraldus Cambrensis, lib iii, c x, the traveller and Archdeacon of Brecon,

---

* December 4th, 1884, examined the aquaria at "the Healtheries" and found that a most interesting alteration of colour had taken place in some Lochleven and brook trout, also in a large male *S fontinalis*   The upper and lower edges of the caudal fin were white in all, and in the fontinalis this was margined internally with red   As all these forms were similarly although unequally affected, such must have been induced by some common cause   In a neighbouring tank were the remains of the Canadian trout, *Salmo purpuratus*, about twelve in number, all with ragged tails and stunted growth, which was possibly partly due to the amount of lime employed for softening the water   It may be that this same agency had occasioned this whitening of the caudal rays

† In the Itchen at Alresford, the keeper recognized two main varieties of marking in the trout, the first with larger spots on the head and gills, a shorter body and redder flesh when cooked, these were said to mainly live on crustacea and did not care for minnows   Secondly, those close to Alresford where crustacea are not numerous, but they devour large numbers of minnows

who attended Baldwin, Archbishop of Canterbury, in a progress through Wales in 1188, tells us of eels, trout and perch existing in the lakes of Snowdon which only possessed the right eye they being invariably blind with the left The Fischan, near Mandorf in Germany, was reputed to contain blind trout (V Ern Bruckmann Epist Itin xxxvi, Wolfenb 1734, p 10). A deformed race of trout are asserted to exist in a small loch in Inverness-shire near Pitmain, among them there appears to be an arrest of development in the upper jaw, giving their heads a slight resemblance to those of bulldogs (see plate xu), due to the projection of the lower jaw (Encyc Brit 7th ed, art Ang) Similar malformations are seen in the "ground trout" of Penyghent (Yorkshire Vertebrata) and many other places

In the British Museum is a specimen nearly six inches long to the fork of the tail, from the Okemont river, presented by Mr Tegetmeier It is almost toothless, there being only a few in the gums of the premaxillary bone of the right side near its external angle, one on the vomer, and a few others in the mucous membrane Corners of tail chipped, length to fork of tail 5 8 in, of head 1 5, eyes 0 3, apart 0 2, from end of snout 0 3 inches

In Loch Islay exists a race of tailless trout, Salmo Islayensis, Thomson (Tranquair), Journ Anat. Phy. vi, p 411, pl xix, and Thompson, Science Gossip, 1872, p 85, asserted that in some streams such had been traced to be due to the action of deleterious matter in the water (see Angler's Note Book, 1880, p 66) Mr J. Harvie-Brown observed, about 1876, that a contraction of the rays of the tail fins of the trout in the river Carron occurred, and was believed to be due to continuous pollution of the water through the agency of paper mills. At Malham Tarn, in Yorkshire, 1240 feet above sea level, the trout are distinguished by a deficiency or malformation of the gill-covers in about one in every fifteen captured As I have seen the same result due to gill-fever or consequent on breeding in confined places, I believe this to be at least one of the causes On Plinlimmon, and in adjacent parts of Wales, are "hunchbacked" trout, having deformed vertebral columns as already alluded to (see plate xii) In some, at least, of these instances the young are reared where cascades are falling over heights into a series of pools, and the egg coming within the reach of these, suffers injury, and consequently disease of the spine (so common in fishes) is set up Barrington (Phil Trans 1767) remarking upon some examples crooked near the tail continued, "These trout are only caught in a small basin, eight or nine feet deep, which the rivers form after a fall from the rocks" Perch were found to be similarly affected, the same cause acting apparently on either form. There are likewise races in which some local cause has set up local action, as of the stomach alone for instance, the gillaroo (see p 194), due to the food it indulges in, has the muscular coat of its stomach thickened, which abnormal structure has been reproduced in succeeding generations For it must not be assumed, because in certain examples we are unable to find Limnea and other shells, that the fish has never consumed any; they may have been digested, or it may have varied its food, or the shells may have been temporarily unobtainable In County Derry, in the river Glenlark in the Munterloney Mountains, "Mr Sinclaire states that the water abounds in stones are deeply tinged with a rust colour, of which the trout likewise partake. Their flesh is very bad and of a metallic flavour, so bad are they that the country people will not eat them, and as they are not fished for, the river abounds in them" (Thompson, Nat Hist Ireland, iv, 153)

Names *—Brook trout, burn trout, brown trout, yellow trout, eldrines (Esk) The Botling of Wastwater in Cumberland, Yarrell suggested must be a male trout, black nebs, and many other local names have been already alluded to Aller-float or aller trout, refers to a large one frequenting a hole in a retired or shady

---

* In Austria varieties of the brook trout are distinguished as forest- or stone trout, alpine- or mountain-trout, gold- or pond trout, and, according to the lighter or darker colouring, the white trout, the black-trout, &c Some are said to be always barren, while the breeding season is from September to January (United States Fishery Report, 1876, p. 609)

portion of a brook under the roots of an alder tree   In Herefordshire there is a country proverb respecting the "aul" or "alder"

> " When the bud of the aul is as big as a trout's eye,
> Then that fish is in season, in the river Wye "

Rack (Northumberland), also *rack-rider*, a small trout   *Shot* (Westmorland)   *Breac-precht*, Highlands of Scotland   *Alevin* try still retaining its yolk sac and before it commences to feed by the mouth   *Sreota*, Anglo-Saxon a ' shooter   or " darter "   also *trukt*   *Trrotht* is an old mode of spelling the name of this fish

Habits—Bold, voracious, cunning and shy, they possess keen sight, and appear to be suspicious of anything novel they may observe   In some of our streams which are constantly fished they have become almost insensible to the charms of the artificial fly, while if they have once been hooked, they would often seem to remember the circumstance   Should an outlying fish be disturbed it dashes away, and this flight warns and alarms its neighbours   Although they evidently like rapid streams, the largest fish are often taken in sluggish spots, where they mostly move about in search of food of an evening and during the night-time, swimming low, especially in cold weather   A favourite haunt or place of rest is often behind a stone or bank, or heavy weeds or a root, and they appear to prefer a bank or bush which gives shade from overhead   Sometimes trout are so hungry that they appear to take almost anything   thunderstorms or darkness may cause them to cease from feeding but on cool days it may have the reverse effect *   A correspondent of *The Zoologist* (1847 p 2030) remarked upon a trout kept in confinement, and on a minnow being thrown in it would immediately ascend nearly to the surface, hover over its prey like a hawk for a few seconds, then dash down and seize it by the head   They require moderately pure water, for a carp will live where a trout will die   They are alarmed by shadows falling over their haunts, and the presence of pike, which takes a heavy toll from these fish, in the waters in some localities prevents them feeding freely, causing their condition to be poor and the sport they afford to be small   It used to be said that chub drive out trout during the four hot months

It some trout prefer food which causes their flesh to be tinged with red,†

* Mr Findlay Purdom, *Land and Water*, August 7th, 1886, observed, "I notice in your last issue, in an article entitled 'At the Burnside in the Lammermoors,' that the two gentlemen mentioned therein gave up fishing as there was thunder in the air, and one remarked that trout would not look at a hook under such circumstances   I have seen this opinion expressed several times, but from experience ha e found it incorrect   On one occasion a brother and myself were caught in a severe thunderstorm whilst starting to fish in the Ale, in Selkirkshire   When the rain had ceased we began, and the trout took splendidly, though it thundered loudly all afternoon   We got over six dozen, the biggest catch we ever had in that river   The second biggest basket there was also made during a bad thunderstorm, and one big trout was missed, whilst we were sheltering under a bridge till the worst was over   The bait in both cases was worm   Several other instances of good takes during thunder have also come under my notice, but would take too much space to detail here   I would like to know if any of your readers have had similar experiences '

† Mr J Harvie Brown, in *Land and Water*, 1881, observed that "Trout abound in nearly all the innumerable lochs of North Uist   In those near the sea on the west coast of North Uist they are usually of a good size, often running to ¾ lb and larger, but on the moor lochs with few exceptions, they are much smaller   Into many of the lochs the sea enters regularly at high tide, or occasionally at spring tides, and the water is consequently brackish, or very slightly mixed with salt water   At the time of the inflowing tide brown trout are often killed in the strong stream way amongst almost perfectly pure salt water—the fresher water being, however, nearest the surface   Often at the same place, and sometimes at the same cast, a trout and a lythe may be caught   This brackish water does not appear to affect the growth or condition of these brown trout, indeed, they are usually larger and of finer quality than those obtained in the inland lochs, which have only occasional communication with the sea at spring tides, or are completely shut off from the sea

" In Loch Hosta, which is now quite fresh   the trout are very silvery, like Lochleven trout, but of a different build, being shorter and thicker   But another loch between Trumisgarry and Scolpig contains much more silvery specimens, though it has had longer separation from the sea   It is called Loch Beck   Most of these lochs where the very silvery trout occur are sandy-bottomed, and not rocky, which no doubt, partly accounts for the silvery colour   In the same way, at a far inland locality in Sutherlandshire, burn trout, dark and spotted which were caught

while others in the same water appreciate a different sustenance, and consequently are not thus tinged, if the gillaroo eats shells, occasioning thickening of the middle coat of its stomach, while such diet, as a rule, is rejected by the common variety of *Salmo fario*, it appears to point out that the tastes of some differ from those of their companions, while it is a well-known fact that certain forms of food promote fish-growth more rapidly than others. As already observed, those trout which principally subsist upon fresh-water shrimps, *Gammari*, are generally of the most brilliant tints, and the most pinky-coloured flesh, while vegetable diet appears to mostly cause a silvery hue and sometimes a dull appearance *

and introduced to a chain of lochs in the same county which have their sources in innumerable springs of clear water from granite and limestone mountains—principally the former, as the limestone for the most part lies at a lower level—became in a single year silvery and covered with minute bright scales like sea trout, and grew to the size of I lb. weight in twelve months from at most ¼ lb. This experiment was made by our fishing party in 1877-78-79. The specimen first caught after the introduction in 1878 is preserved in the collection of Dr W M Mackintosh, of Murthly. The food in this loch are shell-fish and tadpoles, and the bottom is granite, gravel, and sand. On the other hand, trout are often caught in sandy lochs or bays at far inland localities which present nothing of this silvery character at all. Thus those of the sandy or granitic pebbly bays of Loch Errochd, in Perthshire, are golden yellow trout.

"But to return to North Uist. In most, if not in all, of the sandy-bottomed lochs of the west coast the trout are more or less silvery. We do not with certainty know the favourite haunts of the sea trout and other migratory fish *whilst* in the sea, but it is not, perhaps, unreasonable to suppose that sandy bays, or patches of sand amongst the rocks, give them most harbourage, whence, perhaps, their silvery colour, which they rapidly lose upon entering peaty or rocky streams and lochs, and never perfectly recover until they return to the sea.

"In many of the larger lochs of North Uist—as, for instance, Loch Ghearn in the west and Loch Scatavagh entering from the east, where the sea has regular or occasional access, sea trout are known to ascend, but many, if not all, fail to return to the sea. These fish, however, do not easily succumb and die, but live, at all events for a considerable time, but are seldom caught in good condition. Such fish are taken at all seasons of the year. In some lochs no doubt they do finally succumb. Loch Scatavagh is a very large loch, and swarms with small ill conditioned brown trout. All these lochs where the sea trout fail to return to the sea are *rocky and intricate in their* shore-lines. The general belief amongst the natives is that the sea trout and bull trout which ascend lose their way, and cannot again find the exit, or, in some cases, enter during high water tides, and cannot escape during the lower summer tides.

'Now, in Loch Hosta and other lochs on the west coast, which either have regular or occasional connection with the sea, or which, like Loch Hosta itself, had *at one time* communication, and the banks and bottom being sandy or loamy, and having better feeding, it seems just possible that sea trout ascending to these lochs in former times, or in exceptional and occasional times at present, may have become acclimatized and have added to their stature, and even changed their nature and appearance, and multiplied in number. It is evident from the sea levels at various localities along this west coast of Uist, that one of two changes has taken place. Either the land has actually risen, or, what appears more likely, the land has gained upon the sea by reason of the shifting sand upon the coast. Below Newton Farm the former sea level—remembered by people still, or lately, living—is remarkably patent.

'In the same way Loch Hosta has become sanded up at its exit, or at least sufficiently so to prevent sea trout from ascending the shallow sand-stream which still unites it with the sea. The present tides rise to within a hundred yards of Loch Hosta, but no sea trout enter it now, though there is every reason to believe they must once have done so. At present, even during a spate coming down the burn, sea trout could not get up, as the water debouches upon the level sand and spreads all over it, having no defined channel.

"Questions arise regarding these sandy lochs and their inhabitants which are curious, if not also instructive.

"At one time in the world's history possibly, indeed probably, not very remote—I speak in the geological sense of remoteness—some of these lochs must have been bays of the sea. The small, ditch like burns now entering them show no appearance of ever having been any larger than they now are, and in most cases are too insignificant to harbour the smallest adult brown trout even at the present time. Hence comes the question, How came these lochs, once bays of the sea, to be inhabited by *Salmo fario* ?

"In the island of Daria, on the west coast, is a loch famous for the quality and beauty of its trout, which are said by Wilson to resemble exactly the famed Lochleven variety. Mr Wilson says —'This loch, called, we believe, Tangéstal, has one side of its shores flat, shallow, and sandy while the other is, at least in parts, more stony and abrupt.' Describing the trout further, he calls them 'trouts of outward pearly lustre, and flesh of roseate hue.'

Another question is, have the sea trout (which at a remote date entered these sandy, loamy lochs) all *died out*, or have the fittest survived their change of residence and confinement to fresh water, reproduced, and in course of ages changed their nature and appearance to suit the new conditions ? "

* T Dougal, *Fishing Gazette*, May 29th, 1886, remarked that " I have frequently seen well-

Stoddart, *Angler's Companion*, observed that a trout "when taken from a river or streamlet (where, if suffered to remain season after season, it would assume no tinge of redness whatsoever) and transferred to a lake or pond containing marl or other rich food, speedily acquires the high complexion in question" (p 173)

They are out of condition subsequent to the breeding season, and in England Devonshire is considered about the earliest county in which they come into condition and are fished for from the commencement of February, which is generally about a month too soon, but elsewhere, as in the Cardiganshire Teifi, there are rivers equally forward

Irrespective of residing entirely in fresh waters, some would seem to prefer estuaries, or being within tidal influence, at least during certain portions of the year, for it is not unusual to observe brown trout being captured in salt water, while even in fresh water they have been taken on their return and with sea-lice still present on them

The food which trout consume is of various descriptions One about 1½ lb weight, taken in June, 1882, in the Tweed, was found to contain 11 small trout and one minnow They do not object to little fish, as the minnow, loach, sticklebacks, &c , water rats, young birds, frogs, snails, slugs, worms, leeches, maggots, flies, beetles, moths, water spiders, and even a lizard (*Field*, Oct 1885) They will swallow one of their own kind two-thirds as large as themselves In Mr Buckland's museum was an example, the stomach of which was distended by 2470 eggs of apparently the salmon

Fish-culturists find that artificially fed trout often will not readily exchange their accustomed food, and likewise that fish do not fatten so well on artificial as on natural food while thinner ones have the par bands less marked * Should the amount of natural food be insufficient, it ought to be cultivated, for it has been asserted that in some localities there has been a gradual extermination of the larger forms of water-fed flies, but in wilder streams less interfered with by farmers and millers, there has been no such change

Many instances are on record of trout seizing their own species when they have taken a bait Thus in *Land and Water* it was observed by "Sprint," that "Mr W Atkinson, of Kendal, was angling in the Lune, above Kirkby Lonsdale, when with a fly he hooked a small trout of about 1½ oz Before he could draw it quickly to land it was seized by another and a much larger fish For some time the angler played the fish without seeing what it was, but in a minute or two got sight of what he had hold of, and found that a large trout had seized the smaller one, which had, in the first instance, taken the fly In due course the big fish, keeping his hold, was, at the first opportunity, quietly secured in the landing net, and immediately he felt the touch of the net gave up hold of his would-be prey, but too late to escape This unusual capture was duly basketed, weighed 21 oz and was in moderately good condition The small trout on the hook was, as might be expected, sadly mauled by the teeth of his big brother, and was quite dead when taken off the hook Mr Atkinson says that at least three minutes elapsed from the time the large trout seized the smaller one and then being landed in the net On being opened, the large trout was found to contain another trout, about 1½ oz weight, in a partly digested condition"

coloured Highland loch trout in which the skins—not the flesh—became black a few hours after capture　　I have seen all the trout on one side of a loch, not over 300 yards wide, very black, in correspondence with the hue of the rocky sides and bottom, and all those on the other side of a lively greenish hue, like that of the bottom there, which is covered with short grass for a few yards from the bank "

* Stoddart, *Art of Angling*, mentioned an experiment made in the south of England in order to ascertain the value of different forms of food 'Fish were placed in three separate tanks, one of which was supplied daily with worms, another with live minnows, and the third with those small dark coloured water flies, which are to be found moving about on the surface, under banks and sheltered places The trout fed with worms grew slowly, and had a lean appearance those nourished on minnows, which it was observed they dashed at with a great voracity, became much larger , while such as were fattened upon flies only, attained in a short time prodigious dimensions, weighing twice as much as both the others together, although the quantity of food swallowed by them was in nowise so great "

Early in 1885, Sir M Gordon hooked a female trout 3 lb 9 oz in the Test, another, a male 3 lb 11 oz followed it, and both were secured in a landing net, the free trout never left its companion (*Land and Water*, June 6th, 1885) At the end of May, 1885, a trout 1 lb. 5 oz was followed in all its twists and turns by a roach that was probably a few ounces heavier than itself, but it scuttled away at the sight of the landing net It has been questioned whether this was sympathy or curiosity ?

" As to the time when fish feed most and least respectively, the returns show that they feed most in April, May, and June, and least in December and January, although they have been known to feed greedily in those months."—*Fourth Ann Report Scotch Fish Imp Assoc* 1882

Parfitt found river molluscs, as *Valvata piscinalis, Planorbis marginalis, Physa fontinalis,* and *Limnea peregra* in the stomachs of some taken in May, in Powderham Park, Devonshire but food varies' with streams, &c Respecting Loch trout, " The examination of the contents of the stomachs of the trout taken from it (Loch North-Maben district), showed that they fed largely on *Gammarus pulex*" (Gordon, *l c*, p 94 *Scottish Naturalist*). In Sutherlandshire, I found loch trout fed largely on *Limnea, Gammarus,* &c Mr George Sim, A L S, examined the contents of the stomachs of fifty-two fresh-water trout taken in Aberdeenshire and Kincardineshire during March and the first half of April, 1887 twenty-eight had the remains of caddis or May-flies, fourteen of beetles, eight of small stones, five bits of straw or grass, four of water shrimps, *Gammarus pulex,* four of insects and flies, one of *Cyclas flavescens,* one of a leech *Piscicola geometra,* one of a snail, *Limnea peregra,* one of a caterpillar, one of a small fish, one of a fresh-water limpet *Ancylus fluviatilis,* while three were destitute of food

In 1886, I had several opportunities of examining the food* consumed by trout in the Windrush, and found that during April and May they mostly fed upon *Limnea,* the caddis worm, and the larvæ of Ephemeridæ, a few beetles, and one had a bull-head, *Cottus gobio,* in its stomach In June they appeared to restrict themselves to May-flies, with which they were gorged

Modes of capture —These may be either netting, spearing, tickling, poisoning, angling, or other methods which do not come within the scope of this work For the plans of netting these fish are in many respects similar to those referred to under the head of Salmon (pp 135-141) Spearing is not now permissible, although it used to be employed by torchlight Tickling for these fish in small streams is occasionally employed with success The use of the otter is illegal, but in Ireland cross-line fishing† is licensed The angler has several modes of procedure at his command, if the fish are large, spinning bait may be employed , or ground fishing with worms, or fly-fishing either with the real or imitation insect Different rivers, seasons, and even periods of the day have their peculiar varieties of winged insects acceptable to these fish , as a rule if the water is clear and low, and wind is absent, small ones are most suited if clearing after a flood, or full but not discoloured, the fly-fisher has more chance of sport,

---

* Marston, *Fishing Gazette*, January 9th, 1886, p 23, observed that " trout get fat on grayling ova and fry, but grayling do not feed on trout ova or fry They would eat the ova if they could get it, but they stop in the main stream, while the trout goes up the brooks to spawn "

† T Hearne, *Land and Water*, June, 1885, observed respecting the river Moy (Dalhna) and Lough Conn that :—" In one of my notes to *Land and Water* some time ago, I said there were bailiffs, with boats and crews, appointed to put down illegal fishing with otters on Lough Conn That has been done, but what was never dreamt of, or ever known to be used before on the Lough, has taken the place of the otter, that is, cross-line fishing There are five cross lines fishing the Lough Two go from " Cloghan's " shore, two at Poutoon (from Glass Island), and one at the lower end of the Lough, on that splendid salmon and trout ground called the Strand, near the mouth of the Deel river I only wish that cross line fishing was made illegal, as I am sure that five more cross lines will be added to the number already on the Lough next fishing season This day I asked the owner of one of the cross lines, who was selling his fish in town, what was his best day on the Lough I tremble to give his answer —97 good trout and two salmon I met the owner or part owner of another cross line, who was also selling fish in town He told me he got 32s for the trout he had, and sold them at 6d per lb , and killed them all one day, with a salmon to boot Good-bye to angling with rod and line on Lough Conn. It's done, at least for some time "

as well as if late in the season when few flies are born   When the water is
opaque a worm or spinning bait may be employed with success   In small streams
real flies and grasshoppers may be used as bait for hooks and a short line which is
bobbed on to the surface of the stream from over a bush   If once pricked by the
hook it is generally but not invariably shy   while it is disturbed by flies clum-
sily thrown or splashing into the water   Frosty weather checks trout moving,
and while snow water or that derived from the melting of snow, is running into
a stream it is almost useless attempting to fish with the rod

In the dry weather, at the Orkneys in 1882, the water in the Loch of Harray,
on the west mainland, was reduced in volume and rendered tepid by a succession
of hot days   The trout assembled in shoals at the mouths of the burns and were
slaughtered in thousands by netting

As regards angling, Mr Francis observed in *The Fishing Gazette* that " the flies
which I now use at Driffield are hardly ¼ of the size with which I used to kill
nearly fifty years ago, and there is no small difficulty in obtaining undrawn gut
fine enough for the angler's purpose   But Mackintosh, who fished the same
waters at the beginning of the century, tells us of a time when the flies thrown
there were almost of lake size, and when he found it a good plan to tie his
droppers on hog's bristles "

Baits —Worms as brandling, gilt tail meadow-worm, tug-worm and red-
worm—for a large one a well scoured dew-worm   A minnow or any small silvery
fish, a loach, or a bullhead with its fins removed

Breeding —Trout commence breeding in their second year or prior to their
attaining 24 months of age, and often later in the season than their parents   The
males are more forward than the females, but at this early period of their lives
the probabilities of the ova being healthy and fertile are less than in somewhat
older examples   At first the number of males appears to be in excess of the
females, but the mortality among them is greater than in those of the other sex,
until at 3 or 4 years of age the proportion may be expected to be about the same,
and subsequently females preponderate   The number of eggs produced by each
female trout has been roughly estimated at 800 for every pound's weight of the
fish, which computation has been observed at the Howietoun breeding ponds to
be fairly accurate   But the size of the parent exercises a considerable influence
on that of the eggs, thus in Sir J Gibson-Maitland's fish farm we found the
following average numbers to be present—in 2 and 3-year-old fish, 0 17 of an inch
in diameter, in 6-year-olds, 0 18 to 0 19 inch , and in 8-year-olds 0 20 to 0 22
inch (see p 25 *ante*, also under the head of Lochleven trout, p 228)   The colour
of the eggs are as various as observed in the salmon, and I have seen some
orange, others straw-coloured, from two fish taken together out of the same
breeding pond *

As the young trout, unless due to exceptional circumstances, grow more quickly
the earlier the spawn has been deposited, or rather get a better start early in
the season, it is advisable if possible to get young from November eggs rather
than those from January and February

The period at which these fish breed varies in different rivers and districts,
extending from October until February and even, although rarely, to March.†

---

* Jacobi's paper on *Trout Hatching*, 1763, appeared in *The Hanover Magazine*, it was trans-
lated and reproduced in Yarrell's *British Fishes*

† Col Whyte writing to *Land and Water* observed, "I visited the spawning ground for a trout
lake of mine on February 10th, and there were not one-half the usual number of redds   Again
I went there one month later, and found the usual number, and the trout were seen spawning
there during the first week in March   Generally speaking, the spawning is finished in November "
W B Scott, *Field*, March 22nd, 1884, stated, " Trout in the river Teign and its tributaries, also
in the river Kenn and several other streams in this neighbourhood (Chudleigh), are now full of
ripe spawn   I have known the streams here for fifty years and I never heard of such a circumstance before   The proper time for trout spawning used to be in the late autumn months,
October and November "   R N , *Field*, February 9th, 1881, remarked, ' I have this morning,
February 2nd, taken out of my trap two pairs of spawning fish, one of the males being nearly
3 lb   One pair had partly spawned exactly in the same spot where some of the November fish
had spawned, whose eggs are now just hatching and not likely to be improved by being
disturbed '

Mr Harvie-Brown at Loch Gorm, in Sutherland, which is greatly fed by snow water from the Bucht of Benmore, has taken trout heavy with spawn in June and July * It has been questioned whether these fish are annual or biennial breeders,† and Dr. J. Davy came to the conclusion, after examining a large number captured in open streams, that only half spawned annually ‡ At Howietoun, it has been found that some at least are annual spawners there It is also clear that in some waters a portion at least of these fish are not annual breeders A marked example of Lochleven trout was spawned at Sir J Gibson-Maitland's on November 27th, 1874, and again on November 25th, 1875 In ponds destitute of streams, no young, as a rule, are produced, either due to spawn not being developed, remaining unfertilized, or else deposited in an unsuitable place It has been generally considered that when the ova of these fish have arrived at a certain stage the female has no power to retain them but they must be extruded, a conclusion which there is reason to doubt, as it has been found possible to retard the deposition of the eggs for as much as a fortnight or even three weeks, by placing the fish in a wooden box through which a current of water flows

To my mind, the experiments in breeding trout (*see* p 26 *ante*) should teach a most important lesson to all who desire to stock their waters with a healthy and large race The parents ought to be selected from fish that are in full vigour and of mature age, which can only be attained where segregation is properly carried out Netting breeding fish in streams at haphazard and collecting them

---

* One taken by Mr Fowler in Loch Toll an Lochain, in Ross shire, on June 17th, 1885, weighed 14½ lb It contained numerous ova so ripe that they were running out when received by Mr Eden in London to be cast.

† R B L, in *The Field*, January 20th, 1886, remarked, "In the very first week in this month one is always attracted by unusually fine trout displayed on the stalls of the metropolitan fishmongers The majority of such fish are in perfect condition some of them as fat and broad, and firm and bright, as if they had fed on the daintiest and choicest of the ephemera during the winter months The Irish lakes produce these charming fish It would be interesting to know when these trout spawn, or are they spawning fish at all ? Certainly, those in such prime order now, never either shed milt or ova during the last season, if they had, their condition would not be what it is at present The lakes of Killarney and other districts appear to produce these irregularly breeding trout in greater numbers than our English waters In Windermere, Westmoreland, the large trout netted early in the season—and the smaller ones too, for that matter—are, as a rule, poor lanky things, ill mended kelts, in fact On the contrary, badly-fed early spring fish from the Irish lakes are exceptional Every river contains barren trout in certain numbers, but such are generally of small size, bright fellows, that may even be seen rising during any mild day throughout the winter, when the little black midges come on the water during the early afternoon No doubt these Irish lake trout, like the chars and gillaroos, feed in the deep water on the larvæ and various water beetles and insects found in such places, but how often do these choice specimens spawn, if at all ? This would no doubt be welcome knowledge to many readers "

Mr E T Danbury, Bedhampton Rectory, in *The Field*, January 19th, 1884, remarked on having placed a pair of trout in a good sized hamper in the water, intending to take the spawn when the female was ripe Next morning he found the female had been so maltreated by the male during the night, as to be completely disfigured and in a dying state. Obtained about 2000 ova The male was larger than the female

Mr J Douglas Ogilby, Altnachree, observed, March 9th, 1884, "I got leave from the Irish Fishery Commissioners to catch brown trout, and since that date have obtained and examined sixty trout varying in size from 4 in to 10 in of these 18 males and 26 females had the spawn plainly visible perhaps my meaning will be better conveyed when I say that in a 6 in fish the lobes of ova would average 1½ in long The remaining 14 were without any symptoms of breeding at all

" I have remarked several things during the course of these investigations (1) That in the spring months the female fish preponderate in number and are seemingly further advanced in spawning, while the reverse holds good in the autumn and (2) that the very small trout are as a rule more advanced than the larger and show a much higher percentage in the numbers in which spawn is visible, especially again among the female fish (3) I frequently find at the posterior end of each lobe of ova, one or two fully developed ova evidently of last year, but I presume this is of little consequence The trout in these burns average six to the lb "

‡ On June 12th, 1856, opened a female trout taken yesterday in the Windrush with the May-fly, and which was gorged with these Ephemeridæ I found two trout eggs in its abdomen, one nearly as low as the ventral fin, the other with numerous blood vessels going to it from the surface of the liver and intestines The fish was in good condition and eggs for the next season visible, 0 02 in in diameter in this case it would appear that the trout, if it had lived, would have bred two seasons consecutively Probably food is a considerable factor regulating capability of breeding

14

eggs may give a good show as to numbers, but not in the size of the ova and the subsequent condition of the young fry. To obtain the best results numerous ponds must be under the sole control of one management and means taken to prevent their contents being tampered with, and in this way only can the breed of trout be gradually improved. The argument may be advanced that young fish reared in England are larger at one or two years old than are those raised in the colder North, but such does not prove them to be more adapted for stocking pieces of water. It is more probable that those raised in colder places have hardier constitutions and are better able to fight the battle of life, while they certainly grow much more rapidly when removed to a warmer spot than if left in Scotland, and perhaps in a short time attain to a greater size than their relatives reared in warmer southern streams will.

Lochleven trout at Howietoun cease to be prolific breeders at eight or ten years of age, and the late Mr Arthur, writing from Otago (February 10th, 1885), observed, " For what it is worth we find trout breeding every year. Certain lean and moribund males however, caught in 1875 and 1876, had no doubt ceased to be fertile and these were seven to eight years old "

I have seen trout in good condition near the end of the year in which no seasonable augmentation in the size of the breeding organs had commenced and they must necessarily have been sterile that season, but were in excellent condition for the table.* On the other hand I have observed some badly-nourished forms likewise sterile, and probably from this cause, while I have been unable to discover any evident difference in the lengths of the fins of sterile and fertile fish as observed by Widegren.†

Although trout generally migrate into the smaller contiguous brooks to breed, large ones are more frequently found forming redds in the broader and deeper streams than are smaller fish. But it is by no means rare to find large examples having taken possession of pools in burns.

A trout's redd or nest is a mound of gravel which would fill one or even two wheelbarrows, and when by probably causing a shallow may assist in aerating the water. The eggs themselves lie loose among the gravel at from one to two feet below the surface. Eggs when shed are elastic, but soft, and sink in water, when artificially propagated, the milt of the male is added to the eggs as described at page 31 *ante*. The period for which milt will remain serviceable after removal from the fish is an interesting subject. On October 23rd, 1874, some was obtained at Howietoun at 9 A.M. from a *Salmo fario*, then carried to Loch Leven in a tightly corked phial, and used at 1.20 P.M. the impregnation turned out to be perfect. Ova or milt may be kept alive for some hours, but the addition of water is rapidly fatal.

April 8th 1887, at Delaford Fish Farm, I observed a very considerable difference in the colours of the alevins, the sac of those from the Colne trout eggs were red, whereas others from elsewhere were more or less straw-coloured or pale. The adipose dorsal fin of Kennett trout showed very slight orange, so also did both edges of the caudal while there was none on the adipose fin of the Lochlevens. Two days previously I had visited Mr Andrews' famous establishment at Guildford, where in some yearling Lochleven trout raised from Howietoun eggs I found as follows —8, 8, 9, 9, 9, 10, 10, 11, 13, 13, par bands. In all the adipose dorsal was tipped with orange and caudal red margined. Also the alevins showed orange on the adipose dorsal not only as soon as the sac was absorbed, but even previously. I also examined a number of brook trout from the local race and found 9 to 10 bands normal, but one had 15. They had the orange on the adipose dorsal fin very unequally distributed, and one had three beautiful vermilion spots on it. A

---

* Taylor in *Angling in all its Branches*, 1800, observed that in the Clun, Shropshire, there are a number of trout which do not grow very large but the angler will often take barren trouts, that are excellent in winter, when other trouts are good for nothing. See also F. Gosden, *Fishing Gazette*, 1886, p. 28

† Widegren observed that in Scandinavia sterile trout were more silvery than specimens of the same age and size which had ova and milt developed

yearling of the local brook trout which I measured was 9¾ inches in length, and was said to be by no means the largest of the lot

Respecting the artificial breeding of these fish, whether for stocking depleted waters, keeping up the supply, or the introduction of trout to localities from which they had been previously absent, several questions have to be considered Are the eggs to be locally obtained, fertilized, and incubated? (*see* p 29 *ante*) or is it intended to obtain eggs from elsewhere? What breed would be most suitable? and at what stage of incubation are the eggs going to be procured? (*see* pp 31, 32 *ante*) If it is intended to obtain them in the eyed stage, are they going to be hatched in boxes or in redds (*see* p 43 *ante*) in the stream? Lastly, if stocking is to be effected by means of the young, are one or two-year-old fish to be selected for the purpose?

The race of fresh-water trout that has been most cultivated in Britain is that of the Lochleven at Howietoun, but doubtless were the brook trout similarly treated and its pedigree breeding equally well carried out, there would be little to choose between the two races, but as at present such has not been attempted, so practically the proprietor who wishes for a fine breed has no selection In small streams, where food is not abundant, it is probably better to supply eggs or young from small forms, and not from the larger framed races, which would be comparatively starved in such localities Some practical fishermen are of opinion that a naturally-fed trout* is worth at least three artificially reared, for stocking the majority of waters, and that fish which have daily received a plentiful supply of artificial food, without trouble on their part, deteriorate seriously in condition, if some do not even die, when they are suddenly turned into a stream where food is not too plentiful, and is obtained with some difficulty But this is certainly not the case in some localities, and full particulars of the best course to pursue under different conditions is to be found in the history of Howietoun and other similar publications on the artificial breeding and stocking of waters with trout (*see also* pp. 44 and 45 *ante*), while it may be considered an almost invariable rule never to change water in which young trout are being carried during transit

In some instances it has been surmised that floods, as in the Thames, occurring just after the spawning season, are occasionally productive of mischief, by carrying off the weak fish, but in most cases it is probable that they seek safety in some local place of security If carried over embankments, especially those made by railways, there is more risk of them not being able subsequently to regain the river

As regards the cultivation of trout streams much may be accomplished, but degeneration of stock generally will not be arrested by introducing larger forms of trout, for the cause is, as a rule, to be found in absence of sufficient food or some local prejudicial agent, and larger frames require more—not less—diet Mr Francis, *Fishing Gazette*, July 10th, 1886, remarked " that in contrasting my early days of English fly-fishing with my more recent experiences, nothing strikes me more than the different ages at which I have found trout at their best To particularize streams would involve me in tedious detail, but I have fully a dozen first-class trout streams in my mind's eye in which the big fish, especially after May, used to be the best for the table, whereas now the judicious *gourmet* would almost always select for his breakfast or supper the smallest trout which the rules permit to be killed Where the 2 lb used of old to be red-fleshed, firm, and combative, I find, except in a few specially favoured reaches, that hardly a fish over 20 oz is worth cooking, and that a ½ lb is better for the table, as well as livelier on the hook than his seniors "

* " Green Wren," in *The Field*, Dec 4th, 1886, referring to the greater difficulty which is being yearly observed to get trout to rise and take the fly, suggested that this may be due to inherited instinct, and has been universally attributed to education from over fishing and a bad habit of bottom feeding or preying on the half developed fly As a remedy he proposed " to breed trout artificially as much as you possibly can, but do not breed from a single fish which has not been captured by the fly By this means you would secure a progeny whose inherited instinct, if such a thing exists, would be a taste for the fly, and, let us hope, a distaste for the vulgar and plebeian habit of bottom feeding "

Similarly in Wales, it has been found that the great increase in the numbers of fly-fishers has been coincident with decreased size of flies and diminished baskets of fish. In some pieces of water one sees thousands of small trout and no large ones, and it would seem as if the general size is such that they are unable to prey upon one another; consequently, all starve together *

For good fishing, it is necessary to have a good breed of trout and plenty of food. If there is a large stock by consuming the food and producing a famine, some, if not all, must be kept out of condition; and in such cases it is necessary either to increase the food or decrease the stock. While pike in waters will often prevent trout feeding, even large trout of a kelt-like form may be as injurious as pike by eating the smaller fish. Streams coming from a limestone formation and high hills generally give smaller fish than those which pass over rich meadows, where the water is warmer and the food superior.

It has been observed in Germany, that young trout thrive best in natural streams for the first six months of their lives, and subsequently best in trout ponds from 5 to 10 feet deep, and ⅛ to ⅔ of an acre in extent. Shallowest at the inlet to allow the water-weeds to grow and thus furnish animal life; deepest at the other end to permit the temperature to be low (see *Fishing Gazette,* May 8th, 1886)

That the existence of places in a clear stream where trout can conceal themselves are almost a necessity, must be admitted by every fisherman. The wave of a fishing rod, the appearance of some unusual phenomena will make the fish either rush to their accustomed haven of security, or dash away to and alarm the shoal. Also, when from some cause, as a miller cutting the weed, these hides have been destroyed or are deficient in a stream, an angler has but little chance of making a capture, and as a result the trout increase in numbers more than in size. The following plan has been found by Mr Francis in some streams to prove efficacious: nail some inch deal boards, 7 feet long, to three cross pieces of ash, 6 feet long, and three inches by two inches, making a kind of table 7 feet by 6. Then drive four plugs into the centre of the stream about 5 feet apart, square, and standing eight inches from the bottom. The table to be nailed to the plugs.

Many of the agencies which destroy the ova or young of these fishes have been detailed (pp. 28, 45, &c.). Robins, hedge-sparrows and water ousels are not harmless, but have been observed carrying off eggs and young fish (Beresford, *Field,* July 2nd, 1884), the wagtail has likewise been accused of the same practices. In the United States, mosquitoes† have been observed killing young fish, while an external parasite *Argulus foliaceus,* is not rare in our fresh waters, and is also destructive. In some places I have known the bed of the stream, when the water has been run off, absolutely swarming with bull-heads, *Cottus gobio,* which fish are most destructive to young trout.

Mr Hutton, *Fishing Gazette,* July 17th, 1886, gave an account of seeing in the backwater of the Dove, a trout of about 1 lb struggling with an eel 8 or 9 inches

---

* Mr Francis, *Fishing Gazette,* July 10th, 1886, observed that "in Llyn Ogwyn years ago, from May to September, a good hand on any fair day might take from three dozen to four dozen vigorous red-fleshed trout, averaging about 10 oz." Twenty-five years later he found baby trout, due to the owner ceasing a practice long in existence of periodically netting the shallow end of the lake, as a result of which, the trout have multiplied beyond proper limits, causing a disproportion

† A recent *Bulletin* of the *United States Fish Commission* contains the following:—'In the middle or latter part of June, 1882, I was prospecting on the head waters of the Tumichie Creek, in the Gunnison Valley, Colorado. About nine o'clock in the morning I sat down in the shade of some willows that skirted a clear but shallow place in the creek. In a quiet part of the water, where their movements were readily discernible, were some fresh hatched brook or mountain trout and circling about over the water was a small swarm of mosquitoes. Every few minutes these baby trout—for what purpose I do not know, unless to get the benefit of more air—would come to the surface of the water, so that the top of the head was level with the surface. When this was the case a mosquito would light down and immediately transfix the trout by inserting its probosers, or bill, into the brain of the fish which seemed incapable of escaping. The mosquito would hold its victim steadily until it had extracted all the life juices, and when this was accomplished it would fly away, and the dead trout would turn over on its back and float down the stream. In half an hour, over twenty trout were sucked dry, and their lifeless bodies floated away with the current"

long   It worried it as long as seen, like a terrier at a rat   A few years previously Major Tarie found a fine Test trout choked by an eel it had attempted to swallow   Mr Francis Francis witnessed the river lamprey removing the stones over trout redds, and doing incalculable injury to the ova

Life history —All the various forms of trout have their par stage *   The size to which the adults attain, depends upon the suitability of the water inhabited and the amount of available food   Thus, as already observed, in some mountainous districts they may never exceed three or four ounces in weight, while young hatched from the same batch of eggs may attain to pounds   They are said to be long-lived fish , one was stated to have been kept twenty-eight years in a well in Dumbarton Castle , another is said to have been fifty-three years in a well in the orchard of Mr Mossop, of Board Hall, near Broughton-in-Furness   While in *The Field*, February 9th, 1884, will be found the account of a trout taken from the river Sliting about thirty years previously, when it was put into a spring well in the garden of Mr W Leithead, Crowbyres, and lived there until the first week in February, 1884, when it died   During its lifetime it was well fed and kindly treated, but never weighed more than a pound. Possibly these forms were sterile as such an age in stock ponds is unheard of †

Inherited instinct may induce trout, as at Loch Leven, to ascend streams to breed as their ancestors did before them   but it would not lead them to understand that the conditions of those streams, due to drainage works, were altered, so that rapid subsidence ensues, leaving the ova dry

In 1875 ten small trout from Lochy Bhravin were introduced into Loch Toll an Lochain, Ross-shire, 2250 feet above the sea, and up to that time entirely destitute of fish   On September 2nd and 3rd, 1884, Mr J Fowler and the Rev M Fowler took seventeen with a fly weighing 30 lb   The two largest were, one 23 in long, weighing 5 lb 13 oz , the second 22½ in long, weighing 5 lb 5 oz , the remainder varied between 1 lb 13 oz and 1 lb 1 oz   In these fish were beetles, flies, fresh-water shrimps *Gammarus*, and various insects   Shell fish as *Ancylus*, and snails *Limnea*, are found in the Loch

As food —Its value differs with the localities from whence it has been taken   Its old name was "the venison of the waters," and denoted the general estimation in which it was, and is still held   It is in its primest season from May until the end of September, deteriorating in and after the breeding period unless among such as are sterile   Some consider the females as food to be superior to the males

The difference in the colour of the flesh of trout is interesting for several reasons, and may be seen from as highly coloured as in a salmon to being perfectly white, but this colour is not invariably a test as to its suitability for the table, for some white-fleshed forms are excellent, and those which are rosy-fleshed not invariably so, still the reverse is generally the case   I carefully examined a large number in Sutherlandshire, mostly from Loch Assynt, in June, 1886, and found the flesh to be of all colours, from as red as a salmon to quite white, but as food they seemed all equally good   Although, as I have already stated, in some places

* *Yearling trout* are such as are hatched in the winter, say of 1884 85 (i e February), and which cease to be yearlings at the commencement of the following spawning season '86   Mr Andrews, of Guildford, in the first week of October, 1884, sent Lochleven trout and brook trout hatched January and February the same year to the Exhibition tanks, South Kensington, and on arrival they measured up to 6¾ in in length

† " June 1st, 1876, a trout about 3 in long was taken from the Moouzie burn by Mr James Gray, of Lauchons in Fife, and placed in Lady Well, which is situated at the east end of the village, and it is now over 17 in long and weighs about 2 lb   The children feed it with worms and bread   In 1835 a trout about 5 in long was taken from the river Leader by a man named J Crossley, and put into a well in the town of Earlston, where the village children fed it many years   It grew well for some time, then got emaciated, and died in 1869, but never increased in weight over 1½ lb " (Greville P , *Field*, November 22nd, 1884)   A correspondent of *The New Sporting Magazine*, for November, 1840, observed " that a friend of his has kept trout in a kind of store stream, and having fed them with every kind of food, has had some increase from 1 lb to 10 lb in four years   Mr Toomer placed in a pond a trout of 3½ lb which he caught in the river in a storm, and in about a year it had grown to about 9 lb " (Daniel, *Rural Sports*)

the redness of the flesh appears to be caused by the diet of the fish, and that fresh-water shrimps, *Gammari*, are one of its causes, such does not seem to be always the case In the stream Churn, passing Cowley and Colesbourne, an affluent of the Gloucestershire Colne, there are quantities of these *Gammari*, but the flesh of the trout is white, and it is not until they near the Colne that they get a slight pinkish tinge, yet all are equally good T Medwin, *Angler in Wales*, remarked that "trout which feed on leeches eat up red "

A correspondent of *Land and Water*, June 14th, 1884, observed that ' hitherto it was a very exceptional thing to take any other than white fleshed trout (above Totnes weir) now, however, that the dapping season has commenced the large fish in the deep water above the Totnes weir have been taken in considerable numbers similar sized fish were last year all white-fleshed trout, but now a large proportion of them are pink I consider this is caused by the fish feeding in the tidal waters below Totnes weir on shrimps and other salt-water food, and they are able by means of the fish pass to get up again to the fresh water which formerly they could not do except in floods, and then rarely "*

The month at which trout get into condition is a question that is of considerable interest to the angler as well as to the housekeeper In the southern rivers† which are rapid, of no very great size, and descend from hills, the small and resident trout generally afford sport to the angler as early as March and April,‡ possibly these small forms rapidly mend subsequent to the breeding period But

---

* At a meeting of the *Scotch Fisheries Improvement Association* in 1884, a letter was read from Mr Harvie-Brown respecting some experiments regarding the colours of fish, observing that " The subject of coloration of flesh of trout is a much more intricate one than at first appears I know of trout holding largely developed spawn in June and July in a loch in Sutherland whose flesh is not pink only, but bright red, like a salmon's, and yet they are not fit to be eaten I know, also, in a limestone burn the very finest trout, which on the table are perfectly white in the flesh, whatever size they grow to, but in another limestone burn from the same source, or nearly so the trout are quite different in appearance externally, but equally white in flesh and equally delicious for eating I put a ½ lb trout, along with others, into a previously barren loch, in two years some of these trout attained to 4½ lb weight, developed huge fins and square or rounded tails, lost all spots, took on a coat of dark slime, grew huge teeth, and became *feroces* in that short time The common burn trout, taken from a very high rocky burn up in the hills, in two years became indistinguishable from *Salmo ferox* The first year they grew to about 1 lb or 1½ lb, took on a bright silvery sheen of scales, were deep and high shouldered, lusty and powerful, more resembling Lochleven trout than any others This was when their feeding and condition was at its best, but as food decreased, and they rapidly increased in number, spawning in innumerable quantities, and with no enemies, the larger fish began to prey on the smaller, grew big teeth, swam deep, and lost colour, grew large fins and a big head and became *Salmo ferox* so called In two years more the food supply became exhausted, and now the chain of lochs holds nothing but huge, lanky, kelty looking fish and swarms of diminutive ' black nebs,' neither of the sorts deserving of the angler's notice The first year they were splendid fish—rich and fat Now they are dry and tasteless "

† Respecting early trouting around Dartmoor the following appeared in *The Field* —" Mild weather being granted—a condition not uncommonly conspicuously wanting—the angler cannot get to work upon the moorland streams too early after February 1st The fish being always in season, so to speak, always on the feed, are eager to accept such lures as the March brown, February red, blue dun, blue upright, or anything in red, brown, or rusty with gilt twist, or blue with silver twist " On January 29th, 1887 J D B wrote saying that " trout fishing in North Devon begins February 18th," and R N , *Field*, February 12th, 1887, replied, " I have always maintained that this is at least a month too early Trout fishing should not legally begin till March 1st, and no one with any regard for his fishery should allow it till April 1st To day, February 5th, I caught a trout 15 in long, 1 lb 4¼ oz , with the milt running from him, and within two yards of the spot was a newly made redd On dissecting him I found about two-thirds of his milt remaining, and in his stomach a minnow Now, it is a well known fact that the colder the water and climate the earlier the trout spawn, but I do not think that they vary much in their time in any district The bulk spawn at the end of December and beginning of January, the earliest I ever knew were November 13th, and the latest the first week in March " J D B answered February 19th, " W C , writing last week from Exeter, says that some few trout have been taken in capital condition R N has the mistaken idea that the cold weather acts upon the spawning of the trout Now if we had summer weather all through the winter, they would have to spawn when their natural time came Everything has its times and seasons Trout spawn mostly in the Devon streams the latter end of November and beginning of December I believe that holds good for every county in England, Ireland, Scotland, and Wales "

‡ As early as February in some Cardiganshire and Montgomeryshire streams

where fish are larger they seem to take longer attaining a fit state for the angler,* and in some waters all are not in condition by the middle of April Ephemera (1853) observed, " I never saw a trout in prime season before May   The trout season ought to be fixed from 1st April to 13th August" (p 274)

Streams differ considerably as to the time at which the trout in them recoup themselves, partly consequent at the period they spawn, and partly owing to the amount and variety of their food, for this may be natural or even artificial as when obtained from sewers emptying into rivers   Early spawners without good and nourishing food on which to mend are not early ready for the table

Diseases and injuries —These have already been considered, first when in the young stage (p 45 *ante*) and under the head of Salmon (p 109 *et seq*) and sea trout (p 180 *ante*)   Some coarse fish, as roach,† are sometimes found to be injurious to trout, for they may augment in such numbers as to consume the food which would otherwise form the diet of the Salmonidæ   similarly minnows may starve young trout In *Land and Water* May 6th, 1882, Mr Header of Plymouth, described how a trout about 11 in long was hooked in the Plym, and which on being landed was found to have an india-rubber band over the head   It had slipped backwards and had got partly under the gill-covers where it was compressing the gills, and had deeply furrowed the isthmus   The fish was in splendid condition   Leeches, *Piscicola geonutia*, are often injurious to trout

Legislation —Many anglers in England are of opinion that it would be better for sport were the opening of the trout season never to commence before the middle of March, which even then is early, except for some streams in Wales and Devonshire ‡

Salmon preservers seem to generally believe that the trout by consuming salmon eggs and the fry, becomes one of the greatest enemies they have, but it is not very probable that any considerable number of the former are extracted from redds if such are at the usual depth   but that they will eat salmonoid ova if they get the chance is well known, even parent fish having been observed to devour their own eggs as they were being deposited—while salmon kelts kill numerous small trout

* It was also observed in *The Field* that, " Perhaps these conditions are exactly reversed in the case of the rich and luscious chalk streams, where the trout are almost of a different species running to a much larger size, breeding later and more sparingly, and requiring a long rest and some nutritious feeding to regain their grand proportions of fine condition I can easily imagine how the happy members of the Houghton Club, who patiently bide their time for the well-nurtured and highly educated leviathans of the Hampshire rivers, might look down with contempt upon the easy sport of March fishing on Welsh or Devonshire streams, and jeer at impatient anglers who rejoice to face an easterly wind for the capture of a dozen or two of small but delicious trout that scarcely make up a satisfying dish for a rustic appetite "

† " Roach r Trout A 7 acre artificial lake was stocked with these two forms As the former have increased in numbers the trout seem to diminish in size Some time ago when the roach were very scarce, there were trout up to 3 lb, and the average was over 1¼ lb Now it is very seldom that a trout is got over 1 lb "—*Field*, April 26th, 1884

‡ Mr Pritt, in *The Field*, April 17th, 1886, observed, " Referring to the letter of 'Amicus,' in *The Field* of the 10th, your correspondent speaks of the ' few rivers where trout are allowed to be taken on Feb 2nd ,' he is possibly unaware that, so far as the conservators are concerned, this is the case with some rivers in Lancashire and with every river in Yorkshire, and the streams of the latter county alone are more than can fairly be called ' a few ' Where a later date for opening has been fixed in these rivers it is through the action of the local clubs, and these do not by any means cover the whole length of the fishable water The result is that, on those stretches which are protected neither by the water bailiffs of the conservators (who devote their attention mainly to salmon) nor by the rules of the local associations, an amount of fish destruction goes on in the earlier part of the season which it is pitiable to hear of Neither size nor condition is allowed to overrule the belief that all is fish that comes to the net "

Mr J Naden, *Field*, March 5th, 1887, writing from Hartingdon, Derbyshire, remarked, " I think (at least for this part of the country, North Derbyshire and North Staffordshire) the fishing season both closes and opens too soon The trout here are in good condition till the middle of October They are in as good condition at the end of October as they are at the beginning of March At the time I am writing this (February 24th) numbers of them are in the little rivulets spawning But unless in other parts of this river, and in other rivers the trout spawn much earlier than they do here, I think the Board would do well to reconsider the close time for them —i e , if the time is fixed by the Board, and not by the Imperial Legislature "

In some waters it has been held that not killing eels is very destructive to trout, consequently night-lines should be permitted. Eels in some localities are more mischievous than in others, while otters are said to be very partial to eels. It is stated, in the forty-sixth Report (1883-84) of the *Thames Angling Preservation Society*, that, "as regards the trout, which, previous to the abolition of night-lines, were gradually diminishing, there is now an abundant supply, and the past season has afforded substantial evidence that those fish are yearly increasing in numbers and the prestige of former days returned."

Habitat.—The colder and temperate portions of the northern hemisphere, descending in Asia as far south as the Hindoo Koosh, but not normally present in any portion of Hindostan. Heber, mistaking a spotted carp, *Barilius*, for a trout, asserted they were found on the Himalayas, on which authority Conch gave India as one of its habitats. It has been introduced on the Neilgherry range of hills in Southern India, where most of the examples were transferred to the rivers on the Koondah range. It has also been artificially introduced into many countries in the southern hemisphere. In the Orkneys it is found in great numbers in every burn, and generally extended throughout the rivers and lakes of the British Isles when unchecked by pollutions. Some exceptions, however, to this general rule would seem to occur. In Norfolk it is found in small numbers in the higher parts of the Bure, the Ware, and some of their tributaries, but not in the Waveney (Lubbock).

As to the size it attains, in 1880 Buckland made a cast of one 17 lb weight, captured at Reading. July 11th, 1882, one 20 lb weight was secured in Lough Derg, an expansion of the Shannon (S. Hailey); while the so-called *S. ferox* has been taken up to 50 lb weight or even more. In the Thames, close to the mouth of the Kennett, one was taken on April 24th, 1880, weighing within one ounce of 17 lb., on May 18th, 1863, a 15 lb one was caught in Marlow Weir pool, and on May 21st, 1883, Mr Ross Faulkner caught a 14 lb fish at Hampton Court. If this fish has abundance of space, unlimited food, and is permitted to live out its existence, it would doubtless arrive at as great a size as was formerly recorded from Irish lakes.

ADDENDA

Since the foregoing went to press, through the kindness of Mr Willis-Bund, Lord Lisburne and Dr Rowland, I have been enabled to investigate in Cardiganshire some of the apparent causes affecting the number of cæca, a detailed account of which will be published. In the three lakes situated in the hills and which form sources of the Teifi we found in five from Llyn Tuifi, two *males* 33, 40, three *females* 35, 39, 41. in five from Llyn Hir, three *males* 37, 41, 43, in two *females* 48, 52. in five from Llyn Egnant four *males* 33, 43, 44, 48, one *female* 42. In the upper portion of the Brefi where the stream is narrow, running between rocks, and the contiguous land is uncultivated, five trout, with very little fat on their cæca, one *male* 35, four *females* 34, 35, 36, 41. In the last two miles of the Brch, the sides of which are cultivated, six fish, three *males* 33, 38, 45, three *females* 41, 41, 50. In the Teifi, fourteen trout, seven *males* 38, 41, 41, 41, 46, 46, 48, seven *females* 39, 40, 42, 45, 45, 47, 49. Average in Teifi fish, 13, in lower or cultivated portions of its affluent, the Brefi, 41, in its higher or uncultivated part, 36, in lakes at its commencement, Llyn Teifi, 37, Llyn Hir, 44, Llyn Egnant, 42. or the least number being where the least amount of food existed. In Llyn Berwyn, a lake at the head waters of one of the tributaries of the Towy, of two fish, a *male* had 42, a *female* had 42. in the narrow and rocky Pysgotwr having uncultivated sides, and which flows into the Towy, out of nine fish, five *males* had 28, 35, 35, 35, 37, and four *females* 32, 35, 36, 40, or a general average of 35, again showing that with paucity of food a diminished number of cæca co-existed (*See* p. 109 *ante*). In three of the Teifi trout I found two had each 56 + x vertebræ and one had 57 + x.

Lochleven Trout, Plate VI and VII, fig 1 and 2

(For synonymy, *see* p 190, *ante*)

It has, from almost immemorial time, been a subject of argument as to whether the Lochleven trout should be considered a species distinct from the burn trout (*Salmo fario*) , and also, supposing it to be a distinct species, whether it might not be the descendant of a marine form which, having ascended the river Leven and obtained access into the loch from the sea has been unable to return there For tunately for investigators, in the year 1873 Sir James Maitland turned his attention at Howietoun to fish-culture, the race of trout which he selected for stock was that of Lochleven, from which he was only 25 miles distant and it about the same elevation

The question of whether the Lochleven trout is a local race or a distinct species, is one which is of considerable practical importance to the fish-culturists of this country, quite irrespective of its scientific interests If it is a species distinct from our brook trout, its introduction into our streams and dissemination through our fresh waters, would be a great source of hybridization with our indigenous forms, and such would tend towards sterility of the offspring On the other hand, if it is merely a local race, its crossing with the brook trout would be merely the inter-breeding between two varieties of one species, which, instead of being a cause of sterility, becomes mere commonly a means of improving a breed

In Sir Robert Sibbald's *History of Kinross-shire*, 1710, we read —" Loch Leven abounds with fine fish, such as the salmonds,* taken in the summer   The gray trout or bill trout, some of them as big as a salmond , grayish skinned and red fished, a foot long, taken all the year over Cenduc or Camduc in Irish, 'blackhead,' having a black spot on the top of its head, is fat, big as a Dunbar herring, red fished, much esteemed "

Pennant, in 1769, visited Loch Leven, and observed —" The fish of this lake are pike, small perch, fine eels, and most excellent trouts, the best and the reddest I ever saw , the largest about six lb in weight" (*Journ* 4th ed p 69). In his *British Zoology*, 1776, he did not refer to any distinct species existing in Loch Leven , but after remarking on the large trouts of Lough Neagh in Ireland, locally termed Buddaghs, he continued, " Trouts (probably of the same species) are also taken in Hulse-water, a lake in Cumberland, of a much superior size to those of Lough Neagh These are supposed to be the same with the trout of the lake of Geneva, a fish I have eaten more than once, and think but a very indifferent one ' (iv, p 299)

The Rev A Smith, *Statistical Account of Kinross*, 1793, remarked that, " In Loch Leven are all the different species of hill, burn, and muir trout that are to be met with in Scotland, evidently appearing from the diversity of manner in which they are spotted , yet all three different kinds, after being two years in the loch and arriving at three-quarters of a lb or one lb in weight, are red in the flesh, as all the trout of every kind in the loch are, except, perhaps, those newly brought down by the floods, or such as are sickly The silver-gray trout, with about four or five spots on the middle of each side, is apparently the original native of the

---

* The term *salmond* was employed so vaguely by some authors as applicable to both the salmon and sea trout, that the simple name being used is hardly sufficient evidence of the presence of *Salmo salar* Thus Sir R Sibbald, in his *Scotia Illustrata*, 1684, divided salmon from salmoneta, and referred to the latter as follows —" Salmoneta, qui nostratibus the *Salmon trout* " (p 25) He also observed, " The Gray trout, or Bill trout, some of them as large as a salmond ," but as I shall show, this gray stage is not the livery of old specimens, and none have been recorded over ten lb in weight, it would seem he referred to sea trout, again, silvery trout in Scotch lochs are often classed as sea trout

loch, and in many respects the finest fish of the whole   The fry of all kinds are
white in the flesh till they come to the size of a herring, about the beginning of
the third year   Those called bull-trout are believed to be the old ones   In
spring 1791, a large one was caught that weighed ten lb '

Dr Walker, in his posthumous *Essays on Natural History and Rural Economy*,
1812, observed of the trout in Loch Leven —"The first most frequent is called at
the place *Grey Trout*, and is a fish not distinctly described by naturalists, it is
found usually from one lb to two lb in weight, at times considerably larger   This
is supposed to be *Salmo levenensis*, N   The second, called by the inhabitants bull-
trout, *Salmo taurinus*, N , supposed to be a distinct species , but there is reason to
suppose this is the male of the above   These two are generally known in Edinburgh
as Lochleven trout   The third is called at Kinross the *Camday* is eight in to
ten in long, and reckoned a distinct species   but is only the gray trout at an early
age "   He likewise referred to three more species as the burn trout and the highland or muir trout; and another form of bull trout, which he does not appear to
have seen, found in the deep parts of the lake, attaining to seven lb or eight lb in
weight, and with yellow flesh

Graham, *General Review of the Agriculture of Kinross and Clackmannan*, published towards the commencement of the present century, after giving an account
of the fish found in Loch Leven, remarked, "Flounders are also found in Loch
Leven," which demonstrated that at this period sea-fishes were able to obtain
access up the river Leven into the lake   As the weirs on the Severn passable
to Salmonidæ, shad, and eels, appear to be impassable to flounders, the ascent to
Loch Leven in those days could not have been very difficult

In the year 1874 Mr R Burns Begg, the ex-president of the Kinross Fishing
Club, compiled an interesting account of this fish, and of the locality which it
inhabited   The Lochleven lake, prior to 1830, covered a superficial area of 4312
acres, it is situated 300 feet above the sea-level, and receives the waters of the
Gairny and the north and south Inench , while the mean flow from it throughout
the year amounts to 4000 cubic feet a minute, which goes into the river Leven,
and this river, after a course of fourteen miles, falls into the Firth of Forth   In
December, 1830, the loch was diminished to three-fourths of its original dimensions, to 3543 acres, by an extensive drainage operation, which permanently
reduced its natural level to the extent of four-and-a-half feet, and means were likewise devised by which, when desired, another four-and-a-half feet can be drawn off *
Fleming made a careful inspection of the loch during the years 1831 and 1835, in
order to ascertain what effect the drainage had had upon its fisheries, and he concluded that they were permanently diminished one-third in their value , the sluices
acting injuriously to young fish by the strong current at its outflow   that the
margin of the lake had undergone a change unfavourable to its piscine inhabitants,
owing to the peculiar barrenness of the shore, rendering the new margin ill suited
for supplying them with food   But in the lake itself the water-snails were found
not to have been destroyed

Many have supposed that the superior flavour of Loch Leven trout‡ is a consequence of the quality and abundance of the food which they could obtain there

---

* Dr Gunther wrote in 1886 to the Secretary of the *Glasgow Trout Preservation Association*,
stating that there was a question, " Whether the celebrated Lochleven trout of old Scotch
naturalists is still in existence in its purity   If I recollect rightly Lochleven was, according to
the reports of the time, nearly depopulated some twenty years ago, and replenished with stock
taken from other localities " (October, 1886)   The committee of the above association observed,
" This statement as to the mixing of the breed was a surprise to the committee, and on inquiry it
was discovered to have no foundation ' (*Report as to Stocking Loch Ard with Lochleven Trout*,
1887, p 7)   Mr David Marshall, of Kinross, remarked that " the date of the connection of the
late Mr Campbell Marshall, my father, and myself as tacksmen of Loch Leven, begins with 1st
September, 1839, and ends with 1st September, 1874, and certainly no such piece of work was
done during those years   and if anything had been done previously, we were sure to have
known it " (l c pp 7, 8)

† Whether this form is or is not *Salmo cumberland* of Lacépède, in his *Histoire Naturelle des
Poissons*, vol v, p 696, cannot now be determined from the meagre description which has been
handed down to us , but that author described it as having a small head, white flesh, and being
externally of a gray colour   A correspondent of Loudon's *Magazine of Natural History*, vol v,

In the *New Statistical Account of Scotland* mention is made of a trout taken April 27th, 1841, that weighed ten lb., being twenty-seven inches long and seventeen inches in girth We are likewise told of the fish in this lake, that their superiority in quality is not confined solely to the Lochleven trout proper, but is to be observed in the common trout, and even in the pike, perch, and eels, also that the trout of Loch Leven do not continue to exhibit the same distinctive superiority should they be removed to other waters In new quarters, however favourable such may appear to be, they are said to invariably deteriorate and lose much of their quality

The peculiarly excellent food in the water at Loch Leven has been supposed to consist of a small reddish-coloured shell-fish, believed to be restricted to the shallow shingly beds lying near to the shores (the form here alluded to would seem to be the *Limnea*) , also the sessile-eyed crustacean "screw," or "water-shrimp," *Gammarus*, and Mr Wilson concluded that it was owing to the abundant and perpetual breeding of these and other living creatures that the trout in question owed their superiority But a fisherman who had the management of the curing of the trout, and had observed the food taken from their stomachs, remarked that he had never observed any small shells, but mostly worms, minnows, perch, and young trout, while evidence was adduced by fish-dealers and others who had been regularly supplied with trout, both before and since the draining, and who distinctly stated that they could observe no deterioration whatever in the fish Parnell, however, held a different view, while there cannot be a doubt but that the stock of fish was largely diminished from some cause I will now pass on to a description of these trout as well as the inquiry into the reasons why the Lochleven trout has been regarded as a distinct species, and whether any persistent differences from other trout can be shown in its external form, its internal organization, its tints, or the colour or taste of its flesh ?

B x-xii, D 12-13 ($\frac{2\frac{1}{2}}{8-10}$), P 12-14, V 9, A 10-12 ($\frac{2-3}{8-9}$), C 19, L l 120-130, L tr $\frac{2\frac{1}{2}-3\frac{1}{2}}{5\frac{1}{2}-7\frac{1}{2}}$, Cæc pyl 47-90, Vert 56-59

Body rather elongate,* with the abdominal profile a little more curved than that of the back Length of head about $4\frac{1}{4}$ to $5\frac{1}{4}$, rather longer in the males · of caudal fin 8 height of body $4\frac{1}{2}$ to 5 in the total length.

As to external form, it has been said to be less stout, and its head shorter than

---

1832, p 317, observed upon a form of trout which was found in Ulswater and Windermere, termed by the residents a "gray trout," and having the habits of a char, and which he asserted was captured up to twenty lb weight he likened it to Lacépède's fish
* Parnell in the *Transactions of the Royal Society of Edinburgh*, 1837, p 154, appears to have been the first who scientifically investigated this form of trout, and he remarked as Jardine had previously done respecting the "par," and as Gunther subsequently did of the "huling," that "I consider it, however, not only as distinct from *S fario*, but as one of the best defined and most constant in its characters of all the species hitherto described "
From his remarks, we learn that he thought " the differences that exist between *S cæcifer* (as he termed this form) and *S fario* are very striking The pectorals of *S cæcifer*, when expanded, are pointed , in *S fario* they are rounded The caudal fin in *S cæcifer* is lunated at the end, in *S. fario* it is sinuous or even *S cæcifer* has never any red spots *S fario* is scarcely ever without them The caudal rays are much longer in *S cæcifer* than in *S fario*, in fish of equal length In *S cæcifer* the tail fin is pointed at the upper and lower extremities, in *S fario* they are rounded The flesh of *S cæcifer* is of a deep red, that of *S fario* is pinkish or often white The cæcal appendages in *S cæcifer* are from 60 to 80 in number , in *S fario* I have never found them to exceed 46 " He also observed that this fish does not appear to be peculiar to Lochleven, as he had seen specimens that had been taken in some of the lakes of the county of Sutherland
Sir John Richardson, in the *Fauna Borcali Americana, l c*, remarked that in "external form, the proportional size of various parts of the head and gill covers, the size of the scales and the dentition, agrees with *S lemanus* . Three individuals of the Lochleven trout that were dissected had each 73 pyloric cæca, and in one of them 59 vertebræ were counted " Yarrell added nothing to the previous descriptions Knox, *Lone Glens of Scotland*, 1854, observed of this trout of Lochleven, that it "is a beautiful silvery dark-spotted trout, imagined by some to be peculiar to the lake This, however, is not likely since trout quite resembling those of Leven are found in many northern lakes " (p 36) He concluded, after citing some of the opinions of others, that he was "disposed to think that two species of trout inhabit Loch Leven, independent of the common river trout, namely, the trout which lives on entomostraca, and comes into season in December, January, and February , and the trout, which, feeding on the buccinum, and on flies, worms, and all the common food of the common river trout, comes into season later in the

in the brook trout   Although certainly this is sometimes the case, such characters are not persistent

In measuring a number of Howietoun examples, I find that in specimens from 3 to 4 inches in length, the head is from 4¾ to 5 in that of the entire length   In *males*, from 7 to 10 inches in length, it is from 4¼ to 4½, and in examples from 14 to 15 inches, it is from 4 to 4½ in the same length   In *females* from 8 to 10 inches, the head is 4¾ to 5 in the entire length, from 13 to 14 inches, about 5½ in the same distance, and at 20 inches one-fifth

In form of the body there is no difference perceptible in those fishes reared in Gloucestershire or at Guildford, from eggs obtained from Howietoun, and young of brook trout raised from local brook trout eggs   It is thus seen that this ultimately depends upon local circumstances or conditions   for if they are removed to another locality where these conditions are different, they assume the local brook trout form   The same observation applies to the length of the head, which in some well-fed examples, and, in fact, generally so in the young raised at Howietoun, is a little shorter in proportion to the length of the body than is usually seen in the brook trout, but this likewise alters on their being transferred to a new home

Eyes —Diameter in an example about ⅛ lb weight, 5⅛ in the length of the head, 1½ diameters from the end of the snout, and behind the same distance apart it is of greater comparative size in small specimens, but smaller in larger ones   Interorbital space convex   The lower limb of the preopercle is rather short, as will be seen in the examples shown in figure 18, and on comparing them with examples from Loch Assynt, in Sutherlandshire, the differences were very slight, but in

Fig 18   Preopercle of Lochleven trout   1, *female*, 10 9 in long 2, *male*, 11 in long 3, *female*, 19 2 in long 4 *female*, 20 in long 5, *female*, 23 in long

some specimens from the south of England, the lower limb of this bone was longer   Maxilla rather feeble, it reaches to slightly behind the hind edge of the eye lower jaw with a hook or knob at the upper end of its extremity   It has been said that the maxillæ of the Lochleven trout are weaker than seen in the brook trout, and this is correct to a great extent if we compare forms from the South with undoubted Lochlevens   But if the comparison is made with loch

spring" (p 37)   In the *Journal of the Linnean Society* (Dec 19th, 1851), Dr Knox remarked, that at first he thought this a specific form, "although anatomical investigations had not hitherto confirmed it"

Dr Gunther *l c*, gave a fuller description than the previous authors whom I have quoted He observed of this fish that it has the "body much less stout than in *S fario*   In the male sex a mandibular hook has never been observed   Maxillary much longer than the snout but much narrower and more feeble than in *S fario* (*see* figures, p 6), in specimens 13 inches long, it extends to below the hinder margin of the orbit, and at no age does it reach beyond it The teeth on the body of the vomer form a single series and are persistent throughout life   Fins well developed, not rounded"   He found from 19 to 90 cæcal appendages, while at p 6 are figured two maxillary bones, stated to be from *S fario* and *S levenensis*, but not being completed at their proximal extremities renders it almost impossible to understand for what they are intended to represent   The supplementary bone would seem to be where the most difference exists

In giving a decision on the well-known 'Orange fin ' case, in 1872, the Sheriff Substitute found "in reference to the outward silvery appearance of the fish in question, both Dr Gunther and Professor Young state that the silvery coat with which these fishes are clothed is to be regarded as a distinctive mark of their being migratory fish of the salmon kind   The assumption of the silvery coat   in the case of river fish, is to be held an almost infallible test of a migratory and sea going habit   Nor is this inconsistent with the well-known fact, that in the case of certain fish which inhabit lochs having now no communication with the sea, a similar silvery appearance is to be seen   In the case of the Lochleven trout, which affords the most notable example of the phenomenon referred to, it must however, be kept in view, as having an important bearing on the character of this fish, that the loch which it inhabits had, most probably, at one time a communication with the sea, and that the fish themselves possess in a most remarkable degree

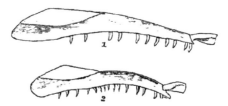

Fig 49   Maxilla of female trout   1, specimen from Otago, 19 2 in
long   2, specimen of Lochleven trout from Howietoun, 20 in long

tront, as, for instance, those in Sutherlandshire, this difference is not so striking
It will similarly be seen to be the case on comparing the jaw of a large female
brook trout with that of a Lochleven   But it is evident that in Lochlevens
reared at Howietoun, the males have not such strong jaws or teeth as those living
in a wild condition, which is probably owing to their having from their earliest
existence had food provided for them   Also as regards trout, very probably age
should also be taken into consideration as well as size, for a large four-year-old
Howietoun male would probably be less strongly armed than a similarly sized fish
which had been reared in a loch or stream, and which had most likely taken a
greater number of years to attain to the same size   Likewise, when examining
this subject, care must be taken that the accessory bone of the maxilla does not
by its position make it appear in a figure that the jaw was exceedingly strong, for
this in reality has but little to do with strength, in fact it has been considered
as probably homologous to an ossified labial cartilage   As to the male having
no knob on the lower jaw, that likewise is a most erroneous assertion ; in the one
figured in Plate VI, fig 1, and which fish measured 14 6 inches in length, and was
44 months of age when caught in October, 1886, the knob was very well developed
This knob is constantly seen in all old males of this form ; while even in some old
females at Howietoun a small one has occasionally been observed

As to the maxillary bone being "much narrower and more feeble than in
S fario, in specimens 13 inches long it extends to below the hinder margin of the
orbit, and at no age does it reach beyond it "* (Gunther)   This statement as to
where the maxillary bone extends posteriorly, and first made by Dr Gunther, is
not borne out by an inspection of Howietoun fish or those from Lochleven, in
which in large specimens it extends from one to two diameters of the orbit
posterior to the eye and this is of normal occurrence   In a Howietoun example
26 inches long, it reaches to 1¼ diameters of the orbit behind the eye, while a total
length of 27 inches is that of the longest fish which has been captured in that
establishment   For as they become more or less sterile at from 8 to 10 years of
age, a time to which breeding males rarely attain, they are no longer profitable,
and therefore older fishes are not kept

The male figured (Plate VI, fig 1) was 14 6 inches long, and captured at
Howietoun, September, 1886, it was 3½ years old, length of head 4¼† in that of
the entire length of the fish   Maxilla rather narrow and extending to behind the
hind edge of the orbit, consequently in this specimen it must have grown rapidly,
raising the question of whether it would not have become thicker with age

the features of a salmon and the sea trout   The fact of one of these trout having, in the
course of the present trial, been regarded by Professor Young as a sea trout, after examination, is
a very strong testimony to the difference between the characteristic features of the Lochleven
trout and those of all the non migratory river fish " (pp 166 167)

* The teeth in the maxilla of S levenensis, in Dr Gunther's figure, are shown as directed
forwards and upwards, the base of each tooth appears as if resting on the skin with its point
turned towards the maxillary bone ! (See page 146 ante)

† In a female from Lochleven 14 4 inches in length captured about the same time, the head
was 5¼ in that of the entire length of the fish

Teeth.—Of moderate strength, and which it has been asserted exist in this form on the vomer in a single series, and persistent throughout life, but in a double row in burn trout of the same size, but we have first to consider whether the facts as stated are correct. All trout and salmon (not chars) when young, irrespective of the teeth on the head of the vomer, have (as has been already remarked) a double row along its body, but these in all, dependent on age or rapidity of growth, fall out, commencing behind and extending forwards. In salmon and sea trout, which are forms which grow most rapidly, these teeth are shed the earliest, while the Lochleven trout, which is likewise a rapid grower, loses them rather sooner than the burn or loch form, while to say that in the mature they *are invariably* in a single row is erroneous. At the same time it is not here advanced that rapidity of growth is the sole cause of this, but the deciduousness of the teeth appears to be owing to the absorption or narrowing of the tooth-bearing ridge on the vomer, in consequence of which, first from being in pairs, they become in a single row and finally fall out. (*See* fig. 45, page 197 *ante.*)

In the following seven specimens of Lochleven trout the condition of the vomerine dental system was as follows :—In a *female* 20 inches long, 2 teeth exist on the hind edge of the head of the vomer, and 3 along the front half of its body, the two first of which are almost opposite one another. (2) In a *male* 9 inches long, 2 teeth at hind edge of vomer, 2 at the front end of the body, and 7 in an irregular zigzag line, almost in one continuous row, while their points turn

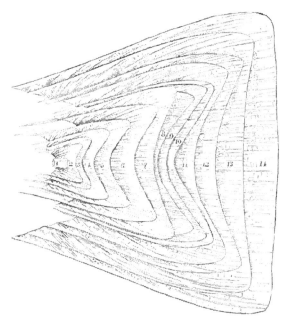

Fig. 50. Outlines, life size, of tail fins of Lochleven trout reared in ponds at Howietoun. 1, at 2 months old : 2 and 3, at 13 months : 4, male, 16 months : 5, 6, 7, males, at 30 months. From specimens in the British Museum collection : 8, female, 12 in. long : 9, female, 13 in. long : 10, female, 13·6 in. long : 11, female, 15·4 in. long : 12, male, 17 in. long. From Howietoun fish : 13, female, 7 years old, 22·7 in. long : 14, male, 7 years old, 22 in. long.

alternately to the right and left   (3) In a *female* 10 9 inches long, 2 at hind edge of head of bone, 2 in a line at the commencement of the body, and 8 as in the last specimen, but more distinctly in pairs   (4) In a *female* 13 5 inches long, 2 at hind edge of head of vomer, then 4 in a single row, next a pair turning one to either side, and lastly, 4 more single ones   (5) In a *male* 14 inches long, 2 teeth at hind edge of body of vomer, 9 in a single row along the body of that bone, of these the two centre ones form a pair   (6) In a *female* 19 2 inches long, 4 teeth at hind edge of body of the vomer, 12 along the body, among which are three pairs   (7) In a *female* 23 inches long, 3 at hind edge of body of vomer, 8 along its body in a single row, some turning one way and some another   The foregoing would seem to prove that it is by no means an invariable rule that all the teeth along the body of the vomer are in a single row, in fact they are similar to what is seen in trout in many Scotch and Welsh lochs

Fins —These vary in the Lochleven as well as in other forms of trout, which is due to the same causes   The pectoral may be more pointed in the young than is generally seen in the brook trout, but similar to the white sea trout, and reaches to about half-way to the base of the ventral, which latter fin is inserted under the middle or hind third of the first dorsal, and extends above half-way to the origin of the anal   The caudal fin has been stated to be much longer[*] than seen in the burn trout and its posterior end to be truncated and pointed at both its upper and lower angles   But it will be seen on referring to fig 50 that such characters have been given because the observers have examined young examples, the fin becoming convex posteriorly with age (*see* no 14 at 22 inches in length)

The statement that the pectoral fin is pointed is partially correct in small specimens, as it also is in small brook-trout, but in old and well-preserved examples it is similar to what is found in other races of fresh-water trout, as may be seen in figure 42, p 187

Scales —There are 13 to 15 rows in an oblique line running from behind the base of the adipose dorsal fin downwards and forwards to the lateral-line   *Cœcal appendages*   Richardson found 73, Parnell 80, Gunther 49 to 90, due either to several becoming confluent into one stem, or one subdividing into several, but anyhow demonstrating inconstancy in numbers   The number of these appendages are exceedingly varied, and from the time Parnell first ascertained that these trout often possess a larger number than are usual in brook trout, until the present day this has been held conclusive evidence as to their specific difference from other races.   Many who would admit that variations in external colour or that of the flesh, or even alterations in form, may be dependent on local surroundings, will be slow to believe that structural differences are not of much greater value   Here we must first inquire whether the number of these pyloric cœca are constant in the Lochleven race of trout, whether they ever vary in the brook trout, and, lastly, if any facts can be produced proving them to be inconstant ?

Having thus shown that these appendages in the Lochleven trout have been recorded as between 49 and 90,[†] while in other non-migratory fresh-water forms they have been found to be between 27 and 69 (*see* p 188 *ante*), I propose

---

[*] As to the rays of the caudal fin being longer than is seen in the brook trout, I have been unable to find that such is the case, either in Howietoun specimens, those from Lochleven, or those in the British Museum as they seem to be absolutely identical in the two forms   In the skeleton of a female 20 inches long, I find the middle caudal ray is 2 1 inches in length, and the longest outer ray 2 9 inches , but were Dr Gunther's figures to be applicable to these fishes, the outer ray should be 4 1 inches in length , but such proportions I have never seen in the thousands of these fish I have observed at Howietoun or elsewhere, not omitting those in the British Museum   Specimens having the angles of this fin pointed would appear to be young fish, often males, kept, as at Howietoun, where they are not disturbed , but in the old fishes this fin is invariably rounded at its posterior extremity   The statements in the British Museum catalogue alluded to are that—" In specimens 13 inches long, the middle caudal rays are not quite half as long as the outer ones, and in older ones they are half as long " (*Gunther*)   Also that in a specimen 13½ inches long, the middle caudal ray was 1 inch in length and the outer or longest one 1½ '

[†] Among the local Lochleven forms (*see* p 188 *ante*) Parnell found 60 to 80 cœca, Sir J Richardson 73, and Gunther from 49 to 90 , but although the last author in his description of the species says, " Cœcal pylori normally 60 to 80," he instances seven females in the British Museum

enumerating some which I have counted in examples of this fish   Among *males*
I have found them as follows —In specimens varying from 7 to 20½ inches in
length   At Howietoun, among fertile fish 8 examples averaged about 67 cæcal
appendages being one of each of these numbers—82, 75, 74, 73, 65, 62, 62, 48   At
Cowley, in Gloucestershire, one fertile male had 62, one which was sterile 52
Among *females* the number among fertile fish varying in length from 12 to 3 2
inches   7 examples averaged about 58 of the appendages, being one of each of
the following numbers—66, 64, 62, 59, 57, 55, 45, while one large female from
Loch Leven had 17, another 57   As a rule the size of these cæca in females
appear to be larger than is seen in the males, while in one of the latter a single
one of these tubes was abnormally shortened near the pylorus

The foregoing figures show a variation of these appendages at Howietoun
from 45 to 82 in *male* fish, and from 45 to 66 among *female* fish, while in one
fertile male which was examined in Gloucestershire, there were 62, and in
another, not so well fed, from the same locality, and sterile, there were 52   In
only one do we see the numbers approaching to 90 (82) as given by Dr Gunther,
and with that exception 75 were the greatest amount counted, and from that
down to 45, clearly showing that this is an unstable character, prone to change,
and consequently unsuitable for characteristics wherewith to discriminate species
Also, that, away from Loch Leven, these appendages have diminished in number,
and still more so in those from the ova hatched at Guildford and reared in
Gloucestershire, where likewise the smallest fish were sterile, and had the fewest of
these appendages   As to the difference in the diameter of these cæca such was
not usually apparent, except so far as I have mentioned above

Having thus seen that in its external form either the differences which have
been stated to exist between this fish and the brook trout are erroneous, or else
they are liable to alteration when the fish is removed to another locality, I think
all must admit that such unstable differences are insufficient for the purpose of
constituting species

As to external colour we find Parnell asserting as among its specific characters,
" body without red spots," and that these fish are generally seen without these
up to a certain age is of very common occurrence   The alevins and young par
raised at Howietoun are very similar to the young of the burn trout, but are
normally wanting in any orange to the adipose dorsal fin, it is rare for the
dorsal, ventral or anal to be margined with a white, black-based edge, and the
par bands are mostly more numerous, sometimes being from 16 to 17.   As the
fish become older three main types of colour are observable, a slaty or greenish
gray, becoming lighter beneath, and the upper two-thirds of the body and dorsal
fin spotted with black, and the fins generally grayish black   This form of colour
is prevalent up to the end of the fourth season, and may almost be looked upon
as equivalent to the silvery stage of the salmon smolt, or grilse,* but I have never

---

collection as follows —" Females, from 12 to 18 inches long   Purchased, said to be from Loch
Leven   Caught in April   Cæcal pylori 65, 63, 60, 54, 54, 53, 49, vertebra 58 59   These
specimens have the pyloric appendages fewer in number than is generally stated, yet these cæca
are so wide—so much wider than in *S fario*, that the reduction of their number has evidently
been caused by a confluence of several cæca with one " (Catal vi, p 101)

From the foregoing it is evident that the number of these appendages is very variable, for in
this race they have been recorded as being from 45 to 90   If, however, we turn to the writing of
most authors that have counted those existing in the *S fario*, we find them enumerated as follows
—' I have never found them to exceed 46 " (Parnell, p 308)   Thompson in 1836 examined
the so called *S ferox*, and found in four examples 49, 45, 39, and 36 (*Nat History of Ireland*,
iv, p 157)   Gunther among his other five non migratory fresh-water forms enumerated them as
varying from 33 to 49   While Sim as already observed found them in 52 examples of Aberdeen
shire and Kincardineshire specimens of burn trout to vary between 30 and 69   (See also p 216)

* On September 8th, 1865, captured with a fly from one of the Howietoun ponds, a two year old
male Lochleven trout, the young of the 1875 fish, or one generation removed from those of Lochleven   Length 7 4 in, of head 1 6 in, diameter of eye 0 3 in, its distance from the end of the
snout 0 4 in, and 0 5 in apart   Cæcal appendages 73   Colours—silvery with black spots which
are largest on the head and opercles where they are encircled by a light ring   Dorsal an very
spotted, and with a dark upper fore edge with traces of white, front margin of anal the same
Other fins grayish   Maxilla reaches to beneath the hind third of the eye

seen one over four years of age continuing this livery   The second is that of an older form, and a general purplish golden, densely covered with black spots, among which some red ones are usually to be seen, while in many old females a dark line shows itself along the middle of the belly, which, as well as the under surface of the head, is more or less black in males at the breeding season   In one female 18 inches long, on November 24th, 1886, three bright orange spots were present on the adipose dorsal, which fin as a rule is of a lead colour, with two or three black spots   Males appear generally to have the pectoral, ventral, anal, and end of caudal fin darker than the females.*   The third form, which will have to be again referred to, consists of small undersized fish, which, owing to sickness or some other cause, have the colours of the brook trout, with orange-tipped adipose dorsal fins   The most distinct white edging to the fins, when it exists, appears to be seen in males, but the amount of spots in all is very various

Here the question again arises (see p 83 ante) whether any alteration in the colour occurs, if these fish are transferred to new localities† dissimilar in some respects to where their parents reside?   Ten thousand yearlings from Howietoun were turned into Loch Goldenhoof, about two miles away, and fed by the same stream, which passes through the fish farm; this loch is nine acres in extent, and averages six feet in depth   In July, 1886, I examined some of these introduced fishes, and found them of a purplish colour shot with gold, and covered with black ocellated spots, but rarely red ones.   Dorsal fin spotted with black, but without any white edging, its outer surface grayish, a little orange upon the adipose dorsal fin   The colours, in fact, of these fish were not what is seen in the Howietoun ponds, but nearly approaching those in the Loch where they had been placed, a few had some red spots   As the water in the two localities was the same, food, possibly deficiency of it, would seem to have been the principle reason of this change in colour

The last experiment shows that some alteration in colour may follow new environments,‡ but a still more conclusive result as to the change in colour which may take place in these fishes under like circumstances occurred in Gloucestershire   The proprietor of Cowley had two ponds in a wood on his estate, each about an acre in extent, situated one above the other, and from the lower of which emerges a small stream, these he wished to have stocked with sporting fish   The two ponds are supplied by underground springs, while there is a fall of about 16 feet from the outlet of the upper pond, and a rather greater one from that of the lower where the stream commences   It will be apparent that no fish could obtain access from above, there being no water there, neither could they ascend the 16-feet perpendicular fall from the stream to the lower pond   It was determined to try the Lochleven trout, so these ponds were drained, mudded, and then puddled with clay

During December, 1884, and January, 1885, one thousand yearling Lochleven

---

* The upper anterior angle of the dorsal fin rarely has a light black-based edging in these fishes, and Parnell in figuring it and the burn trout correctly gives it to the second but not to the first   However, it is seen like this elsewhere

† In the year 1868, the late Mr McIvor, of the Government Gardens at Ootacamund in the Madras Presidency, succeeded in introducing some Lochleven trout and other European fish to that elevated region, where they are, or were, doing well (see Journal of the Linnean Society, Zoology, vol xii, p 562)   In January, 1876, Mr Thomas, F L S, of the Madras Civil Service, sent me a specimen from the Hills which was 6¼ in long, and on its body were red spots   In this instance it was clear that if a young Lochleven trout could assume red spots when removed to Asia, there was no reason why any similar movement in Europe might not occasion the same results

‡ The assumption of the general colours of the trout in any given locality by introduced breeds is of very common occurrence, at least after the third year   Now this is the period at which the young of the imported forms would be in a condition to be observed by the fisherman, whether angler or netter   This is generally asserted to be owing to the imported fish having interbred with the local race, and the hybrid (as it is wrongly termed) or mongrel form has the local colours   It is therefore interesting to ascertain whether, were eggs removed to a given spot quite distinct from the waters where the parents reside, the young which emerge from those eggs would retain the colours of their parents, or assume those peculiar to the locality, for if this latter occurs, it must be evident that such has been consequent upon local surroundings

trout were received from Mr. Andrews of Guildford,* and these were placed in the
ponds by Mr Ogden, of Cheltenham   In August, 1886, I was informed that, it
having become necessary to remove these fish to a more suitable locality, they had
been capturing them, and very great differences were perceptible both in size and
colour among these two sets of fishes—those in the upper pond being silvery with
a few black spots, whereas those in the lower pond were of a much larger size,
covered with spots, and having purple and golden reflections   Having obtained
leave, I visited these ponds, accompanied by Mr Ogden, on August 25th, 1886, and
found the temperature of the water at 2 45 P M to be from 57° to 65° Fahr in
accordance with depth and the side of the pond investigated   The lower pond
was the deeper, and in it were large quantities of the American weed, *Anacharis
alcinastrum*, also some of the *Chara*, while on the surface was a considerable
amount of the water crowsfoot (*Ranunculus aquatilis*), whereas in the upper pond
there were fewer weeds, but some of the *Pimpinella saxifraga* was present near its
upper end

It seemed, so far as we could ascertain, that more animal pond-life was present
in the lower pond among the greater amount of vegetation, especially in the
sessile-eyed crustaceans *Gammarus pulex*, and water-snails *Limnea ovata* variety
peregra   These forms were, however, also present in the upper pond, where a
small water-newt was also netted   During the month of April, 1866, when
investigating the stream which issues from the lower end of these ponds,
I found enormous numbers of tadpoles and the larvæ of Phryganeidæ and
Ephemeridæ

A fish captured from the upper pond (plate vii, fig 2) was 7 inches long, its
colours generally silvery with a golden abdomen, and a few black spots along the
sides, three of which were below the lateral-line and two on it, as well as three
red ones, cheeks silvery yellow tinged with gold   Some spots on the rayed dorsal
fin, which had a white black-based edge at its upper angle, while the ventral and
anal fins had a very distinct white black-based edging   Upper and lower rays of
caudal fin, and the upper end of the adipose dorsal, orange-edged   Fifty-two
cæcal appendages   A male, but sterile   The appearance of this fish was to colour
was, Mr Ogden observed, similar to the others previously removed from the
pond

Two male fishes were taken from the lower pond, one ten, the other eleven
inches long   They were generally purplish, with golden reflections   The side of
the body (of one which was most critically examined) from the upper edge of the
pectoral fin to and above the lateral-line, was closely dotted with ocellated black
spots, while there were also some red ones, five of which were on the lateral-line
Cheeks and abdomen golden, becoming white on the chest   Dorsal fin with
numerous spots, and a pink black-edged upper angle   Adipose dorsal with a red
edge and several black spots   Pectoral and ventral chrome with white edges, base
dark   Sixty-two cæcal appendages   The generative organs well developed
Twenty-two small *Limnea*-shells in its stomach

Near the end of the year 1886 an interesting occurrence occurred among these
fish, which would seem to prove that Lochlevens throwing back to brook trout,
may be consequent upon a diminished supply of food causing deterioration
During the last week in November Mr Ogden was near this lower pond, and saw
a large trout rise, so he returned to the house, and having obtained his fishing-
tackle, made a cast over it and captured it at the first throw   It proved to be
15 oz in weight, in good condition, but was described to me as having been
nearly black (similar to plate vi, fig 1), while it was the largest fish that has been
seen there   In fact this pond latterly had very few fish in it (most having been
removed), leaving a more abundant supply of food for those which remained,
consequently this fish had grown larger and taken on the Lochleven trout colours

---

* Mr Andrews, of Westgate House Guildford, wrote (September 14th, 1886) —" The yearling
fish supplied to Mr Ogden, of Cheltenham, in 1885, were Lochlevens reared from eggs which
were sent me from Howietoun   There can be no doubt of their being from ova from Stirling, as
they were put in a pond quite distinct from the others on a different water shed."

As regards the colour* of the adipose dorsal fin, on June 5th, 1886, I examined this in many Lochlevens, from pond 9, the first was rising 2 years, and 5 inches long It had two black spots on the adipose dorsal, but not a trace of orange and no red spots on the body , and several more subsequently looked at were the same. Three had a slight orange tinge on the adipose fin, and likewise a few red spots on the body , in fact this fin was orange-tinted in all wherein red spots existed on the sides, and the presence of these red spots was the exception, not the rule Passing on to the nursery ponds, we examined a few under-sized Lochlevens which had not fed well; all had their bodies red-spotted and also red on the adipose dorsal fin, while the rayed dorsal had a more distinctly black white-edged margin than was generally seen Some of the fish had two, three, or four black spots on this fin These fish would at once have the brook trout livery and not pass through the normal silvery stage—a stage that has been erroneously asserted to be an infallible test of whether a trout is migratory and sea-going In August I examined a number of the two-year-olds of these fish, which were removed from the Howietoun ponds, and only a trace of orange was apparent in the adipose fins of some, but the white front edge to the dorsal and anal fins was not uncommon

Many statements have been made as to the number of the par bands extending along the sides of trout, and some naturalists apportion two or three more to the anadromous than to the fresh-water forms (p 158 ante) But I have already shown (p 172) that those numbers are inconstant, and that I have counted from eight to seventeen, and all the intermediate numbers, in undoubted young Lochlevens.

I have already (p 145 ante) referred to how a hybrid between a Lochleven trout and salmon par showed an orange edging to the adipose dorsal fin, whereas not only is such absent in both young salmon and young Lochlevens, but present in many sea trout with which young Lochlevens have been compared

I assume it cannot be denied that the Howietoun fish are in every respect similar to those of Loch Leven, from whence the breed was derived This variety is sometimes, not always, finer shaped towards the tail, and when young has a rather shorter head than is seen in the ordinary brook trout Its maxillary bones, when it remains in its native locality, are somewhat finer than in our ordinary river trout , its cœcal appendages are more in number, while its colour differs, being as a rule silvery with black, but no red spots up to its fourth or fifth year, but as already remarked, all these characters are liable to change if removed to a new locality This fish doubtless is a rapid grower in its northern home; and the race at Howietoun has been much improved by selection of breeders , but removing the eggs to a new locality and then rearing the young has shown that the form and colour of the local race of trout is, as a rule, assumed, while even the number of cœcal appendages becomes altered, owing to changed condition of life †

Variety —One was taken, October 15th, 1886, at Howietoun, which had the basal half of its caudal fin spotted with black, otherwise it was slate-coloured

Habits.—These are similar to what have been remarked in the brook trout (see p 204 ante) During the breeding season it has been observed that some adults have abraded snouts, apparently due to rubbing or routing up the ground for eggs, but as such is not seen among unripe fish, it has been suggested that it may be consequent on their searching for suitable places in which to form redds, and

---

* A brook trout 5 inches long, taken from the brook, had 10 vermilion spots along the lateral-line, and two rows below it, also some irregularly disposed ones on the body with a considerable number of black spots , and black and red ones on the dorsal fin, which, and also the ventral and anal, had a white dark-based front edge (see also p 172 ante)

† Mr Andrews (MSS Nov 1886) finds in his " Fish Cultural Establishment " at Guildford that " eggs of the Lochleven trout from Howietoun do very well with him , they are hatched in water coming from chalk, and reared where it comes from a gravelly soil The young grow more rapidly, and are deeper in form than seen at the same age in their native home The yearlings have the tip of the adipose dorsal fin and edge of the tail fin red, and there are also some red spots on the body, in common with young of the brook trout and some reputed as *S feroa* ' Mr Andrews continued that he " knows of no *unmistakable peculiarities* observable in the foregoing three varieties of British trout ," and I question if anyone else is able to point such out

15 *

pushing up places where the entrance is more or less impeded, and thus causing them to employ their snouts for this purpose.

At the Howietoun fish-farm, one fact used to be very patent, that the form of trout least alarmed at the presence of strangers was the Lochleven, which had been hatched and reared there, coming immediately to the surface for food, making the water bubble with their numerous forms, while they allowed themselves to be removed by means of a hand-net, the American char kept more to the mid-water, while the common brook trout, which had been obtained when young from the burns, were so cunning that the very sight of a net caused them to dive down and remain at the bottom. Some of the young raised at Howietoun are observed to take on cannibal propensities, when if small their colour becomes yellow, their teeth abnormally developed, while they rapidly augment in size. At Loch Leven during the breeding season these fishes are observed to push up rivers to deposit their spawn, and in these localities the young are hatched and the parr reared. In fact their habits appear to be migratory to a qualified extent, the parr not leaving the burns for the loch until they are from ten to eighteen months of age.

This form of trout agrees, in many respects, with the variety of the sea trout termed Whitling, *Salmo albus* (see p 159 *ante*), for in the young state it usually has the same short head, preopercle with a very indistinct lower limb, and a number of cæcal appendages. Unless the examples from Howietoun which I have dissected are exceptions, it would seem that change of locality to a smaller piece of water has been coincident with a decrease in the number of the pyloric appendages, coupled with a decided lengthening of the head.

Breeding.—Similar to the brook trout elsewhere, these fish at Loch Leven ascend the streams for the purpose of spawning towards the end of September or commencement of October. The size of the eggs of these fishes has already been referred to (pp. 25, 208), but it would seem that there may be slight yearly variations, thus in 1885 they were slightly smaller at Howietoun than in 1884, for in February, 1885, I found the average size of the eggs from seven-year-old parents was 0.24 in., but some were 0.20 in., others 0.22 in. in diameter. In some seasons, however, among those spawned the second week in December, a considerable percentage were observed larger than the eggs obtained earlier in the season, thus the average size from old fish was 0.21 in., the largest was 0.27, and the smallest 0.175. This leads one to believe that both the age of the fish and the period of the season have to be taken into account when considering the size of the eggs. Probably one reason why young fish do not give such large eggs as older parents is, that in the first the nutrition, which is consumed, goes both to assist in the growth of the parent fish and the formation of the ova, whereas in old fish their growth has not to be taken so much into account. The disastrous results of employing the eggs or milt from young parents, has been already referred to* (see p. 26 *ante*). At Howietoun the milt of the males appears to be ripe at least three weeks prior to the eggs of the females, and although among the young, males are the predominant sex, at five years old they are commencing to be scarce, and become very rare at six.

September 3rd, 1884, a Lochleven trout hatched in 1878, in pond twelve, was accidentally killed, and it weighed with its ova 2 lb., the eggs comprising ¼ lb of that weight. These eggs were carefully counted by Mr Thompson, and found to be 1944 in number, or 1296 to each pound's net weight of fish after removing the eggs, or 972 to each pound's gross weight of fish, or before the removal of the eggs.

In October, 1866, in one which died of fungus, I found three eggs from the previous year adherent to the pyloric cæca. In one fine female the right ovisac was full of healthy looking eggs, while the left had merely its upper two-thirds full, and from its lower portion depended a whitish membrane, containing some eggs from the preceding season.

These fish about the breeding time spring out of the ponds, and rush over their

---

* In 1881 Sir James Maitland fertilized the ova of the Lochleven trout with the milt of the sea trout, and 95 per cent hatched (*see Professor Rasch's Experiments*, note, p 48 *ante*). The colour of the eggs has been referred to at p 208

surface as if they were very uneasy   Should they be much fed at this period it has been thought that distension of the abdomen from food sometimes causes them to prematurely extrude eggs   Sometimes the old fish will even spring on to the banks of the ponds, and so meet with their deaths   The kelts at Howietoun commence feeding about a month after breeding

Life history —It will be very important to follow this out in the Lochleven trout, showing how it may vary with changing circumstances, and consequently supply an excellent example of how very variable are these unstable forms, not only in their external appearance, but also in their internal structure   The alevins at Howietoun do not show a trace of orange on the adipose or dead fin of the back, nor is it seen on either edge of the caudal   at Delsford, in April, 1887, I similarly observed that this orange colour was absent   But at Mr Andrews' at Guildford, among those hatched from Howietoun eggs it was present in all (April, 1887), similarly to what existed in the brook trout raised from eggs obtained from local forms   This must conclusively show that certain causes will occasion the adipose dorsal fin* and the upper and lower margins of the caudal to take on an orange colour similar to the common brook trout   Passing on to the fry, or those which have absorbed the yelk-sac, we find that at about two months of age, or even less, the finger marks show themselves on the sides, and that prior to the appearance of the scales

Lochleven Fishery —At Lochleven the drainage works do not appear to have proved beneficial to the trout in the loch, where from 1846 to 1855 the captures principally taken by net averaged annually 13,200, subsequent to which figures have not been obtained until 1872, when 18,000 were taken by anglers and 2000 by net   and in 1873, when 13,394 were taken by the rod   Latterly this loch has been much frequented by anglers, and as the fish (probably due to the excessive lowness of the burns) appear now to be less favourable for breeding, artificial stocking has been resorted to †

Sir J G Maitland (*Field*, September 23rd, 1882) showed the results of stocking this loch from his establishment at Howietoun —

Year	fry turned in	captures	average weight each
1875,	9000	5093	1 113 lb
1876 ,, ,,	22,000	3227	1 086 lb
1877 ,, ,,	70,000 ·	6286	901 lb
1878 ,, ,,	45,000	13,519	685 lb
1879 ,, ,,	none	21,491	777 lb
1880 ,, ,,	none	19,642	960 lb
1881 ,, ,,	none	16,811	1 050 lb
1882 ,, ,,	50,000 ‡	9415	1 011 lb
1883 ,, ,,	none	14,227	913 lb
1884 ,, ,,	none	15,940	874 lb
1885 , ,,	200,000	16,775	873 lb
1886 ,, ,,	240,000	12,157	956 lb

Mr Francis (*Field*, October 1st, 1881) observed that he was shown small ponds at Sir James Maitland's at Howietoun, proving most conclusively that —

* Although I am unable to satisfy myself of the existence of rays in the adipose fin of young trout, still they have been asserted to be present   Mr Gorebwer observed, in the Transactions of the *East Kent Natural History Society*, that this fin is "small and rudimentary, not unlike a fatty layer in a thin skin-film, it is quite destitute of fat, and is kept extended by a thickly crowded set of parallel and very delicate rays, extending from the back of the fish upwards to the free margin of the fin, and often projecting a little beyond it, as one may witness by the help of an achromatic object glass of half an inch focal length   These rays are indeed composed of a peculiar glassy and homogeneous matter, like the intercellular part of true cartilage, quite structureless, and devoid of cells , nor have these rays any muscular provision for their motion which we know to belong to true fins, neither have the rays of the adipose fin any resemblance in structure to the bony rays of other fins "

† It was pointed out that it takes two seasons for the fry to attain to a useful size, a conclusion which agrees with the figures, also that with the increased takes at first there is a diminution in the weight of the individual fish

‡ Also in 1882, 3000 two-year old fish from Howietoun were placed in the loch   Knox found that Lochleven trout were filled with entomostraca in the month of January, but that during the remainder of the year they lived on *Buccinum*   at Howietoun they thrive on clams, or horseflesh.

"A small pond, 70 yards by 30, and in it you can maintain 1400 trout, averaging 4 lb each, in the height of condition, and in beautiful order, and fit for the table   Is it not clear from this that any ordinary lake in a nobleman or gentleman's grounds can be made to carry any number of fish you require for either sport or table, provided they are properly and duly fed ?   It is, as I have always maintained, wholly and solely a question of feeding and what so easy as to feed a trout ! he will eat nearly everything from bread to cockroaches, and even clover heads do not come amiss to him   he picked half a dozen heads of red clover from the grass, and then threw them on the water, and the big fellows came at them like tigers, and even when you pulled the heads to pieces, and scattered the petals on the other ponds, the small fish would take them just as greedily "

Diseases —These fishes are affected with disease similarly to the salmon and the trout, while bay-salt has been used with success at Howietoun in order to arrest a fungus which has from time to time appeared in the ponds *

As food —The Lochleven trout is generally very highly esteemed, not only for the red colour of its flesh, but because it possesses a peculiar delicacy of flavour, most probably the result of the food upon which it lives, for, remove it to another locality, and the flesh will often become white   Whether the flavour of these fishes now found in the loch has or has not deteriorated since its partial draining, as asserted by some and contradicted by others, must ever remain unsolved, because the manner in which the fish were cooked, the amount of hunger in the partakers of this food, and many other circumstances would have also to be taken into account, while deciding such a question from recollection would be a rather doubtful proceeding   There is a legend that in olden times these fish never took a fly , and an anonymous writer in 1886, commenting upon the bad luck which had attended an angling competition, observed that fly-fishing on the Loch Leven had been in existence for about twenty-five years, but previous to that time these fish showed no disposition for winged prey   Granting the general accuracy of this statement, such would seem to partially confirm the opinion of Parnell and some others, that the local food has diminished in amount, therefore these fish will now take the fly

Parnell held that at Lochleven the flesh of this form of trout is of a dark red, but in the common loch or burn trout pinkish or often white   But this cannot be held as distinctive of species, for in the same day in Sutherlandshire, at Loch Assynt, some trout captured showed all variations in the colour of their flesh, from white to red, but were all equally well tasted   And Parnell observed that " James Stuart Monteith, Esq , of Closeburn, caught a number of small river trout, and transferred them to a lake (Loch Ettrick), where they grew rapidly , their flesh, which previously exhibited a white chalky appearance, became in a short time of a deep red, while their external appearance remained the same from the time they were first put in " (p 370) †

Habitat —Loch Leven in Fifeshire, and other lochs in the south of Scotland and the north of England , while Parnell recorded having met with this form so far north as Sutherlandshire

As to the size this fish attains, six-year-old examples, some weighing as much as 7 lb , were found at the Howietoun ponds in 1882, since then they have been captured up to 10 lb in weight   In Loch Leven on April 27th, 1810, one 10 lb weight was netted , while in the *New Statistical Account of Scotland* mention was made of two examples captured previous to that date, one being nearly 9 lb , the other almost 18 lb.

---

* I was informed that crows at Howietoun, after having eaten diseased fish, moulted and became most miserable objects, and three or four were thought to have become leprous

† Mr Ffennell, writing of the Lochlevens at Mr Andrews (*Times*, Oct 14th, 1886), observed, " I certainly think that those I took from the roadside pond in Surrey were the very best I had ever placed before me "   Elsewhere these fish have been used for stocking pieces of water, but with varying success   Thus Knox, *Lone Glens of Scotland*, 1854, remarked of those introduced into the artificial Lake of Prestmarman, under circumstances highly disadvantageous they thrive tolerably well (p 35)   They have also been transferred from Loch Leven to the county of Renfrew

CHAR.

When treating of the group *Salmones*, or forms among the genus *Salmo*, wherein teeth are found present at some period of their lives on the body as well as on the head of the vomer, I gave (pp 10 to 11) a synopsis of the views held by British Naturalists respecting what they each deemed to be species or else referred to varieties. I propose taking the same course with the chars, a subgenus of *Salmo*, wherein the vomerine teeth are restricted to the head of that bone (*see* fig 3, p 10)

Although char do not differ so much in colour among themselves as do our trout, partly owing to their not frequenting salt water, still, at various ages, their forms are so diversified, and sexual distinctions so considerable, as to have deceived many ichthyologists who have studied these fishes more in museums than in their natural haunts. Fish culture has, however, proved of great service in eradicating from systematic zoology a large number of species, which must, however, unfortunately continue for years encumbering the pages of ichthyological literature *

---

* Willoughby (1686) placed under one head *Umbla minor*, Gesner the *Reutele* of South Germany, the *Torgoch* of Wales and Westmoreland, and the *red char* of Windermere, table no 7 He also alluded to the *gilt* or *gilt char* of Westmoreland, which he referred to *Carpio lacus Benaci* of Rondeletius, he likewise figured it, table no 5

Ray (1713) held the same views as Willoughby

Pennant (1776) figured the char, and asserted his opinion that the *case char*, the *gelt* or *silver char*, i e , a barren fish or one which has not spawned the preceding season, and on that account is reckoned to be in the greatest perfection, the *red char*, and those of Loch Inch in Scotland, were probably all one species. He observed that the variety *case char* spawned about Michaelmas, while the *gilt char* did so from the beginning of January to the end of March. He also alluded to the Welsh char

Donovan (1804) gave a figure of what he considered the *gilt char* of Pennant, *Salmo alpinus*, Linn , also a plate of *Salmo salvelinus*, Bloch, the *torgoch* of the Welsh, then said to be confined to the waters of Llyn Quellyn, one of the Alpine lakes situated in a deep valley on the west side of Snowdon. He considered that it differed from the chars of Windermere

Turton (1807) agreed with Donovan, as did also Fleming (1828). Jenyns (1835) held identical views, but termed the Alpine char of Donovan *S umbla*. Yarrell (1836) held the same opinions as Jenyns, but in his second edition (1841) as well as in his third (1859), all our British forms were held to be varieties of one species

Agassiz (1834) believed that all our British forms were identical with the *Ombre chevalier* of the Lake of Geneva, observing that naturalists " have especially attached themselves to the form of the head and the arrangement of the colours but these two particulars are much too variable to supply precise characters, as to the variations in colour we may say they are infinite" (*Brit Assoc Report*, 1834, p 619)

Richardson (1835) placed (1) *S umbla* as synonymous with *S alpinus* and *S salvelinus* of Linnæus, and also with the species found in the Lake of Geneva, but he desired his readers to remember that the history of the char, whether single or distinctive, had not up to that time been clearly made out. In Windermere he continued that the case char ascended rivers, spawning about Michaelmas, while the red char deposited its ova along the shores of the lake, and not until the end of December or the beginning of the year

Parnell (1838) classed our northern char as *S umbla*, Linnæus.

Thompson (1840), and subsequently in 1851, held that all the forms of British and Irish char were varieties of one species, the *S umbla*, Linnæus

White (1851) placed all the British examples in his catalogue of the fish in the National Museum as pertaining to *S umbla*

Dr J Davy (1857) said of the char, "so various are they, indeed, that in no two lakes do they perfectly agree, either in their average size, form and colouring, or even in their habits. Compare the char of Windermere and Hawes Water were it not for their scales and other distinctive features there would be little hesitation in saying that they were different species, the char of Hawes Water is so much smaller and thinner and differently spotted the one taking the artificial

S fontinalis, or the American char, has likewise been added to the British fish fauna, having been introduced and being now extensively distributed throughout the country, but with varying success, as will be alluded to

Up to 1866 Pennant, Agassiz, Yarrell, and White only admitted one form of char as British, while Donovan, Turton, Fleming, and Jenyns believed in two Gunther increased them to six, subsequently *S struanensis* was added, and the American char widely propagated

Widegren (1864) asserted that in Scandinavia there existed two races of char, the larger being found in Lapland, Lake Wetter, and other lakes, while the smaller was present in pieces of water of less size, as those of Jemtland, Wermland, Smaland and Norway.* These two races he held to be simply modifications of one species, *Salmo alpinus*, the sæbling of South Germany, of which *S umbla* is a synonym Holding these opinions, which were identical with those of Agassiz and others, he entered his protest against the validity of Dr Gunther's new species, which he deemed as merely so many additions to the synonymy of *S alpinus* Collett, *Norges Fiske* (1875), considered all the char pertained to one form, so also did Malm, while Moreau, in his *Fishes of France* (1881), arrived at the conclusion that all the chars of that country were a single form, *S umbla*, which he considered identical with *S salvelinus*

In the Zoological Record of 1864, Dr Gunther disputed the possibility of the size of the teeth having any bearing on the food these fish consume, maintaining that such may even be a reason towards instituting a species However, in the artificial rearing of Salmonoids it has been found that some young do take on cannibal propensities, and are furnished with larger teeth than their neighbours Referring to the size of the eggs, I have already shown (pp 24, 25, 228) that such may depend on the age of the fish, and other circumstances

There appears to have been three different main reasons for dividing the British chars into several species, their colour, the number of their vertebræ, and also of their cæcal appendages

The colours in the British char do not vary to so great an extent as in the trout, owing to their residing in deeper waters and usually merely ascending towards the surface at night-time to feed, while other changes in tint are consequent upon the breeding season In the Lakes of Cumberland, Westmoreland, and Lancashire, observed Jenyns, this fish in its ordinary state is the *case char* of Pennant, when exhibiting the bright crimson belly which it assumes before spawning, it is called the *red char*, when out of season the spawn having been shed, it is distinguished by the name of the *gilt char* Thompson remarked that he had examined in a fresh state char from Windermere, from Loch Grannock (Scotland), and Lough Melvin (Ireland), and preserved in spirits or dry from nine other lakes in Scotland or Ireland Examinations of these had led him to believe that there existed but one species which, however, like the *Salmo fario* is subject to extraordinary variations In one lake he observed that the male fish can at a glance be distinguished from the female either by colour or by the many characters which are comprised under 'form " In another, so similar are the sexes in every external character, that without the aid of dissection they cannot be determined In size we find the species ordinarily attain twice the length and several times the weight in one lake that it does in another, although the area of their waters is of similar extent, indeed, in some of the largest lakes this fish will be found not to attain near the size it does in some others which are but pools in comparison, there are, however, various influences, as seen in trout, which account satisfactorily for such differences In the form of the

---

fly of the angler freely, the other—that of Windermere—is seldom caught except by trolling with he minnow "

Dr Gunther (1866), as in the *Salmones* so in the *Salvelini*, largely augmented the number of what he considered British species, although he rejected *S umbla* and *S salvelinus* as British forms He gave (1) *S alpinus*, vertebræ 59-62, cæcal appendages 36-42, (2) *S Killinensis*, vert 62, cæc pyl 44 52, (3) *S Willoughbii*, vert 56 62, cæc pyl 32 44, (4) *S perisii*, vert 61, cæc pyl 36, (5) *S grayi*, vert 60, cæc pyl 37, (6) *S colii*, vert 63, cæc pyl 42

Sir J Gibson Maitland (1881) added *S struanensis*, cæcal pyl 28

* For contrary views, as observed in Ireland, *see* Thompson's remarks

body again we find this species, when in equally high condition, to be in one lake herring-like and in another approximating to the roundness of the eel   So manifold are the differences presented by the char from various localities, that it would be tedious and perhaps useless to point them out in every case   A correspondent in *The Field* (April 22, 1882), speaking of the white trout of Quebec, observed that the best authorities seemed to agree that the sea trout of the provinces is simply a *Salmo fontinalis* that had emigrated into salt water and changed its colour by that means   This leads us to ask whether we ought to agree with Agassiz, Thompson, and others, that the number of species of char in these islands is limited to one, but that subject to great variations in form, in colour, and other characters due to physical causes ?   Or should we adopt the theories of those who see at least half-a-dozen species in the British Isles, and anticipate many more being discovered when the lochs of Scotland and the loughs of Ireland have been exhaustively explored ?

The *number of vertebræ* in examples of the British char have been recorded as varying between 59 and 63, while the *cæcal appendages* differ greatly, but not so widely as in the fresh-water trout, having been observed varying between 28 and 52   As to the number of *scales* along the lateral-line, it is remarkable that in the American *Salmo fontinalis* they would seem to have decreased in numbers in some which have been introduced into the fresh waters of this country and bred artificially   this is a subject which requires being closely watched before a very decided opinion can be given

If we seek to investigate the history of these fishes from the earliest times, and inquire of geologists as to what account they are able to furnish, we are told that the *Salmonidæ* are a comparatively recently evolved family (*see page 4 ante*), while they are now very locally distributed in our lakes of Wales, the north of England, Scotland, and Ireland   Mr Symonds, in the last edition of the *Records of the Rocks*, observed   " I have fished in and visited many of the lakes in Great Britain where the char, *Coregoni*, and great lake trout (*Salmo ferox*) are known, but I never saw one in which they still exist that is not either a glacier lake, or rock basin, or that is not dammed or otherwise surrounded by glacial moraine matter   They are also inhabitants of the lakes of Sweden and Norway, which everywhere bears traces of the glacial epoch and its close, and seem to me to be (like the Alpine plants that still linger among the mountains), fishes of that colder period when the last of the glaciers still hung to the combes of the Highlands of Scotland and Wales "   But other geologists have shown that they are not now restricted to lakes of glacial origin   Mr Brooke, writing respecting a species of Irish char, observed that " Lough Eske (where it was captured) was the crater of an extinct volcano, as suggested by Dr Wilde, of Dublin "

Doubtless the char prefer the colder north to the more temperate portions of the globe, and also moderately still waters   Among the fishes brought by the late Arctic expeditions were examples of char very similar, if not identical with British forms, thus seeming to show a near relationship one with the other   While in Nordenskiold's Arctic voyages it was recorded that the young of *S alpinus*, three inches long, were captured on the eastern side of Widje Bay in June, 1861

Char are a more delicate and apparently shorter lived fish than trout, they require deeper and stiller pieces of water and a colder temperature   they have even been recorded as residing in lochs where the sun never reaches the surface of the water   They are readily destroyed by poisonous substances, while attempts to introduce them to fresh localities have not been so uniformly successful as with the trout   The very young, as up to twelve months, will thrive in boxes under cover where trout would dwarf, while they seem to be rather intolerant of heat, and the American form, at least, is of a roving disposition

Many and various reasons have been advanced by different persons for and against the enactment of laws for the protection of fish, especially char   The following remarks of the *Salmon Commissioners* of 1860 are of interest —" This delicate fish is also decreasing in number and the cause is obvious   They are fished for and taken only late in the season and during their spawning time   The excuse for this is that they then only come to the shallow parts of the lake and cannot be taken at other times from the depth of water they frequent This, however, is not really the case In October they are taken at a depth of 40 yards or more, and the best fish are got then The fact is, that in summer when they are in full season, it is more profitable for the boatmen to attend upon tourists and anglers, and the difficulty of deep-water fishing is made the excuse for taking them after the spawning season has begun This fish is in great demand at all the hotels near the lakes, but if some check be not put upon their destruction at improper seasons they are likely to disappear altogether " (Report, p v) While Mr Houghton in his *British Fresh-water Fishes*, considered that the extension of the Salmon Act to char was a great mistake " The only time—and that time is of short duration—when char can be taken in any numbers is in October and November, when they leave their deep-water haunts for the shallower parts of the lakes The destructive agency of man, limited as it was to one or two months' duration, could have but little effect in causing a diminution of the species in the extensive depths of our great lakes, which, for five-sixths of the year, provide safe and unassailable harbours " On the other hand it has been asserted that the char of Lough Neagh, in Ireland, have been exterminated by man within the last forty years, showing his power, when unchecked by legislative enactments, of effectually accomplishing such a destruction In *Land and Water* for December 27th, 1879, is an interesting article upon the result following the preservation of the Llanberris char. Two large fresh-water lakes exist, joined together by a small river In November the char pass up this stream to the lower portion of the upper lake to spawn, having accomplished which they return to the lower lake The proprietors acting on the principle enunciated above, used to net them at the spawning period, but the Salmon Act of 1873 prohibited the capture of these fish between October 1 and February 1, so the killing of these spawning char has been stopped Prior to 1874 they were only to be seen here and there in shoals of a score or so, whereas now they may be observed in hundreds, averaging about nine fish to 2 lb weight In September, 1879, an angler, with a worm bait, captured in one evening 23 lb weight of char,* and as

* H H , writing in *Land and Water*, observed of these Llanberris lakes, that " the fact is, the lower lake, in which these interesting fish make their home, is so deep, and the bottom so rocky and uneven, that it is impossible to net them, hence the reason for netting them when spawning, for in those days there was no close time for char, but they could be taken either in or out of season The Act of 1873 has changed all this, and appointed a close time for char as well as trout, therefore, it is illegal to take char or trout between October 1 and February 1 which is just a month too soon to be able to net char in this particular lake But since the Act of 1873 came into force (five years) the present proprietor of those lakes, like a thorough sportsman, has not attempted to net char during close time (it is private property), although, as I said before, it is the only time they can be netted The consequence is that char are now to be seen in Llanberris Lake in shoals Prior to 1874 they were only to be seen here and there in shoals of a score or so, whereas they are now to be seen in hundreds What is the cause of this great increase of char ? There is only one answer, viz , the preservation of the fish Now for the mode of angling for those fish at Llanberris At the commencement of last September a gentleman from Llanberris went one evening with his rod to the upper end of the lower lake, baited his hooks with worms, expecting to get a large trout , so, after testing his casting-line and reel he made a cast and in a few minutes there was a tug, then a pull, and the fish was landed, but only weighed a quarter of a pound Fresh bait, another cast, but this time a different tug, so he muttered to himself, ' A big fellow at last ! ' However, when landed, there were two fish, but instead of the nice yellow trout, he beheld two red fish He could not understand it, but at last exclaimed, ' Char ! ' and was over joyed at his new discovery—viz , the worm bait He went on fishing, and landed during the evening 23 lb of char, returned to Llanberris, and found a ready sale at one shilling per lb The news spread, and the next morning there were several anglers at work, and all had good sport This continued until close time, and some days hundreds of quarrymen might be seen fishing, some in boats, others from the shore, some of them taking as much as 45 lb in the day, a few were also taken with the fly , but I am sorry to say another mode of fishing has been practised— viz , ' snatching ' It appears at times those fish are to be seen in shoals on the surface of the lake, and as they will not then take a bait, bare hooks are thrown amongst them and suddenly snatched, often getting two or three fish at a cast It is a great pity this practice is not put a stop to The char in this lake are not large, some a quarter of a pound, but the average is nine fish to the two pounds "

R H B remarked in *The Field*, January 15th, 1887, that " with regard to the Windermere char, one wonders that it has survived and multiplied under the surroundings of destruction which

soon as the news got abroad many others took to angling for these fish, and all had good sport This continued until close-time, and some days hundreds of quarrymen might be seen fishing, some in boats, others from the shore, while as much as 45 lb a day has fallen to the share of one rod, a bait having been almost invariably used, although a few were taken with a fly

A correspondent of *The Field*, October 28th, 1882, remarked upon night fishing for char with well-scoured brandlings and fine tackle in North Wales All is done by feel, and, when a vigorous tug occurs at your line, the angler has to strike, at the approach of day the char begin to bite savagely, as dawn commences the biting ceases, and the fish disappear as if by magic

Respecting the Windermere fishing for 1881 it was remarked in *Land and Water*, November 26th, 1881, that " the char fishing was, as usual, very profitable " There can be no better argument in favour of a close season and protection than the great increase in the value of the char fisheries since such was applied and protection afforded to these fish The fishing is free to all, and a great number of the natives on the shores of the lake gain a good livelihood by supplying the strangers and hotels with the fish The mode in which it is generally carried on by the fishermen as described in *The Field*, is with what is termed a plumb-line

Fishing with the plumb-line usually commences about the beginning of March, and at that time the fish are got about thirty yards from the surface and in the deepest parts of the lake As the weather gets warmer they gradually approach the top, and although they are frequently to be seen on a warm day leaping at the flies on the water, yet it is an almost unheard-of thing on Windermere to cast for them with a rod The plumb-line for char is made of strong cord, and varies in length according to the number of baits which are to be put on it, but it is usually between forty and fifty yards long, and this is sufficient to carry five baits At the end of the line is a lead sinker, weighing about 1¼ lb, having a small wing fixed in it, which assists in preventing it from revolving, although it is fixed to the main line with a strong swivel To this line is attached at intervals of six or seven yards, short lines, or, as they are called by the fishermen, droppers, varying in length from six to ten yards, the shortest being that nearest the bottom of the line What is generally used at Windermere, is a " phantom " made by the fishermen themselves, from sheets of metal coppered on one side and silvered or coloured on the other, which can be procured from any coppersmith or

---

encompassed it for so long Little was known of its habits, and because some were ill-conditioned and lean and others well fed and plump, it was long argued that two varieties inhabited the lake— the ease char and the gilt char, some even argued there was a third variety—the silver char We had, at the end of November, 1862, Dr Gunther writing for specimens of the Windermere char, ' as they are just now, and for a short period only, in season ' They were then on the spawning beds ' and it was when thus engaged that such destruction was played upon them There was no Act of Parliament for their protection, they were killed all the year round, and especially in the late autumn and winter months, when they came on to the shallows Still gregarious, they spawned together in infinite numbers on the gravel beds near the shore or in the river Brathay From the beginning of November to the middle or end of January they were netted, ' hooked foul,' and caught with a bait of salmon roe or worm One net could sweep up a whole school, and three hooks, tied triangle fashion and skilfully manipulated, might account for half a hundred fish during a day These were the halcyon days for potted char The poor sickly fish were so soft and flabby that they could not be eaten cooked otherwise Some people now cry out because they cannot obtain this dainty as freely as heretofore, and say that preservation has not made char more plentiful Generations of destruction cannot be remedied all at once, but such people should be reminded that even in 1860 char, when in season during spring and summer, realized a shilling each all round at Bowness, irrespective of their size They do not fetch more than that price now The spawning habits of the char have been said to be peculiar, but we do not consider them very much more odd than those of either Salmo salar or Salmo fario Some spawn on the shallows of Windermere, whilst others run up the Brathay for a similar object, but neither in Rothay nor Troutbeck—both, to all appearance, likely breeding places—do they ever form their redds The Ennerdale char spawn both in the lake and in the Liza, a river that is one of its main feeders Most of the char in the Scotch lochs spawn therein, though there are cases where they prefer a stream for that purpose, those of Loch Eurick to wit, and in Wales, too, they usually seek the shallows of the lakes when the period for depositing their ova and milt approaches The spawning season commences in November, and continues more or less, according to the season, into February, seldom later, and it has been noticed that those char which enter the tributary streams are more forward in their operations than the fish that remain in the lakes "

ironmonger   The fishermen cut them out with a pair of strong scissors, shaping them to their taste   A small treble hook is put on the phantom, and two yards of strong gut, having at least two swivels, and the remainder of the short line, or " dropper," may be of fine cord   Two lines such as are here described are used in fishing char, one on each side of the boat

Having reached the fishing ground, the boat must be rowed slowly, and the sinker is dropped over the side, and the line allowed to sink until the dropper next to it is reached, when the main line is temporarily fixed, until the " dropper" and phantom is put out, the main line is then loosened and sunk farther, until the next ' dropper " is reached and put out, and so on until the whole line is out   This having been done, the end of the main line is attached to the top of a strong rod (a young sapling does very well), about fourteen or sixteen feet long, supple at the top, but not too much so, and then the rod is made to rest over the stem of the boat at the side upon which the line has been put out, and the butt end securely fixed in the bottom of the boat   When this has been done the second line may be put out at the side of the boat, in the same way as the first line, and secured with a rod   Care must be taken to have the boat always moving, otherwise the lines will foul

It would appear that the preservation of char leads to a substantial increase in their numbers, and augmentation in the food-producing property of the lake where such is carried out   While these fishes are not so very indifferent to bait and flies as some persons would lead us to believe, the angler with a bait appears in most waters to have more chance of sport than the fly-fisher, thus although the char of Windermere usually will not rise to the fly, the Welsh *torgoch* takes it freely

Mr Harvie-Brown observed respecting a char of lochs in Scotland containing char, that in one small, deep pool of crystal-clear water they are of a larger size than those inhabiting the lochs lower in the valley   In a perfectly dead calm they rise, sometimes freely to a certain fly, but cease whenever a ripple disturbs the surface   As many as six dozen have been taken by one rod in a single day   One can see several feet down into this basin of pure water in a calm, and perceive the fish floating upwards and sucking in the fly, as they seldom dash at it like a trout

Char, says Mr Jackson, except for a few weeks in the year when they appear to live on flies, prey on all small fish and capture them, even larger than would be supposed possible by any one who had not taken (as I have) a perch nearly two inches long out of a char about nine inches in length

R H B remarked of the char in *The Field*, January 15th, 1887, that " those of other waters in the North of England, excepting, perhaps, Buttermere and Ennerdale, are smaller in size, and, in place of averaging about three to the pound, vary in weight from two ounces each to about four ounces   This smaller size is particularly striking with regard to the char of Goats Water and Hawes Water   Numerous enough in the latter, specimens of four ounces each are rare, and the usual average is of from two ounces to three ounces   In the other sheet of water they are smaller still, and fairly plentiful, some eight to the pound being the ordinary size   From this it may be safely inferred that at some time or other, these smaller waters have been artificially supplied with char from the larger ones, which thus, as it were, become acclimatized   They can scarcely be said to have flourished, for, failing to find the minute larvæ upon which the char waxes fat, they have degenerated into little lean creatures, and are to the ordinary char, just what the burn trout is to the handsome brown fellow from the richest streams   Another interesting circumstance in the life history of these small ill-fed char, is that they rise to the artificial fly both in Goats Water and Hawes Water, far more readily than elsewhere ; indeed, they seldom, in late years at least, are taken from the other English lakes by such means   Considerable numbers may be caught on almost any favourable day during the season with rod and line in either Hawes Water or Goats Water, thus a tendency to feed on the surface is shown, and similar remarks apply to the char of Loch Dochart in Scotland "

CHAR.

1. British Char, Plate IX, fig 1 and 2

Umbla minor, Gesner, p 1201, Willoughby, p 196, t N. 7, Ray, p 65 *Salmo Lemani lacus seu Umbla*, Rondel ii, p 160, Willoughby, p 197, t N 5, Ray, p 66 (*Gilt charre*) *Charr*, Pennant, Brit Zool (Ed. 1776), iii, 305, pl lx and (Ed 1812) iii, p 407, pl lxi, Low, Fauna Orcad p 234

Salmo alpinus, Linn Faun Suec p 117, no 310, Syst Nat i, p 510, Gmel. Linn p 1370, Bonn Enc Ich p 162, pl lxvii, f 272, Nilss Skand Faun Fisk p 426, Jardine, Brit Ass vol iv, p 614, Gunther, Proc Zool Soc 1863, p 8 and Catal. vi, p 127, Collett, Norges Fiske, p 160, Day, Brit and Irish Fish ii, p 112, pl cxvii, f 1

Salmo umbla, Linn Syst Nat p 511, Bloch, t ci, Gmel Linn p 1371, Bonn. Enc Ich p 164, Jurine, Poiss Lac Leman, pl v, Agassiz, Poiss d'eau douce, pl ix, x and xi; Cuv and Val xxi, p 233, Parnell, Mem Wern Soc vii, p 308 and Fish Frith of Forth, p 148, White, Catal Brit. Fish p 78, Thompson, Nat Hist Ireland, iv, p 160, Heckel and Kner, Susswasserf p 285, Gunther, Proc Zool Soc 1862, p 39 and Catal vi, p 125, Moreau, Poiss France, iii, p 530, f 207

Salmo salvelinus, Linn Syst Nat p 511, Bloch, t xcix, Gmel Linn p 1370, Bonnaterre, Ency Ich p 162, pl lxvii, f 273, Cuv and Val xxi, p 246, Yarrell, Brit Fish (Ed 3), i, p 241; Gunther, Proc Zool Soc 1862, p 38, 1863, p 7 and Catal vi, p 126, Blanchard, Poiss France, p 444, f 115

Alpine charr, Couch, Fish Brit Isles, iv, p 272, pl ccxxvi

Salvelinus alpinus, Malm, Bohuslaus Fauna, p 540 *

Variety TORGOCH OR WELSH CHAR †

Torgoch, Willoughby, p 196 *Umbla minor*, Gesner, Farrington, Phil Trans Roy Soc 1755, p 210 *Torgoch*, Pennant, Brit Zool 1 c, *Red Charre or Torgoch*, Ray, 1 c

Salmo salvelinus, Donovan, Brit Fish v, pl cxii, Turton, p 104, Jenyns, Brit. Vert p 428, Yarrell, Brit Fish (ed. 1), ii, p. 70, c. fig (ed 2), ii, p 121.

Salmo umbla, Jenyns, p 427

Salmo cambricus, Gunther, Proc Zool Soc 1862, p 49, pl vi (not Donovan)

Salmo perisii, Gunther, Ann and Mag Nat Hist 1865, xv, p 75, and Catal vi, p 133, Houghton, British Fresh-water Fishes, p 141, c fig, Day, Brit and Irish Fish ii, p 112, pl. cxix, f 2

Torgoch, Couch, Fish Brit Isles, iv, p 264, pl ccxxiii

Variety WINDERMERE CHAR ‡ Plate IX, fig 2 and 3

Charr of Windermere, Willough 1 c, *Case charr*, Pennant, 1 c and Ray, 1 c

Salmo alpinus, Donovan, Brit. Fish pl. lxi, Turton, Brit Faun, p 104, Fleming, Brit An p 180

---

* While this work was going through the press I received a copy of Dr F A Smith's magnificent monograph on Salmonidæ (*Till kongl Vet Akad* Inlemnad den Jan 14th, 1886), in which the text, the elaborate tables of measurements, and the beautiful plates are worthy of great praise

† D 12-13 $(\frac{3}{54})$ | 0, P 12, V 9, A 11-12 $(\frac{3}{54})$, C 21, L 1 125 135, Vert 61, Cæc pyl 36 This form has moderately-sized teeth, pectoral fin extending more than half way to the base of the ventral It is said to have 170 rows of scales descending to the lateral-line, and to be a smaller form than the char of Windermere Numerous red spots on its sides, belly red in the adult pectoral, ventral and anal fins with white upper and anterior edges *Name—Torgoch* in Welsh signifies *tor*, "a belly," and *goch*, "red" It is said to emerge from the depth of the lakes seeking the shallows for a short period in winter It rises to a fly

‡ D 12-13 $(\frac{11}{10})$ | 0, P 13-14, V 9-10, A 11-12 $(\frac{3}{39})$, C 19, L 1 126, Vert 59-62, Cæc pyl 28-44 *Teeth*—of moderate strength, 4 in each premaxillary, 20 in each maxillary *Fins*—pectoral reaches more than half-way to the root of the ventral *Colours*—sides with red dots belly red pectoral, ventral and anal with white margins *Scales*—from 118 to 128 along the lateral line, and a larger number (180) have been recorded in rows descending to it In an example 7 2 inches long, from Windermere, there were 10 finger marks on the left side and 11 on the right Vertebræ 60 + x, and 13 gill rakers on the outer branch of the lower branchial arch, in the two males figured one had 33, the other 42 cæcal appendages

Salmo umbla, Jenyns, Brit Vert p 427, Thompson, Ann and Mag 1840, vi, p 430

Salmo Willughbii, Gunther, Proc Zool Soc 1862, p 46, pl v, 1863, p 11, and Catal vi, p 131, Day, Brit and Irish Fish ii, p 113, pl cxvii, f 2.

Salmo strivanensis, Gibson-Maitland, Field, Oct 8th, 1881, p 516

Willoughby's char, Couch, Fish Brit Isles, iv, p 262, pl ccxxii

Variety LOCH KILLIN CHAR [*]

Salmo killinensis, Gunther Proc Zool Soc 1865, p 699, pl xl, and Catal vi, p 130, Houghton, Brit Fresh-water Fish p 145, c fig, Day, Brit and Irish Fish ii, p 113, pl cxviii, f 1

[?] *Salmo arcturus*, Gunther, Proc Zool Soc 1877, p 294, pl xxxiii

Variety. GRAYS CHAR [†]

Salmo alpinus, Dubourdieu, Hist Co Antrim, i, p 119, Thompson, Ann Mag Nat Hist 1840, vi, p 448

Salmo umbla, Thompson, 1 c p 439 *(young)* and Nat Hist Ireland, iv, p 160

Salmo Grayi, Gunther, Proc Zool Soc 1862, p 51, pl vii, and 1863, p 12, and Catal Fish Brit Museum, vi, p 136, Houghton, Brit Fresh water Fishes, p 139, c fig, Day, Brit and Irish Fish ii, p 114, pl cxix, f 1.

Gray's char, Couch, Fish Brit Isles, iv, p 267, pl ccxxiv

Variety COLES CHAR [‡]

Salmo Colii, Gunther, Proc Zool Soc 1863, p 12, pl ii, and Catal Fish Brit Mus vi, p 138, Houghton, British Fresh-water Fishes, p 138, c fig, Day, Brit and Irish Fish ii, p 114, pl cxviii, f 2

Coles Charr, Couch, Fish Brit Isles, iv, p 269, pl ccxxv.

B x-xi, D 12-14 ($\frac{3-4}{8-10}$) | 0, P 12-14, V 9-10, A 11-13 ($\frac{3-4}{8-10}$) C. 19-21, L l 125-145, L tr 25-31/30-40, Cæc pyl 28-62, Vert 59-63

* D 14 ($\frac{4}{10}$) | 0, P 13, V 9, A 13 ($\frac{4}{10}$), C 19, L l 135, Vert 62, Cæc pyl 41-52

Length of head 4½, of caudal fin 6¼, height of body 4½ in the total length *Eyes*—diameter about 1/6 of the length of the head, 2 diameters from the end of the snout, and also apart Form of preopercle varies in different specimens, subopercle mostly short and high Maxilla reaches to behind the orbit *Teeth*—small *Fins*—dorsal, pectoral, and ventral well developed *Scales*—Dr Gunther counts 180 rows descending on to the lateral-line, in an example examined there were 135 pierced scales along the lateral-line *Colours*—dark sides with few light spots In some the anterior edges of the lower fins are lightly coloured *S arcturus*, Gunther, the most northern Salmonoid recorded N lat 80° 28′ by 34′ is differentiated from *S killinensis* owing to its being a little more slender ! Malmgren (Ælv Sven Vet Akad Furk 1865 p 534) remarked upon an example of *Salmo alpinus*, 76 millim long, found in a river in Northern Spitzbergen

† D 13-14 ($\frac{2-4}{9-10}$) | 0, P 13-14, V 9, A 12 ($\frac{2}{3}$), C 21, L l 125-140, L tr 31/30, Cæc pyl 37, Vert 60

Lower jaw feeble *Teeth*—small, 4 on each premaxillary and about 16 on each maxillary *Fins*—dorsal commences slightly nearer the snout than in the other forms, the fin being in the centre of the length of the back Pectoral terminates at no great distance from the ventral fins well developed —*Scales*—19 rows from the hind edge of the adipose dorsal fin downwards and forwards to the lateral-line, 25 rows beween the lateral line and the base of the ventral fin 125 to 140 rows along the lateral line *Colours*—sides with orange dots fins with or without a light edge

Thompson observed of the char of Lough Melvin, that " the males are generally more gracefully formed than the females, and most of them are rather brighter in colour, but there is no external character so strikingly different as to lead to a certain knowledge of the sex some of the largest finned are females " They are termed " *fresh water herrings* " in Lough Melvin When cooked the flesh is pale and its taste insipid As to their *breeding* Mr Houghton received some from Lough Melvin in November, the males had not parted with their milt, nor the females with their ova

‡ D 13-14 ($\frac{2-4}{9-10}$) | 0, P 13, V 9, A 12 ($\frac{2}{3}$), C 19, L l 125-128, L tr 31/30 Cæc pyl 42, Vert 63

Teeth—very small, 4 to 6 in each premaxillary 14 to 17 in each maxillary *Fins*—pectoral not reaching nearly to the ventral Ventral and anal fins with a narrow white anterior edge *Scales*—125 rows along the lateral-line, and 160 descending to it 18 rows between the hind edge of the adipose dorsal fin and the lateral-line and 25 from the lateral-line to the base of the ventral fin The form of *S Colii* appears to be principally distinguished from *S Grayi* by the comparative shortness of its pectoral fins It has been recorded from Lough Eske (*Esk or Yesh*, " a fish "), the crater of an extinct volcano, and L Dan

Length of head $4\frac{4}{5}$ to $5\frac{1}{4}$, of caudal fin 6 to $6\frac{1}{2}$, height of body $4\frac{4}{5}$ to $5\frac{1}{2}$ in the total length Eyes—size depends much on age, sex, and nature of locality from whence procured usually situated just in front of the middle of the length of the head, from $1\frac{1}{4}$ to 2 diameters from the end of the snout and the same distance apart In some the comparative height of the body is much greater than in others, and dependant on food, health, and the vicinity of the breeding season, the kelts becoming emaciated The maxilla in some extends to beneath the last third of the orbit, in others to beyond the vertical from its hind margin, while it is likewise slightly more strongly developed in some than it is in others The lower jaw in some varieties, as the torgoch of Wales, may be longer anteriorly than the upper jaw (see p 220 ante) The opercular pieces are of as diverse shapes in the char as described in the trout, and frequently are dissimilar on the opposite sides of the head, while in old males there may be a concavity over the occiput Teeth—present in the jaws and on the head of the vomer, but none along the body of that bone Fins—dorsal usually commences about midway between the end of the snout and the base of the caudal fin, in some examples a little nearer the snout The pectoral and other fins are of varying lengths in accordance with locality, sex, and other varying conditions Scales—small, and a much larger number of rows descending from the back of the lateral-line, than there are of pierced rows along its whole extent Cœcal appendages—these vary considerably, and in a few examples have been found as follows —in Loch Inch 38 (Thompson), L Rannoch, 28, the Lakes, 28-44, Dr Gunther detected from 36 to 52, and the smallest number in those from Windermere, 36 From the same locality I possess examples with 33-42, another with 28, and found the same number in a specimen received from Loch Rannoch as S struanensis It is evident they are as inconstant as in the trout (see pp 199, 216) Colours—these again vary, but as a general rule the belly, prior to spawning, becomes of a scarlet or claret colour, while there are usually some light-coloured orange or red or black spots on the body and head The front edge of the dorsal, ventral and anal, as well as the upper edge of the pectoral, are often of a pure white or orange colour The variation in tints and shades are not so great in char as in trout In some, the ventral, anal, lower portion of the pectoral, and hind edge of the caudal partake of the scarlet colour of the abdomen In three specimens captured for me in Loch Altnagallach, in Sutherlandshire, June 30th, 1886, the belly in all was tinged with yellowish-pink, paired fins with a reddish inner edge, spots on body tinged with red Back, bluish-purple glossed with gold, which faded gradually into the belly, eyes golden One from Windermere had 11 par bands.

Varieties in colour —"By such alone," Dr Gunther observed, "fresh specimens of Salmo salvelinus and S umbla, of S Grayii and S Willoughbii, may be always distinguished," and in his division of the British species into many, he divided it first in accordance with the development of the jaws and size of the teeth, which are inconstant characters He then sub-divided it in respect to the length of the pectoral fins · but here it is evident that the question of sex, locality where hatched and reared, and many other local circumstances, should be taken into consideration I examined eight specimens received from the lakes, and found as follows —All were from $8\frac{1}{2}$ to 9 inches in length, in two the pectoral extended just half the distance to the base of the ventral, and in the remainder $1\frac{2}{5}$, $1\frac{8}{11}$, $1\frac{11}{14}$, $1\frac{8}{9}$, $2\frac{3}{13}$, and $2\frac{1}{4}$ in the interspace, clearly showing that this is not a character on which very great reliance should be placed *

The next subdivision insisted upon was whether the dorsal fin contained 13 or

* Hamilton, History of British Fishes, ii, 1843, p 143, observed that "this pretty and fine flavoured fish is liable to great variation, and this has rendered its synonymy and history somewhat confused It was for a time supposed that the Welsh char was distinct from the char of Cumberland, Westmoreland, and the Scottish lakes, and they have actually been described as separate species by Mr Jenyns Mr Yarrell, too, at one time favoured this view, but a more careful examination has led him to the opinion that all are referrible to one variable species The different states and varieties are known in this country by the names of Case Char, Gilt Char, Red Char, Silver Char, &c " Mr W Kinsey Dover, in his recent Natural History of the Lake District, considered there were two distinct varieties of this fish, one the "silver char," the

14 rays Such an enumeration, however, is evidently open to uncertainty, unless it is taken into consideration and recorded how many undivided and how many branched rays are present (see fig 36, p 163 ante) The first few which are undivided are minute, one or two may even be wanting Thus in the 8 examples from the same locality already referred to, I found from 3 to 4 undivided, and 9 to 10 divided rays in the dorsal fin, and similarly in the anal, 3 to 4 undivided and 8 to 9 divided rays Moreau, in France, finds D $\frac{3-4}{9-10}$, A $\frac{3}{7-8}$ This character, therefore, is not reliable

As to the comparative height of the body, that varies with sex, season, food, and condition, and cannot be otherwise than a very uncertain element in the discrimination of a species

Although the difference in the size of the scales has been held as one of the most constant and important characters in salmonoids, one cannot resist the conclusion that such a belief is founded on error Possibly in no family of fishes are greater variations perceptible in the relative size and number of scales among individuals

In examining numerous examples of *Salmo fontinalis* reared in this country, and counting the pierced scales along the lateral-line, I have found specimens which have from 122 to 142 but it is in the number of irregular rows which descend from the back to the lateral-line where the greatest diversity occurs, while it is here some naturalists count Although in 8 of my British char the difference in the number of pierced scales along the lateral-line does not exceed 20, I find from 185 to 235 rows descending to the lateral-line, or a variation of 50 scales Taking the whole of the reputed British species, the extreme variation recorded is 70 rows If, therefore, among 8 examples of American char received from two localities I can observe a difference in number of at least 50 rows of scales descending from the back to the lateral-line, the extreme variation of 70 among specimens of char obtained throughout the extent of Great Britain and Ireland, appears hardly sufficient ground for instituting distinct specimens Sir W Jardine considered that "the northern, or Sutherland char," has more elongated scales than the "southern char," the scales of which he described as being more orbicular, but having obtained and examined some I do not find such to be the rule

"The char of Hawes Water," observed Dr Davy, "which is known to feed a good deal on insects, is a small and slender fish in comparison with the char of Windermere, which feeds more at the bottom and has a less precarious supply, especially of *Squillæ*, which abound in the lake * The one takes the artificial fly freely, the other —that of Windermere—is rarely so tempted and seldom caught, except by trolling with the minnow In short," he remarked, "so various are they that in no two lakes do they perfectly agree, either in their average size form, colouring, or even in their habits" In examining 8 examples from the above locality I found the following variations —D $\frac{3-4}{7-10}$, A $\frac{4-5}{8-9}$, L l 118-128, Cœc pyl (in three examples) 28-42 The number of rows of scales descending to the lateral-line varied from 166 to 180

Names —*Charre, chars* or *char torgoch,* "red belly " (Wales) *Gally-trout* "red bellied trout" (Windermere, Lochleven, &c), while it is also termed at the latter place *gelly-troch trout* (Lochleven Angler), which is said to signify a black leech which abounds in this loch and upon which it feeds *Red-wame,* Scotland *Tarr-dheary* and *dearg-bhlian* (Gaelic in the Highlands of Scotland) *Murneen* in Galway and the loughs of Mayo in Ireland (Wilde) *L'ombre chevalier,* French

In olden times that three sons of the Church introduced these fishes into Wales from Rome, and placed two in each of the lakes of Llanberris, Llynumba, and Trevennyn While those in Windermere and

other the "gilt char " the former keeping chiefly to the upper part of the lake above Bowness Continuing, "Mr Braithwaite, of Kendal, who has recently published a treatise on the Salmonidæ of Westmorland, has informed me that he believes in only one species existing in Windermere Lake" (p 13)

* Finding the stomach of the char figured in plate ix rather hard, I opened it, but only found two stones which measured as follows in inches, 0 3×0 3×0 2 and 0 2×0 2×0 1.

Coniston, then termed Thurston Water, were similarly ascribed to the monks of Furness Abbey, who were said to have brought them from near the Alps But as this legend attributed their introduction to only about two centuries since, we are met by a statement which was made three or four years ago of the discovery of a MS bearing date A D 1535, wherein a certain Jacques Tallour was permitted "to catch and tol the fayre fish char in Wynandermer, and also hys sonne Gerald," but we have no evidence of the genuineness of the document However, Isaak Walton, in 1653, mentioned the existence of char in Winander Mere, and did not refer to it as being of any recent introduction

Habits—A gregarious and usually deep swimming fish, but in warm weather coming nearer to the surface, they are mostly shy of taking a bait and feed largely at night-time The common food of the trout has been found in their stomachs, while when in confinement they can be similarly fed They appear to require very pure and mostly deep water for their residence, but are found in some Irish lakes which are not of great depth They feed upon aquatic insects and fish, and appear to be most lively during the night-time

They have been observed to have disappeared from some lakes due to the entrance therein of poisonous matter, as from lead mines,* but in other localities where no such deleterious substances have obtained access, as Loch Leven, and some of the Irish loughs, where they have likewise disappeared, it has been suggested that such may partly be dependent upon the diminution or disappearance of such eutomostraca as previously formed their natural food When half or full grown they do not bear confinement well,† but may be kept for a short period in troughs through which a supply of water flows Thompson, in 1835, observed that they were thus kept at Coniston Water at the hotel and sold at 10s a dozen

O, in *Loudon's Mag Nat Hist* v, p 317, observed of the Windermere fish that "about the beginning of April, when the warm weather comes in, they retire into the deep parts of the lake, where their principal food is the minnow, of which they are very fond," while they are captured with spinning bait

As food—The flesh of these fishes varies, in some localities it is pink in colour,

---

* It has been stated to descend to the sea, and it has been asserted that some were captured there or at the mouths of rivers on the Welsh coast after they had been driven out of Llanberris by poisoned waters Further evidence on this point is required

† Yarrell asserted that in the autumn of 1839 several char of some half pound weight each were placed in Lily Mere, a secluded sheet of water not far from Sedburgh in Yorkshire, and the property of the Uptons, of Ingmire Hall It was further said that some twelve months later two of these fish, weighing 2 lb each, were caught with the fly, admirably fed and well shaped, in the pink of condition They were served at the Queen Dowager's table at the Rose and Crown Hotel, Ky Lonsdale, where doubtless Her Majesty was staying A writer in *The Field* remarked that "the story may be true or not Lily Mere, from its small size and general surroundings, is not a likely place in which char would grow to so very unusual a size in so short a time Probably the so called char were nothing else than two fine trout with which the mere was then well stocked, and is so in a lesser degree at the present day."

‡ "Some years ago a number of char were placed in Potter Fell Tarn, some four miles from Kendal, a sheet of water situate at a great height above the sea level, and abounding with trout. Occasionally a char or two were caught with the fly, and rigorously returned to the water But they made no headway, and Mr Banks, the owner, tells me that not one has been caught for some years However, a strange occurrence following this attempt at acclimatization did take place Some twelve months after the fish were placed in the tarn, an angler, below Burneside, on the Kent, took from the river, with fly, a nice char of half a pound weight No doubt this was an escaped fish from the Potter Fell, and there is a narrow mountain beck which runs direct from that tarn into the Kent There was no mistaking the identity of the fish, for it was brought to Kendal alive, given to Mr Banks, who returned it in due course to the place from which it had strayed, quite two miles away The fact of this fish taking an artificial fly in a stream suggests that the char might thrive if introduced into some of our rivers There is no proof that it is destructive to other fish, and though its nature is that of a bottom or at least a mid water feeder, the instances of Hawes Water, Goats Water, and of this one in the Kent, are presumptive proof that, with altered conditions, the char adapts itself to circumstances, and feeds freely at the surface of the water The fact is, both trout and char 'feed' where they find the choicest morsels, and these so-called 'bad rising' trout in certain lakes are only such because their epicurean tastes are better suited by the food found below the surface In other instances than the one mentioned are char caught by rod and line in the streams flowing into or out of the various lakes they inhabit, and though usually, not always, stray specimens, still they afford proof of the possibility of the race becoming settled inhabitants of at least some of our rivers" (R. B. L, *Field*)

16

in others white at the lakes they are in the greatest perfection from July until October while in Sutherlandshire they are said to be in best condition during June and July (*Reports British Association*, 1834), and I have found them in that county at this time with a tinge of orange all over the abdomen In the lake district those from Windermere are most prized, while in Hawes Water and Goats Water they are small, in poor condition, and generally of inferior flavour Potted char has been held in great esteem from very early times, and a writer in *The Field*, October 6th, 1883, remarked upon having come across a reference to it in one of the earliest *Gazetteers* ever published in England It is a small duodecimo entitled *An Historical Dictionary of England and Wales*, published anonymously in London A D 1692 * As they soon lose their delicate flavour after removal from the water they are potted and thus considered a great delicacy They should be simply fried if fresh caught

Migrations —These may be simply from deep to shallow water at different periods of the year, or they may be undertaken at the breeding season to reach suitable spots, or these fish may disappear from one place where they had been planted, apparently owing to the unsuitability of the locality

If we investigate the history of the Lochleven char we find materials at hand on this subject respecting these fishes which are interesting Commencing with Sibbald in his *Scotia Illustrata*, 1684 he observed among the loch fish "Salmerinus, An Trutta parenchymate rubro, the *Red Trout?*" and in his *History of Kinross-shire* 1710, he referred to "the gelletroch or red-womb trout it hath a small head, it is usually eighteen inches long The speckled trout red-womb with white fins, taken in October with nets—some are reddish within, some whitish" Pennant, *Tour in Scotland*, 1775 observing of Lochleven, "the fishermen gave me an account of a species they called the *Gally* Trout, which are only caught from *October* to *January*, are split, salted and dried, for winter provision by the description, they certainly were our char, only of a larger size than any we have in *England* or *Wales* some being two feet and a half long " (p 69) In Mr R Burns Begg's *Lochleven Angler* (1874), it was remarked that "char seems to have been by no means uncommon about the commencement of the present century, and several of the witnesses (before Professor Fleming and the sheriff and jury) referred to them as having been regularly taken in considerable numbers with the net The Rev Mr Smith, who towards the close of the last century officiated as minister of the parish of Kinross for upwards of twenty years, thus referred to it in his *History of Kinross-shire*, 1793, "The gally-trough or char abound in the loch What is remarkable of them is the size to which they often grow, some of them weighing near 2 lb, and they are never known to rise to a fly or to be caught with a hook baited in any way whatever " The weight here stated by Mr Smith being the 'old pound ' is equal to nearly three modern pounds ' From some cause, which has never been satisfactorily ascertained, the char has for a considerable number of years entirely disappeared from Loch Leven, not a single specimen having been caught either with rod or net for upwards of thirty years The very 'last of the race ' is believed to have been caught with the net in the latter part of the season of 1837 at 'the Old House set,' near the present Kinross House Pier" (pp 23 24)

I have already referred (p 218 *ante*) how in 1830, by a system of drainage, the depth of Loch Leven was reduced four feet and a half, and that the last of the chars was captured in 1837 But even in 1833 an old fisherman, Peter Whyte,

---

* The same writer gave the following receipt for potting these fishes —"Do not wash but only wipe the fish with a moist cloth Get a sieve basket similar to those used to convey fruit to market Place the fish in it layer upon layer, sprinkling, as you proceed with the packing, coarse salt between each layer They must not be packed tight, so as to allow the brine to run off Leave them so for a couple of days or less, according to taste, some palates preferring pungency, others mildness Then take the fish out of the basket, wipe them, take off the heads, and extract the entrails Re pack them loosely in layers, applying spice and bay leaves to taste, in a pan or some other baking utensil Cover the top over with plenty of fresh butter put the pan in a moderately heated oven, and bake for two hours Finally, take out the pan, drain off the surplus grease, and, having provided some clarified butter, conclude the process by potting the fish Thus you have a dish fit to set before a king "

asserted that these fish were scarcely to be found, but continued that this had happened before, and his father had told him that they had been absent for seven years at a time Although it has been observed that they never were very plentiful in Loch Leven, we have James M'Gill's evidence that he had seen two half-boll sacks filled with char caught by poachers during the spawning season in the North Queich between Lethangie and Lathro

It would seem to be by no means unlikely that three causes have been at work to destroy these fishes from Loch Leven (1) indiscriminate slaughter, especially during the spawning season, (2) decrease in the depth of the water of the lake following the drainage works, and (3) diminution of food occasioned by the drying up of the margins of the loch where snails and other suitable nourishment was previously in abundance

Means of capture—Char are not so sporting a fish as trout, being more nocturnal in their habits and living in deeper waters But in some localities they are found feeding at the surface and taking artificial flies* or other lures † In Windermere they are netted in deep water, *cubbles* being the name applied to these fisheries ‡ R B L in *The Field* (January 22nd, 1887), observed—"All the earlier fish appearing in the markets are so taken, but as the weather becomes milder (say towards Whitsuntide), the nets are used in a different manner, so manipulated as to fish in mid-water only, the char having now come nearer the surface But by far the most important and interesting means of taking char here is by means of the plumb-line (*see* p 235 *ante*) The baits usually used are artificial, pieces of metal silvered on one side, copper, red, green, or brown on the other, spinning from either the head or tail Minnows can be used in the same way, spoon baits too, and both the blue Phantom and Garnet-quill minnows have been tried successfully Still the natives prefer the metal baits, and the sizes used for ordinary trout are of course the correct ones Usually two such lines as the above are worked by each boat, and the fisherman shows considerable skill in his manipulation of them and rowing his craft along at a proper speed at the same time—the latter is just sufficient to keep the baits spinning and the tackle taut The boatman knows the ground char frequent, and the nature of the bottom too, for should he come upon rocks and weeds his tackle gets entangled, and a big smash must almost inevitably result In Coniston Water, Bassenthwaite, Ennerdale, &c, this fish is taken by similar means, but in smaller quantities In Hawes Water and Goats Water, as already stated, it rises to the fly pretty freely, but it is seldom caught in any other north of England lake, excepting by nets and with the plumb-line In the lake of Llanberis, where char are likewise fairly numerous, they are usually taken in nets, as they are in Lough Esk (co Donegal) and in many other waters In *The Field* of August 6th, 1883, a description of a night's char fishing appears, the correspondent using worms as bait He appears to have had good sport, fishing from a boat, using two hooks properly baited about half a yard apart Many years ago char were taken in the English lake district both with worm and salmon roe, but this was when they were spawning I believe that the char rising best to the fly in Scotland are those of Loch Doon, in Ayrshire, but they also take fly fairly freely in Loch Knockie, Inverness, during October, in the Tarff, Kirkcudbright, also late

---

* Mr Bantock, *Lochs and Rivers of Sutherland*, observed "char abound in scores of the Sutherland lochs, but they are very rare risers to the fly, and have never been taken by any other lure"

† R B L likewise observed that "some thirty years or so ago most of the char fishing on Windermere, &c, was done by means of the 'otter' or 'lath,' as it was locally called Both flies and spinning baits, natural and artificial, were attached to the line, but, the fish being near the surface only during the summer months, such mode of fishing had but a short season It will be between forty and fifty years ago since a Mr Spencer, from Manchester, first introduced the plumb-line into the Lake district, no doubt his method being an adaptation from the one used in mackerel and some other sea fishing Mr Spencer, a capital angler himself, had the best of tackle, and contrived to kill large quantities of char, his success, season after season, speedily induced imitators, and the plumb-line did not take long to become established"

‡ Fraser, *On the Salmon, &c*, 1833, p 71, remarked, "I find that last season a man having a blaze of fir broom or heather in the left hand and a hoop or peck-net in the right, could fish up as many (char) as a net can do"

16 *

in the season, in Corry Lau, and in Lochs Ericht and Fruchie Borley Loch, in Sutherlandshire, is noted because it contains no other fish than smallish char, and in Loch Doule, it is said, this fish sometimes attains the unusual weight of $2\frac{1}{2}$ lb In some of the Irish loughs char have been caught by anglers when salmon fishing with fly, and a specimen so taken from Lough Conn in 1867 was the means of determining that char were present in that water A similar remark applies to a char caught in Lough Inagh about twelve years later, and a writer in No 504 of *The Field* says in Lough Moy they are caught both in nets and on night lines, and in the same paper of December 25th last, a correspondent writes of having killed char with fly in loughs Ennel and Owel, Westmeath, Glendalough, Derry, Clare and in Connemara, and Cuilane at Ballinahinch "

Breeding —That char may be annual breeders was shown at Howietoun where a Loch Rannoch male was successively employed for this purpose in the season of 1882, and again in 1883, but it died prior to the season of 1884 The time of breeding is from* about November to February or March At this time, at least in Windermere, their colours and spots are more intense, the mouth and fins become of a dark yellow or orange, and they are covered with a thick slime These fish form a redd similar to salmon or trout †

Davy observed that the char more commonly avoids than seeks running water for the purpose of breeding, and that the gravelly and rocky shoals of the lakes it inhabits are its favourite breeding localities, rather than the bed of a river or brook where the water is in rapid motion (*Physiological Researches*, p 272) Artificially changing the water duly has been found sufficient in order to hatch the eggs of these fish He also tried two lots of young char from January 31st to April 1st, one brood in its globe was shut up in a dark cupboard, and only taken out for a minute or two daily to change the water and give food The second was kept in the light, but no difference in size could be perceived

The following is an extract from *The Field* (March 29th, 1884), of an account

---

* "The remarkable fact is reported from Transtein, in Bavaria, of a number of char (*Salmo salvelinus*) having been captured from the large char species kept in the Koenigsee, near Berchtesgaden, which, upon examination, had been found ready for spawning About seventy six of these fish varying in weight from 6 lb to 14 lb, have been caught towards the latter part of June, and during the months of July and August, upon all of which, spawners and milters, the signs of immediate spawning were clearly observed The usual spawning season of the char, according to the classification of the *Salmonidæ*, being October and November, leads to the question whether there exist now two species of char, and how the spawning in Midsummer of some of them can be explained The German *Fishing Gazette* states that the ova derived from the giant char fish lately caught, have been sent to the fish-hatching establishments of Saint Bartholomae, after the young fry acquired from the ova of the char during the spawning season of November and December last, had been first removed The hatching of the ova from the summer spawning is proceeding quite satisfactorily at St Bartholomae and Transtein" A writer in *London's Magazine of Nat Hist*, 1832 v, p 316 (signing himself O), stated, "Windermere is fed by two streams, which unite at the head of the lake, named the Brathy and the Rothay, the bottom of the former is rocky, and that of the latter sandy On the first sharp weather which occurs in November, the char makes up the Brathy in large shoals for the purpose of spawning, preferring that river to the Rothay, probably owing to the bottom being rocky, and resembling more the bottom of the lake, and it is singular that those fish which ascend the Rothay, invariably return and spawn in the Brathy, they remain in this stream and in the shallow parts of the lake until the end of March " Mr Braithwaite, *Salmonidæ of Westmoreland*, 1884, p 7, observed of the "gilt char" and "case char," ' it is well known that they spawn at different periods between the end of September and beginning of March " (p 7)

† Mr C I Jackson, *Land and Water*, August 14th, 1884, observed, " I have seen salmon on the redd, but could not say distinctly how they were working Lately, however, I had a very good chance of watching char in one of the Southport Aquarium tanks—a far better opportunity than can possibly be afforded by looking down upon a fish in a river We obtained a fine shoal of char from Windermere at the opening of the season this year Soon after they came, I saw one of them had not spawned, and was busy making its nest Its *modus operandi* was exactly as described by Mr Buckland It swam slowly down towards the selected place as though concentrating its energies, when it arrived over the spot, it threw itself partially on its side, and dropping the hind part of the body, it gave several violent blows (three or four) with its tail, scattering the gravel right and left The impetus of the blows not only scattered the gravel, but drove the fish upwards in a slanting direction Quietly allowing the force to expend itself, it then turned round, swam slowly back, and repeated the process time after time, until it had made quite a large hole."

of a visit paid by Dr Leitch, of Keswick, in 1850, to inspect the "Char Dub," as
it is called, in the river Liza —"We went down the pastures by the little river
side, circled by the grand snowy mountains, the pillar, the steeple, red pike, and
the dark walls of abrupt high land that shut in the gleaming steel mirror of
Ennerdale lake About three hundred yards above the lake, where a stone wall
runs down to the river Liza, is a long 'dub' or pool, one part of which is very
deep This is the famous 'Ennerdale Char Dub' The fish had not yet gone
down (the 25th of November), and we saw the bottom of the pool blackened with
them Many thousands certainly were there, and in a proper light the gleam and
twinkle of their multitudinous white-edged fins was a pretty and singular
spectacle As they refused the rod rag fastened, for want of hooks, to a pin, and
with a thread flung by means of a fishing rod into the midst of them, we took
means to drive them downward, and by-and-by procured two or three for the
artist (Mr Pettitt), who had remained at Buttermere to paint one of the char of
that lake Small as they looked in the water, they yet were occasionally as large
as the Buttermere char One or two were about eight ounces, king fish, most resplen-
dently coloured, red and gold bellied, fins with a pink shade in the centre, shaded
into a brown ash hue, and edged with pearl colour, as they lay on the grass fresh
from the stream—a most brilliant and elegant creature, wanting, however, the
regular white spots, 'bediopt in hail,' which add so much to the beauty of the
Buttermere char On only one fine king fish I observed some dusky red spots
below the median line Their form is more like that of the Welsh than Crummock
char, not so rounded in the outline The rennal or she fish, were much smaller
and poorer in colour than those of Buttermere, their were of an ashy, greenish
hue, almost the colour of the robin redbreast's back, deepened by dark shadowy
marks They seemed almost all to have finished spawning, and, no doubt, in a few
days will descend to the lake In that dub must be deposited millions of ova,
and it perhaps might be worth the while of the owner to preserve them by means
of a dam, or temporary breakwater of any kind above, from being washed out of
the 'ruds' by floods, while a grating placed below might keep away pike or other
fish likely to swallow the ova or young before they reach the lake "

Diseases and causes of destruction—These are similar to what are perceived in
trout, except that it seems to be a more delicate fish and requires deeper water,
as will be referred to under the American char, *Salmo fontinalis* Ullswater,
forty years ago, was the best angling lake in the north of England From the
middle of April to the middle of September, unless the elements were decidedly
adverse, the angler might be sure of a fair basket, either with the fly or with the
minnow Then the fishing became very bad about 1860 For many years prior
to 1860 the Glenridding mines were worked without producing any striking injury
to the fish, except to char, which, according to the best evidence attainable,
spawned principally in Glenridding Beck About 1860 a weir was placed across
the Eamont, a little above its junction with the Lowther Trout used to descend
the Eamont in order to spawn in the Dacre and Lowther This weir prevented
those which went up the Lowther returning, and it was noticed that after that
period the trout in that river increased rapidly About this time an increase from
the lead mines of twenty-five per cent of *debris*, crushed and pounded rock, was
discharged into the lake Dead skellies, rarely seen, were after this often found
on the shore and char appear to be extinct

Habitat—In Norway the red char lives from a sea level up to 600 metres
above it in the S E portions of the country it is rare, in West Norway more
common and captured in large numbers with a fly Its flavour varies as greatly
as does that of the trout, and it appears to thrive best in lakes where the temperature is somewhat uniform, without bottom springs and not having too large
an amount of brook-water flowing in It extends to Great Britain and Ireland,
France, Southern Germany, and in the clear lakes of the Alps of Upper Austria,
Tyrol, Bavaria, Switzerland, also in the Carpathian lakes up to 6000 feet above
the sea

The Orkneys, at Hoy and Hellier, also being occasionally captured in Loch
Stennes, and three were obtained in Waas, in 1832 (W Baikie) also from North

Uist in the Hebrides   Examples from Sutherlandshire are in the British Museum, while Mr J Harvie-Brown informs me that there is a char loch about twenty-five miles from Durness, on Ben Hope, where they are taken up to $1\frac{1}{2}$ lb weight   At Midsummer they are only known to rise at one part of the loch, on its S E side, between the exit of the stream and the island, Druck Doon (Ayrshire)   In September numbers are taken with both worm and fly   Mr Bantock says that char abound in scores of the Sutherlandshire lochs, and mentions the one referred to on Ben Hope, and another small loch (Borley) near the Manse at Durness   they are also found in the upper end of Loch Assynt, Loch Altnagillach, and another near Oykell   Thompson recorded their existence and obtained specimens from Loch Corr, Loch Moy, and Loch Killin, Inverness-shire, Loch Tay and Dochart, in Perthshire   Sir J Gibson-Maitland has taken them in Loch Rannoch, they are also recorded from Loch Ericht   Pennant reported their occurrence in Loch Inch, Wigtownshire, and Thompson in Loch Giannoch, Kirkcudbrightshire   Also an example from Loch Biuiach is in the national collection   Black, 1844, observed that this fish had of late years disappeared from Loch Leven

In England the lake districts of Cumberland, Northumberland, and part of Lancashire, more especially in Windermere Keswick, Crummoch Water, Buttermere, Ennerdale, Coniston Water, Bassenthwaite lake, West Water, Hawes Water, and occasionally one is now found in Ullswater, the area where char do or did frequent was estimated at 35,320 acres   Windermere, we are informed (1878), is very productive, while in Coniston the fish have been poisoned by the mines, they are also found in Rydal   In Windermere they are somewhat restricted to the deep waters, and spawn in the River Brathay, avoiding the Rothay, which is more frequented by trout

In North Wales* this fish is still found near Snowdon, in the Lakes of Llanberris, Llyn Cawellyn, Llyn Coss-y-gedawl, Bala and Bettew Festiniog in Merionethshire

In Ireland   In the county of Donegal it has been taken in Lough Esk (Camden), also from near Dunfanaghy, probably Lough Sessagh, where they are still found (Templeton), L Gartan, L Kindun, L Shessuch, L Keel (Thompson), and L Derg (*Field*, June, 1879), L Elvyn (Couch), and Lough Veagh while many of the Donegal loughs which have no appearance of a glacial origin, and in some cases, as in the small bog loughs of Innishowen, they are nowhere deep (Ogilby)   In Antrim from L Neagh (Dubourdieu)   Thompson visited this place in 1834, and was informed that none had been captured for the last ten years, although twenty years previously they had been abundant   An old fisherman explained the reason as follows —"That they once went down the River Bann to the sea and never came back again"   In Monaghan at Lough Eaglish (incorrectly spelt Esk) according to Templeton, who stated they had become very rare and were all but extinct   In Fermanagh at Lough Melvin and L Erne (Thompson), Westmeath in Belvidere Lake (Ball), loughs Eunel and Owel, county of Cavan in Drumlane Lake (Thompson), in county of Mayo, Castlebar (Daniel) and Lough Conn, county of Galway in Lough Corrib, and L Bofin (Thompson), Longford at Lough Nabrach (Ball), Connemara in Lough Ourad (Davy), and Lough Inagh; Wicklow in Lough Dan (Thompson) and L Lada (Couch), Waterford in four mountain lakes (Smith), Lough Currane, County of Kerry, and at Inchigeelagh in the county of Cork (Vyse), Loughs Mindorm and Minteagh of Innishowen (Ogilby)

These fish usually average about 6 or 4 to a pound, or in the best water about six ounces each   but they have been captured in the lake district from $1\frac{1}{2}$ to over 2 lb and elsewhere been obtained heavier

The figures in plate IX are both from Windermere char captured at the same time, March 31st, 1887   No 2 is a male 12 inches long, with 33 cæcal appendages, and nineteen rows of scales between the base of the adipose dorsal fin and the lateral-line   No 3 is likewise a male 11 3 inches long, with 42 cæcal appendages

* It is rare to find char in Wales in situations under 1500 feet in altitude

2. American char, or Salmo fontinalis, Plate IX, fig 1 (*Male*)

Salmo fontinalis,* Mitchell, Trans Lit and Phil Soc New York, 1814, 1, p 435 Richards Faun Bor-Amer iii, p 176, pl lxxxiii, f 1 and pl lxxxvii, f 2 (head), Storer, Report Fish Mass p 106, Kirtl Report, Zool Ohio, p 169, and Boston Journ Nat Hist 1843, pt iv, p 305, pl xiv, f 2, DeKay, Fauna New York Fish p 235 pl xxxviii, f 120, Ayres, Boston Journ Nat Hist iv, 1843, p 273, Cuv and Val xxi, p 266, Bingelow, Bost Journ Nat Hist vi, 1850, p 49, Gunther, Catal vi p 152, Day, Brit and Irish Fish, ii, p 119, pl cxx, f 1, 2

    Salmo hoodii, Richards l c iii, p 173, desc part (spec from River Mingan)

    Salmo nigrescens, Rafin Ichth Ohiens p 45

    Baione fontinalis and *erythrogaster*, DeKay, Faun New York Fish pp 236, 244, pl xx, f 58 and pl xxix, f 126

    American char, American trout, Fontinalis and in American works as *red-spotted trout, speckled trout, spotted troutlet brook trout, common brook trout*

B x–xi, D 12-13 $\left(\frac{3-4}{9-10}\right)$ | 0, P 12-13, V 8-9, A 10-11 $\left(\frac{3-4}{7-9}\right)$, C 19 L l 122-140, L tr 36-50/51-63, Cæc pyl 25-40, Vert 57-62

Length of head $4\frac{1}{4}$ to $5\frac{2}{3}$ ($4\frac{1}{3}$ in a male), of caudal fin $6\frac{1}{4}$, height of body $4\frac{2}{3}$ to 5 in the total length   *Eyes*—in anterior half of head in adults—diameter of each from $4\frac{1}{4}$ to 5 or $5\frac{1}{2}$ in the length of the head, 1 to $1\frac{1}{2}$ diameters from the end of the snout, and from 1 to $1\frac{3}{4}$ apart   Hind edge of preopercle regularly curved and with a very short but distinct lower limb   Height of opercle equals twice its greatest width, height of subopercle equals half the length of its lower edge which, with its hind margin, forms a regular curve   The form of the various opercular pieces in these fishes is liable to great variation, frequently due to an apparent arrest of development, this is also seen at Howietoun among examples which have had gill-fever in their infancy, and is considered to be one of its results   In one example the subopercle differs on the two sides of the same fish   The maxilla reaches to beneath the hind edge of the eye, or even a little beyond   *Teeth*—about six in a triangular band on the hind edge of the head of the vomer, but none along its body   Those in the jaws rather stronger than seen in brook trout of similar size   The head of the vomer extends more than half-way along the body of that bone, and posteriorly becomes somewhat blunted with age (*see* fig 51)   *Fins*—the rayed dorsal commences slightly nearer to the end of the snout than to the base of the caudal fin   its third or fourth ray is the longest and somewhat exceeds the length of the base of the fin   ten branched rays, the last being divided its base, are not rare   Pectoral extends about half-way (in some examples more in others less) to the base of the ventral, which latter is inserted below the centre of the rayed dorsal fin, laid flat it does not quite reach the vent in young fish, nor nearly so in adults   Caudal forked in the young, but becoming square with age, similar to what takes place in the trout.   *Scales*—40 to 49 rows from the lateral-line to the base of the ventral fin   21 to 26 rows from the hind edge of the base of the adipose dorsal fin downwards and forwards to the lateral-line, from 185 to 235

---

* In the following pages I omit the consideration of several forms which have received names in the United States, as being scarcely subjects of sufficient interest in a popular work in this country, also, as to whether the American great lake trout, *Salmo namaycush*, and its several varieties, is or is not identical with, or very closely allied to, the *S fontinalis*, as such will have to be proved or disproved by the fish-culturists who are able to obtain these eggs from the former fish residing in its native home   Dr Gunther divided *S namaycush*, "Catal Fish Brit Mus" vi, 1866, pp x and 123, as a true trout with teeth along the body of the vomer, from *S fontinalis*, l c pp x and 152, as a char, with teeth on the head of the vomer only   Again, in his "Introduction to the study of Fishes," 1880, pp 645, 646, he reiterates this, although in the intermediate period the error had been clearly exposed   Among various other erroneous statements, this mistake of Dr Gunther's has been reproduced by the compiler of the remarkable article *Salmonidæ*, in the present edition of the *Encyclopedia Britannica*

rows pass from the back to the lateral-line   *Colours*—greenish along the back,
becoming lighter on the sides and beneath, the whole being beautifully shot with
purple and gold   Numerous round or oval spots along the back becoming fewer
below the lateral-line , anteriorly from the head to the dorsal fin many coalesce
Red spots above, on, and sometimes below the lateral-line   White edges with
black bases to the upper margin of the pectoral and the anterior edges of the
ventral and anal fins   Sinuous bands of black or rings on the dorsal fin the upper
and lower edges of the caudal barred   During the breeding season the male is
black along the centre of the belly, and on turning the fish wrong side up this
appears like a black central band (interrupted by the yellow margins of the
ventral and anal fins) with a brilliant yellow one along either side of it   In some
the sinuous lines of the back merely extend half-way down to the lateral-line
The female is rather more green, the sides lighter, and it is usually more spotted
In the month of May, 1887, I was at the South Kensington Museum, and Mr Eden
showed me some of these fish kept in darkish tanks   They were of a lovely
greenish purple, with two or three rows of small but intensely scarlet spots below
the lateral line the bands over the back were not well seen, but the parr marks were
distinct in nearly all   They were three-year-olds and well grown   One male was
so pugnacious that he had to be confined in a separate aquarium   In these tanks
the water was kept clean and a tussock of grass with its roots put in every third
day.*   The number of parr bands in the young at Howietoun vary between seven
and eleven or twelve, but in some specimens they are much broken up—in others,
those on the lower half of the body are intermediate between the lower ends of
those of the upper half of the body

When the New England States were first peopled from Britain this fish was
called a "trout," for but few of the early emigrants could have had an opportunity of observing a "char," and they gave it the name that most nearly
reminded them of a form which existed in the mother-country

Mitchell, who first described it scientifically in 1814, remarked that this fish
"lived in running waters only, and not in stagnant ponds, and therefore the
lively streams descending north and south from their sources in Long Island
exactly suit the constitution of this fish   The heaviest Long Island trout that I
heard of weighed 4½ lb "

Mr Perley, *Catalogue of the Fishes of New Brunswick and Nova Scotia*, 1851,
considered "that there is but one distinct species of the brook trout in North
America "

Without following out the various and interesting accounts which have been
given of the *Salmo fontinalis* in the United States and Canada, I propose to offer
a brief synopsis of Mr Brown-Goode's excellent report on the subject in
Scribner's *Game Fishes of the United States*   It has its home between latitudes
32½° and 55° in the lakes and streams of the Atlantic watershed, near the
sources of a few rivers flowing into the Mississippi and the Gulf of Mexico, and
in some of the southern affluents of Hudson's Bay   Its range is limited by the
western foothills of the Alleghanies, and nowhere extends more than three
hundred miles from the coast, except about the Great Lakes in the northern
tributaries of which trout abound   At the south they inhabit the headwaters of
the Chattahoochee in the southern spurs of the Georgia Alleghanies, and
tributaries of the Catawba in North Carolina   They also occur in the Great
Islands in the Gulf of St Laurence, Anticosti, Prince Edward's, Cape Breton,
and Newfoundland   They do not appear able to thrive in water warmer than
68° Fahr , although they have been known to live in swift running water at
75°   With water below 36° they are torpid and refuse to feed   The identity of
the Canadian Sea Trout and the Brook Trout has been settled beyond a doubt
There are many variations and local races of these fish, the same stream often

---

* Livingston Stone, *Domesticated Trout*, ed 2, p 296, observed, respecting this fish, that " if
you want to make the colours of trout deep and dark, grow them over a black muddy bottom, well
shaded   If you want to cultivate light and delicate tints, grow the trout on a light, open, gravelly
bed "   Also, as to *shape*—" If you wish to have trout short and deep, grow them in a deep still
pond   If you want to have them long and slim, grow them in a shallow swift current "

contains dissimilar forms and those bred in different hatcheries may easily be distinguished

The same author observed that the Lake Trout or Salmon-Trout, *Salmo namaycush*, inhabiting the chain of Great Lakes from Superior to Ontario, as well as Lake Champlain and many other smaller lakes of the United States and of British America, has as its nearest relative the *S fontinalis*   The Lake Trout appears to have undergone modifications, being a char not land-locked, but placed under conditions directly opposite to those connected with those which are land-locked   It would perhaps seem like a hasty generalization to point to *S fontinalis* as the form from which the Lake Trout has been developed, but one may fairly take into consideration the fact that this species alone, of all the group of *Salmo*, is usually associated with *S namaycush*   Professor Brown-Goode considers that "the popular and scientific names which have been given to this species are due to the wonderful tendency of variation in size, shape, and colouration, which this species, like the Brook Trout, exhibits   Every lake in which they occur has its own varieties, which local authorities believe to be quite peculiar   Some are black, some brown with crimson spots, some gray with delicate reticulations like those of a pickerel"

The fontinalis has been introduced from America into this country, and Frank Buckland, *Land and Water*, 1871, among other fish remarked, "American brook trout brought over by Mr Parnaby, of Troutdale Fishery, Keswick," also in his *Natural History of British Fishes*, 1880, p 345, he remarked, "The first specimens ever seen in this country were sent to me beautifully packed with moss in tin boxes, by some friends in America.   The parent fish were obtained from Lake Huron, in Canada   Since that time the import of eggs of fontinalis has become a regular business," and Livingston-Stone observed that in 1868,[*] "one lot was sent to England to Mr Frank Buckland, and was favourably noticed in the London *Times*" (p 311)

Varieties —DeKay, *Natural History of New York*, asserted that there were two distinct species, *Salmo fontinalis* and *S erythrogaster*, the first without, the second with red spots   A local observer remarked that in its native habitat, it "affects every forest pond, with its 'runs,' affluent brooks and larger rivers, presenting a large series of varieties in colouring, with, however, certain prominent marks by which they are always referable to one species   In the deeper parts of large lakes, it has for company two other species—*S confinis* and *S amethystus*, both much larger fish, *S confinis* attaining a weight of 20 lb   Both are coarse fish and bottom feeders," and General Hardy, *Land and Water*, November 23rd, 1885, observed that "of course, it is subject to variation in the brooks, rivers, and lakes of its extensive range (I have known lakes, separated by a narrow ridge of a few yards wide, containing trout so different in colouring and shape as to cause an impression of existing specific difference) '

"Fish inhabiting swift streams have lithe trim bodies and long powerful fins, those in the quiet lakes are stout, short-finned, and often overgrown   In cool, limpid brooks, with sunlight, much oxygen and stimulating food their skins are transparent and their hues vivid   in dark, sluggish pools they are sombre and slimy and are called black trout" (*Brown-Goode, Nat Hist Aquat Animals*, p 500)

"Mic-Mac" writing from Boston, in *The Field*, April 22nd, 1882, observed, "One word with regard to our white trout   They certainly are not identical with the white trout of the Irish lakes   There has been a great deal of discussion and disagreement on the subject of this fish, but at the present date the best authorities seem to agree that the sea trout of the provinces is simply a *Salmo fontinalis* that has emigrated into salt water, and changed its colour by that means   Anatomically they are identical with, externally they are very different from, a river fish—so much so that the veriest tyro will, after a day's fishing, be able to

---

[*] Mr Parker Gillmore, *Times*, October 28th, 1885, claimed to have been the first who proposed the introduction of this fish into our waters in 1866-67, and at the termination of the latter year went to America, collected and shipped them to this country (that would have been in 1868), for which he had not only been left a pecuniary loser, but also that he had never been credited with his work

tell at a glance a river from a sea trout   In the early summer or late spring they
appear on the coast of Nova Scotia, New Brunswick, and the province of Quebec,
running up the St Lawrence in countless myriad   Into every 'gully' and mouths
of every river or good-sized brook they crowd, so that I have known of a man
standing on the sand beach of the gully at Pokemouche, with a red hackle,
taking them just as fast as he could land them and re-cast   They run quite
even in size, from 1 lb up to 3 lb, or more, but averaging about 1½ lb to 2 lb
They are bright and silvery, showing some red spots, but rarely any blue,
and their flesh is deep red and very fine flavoured   The motive for this
appearance of the schools seems to be to follow up the caplin that run up
the rivers at this season to spawn   In some of the Canadian rivers these
sea trout are found more or less through the summer, but, although I have been
on or near several of the rivers, I have never been able to satisfy myself that there
was an autumn run of sea trout, that is at spawning time, to be compared at all,
in point of number or regularity of time of occurrence, with the spring run   In
fact, I doubt whether they do spawn in fresh water, and yet, if they do not, it
would be a most remarkable exception to what we know of the habits of the Salmo
family   We have here in Massachusetts a sea trout that is well known on the
south side of Cape Cod, and called by the natives 'salters,' that also run up the
mouths of the brooks in early spring, in this case coming up after the shrimps
Although evidently of the same family as the regular brook trout that are caught
in the same waters, they differ from them even more than the Canadian sea trout
do from their river confrères   The main difference between the latter lies in
colour, whereas our salters not only are as silvery as a salmon, but their shape is
very different—they have very small heads, are roach backed, very deep, and
weigh nearly twice as much as a brook trout of the same length   That they are
more palatable to the gourmet is proved by the fact that they easily command a
dollar a pound in the market, where the others will sell from 37½ to 50 cents,
Their flesh is very red, and the firm flakes are separated by a layer of fatty curd
such as we find in a fresh-run salmon with the sea lice still on him "

Habits —Similar to our char and, like it, appears to prefer deep water, ponds
under eight feet in depth being unsuited   Is generally considered to have great
roving propensities, and is not often found rising to the fly after having attained
a pound in weight   It is somewhat a greedy feeder, and when artificially fed will
often eat to repletion   A "*Conservator*" writing from Shropshire to *The Field*,
remarked that he considered it useless for turning into a running water, as it
drops down stream, while it does not attain to the size of our brook-trout, and in
a lake will not rise well to the fly   He thought it as bad as pike in destroying
other fish, consequently he did not recommend it, although it is excellent eating,
and fights well when hooked

It had been observed at Howietoun that these fish, as well as the trout, were
much more shy* on Sundays than on any other day of the week, and this was
ascertained to be simply owing to the attendants on that day being differently

---

* Mr Seth Green, superintendent of the New York State Fish Hatchery, says that in the
fish pond at the hatchery there are 5000 large brook trout that were all captured with the fly in
unfrequented streams and lakes of the Adirondack region   These trout, he says, have convinced
him that fish have reasoning powers and memory   When they were hooked and reeled slowly to
the boats, they had time and opportunity to note the form and character of the tackle that made
them prisoners   They have never forgotten that   They will follow Mr Green as he walks about
the pond   Let him have a walking-stick and a fishing-rod hidden behind his back, if he reveals
the former to the fish, by holding it over the water, they pay no attention to it   But the moment
he produces his rod with the tackle, away they all scamper to distant parts of the pond   Mr
Green says he will permit any one to cast a fly in that pond to his heart's content, as he is satisfied that not one of the trout will come near it, so vividly do they remember their enemy of five
years ago   At a recent meeting at New York, Mr Green stated that he was trying to see if
brook trout can be improved by mixing different kinds, since it is known that constant inter
breeding of animals deteriorates them in size and intellect   Mr Green rather amused the
meeting by maintaining that fish had reasoning powers, and that he did not see why they could
not be improved in point of intellect   "If," said he, "we can breed a trout that has sense
enough to avoid the nets of the poachers on Long Island, I am under the impression that some
clubs that I know of would be willing to give somebody a chrome "

dressed* from what they were on week-days   While Livington-Stone (p 297) advised that if you wish to prevent a lot of trout being hooked out in the night by poachers, they should be well fed towards evening, and then two or three be captured by a small hook, and after a moment or two thrown back into the pond   They will create a panic amongst the rest so that there will be no more fishing that night with a hook

In the United States we are told that this fish cannot thrive in water warmer than 68° Fahr, though they have been known to live in swift-running water at 75°, but Brown-Goode remarks this higher temperature has been among those in fish-cultural establishments, and "fishes hatched in artificial ponds may probably be inured to greater warmth than wild fishes can endure, and it is doubtful whether the latter are often found in warmer water than 60° or 65°."   Below 36° they become torpid and refuse to eat

Breeding—The eggs, as already remarked, are only about half the size of those of the brook trout, and although in some localities it has been observed to deposit its ova earlier than the trout, it does so mostly at about the same period At Howietoun reducing food has been followed by decreased yield of eggs, and if the food is very much diminished to prevent fungus, such has been followed by temporary sterility.   A very small amount of milt in these, and I believe likewise in the British char, is sufficient to fecundate a large number of eggs †   At Howietoun the later in the season the eggs are obtained the larger seems to be the mortality among them   While fish, the first time they breed, do not spawn quite so soon as the older ones, they have not only a smaller‡ but a less number of eggs in proportion to their weight and size

8 eggs from a 4-year-old averaged 0 18 of an inch each in diameter
8   „   „ 3   „   „   0 17   „   „   „   „
8   „   „ 2   „   „   0 14   „   „   „   „

The redds are not infrequently found in very shallow water§ and for this purpose they commence running from about the middle of September, but there is often a considerable difference as to the time when all spawn, while naturally they take from five or six to eight or ten days in the process

Milner in the United States tells us that at Waterville, Wisconsin, a pair of these fishes had selected a spot near the banks of the stream where the water was about 10 inches deep   The female had fanned the gravel with her tail and anal fin until it was clean and white, and had succeeded in excavating a cavity   The number of days the eggs take incubating at Howietoun in water from 43 to 43½ degrees Fahrenheit is from 79 to 81

Mr S H Ainsworth has compiled a table respecting the incubation of these fish in the United States, from which I extract the following —

Average temperature of water	No of days to hatching.	No of days subsequently before feeding
37 0	163	
38 5	135	77
39 0	121	
40·2	109	60
41 0	103	
42 5	96	

* Livingston-Stone, *Domesticated Trout*, ed 2, p 219, observed that "their sensitiveness to colours is seen every week at the ponds where trout are domesticated, especially when their keeper changes a dark coat for a light one, or leaves it off altogether   The appearance of the unaccustomed light coat or white shirt will often frighten well-tamed trout into a panic "

† Mr M. informed me (April 24th, 1884) that late in the season he found some female fontinalis with ova, but possessed only two males, one of which was spent, and he merely obtained about two drops of milt from the other for between 3000 and 4000 eggs   out of these from 94 to 96 per cent hatched

‡ *See* Livingston Stone s observations as to the cause why the eggs of these fishes from some localities are smaller than in those from others (p 25 *ante*)

§ The secretary to the *National Fish Culture Association* informed me (Nov 4th, 1886) that some of these fish hatched in March, 1885, from eggs received from the United States, were now 9½ inches long (having been measured by himself) and that between October 22nd and 29th, 47 fish, males and females, had already spawned, and between the last date and Nov 1886, 20 more, from which he had obtained 8000 small eggs

Average temperature of water	No of days to hatching	No of days subsequently before feeding
43 3	89	45
44 0	81	
45 5	73	
46 5	65	
48 0	56	
50 0	47	30
52 0	38	
54 0	32	

Seth Green's rule is that these eggs hatch in fifty days, every degree warmer or colder making a difference of five days

Hybrids—These have been made among these fishes as observed (at p 49 *ante*), and will be further referred to in detail

Life history—Although when a few months old they do not require such a depth of water as trout, and do well kept indoors in rearing-boxes, it is not so as they get older, when, should the ponds in which they are be too small, they seem to stunt the subsequent growth of the fish   But, although it is evident to every fish-culturist, that among the same batch of young fish of every species of this family, some grow more rapidly than others, even when kept under identical conditions, the cause of this is not so apparent   Soon after these fish have absorbed the yolk-sac, it is common to observe how the larger ones take the best spots and strongest current of water, while the smaller ones congregate nearer the lower end of the trough where they will be least interfered with, the consequence being that the largest fry live where the most food is to be obtained, thus giving them another advantage over their smaller and weaker brethren   Also, fish of different sizes keep together   Over-crowding certainly does much damage (*see* pp 43-46 *ante*)   Other things being equal, such fish as have the largest supply of water grow the fastest, while they do better in moderately warm than in cold water, and they should be well fed   In ponds, unless the food is properly distributed, some may be insufficiently fed, when, becoming weak, they do not collect at feeding time   Means have to be taken to obviate this (see *History of Howietown*, p 72)

Mr Andrews at Guildford, states that he found that his yearlings ran from 8 oz to 10 oz and two-year-olds from 1¼ to 2 lb each, three-year-olds averaged 4 lb, and four-year-olds go 5¼ lb to 6½ lb   (*Land and Water*, July 22, 1882)   Livingston-Stone, *Domesticated Trout*, p 253, remarked " I have seen a trout that was reasonably believed to be but two years old that weighed a pound, and I have seen one of the same age that barely turned the scales at half-an-ounce '   " If you want to dwarf trout, keep them in cold sunless water, in close confinement, and with little food, and you will do it "

Diseases—Seem to be very amenable to *Saprolegnia ferax*, and it is very common to see the opercles shortened, apparently owing to having had gill-fever when young   At Howietown many are believed to suffer from enteritis should the temperature suddenly fall

In American streams they are said to generally disappear when the trees are cut down, probably because their constitutions are unsuited to waters subject to rapid changes of the temperature, although they are able to stand a considerable heat at times

As food are excellent, the flesh may be white, perfectly pink, or of a deep red *

* Mac Mac, writing from Boston to *The Field* of April 22nd, 1882, observed, " By the-bye, I see that Mr Francis Francis speaks well of our trout, i e , Salmo fontinalis, as a table fish   If he found the ones he had, which he says were white-meated, good, I only wish I could send him a brace of good Cape ' salters '   We do not consider a white-meated trout as fit to eat, although I have eaten some, when taken out of a cool pool with rocky bottom and white sand margins, that were white in colour and with white flesh, but yet sweet and palatable   But I think there can be no doubt that to get them in their perfection the flesh should be red, or at least pink   We have a theory that feeding on shrimps has a great deal to do with the colour of the flesh, it most

Habitat —The fresh waters of British North America, and contiguous portions
of the United States   It has, during the last twenty years, been acclimatized in
this country, and thrives in some of the places where it has been turned out, in
Scotland England, or Wales   Although in Norfolk it has been stated to have
done well, and grown twice as quickly as the brook trout, this is denied, and
Mr Southwell informed me (December 6th, 1886) " The remark that *S fontinalis*
' thrives well ' in Norfolk (among other places) is quite incorrect, of all those
which have been introduced I doubt whether any survive   A few lake trout
turn up now and then, but I don't believe they breed, and the only introduced
fish which has done any good is *S fario*, already a native species, and even this
finds but few of our rivers suitable for its reproduction "   At Howietoun it has
done fairly well, but does not often seem to live over its fifth year, being very
susceptible to atmospheric changes and needing deep water   In Mr Andrews'
ponds, in Surrey, it is said to have done well, while in Bagshot Park it is likewise
stated to have thriven   But although there are many waters suitable to these
fish in the British Isles, there are more where it cannot be expected they could
thrive—quantity, depth, temperature, and purity having all to be considered
(*see* how char in Loch Leven have disappeared, p 242 *ante*)

As to the size the *Salmo fontinalis* attains, we are told that in the Rangely
Lake, in the U S A , Mr Page, in 1867, took one 10 lb , but they seldom exceed
2 lb or 3 lb , and a 5 lb one is considered a monster   In August, 1886, Mr F
Grote took one at Megantic, Me , which weighed 12¼ lb   Brown-Goode, remarking on these fish, observed that the Lake trout, *S namaycush*, sometimes attains
the weight of 120 lb , while the common char, *S fontinalis*, even under similar
conditions, never exceeds 14 lb or 15 lb

In one of Mr Basset's ponds, at Tehidy, near Camborne, in Cornwall, Mr
Cornish (*Land and Water*, May 1st, 1886) tells us that a 9¾ lb one was captured
in April, 1886, also that with this species, " Mr Basset stocked his ponds some
nine years since   This one was taken on a ground line, but the fish is said to show
excellent sport when taken on a trolling bait, and it is an exceedingly voracious
feeder   I apprehend, however, that its presence in a pond probably means the
extermination of all common trout in it "   The Maclaine of Lochbuie has acclimatized this fish in a moor loch about 1000 feet above the sea, near Loch Uisk, in
Mull , in 1884, one was captured 2¼ lb in weight, and they are said to have
attained to 5 lb

The example figured Plate ix, fig 1, is from a male specimen 9¾ inches long,
from the Howietoun stock ponds

certainly has with the flavour   But on the other hand, I fish every spring a lake that is up on
high land, fed entirely by springs, whose outlet runs into Lake Umbagog, thus forming one of the
chains of the head waters of the Androscoggin, the trout of which are celebrated throughout the
State of Maine for their size, deep colour, and flavour   In this lake, up to five years ago, there
were no fish of any species except trout, and consequently they must have fed on flies, the larvæ of
water insects, &c   It used to be poached through the ice in winter, when the only bait used was
live bait—i e , minnows, shiners, dace, &c , and either from the ones that escaped, or from the
fact that after their day's fishing they put what live bait they had left into the pond, it now is
quite full of small fry "

In the *Bulletin of the United States Fish Commission*, 1882, ii, p 10, we are told that in
America the fontinalis " takes the first rank as a fish to be cultivated in ponds, provided the
ponds are fed by springs or cold running water   Ponds not possessing these qualities are unsuited
for them "

HYBRIDS

A brief account of hybridism among fishes, more especially as observed in the salmon family, has been already given (pp 46-50 *ante*), and it has been shown that the existence of hybrids in this country has been recorded for at least the last two centuries   But, nevertheless, various authors now and again, even at the present day, have ignored the labours of their predecessors, and while admitting the existence of these salmonoid hybrids, have boldly asserted that they were their first undoubted discoverers! Another class has maintained that hybrids are unable to breed (*see* p 49), for how else could the commingling of genera and species be obviated ? Again we have an intermediate class, who, admitting the existence and fertility of hybrid races, hold to the opinion that we have yet to learn through how many generations such fertility can extend , and what will be the effect of intercrossing these hybrids among themselves, or re-crossing them with one of the original parents or any pure breed ?

To partially solve some, at least, of these interesting questions, Sir James Maitland, 1 7 s, at Howietoun, has devoted a very great amount of trouble, and gone to great expense during the last eight years or more, and when carrying out his experiments has given me the opportunity of being present while the crosses were being made, permitted me unlimited access to his hatching-houses and fish-ponds, and has supplied me with specimens whenever I have required them Consequently, unless otherwise expressed, all the following experiments were made at the private fish farm at Howietoun by the owner himself

Of course, on obtaining a fish from a stream of certain appearance, it may convey to a competent naturalist the belief that it is undoubtedly a hybrid, but we require conclusive evidence first that such can occur between two distinct species, and secondly proof as to what will be the appearance of these hybrids Here fish culture gives us undeniable evidence that hybrids can occur, that they are not necessarily sterile, and also what their appearance may be From these we may decidedly recognize some forms by their colours, as those between trout and American char, one of which I received in 1882 from Sir Pryse Pryse, of Goggerddan, in North Cardiganshire , whilst we have instances recorded of these two species of fish having been observed forming redds together in this country * when in a wild condition, and several anglers have informed me that they inter-breed in the Wandle as well as in Cardiganshire and elsewhere

If hybrid salmonidæ are to be worth cultivating, the first question which arises must be which is the finest breed to employ, and whether the size of the parent has any peculiar modifying influence on that of the offspring ? In the British Museum collection are very fine examples, some termed ' Bull-trout, ' others, " male salmon " I have never observed in rivers yellow bands on the cheeks of any except pure salmon, but they are distinctly visible upon a 43 lb fish labelled " Bull trout of the Tweed " (Gunther, *Brit Mus Catal* vi, pp 25-28), while this specimen has thirteen scales passing downwards and forwards from the adipose dorsal fin to the lateral-line, and only forty-three cæcal appendages In this case the question arises whether it might not probably be a hybrid, and in another fish

* During Christmas week, 1885, Mr Thomas Ford observed in a stream at Caistor, in very shallow and perfectly clear water, a female brook trout which had made a large hole, and a male *fontinalis* There were half-a-dozen more common trout in the pool, but the *fontinalis* drove them all away, although they were the larger fish   " When shooting its eggs the body of the trout was subject to a tremulous motion, whilst its back fin was occasionally out of the water At times the *fontinalis* remained almost immovable just above the trout, but now and then it would go completely over and under the female fish It was quite evident that the female trout preferred the company of the *fontinalis* to that of its own species This is the second time that I have observed the crossing of the species in a state of nature " He watched it a quarter of an hour (*Field*, Jan 9th, 1886)

46 inches long from the Tweed, the cartilaginous hook on the lower jaw is very slightly developed, yet it was a male* (*see* p 58 *ante*) As I shall show that salmon and trout may interbreed and produce fertile offspring, it would become interesting to ascertain how such hybrids could be differentiated from the pure races, and whether the species which forms the male or female parent occasions perceptible differences in the young. I have already shown cause for supposing that hybrid salmon and trout do not lose their anadromous propensities

HYBRID BETWEEN SALMON AND LOCHLEVEN TROUT

Day, *Proceedings Zoological Society*, 1882, p 751, and 1884, p 18

Maitland, *History of Howietoun*, 1886

On November 25th, 1879, a man arrived at Howietoun with some salmon milt which Mr Napier, the local inspector of fisheries, had despatched the previous evening from Stirling in a tightly corked soda-water bottle, that had been kept during the night in snow, and which seemed on arrival as if it had been frozen This milt was employed for fertilizing ova taken from a four-year old Lochleven trout, and a few of the progeny were successfully reared November 14th, 1882 one, eleven inches long, was taken in my presence, it was a male which I described in the P Z S, 1882, and likewise gave a woodcut of its head

Some of these fish when young were placed in the island pond along with the trout, and when that pond was drained in my presence, November 28th, 1883, several were obtained, three of these I sent to the *Economic Fish Museum* at South Kensington, one I retained and examined, it also was a male (*see* P Z S, 1884) Several were transferred to pond No 11

November 14th, 1884, on pond No 11 being drawn, three of the above hybrids were captured, the largest being 16⅓ inches long, they appeared to be in good health, but none had shown any tendency to spring out of the ponds at the spawning time A specimen I retained was eleven inches long, or similar to the first taken the previous year They were as follows —

B x, D 12 (⅜), P 12-13, V 9-10, A 11 (⅜), C 19, L l 114-118, L tr 24-25, 30 32, Cæc pyl 62-69

In the first the length of the head was 4½, of pectoral fin 6⅓ in the total length, while in the second the length of the head was 5½, and of pectoral fin 7¼ in the total length Both were males Teeth in an apparently double row along the body of the vomer, and in both twelve rows of scales were present in a line passing from the adipose dorsal fin downwards and forwards to the lateral-line, and from twenty-one to twenty-five from the lateral-line to the base of the ventral fin In the first the rows of scales in the upper half of the body were very irregular, and in the second in the tail portion of the body *Colours*—on removal from the water silvery, with a rich purple gloss, and from six to eight irregularly placed rows of black spots on the fore-part of the body, decreasing to three, or even two, in the caudal portion no par bands, two to five black spots on opercle, one or two on preopercle, some on cheeks and top of the head Lower two-thirds of dorsal fin with large black spots, and white anterior upper edge the fins generally grayish and darkest in the centre, the anal having a light front edge Generative organs rudimentary

HYBRID BETWEEN SALMON AND LOCHLEVEN TROUT

Day, *Proceedings Zool Society*, 1882, p 752, and 1884 pp 19, 376, and 1885, p 241

December 24th, 1881, about 20,000 eggs of Lochleven trout at Howietoun were fertilized with salmon milt obtained from the Teith They hatched on

---

* Professor Flower, c n, the obliging Director of the Natural History Museum, at my request had the example opened, and it was undoubtedly a male

March 9th, 1882, or in 75 days In due course the fry were removed to a planked pond at Howietoun, 20 ft long by 5 ft wide, and 1½ ft deep Through this a stream flows, entering at its upper and making its exit at the surface at its lower end On Nov 15, 1882, we examined them, and the largest fish was 4½ inches in length

B v, D 13 ($\frac{3}{10}$), P 13-14, V 9, A 11 ($\frac{3}{8}$), C 19, L 1 116-118, Cæcal pyl 61-78

The length of the heads of these hybrids were about ⅕, and of pectoral fins from 5¼ to 6⅔ in the total length of the fish * The maxilla in these fish extends posteriorly to beneath the hind third of the eye The preopercle has a distinctly oblique lower limb in no 1, but it is less strongly marked than in no 2, while merely a simple curve exists in nos 3 and 4 The cæcal appendages were examined in two, one (no 3) had 78, the other (no 4) had 61 and when hybrids between the same parents show such variations, it demonstrates the inconstancy in the number of these appendages Colours—were nearly identical in all, from 12 to 13 par bands and the sides closely sprinkled with small black spots and a few red ones, some black spots on the head, while in all the front upper edge of the dorsal fin was white with a dark intramarginal band,† and from 11 to 13 black spots on or between the rays In November, 1883, three more of these fish were captured, which measured in length 5 4 5 7, and 7 3 inches respectively,‡ while the numbers were supposed to be about eight hundred In these three specimens the number of par bands along the sides varied from 10 to 12, while the direction of the rows of scales showed great irregularity, and those between the adipose dorsal fin and the lateral-line varied from 12 to 14

On March 13th, 1884, these hybrids, numbering 212, the largest six being over 10 inches in length, the majority smaller, while a few did not exceed 2¼ inches, and all apparently in excellent health, were transferred to the octagon pond at Craigend, the diameter of which is 20 ft, and its depth 4 ft, its sides and bottom are planked, while the stream which supplies it flows in at about 1 ft below the

	No 1 Inches	No 2 Inches	No 3 Inches	No 4 Inches
* Length of example	4 3	3 4	4 1	4 0
,, ,, head	0 9	0 7	0 8	0 8
,, ,, pectoral fin	0 8	0 6	0 6	0 6
,, from snout to base of dorsal	1 7	1 1	1 7	1 6
,, ,, ,, ,, caudal	3 8	3 0	3 6	3 4
Diameter of eye	0 2	0 15	0 2	0 2
From end of snout	0 25	0 2	0 2	0 23
Apart	0 3	0 27	0 3	0 3
Height of body	0 8	0 65	0 7	0 7

† As no white dark based edging exists on the anterior superior edge of the dorsal fin in the Lochleven trout bred at Howietoun, but is present in most burn trout, this forms another link in the chain of facts, that these two forms of trout are merely varieties of one species

	No 1 Inches	No 2 Inches.	No 3 Inches.
‡ Length of example	7 3	5 7	5 4
,, ,, head	1 6	1 2	1 15
,, ,, pectoral fin	1 05	1 0	0 9
,, ,, caudal fin	1 8	0 9	0 9
,, from snout to base of dorsal fin	2 8	2 2	2 2
,, ,, ,, ,, caudal ,,	6 2	4 9	4 6
Diameter of eye	0 3	0 23	0 25
From end of snout	0 5	0 33	0 3
Apart	0 6	0 4	0 4
Height of body	1 5	1 2	1 0

Specimen No 1, had the teeth in a double row along the body of the vomer, scales in irregular rows in places, the upper two thirds of the body spotted with black, some large red spots along the lateral line, three black spots on the opercle and a fourth at its upper corner, one on the preopercle, twelve par bands along either side Dorsal fin gray with a white edge at its upper anterior margin, the lower half of the fin spotted with black, adipose dorsal orange with a gray front edge Specimen No 2, nearly similar but a little more yellow, and with ten par bands on one side, twelve on the other Specimen No 3, had ten par bands on one side and eleven on the other, many red spots on the body

surface and passes out at the lower end at the same level This stream rises from springs about half a mile away, and before reaching the octagon pond goes through the two 100 ft. ponds, which are stocked with Lochleven yearlings, consequently anything deleterious in the water must first affect these small fish

On one 6½ inches long being removed, on Aug 26th, when it was about twenty-nine months old, it was found to be a female, but sterile The dorsal fin had three rows of black spots along its lower half On Nov 14th, a net was put into this pond, and the specimen 10 inches long, which outwardly looked most likely to prove fertile, removed, it was a sterile male On Feb 12th, 1885, one 9½ inches long was captured with a fly, to which it rose well Its dorsal fin was spotted, there were 7 large black spots on the opercles on the right side, and 8 on those of the left, a row of red spots along the lateral-line, and a second above it A slight appearance of par bands was still visible The fins anteriorly were white edged

These fish did not attempt to spring out of the pond until May, 1885, or when thirty-eight months of age, and in a similar manner to smolts when becoming grilse On May 24th, one which was found dead was opened, and proved to be a female with the eggs developing, and which, had it lived, would evidently have bred that winter

In June, 1885, the water in the Craigend burn which supplies this pond, became very low, although during that month it never quite ceased flowing That in the pond became so discoloured, it was impossible to see the fish unless they came to the surface, and then existence could only be demonstrated by throwing a very little food in, when they rose to take it

On July 3rd, a slight shower occurred, but rain still held off, and the fish appeared to be livelier than they had been for several days previously, and when fed at 6 30 P M , some of them jumped quite out of the water at the little food thrown to them The temperature at the surface was 64°, and experiments made since, show that it is 2° colder at the bottom On July 4th, at 8 30 A M , on Mr Thompson, the manager, going to feed these fish, one was observed dead on the surface, while none of the others could be seen to move. The water was at once drawn off, in order to shift any that might chance to be alive, but only two were found to be so, and 142 were dead * Some appeared as if they had succumbed more than twenty-four hours, the two which remained alive, subsequently quite recovered, and were put into another pond The largest of the hybrids was 13½ inches long, and weighed just over one pound †

In both examples the maxilla reached to beneath the hind edge of the eye · there were in one eleven, in the other twelve, rows of scales between the adipose dorsal fin and the lateral-line Eggs small, but very distinct in both, as if the fish would have bred during the ensuing season , in no 2, in which the ova were largest, they measured 0 1 of an inch in diameter. It should be mentioned that in the 100 foot ponds above the one in which these fish died, none of the Lochleven fry succumbed

The cause of this unfortunate termination of a most interesting experiment must probably be sought for in the size of the pond and insufficiency of the

* Two examples gave the following results ,—

	No 1, in inches		No 2, in inches
Length of example .	10 4		10 1
,, ,, head	1 9		1 8
,, ,, pectoral fin	1 5	.	1 5
,, ,, tail	1 4	.	1 3
,, ,, eyes	0 4	.	0 375
Eyes apart	0 7	.	0 7
,, to end of snout	0 6	.	0 5

† Mr Thompson observed (July 10th, 1885), that among these dead fish " there were more males than females, I think, but there were a good many, I was not quite sure of their sex (apparently barren), as in most hybrids some bore resemblance to the male parent and some to the female, these last were fattest "

amount of running water to carry enough air in solution to equal the requirements of the fish Temperature alone can hardly be the reason, because that of the water in the Howietoun ponds on the same day was 66°, but there the supply, coming down the burn from Loch Coulter, was ample The foregoing, however, proved one fact, that fertile female fish may be raised by hybridizing the eggs of trout with the milt of salmon par that females so raised may breed in their third or fourth season, similarly to salmon, but later than in the generality of trout

One of the fish that survived was a male, employed Nov 6th, 1886, to fertilize 3000 Lochleven trout eggs on January 25th, 1887, about 80 hatched, and on June 27th the lot, numbering 55, were put into pond no 2 at Howietoun, they were strong and from $1\frac{1}{2}$ to $1\frac{3}{4}$ inches in length

The other, also a male, was likewise employed on Dec 5th, 1886, for this purpose to fertilize 7000 eggs of a Lochleven trout, but on Feb 27th, 1887, only one or two hatched But these instances proved that this class of hybrids may be fertile *

Hybrids between Lochleven trout and Salmon

December 27th, 1884 —Seven thousand ova from a Teith salmon were milted from a Lochleven trout, and about 5000 hatched in the old house on March 11th, or after incubating 75 days There was a great mortality from when they had attained to a month old and continuing up to the time of feeding, many being weak and dropsical June 30th, 1885, about 2000 were transferred to pond 4, Feb 22nd, 1887, about 1000 remain, and they look very well, they have 13 par bands, a white edge to dorsal and anal fins, and a slight one to the ventral Not many red spots One measured $5\frac{1}{2}$ inches long March 1st, 787 were shifted to pond no 7, the largest being from seven to eight inches long, but several were merely from two to three inches in length

Hybrids between Salmon smolts and Lochleven trout †

Day, *Proc Zool Soc* 1885, p 242
November 11th, 1884 —About 12,000 eggs of the Lochleven trout, having an average diameter of 0 21 inches, were milted from three male Howietoun-bred smolts, the largest of which was twelve inches long and the shortest ten inches, all being silvery, but showing the remains of par bands The following were the number of eggs picked out as dead —November 34, December 28, January 25, while 2295 were found to have escaped impregnation The rest hatched January 28th, 1885, or in 78 days, but between then and February 25th about 1000 died, for although the alevins looked well for the first three weeks (except that their eyes were rather small), a large percentage then showed signs of deficient vitality, the yolk-sac did not absorb, the young fish became dropsical, and nearly 2000 died On June 19th about 5000 were transferred to pond no 1 at Howietoun, along with some similar hybrids In all these fish the adipose dorsal fin was lead-coloured On July 26th, 1886, 1260 fish were shifted from no 1 to no 8 pond, and on October 12th one which was measured was $5\frac{1}{4}$ inches in length July 5th, 1887, another taken with a landing net, measured ten inches.

* At p 103 I have already recorded how 100 eggs from a dead or dying grilse were milted Nov 7th, 1884, from a male Lochleven trout, and eighteen hatched January 23rd, 1885, or in 77 days, seven remained July 4th, 1885, and were put with hybrids of the same description into pond no 1

† On the same day about 800 eggs of Lochleven trout were milted from three Howietoun raised pars and smolts A fair number hatched on February 5th, or in 90 days, but subsequently many succumbed to dropsy June 19th, 1885, about 400 were shifted to pond no 1 at Howietoun, along with some other similar crosses

Hybrid between Salmon par and Lochleven trout

Day, *Proceedings Zool Soc*, 1884, pp 40, 376, and 1885, p 241

November 29th, 1883 —About 4500 eggs were obtained from a Lochleven trout which had been hatched early in 1875, and these were milted from a par of the salmon which had been hatched in March, 1881, consequently was 32 months of age, and showed all the par colours The number of eggs removed as dead during the 78 days they took incubating, were as follows —December 65, January 18, February 4, or a total of 87 deaths, while in addition 199 eggs were found to have escaped impregnation Consequently although the mortality was small, it by no means gave a true index to the result of the experiment, for it was soon perceived that the young were not a strong and vigorous brood, while weak ones are useless for stocking purposes, even should they surmount the diseases and dangers of their youth

On February 15th, 1884, some thousands were hatched from these eggs, but nearly all were seen to be suffering from what has been termed dropsy, or blue swelling of the yelk-sac, probably due to insufficient vitality in their constitutions On March 12th, 1884, I first saw these young fish, then nearly a month old, and their average length being 0 8 of an inch, but what at once struck an observer was the large pyriform umbilical sac, which seemed to anchor them to the bottom of the tank Some were seen singly, others in groups, while every now and then one would start up and swim a short distance in an irregular or spasmodic manner, and then sink to the bottom. This dropsical enlargement in a considerable proportion of the fish was 0 35 of an inch in length, and 0 2 of an inch in diameter at its widest part, while it stood out in tolerable relief from the enclosed yelk-sac, showing the existence of two coats, separated one from another by an accumulation of clear fluid Under a strong glass there appeared to be a want of vitality in the fish, the pulsations being weak, the activity of the heart being feeble, and the blood wanting in red corpuscles Due to this dropsical distension, the pectoral fins were much impeded in their movements, which is a very material consideration, because in the young fish these fins are in constant motion, in order by keeping up a continuous current to assist the gill-covers in aerating the blood at the gills June 24th, shifted from the house to the 20-feet pond at Howietoun, close to despatch house, on August 29th, 1884, about 100 were alive May 6th, 1885, temporarily placed in no 4 pond, and on June 20th to pond 32, only 53 fish remaining June 17th, 1886, they were about two dozen in number, and shifted to pond 16, all being small except two, one of which was twelve inches long, and ¾ lb weight At this time some had one, others two rows of rather large pinkish-red spots along the lateral-line, and also above and below it

On November 23rd, 1886, 1000 eggs obtained from one of these fishes* were milted from a Lochleven trout, and about 700 hatched on Feb 10th, 1887, or in 79 days, they looked well June 27th, 667 fish were removed to no 1 pond at Howietoun

Crossing eggs of burn trout with milt from dead par

Day, *Proceedings Zoological Society*, 1884, p 378.

November 29th, 1883 —About 1000 eggs taken from a burn trout, *S fario*, which had been some years in the pond, were milted from a par 32 months old, which had been a few hours dead But not a single egg fructified Only three turned white in December, three in January, and fifteen in February, or a total of 21 On March 12th the remainder were still clear, but without any signs of an embryo within, having evidently been unimpregnated.

---

* Length of example, 9 1 inch, length of head, 1 9 inch, length of pectoral, 1 4 inch Lower jaw short Scales near pectoral fin and along the back to end of dorsal fin very small eleven rows between adipose dorsal fin and lateral line Black spots on the dorsal fin, having a light ring round them anal with a white front edge Tail very jagged

As bearing on this, Mr. Buist filled a box with unfertilized salmon ova, and treated them as if they were fertile and he observed that they never turned white or opaque, like ova which had been impregnated, and subsequently died (Brown, *Stormontfields Experiments*, pp 39-40, *see* also p 32 *ante*)

Hybrid between Lochleven trout and Salmon smolt

Day, *Proc Zool Soc* 1885, p 242

December 9th, 1884.—About 400 eggs, averaging 0 22 inch in diameter, of a Howietoun raised grilse, were milted from a Lochleven trout, but only half the eggs were impregnated   About 150 hatched on February 25th, 1885, or in 78 days, and were turned into pond no 4 on June 30th, very few having died   On February 27th, 1886, some measured 3½ inches in length

Hybrid between Salmon par and American char

Day, *Proceedings Zoological Society*, 1884, pp 40, 378

Nov 29th, 1883 —Three thousand six hundred and ninty-five eggs of an American char, *Salmo fontinalis*, were milted from a salmon par 32 months old some hatched Feb 20th, 1884, or in 83 days   The deaths among the eggs in December were 144, January 1527, February 401, or a total of 3372   On March 7th, 1884, only seven were alive, and these subsequently succumbed   The amount of fertilization received in this instance by char eggs from salmon par milt was evidently less than that afforded to the larger eggs of the Lochleven trout

In the foregoing accounts of experiments on hybridism carried out at Howietoun, instances have been given of cases between the salmon *Salmo salar* in all its stages with the Lochleven trout,* and also with the American char   It now becomes necessary to follow out the crossings of the trout with the char

Zebra Hybrids, or between American char and Lochleven trout, Plate XI, fig 2

Day, *Proceedings Zoological Society*, 1884, pp 30, 378, 585, plate lvi

November 15th, 1882 —About 3000 eggs of the Lochleven trout were fertilized at Howietoun with milt from an American char, *Salmo fontinalis*, they hatched on February 8th, or in 85 days   The mortality among the incubating eggs was as follows.—November 68, December 142, January 89, and February 41, or a total of 340 eggs, or a proportion of about 1 death to every 6 ova   The young were much malformed, monstrosities being numerous, some had blindness in one or both eyes, others had bull-dog deformities of the snout   Some were very light coloured, but not quite albinos, as the markings though pale were visible In May, 1883, I received from Howietoun one of the specimens, it was 0 8 of an inch in length, the anterior portion of its head was deformed owing to want of development of the premaxillaries and contiguous bones, while its colours were white without any markings

July 20th, 1883 —I took four more specimens from the hatching box, and they varied in size from 1 6 to 1 7 in in length, while the number of par bands varied from 8 to 11   The remaining fish were transferred to a large wooden tank raised off the ground and supplied with water from a stream, but was rather exposed to the east

* November the 27th, 1884 —1296 eggs taken from a Lochleven trout were milted from a male sea trout, *Salmo trutta*, and on March 20th, 1875, in the afternoon, or in 113 days, about 900 eggs hatched, and on the 21st only 10 remained to hatch. *See* also experiments of Shaw, Young, and Rasch (p 48)

On November 29th, three more* were removed for examination, and with the following results —*Specimen no* 1 was blind of the left eye, but the colours on its two sides were similar, and like no 2, except having two instead of one band across the dorsal fin   Seventeen rows of scales between the adipose dorsal fin and the lateral-line   *Specimen no* 2, eyesight normal   The finger-marks were broken up into arched bands, or circles enclosing spaces, the ground colour being yellowish   the upper surface of the head and back spotted and marked with black dots   the dorsal fin with a dark band across its centre and a dark spot at the base of its first ray   Twenty-two rows of scales between the adipose dorsal fin and the lateral-line   *Specimen no* 3 had the right eye absent, the ball having retracted into the socket, while the left eye was almost blind, the pupil being reduced to a narrow slit, and a black spot was present on the sclerotic   When alive this fish appeared as a semi-albino, markings were present, but light in colour on both sides, more especially so on the right   Fifteen rows of scales between the adipose dorsal fin and the lateral-line

March 12th, 1884 —Upwards of 20 were found to be dead, so the next day they were removed to the upper planked pond† at Howietoun, into which 211 were turned, but some appeared to be very weakly   In three of these fish a remarkable change had occurred in the colour of their fins, the ventral, anal and caudal having become of a carmine red   One which was 2½ in long happening to die, I found that its left eye had never been developed, while in the right one there were adhesions between the iris and subjacent structures   In a second the left eye had not been developed, while the right eye had suffered from congenital malformation   The longest fish was a little over 3¾ in in length

August 28th, 1884 —About 190 of these fish existed and were in excellent condition, and their appearance was very beautiful ‡

Teeth —In a triangular transverse row across the hind and lateral margins of the head of the vomer, followed by three or four more teeth placed in a single series along the anterior half of the body of that bone   these posterior teeth, which may be four in number, are in a single median line, so far as I have had the opportunity of examining and are always present as seen in fig 52, 2 and 2a (p 270), showing either that deciduous vomerine teeth may exist on the body of the vomer in char crossed by trout   or else, that instead of a double row of teeth along the body of the vomer, as seen in trout, they may be reduced to a few placed in a single row should such fish be crossed with char   *Scales*—18 to 22 rows between the base of the adipose dorsal downwards and forwards to the lateral-line   *Colours*—yellowish shot with purple and reticulated with irregular black bands, spots, and markings along the body, but most spotted on the upper surface of the

	No 1, in inches	No 2, in inches	No 3, in inches
* Length of example	2 7	. 2 6	2 2
„ „ head	. 0 6	0 6 .	0 4
„ „ caudal fin	0 4	0 5	0 3
Height of body	0 5	0 55	0 4

† Pond no 3, twenty feet long, five wide, and containing about 36 inches of water
‡ The following is a description of two specimens removed from the pond, the second being the one figured on plate xi

B x, D 13 ($\frac{1}{13}$), P 13, V 9-10, A $\frac{3}{9}$, C 19, L l 128 140
Cæc pyl 37 39, longest ½ inch

	Inches	Inches
Total length	6 7	16 0
Length of head	1 3	2 5
Length of pectoral fin	1 0	1 6
Length of ventral fin	0 8	1 3
Length of caudal fin .	1 0	2 1
Height of body . .	1 5	2 8
Eyes, diameter of	0 3	0 5
Eyes from end of snout	0 4	0 9
Eyes apart	1 5	1 0
Distance from snout to dorsal fin	2 8	5 3
Distance from base of pectoral to base of ventral fin	1 3	3 7
Distance from base of ventral to base of anal fin	1 2	2 0

head and back, a few dark marks also on the sides of the head   Dorsal fin yellow, with black spots and irregular bands, the upper portion of its anterior edge being rather light with a dark base   Adipose dorsal with a black base and two black spots one above the other   Pectoral black-tipped   Anal with the three first rays white, posterior to which the fin is stained with dark gray, especially in its outer portion   Caudal dark-edged, and with a few indistinct bars at its base   It was a male with the milt very fully developed

November 12th, 1884 —Pond no 3 at Howietoun was examined, and the females of the zebra race were not quite ready for breeding, while they appeared to be fewer in number than the males, some of which were ripe   On December 24th they were shifted to pond no 5, and 146 fish were present. September 8th, 1885, the largest removed with a landing net was $9\frac{1}{2}$ in long   November 5th, 1885, on netting pond 5, all those examined appeared to be sterile, the largest fish being $12\frac{1}{2}$ in long

Zebra Hybrids, or between American char and Lochleven trout

Day, *Proc Zool Soc* 1884, p 379

November 29th, 1883 —Three thousand ova were taken from a Lochleven trout of the season of 1875, and milted from a *Salmo fontinalis*   The number of dead eggs removed was as follows —December 80, January 56, February 25, or a loss of 161, while 296 were found not to have been impregnated, or a proportion of one death to every 17 ova   These young fishes, in March, 1884, were much more advanced than the young diopsies (see p 259 ante)   June 24th, they were removed to the 20 ft tank near the 'Despatch House," where they continued until May 6th, 1885, when they were shifted to pond no 3, on June 20th, they were again moved to pond no 8, they now numbered 161   September 8th, a net full was removed, and the largest fish in it was $6\frac{1}{2}$ inches long, on November 26th, they were transferred to pond no 5. On October 15th, 1886, one 15 inches long, which died of fungus, had milt fairly well developed *

Leopard Hybrids, or between Lochleven trout and American char

Day, *Proc Zool Soc* 1884, pp 31, 32, 379

November 15th, 1882 —Eight thousand ova of an American char, *Salmo fontinalis*, were fecundated with the milt of a Lochleven trout   They hatched on February 7th, or in 84 days, the mortality during incubation was in November 28, December 575, January 1818, February 297, of a total loss of 2718   The young fry were greatly deformed, many had their spines crooked, atrophy was present in the posterior portions of some, and a deficiency of the fins generally, more especially of the caudal   In May, 1883, the young were about 1 inch in length, and had about 11 par bands, the foremost four of which were mostly below the lateral-line, while the remainder generally crossed it †   On July 20th, the cross bands had become wider passing downwards to the belly and upwards to the back, which, however, they did not extend on to, but small and irregular bars descended towards the interspaces between the cross bands   The broad cross bars on the body were twice as wide as the interspaces, generally about nine in number,

---

* December 13th, 1884 —Five hundred eggs, having a diameter 0 18 inches each, were obtained from a dead sea trout which had been gaffed, the wound having extended into the ovary, and possibly water also   The milt of a Howietoun grilse was added, they were put in box 64 on March 1st, one hatched, and it was turned into box 92   On February 24th, 1887, this fish was alive and well along with *Salmo irideus*

† Sir James Maitland sent me one specimen 0 8 of an inch long, its head and the anterior part of its body were normal, but posterior to the dorsal fin a general atrophy had taken place, and although the anal fin was fairly developed, the caudal portion was embryonic   It had six bars along each side

while another crossed the head, and a dark band ran across the middle of the dorsal fin. I removed three from the box *

On November 29th, an example 2 1 inches in length was taken from the remaining 16, the finger marks in this specimen appeared to have been about 12, but were broken up into irregular shapes, reticulated over a yellow ground colour The back was black spotted Dorsal fin with two oblique black bands, a light upper edge and a dark spot at the base of its first dorsal rays , 15 rows of scales between the adipose dorsal fin and the lateral-line These fish were kept under the same conditions as the Zebra breed, and on March 13th, 1884, only 8 remained and they seemed in rather an unsatisfactory state, and on December 24th, the last eight were shifted to pond 24, and again in 1886, to pond 16

Hybrid between British char and Lochleven trout.

December 5th, 1885 —About 6500 eggs of *S levenensis* were milted from a Windermere char which had been kept too long, for although the impregnation was considered good, there was a deficiency of milt, in 84 days, or on February 27th, about 30 hatched , and on July 30th, 20 were moved to pond 4 December 17th, 19 remained and were shifted to pond 23 They were fully as large as yearlings of the true Lochlevens and much more silvery May 30th, 1887, moved to pond 32

Struan Hybrid, or between American and British char, Plate XI, fig 1

Day, *Proceedings Zool Soc* , 1884, pp 38, 379, 586, and plate lvii

November 15th, 1882 —About 9000 ova of an American char, *S fontinalis*, were fertilized with the milt of a Scotch char, which had been termed *S struanensis*, obtained from Loch Rannoch, and which had been retained in one of the boxes The milt seemed rather thick, they hatched on February 9th, or in 86 days The mortality among the eggs was November 28, December 309, January 1907, February 130, or a total loss of 2104 eggs, or nearly 1 in 4¾, due probably to the insufficiency of fertilization There were no considerable amount of monstrosities or malformations On May 20th, 1883, I received one 1¼ inches long, having 8 broad cross bands and many intermediate smaller ones, no band on the dorsal fin On July 20th, I received four more of the following dimensions 1 3, 1 8, 2 0, 2 1 inches in length, and with from 8 to 11 par bands In some, these par bands were much more broken up on one side of a fish than they were on the opposite, one had 9 wide ones, another had 6 to opposite the end of the dorsal fin, after which they were broken up All had the light anterior edge to the first dorsal fin. November 29th, 1883, two more were removed from the tank of 2 8 and 3 0 inches respectively in length † From 20 to 28 rows of scales between the base of the adipose dorsal fin and the lateral-line Teeth along the head of the vomer, none along its body These were kept under the same conditions as the Zebra and Leopard breeds On March 13th, 1884, 91 lively young fish were transferred to a planked pond at Howietoun, and from among these

	No 1	No. 2.	No 3
* Total length	1 8	1 6	1 5
Length of head	0 5	0 35	0 4
,, ,, caudal fin	0 3	0 25	0 3
Height of body	0 5	0 3	0 3
Number of bars	8 & 10	10 & 11	9 & 8

	No 1	No 2
† Length of example	3 0 inches	2 8 inches
,, ,, head	0 6 ,,	0 6 ,,
,, ,, caudal fin	0 5 ,	0 15 ,,
Height of body	0 5 ,,	0 5 ,,

one 7 3 inches long* was removed for examination The lower jaw was slightly deformed, being unnaturally shortened   *Teeth*—in a transverse row across the head of the vomer, but none along the body of the bone   *Scales*—23 rows pass from the base of the adipose dorsal fin downwards and forwards to the lateral-line.   The dorsal, anal, and other fins are much more developed in these pure char hybrids than in the Zebra, wherein the char was crossed with a trout *Colours*—of a beautiful iridescent purple, with thirteen transverse or par-bands along the sides, the whole of the body covered with small light spots, none on the fins   Anterior edge of the dorsal, ventral, and anal white, also the outer ray of the pectoral.   A few dark marks along the base of the dorsal fin, all the fins darkest at their outer edges   The specimen was a male with the milt very fully developed

November 12th, 1884 —Pond no 4 at Howietoun was again examined, and 91 fish were present   the largest fish was 8½ inches long , most of the females were not quite ready for breeding, as December set in they began to be languid , and one or two having died, they were shifted into pond no 5, on December 21th, when 71 fish were transferred   The next day fifteen died, and two on the 26th Subsequently few succumbed , but one on February 12th   These fish seem, in their shallow pond, to have felt atmospheric changes very severely, requiring deeper water into which to descend, while it is very remarkable that the hybrid crosses between the American char and the Lochleven trout (9 leopards and 116 zebras) were not so affected, although kept under precisely similar surroundings

November 25th, 1885 —The largest was 10½ inches in length, many were found to be ready to spawn, some not quite so, but from thirty-five fish from 10 to 12,000 eggs were obtained, some were crossed among themselves, as will be detailed. There were not so many males with ripe milt as there were females with ripe ova

February 27th, 1886 —A good many of the old struans have died since spawning, they appear to be a delicate fish , found four dead to-day , it seems this frosty weather kills them, as was observed last year   The hybrids between *S fontinalis* and *S levenensis* are in the same pond, but none have died, so I conclude the cross with the trout has enabled the breed to stand the cold   Water is four feet deep

Struan Hybrids, or between American and British char.

Day, *Proc Zool Soc* 1884, p 379

November 12th, 1883 —Some eggs of the American char, *Salmo fontinalis*, were milted from a Scotch char, *S. alpinus*, the deaths among the incubating eggs were, in November 28, December 193, January 1028— or a total of 1449 deaths   On March 13th, 1884, there appeared to be about 500 alevins doing well, and on April 24th, 1885, they were mixed with the other struans in pond no 5

Struan Hybrids, or between American and British char

Day, *Proc Zool Soc* 1884, p 379

December 1st, 1883 —Some eggs of the American char were milted from a

* B xi, D 13 ($\frac{1}{10}$), P 13, V 8 9, A $\frac{1}{29}$, C 19, L l 158, Cæc pyl 32-37 —

			7 3 inches		10 5 inches	
Length of example			7 3 inches		10 5 inches	
,,	head		1 5	,,	2 7	,,
,,	pectoral fin	.	1 2	,,	1 9	,,
,,	caudal		1 2	,,	1 5	,,
,	ventral		0 9	,,	1 5	,,
Height of body		.	1 9	,,	2 9	,,
Eyes, diameter of			0 3	,,	0 4	,,
Eyes from end of snout			0 1	,,	0 8	,,
Eyes apart			0 5	,,	0 8	,,
Distance from snout to dorsal fin		.	3 0	,,	4 6	,,
,,	base of pectoral to base of ventral		2 2	,,	3 1	,,
,,	base of ventral to anal		1 1	,,	1 9	,,

The larger of these two examples was a male taken October 15th, 1886, and is figured on plate xi

Scotch char, the deaths among the incubating eggs were, in December 138, January 737, February 194—or a total of 1119, they hatched on February 16th March 13th, 1884, upwards of 100 were present   On April 24th, 1885, they were shifted to pond 5, along with similar hybrids

Struan Hybrids crossed

Day, *Proc Zool. Soc.* 1885, p 243
November 12th, 1884 —A female struan hybrid, twenty-one months old, gave 146 eggs, which were milted from a male of the same breed   Only six hatched on February 3rd, 1885, or in 84 days

Struan Hybrids crossed

November 24th and 25th, 1885 —About 17,500 eggs were obtained from struan hybrids, and crossed by males from the same breed, they being at that time thirty-three months old   The mortality from the two lots was, in November 5735, January 5635, and February 393, 1034 were unimpregnated   They commenced hatching February 11th, and about 2000 young came out   Many were very weak, and the mortality became considerable.   July 30th, 689 fish were shifted to 20 feet pond no 3, and on December 27th 450 were moved to the botanical pond, which is about four feet deep   About the middle of June, 1887, and the subsequent three weeks when the weather was scorching and the glare great, many were observed to commence to lose their colour, to become somewhat similar to albinos, with the pectoral, ventral, and anal still showing the red colour   On a net being placed near them they did not move unless touched, and on being taken out of the pond were found to be blind   in those slightly affected in colour the pupil was fixed and the colour dull almost opaque, in those fully affected it was quite opaque   At the commencement of July some wood was placed over the inlet end of the pond under which the fish crowded, but the temperature of the water did not fall until some rain fell on the 5th and 7th, when the fish seemed more lively   Some boards were now placed over a portion of the pond for the char to get under, but no other locality was available in which to transfer them   This instance is interesting, as showing how excess of light and heat, added to insufficient depth of water, causes mortality among these fishes

Struan Hybrids crossed

November 5th, 1886 —Twenty thousand eggs of this form of hybrid, 45 months old, were milted from males of the same race, the mortality being, in November 6895, December 4397, January 1503   This cross was repeated next day with 6000 eggs, and the mortality among them was, November 2526, December 1257, January 657, and 675 were not impregnated   They commenced hatching January 13th, and continued doing so for several days   Some of these hybrid parents were two years old, others a season older   As a rule, to which there were exceptions, these fish were weak   On June 14th, 1887, 1250 were placed in box 4, and 1000 in box no 5 in the hatching-house

Struan Hybrids breeding

December 6th, 1884 —Six hundred ova were obtained from a 22 months old struan hybrid   These ova had an average diameter 0 15 inch, and were milted from another struan hybrid and placed in box 104b   February 23rd, or in 79 days, 50 hatched and were transferred to box no 92, but only one lived, and it was placed in pond 3.

Struan hybrids breeding with Lochleven trout, Plate XI, fig 3 *

Day, *Proc Zool Soc* 1885, p 243

November 12th, 1884 —Four thousand five hundred eggs from two Lochleven trout were milted from a male struan hybrid and placed in box 88 , 1292 eggs were picked out during incubation, 1568 were unimpregnated, and the remainder hatched on February 2nd, 1885, or in 83 days, among them were many deformities, a few diopsics, and subsequently a high mortality On June 30th, 320 were placed in pond 3 Some were albinos, one especially was not blind at all there was a black hue along the top of the dorsal fin, the largest fish was four inches long July 5th, 1886, doing well November, 1886, then colours were very similar to those of the "zebra" breed, only being a little more plum-coloured along the sides, the dorsal fin less marked, and the head darker , consequently, those hybrids which contain one-fourth of Lochleven trout blood and three-quarters of that of British and American chars commingled, have adopted the colouring previously observed in hybrids between the American char and the Lochleven trout, while the tints of the British char are almost absent These forms are not sterile March, 1887, there were 157 of these fish alive, the longest being 11 inches July 7th, 1887, they were looking exceedingly well

Struan hybrids breeding with Lochleven trout

December 5th, 1885 —Seven thousand eggs of Lochleven trout were milted from struan hybrids, and on February 20th, or in 77 days, about 1500 hatched July 30th, 1886, shifted 620 fish to no 5, or 20-feet pond Many were albinos The mortality was as follows December 63, January 311, February 1531, unimpregnated 3782 March 17th, 1887, they now numbered 500 and were moved to pond no 4, and on June 14th to pond no 13, there being 413 good and strong fish

Struan hybrids breeding with British char

December 5th, 1886 —About 1200 eggs from struan hybrids were milted from a char received from Windermere, but the fish was nearly spent, and only two hatched, on February 20th, or in 77 days, the impregnation being possibly bad owing to deficiency of milt The following eggs were picked out December 322, January 1335, February 223

Zebra† hybrids breeding with Lochleven trout

Day, *Proc Zool Soc* 1885, p 242

November 12th, 1884, pond no 3, at Howietoun, was examined, and the females of the "zebra" race were not quite ready for breeding, while they appeared to be fewer in number than the males, some of which were ripe 1350

* B xi, D 13, P 16, V 9, A 11, C 21, L.1 133, L tr $\frac{27}{40}$, Cæc pyl 45

	Inches
Length of example	7 5
,, ,, head	1 4
,, ,, pectoral fin .	1 1
, ,, caudal fin .	1 15
,, ,, ventral fin	0 8
Height of body	1 8
Eye, diameter of	0 3
Eyes from end of snout	0 1
Eyes apart	0 15
Distance from snout to dorsal fin	3 3
,, ,, base of pectoral to base of ventral	2 0
,, ,, ,, ventral to anal	1 4

This example was captured October 13th, 1886, and is the one figured

† Zebras are a breed of hybrids in which the American char is the male and the Lochleven trout the female parent (*see* pages 260 262)

eggs were taken from a Lochleven trout and milted from a ' zebra '' 8½ inches long These were placed in box 92a Only about 12 of these eggs eyed, and merely 3 embryos developed, while they died unhatched As a rule the eggs appeared not to have been impregnated On measuring them I found that the majority averaged 0 24 of an inch in diameter The cause of failure in this instance was probably due to the young age of the male

Hunter, as we know, was of opinion that hybrids in the higher forms of vertebrates were not productive, except in cases where the generative organs were in a condition of perfection, a state which might be considered unnatural in hybrids But in fishes, the lowest of the vertebrate orders, the labours of fish-culturists lead one to modify those views, while Darwin and others have pointed out that domestication tends to eliminate sterility It will now be interesting, first, to ascertain the average percentage of salmonoid eggs which are successfully incubated in a well-appointed fish-cultural establishment, and then to compare these with what takes place among hybrids

If we place the average proportion of salmon or trout eggs dying during incubation at 5 per cent , such is in reality more than usually occurs at Howietoun, but this figure gives us a basis from which to calculate losses by But, as I have already observed (p 26 ante), eggs from young mothers are subject to a greater percentage of deaths during incubation than such as are (to a certain extent) obtained from fish three or four seasons and upwards of age While similarly milt from young parents may be a cause of failure in impregnation or mortality among the alevins and springlings

In first crosses for forming hybrids, and the first crosses of hybrids, we have the following records —

			Description	No of eggs incubated	Failures		No of days incubating
1881	Dec	24th	Male salmon (adult) and Lochleven trout	20 000			75
1884	,,	27th.	,, (,,) ,, ,, ,,	7000	about 28 per cent		76
1884	Nov	11th	,, (young) ,, ,, ,, ,,	12,000	,, 19	,,	78
1883	,,	29th	,, (,,) ,, ,, ,,	4500	, 6	,,	78
1884	Dec	9th	Male Lochleven trout and salmon (young)	400	,, 62	,,	78
1883	Nov	29th	Male salmon (young) and American char	3695	,, 93	,,	83
1882	,,	15th	Male American char and Lochleven trout	3000	,, 17	,,	85
1883	,,	29th	,, ,, ,, ,,	3000	,, 15	,,	—
1882	,,	15th.	Male Lochleven and American char	8000	,, 32	,,	84
1885	Dec	5th	Male British char and Lochleven trout	6500	,, 90	,,	81
1882	Nov	15th	Male American char and British char	9000	,, 23	,,	86
1884	,,	12th	Male struan (young) and struan	146	,, 99	,,	83
1885	,,	25th	,, ,, ,, ,, ,,	12,000	,, 83	,,	—
1884	Dec	6th	,, ,, (,,) ,, ,,	600	,, 91	,,	79
1884	Nov	12th	,, ,, ( ) ,, Lochleven	4500	,, 63	,,	—
1885	Dec	5th	,, ,, ( ) ,, ,,	7000	,, 78	,,	77
1886	,,	5th	,, ,, ( ) , British char	1200	,, 99	,,	77
1884	Nov	12th	,, zebra ( ) ,, Lochleven	1350	,, 100	,,	—

Of course one must not lay too great a stress upon the percentage of losses of eggs during incubation from the number of experiments here recorded, but taking them for what they are worth they would seem to point to the following results Employing the milt of adult salmon to fertilize trout eggs the loss was as much as 28 per cent and though the mortality among the yearlings and young fish was considerable, such must have been partly owing to the small amount of space which could be accorded to them

When we investigate the figures respecting Lochleven trout crossed by salmon smolts or par we find what at first appears strange, that the loss during incubation was far less than when the milt of adult fish was employed This seems to be probably owing to mechanical causes, as I have already alluded to the size of the micropyle in the trout ova being of barely sufficient extent to admit the spermatozoa of salmon, but owing to the large size of the eggs of these trout at Howietoun this difficulty has been partially overcome But employing young male salmon fertilization must be more readily effected, still one point requires elucidation, which is, provided the mortality during incubation is not great, what is it among the alevins, springlings and yearlings? In the first lot (laid down Nov 11th, 1884) there was a great deficiency of vitality among the alevins, which suffered extensively from dropsy of the sac, about 10 per cent dying during the first month and another 20 per cent subsequently before June A similar result occurred in the second lot (laid down Nov 29th, 1883) wherein in fact by August, 1884, only 100 remained alive

Next we see (Dec 9th, 1884) a few eggs of a salmon grilse which it was attempted to fertilize by means of the milt of an adult Lochleven trout, and here doubtless the same mechanical difficulty already alluded to would take place, the number of eggs lost during incubation being 62 per cent, only about one-half having been impregnated

Passing on to still smaller eggs, as of the American char, the attempt to fertilize them (Nov 29th, 1883) with even young salmon was a great failure, as many as 93 per cent being lost during incubation in fact all but 21 out of 1000 appear to have escaped impregnation

In the next two experiments (Nov 15th, 1882, and Nov 29th, 1883, zebra hybrids) eggs of Lochleven trout were fertilized by American char and here no mechanical difficulty could be present, and the deaths during incubation were from 15 to 17 per cent, while comparatively very few were lost from want of impregnation With two such distinct species as a char and a trout, crossed as described we find deaths and deformities due to hybridizing, in fact to some physiological not mechanical cause, while as the parents were both of pure breeds and no reason existed to suppose that the generative organs of either were affected this would seem to point out that crossing these two distinct species was calculated to occasion deformities or monstrosities in the resulting offspring

Similarly fertilizing American char eggs with milt from the Lochleven trout (Nov 15th, 1882, leopard hybrids) the mechanical difficulty would seem to again occur and the mortality during incubation was about 32 per cent or double what took place in the preceding cross As might be anticipated the physiological deleterious cause was likewise present in this instance, consequently deformities were numerous

If we, however, pass on to a cross made between a male American char and a British char (Nov 15th, 1882, struan hybrids) we see an almost intermediate condition Here we can hardly suppose that the mechanical difficulty would be present, yet the mortality was as great as 23 per cent, pointing to the physiological or pathological question, but the young were not so malformed as in the preceding crosses But it may be a subject that has yet to be solved as to what is the relationship between the British and American chars ?

This brings us to the consideration of *are hybrids fertile ?* and in the preceding experiments it has been shown that they are But mere possibility of fertility from the males or females of these hybrids, however interesting physiologically, is not so much so to the fish-culturist and riparian proprietor who wishes to know the amount of fertility which might reasonably be anticipated, and through how many generations ? Also whether fertility decreases with increased hybridization ?

Doubtless the amount of mortality among the eggs of hybrid *Salmonidæ* is, as has been shown, very great, but the age of these fish is one factor that has also to be taken into consideration

First as to the interbreeding of struan hybrids, in the first year when this was carried out (Nov 12th, 1884) or when the fish were 21 months old, the mortality was over 96 per cent of the eggs, in fact out of 146 eggs only six hatched On December 6th of the same year this cross was again made, but the mortality was over 91 per cent, and of the 50 which were hatched only one lived, these fish had no stamina

Breeding these struan hybrids among themselves when a year older (33 months old) gave the following result (Nov 25th, 1885), a mortality of 83 per cent, but the deaths among the young, although considerable, did not reach to what occurred the previous year

The next set of experiments consisted in crossing hybrids with pure breeds On Nov 12th, 1884, when the strains were only 21 months old their milt was used in order to fertilize some Lochleven trout eggs, and the mortality during incubation was 63 per cent It has been previously pointed out that male salmonoids are mostly more advanced for procreative purposes than females are There were many deformities and albinos among these offspring This cross was again tried, Dec 5th, 1885, when the mortality was about 78 per cent and many of the offspring were albinos

It would appear from the foregoing, it is probable when crossing two races of which the male belongs to the larger breed, that fertilization of the ova may be prevented owing to the size of the micropyle being insufficient to freely admit the entrance of the spermatozoa

That some physiological cause must be in existence which occasions deformities or monstrosities, and many eggs are unfertilized Also that in such crosses the offspring are very weak

The colours in hybrid (zebra) offspring crossed by a race of pure Lochleven trout have not reverted to those of either of the original parents, but appear to be forming these of a very distinct and separate kind

It will now be necessary to notice the number of days the eggs of hybrids require for incubation and to compare them with what takes place in those of the parent species kept distinct but under similar conditions * December, 1881, Lochleven trout eggs milted from salmon hatched in 75 days, and in December, 1884, salmon eggs milted from Lochleven trout took 76 days December, 1884, some salmon ova were milted from salmon and incubated under the same conditions as the hybrids, and they hatched in 79 days In fact the hybrids, whichever species was the male parent, hatched four or five days before the home-bred fish

On each occasion of the milt or eggs from a Howietoun raised grilse being crossed by Lochleven trout they took 78 days in incubating

It must be self-evident that should any cause occasion salmon or trout or char eggs to be hatched prior to the normal number of days of incubation having elapsed, such cannot conduce to the strength of the offspring We know this may be effected by elevating temperature (see pp 35, 36 ante), and that weak alevins are the result But when this is done by other means, as employing the male of a species (admittedly healthy) wherein incubation requires a moderate number of days to fertilize eggs from a healthy female of another species which requires a much larger number of days, and the period of incubation becomes reduced, it would seem to be a most probable result that certain pathological conditions would be set up in the offspring, such as were perceived in some of the hybrids already referred to

The American char, Salmo fontinalis, at from 43° to 43.5° Fahr requires from 79 to 81 days for incubation, and crossing a female with a young salmon the period required was 83 days, and in two other instances where Lochleven trout were the male element 84 and 85 days when the British char was similarly employed 86 days But when we examine the period required for the eggs of hybrids inter-bred among themselves we see another alteration, almost a regular diminution in the number of days, as among the strains they varied from 79 to 83 days, but crossing these hybrids with British char or Lochleven trout only 77 days were required

Respecting the number of par bands† on the sides of young hybrid Salmonulæ

* During the winter of 1886-7, at Howietoun, with the temperature of the water kept at 43° or 43.5° Fahr, the following number of days was found necessary for incubating the eggs of the following fish —Salmon, pure, hatched at Howietoun, laid down in November, 81 days sea trout, S trutta, laid down in November, 81 days burn trout, Salmo fario, not above 3 years of age, laid down November 11th, 79 days in one lot, 74 in another Lochleven trout, pure 10 year old fish, laid down in November, 76 days Lochleven, 8-year-old, milted in November by young burn trout, 75 days Lochleven, 3-year old, milted in November by burn trout, 76 days. American char, S fontinalis, laid down in November, from 79 to 81 days

† The number of bands appears to be in some way modified by locality, if the young at Howietoun are reared in water coming from Loch Coulter they have about 17, if from the small

(*see* pp 158, 227 *ante*) the following are some of the observations made at Howietoun —

	Average length	Most bands	Least bands	Greatest difference in a single fish
7 hybrids of Salmon and Lochleven	11½ inches	12	10	2
4 ,, Zebra breed	9¼ ,,	11	8	2
3 ,, Leopard breed	9¼ ,,	11	8	2
6 ,, Striuan breed	9¼ ,,	13	8	3

This would appear to show that the difference in the numbers of these par bands in these fishes may be comparatively considerable

The number of rows of scales I have found existing in the various chars have been as follows —

British char	Scales along lateral-line 125-145	from adipose dorsal to	11	18-23
American char	,, ,, 122-142	,,	,,	,, 21-26
Hybrid char	,, ,, 124-136	,,	,,	,, 20-28

The mode of dentition on the vomer alters in hybrids, as will be seen in fig 52, showing how the teeth in the char, *Salmo fontinalis*, are restricted to an angular band of about six or eight situated along the hind edge of the head of that bone   But in crossing with trout the number of teeth on the head of the bone decreases   while the knob at the inferior end of the head lengthens along the central line of the vomer, where teeth in trout are situated, and this elongation serves as a dental ridge showing three or even four teeth along it

It may be a question whether any prepotency of sex among the parents of hybrids can be detected in the offspring, exhibited either in sexual development or in external characters ?

Of course as trout and char may equally commence breeding when just under two years of age we cannot expect to find any prepotency of parental sex to be thus shown among the offspring, but it is different with the salmon, among which we may anticipate spawning at a year later than in the trout

In the cross made December 24th 1881, between salmon and Lochleven trout, and which hatched in March, 1882, the fish were suffocated in July, 1885, but some would evidently have bred that winter or in their third or fourth season similarly to salmon   two which survived, and were males, were employed for breeding, November and December, 1886

November 29th, 1883, a salmon par was employed to fertilize milt of a Lochleven trout, and among the few survivors of the diopsical offspring one female gave eggs November 23rd, 1886, or at 33 months   Consequently in all those instances where the male parent was the salmon the young did not breed before the 33rd month, or similarly to salmon bred at Howietoun, but twelve months later than trout or char

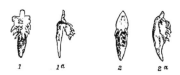

No 52   Teeth on vomer of American char   1 front view,
1*a*, side view   of hybrid between American char and Lochleven
trout   2, front view, 2*a*, side view.

Craig end burn only from 12 to 14, and those much broken up, the food being the same in both localities   The young of sea trout *Salmo trutta* (*see* note in p 146 *ante*), on July 6th, 1887, in pond 3 at Howietoun, were found to have 9 complete and some incomplete par bands, while some young of S *fario* in the next pond, no 4, and of similar age, had from 10 to 12 of these bands.

MONSTROSITIES

The subject of monstrosities or abnormal variations among men and the lower animals, has always excited attention in every class of the community, for in times gone by they were considered, even by educated persons, as mysterious portents of events which would shortly take place, or else the result of diabolical influences And even now, in some districts, such ideas are observed to linger among the uneducated or the credulous, while they are more widely disseminated in Eastern climes

The very term monster has been derived either from the Latin term "monstro" *to show*, or from "moneo" *to warn*, in accordance with the views held by different schools of thought or superstition For some imagined that these abnormal creatures showed the results of witchcraft, or the direct effects of evil agency as one may observe by referring to Rueff's work, *De Conceptio et Generatione Hominis*, A D 1580, wherein he devoted a chapter to the question "An homines ex dæmonibus et rursus dæmones ex hominibus infantes concipere possunt ?" And here he gravely arrived at the conclusion that these monstrosities had not really demons for their fathers Even at the present day, in some portions of Hindustan, the natives deem it no crime to destroy such creatures at the time of, or shortly after their birth, as they hold contrary views to the conclusions arrived at by Rueff Individuals of great intellect as Aldrovandus, Ambrose Paré, and many other illustrious men have held that these monsters being presages of Divine vengeance, were sent into the world in order to warn people of impending disasters, and Lycosthenes went so far as to add pictures to his descriptions of each variety of monsters, and which he believed showed the calamity which its birth was intended to foretell

Violik observed that monstrosities were most numerous among domesticated animals, but "they seldom happen among Reptilia, still less frequently among Fishes, Molluscs, Articulata, and Radiata" Thompson remarked that they do not come by chance, but the laws regulating their occurrence are still undiscovered,[*] while monsters in a wild state have less chance of survival than perfect animals, being more or less unable to escape from their enemies

The period at which original malformations commence, may be at or prior to the time of fertilization of the ovum, for they may be congenital or acquired Or it may be some cause affecting the development of the embryo from its earliest stage subsequent to fertilization, and these last may be again subdivided into causes affecting the development of the embryo or fœtus from within, or such as accidents, &c, which may occur from without

It has been remarked in the higher forms of vertebrate life that malformations or an influence originating such, may exist in either the ovum or spermatozoa prior to fertilization, as was observed in the case of a female cat at Cheltenham possessing an abnormal number of toes, which were reproduced in her young, and for several successive litters Similarly, the father may be the origin of malformations thus an otherwise well-formed man has been known to procreate with different women, children having the same deformity, or even the malformation may miss one generation to appear in a subsequent one These instances, which might be increased indefinitely, are only adduced to show that the

[*] The observation " law of nature" simply, as Carpenter remarked, expresses a set of uniformities in the surrounding universe which man assumes to hold good just so far as they have been verified, but not necessarily any further, while it accounts for nothing and explains nothing

elements of deformity may be present either in the germ from the father* or the mother, and be communicated to the offspring, occasioning hereditary deformities which may extend over more than one generation †

Everyone who possesses even a very limited acquaintance with fish-culture, must be aware that monstrosities among the young as they emerge from the egg are by no means rare, and likewise that such can be hereditary as may be seen in the race of gold-fish, *Cyprinus auratus*, bred by fish-culturists Now and again we find reference made to these monsters in the public press with surmises as to their cause, and then the matter drops until another is recorded and furnishes material for further discussion The subject, however, is one that has engaged the attention of some of the foremost men in science, and that from almost immemorial ages, and if opinions are still divided as to the exact process of how these abnormal forms arise, still very much information on this point may be gleaned from the pages of scientific journals I have, therefore, thought that it might be interesting to bring together some notes on this subject which more especially have a bearing on the monstrosities, and some pathological changes as seen among the young Salmonidæ, whether *congenital*, or occurring during inter-ovarian life being *acquired*, or arise subsequent to that period and during extra-ovarian life These divisions must therefore be restricted to the embryo within the ovum, or subsequent to its extrusion, while the yelk-sac or alevin stage, may properly be referred to the latter of these periods

Monsters, as a rule, succumb as soon as the alevin absorbs its yolk-sac, and although it has been asserted that all the layings from certain females produce monsters, I have not as yet had the opportunity of showing such an instance, but have observed the contrary, e g all the young produced from a mother with bull-dog deformity being perfect

The following divisions of monstrosities and deformities, as seen among fishes, may be observed (1) due to *constitutional causes* as from young parents, hybridi-zation, &c (2) *Congenital or hereditary causes‡* as hereditary monstrosities such as the various races of gold carp (3) *Acquired* causes or *accidental circumstances* as arrest of development or accidents to the embryo§ prior to hatching

As regards the effects of constitutional causes on the proportionate number of monstrosities and malformations, such appears to be greater in hybrid fish, or when bred from pure parents, but distinct species, than when the breed is kept pure, or both parents are of one species It thus seems clear that the element or cause of malformation must exist at the period of, or subsequent to the fertilization of the egg. As these monstrosities, &c, increase in hybrids interbred with hybrids, if the parents are very young, the same results are seen (*see* p 265 *ante*), and the alevin may suffer from dropsy of the yelk-sac (plate XII, fig 16), (*see* p 261 *ante*)

---

* This may be seen in an excessive number of fingers, harelip, etc

† Dr E Cutler, *Medical World*, 1886, iv, pp 18 20, suggested that abnormal forms of sperma-tozoa are sometimes the cause of teratological conditions in the children, and stated that abnormal forms of the following character have been observed in the sperm of man Spermatozoa with two or three bodies, with one body and two or three tails, with two bodies and two tails, and with two bodies and three tails The average proportion of these monstrous spermatozoa is about 1 in 50,000, their movements are slower, but more vigorous than the normal forms

Monsters have been considered to be sometimes formed by an excess of development, one fœtus may be contained within another in almost every part, or a more or less developed rudi-ment may adhere as a tumour to the outer surface of another body, and be even covered by the integument Some have been compared to parasitic disease formed in the interior of the body of the fœtus as hair or teeth, or rudiments of a second fœtus internally or adherent externally Vrolik mentioned a fœtal calf being born, the tongue being the sole developed portion, demon-strating that merely a single well defined organ may be present

‡ Gegenbaur has divided atavistic phenomena, or the reappearance of a more primitive organization, or a reversion to a primary condition into (1) Palæogenetic if present in the germ, or by law of inheritance, and (2) Neogenetic if absent in the germ The existence of this last phenomenon is denied by Mr Bland Sutton (*Proc Zool Society*, 1886 p 551)

§ It would, perhaps, be useful in this class of fishes, to separate the embryo from the fœtus in description, but in practice such would be difficult, for although such might define a period before and subsequent to the eyed period, but few would agree as to the precise time at which such occurs, or what position the alevin would hold

As already observed, there are doubtless congenital or hereditary causes occasioning monstrosities, and which latter may be divided into double and single ones The chief hypotheses which have been offered to account for double monsters are (1) by *fusion*, or that they have been formed from two distinct embryos which have become united or fused together   (2) By *fission*, or that they have sprung from a single germ, which has doubled or become sub-divided   (3) That the germ itself was abnormally compound from the very first

It has been observed that we may arrange these monsters as existing in the higher forms of vertebrate animals in a continuous series from such as possess an extra finger or toe, to those in which two or even three heads have been present While the examination of a large number of specimens has led to the conclusion that superficial portions of animals are more liable to multiplication than are internal organs, and those of the upper or anterior half of a body than its inferior or posterior extremities *

If, however, we restrict ourselves more to fishes† we can observe monsters with three heads (plate xii, fig 11 and 11a), or with two heads (plate xii, fig 8), or the chest may likewise be doubled , or twin fish completely developed, but possessing a single yelk-sac (plate xii, fig 10), or only one is completely developed, the other being more or less in a rudimentary condition (plate xii, fig 6)   Or monsters with three or two heads may only possess one tail (plate xii, fig 11), or they may be united by their tail portion (plate xii fig 9)   Or the head and body may be single anteriorly, but the tail portion may be double (plate xii, fig 4)   Or there may be three eyes (plate xii fig 1), or even four, and these may be variously situated

M de Quatrefages‡ considered, *Annals of Natural History*,§ xv, 1885, p 47,

* Among vertebrates double monsters have been thus divided —1 *Anterior duplicity*, when two bodies become adherent to one another by their anterior surfaces (as by the sterna)   2 *Lateral duplicity*, as a common thoracic cavity   or it may be in two principal divisions, as duplicity of the entire body, terminating in singleness, or duplicity of the remaining entire body, but the head continues single   Or in some cases the two heads begin to coalesce   then only one ear remains between the adjacent surfaces of the two heads , or both ears may become lost , or the two adjacent and middle eyes approximate; next there may be only one orbit , or union of the heads , or the head merely doubled in individual parts   The body may be single in the middle, but double above and below , or the body may be single above and double below   3 *Inferior duplicity*, or two bodies with their lower ends united, a head above and another below. 4 *Posterior duplicity*, two bodies united by their backs, or portions of them   5 *Superior duplicity*, as two children which have been born connected by their skulls   It has been remarked that there has been only one triple human monster recorded

† See M Girdwoyn, *Pathologie des Poissons*, 1880

‡ A commonly expressed error is that double yolked fowls' eggs always contain two embryos, and that during incubation one generally develops to the partial or entire destruction of the other, and that thus extra heads or organs are produced   Thompson, however, *London and Edinburgh Monthly Journal*, July, 1844, tried to hatch examples of these eggs, but failed , in some it was evident that only one yolk was productive, and it would appear that double monsters are not dependent upon double yolks, although it has been thought that from such possibly twins might be produced

§ M de Quatrefages exhibited at the French Academy of Sciences, March 19th, 1854, a double monster which he kept alive nearly two months , it consisted of two fishes completely separated one from the other, and adhering to the opposite sides of a vitellus, which showed a deep notch in the front   Of these two fish the largest had its face deformed, its eyes were absent, but the remainder of its body was perfect   The second or smaller fish had its head well formed, but its body was humped and its tail twisted   The abdominal veins (afterwards converted into the *vena portæ*) were in their normal situation, their ramifications spread over the whole surface of the vitellus, communicating at their extremities with the roots of the vitelline veins, which subsequently form the hepatic veins   Also numerous anastomoses connected the last ramifications of the abdominal vein of each embryo with those of the vitelline vein of the other, so that a continual interchange of blood took place

On February 19th, nearly a month after the specimen came into M Quatrefages' possession, and about six weeks after exclusion from the egg, the two embryos were close together, and ready to unite on one side of the abdomen, while on the other they were still separated by a considerable space occupied by the vitellus   The larger embryo had originally been situated to the right of the vitellus, but had become superior, lying somewhat across the smaller and more deformed individual, which it carried about with it

M de Quatrefages, as well as M Serres, concluded that this monstrosity had been formed by the coalescence or fusion of two originally distinct embryos, and that the vitellus from which it

that these double monsters are formed by a coalescence of two originally distinct embryos, and that the vitellus from which his had been developed had also been double, the point of junction being in his opinion indicated by a deep notch at the anterior part of the vitellus. He also thought that certain living alevin monsters upheld his opinion. On the other hand, M. Coste believed that the vitellus was invariably single, and that the circulation in double monsters was common to the two embryos.[*] Thompson observed a double primitive groove in a single ovum which would probably have developed into a double monster.

M. Lereboullet's observations[†] appeared to demonstrate that double monsters

had been developed, had likewise been double, the point of junction being indicated by the deep notch in the anterior part of the vitellus, which has been already referred to

[*] M. Coste asserted that the incubation in double monsters was common to the two embryos, that the greater part of the blood which had circulated in the body of one passed into the vessels of the umbilical vesicle (abdominal vein), whence the greater portion of it was carried by the vitelline vein to the auricle of the other embryo, and so on, and that, in accordance with this reciprocal circulation, the contractions of the two ventricles takes place alternately   (M. Quatrefages believed that he did not find this to be the case in the two instances observed by him.)

M. Coste maintained that in double monsters there was only a single vitellus and umbilical vesicle, because at whatever age these monsters were examined, the vesicle was invariably simple, a view further supported by the condition of the circulation That as the external lamina of the umbilical vesicle formed a common abdominal wall, enclosing the vitellus, it was impossible to regard the two embryos as distinct individuals developed at the poles of a double vitellus, and becoming coalescent at a late period of their youth, as they were actually united from the first into a single organism by this membrane, and their subsequent union was effected by the gradual contraction of this membrane as the vitellus became absorbed This conjugation was consequently a primordial phenomenon and of a more intimate nature than one of simple adherence, as was described by M Geoffroy Saint-Hilaire, wherein two chickens, hatched from two separate yolks contained in one egg, were found to adhere to one another by the belly

[†] He coincided with M. Coste's views, and his experiments made on the eggs of the pike, *Esox lucius*, showed that the development of the embryo commenced at the moment when the blastoderm had almost completely enclosed the vitellus, by the formation of a triangular tubercle on the blastodermal ridge, and that from this centre the embryonic fillet took its rise. In many cases this ridge of the blastoderm bears two tubercles, from each of which an embryonic fillet was produced, and the further development of these gave rise to double embryos of various kinds He found that the formation of monsters could be determined at pleasure by placing the eggs in unfavourable conditions for development. He described the formation of several varieties of these double monsters. (1.) In some two tubercles budded out from the margin of the blastoderm, from each of which proceeded a fillet, furnished with a dorsal furrow, forming two embryos adhering to the marginal ridge Soon afterwards the divisions of the vertebræ appeared, the external ones having their ordinary form and dimensions, while the internal gradually became confused, passing from the body of one embryo to that of the other, thus causing the partial amalgamation of the two embryos In this way a double fish was formed, arising from two primitive germinating points, produced on the blastodermal ridge, so as to become partially joined ; it had therefore two separate bodies with a common tail

(2.) In other eggs the blastodermal ridge gave rise to a long and broad fillet terminating anteriorly by two rounded lobes. Two parallel furrows appeared in the fillet and soon developed the vertebral divisions, while the anterior lobes acquired a determinate form, and each produced two ocular vesicles, constituting a single body with two distinct heads In these cases, however, the duplicity was transitory ; the two heads soon came into contact, and became fused together in such a manner as to form only a single head The mode in which this fusion occurred he had been unable to ascertain In some cases the two heads appeared to remain distinct

(3.) Some embryos had a single head, two separate bodies, and one or two tails, they were thus formed —The ridge of the blastoderm, which had the form of a gaping button hole, produced a single cephalic tubercle, but the formative process goes on in the whole circumference of the margin, each half of which acquires a *chorda dorsalis* and a nervous cord, and soon exhibits the divisions of the vertebræ When the cephalic tubercle was short, and merely gave origin to the true head, each of the two bodies was furnished with two auditory capsules, two pectoral fins, and a heart, but when this tubercle was more elongated the anterior part of the body was simple and bore two eyes, two auditory capsules and a single heart, and the body terminated posteriorly in two short branches.

(4.) This organization of the ridge of the blastoderm into a double embryo, seemed to explain the formation of a simple embryo, bearing on the right side of its body a small tubercle directed backwards and terminated by an auditory tubercle and an active heart Here the resorption of the parts of the body posterior to the heart in one of the embryos was considered the reason, while he witnessed the complete disappearance of one of the bodies in the other instance

(5.) In another egg the ridge of the blastoderm showed two contiguous tubercles, one of which had the ordinary form of the cephalic tubercle, while the other was smaller and irregular. The first alone acquired a furrow, and gave rise to an embryo, on one side of which the smaller tubercle was borne

were produced by fusion of two embryos, and the theory that attributed a separate vitellus to each embryo was incorrect He believed there was only a single germ, but that this, by becoming developed in two directions, instead of one (as normally), gave rise to two more or less distinct embryos That the blastodermal ridge plays a most important part in the formation of these embryos, and in fact constitutes the "true embryonic germ, which is always simple and single, like the vitellus which is covered by the blastoderm but when its development is deranged from its regular course, is capable of vegetating like the substance of which the bodies of polypes are composed, so as to produce various forms, which however, in their subsequent development, always show a tendency to return to the original type of the species "

Vrolik likewise remarked, as an objection against the hypothesis of fusion of two originally perfect and separate embryos, that double monsters "form one series, among whose several members the degrees and modes of deviation from singleness gradually increase, and pass without one abrupt step from the addition of a single ill-developed limb, to the nearly complete formation of two perfect beings " He considered one germ being provided with an excess of formative power becomes the cause and origin of every double monster In fact, we do not see fusion, but an excess or irregular distribution of developmental power, and instances of singleness tending towards reduplication and not of reduplication to singleness

Valentin concluded that an injury inflicted on the caudal extremity of an embryo on the second day, had been found on the fifth to have produced the rudiments of a double pelvis and four inferior extremities. But Vrolik said, if we admit this cause for those large and principal types, we must acknowledge that such is insufficient to account for those cases in which, the body remaining single, some parts are double, and here excess of formative power is the sole explanation we can offer In many double monsters there may be excess in one part and defect in another, the power being more or less excessive in quantity and being also wrongly distributed "It is not impossible," observed Vrolik, "that excess of power in the ovum, which all admit can alone explain the lower degrees of duplicity, may, in proportionally higher degrees, perhaps by the formation of two primitive grooves, produce the most complete double monster, or even two such separate individuals as are sometimes found within a single amnion "

The eyes may be modified in various ways, for some fish are born blind owing to entire absence of the eyeball, or it may be present on one side of the head but not on the other In many cases the eyeball may be present, but in a more or less rudimentary or abnormal condition Or there may be a single eye situated on or near the top of the head Two eyes may be merged into one, or we may have three eyes, or even four eyes on one head (plate xii, fig 1 and 1a), while in such as have additional heads the eyes may be normal in each, or, as in the example figured (plate xii, fig 11), one eye may be absent from one of the heads, while a double optic nerve has been observed with a single eyeball, or even a single optic

(6) Sometimes three heads were present, one of these was thus described by M Lereboullet It was a double embryo, composed of two bodies united behind, but quite free in front One of these bodies was of the normal form, the other bore two heads, of which that on the left was of the normal form and furnished with two eyes, while that on the right only bore the right eye, the union of the two heads being effected at the point where the left eye ought to have been This embryo was still within the egg when described, it had two hearts, one common to the two principal bodies, situated at their bifurcation, the other placed in the angle of union of the two heads He considered that two fillets had been formed, one of which had been terminated by two cephalic lobes and acquired two furrows (as in no 2), while the other continued simple These two embryos thus united posteriorly (as in no 1) producing an embryo with one tail, two bodies, and three heads

(7) When the development of the egg was retarded by means of a low temperature, the ridge of the blastoderm produced no embryo, but contracted gradually like the opening of a bag, its substance became condensed and formed a mammillated tubercle projecting from the surface of the vitellus This tubercle continued living, rose more and more from the surface, acquired a linguate form, and at last constituted an elongated body, narrowed in front, divided transversely into vertebral lamellæ, *without dorsal chord or sensitive organs, but furnished with a heart* of which the contractions were sometimes very lively

nerve with a double eyeball, or the nerves may be present but the eye absent
How these additional eyes have been developed has been a cause of dispute *

The types of simple monsters may generally be classed under one cause, arrest
of development† occurring in the normal course of embryonic life. And these
may be shown in the head wherein the eyes, mouth, upper jaw, lower jaw, or
opercles may be affected or in some portion of the vertebral column,
or in the fins which may be shortened, lengthened, or the rays in an abnormal
condition

Sometimes the upper jaw is the shorter, sometimes the lower, as may be seen
figured in plate xii, and these monstrosities, especially the latter, are common
among hybrids and fish raised from young parents. Although these monstrosities
may be occasioned by increased growth, they are more commonly due to the arrest
of development in some of the bones of the head

The bull-dog deformity of the snout or an arrest of development in the
premaxillaries (plate xii, fig 19) is by no means rare, more especially in fishes
raised by the fish-culturist The example figured was sent me from a burn near
Perth, but I have also examples of *fontinalis* from Howietoun with a similar
deformity, one of which was a female, from it many eggs were obtained, but none
of the young were thus malformed, it not being inherited ‡

There may be an apparently shortened lower jaw, as is more commonly seen
in hybrids or in fish artificially raised, than in those in their natural condition
Many, however, do not seem to be born thus, and at Howietoun it has been
observed to be most common in such as are kept in wooden tanks, and supposed
to be owing to their using their lower jaws with injurious force against the

* M Camille Dareste (*Arch Zool Expér et Gén* x, 1876) entered very fully into this question,
least, among the higher vertebrates The type of monsters, as he observed, which appear first in
the embryonic evolution is that characterized by an arrest of development in the head, which shows
neither eyes, nose, or buccal apparatus This is rather rare The head consists of a single bud,
presenting in its lower part a *cul-de sac* the pharynx He had observed, in fact, a great number
of times, very diverse anomalies of the primitive groove in the region of the head In many of
these he saw that the primitive groove had not attained to the anterior extremity of the head
It is evident that under such conditions the anterior cerebral vesicle and the ocular vesicle
which are dependent on it, cannot be formed , or else that the vesicle is incompletely formed and
becomes constituted as a simple rudiment If the embryo continues to develop it presents the
fundamental character of an undeveloped head

The next type, cyclops, or a single eye in the median line of the face, or formed of two
conjoined into one, or two eyes in one orbital space, or even in two orbits placed very close
together or nearer than in a natural state, are merely degrees of one type Geoffroy Saint-
Hilaire, relying solely on the study of these monsters themselves, gave an account of cyclops
formed by atrophy of the nasal apparatus and a more or less complete fusion of the eyes Husche,
on the contrary, began by observations of facts in embryology, and explained all these forms of
cyclops by an arrest of development He believed that he had observed the ocular apparatus was
single in its origin, and formed a vesicle situated at the extremity of the cerebro-spinal tube
immediately in front of the first cerebral vesicle This single ocular vesicle enlarged in size
transversely, and then divided into two parts and finished by constituting two distinct ocular
vesicles, and situated on the two sides of the head The interspace between the two ocular
vesicles became occupied, little by little, by a prolongation of the cerebro-spinal tube, which first
formed the vesicle of the third ventricle, afterwards the vesicle of the cerebral hemisphere

M Dareste, however, considered that the ocular vesicles are separated from their first
appearance, and that the cyclops is not the persistence of certain embryonic conditions but an
arrest of development

† One very general cause of malformation is attributed to impeded circulation in the fœtus
possibly first through the circulation, and subsequently through the nervous system Vrohk
remarked that "I presume to conclude that no malformation whatever proceeds from a central
system, but is occasioned merely by impeded development, the cause of which remains concealed
This impediment may be confined to one part, or may be extended over more " Abnormal
development gives monsters wherein there is a deficiency if impeded, and excessive formation
when such is in excess

‡ Mr Eagle Clarke sent me, 13th November, 1885, a specimen of trout from Penyghent (*see
Yorkshire Vertebrata*, p 127), with the under jaw projecting beyond the upper All the fish in
the beck (which is on the mountain side and has only a course of a short half mile, when it
disappears into a deep abyss in the limestone), are of the same variety, and locally termed
"ground trout "

The late Mr Arthur writing from Dunedin, April 2nd, 1885 remarked of Lochleven trout
which arrived in New Zealand " a year ago, a Government lot, have developed a singular deformity
in the shortening of the lower jaw "

sides occasioning some deleterious effect Sometimes the lower jaw is twisted round to one side, and may likewise be lengthened

Among single monsters the tail fin may be more or less horizontal like that of a shrimp (plate xii, fig 5), or the body may be curved so as to form a circle round the yelk-sac (plate xii, fig 12), or laterally (plate xii, fig 13) Or the head may be much developed while the remainder of the body is rudimentary and much resembles a tadpole The head may be variously malformed

In some forms we may observe distinct pathological changes in the spinal column as has been observed by several authors as " The Hog-backed trout of Plinlimmon," *Cambridge Quart Mag* 1833, p 391 , Cobbold, *Edinb New Phil Jour* ii 1855, plate vi In plate xii, fig 12 is the figure of a young trout in which the spinal column is bent into an almost semi-circular form and is of very great interest It has been observed among the eggs transmitted to long distances that there are always some alevins born with spines curved into a more or less circular form Attempting to swim they go round like dancing dervishes and die on the absorption of the yelk sac If, however, they are malformed to a lesser extent we find spinal disease and a hunch-backed fish resulting In 1747 Mr Barrington sent a paper to the Royal Society on the *Hog backed Trout of Plinlimmon* He remarked that they occurred in watersheds where there were considerable falls, and theoretically it seemed probable that such might be occasioned by injuries occurring to the embryo, and in 1886 I tried what would be the effects of concussion on eggs and their contents* (*see* p 41 *ante*) and while the embryo was still unhatched and assisted by Mr S Wethered, F G S , we ascertained that concussion had occasioned spinal injury (plate xii, fig 15) In accordance with its extent the young fish has curvature of this portion of the body, and in the slightest cases they recover but with shortening of the spinal column, occasioning hog-backed deformity (plate xii, fig 14)

* The concussion of water falling from an elevation would act very similarly to the eggs being dropped from a height and might occasion spinal irritation with subsequent disease and absorption of the bodies of the vertebre, thus reducing the length of the spinal column as figured, and, as is also very commonly seen in members of the cod family, but in nature these are soon eaten up

Genus 2.—THYMALLUS, *Cuvier*

Branchiostegals seven to ten · pseudobranchiæ well developed. Body somewhat elongated and compressed. Gape of mouth small, maxilla short, rarely extending to beneath the middle of the orbit. Minute teeth on the jaws, near the head of the vomer, and on the palatines, none on the tongue. First dorsal with many rays (20-24 rays), second dorsal fin adipose. caudal forked. Stomach siphonal. Scales rather large. Lateral-line well marked. Cœcal appendages rather numerous. Air-bladder very large.

Geographical distribution.—In the northern hemisphere, generally restricted to fresh waters. in Europe, it appears to prefer cold and mountainous streams to more temperate climes, and abounds in Scandinavia and Lapland, the east of France and the north of Italy.

The Grayling, Plate X, fig 1

Thymallus seu Thymus, Belon De Aquat p 184, Silvian fol 81, t xvi, Rondel ii, p 187, Gesner, pp 978, 979, Aldrov v, c 14, p 594, Jonston, iii, tit i, c 3, p 128, t xxvi, f 3, 4, and t xxxi, t 6, Willoughby, p 187, t N 8, Ray, p 62. *Coregonus*, no 3, Artedi, Synon p 20, Genera, p 10, Species, p 41. *Salmo*, Gronov Zooph no 375. *Trutta*, Klein, Pisc MSS v, p 21, no 15, t iv, f 5. *Grayling*, Pennant, Brit Zool (Ed 1776) iii, p 311, pl lvi (Ed 1812), iii p 414, pl lxxii, Low, Fauna Orcad p 224, Davy, Salmonia, 1832, p 198, Duhamel, Pêches, ii, p 218, pl iii, f 2.

Salmo thymallus, Linn Syst Nat i, p 512, Bloch, Fische Deuts i, p 158, t xxiv, Gmel Linn p 1379, Bonn Ency Ich p 167, pl lix, Bl Schn p 410, Donovan, Brit Fish, v, pl lxxxviii, Pall Zoo Ross-As iii, p 364, Turton, Brit Fauna, p 101, Gronov ed Grav, p 153.

Salmo thymus, Bonnaterre, l c p 167.

Coregonus thymallus, Lacép v, p 254, Flem Brit An p 181; Jurine, Poiss Lac Leman, page 170, pl x.

Thymallus vulgaris, Nilss Prod Ich Scan p 13, and Skand Fauna Fisk p 417, Jenyns, Manual, p 430, Bonap Pesc Eur p 23, Kroyer, Dan Fisk iii, p 35, c fig, Yarrell, Brit Fishes (ed 1), ii, p 79, c fig (ed 2), ii, p 136 (ed 3), i, p 304, White, Catal p 80, Thompson, Nat Hist Ireland, iv, p 167, Schlegel, de Dier Ned p 133, Siebold, Sus w f Mit Eur p 267, Gunther, Catal vi, p 200, J Wrummont, Pub de l'Inst de Luxen xi, pp 1-48, Collett, Norges Fiske p 171, Feddersen, p 78, Canestrini, Fauna Ital i, Pesc p 23, Houghton, Brit F W Fish p 119, c. fig, Moreau Poiss France, iii, p 543, Gigholi, Cat Pesc Ital p 42, Day, British and Irish Fish, ii, p 131, plate cxxii.

Thymallus vexillifer, Agass Mem Soc Sc Nat Neuch i, t B, t D, f 5-8, and Poiss d eau douce, pls xvi, xvii, xviii, Cuv and Val xxi, p 438, Heckel and Kner, Suss w f p 242, Blanchard, Poiss des eaux douces, France, p 437, f 113.

Thymalus gymnothorax, Cuv. and Val xxi, p 445, pl. 625, Gunther, Fische des Neckars, p 117.

Grayling, Couch, Fish Brit Isles, iv, p 280, pl ccxxxvi.

B viii-x, D 20-24 ($\frac{4-6}{14-19}$) | 0, P 15-16, V 10-11, A 11-14 ($\frac{1-4}{6-10}$), C 21, L l 1 75-85, L tr $\frac{9-6}{14-15}$, Cæc p¹ 22-30, Vert. 39/22.

Length of head 5¼ to 6, of caudal fin 6, height of body 4¼ to 5 in the total length. *Eyes*—diameter of each 4 in the length of the head, 1¼ diameters from the end of the snout, and about the same distance apart, pupil pear-shaped or transversely oval. Its form is rather elongated and very graceful, dorsal profile more curved than the abdominal   Upper jaw very slightly the longer, the posterior extremity of the maxilla reaches to beneath the anterior edge or first third of the orbit   Teeth—fine ones in the jaws, near the head of the vomer, and on the anterior portion of the palatines, none on the tongue   Fins—these vary with the sex, the last dorsal rays are somewhat produced in adults   The first dorsal fin commences midway between the end of the snout and on a line above the front edge of the anal fin, the height of its rays being about two-thirds of that of the body below it   Pectoral inserted in the lower fourth of the height, and as long as the head excluding the snout.   Ventrals situated beneath the middle of the rayed dorsal fin, and comparatively small, terminating on a line below the hind edge of the adipose dorsal   Caudal forked   Scales—in regular rows, some small ones being present over the basal portion of the caudal fin   The chest, or that portion of it as far as the pectoral fin, may be entirely destitute of scales or else scaled   In the example figured there were thirty rather short cœcal appendages   Walls of the stomach thickened   Intestines—with about 17 transverse valves, rather more complete than in examples of Salmo   Colours—these during life are beautifully changeable, head of a bluish purple and a golden tinge along the back, while the horizontal lines along the body are dark, and each of the scales has a golden tinge   Dorsal fins with purplish bands and ocelli which have a purplish red centre, and there are likewise some purplish streaks along the course of the rays, while the outer edge is likewise purplish   Black spots scattered over the body, occasionally there are some on the fins   In some specimens spots are absent, which, though rare in this country, appear to be more common in France, as Valenciennes had many such examples   The brighter colours decrease with age, and gray lines show themselves along each row of scales, while the young have transverse bars or bands

Names —Thymallus was given to this fish by Ælian and also by Ausonius, from the fancied resemblance of its odour to that of the water-thyme,* upon which it was supposed to feed, an odour which many of the present day fail to detect,† and others consider that they can observe a likeness in its smell when first captured to that of the cucumber   Some who imagine they are able to recognize this odour have suggested that the varying nature of its food may cause the grayling to occasionally possess a strong smell which at other times is almost or quite absent   Salviani in the sixteenth century observed, that being a swift swimmer it disappears like a shadow, from whence it derived its name umbra   "Grayling" is said to be a corruption of Gray lin or line referring to the longitudinal lines along its gray body   Oumer, Northumberland. Shutts, Sheets, Shott, or Shot, young in the Teme as in their second year   While St Ambrose of Milan is recorded to have termed

---

* Dr Hamilton observed that it was named from wild thyme, Thymus serpyllum, because the water thyme is not British and has no smell   Ausonius, however, named it after a plant from the Ticino and Adige   Donovan remarked that at the beginning of last century or earlier, it was indeed imagined by fanciful writers to subsist, at particular seasons, on what they denominated water-thyme; they seem persuaded the powerful aromatic smell of the fish was contracted from this species of food, an idea apparently borrowed from Ælian

† In Walton's Angler we find it remarked that "some think that he feeds on water-thyme, and smells of it at his first taking out of water, and they may think so with as good reason as we do, that our smelts smell like violets at their being first caught, which I think is a truth"   Pennant "never could perceive any particular smell"   Donovan likewise "never ourselves observed any such smell"   Sir H Davy considered that it had "an agreeable odour"   Valenciennes "never remarked this thyme-like odour in individuals which he had seen alive" (Vol xxi, p 480)   Dr Hamilton asserted, ' I can distinctly aver that most grayling, when in season, have decidedly a thymy smell, very different to that of the smell which has the odour of cucumber   I think the larger fish, and when not in season, are devoid of it, but in a ¾ lb grayling it is nearly always present" (Fishing Gazette, Feb 13th, 1886)   Mr Senior remarked (Waterside Sketches), "A fish taken from the Teme I once thought had a decided smell of cucumber, another from the Itchen was redolent of thyme, the first which the Wharfe yielded me smelt of something which the keeper said was cucumber, while I equally maintained it was thyme"   The Gyrinus natator, Linn , has so strong an odour, that, when several of these insects are collected together, they may be scented at a distance of 5, or 6, or more paces (Roesel)   It is to the eating of these insects that Mr Lloyd (Scandiv Ad 1, p 128), is inclined to attribute the remarkable odour emitted by the grayling

it the "flower of fishes" Aubrey in his MS said that in his days the umber was caught in the Madden, between Wilton and Salisbury, &c "This kind of fish (he remarked) is found in no other river in England except the Humber in Yorkshire From that river, therefore, I conclude it takes its name of *umber*" (Maton, *Nat Hist of Wilts*) Cotton, however, says this name is derived from its being very black about the head and gills and down the back, and has its belly of a dark gray dappled with black when in the season One-year old fish are in some places known as *pinks*, at about ¼ lb weight *shot* or *shut*, or those not breeding *Grayling* or *graul* is another name for grilse in Lough Foyle, Ireland (*J Johnstone*) *Brithyll rhestrog* and *Glasgangen*, Welsh *De Vlagzalm*, Dutch *Ombre*, French

This fish is another whose introduction has been ascribed to the monks, and many of the local grayling fisheries are found in the vicinity of where monasteries formerly stood, as in the Ure near the site of the Jervaulx Abbey But it would be difficult to convey this fish from the continent with the means then at their disposal, while in Kent, Dorsetshire, Devonshire and Cornwall, where there were many monasteries, grayling are not found, also it is only this century they have been introduced into Scotland, while they have not yet been acclimatized in Ireland, but their propagation there is about to be tried

Habits —Although found in many of our rivers, and in some abundantly, the grayling is certainly a local fish, while at times it appears to be gregarious, showing a tendency to congregate in small shoals, which often drop down stream In this country it would appear to be strictly fluviatile and fresh-water in its habits, never migrating to the sea, but in Scandinavia it is found in lakes also in the North Sea, Cattegat, and Baltic Sir Humphry Davy tried it in brackish water but without success It prefers clean streams, in which there are a succession of sluggish pools and shallows, with sandy, gravelly, or loamy beds, rocky or stony bottoms being unsuitable * The larger ones seem to resort more to the deeper and quiet spots, the moderately-sized and small ones to the shallows, taking their post behind a rock or a bunch of weeds Although clean streams are preferred, still a moderate or cold temperature of the water seems to be of more consequence, but too much cold or too much heat are asserted to be equally fatal to it It is not every river that appears suited for the grayling, thus the attempts to acclimatize it in the Thames do not appear, so far, to have been a success although a few have been captured there It lives somewhat deeper in the water than the trout,† and although in some streams the two forms reside together on not unfriendly terms, should food be abundant, such is not invariably the case, as in some localities it is popularly said to bully the trout ‡ it may be

---

* Dr Hamilton says, "that grayling require rivers that are rather sluggish than swift, with deep pools connected by moderate rapids, subject to no very great fluctuations either as regards volume of water or temperature, and running through limestone districts is far from being the right one No grayling grows to such a size or increase faster than those in our chalk streams, and no river fluctuates and changes its condition as regards volume of water more than the Teme '

† Although it has been asserted that grayling do not feed upon the eggs of the trout (*see* p 207 note *ante*), Mr Currell (*Fishing Gazette*, March 6th 1886) observed, ' I have seen a shoal of grayling following trout and digging up the gravel, and have seen the trout rush open mouthed at them and drive them off again and again "

‡ The secretary to a *Glasgow Angling Club* once wrote asking how to destroy grayling, as since their introduction the trout fishing had very much decreased In other localities, as the Windrush in Gloucestershire, the Corve in Shropshire, &c, the two forms do not appear to interfere with one another A correspondent of *The Field* (March 24th 1883) observed, " Last August I had a few days' fishing on the Kennet I was greatly interested in the history of the Hungerford Club, and one of the secretaries (with whom I was fishing) furnished me with the following facts, giving me full permission to make them public In 1877, when the club was formed, the water contained a limited stock of very large trout, which were rarely caught except in the May fly season, but it swarmed with coarse fish of all sorts A war of extermination was commenced at once, and it has been so systematically kept up ever since, that up to the present time the club has killed 2745 pike, and 8273 other coarse fish on their own fishery, and, on the water immediately below this, 696 pike, and about 2000 coarse fish of other kinds This in itself is a wonderfully good work, but it is not all, for in 1879 fifteen brace of half pound grayling were introduced from the Derwent, together with 2000 fry The experiment has been watched with much interest and each periodical netting has given evidence that the new stock is rapidly taking root The wide, extensive shallow above and below the town bridge at Hungerford is the perfection of grayling water, and all down

that being to a great extent a ground feeder, it helps itself to the eggs' from the trout's redds while the trout is breeding   It is not of a roving disposition and generally limits its range to within a few miles   it is generally reputed that it cannot spring out of the water like the trout, consequently it is unable to surmount barriers, a conclusion denied by Dr Hamilton who says it can do so when hooked, but its large back fin, aided by its well-developed air-bladder, would seem to show that its formation is that best adapted for rapidly rising or sinking in the water   In early spring months it returns to deeper water and seems almost to cease to feed, possibly due to the nearness of its breeding season   It has been found to live in newly-made ponds, constructed in hard soil, where, however, it is said not to breed, but more investigation is required on this question, as the same was formerly believed of the trout   old and muddy ponds are not suited for its existence, for there it rapidly succumbs   It eats insects and their larvæ, small molluscous shell-fish as *Physa* and *Neritina*, also *Crustacea*, and is fond of the larvæ of the caddis fly, in swallowing which it likewise takes in the pieces of stick, stones, &c, which are attached to them   But it seems to prefer water-shrimps, beetles, spiders, and such food as it can obtain at the bottom, to the fly

*Migrations —*I have already stated that occasionally these fish congregate in shoals and generally drop down stream, in fact, it used to be considered that they never headed up   Mr Francis Francis (*Field*, May 28th, 1881) observed, upon one being taken in the Anton, continuing, that "only a few years ago there were none much above the sheep's bridge at Houghton   This year there are many in the Machine Barn shallow, two miles up, but that they should have headed up something like a distance of ten miles, and out of the Test into another stream, is astonishing" Mr Wibram (*Fishing Gazette*, March 13th, 1886) remarked on having found them working both up and down stream in Yorkshire   Mr Brotherston, of Kelso, observed that this fish was introduced there by the late Marquis of Lothian, and it appears to be particularly suitable to its habits, as it is increasing rapidly, and also spreading down into the Tweed

*Breeding —*Generally spawns on the shallows in April or May,* or even earlier, while at a little distance the eggs somewhat resemble frog-spawn   Fish under half-a pound weight do not appear as a rule to spawn, rendering it probable that they do not commence to do so until their third season, or possibly the fourth   On February 26th, 1881, Mr Bowle Evans sent me two examples from Hereford-shire, and I found the ova almost ready for extrusion (the preceding winter had been a very mild one)   The ova are smaller than those of the trout, and transparent, while the interior may be white, opalescent, cornelian colour, or even deep orange, the eggs are deposited on the gravel near the tails of shallows, and in shallow nests or redds, like the salmon, trout, or char, but not to so great

the broad water below they are already present in sufficient numbers for the angler to come across several in one day   For instance, on August 16th, on this water, I had a brace of nice trout, weighing 3¼ lb, and three grayling, all of which went back again   But the way in which the grayling have prospered and increased may be better judged by the record of the last summer's netting, which shows that they took and returned to the water—

Over 2 lb	From 1½ lb to 2 lb	From 1 lb to 1½ lb	From ½ lb to 1 lb
6 brace	15 brace	50 brace	70 brace

and quantities of little ones   One fish of 3¼ lb has already been found, and grayling have been met with at Newbury which must be eight or ten miles from Hungerford   Now, even if there be truth in all the evil things which are said of grayling, it is quite certain that they cannot injure the trout, in season or out of season, to anything like the extent that the 11,000 coarse fish would have done if they had been left unmolested   Moreover, the stock of trout is increasing enormously on the Kennet, and the water in some places swarms with store fish (I put back four brace one day, only keeping two fish above the 12 in limit)   Prudent conservators of any fishery will always bear in mind that it is quite possible to have too many trout in a river   However, in the Kennet there is ample room for a very large and good stock of both trout and grayling, and, in another year or two, anglers who have access to this splendid river will find that their sport is just about doubled "

* The Rev L Bagot (*Field*, September 22nd, 1883) recorded the capture of a half pound fish in the Corve on September 5th, full of spawn   and Mr Webb, of Trowbridge, when fishing near Salisbury, on September 15th, among his captures of 7½ brace of grayling took two of 1½ lb each which were full of spawn, the smaller ones were quite clean

a depth Neither do these fish attempt to pass up to the heads of streams for breeding purposes, but select shallow localities near where they usually reside, and where females may be seen waited on by two or even three males The ova are more delicate than those of the trout or char, and it has been remarked in Herefordshire that should a severe frost occur during their spawning season, the succeeding year's supply of young fish appears to be deleteriously affected The body of the embryo is visible in the egg on the ninth day, and usually hatches from about the twelfth to the twenty-fifth day due to this rapid development, it becomes difficult to transmit eyed grayling ova to any distance, as but few days elapse between the appearance of the eyes of the embryo and the eggs hatching The young when hatched must be kept in very pure water, for that which is sufficiently good for a trout alevin is not always suitable for grayling At the hatching time the egg-shells should be at once removed as they are found to be very deleterious. About the end of July or commencement of August the fry are about four or five inches long In aquaria it has been observed that young salmon or trout will readily eat young grayling

During the breeding season the grayling loses much of its natural timidity, thus we are told by "Southwest" in *The Field*, January 30th, 1886, that in the Test "About eighteen brace of grayling were removed on Wednesday, and laid down higher up the river, where they will probably spawn They were conveyed to their destination in a punt half-filled with water, and as a proof of how little the nerves of grayling are disturbed by the somewhat rough handling they must receive from netting, I may mention that one of the fish in the punt actually rose at a tiny black fly that happened to appear on the water therein I have noticed this singular absence of fear on the part of grayling on another occasion We had netted out a considerable number, and placed them in an abandoned unreserv, through which the stream ran Certainly not more than an hour after their capture, they rose to the flies just as if nothing had happened "

Hybrids have been raised between the grayling and the trout, thus it was stated in the *Journal of the French Société d'Acclimatation* (1877, p 495), that grayling eggs from the Lake of Pavia, were during the months of November and December 1872, fertilized with the milt of the salmon-trout, and batched in January, 1873, at the School of Fish culture The alevins grew well, so that at 6 months of age they were 3½ in long at 22 months, 7 in long , at 32 months, 11 4 in in length , and at 42 months, 13 4 in long They were of a slate-colour, with greenish reflections, having on the back very distinct, large, and irregular spots and blotches on a light ground, while the abdomen was silvery

They bred at the age of 22 months and 5 days, when it was found that the males were already exhausted, and therefore recourse was had to trout milt On November 15th, 1875, 551 very fine eggs were obtained from a female 21 months and 15 days old , these eggs were hatched between December 30th, 1875, and January 5th, 1876 The alevins were said to have grown more rapidly than trout of the same age, and at 10 months they were from 3½ in to 5 0 in in length In appearance these young differed from the former ones by their coarseness and their habits, but par marks were present Their colours were very similar to those of their hybrid mothers, being superiorly of a greenish tinge with large blotches along the upper half of the body, while the abdomen was of a gray slate colour, becoming ashy-white beneath , adipose dorsal fin clear yellow This

---

* Grayling eggs would seem to occasionally bear removing pretty well April 3rd, 1885, at Mr Andrew's fish-culture establishment at Guildford, I was shown 100,000 grayling eggs obtained the previous evening from Hampshire streams I took twelve in a phial of water to London, and the next day to Cheltenham, and only two died then their size being 0 19 of an inch in diameter On the 6th, C Wethered, Esq , r G s , was good enough to offer to make daily drawings of the development of the embryo under the microscope (the glass-like walls of the ova affording peculiar facilities for doing so) and for this purpose he took two in a tumbler of water to his own house The water was changed twice a day, while each ovum was daily removed to a microscope cell and subsequently returned to the tumbler , one of these hatched on April 22nd, and the other on the 24th On the 23rd those in my hatching house began to hatch, and on the 24th all were out but one which could be seen inside the egg slowly moving its pectoral fins backwards and forwards By May 10th the alevins had absorbed their sacs

cross was again, but unsuccessfully, tried at 33 months and 12 days, for all the eggs, 4153 in number, died

March 31st, 1887, Mr Andrews crossed female grayling with trout Eggs straw-coloured, but not so clear as graylings when I saw them on April 6th, but they did not hatch The difficulty of hybridizing grayling with trout milt arises from two circumstances—first, that trout breeding in many rivers has concluded, or nearly so, prior to that of the former fish , secondly, the size of the grayling eggs is so much smaller than those of the trout

Means of capture —Netting similarly to that employed for trout, but generally grayling is taken by angling and employing fine tackle, and this is principally done either with ground-bait,* or grasshopper (sink and draw plan), or by fly fishing, remembering that they must be delicately handled as their mouths are by no means strong for retaining a hook. Although, as has been frequently observed, this fish is to a certain extent fit for eating all the year round, it is most justly protected throughout the spawning months, while during October and November, into the middle of January, it is in its prime for the table In the Test, although the Houghton Club used to open this fishing from June 1st, the fish were generally in poor condition, but ready to take almost any fly which was offered but in July the case became different, the fish were in good condition and much more difficult to please Still it is generally considered that September and October are the two best months for the fly-fisher, although in November they will take a fly or a bait, more especially in the middle of the day, and even with a shining sun In the Teme the larger fish rarely take the fly, but will take the grasshopper The grayling, although a very capricious fish, is not quite so shy as the trout nor so game when hooked, and often bores with its head up stream in order to get to the bottom, while if baffled it turns down stream still similarly boring . a shorter line may be employed, and fishing down stream is mostly adopted It will often rise when least expected, and when most freely taking the natural fly will frequently refuse the artificial on other occasions it will rise several times in succession at the same fly, and, if not touched by the hook, attempts at its capture may be continued If a rise occurs, the fisherman should strike gently, play his fish quietly, and land it with a net, because its mouth is tender and readily gives way The flies employed are much the same as those for trout, but smaller as a rule, although the May-fly is not always refused The smaller fish are generally taken on the shallows, and with the fly which is usually declined by the larger grayling Introduced from other waters they sometimes lose their game character and refuse the fly Walton says it " is very gamesome at the fly and much simpler, and therefore bolder than a trout * * * yet he is not so general a fish as the trout, nor to me so good to eat or to angle for "

The grayling, however, amongst its other eccentric habits, will sometimes, under the most adverse conditions, " come on " just for an hour or two It may be in the forenoon, or at midday, or in the earlier hours of the cool afternoon , and, should the weather be warm, overcast, or even drizzling, they may sometimes be taken at all hours of the day (*Field*, November 25th, 1884) The largest fish are killed during October and November with the sunken fly Fishing up-stream for grayling is, with the dry fly, a mistake The authorities who recommend the casting of the flies across stream, and the allowing of them to sweep leisurely out (with the line, however, well in hand) and down with the current, after all give good advice, and, in the long run, we are convinced that this is the most paying way of fly-fishing for grayling These fish hold on the shallows, and are very fond of them if they are wide and gravelly, or sandy, and well in the open , but where the stream runs deepest in the middle there the best grayling will be found roaming, it may be, occasionally to the sides, but sticking in the main to the centre This is especially the case in waters like our lowland streams, that do not possess the alternations of rapid and slow currents, pools, stickles, and races, such as are found in the established grayling rivers of Yorkshire, Derby-

* Mr Pritt observed " that in the Yorkshire rivers the grayling will only take a worm *well* in frosty weather " (*Field*, April 17th, 1886)

shire, and Worcestershire   In these latter streams, which may be called natural grayling waters, the whereabouts of the fish may be determined upon with some certainty   Anything in the shape of a glide, before or after rough water, should not be neglected   A gravelly shelf on the edge of a swift, deep stream, is a favourite haunt of the fish   A bit of still, smooth water between two currents formed by an obstacle, and a hollow, worn by deep water out of a loamy bank, giving a lay-by in the nature of an eddy, are also places to which the fly should be introduced   But, as grayling often travel up and down and across in a slow persistent sort of fashion, no labour is lost in fishing down every bit of water , and if it is fished down from beginning to end two or three times in succession, so much the more likelihood of finding fish, as well as of keeping the blood in circulation on a cold day (*Field*, October 25th, 1864)

The larger fish frequent the deeper pools or sluggish portions of the stream, sometimes selecting the vicinity of the roots of a tree which juts into the water, sometimes being more in mid-water   What is termed a grasshopper in Worcestershire, which looks like a nondescript caterpillar, with the point of the hook covered by gentles, is considered to be the best bait there and in the Shropshire and Herefordshire districts, commencing to be employed about September and the two following months on warm days succeeding frosty nights   Having a quill float and a stiffish rod it is worked on the sinking and drawing plan, having sunk to the bottom it is raised about a foot and allowed to sink again, while the stream should suffice to carry it on a little way with each successive jerk   In Derbyshire streams it is said not to be much of a success   The principal ground baits are fishing with gentles, worms are likewise employed *   The grayling occasionally

---

* A correspondent of *The Field* (February 19th, 1887) observed how he has fished in Yorkshire streams by "swimming the worm" during the best months of the year   "The rod best adapted to the purpose is a stiffish fly rod, from 10 ft to 12 ft in length, fitted with upright rings , it should not, however, be too heavy, as such a one becomes very tiring to the wrist at the concluding portion of a long day's fishing   The reel that I prefer is a plain check ebonite one, and it must be kept clean and in good working order, so that the line may run easily from it upon the first rush of a heavy fish   The line should be of tapered, waterproofed silk, say, 25 yards in length   The tackle should consist of a cast from 2½ yards to 3 yards in length, commencing with a couple of lengths of strong undrawn gut and tapering down to the same quantity of the very finest drawn , to the end of this, wrap one no 7 fine wire round bend hook with well waxed crimson silk, but before doing so either heat the shank of the hook in the flame of a candle and bend it slightly outwards with a pair of pliers, or else wrap in at the top of the shank a piece of stiff hog's bristle, this arrangement being intended for the purpose of keeping up the head of the worm , with one small shot about 4 to 6 inches above the hook, your tackle is complete, with the exception of a tiny float about the size of a hazel nut, which you adjust to your cast by means of a small quill plug, having due regard to the depth of stream

"When the angler finds that he is failing to hook fish, and that, after striking at an apparently good bite, the tail of his worm is gone, he should take off the single hook tackle and substitute for it a couple of no 2 fly-hooks, wrapped about one third of an inch apart , but I only employ this tackle under the circumstances named, as in nine cases out of every ten, owing to his rolling propensities, the fish generally contrives to break off one of the hooks either in his mouth or in the meshes of the landing-net, and then you have to waste valuable time in repairing damages   In very bright, low water, I generally commence operations at the extreme tail of a pool, and fish every likely place until I come to water about one foot in depth, so, after you have fished to this point hasten to the next suitable place   In slightly coloured water the angler may fish down stream, casting across a little above him from the commencement of the swim , if, however, snow-water be present, it is very little use to continue fishing, as grayling never take well under such circumstances   Grayling usually take the worm in a very erratic manner , perhaps for two or three hours the angler will never have a single bite, and suddenly he will begin to catch fish almost every swim, and when he is congratulating himself upon his success, the sport ceases as suddenly as it began   My old instructor, Dick Smith, used often to say to me, 'You don't come out to save worms, my lad, but to catch fish,' and many times since then have I fully appreciated the truth of his remark, for a grayling may often be induced to take a lively red worm, when a dead one, hanging like a piece of moss on the hook, will not tempt him at all , always, therefore, have a plentiful supply of worms with you

"In conclusion, let me again impress upon anglers the necessity of sticking to their work, if they mean to make up a good dish of grayling by the above means   Many a time, after fishing for hours without having a touch, have I felt inclined to reel up and wend my way homewards, for you cannot moon about on the bank and smoke your pipe as when in pursuit of the keen eyed trout during the summer months , but patience has prevailed, and perhaps in the last couple of hours in the afternoon I have made up a basket of fish to which is accorded the honour of having a red mark affixed to the account which I have subsequently entered in my angling diary "

may be taken with the minnow, mostly in clear or else very slightly coloured water

During October and November dead leaves are often a great nuisance to the fly-fisher

Life history —Those hatched in June, say 1880, do not as a rule spawn before April, 1883   These fish are rapid growers, attaining to four or five inches in length in a few months   Sir H Davy (*Salmonia*, p 188) believed that such as were hatched in May or June become nine or ten inches in length by September, and weigh from five to eight ounces

We find Mr Willis-Bund, in his editorial note to Section 11 of the Fresh-water Fisheries Act, 1878 (*see* Oke's Fishery Laws, Second Edition, p 60), writing as follows —

"This clause places grayling in an exceptional position, it absolutely prohibits the destruction of grayling, except by angling in private fisheries, during the close season   During their close season, trout or char may not be killed in any way, but grayling may be killed during their close time by angling in private fisheries, even where they are specially preserved   As no one fishes for grayling with nets, it comes to this, that as to them the law is the same as before, and a measure passed for the encouragement of anglers does not make any provision for the fish anglers most value."

Diseases —It was formerly abundant in the Aire above Bingley, but was entirely destroyed in 1824 by the bursting of a peat bog, and subsequent attempts at reproduction have proved ineffectual (*Yorkshire Vertebrata*, p 129)   Mr Francis Francis (*Field*, December 31st, 1881) observed that, although there are no very extreme pollutions in the Wye above Rowsley, yet both trout and grayling have perished from fungoid disease in myriads, indeed, some years ago Rowsley Meadows were pretty nearly cleared out of grayling by it   This fungoid disease, *Saprolegnia ferax*, has been found affecting them in common with trout and other forms   In Jardine's inquiry, in 1860, these fish were said to be almost gone from the Severn, where, up to four years before, they had been abundant, cleared out by disease or dredging the fords for gravel

As food —Its flesh is white, delicate,* and in the best condition about October and November, when the trout are mostly out of season ; in fact, it is not until August, or even September, that it is generally esteemed worth cooking, while it should be dressed as soon as practicable after removal from the water   It is generally boiled   large ones are said to be improved by crimping   Dr Hamilton says, "A grayling over $\frac{3}{4}$ lb. weight is not in condition till the end of July : those of $\frac{1}{2}$ lb to $\frac{3}{4}$ lb are in season all the year round "

Uses —It is stated that in Lapland a substitute for rennet used to be obtained by pressure from the entrails of the grayling, with which they converted the milk of the reindeer into cheese   Gesner asserted that "the fat of this fish, being set with a little honey a day or two in the sun, in a little glass, is very excellent against redness, or swarthiness, or anything that breeds in the eyes "

Habitat —Lapland, Scandinavia, Germany, Britain, France, Switzerland, Italy, and Hungary

They were introduced† into the Upper Clyde in 1855, from three dozen fish brought from Rowsley, Derbyshire, and are said to have thriven well   They have likewise been introduced in the Teviot and Tweed, and are also thriving (Brotherston), one $\frac{3}{4}$ lb weight was taken in the Tay, April 15th, 1884, by Mr. Macpherson, a few miles below Dunkeld   In Cumberland in the Eden, Mr Spence, *Fishing*

---

* "Aldrovandus says that they be of a trout kind   and Gesner says, that in his country, which is *Switzerland*, he is accounted the choicest of all fish   And in *Italy* he is in the month of *May* so highly valued, that he is sold then at a much higher rate than any other fish   The *French* which call the Chub *Un Vilain*, call the Umber of the *Lake Leman, Un Umble Chevalier*   and they value the Umber or Grayling so highly that they say he feeds on gold, and say that many have been caught out of their famous river of *Loue*, out of whose bellies grains of gold have been taken" (Walton and Cotton's *Angler*)   In olden times, in Upper Austria, this fish was greatly valued, and "at times it could only be caught for the Imperial table, for sick persons, or for pregnant women" (Carl Peyrer, *United States Fish Commission Report*, 1876, p 612)

† Orkneys, according to Low, it was common , but he could not have meant this fish.

Gazette (January 30th, 1886) says that he has frequently heard chub called by that name while staying at Carlisle, and he considered that it was absent   Mr Bewley, *Land and Water* (September 9th, 1886), remarked that on May 26th he returned a small one while fishing in some private water near Appleby, some 2000 fry had been put in during 1882-83   in the Esk (Heysham)   while two examples from the Tyne, presented by Mr Knight are in the British Museum   In varying abundance in the middle waters of the Wharpe, Washburn, Nidd, Ure, and Swale,* also in the Cover, Wiske, and Colbeck, the Rye, and other tributaries of the Upper Derwent and the Scalby Beck near Scarborough   In a limited amount in the Tees, and has been introduced into the Esk   Formerly common in the Ribble and Hodder, their extreme scarcity—if not extinction—being ascribed to the great increase of salmon (*Yorkshire Vertebrata*) †   In Lancashire, the Ribble, in Derbyshire and Staffordshire, the Dove, the Wye, the Trent, the Blithe and the Hodder. In Shropshire the Severn, the Teme, the Clun, the Corve and the Onny In Merionethshire, the Dee, and in Montgomeryshire in the Varnuy and the Tanat   In Herefordshire, the Arrow, the Lug, the Dove, the Wye, and the Irwin contain them   The Windrush in Gloucestershire ‡   In Hampshire and Wiltshire in the Test, having been introduced from the Avon (Davy), also present in the Itchen and both the Avons   Hamilton remarked the Dove, the Derwent, the Teme, and the Trent were formerly considered the grayling rivers *par excellence*, but they must now give way to our southern rivers as the Avon, the Itchen, the Test. In the Kennett in Wiltshire they have also succeeded well, also in its tributary the Lamborne

The Swansea Guide stated this fish to be taken in the neighbourhood, but of this Dillwyn doubted the correctness   Mr Harford stocked the Tivy below Lampeter with many thousand grayling which have disappeared   In 1863, 1470 fry were placed in the Lea rather more than three miles beyond Hertford (Wix)   In May, 1866, it was introduced into the Lonan at Tiverton (Parfitt) It appears also to have been introduced into the Thames

Ireland —Rutty, 1772, observes "*Thymallus*, the Grayling or Umber. With us it is a sea fish, and less than Willoughby's, which is a river fish " It seems to me probable that he may refer to *Coregonus oxyrhynchus* as I received an example as a grayling   Brown two years after Rutty (1774) enumerated the grayling but Thompson observed that "the par has been sent to me from the south of Ireland under the name of grayling   Perhaps this name, as applied to the par, may be a corruption of the word *graveling*, which is generally applied to that fish in the southern counties "

Pennant recorded one of 4 lb 6 oz from the Teme at Ludlow   Yarrell mentioned another one of 4¼ lb from the Test, and Daniel one of 5 lb from near Shrewsbury and one of 5¼ lb in the spring of 1887 was caught in a weir trap at the top of the Camlet in Shropshire   In Lapland it is said to reach to 8 or 9 lb weight

---

* A correspondent in *The Field* (November 25th, 1882) denied the present existence of this fish in the Swale, the British Museum possesses four specimens reputed as from that river, received with Parnell's collection

† Mr J A Busfeild, in 1880, remarked that the upper reaches of the Aire are not suited to the habits of grayling   In *Gent's History of Ripon*, published one hundred and fifty years ago, and containing an account of Keighley, it is stated that the River Aire contained, among other fish, "Dares, gralings, perch, eeles, chub, trout, salmon and salmon smelts "   This seems conclusive evidence that in former times the Aire at Keighley contained grayling, that they have been gradually exterminated by pollution, and that the Castlefield Weir has had nothing to do with their non existence above Keighley   Mr Ashton observed (*Field*, October 11th, 1884) seventeen were taken from North Derbyshire, March 31st, 1870, averaging ¾ lb each, in a barrel of thirty gallons, by dog-cart to Sheffield, then by rail to Wymondham, thence by dog cart to Forncett St Peter, and put into the river there   March 17th, 1871, fifteen brace from the same river, all large fish, some full of ova, and turned in at Mr Iliby's, Boyland Hall   April 17th, 1872, thirty-one brace from ¼ to 1 lb 1 Forncett St Peter   April 10th, 1873 twenty and a half brace, ¼ to Forncett, and ⅜ to Boyland Hall   April, 1877, from the Wye to Oakley Park, Suffolk, for the Eye   April, 1879, fifteen brace from the Wye to the Kennett

‡ The Earl of Coventry placed grayling in a tributary of the river at Naunton Bridge, between 1859 and 1864, on different occasions, they are now thriving there

INDEX.

Abramis brama, 48
Acrognathus, 4
acquired monstrosities, 272
Act of 1861, 120
additional scales on par becoming smolts, 90
adipose dorsal in par, colours of, 87
adipose fin, colour of, in trout, 172, 227, 229
adipose fin in brook trout, colours of, 202
adipose fin, rays in, 229
Ælian, 1
Agassiz, 11, 13
Agassiz's trout, 152
agents affecting life in lakes, 183
age when first breed, 76, 77
Agoniates, 3
Ainsworth, Mr, 30
air-bladder, 20
air-bladder in embryo, 20
air bladder, uses of, 20
air in water, 20
albinos among hybrids, 260, 261
Albrecht, Prof, 20
Alburnus lucidus, 48
albus, Coregonus, 47
albus, Salmo, 10, 11, 143, 149, 151, 152, 159, 166, 169, 177, 228
Alepisaurus, 3
Alestes, 2
alevin, 201
alevins, appearance of, 43
alevins breathing, 43
alevins, frozen, 37
alevins of salmon, 82
alevins of salmon for stocking rivers, 106
alevins turned into streams, 11
aller float, 203
aller trout, 203
Allport, Mr, 27
alosa, Clupea, 5
alpine charr, 237
alpinus, Salmo, 7, 10, 11, 231, 232, 237, 238
alpinus, Salvelinus, 237
American char, 11, 217
American char breeding with British, 263, 264
American char breeding with Lochlevens, 260, 262
American char breeding with salmon par, 260
American char, hybridizing of, 268
American trout, 217
Ammodytes, 107, 178
anadromous, 11
anadromous fish, 4

anadromous instinct, 50
anadromous Salmonidæ, 27
anadromous trout changing mode of life, 146
anal fin in sea trout, 170
ancestry of fish, marine, 5
ancestry of fish, freshwater, 5
Ancylus, 177, 181
Andrews, Mr, 8, 23, 29, 44, 226, viii
angling for char, 234 235, 236
angling for trout, 208
angling to continue after netting, 121
Annin, Mr J, 24
apprentices fed on salmon, 112, 113, 114
arcturus, Salmo, 238
are par young salmon? 89
argenteus, Fario, 149
argenteus, Salmo, 11, 51, 55, 105, 149
Argentina, 2, 3, 4, 9
Argyropelecus, 3
Armistead, Mr, 29
Artedi, 27
Arthur, Mr, 7, 145, 183, 187
artificial fish-breeding, vi
artificial propagation of salmon, 78
artificial trout culture, 211
Ashworths, Messrs, 29, 31, 48
atmospheric changes affecting hybrids, 264, 265
atmospheric disturbances, 109
Aulolepis, 4
Aulopus, 3
auratus, Cyprinus, 7, 272
auratus, Carassius, 7
auratus, Salar, 190
ausonii, Salmo, 11, 183
Ausonius, 1
Australasia, trout in, 145
autumn migration of salmon, 66
autumn migration of smolts, 90, 91, 92
Avon and Stem, salmon of, 119

bag net, 140
bag-nets for salmon, 124
bag-nets Scotland, 132
baggit, 54, 98
Barione erythrogaster, 247
Barione fontinalis, 247
baits for trout, 208
Balfour, 22
Baltic, changes in fauna of, 5
Baltic, changes in water of, 5
Bandon, fisheries of, 133
barbatus, Liparis, 5
barbel, 48
barren salmon, 95
barren trout, 210

bass, 5
Beauly, fisheries of, 128
Belone, 18, 107
Belone cancila, 5
Beryx, 4
Bewick, Thomas, 112
bill, 154
bill trout, 217, 219
black fin, 58
black fish, 55
blacknebs, 173, 203
black swan, 28
black tails, 154
black trout, 249
Blackwater, fisheries of, 133
Blanchard, M E, 25
blasting scaring salmon, 68
Blennius gattorugine, 11
bhanag, 59
blindness in hybrids, 260, 261
bhonach, 59
blood discs, size of, 4, 9
blue cap, 150
blue cocks, 162
blue fin, 58
blue-poll, 150, 162
Boards of Conservators, 122
Boccius, 29, 31, 42
body, proportions of, vary, 8
Bond, E, vii
bones, names of, 14, 15
Borgie, fisheries of, 130
botcher, 58
Bothriocephalus, 22, 110
bothing, 203
Bourge trout, 162
box of salmon, weight of, in Tweed, 124
Bowk Evans, Mr, 281
Brachymystax, 3
brachypoma, Salmo, 11, 113, 150, 152, 169, 177
bradan, 59
bradan brionn, 59
brace precht, 204
Braithwaite, Mr, 240
brama, Abramis, 18
brandling, 59
branlins, 83, 84
breac, 154
bream, 48
breathing, 43
breeders selected, 26, 30
breeding affected by temperature, 27
breeding affected by seasons, 27
breeding, age when occurs, 27
breeding, effects of consanguinity on, 27
breeding of char, 234, 244, 245
breeding of fontinalis, 251
breeding of grilse, 94
breeding of Lochlevens, 228, 229

breeding of salmon, 76
breeding of trout, 208
breeding, period of, 24
breeding salmon retained in ponds, 30
breeding trout, pugnacious, 209
brieean, 134
bricein, 59
brill, 48
brith-dail, 161
brithyll rhestrog, 280
British and Irish Fishes, 11
British char breeding with American, 263 264
British char breeding with fontinalis, 263, 264
British char breeding with Lochlevens, 263
British char crossed by struans, 266
British Museum Catalogue, 11
brochyn 162
brood 58, 83
Brook, Mr., 32
brook trout, 6, 190, 196, 203, 217
brook trout, cæca of 199
brook trout, colours of, 200
brook trout, colours of adipose fin, 202
brook trout, descended from, 6
brook trout, gill covers of, 196, 197
brook trout, fins of, 198
brook trout in brackish water, 204
brook trout in sea water, 201
brook trout, jaws of, 199
brook trout old, head of, 117
brook trout, spots on, 202
brook trout, tail fins of, 199
brook trout, teeth on vomer, 197
brook trout, varieties of, 202
Brora, fisheries of, 129
Brown, 28
Brown Goode 218
brown trout 203
Brycinus, 2
Buckland, F., 6, 22 28, 31 34
buddagh, 10, 193, 194, 217
Burst, 28, 260
bull dog deformities, 260
bull dog deformity of trout, 203
bull heads 109, 212
bull-trout, 10, 11, 85, 149, 150, 151, 154, 157, 161 162, 169, 172, 176, 180 218, 254
bull trout and sea trout, how differ, 181
bull trout, angling for, 175
bull trout, few spotted, 11
bull-trout, inferior fish, 179
bull trout, Norway, 11
bull trout, salmon, 11
bull trout salmon spotted, 11
bull trout, thickly spotted, 11
bull punks, 58
bull-salmon, 58
buntlings, 150, 161
bur bolt, 17
burn tails, 154
burn trout, 203

burn trout head of, 147
Burt, 112, 114, 127

cæca of brook trout, 199, 200
cæca of trout, causes of variation, 188
cæca of trout variable in number, 188, 189
cæca in Lochlevens 220, 223, 224
cæcal appendages, 6, 8, 22
cæcal appendages in char, 233, 239
cæcal appendages, sea trout, 157, 158, 164, 171, 177
cæcal appendages in trout, 144, 148, 150, 216
cæcifer, Salmo, 190, 219
Californian trout, 48
cambricus, Salmo, 6, 10, 11, 48, 113, 114, 150, 152, 153, 159, 160, 164, 168, 169, 170, 181, 182, 218, 237
cancila, Belone, 5
candlemass fish, 162
candlemas gray, 154
Capel C., 29
Captain Franck, 129
Caranx, 18
Carassius auratus, 7
Carassius vulgaris, 6
Carl Peyrer, 49
carp, 18
carpio, Cyprinus, 7, 18
carp, varieties of, 7
case char 231, 232, 235, 239
Catoprion, 3
caudal fin of trout, 188
caudal fin, expansion of, 18
caudal fin, how measured, 13, 11
cawg, 58
cemyw hwyddell, 58
cephalus, Leuciscus, 18, 161
Chalceus, 2
Chalcinus, 2
char 6, 11, 48, 231, 237, 240
Characini, 2
char, American, 11
char as food, 241
char breeding 231, 235
char, cæca of, 233
char, causes of destruction, 213
char, colours of, 231, 248
char, dub, 245
char forms vary, 232, 233
char from Arctic regions, 233
char, how breed destroyed, 234
char, how captured, 243, 244
char hybrids, 26, 49
char in hot water, 20, 21
chru, introduction of, 240
char, legislation for, 233, 231
char of Lochleven, 242
chru, potted, 242
char, preservation of, 236
charri 237, 240
charr of Windermere, 237
char, scales of, 243
char, shape of, 248
char, size attains, 246
char, size of, 230
char, Southern Austria, 27

char, species of, 233
char, where captured, 233, 234
char, where found, 213
char, young, how raised, 233
Chauliodus, 3
chub, 18
clean salmon, 59, 106
cinereus, Salmo, 10
Citharinus, 2
clea,s, 2
close time for salmon, 60, 120, 122, 123
close time, varied, 122
close time, Scotch, 131, 132, 133
close time, shortened, 134
close time, weekly, 121
Clupea, 47
Clupea alosa, 5
Clupea finta, 5
Clupea harengus, 5
Clupea sprattus, 108
clupeiformis, Coregonus, 47
cochivie, 154, 158
cocksper, 58
colagan, 154
Coles char, 238
colin, Salmo, 232, 238
Collins, Mr., 80
colour, 18, 19
colours of brook trout, 200, 227
colours of char, 231 248
colour of flesh of trout, 213, 214
colours of trout change after death, 200, 201
colours of trout varying, 196, 200, 201, 202, 225
colours in Lochlevens, 224, 225
colours in trout, 146, 211
common brook trout, 247
compass net 139
concussion, effect of, 41, 277
condition, month when attain to, 214, 215
confinis, Salmo, 47, 49
congenital monstrosities, 272, 273
Connecticut river, salmon of, 115
Coquet, salmon of 117
Coquet sea trout in, 180
Coquet trout, 152
coracles, 137
core, 161, 180
Coregonus, 2, 3, 5, 9, 81
Coregonus albus, 47
Coregonus clupeiformis, 47
Coregonus thymallus, 278
Coregonus oxyrhynchus, 5, 286
Coregonus pollan, 5
Coregoni, 233
Cornish trout, 192
cornubiensis, Salmo, 192, 193
Coste, M., 29, 271
Cottus gobio, 109, 212
Cottus quadricornis, 5
Couch, 11
Couch's trout, 153
Counsell, History of Gloucester, 112
Coventry, Earl of, 286
cowring 139
Crasspuill trout, 190, 191

crooked-tailed trout, 10
cross breeds in trout, 183
crosses of hybrids, table of, 267
cross line fishing, 207
crows eating diseased fish, 230
cruives, Acts concerning, 132
cultivation of trout streams, 211, 212
cumberland, Salmo, 218
Curimatus, 2
cutcutia, Tetrodon, 5
cyclops, 276
Cynopotamus, 3
Cyprinus auratus, 272
Cyprinus carpio, 7, 48
Cyprinus kollarii, 48

Darwin, 50
Dareste, Camille on monsters, 276
Day, F., 11, 26, 29, 30
Davy, Dr J., 9, 20, 30, 40, 41
Davy on hybrids, 48
Davy, Sir H., 10, 27, 34
Davy's trout, 151
dead par used for its milt, 259
decrease of salmon, cause of, 115, 120
decreased size of artificial flies, 211, 212
decreasing length of close season, 131
Dee, Chester, Salmon of, 118
Dee, fine silk nets used by poachers, 137
Dee, fisheries of, 128
deformed trout, 203
dentex, Salmo, 183
dentition of hybrids, 270
dentition in trout, 146
depth of water for eggs, 31
descent of salmon, 74
destruction of char, 215
development of embryo, 32
De Zalm, 58
dhearg bhlian, 240
diœcious, Salmonidæ, 22
diamond scale, 54
Dipnoids, 20
disappearance of char, 241
discoverers of hybrids, 254
disease from immature parents, 78
diseases of char, 245
diseases of fontinalis, 252
diseases of salmon, 110, 111
diseases of trout, 215
Distichodus, 2
distribution, geographical, 4
dogs assisting fishermen, 136, 137
dolachans, 191, 194
dolphin, 18
Don, Fisheries of, 128
Donovan, 10
Donovan's trout, 151
doohulla, 26
dorsal fins of trout, Dr M'Intosh on, 170
dorsal fin in in sea trout, where commences, 170
double-yolked fowls' eggs, 273
Dover, Mr, 289

draft net, 148
draft nets increase with more fish, 134
drainage works, effects on river, 61, 67
drift nets, 139
dropsy, 26
dropsy in alevins, 259
dry seasons, effect on salmon, 68
dry seasons, netting salmon, 137
dubh bradan, 59
ducks 28
Dupplin hatchery, 29
Durham, cost of salmon, 117
dwarf trout, 186

Eagle Clarke, Mr, 276
early close time, 123
early river, how become late, 61
early or late race of salmon, 65
early or late rivers can alter character, 62, 65
early or late rivers cannot alter character, 62, 65
early salmon rivers, 59, 61, 62, 65, 66
ebb tide, effect on salmon, 68
eel choking trout, 213
eels, 216
eel traps, 142
eel weirs, 111
eel worrying trout, 212
eggs, 23, 24
eggs, appearance of while incubating, 34
eggs, artificial incubation of, 29
eggs attacked by fungus, 33
eggs, capabilities for diffusion, 41
eggs, colour of, 24
eggs, concussion, 32, 41
eggs, conveyance, 31
eggs, depth in which can be incubated, 33
eggs, depth of water in, 34
eggs, effect of cold on, 33
eggs, effects of freezing, 37, 38
eggs, effects of peat upon, 38
eggs, effects of paraffin on, 38, 39
eggs, enemies of, 28
eggs, eyed, 32
eggs, fertile from dead salmon, 78
eggs, fertilization of, 24, 29
egg frees, 31
eggs from dead sea trout, 262
eggs from dying grilse, 258
eggs from young fish, 26
eggs, hatching retarded, 43
eggs, how imbibe gases, 39, 40
eggs, how to be unpacked, 48
eggs incubated in moss, 35, 36, 40
eggs incubated in still water, 38, 39, 40
eggs, in dry air, 41
eggs, in dry tube, 36
eggs, influence of light on, 40
eggs in redd temporary dry, 38
eggs in salt water, 32, 36, 37
eggs kept damp, hatching, 32
eggs, milting, 21
eggs, mortality among, 28

eggs, moving of 40 *
eggs, number of days incubating, 269
eggs of fontinalis, 251
eggs, offspring from, 26
eggs of hybrids, mortality among, 268
eggs of land locked salmon, size, 105
eggs of Lochlevens, 228
eggs of salmon, covered in redds, 84
eggs of salmon, enemies of, 82
eggs of salmon, mortality if moved, 81
eggs of salmon, number given, 78
eggs of salmon, proportion hatched, 78
eggs of salmon, size of, 106
eggs of salmon, why covered over, 81
eggs of trout, 210
eggs, packing of, 42
eggs, picking of, 33
eggs retained in ovi sac, 32
eggs sent to Antipodes, 42
eggs shaken, 32
egg shell pervious to water, 40
eggs, size of, 24, 25, 26, 37, 76, 77
eggs, some expand on extrusion, 40
eggs, travelling, 32
eggs turning white, 82
eggs under gravel, 34
eggs unimpregnated, 32, 34
eggs, whence obtainable, 29
eggs when dead, 32
eggs when hatching, 35
eggs, wind, 32
ehoe, 2
eldrines, 208
electric disturbance, 109, 110
elvers, food for salmon, 107
embryo, development of, 32
Encyclopædia Britannica, 247
Engraulis telara, 5
enemies of young trout, 212
entering rivers, salmon, 68
eog, 2, 58
Ephemera, 24, 42, 48
Epicyrtus, 2
Epizoa, 110
errox, Salmo, 10, 11, 143, 149, 150, 151, 152, 153, 159, 169
erythrogaster, Baione, 247
erythrophthalmus, Leuciscus, 48
Esk, fisheries of, 127
Esox lucius, 274
estuaries, effect of, at entrance of salmon rivers 63
estuaries, temperature of, affecting migrations of salmon, 69
estuarius, Salmo, 11, 146, 169, 191
estuary fishermen, 123
estuary trout, 191
Exocœtus, 18
experiments at Howietown, 254
experiments on young trout, 146
eyed ova, 33
eyes badly developed in hybrids, 261

19

eyes, monstrosities among, 275

Fario, 2, 9, 11
Fario argentcus, 119
Fario lemanus, 190, 193
Fario marsiglii, 183
Lanionella, 3
fario, Salmo, 6, 11, 18, 111, 116, 169, 180, 182, 183, 187, 190, 203, 217, 219
fario, Trutta, 190, 193
Far, Mr, 7
fat stored up in salmon, 69
ferox Salar, 194
ferox, Salmo, 11, 148, 187, 192, 193, 194, 197, 198, 233
ferox, Trutta, 193
fertilization, dry process, 31
fertilization, how effected, 269
fertilization, moist process, 31
fertility of hybrids, 268
few spotted bull trout, 11
fiadh bhreac, 193
Field, vii
fine meshed nets for salmon, 137
fingerlins 83
fingerling 78
finger marks, 6
Finland, fishes of 7
Finland, Lake in 21
finnock, 151, 159
fin rays, 12
fins, 12
fins caudal form of, 13
fins characters of, 13
fins in trout, size of 117
fins of sea trout, 157
fins of brook trout, 198
fins of Lochlevens, 223
fins of trout, 187
fins, reproduction of rays, 12
fins, their form symptomatic of sterility, 106
fins, use of, 13
finta, Clupea, 5
fish culture 29
fish deteriorated races of, 27
fish, dropsical 26
Fishenes, Pract Manag of, 29
Fisher Mr, 29
Fishes of the British Isles, 11
fish hatching, 28
fish how marked, 75 76
fishing for char, 231, 235 236
fishing misplaced energy in, 111
fishing with cross lines, 207
fish ladders, 73, 74
fish passes, 73, 74, 121, 137
fish roe, 121
fish, temperature kept in, 36
fission causing monstrosities, 273
fixed engines, for taking salmon, 115
fixed engines nuisances, 110
Fleming, 5 10
Fleming's trout, 171
flesh of char, its colour 241
flesh of Lochlevens, colour of, 230
flesh of trout, colour of, 213
flesh of trout, red, 205, 206

flesus, Pleuronectes, 5
flounders, 5, 18, 217, 218
fluviatilis, Gobio, 12
fluviatilis, Trutta, 10
fly fishing altered of late years, 211
fly fishing for salmon, 136
flying fish, 18
fly nets commenced in Scotland, 132
Fontinalis, 247
fontinalis as food, 252
fontinalis, Baione, 217
fontinalis, breeding of, 251
fontinalis breeding with British char, 263, 264
fontinalis breeding with Loch levens, 260, 262
fontinalis breeding with Salmon par, 260
fontinalis breeding with trout, 251
fontinalis, colours of, 249, 250
fontinalis, habitat of, 253
fontinalis, hybridizing of, 268
fontinalis in sea water, 249
fontinalis introduced into Britain, 219
fontinalis, Salmo 7, 10, 11, 23, 24, 25, 36, 49, 146 202, 232, 233, 210, 215, 217, 219
fontinalis, size it attains, 253
fontinalis shy, 250, 251
fontinalis, varieties of, 249
fontinalis, water suited for, 251
fontinalis, water unsuited for, 252
food for char, 241
Fordwich trout, 10, 154, 170
Forel, fauna of Lake Loman, 183
Forelles, 2
forestinus, Salmo, 190
forket tail, 59
fork tails, 58
forms in char vary, 232
Forth fisheries, 125, 126
foul fish, 98
foul fish, exported, 121
foul salmon sent to Edinburgh, 125
Fowey, salmon off late in year, 68
Francks, Captain R, 112
Francis and trout eggs, 183
Francis Francis, 22, 26, 29
free gaps, 137
fresh run salmon, 70
fresh water fish descending to the sea, 5
Fresh water Fishery Act, 121
fresh water herring, 238
fresh water, salmon raised in, 93
frost, 109
fry, 14, 15, 46
fry, diseases of, 16
fry, food for, 15
fry from grilse and salmon, 86
fry from pure grilse, 86, 93
fry from salmon and par, 86
fungi, parasitic, 110
fungus from overfeeding, 23

fungus on eggs, 33, 34
fungus treated by bay salt, 230
fusion causing monstrosities, 273

Gadus virens, 111
gairardi, Salmo, 11, 111
gairdneri, Salmo, 196
gallivensis, Salmo, 11, 111, 189, 191 194
gally-trout, 240, 212
game fishes, 3
Gammari, 205
Gammarus pulex, 178
gar fish, 18
Gasteropoleous, 2
gastric juices in salmon, 107, 108
gealag banag, 59
geal bhreac, 151
gelly troch trout, 210
generation, organs of, 23
geographical distribution, 1
geological appearance, 1
Geraldin, M, on poisonous waters, 109
gerling, 58
germ origin of deformity, 272
gib-fish, 59
gillaroo, stomach of, 194, 195
gillaroo trout, 10, 11, 186, 194, 195
gill covers affected by sex 169
gill covers deformed in trout, 203
gill covers of brook trout, 196, 197
gill covers of sea trout, 155
gill fever, 44
gilling, 58
gilt char, 231, 232, 235, 239, 240
ginkin, 58
glacial epoch and char, 233
glas bhreac, 59
glasgangen, 280
gleis iad, 162
gleisedyn, 58
Glenlyon, Lord, marking salmon, 129
globe fishes, 5
gobio, Cottus, 212
Gobio fluviatilis, 12, 109
goedenn, Salmo, 119
Gonostoma, 3
gracilis, Salmo, 51, 55
gaalax, 153
gravelling, 58, 161, 286
grayling, 3, 58, 278
grayling as food, 285
grayling, breeding of, 281, 282
grayling, diseases of, 285
grayling eating trout eggs, 280
grayling eggs, 282
grayling, fishing for 283, 284
grayling, habitat of, 285, 286
grayling, habits of, 280, 283, 284
grayling, hybrids of, 282, 283
grayling injuring trout, 280
grayling, laws relating to, 285
grayling, life history of, 285
grayling, means of capture, 283

grayling, migrations of, 281
grayling, names of, 279
grayling, odour of, 279
grayling of Orkneys, 285
grayling, size of, 286
grayling, uses of, 285
Gray's char, 238
gray salmon, 151, 152, 154
gray trout, 10, 149, 172, 217
gratings to intakes of water, 121
gravel-laspring, 58
grawl, 58, 280
grayi, Salmo, 232, 238, 239
great lake trout, 11, 193
grey mullet, 5
grey salmon, 11
grey-schule, 58
grey trout, 11, 150, 151, 218
grilles, glass, 34
grilse, 87, 93, 55, 58
grilse and salmon, difference
    between, 94
grilse ascending rivers, 93, 94
grilse, bait for, 107
grilse bred with salmon, 88
grilse, breeding of, 77
grilse, how ascend, 71
grilse interbred, 88
grilse, rapidity of growth, 93
grilse, remarkable absence of, 72
grisens, Salmo, 10
ground trout, 276
growth of sea trout, 177
gudgeons, 100
gwiniad, 3, 31
gull, great black backed, 111
gull of August, 131
Günther, Dr, vii, 6, 11 13, 22,
    24 25, 48, 182, 184, 218, 219,
    220, 247
Günther's trout, 152
gwiniad, 161
gwiniad ebrill, 161
gymnothorax, Thymalus, 278

habitat of char, 213, 246
habitat of Lochlevens, 230
habitat of trout 216
habits of char, 231, 241
habits of fontinalis, 250
half-fish, 58
half-train net, 138
half-tram net 138
Halladale, fisheries of, 130
halve-net fishing, 138, 139
hamatus, Salmo, 51
Hamilton, 159, 200
hang-nets, 139
hang-nets in Tyne, 118
harengus, Clupea, 5
hardinii, Salmo, 104
harvest fish, 97
harvest Peal, 162
Harvie Brown, 48, 185, 186
hatcheries in Scotland, 29
hatching house, 33
hatching trays, 33, 34
head of salmon trout, 151
head of trout, 147
hearing, 19
heat of water, effects on spawning
    fish, 77
Hemiodus, 2

hepper, 58
herling, 11, 149, 150, 151, 156,
    159
herring, 5
herring sprods, 154
heterocercal tails, 13
hides for trout, 212
Highland trout, 190
high temperature of water, 109
Hippocampi 19
History of Howietoun, 28
hog backed trout, 277
Home Drummond Act, 127, 131
homocercal tails, 12
hoodn, Salmo, 247
hook on lower jaw of salmon,
    96, 97
Hope, fisheries of, 130
horse fishes, 19
horse mackerel, 18
horse rat, 28
Howietoun, 29, 217
Howietoun, history of, 28
Howietoun trout, 227
hucho, Salmo, 10, 149, 151
hunch-backed trout, 203
Huningue, 29
Hunter on hybrids, 267
Huxley, Prof, 36
hybrid between trout and salmon
    parr, 227
hybrid char, 26
hybrid char and trout, teeth in,
    261
hybrid fish, 46
hybridity in salmon, 106
hybridization, 46, 47
hybridization of trout, 141
hybridizing salmon, 267, 268
hybridization of birds, 47
hybridization of horned cattle,
    46
hybridization of horses and
    asses, 46
hybridization of quadrumana,
    46
hybrids, vi, 2, 7, 48, 49, 251
hybrids in trout, 183, 184
hybrid salmon and parr, 88
hybrids, breeding, 265 267
hybrids, fertility of, 268
hybrids of fontinalis, 252
hybrids of sea trout, 176
hybrids, sexes of, 257
hybrids, suffocated, 257
hybrid trout, 144
Hydrocyon, 3
Hypomesus, 3
hypural bones, 15

ice, salmon packed in, 115
immaturity, sign of, 6, 18
incubation of fontinalis, 251,
    252
incubation of salmon eggs, 82
Indian fish and fishing, 27
inherited instinct, 5
injuries caused to salmon, 111
injuries of trout, 215
Inspectors of Fisheries, British,
    29
instinct, inherited, 5
intestines, valves in, 54

introduction of trout into India,
    181
Inver, fisheries of, 134
Inverness, Corporation feast,
    127, 128
Ireland, weekly close time, 134,
    135
Irish laws, introduced into Bri
    tain, 121
Irish salmon, quantity of, 133
Irish salmon Acts, 133, 134
iridens, Salmo, 10, 48, 49, 189,
    196

Jackson, Mr, 7, 139
Jacobi, S, 29
Jardine, 11, 60
Jardine's trout, 152
jaw, lower, 16
jaws, abnormal, 276
jaws of brook trout, 198
jaw, upper, 16
Jenyns, 11
Jenyns' trout, 152
jerkin, 58
Johnson's trout, 151
Johnstone, Mr D, 36
judy, 58
Jurine, 182

kelt, 58, 96
kelts and their destruction, 97,
    98
kelts and their preservation, 97
kelts as food, 113
kelts, capture of, 96
kelts descending, 74, 96
kelts, destructive, 112
kelts die, 96
kelts, is preserving them an
    unmixed good? 96
kelts mending in rivers, 96, 98
kelts mending on salmon fry, 96
kelts of Lochlevens, 229
kelts, perquisites to fishermen,
    96
kelts returning to rivers, 97
Kennet, fisheries of, 280, 281
kidels, 116, 120
killinensis, Salmo, 232, 238
kipper, 58, 96
kippered salmon, 96, 140, 111
kippers, 96, 99
knob on lower jaw of female
    salmon, 58
knob on lower jaw of salmon,
    57
knob on lower jaw of salmon,
    composition of, 57
knob on lower jaw of salmon,
    cannot be shed, 57
knob on lower jaw of salmon,
    falling off, 57
knob on lower jaw of sea trout,
    172
knob on lower jaw of trout, 146,
    186, 187
Knox, Dr, 11
kollann, Cyprinus, 48
kuffer, 45
Kuhn, Professor, 46
kype on lower jaw of salmon,
    96, 97

labels fixed to salmon, 73
Lacépède, 19
lacustris, Salmo, 11, 104, 118, 183, 193
lacustris, Trutta, 183
lakes at head of rivers, effects on migration, 61, 62, 66
lake trout 191
lammasmen, 154 159
land locked salmon, 21, 99, 100, 103, 104, 105
land locked salmon, colours of 105
land locked salmon, how breed, 70
land locked salmon, localities for, 105
land locked salmon, size of eggs, 105
Larus marinus, 111
laspring 58, 83, 85
lateral-line, 18
late salmon rivers, 59, 62, 66
laurel, 58
lave net, 139
laws for protecting salmon 119
law of nature 271
laws Scotch fishery, 125
leaders, 58
leaps of salmon, 73
leeches, enemies of fish, 16
leeches injurious to trout, 215
legalizing nets, 137
legislation on trout, 217
lemanus, Fario, 190, 193
lemanus, Salmo 183 219
Leopard hybrids, 262
Lepeophtheirus stromii, 110
Leporinus, 2
leprosy due to eating stale fish, 112, 113
leprosy from eating foul salmon 98
Lereboullet on fish monsters, 274
Lerneopoda salmonea, 110
Leuchart, 49
Leuciscus cephalus, 48, 161
Leuciscus erythrophthalmus, 48
levenensis, Salmo, 11, 190 198, 218, 220
licenses for taking salmon, 135
life history of brook trout, 213
life history of fontinalis, 252
Lily Mere char, 241
Limnea, 177, 181
Limnea eaten by smolts, 109
Limnea ovata, 109
lingual teeth, salmon, 54
Linnæus s trout, 151
Liparis barbatus, 5
Lisburne, Lord 216
little grebe 28
Livingston Stone, 25, 27, 28, 31, 34 37
loach, 100
local races, 7
Lochlevens bull trout, 190
Lochlevens changed by locality, 220, 225
Lochleven, changes of colour in 145

Lochleven char, size of, 212
Lochleven fishery, 229
Lochleven lake, 218
Lochleven partially drained, 218
Lochleven restocked, 115, 218
Lochleven, stocking of 229
Lochleven trout, 11, 12, 114, 145 146, 190 211, 217, 219
Lochleven trout, cæca of, 188
Lochleven trout, maxilla in, 116
Lochlevens as food 230
Lochlevens breeding with American char, 260, 262
Lochlevens breeding with British char, 263
Lochlevens breeding with fontinalis 260, 262
Lochlevens breeding with salmon 255, 258
Lochlevens breeding with salmon par, 259
Lochlevens breeding with salmon smolts, 258, 260
Lochlevens crossed by salmon, 267
Lochlevens crossed by Struans 266
Lochlevens crossed by Zebra hybrids, 266
Lochlevens descended from sea trout, 220
Lochlevens deteriorate to brook trout, 226
Lochlevens, food of, 219
Lochlevens, habits of, 227
Lochlevens in Gloucestershire, 226
Lochlevens, life history of, 229
Lochlevens not taking a fly, 230
Lochlevens, variety of 227
Lochlevens, vary, 21
Loch Killin char, 248
Lockington, 19
Loch Shin, 60
locksper, 83
locomotion, 14
lower jaw, 16
lower jaw, hook on in male salmon 81
lower jaw of trout, knob on, 186, 187
Low s trout, 151
low temperature, cause of monsters, 275
lucidus, Alburnus 18
Lucioperca, 47
Luciotrutta, 3
lucius, Esox, 274

McCloud river, 25
McIvor, Mr , 225
McIvor introducing trout into India, 184
macks, 58
Magna Charta, on salmon weirs, 120
Maitland, Sir James, V , 28, 29, 30 254
malformations hereditary, 271, 273
malformations, how originate, 271
Mallotus, 2, 3, 4

Malmgren Prof 21
maran, 2, 58
marina, Trutta, 149
marked fish recaptured, 83
marking fish modes of, 75, 76
marking kelts, 93, 95
marking salmon, 73 93, 95, 129
marks of trout, 151
marsilu, Salmo 118
marsigli, Fario, 183
mathaek, 59
maxilla of Lochleven trout, 116, 220, 221
maxilla of sea trout, 155
maxilla of trout, 221
maxilla, strength of, in sea trout, 169
may-fly, grubs of, 28
may-peal, 161
Meckel's cartilage, 16
Mersey, salmon of, 117
mesh, sizes for fishing, 136
microps, Salmo, 119
micropyle in salmon eggs, 77, 106
Microstoma, 3
migrations of char, 241, 242
migrations of salmon, several yearly, 72
migrations of trout 173, 174
Milne Edwards, 29
milter, 58
milt of fontinalis, 251
milt of trout kept alive, 210
milt from dead fish deficient in vitality, 78
milting eggs, 24
milt kept in bottle, 255
minnow in hot water, 21
Mirtern, vii
mistops, Salmo, 104
Mitchell, 248
moff it-men, 58
moudie trout, 154
mongrel fish 48
monks introducing char, 241
monks introducing grayling, 280
monsters among fishes, 273
monsters by excess of development, 272
monsters among alevins die, 272
monstrosities, 41, 271
monstrosities, divisions of, 272, 273
monstrosities, how caused, 50
moon-ged, 58
Morgan, Mr , 144
morgate, 58
mort, 58, 154, 159
Moselle, 1
mosquitoes killing char, 212
muddy water, effect on salmon, 108
Muche, 19
mud in water, 109
mun trout 218
mulach corrie trout, 186
mules if breed, 19, 50
mule trout, 184
murneen, 240
muscles, 17
Musselburgh trout, 179

Mylesinus, 2
Myletes, 2
Myleus, 2
Mytilus, 23

namaycush, Salmo, 247, 249
Natural History of Ireland, 11
Naver, fisheries of, 130
Neilgherry Hills, trout on, 184, 216
Neill, A C Brisbane, viii
Nemacheilus barbatula, 109
nerves, 17
Ness fisheries, 127
nests of salmon, how formed, 81
net-and-cobble, 138, 140
netting trout lakes, 212
New Zealand rivers, 4
New Zealand trout, 198
New Zealand trout, whence originated, 183
Nichols, Mr, 144
night fishing for salmon, 137
nigrescens, Salmo, 247
nigripinnis, Salmo, 11, 187, 192, 198
nobilis, Salmo, 51
North Esk, fishing in, 136
Norway bull trout, 11
nourishment affecting breeding, 70

obstructions, 137
obstructions injurious to salmon, 74
obstructions in rivers, 72
Odontostoma, 3
Ogden, Mr, 35, 226
ombre chevalier, 231, 240
one-eyed fish, 203
Ootacamund, trout at, 184
Ootacamund, Lochlevens at, 225
opercular pieces, 16
orange fins, 154, 177
orange markings on Salmonid v, 143
orange stripes in sea trout, 157
orcadensis, Salmo, 11, 146, 192, 198
Orkney salmon, 192
Orkney trout, 192
Osmerus, 2, 3, 4, 9
Osmeroides, 4
Onchorhynchus, 3
Otago, 145
Otago trout, colours of, 184
Otago, trout in streams, 184
otters killing salmon, 136
oumer, 279
ova, absorption in, 31
ova destroyed by May fly grubs, 28
ova, enemies of, 28
ova, frees, 31
ova, fertilization of, 28, 47
ova, how transmitted, 32
ova of trout, 208
ova on moss, 32
ova, temperature kept in, 36
oxyrhynchus, Coregonus, 5, 286

par, 6, 11, 48, 58, 82, 83, 86, 87, 88, 109, 158, 162
par, ascending rivers, 90
parasites on salmon, 110
parasitic worms destroyed by cooking, 110
par bands, 18, 87, 177
par bands in Lochlevens, 158
par bands in Salmonidæ, 171, 172, 269, 270
par bands in sea trout, 157
par bands in trout, 186, 227
par bands modified by locality, 270
par bands, variation in number, 158
par bands varying, 172
par bands, when lost 87
par becoming smolts, 85, 90
pars, breeding, 26
par, colours of, 6
par descending seawards, 87, 88, 89, 90
pars dying in salt water, 92
parent trout of stock to be selected, 200
par, female never give eggs, 101
par female with ripe ova, 101
par from salmon eggs, 85, 86
par head figured, 52
par, habits of, 84
Parnell, 5, 11, 22
Parnell's trout, 152
par, not related to the salmon, 83, 84, 85
Parodon, 2
par, rate of growth, 85
pars, all males, 89, 85
pars, if able to live in salt water, 92
par, marking, 87
par, teeth in vomer, 102
par, variations of size in, 89
par, various accounts of, 83
par, whether a hybrid, 82, 84, 85, 86
par, young of salmon, 85
peal, 150, 167
peal, food of, 178
peal, head of, 165
peal spawn, 168
pectoral fins of trout, 187
Peel, Mr, 144
Pennant, 5, 10, 47
Pennant's trout, 151
Penobscot salmon, 51, 105
Perca flavescens, 47
Percoglossus, 3
Percy St John, 186
perisn, Salmo, 232, 237
Perley, 248
phinoc, 11, 149, 150, 151, 152, 154, 159, 189
phinoc, Salmo, 10, 143, 150, 152, 169
Physa fontinalis, 100
Prabuca, 2
Prabucina, 2
pink, 58, 82, 87, 100, 280
Piscicola geometra, 46
Pinchon, Dom, 29
plaice, 5, 48
Planorbis, 181

Plenty, River, 28
Pleuronectes flesus, 5
Pliny, 1
plumb line fishing for char, 235, 236
podles, 111
poisoned salmon, 109
poisonous character of water, 109
pollan, Coregonus, 5
pollution of Scotch rivers, 131
ponds, size of, 29
ponds, trout in, 230
Pontoppidan, 37
pool-bound salmon, 75
Pouchet, 18
powan oater, 194
preopercle in adult salmon, 147
preopercle in Lochleven trout, 147, 220
preopercle in Salmonidæ, 147
preopercle in salmon trout, 147
Prochilodus, 2
Proceedings Zoological Society, vii
Pryse Pryse, Sir, 254
pug, 58
pug-peal, 161, 162
pug-salmon, 162
purpuratus, Salmo, 7, 105, 202
putchers, 139
putts, 139
puts and putchers, 68
Pygocentrus, 3
pyloric appendages, 22
pyloric cœca, 21

quadricornis, Cottus, 5
Quatrefages on fish monsters, 273
Queen's gaps, in Irish weirs, 134
quinnat, Salmo, 27, 49

rack, 204
rack rider, 58, 204
rainbow trout, 189
rainbow trout, eyes of, 189
rainfall affecting migration of salmon, 64
Ramsbottom, 31
rappin, Salmo, 183
rapidity of growth of salmon, 95
Rasch, Prof, 48
Ray, 10, 17, 151
rays of tail fin in sea trout, 170
Ray's trout, 151
recruits, 97
red char, 231, 232, 239
red charre, 237
redd of grayling, 281
redd of trout, 210
redd of char, 244
redd of fontinalis, 251
redds, artificial, 44
redds of salmon, how formed, 80, 81, 99
red fish, 55
red flesh caused by food, 211
red-spotted trout, 247
red trout, 242

20

red wame, 210
respiration 20
retrievers, 97
Retropinna, 3 4
Reuter, Dr O , 7
Ribble, salmon of 117
Richardson, 13
Richardson's trout 152
rivers, anadromous period of, 61
Rivers, early and late 59
river and sea trout interchange able, 189
rivers long seasoned, 59
rivers, mode of ascent by salmon, 72
rivers short seasoned 59
rivers suited for grayling, 280
roach, 48
roach injurious to trout, 215
Roccus lineatus, 47
Rondeletius, 36
Roosevelt, Mr B , 47, 49
ronnal chai, 245
round tail, 151 163
Rowland, Dr 216
rudd, 48
runs of salmon in Severn, Forth, Tweed, and Shin, 70, 71

St Hilaire, 50
St Peter and salmon, 116
Sacramento river, salmon of, 115
Salanx, 3
Salar, 9
Salar ausonii 190
Salar ferox, 191
salar, Salmo, 10, 11, 24, 27, 51, 143, 153
salar Salmo, how differs from other Salmonida, 52
salar, origin of, 1
Salminus, 2
Salmo, 3, 9, 241
Salmo albus, 10, 11, 143 149 151, 152, 159, 166, 169, 177, 228
Salmo alpinus, 7, 10, 11, 231, 232 237, 238
Salmo arcturus, 238
Salmo argenteus, 11, 51, 55, 103, 149
Salmo ausonii, 183
Salmo brachypoma, 11, 143, 150 152, 169, 177
Salmo cæcifer, 190, 219
Salmo cambricus, 6 10 11, 48, 143, 144, 150, 152, 153 159, 160, 164, 168, 169, 170, 181, 182, 237
Salmo emereus, 10
Salmo cola, 232, 238
Salmo conhnis, 47, 49
Salmo cornubiensis, 192, 193
Salmo cumberland, 218
salmo dying out 6
Salmo dentex 183
Salmo cilox, 10, 11, 143, 149, 150, 151 152, 153, 159
Salmo estuarius, 11, 146, 189, 191

Salmo fario 6, 11, 18, 144, 146, 180, 182, 183, 187, 190, 205, 217, 219
Salmo ferox 11, 148, 187, 192, 193 194, 197, 198, 233
Salmo fontinalis, 7, 10 11, 23, 24, 25 49, 186, 202, 232, 238, 210, 245 247, 249
Salmo gairnardi, 11, 144
Salmo gairdneri, 196
Salmo gallivensis, 11, 144, 189 191, 198
Salmo glasbach, 162
Salmo goedenii, 110
Salmo graellsii, 51, 55
Salmo grayi, 232, 238, 239
Salmo griseus, 10 150
Salmo hamatus, 51
Salmo hardinii 104
Salmo hoodii, 247
Salmo hucho, 10, 119, 151
Salmo hucho, 10, 119, 151
Salmo nideus 19, 48, 19, 189, 196
Salmo killinensis, 232 238
Salmo lacustris, 11, 101, 148, 193, 194
Salmo lemanus, 18, 219
Salmo levenensis, 11, 190, 198, 218, 220
salmon management, 217, 249
Salmo marsilii, 119
Salmo microps, 149
Salmo mistops, 104
salmon, 10, 192
Salmona, 1
Salmonata, 119
salmonata, Trutta, 10
salmon alarmed, leave their course, 68
salmon, analyses of 141
salmon and grilse how differ, 91
salmon and trout hybrids are migratory, 106
salmon annihilated in rivers, 115
salmon, annual breeders 78
salmon, artificial propagation of, 78
salmon ascending rivers for breeding, 66, 73
salmon ascending rivers on ebb tide, 68
salmon ascending rivers on flood tide, 68
salmon, ascent of, how influenced, 60
salmon as food, 140
salmon is food for apprentices, 112, 113, 114
salmon, autumn migration of, 66
salmon, bait for, 107
salmon bill of Irish nationalists, 134
salmon breed alternate years, 74, 78, 79, 95, 97, 106
salmon breed every third year, 78
salmon breed in first year, 84
salmon, breeding of, 76, 77, 78
salmon breeding with Lochlevens, 255, 258
salmon breed in salt water, 99
salmon breed once in lifetime, 78

salmon breed without going to the sea, 99, 101, 103
salmon brown, 109
salmon bull trout, 11
salmon, causes of destruction among, 109, 110, 111
salmon elk an, ascending river, 69
salmon, close time, 60
salmon, colours of, 54 144
salmon cost of, 112, 113, 114
salmon crossed by Lochlevens, 267
salmon cured, 140
salmond, 217
salmon, decrease of 115
salmon descending rivers, 71
salmon deteriorate in fresh water, 5 6
salmon detained in fresh water, 100, 101, 102
salmon disease, 123
salmon, differences in size 56
salmon do descend rivers 74
salmon do not descend rivers, 71
salmon, do they spawn in the sea, 36
salmon, differences in weight, 55
salmon driven away by sea trout, 67
salmon dying out of a river, 67
Salmones, 2 9, 10, 11, 186
salmonea, Lernœopoda, 110
salmon, early race, 57
salmon eggs fertilized before extrusion, 77
salmon eggs, micropyle in, 77
salmon eggs fertilized by smolts, 81
salmon eggs not hatch in salt water, 50
salmon eggs, number of, 78
salmon eggs, weight of, 78
salmon exterminated, 2
salmon exterminated in rivers 112
salmon, feeding in fresh waters, 108
salmon fins of, 54
salmon fisheries of Scotland, tenure of, 130
salmon fisheries, forces at work in, 119
salmon fisheries in Thames, 116
salmon fisheries, Irish 133
salmon, food of 100, 107
salmon fry, 58, 83
salmon fry, migrations of, 81
salmon fry, penalty for taking, 83
salmon, growth of, 84
salmon, habits of, 59
salmon, homing instinct, 66, 67
salmon, how enter rivers, 68
salmon, how land locked, 5
salmon, how nourished in rivers, 69
salmon hybrids, 49, 83
Salmonidæ, 4
Salmonidæ, ancestry of, 1
Salmonidæ, migrations of, 4
salmon impounded 90
salmon, is the quantity decreasing, 112, 116

salmon, its habitat, 141
salmon, kitted, 114
salmon, knob on lower jaw, 57
salmon, land-locked, 6
salmon, laws respecting, 119
salmon leaps, 73, 128
salmon legislation rumous, 133, 134
salmon, lingual teeth, 54
salmon, local breeds of, 56
salmon, local races of, 56
salmon, marking of, 129
salmon, means of capture, 135
salmon migrating from tidal to fresh water, 69
salmon migrating, sexes distinct, 73
salmon migrating up rivers, 66, 68
salmon, migrations of, 59
salmon, netting in dry seasons, 137
salmon never revert to infantile food, 70
Salmo nigrescens, 247
salmon, night fishing for, 137
Salmo nigripinnis, 11, 187, 192, 198
Salmo nobilis, 51
salmon, oil in, 141
salmon, old male, head, 52
salmon, origin of term, 2
salmon parasites, 59, 110
salmon par in salt water, 185
salmon par breeding with American char, 260
salmon par breeding with fontinalis, 260
salmon par breeding with Lochlevens, 259
salmon peal, 10, 58, 87
salmon, pool-bound, 75
salmon, rapidity of growth, 95
salmon, rate of progress ascending rivers, 73
salmon retained in fresh water, 99
salmon rivers, 2
salmon rivers, stock in, 119
salmon rivers, their preservation, 123
salmon, salted, 114, 115
salmon, scales of, 54
salmon scurf, 154
salmon, sexual distinctions, 57
salmon shoals coasting, 66
salmon, size captured, 141, 142
salmon smelt, 83
salmon smolt, 36, 59
salmon smolts breeding with Lochlevens, 258 260
salmon spawn every third year, 65
salmon spawning time altered, 63
salmon spawn on alternate years, 65
salmon spawn on consecutive seasons, 64
salmon spring, 58
salmon spotted bull trout, 11
salmon, statistics of, 112, 117, 118

salmon strikes, 58
salmon, supply limited, 115
salmon, tail fins at various ages, 53
salmon taken trolling, 108
salmon, temperature of, 9
salmon, term for bull trout, 67
salmon, their limits of reproduction, 106
salmon trout, 11, 149, 150, 151, 154
salmon trout a hybrid, 154
salmon trout from Teith, 155
salmon trout, head of, 154
salmon-trout, tail fin of, 156
salmon, teeth of, 54
salmon-trout, teeth on vomer, 156
salmon, unclean, 98
salmon, unseasonable, 98
salmon, value to rod fishers, 112
salmon, varieties of, 55, 56
salmon, where found, 141
salmon, who obtain them, 112
salmon, with three heads, 55
Salmo orcadensis, 11, 146, 192, 198
Salmo perisii, 232, 237
Salmo phinoc, 10, 149, 150, 152, 169
Salmo purpuratus, 7, 105, 202
Salmo quinnat, 27, 49
Salmo rappii, 183
Salmo salar, 10, 11, 24, 27, 51, 143, 153
Salmo salmo, 51
Salmo salmulus, 10, 51, 86, 91
Salmo salvelinus, 231, 232, 237, 239
Salmo stomachicus, 11, 195, 198
Salmo struanensis, 232, 238, 239
Salmo taurina, 190
Salmo taurinus, 218
Salmo thymallus, 278
Salmo thymus, 278
Salmo trutta, 6, 10, 11, 104, 143, 144, 146, 149, 151, 152, 158, 159, 162, 167, 168, 169, 182, 190
Salmo truttula, 149
Salmo umbla, 231, 232, 237, 238, 239
Salmo variabilis, 183
Salmo venernensis, 51, 104, 148
Salmo willoughbii, 232, 238, 239
salmulus, 10
salmulus, Salmo, 10, 51, 83, 86, 91
salters, 250, 252
salt water and salmon par, 185
salt water bred in by salmon, 99
salt water fatal to salmon eggs, 80
salt water, salmon eggs in, 79, 80
salt water, sea trout eggs in, 79
Salvelini, 6, 9, 11
Salvelinus alpinus, 237
salvelinus, Salmo, 231, 232, 237, 239
samlet, 10, 11, 58, 83, 99
samlets if hybrids, 86
samsons, 91
sand eels, bait for salmon, 140

saprolegnia attacking grayling, 283
Saprolegnia ferax, 33, 97, 103, 110, 111
Saprolegnia ferax, Murray on, 111
saumon, 58
Saurida, 3
Saurus, 3
scagger, 86
scale, diamond, 54
scales, 18
scales of char, 233, 240
scales of Salmonidæ, 271
scales of trout, 199
scales reproduced, 18
sceota, 204
schiffermüllen, Trutta, 183
school peal, 162
Scope, 48
Scopelus, 3
Scotch, crown rights to salmon, 130
Scotch fishery laws, 125
Scotch, free passage for salmon, 131
Scotch salmon fisheries, 121
Scotch salmon laws, 130, 131
scurf, 149, 151, 152, 154, 158
scurf, head of, 158
scurf, tail fin of, 156
scuive, 154
sea fish becoming residents of fresh water, 5
sea and fresh-water trout one species, 143
sea, salmon forced to spawn in, 79
sea, salmon not spawn in, 79
season of char, 242
sea trout, 10, 11, 143, 150
sea trout and bull trout, how differ, 181
sea trout and fresh water trout, varieties of one species, 182
sea trout, angling for, 175
sea trout as food, 179
sea trout breeding, 175, 176, 177
sea trout, close season suspended, 180
sea trout, colours of, 157
sea trout, diseases of, 160
sea trout driving out salmon, 67
sea trout, eggs incubated, 146
sea trout, food of, 178, 179
sea trout, growth of, 178
sea trout, habitat, 180
sea trout, habits of, 173
sea trout, hatched at Howietonn, 146
sea trout in fresh water, 143
sea trout land locked, 190
sea trout, legislation for, 180
sea trout, life history of, 177
sea trout, means of capture, 175
sea trout migrating, 178
sea trout, migrations of, 173, 174
sea trout, names of 154
sea trout, Northern race, 149
sea trout passing into fresh water species, 182

sea trout, some young not migratory, 177
sea trout, Southern race, 150, 160
sea trout, tail fins of, 156
sea trout, variations of colour in, 171
sea trout, varieties of, 172
sea trout, young of, 177
sea trout, Welsh names of, 162
Sebago salmon, 51
segregation of fishes, 30
seine nets, 138
Serrasalmus, 2
Serres on fish monsters, 273
Seth Green, 35, 36
set nets, 139
Severn, river, 28
Severn, salmon of, 118
sewin, 10, 11 143, 144, 150, 151, 152, 161, 162, 176
sewin, habits of, 161
sewin, head of, 160
sewin hybrids, 48, 144
sewin in shoals, 176
sewin selecting rivers, 174
sewin, tail fins of, 163
sewin, teeth on vomer of, 163
sexual distinctions, sea trout, 172
shad, 5
Shannon, fisheries of, 135
Shaw, 29, 31, 48, 158
shed, 58
shedder, 58
sheets, 279
shiags, 58
Shin, captures of grilse in, 94, 95
Shin, captures of salmon in, 94, 95
shot, 204, 279, 280
shrimps for salmon fishing, 186
shutts, 279
Sibbald, Sir R, 217
Sibbald's trout, 151
sil-bodham, 162
silver grays, 154
silver whites, 151
silvery coat in Salmonidæ, 220
silver char, 237, 239
silvery fontinalis, 249
silvery livery of smolts, 90
silvery trout, 190, 191, 195 201
simen, 58
Sim, Mr G , on trout ova, 188
simple monsters, 276
size of Lochlevens, 230
sheggei, 58, 83, 99
skeggei trout, 83
skeleton, 11, 15
skerling, 58, 83, 84, 118
skin, 18
skull, 16
slats, 58, 96
sluggish water, effects of, 35
small meshed nets, 120
smell, 19
smelt, 3, 5, 58, 159
smelt sprods, 154
Smith, Dr F A , 237
smolt, 58, 87, 90, 102
smolts, autumn migration of, 90, 91, 92

smolts, colours of, 55
smolts, descending seawards, 87, 88, 89, 90, 92
smolt eggs fecundated 103
smolt eggs milted from pars, 103
smolt eggs milted from trout, 103
smolts, how descend rivers, 74
smolts, killing of, laws, 131
smolts in sea water, 90
smolts, large, 26
smolts migrating, 93
smolts reascend as grilse, 92
smolts taken in November, 133
smolt with ova, 102, 103
smouts, 83
snow fed rivers, effects on migration, 61
snow water, effects on salmon spawning, 64
soles, 5
Solway, fixed engines in, illegal, 132
Solway migratory trout, 11
Solway, salmon of, 117
sparling, 58
spawn, 23, 58, 162
spawning affected by nourishment, 70
spawning die after, salmon, 96
spawning grounds for salmon, 80
spawning, how artificially done, 30, 31
spawning of salmon, 77, 81
spawning salmon, too many in river, 133
spawning time of salmon, 61, 62, 64
spawning time changed in rivers, 61, 62
spawning trap for trout, 30
spearing salmon, 136
species, 7
species, utility of knowledge of, 50
speckled trout, 247
spermatozoa, 28
spermatozoon deformed, 272 273
Spey, fisheries of, 128, 129
spines affected, 277
splash nets for bull trout, 181
spotted troutlet, 247
sprag, 58
spraid, 59
sprats, 58
spring run fish, 96
spring tides affect salmon in grating, 79
sprods, 58, 150, 154 159
sprod, angling for, 175
sprod, flesh of, 159
stage nets, 139
stake nets, 140
stake nets commenced in Scotland, 132
stake nets for salmon, 124
sterile trout, 144, 210
sterility of eggs due to immature parents, 78
sterility of salmon 106

sterility from deficiency of food, 70
Stoddart, 159
stomachicus, Salmo, 11, 195, 198
stomach of gillaroo, 194
stomach of salmon empty, 107
stomach of trout thickened, 189
stomach thickened in trout, 203
stop net, 139
Stormontfield ponds, 29, 127
stilling, 138
streamer, 58
stocking with young fish, 45
stromii, Lepeoptheirus, 110
struannensis, Salmo, 232, 238, 239
Struans crossed by British char, 266
Struans crossed by Lochlevens, 266
Struans crossed by Struans, 265
Struan hybrids, 263, 264
sturgeon, 141
sucker, 5
summer-cock, 58
Sutherlandshire salmon fisheries, 129
Swaledale trout, 195
sweep-nets, 138
Sweden, breeding of Salmonidæ, 27
swim-bladder, 20

tadpoles, 37
tail-fin affected, 277
tail fins of brook trout, 199
tail less trout, 203
tails, heterocercal, 13
tails, homocercal, 12
tails of Lochlevens, 222
Tahitins locusta, 179
tapeworms, 110
tari dhearg 240
Tasmania, 7
Tasmania, trout for, 22, 27, 23
taste, 19
tarina, Salmo, 190
tarina, Trutta, 180
taurinus, Salmo, 218
Tay, fisheries, 126
Tay Navigation Act, effects of, 127
Tay, river, 20
tecon, 58, 83
teeth in Salmonidæ, 21
teeth nearly absent in a trout, 203
teeth of Lochlevens, 222, 223
teeth of trout, 155
teeth, vomerine, 6, 10
Teith, river, 216
telara, Engraulis, 5
temperature and food, how connected, 63
temperature for incubation, 35
temperature of rivers affecting time of migration, 63, 64, 68
temperature of salmon, 9
tench, 48
Tetragonopterus, 2
Tetrodon cutcutia, 5
Thaleichthys, 3

Thames, salmon of, 116
thickly spotted bull trout, 11
thirst, 17
Thomas, Mr , 225
Thompson, 11
Thompson on monstrosities, 271
Thompson's trout, 152
three heads on salmon, 55
Thurso, fisheries of, 140
Thymallus, 1, 2, 9, 19, 278, 279
thymallus, Coregonus, 278
Thymalus gymnothorax, 278
Thymallus vexilifer, 278
Thymallus vulgaris, 278
thymallus, Salmo, 278
Thyme-like odour, 1
thymus, Salmo, 278
tidal influence, salmon spawning within, 79
tides spring, affect salmon in grating 72
Tinca vulgaris, 48
tobbs, 161
Tometes, 2
torgoch, 231, 237, 240
Totness weir, 179
touch, 18
travelling, preparing fish for, 45
trays, hatching, 32
trottht, 204
troughs, 167
trout, 10, 47, 143
trout alevins, colours of, 210
trout almost toothless, 208
trout annual spawners, 209
trout artificially fed, 206
trout as food, 213
trout becoming sterile, 141
trout breeding, 208, 209, 210
trout, brook, habits of, 204
trout, brook, food of, 204, 205, 206, 207
trout, cæcal appendages in, 148, 188
trout, caudal fin in, 116
trout, colours of, vi, 144, 147, 185, 186, 201, 202
trout, colour of flesh 179
trout, colours variable, 182
trout, crooked backs, 203
trout culture, 29
trout, deformed race, 203
trout divisions of, v vi
trout, domesticated, 28
trout eat grayling ova, 207
trout eggs sent to Otago, 183
trout estuary, 191
trout, Fordwich, 170
trout, forms of in fresh water, 189
trout, fresh-water, 190
trout, fresh-water, colours silvery, 185
trout from Irish lochs, 299
trout from New Zealand, 198
trout, great lake, 11
trout, half annual spawners, 209
trout hatching by Jacobi, 208
trout, how ascend rivers, 71

trout hybrids, 49, 144
trout, increase in size, 184
trout in hot water, 20, 21
trout in mountain streams, 213
trout in sea water, 185
trout in spawn in June, 209
trout, instinct in, 213
trout in Tasmania, 144
trout in thunderstorms, 204
trout, knob on lower jaw, 186, 187
trout, local races of, 162
trout, Lochleven, 8, 217
trout, long-lived fish, 213
trout, many local races, 143
trout, modes of capture, 207
trout, par bands in, 210
trout peal, 162
trout, pectoral fins of, 187
trout, races crossed, 189
trout, races of, vi
trout, scales of, 199
trout, silvery colour, 111, 115, 201
trout, smolt stage in, 145
trout spawning in ponds, 209
trout uneasy at breeding time, 228, 229
trout, varieties of, 185
trout, vertebræ of, 189
trout with deformed gill-covers, 203
trout with one eye, 203
trout without tails, 203
trout yellow from the sea, 191
trow, 138
truff, 150, 161, 166, 167, 168
truff, head of, 166
truff, tail fin of, 156, 163
truht, 204
truites, 2
Truttæ, 2, 9, 11
Trutta fario, 190, 193
Trutta ferox, 193
Trutta fluviatilis, 10, 190
Trutta lacustris, 183
Trutta marina, 149
trutta, Salmo, 6, 10, 11, 104, 143, 144, 146, 149, 151, 152, 158, 159, 162, 167, 168, 169, 182, 190
trutta, Salmo, colours of, 55
Trutta salmonata, 10, 119
Trutta schiffermulleri, 183
Trutta taurina, 180
trutta, Truttæ, 149
truttula, Salmo, 149
turbot, 5, 48
Turton, 10
Turton's trout, 151
twbhyn, 161
twb-y-dail, 161
twbs, 161
Tweed Act, 132
Tweed fisheries, 125
Tweed salmon fisheries, 114
Tweed Salmonidæ, 116
Tyne, salmon of, 117
Tyrer, Mr , 35

umber, 280
umbla, Salmo, 237, 238, 239, 231, 232

unclean salmon, 98
unimpregnated eggs, 260
unseasonable salmon, 98
unspawned salmon, 98, 99
upper jaw, 16
upper proprietors get few salmon, 124
urbhreac, 50
urinary organs, 22
Usk, 118, 119
Usk become an earlier river, 120
Usk, how become an earlier river, 68
Usk not become an earlier river, 118, 120

Valentin on causes of monsters, 275
value of Scotch salmon fisheries, 124
Valvata piscinalis, 109
valves of intestines, 22, 54
variabilis, Salmo, 183
Van Diemen's Land, 42
varieties, 7
varieties of sea trout, 172
venison of the waters, 213
venernensis, Salmo, 51, 104, 118
vertebræ, 15
vertebræ may vary in number, 16
vertebræ, number of, 8
vertebræ of sea trout, 172
vertebræ of char, 233
vertebræ of trout, 189
vexillifer, Thymallus, 278
Vogt 22, 39, 40
vole, 28
vomerine teeth, 6
vomerine teeth falling out, 147
vomerine teeth in brook trout, 197
vomerine teeth in sea trout, 160, 162
vomerine teeth in trout, 146, 147, 155, 156
Vrasski, 31
Violik on monstrosities, 271, 275
vulgaris, Carassius, 48
vulgaris, Thymallus, 278
vulgaris, Tinca, 48

Warkworth trout, 152
water crossing weirs, 121
water fatal to milt or ova, 210
water for incubation, 32
water, high temperature of, 109
water, muddy, 109
water ouzel, 28
water, pollutions of, 99
water rat 28
water, poisonous character, 109
water thyme, 279
water when heated, effects of, 20
weirs, 137, 138, 140
weirs illegal, 120
weirs in Magna Charta, 120
weirs, Ireland, 133
Wenern salmon, 104, 105

Wenern, Lake of, 5
West char, 237
Wethered, Mr., 39, 277, 282
White, 11
white-fish, 150, 162, 167, 168
white-fish, head of, 165
white-fish, tail fin of, 163
white salmon, 10
white trout, 11, 149, 150, 151, 154, 165, 249
White's trout, 152
whitelings, 159
whiting, 154, 159
whitling, 85, 149, 150, 152, 154, 156, 159, 189
whitling, head of, 159
whitling, series of, 159
whitling, tail fin of, 156

whitling, teeth on vomer, 156
Widegren, 13
Widegren's trout, 152, 153
wild thyme, 279
Wilmot, Mr., 30
Willis-Bund, viii
willoughbii, Salmo, 232, 238, 239
Willoughby, 10, 19, 47, 48
Willoughby's charr, 238
Willoughby's trout, 151
Windermere char, 237
Windermere char introduced, 241
Wye, salmon of, 118

Xyphorhynchus, 3
Xyphostoma, 3

Yare, 140
Yarrell, 11, 29
Yarrell's trout, 152
yearling trout, 213
yellow fins, 154, 177
yellow trout in estuaries, 191
yellow trout, young of, 177
Youl and trout eggs, 183
Youl, Mr., experiments by, 42
Young, Andrew, 29, 48
young trout, food of, 211, 212

Zebra hybrids, 260, 262
Zebra hybrids crossed by Loch-levens, 266
Zebras, 266
Zoological Record, 6
zoosperms, 23

ERRATA

Page 32, 14 lines from bottom, *for* "bastoderm,' *read* "blastoderm
,, 95, 19 ,, ,, ,, ,, "next year,' ,, "same year "
,, 111, 35 ,, ,, ,, ,, "beaked," ,, "backed "
,, 125, 28 ,, ,, top, ,, "diseases," ,, "decreases "
,, 183, 20 ,, ,, bottom, ,, "o," ,, 'of "

LONDON
C. NORMAN AND SON, PRINTERS, HART STREET

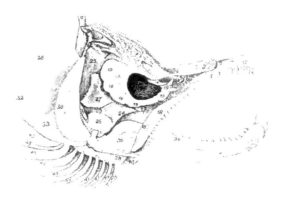

Fig.

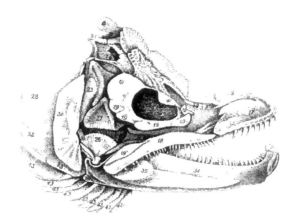

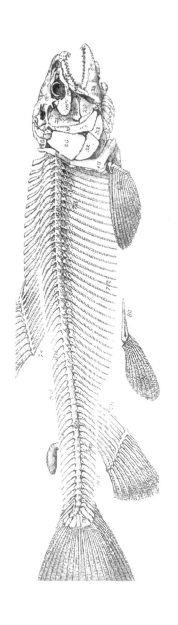

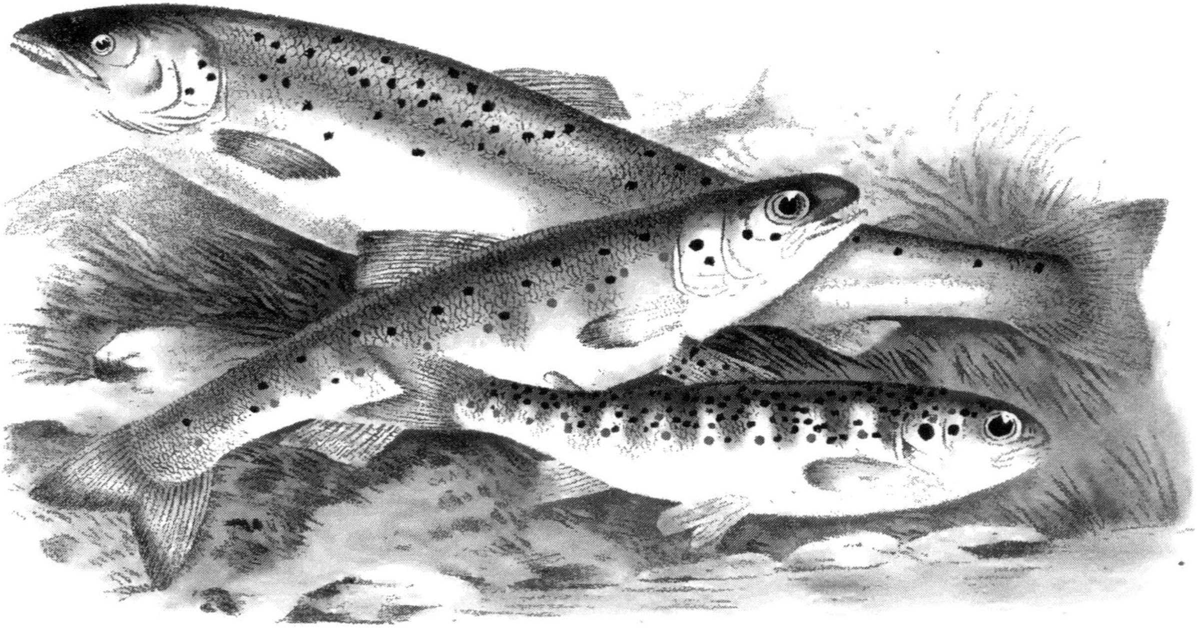

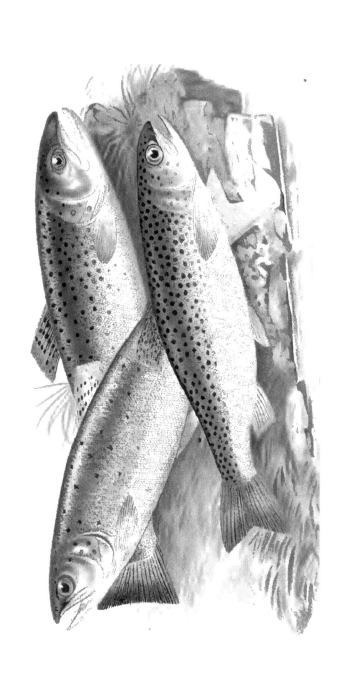

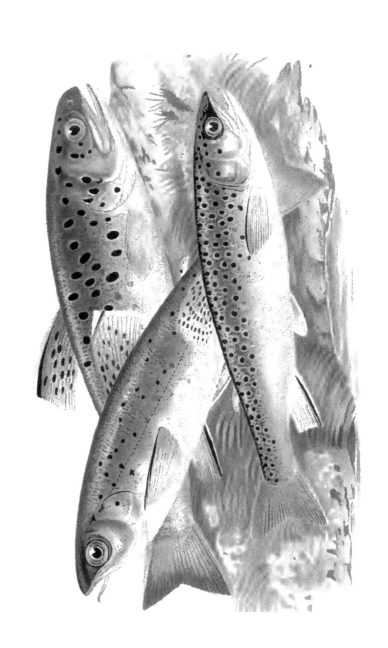

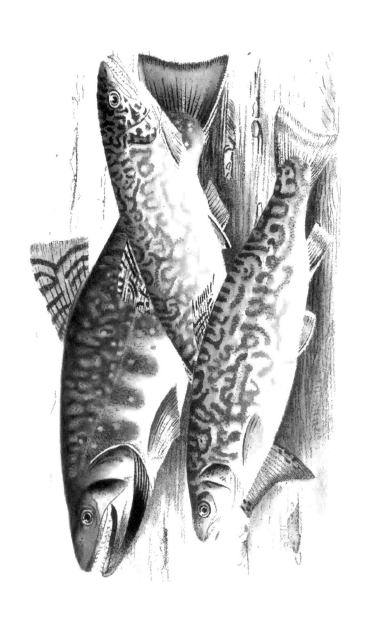

MONSTROSITIES, 1 THREE EYES 2 ONE EYE 3 NO EYES 4 DBLE TAIL 5 DEFORMED TAIL, 6 89:0 ... CLEFT HEAD 5 ... 12 13 +15 CURVED SPINES 16 DROPSY OF SAC 17 DEFORMED GILL COVER 18 SHORT LOWER JAW 19 SHORT UPPER JAW